Lecture Notes in Computer Science　　11245

Commenced Publication in 1973
Founding and Former Series Editors:
Gerhard Goos, Juris Hartmanis, and Jan van Leeuwen

More information about this series at http://www.springer.com/series/7407

Tiziana Margaria · Bernhard Steffen (Eds.)

Leveraging Applications of Formal Methods, Verification and Validation

Verification

8th International Symposium, ISoLA 2018
Limassol, Cyprus, November 5–9, 2018
Proceedings, Part II

 Springer

Editors
Tiziana Margaria
University of Limerick
Limerick, Ireland

Bernhard Steffen
TU Dortmund
Dortmund, Germany

ISSN 0302-9743 ISSN 1611-3349 (electronic)
Lecture Notes in Computer Science
ISBN 978-3-030-03420-7 ISBN 978-3-030-03421-4 (eBook)
https://doi.org/10.1007/978-3-030-03421-4

Library of Congress Control Number: 2018960392

LNCS Sublibrary: SL1 – Theoretical Computer Science and General Issues

This Springer imprint is published by the registered company Springer Nature Switzerland AG
The registered company address is: Gewerbestrasse 11, 6330 Cham, Switzerland

Preface

Welcome to ISoLA 2018, the *8th International Symposium on Leveraging Applications of Formal Methods, Verification and Validation*, that was held in Limassol (Cyprus) during November 5–9, 2018, endorsed by EASST, the European Association of Software Science and Technology.

This year's event followed the tradition of its symposia forerunners held 2004 and 2006 in Cyprus, 2008 in Chalkidiki, 2010 and 2012 in Crete, 2014 and 2016 in Corfu, and the series of ISoLA Workshops in Greenbelt (USA) in 2005, Poitiers (France) in 2007, Potsdam (Germany) in 2009, in Vienna (Austria) in 2011, and 2013 in Palo Alto (USA).

As in the previous editions, ISoLA 2018 provided a forum for developers, users, and researchers to discuss issues related to the **adoption and use of rigorous tools and methods** for the specification, analysis, verification, certification, construction, test, and maintenance of systems from the point of view of their different application domains. Thus, since 2004 the ISoLA series of events has served the purpose of bridging the gap between designers and developers of rigorous tools on one hand, and users in engineering and in other disciplines on the other hand. It fosters and exploits synergetic relationships among scientists, engineers, software developers, decision makers, and other critical thinkers in companies and organizations. By providing a specific, dialogue-oriented venue for the discussion of common problems, requirements, algorithms, methodologies, and practices, ISoLA aims in particular at supporting researchers in their quest to improve the usefulness, reliability, flexibility, and efficiency of tools for building systems, and users in their search for adequate solutions to their problems.

The program of the symposium consisted of a collection of *special tracks* devoted to the following hot and emerging topics:

- A Broader View on Verification: From Static to Runtime and Back
  (Organizers: Wolfgang Ahrendt, Marieke Huisman, Giles Reger, Kristin Yvonne Rozier)
- Evaluating Tools for Software Verification
  (Organizers: Markus Schordan, Dirk Beyer, Stephen F. Siegel)
- Towards a Unified View of Modeling and Programming
  (Organizers: Manfred Broy, Klaus Havelund, Rahul Kumar, Bernhard Steffen)
- RV-TheToP: Runtime Verification from Theory to Industry Practice
  (Organizers: Ezio Bartocci and Ylies Falcone)
- Rigorous Engineering of Collective Adaptive Systems
  (Organizers: Rocco De Nicola, Stefan Jähnichen, Martin Wirsing)
- Reliable Smart Contracts: State of the Art, Applications, Challenges, and Future Directions
  (Organizers: Gerardo Schneider, Martin Leucker, César Sánchez)

- Formal Methods in Industrial Practice—Bridging the Gap
  (Organizers: Michael Felderer, Dilian Gurov, Marieke Huisman, Björn Lisper, Rupert Schlick)
- X-by-Construction
  (Organizers: Maurice H. ter Beek, Loek Cleophas, Ina Schaefer, and Bruce W. Watson)
- Statistical Model Checking
  (Organizers: Axel Legay and Kim Larsen)
- Verification and Validation of Distributed Systems
  (Organizer: Cristina Seceleanu)
- Cyber-Physical Systems Engineering
  (Organizers: J Paul Gibson, Marc Pantel, Peter Gorm Larsen, Jim Woodcock, John Fitzgerald)

The following events were also held:

- RERS: Challenge on Rigorous Examination of Reactive Systems (Bernhard Steffen)
- Doctoral Symposium and Poster Session (Anna-Lena Lamprecht)
- Industrial Day (Axel Hessenkämper, Falk Howar, Andreas Rausch)

Co-located with the ISoLA Symposium were:

- RV 2018: 18th International Conference on Runtime Verification (Saddek Bensalem, Christian Colombo, and Martin Leucker)
- STRESS 2018: 5th International School on Tool-based Rigorous Engineering of Software Systems (John Hatcliff, Tiziana Margaria, Robby, Bernhard Steffen)

Owing to the growth of ISoLA 2018, the proceedings of this edition are published in four volumes of LNCS: Part 1: Modeling, Part 2: Verification, Part 3: Distributed Systems, and Part 4: Industrial Practice. In addition to the contributions of the main conference, the proceedings also include contributions of the four embedded events and tutorial papers for STRESS.

We thank the track organizers, the members of the Program Committee and their referees for their effort in selecting the papers to be presented, the local Organization Chair, Petros Stratis, the EasyConferences team for their continuous precious support during the week as well as during the entire two-year period preceding the events, and Springer for being, as usual, a very reliable partner in the proceedings production. Finally, we are grateful to Kyriakos Georgiades for his continuous support for the website and the program, and to Markus Frohme and Julia Rehder for their help with the online conference service (EquinOCS).

Special thanks are due to the following organization for their endorsement: EASST (European Association of Software Science and Technology) and Lero – The Irish Software Research Centre, and our own institutions: TU Dortmund and the University of Limerick.

November 2018   Tiziana Margaria
                                                                                 Bernhard Steffen

Organization

Symposium Chair

Bernhard Steffen   TU Dortmund, Germany

Program Chair

Tiziana Margaria   University of Limerick, Ireland

Program Committee

Wolfgang Ahrendt	Chalmers University of Technology, Sweden
Jesper Andersen	Deon Digital AG
Ezio Bartocci	TU Wien, Austria
Dirk Beyer	LMU Munich, Germany
Manfred Broy	Technische Universität München
Loek Cleophas	TU Eindhoven, The Netherlands
Rocco De Nicola	IMT School for Advanced Studies, Italy
Boris Düdder	University of Copenhagen, Denmark
Ylies Falcone	University of Grenoble, France
Michael Felderer	University of Innsbruck, Austria
John Fitzgerald	Newcastle University, UK
Paul Gibson	Telecom Sud Paris, France
Kim Guldstrand Larsen	Aalborg University, Denmark
Dilian Gurov	KTH Royal Institute of Technology, Sweden
John Hatcliff	Kansas State University, USA
Klaus Havelund	Jet Propulsion Laboratory, USA
Fritz Henglein	University of Copenhagen, Denmark
Axel Hessenkämper	Hottinger Baldwin Messtechnik GmbH
Falk Howar	Dortmund University of Technology and Fraunhofer ISST, Germany
Marieke Huisman	University of Twente, The Netherlands
Michael Huth	Imperial College London, UK
Stefan Jaehnichen	TU Berlin, Germany
Rahul Kumar	Microsoft Research
Anna-Lena Lamprecht	Utrecht University, The Netherlands
Peter Gorm Larsen	Aarhus University, Denmark
Axel Legay	Inria, France
Martin Leucker	University of Lübeck, Germany

Björn Lisper   Mälardalen University, Sweden
Leif-Nissen Lundæk   XAIN AG
Tiziana Margaria   Lero, Ireland
Marc Pantel   Université de Toulouse, France
Andreas Rausch   TU Clausthal, Germany
Giles Reger   University of Manchester, UK
Robby   Kansas State University, USA
Kristin Yvonne   Iowa State University, USA
  Rozier
Ina Schaefer   TU Braunschweig, Germany
Rupert Schlick   AIT Austrian Institute of Technology, Austria
Gerardo Schneider   University of Gothenburg, Sweden
Markus Schordan   Lawrence Livermore National Laboratory, USA
Cristina Seceleanu   Mälardalen University, Sweden
Stephen F. Siegel   University of Delaware, USA
César Sánchez   IMDEA Software Institute, Spain
Bruce W. Watson   Stellenbosch University, South Africa
Martin Wirsing   LMU München, Germany
James Woodcock   University of York, UK
Maurice ter Beek   ISTI-CNR, Italy
Jaco van de Pol   University of Twente, The Netherlands

Additional Reviewers

Yehia Abd Alrahman   Neil Jones
Dhaminda Abeywickrama   Sebastiaan Joosten
Lenz Belzner   Gabor Karsai
Saddek Bensalem   Alexander Knapp
Egon Boerger   Timothy Lethbridge
Marius Bozga   Chunhua Liao
Tomas Bures   Alberto Lluch-Lafuente
Rance Cleaveland   Alessandro Maggi
Giovanna Di Marzo Serugendo   Dominique Méry
Matthew Dwyer   Birger Møller-Pedersen
Benedikt Eberhardinger   Stefan Naujokat
Rim El Ballouli   Ayoub Nouri
Thomas Gabor   Liam O'Connor
Stephen Gilmore   Doron Peled
Emma Hart   Thomy Phan
Arnd Hartmanns   Jeremy Pitt
Rolf Hennicker   Hella Ponsar
Petr Hnetynka   Andre Reichstaller
Reiner Hähnle   Jeff Sanders
Patrik Jansson   Sean Sedwards
Einar Broch Johnsen   Christoph Seidl

Contents – Part II

Statistical Model Checking

RERS 2018

Doctoral Symposium

A Broader View on Verification: From Static to Runtime and Back

A Broader View on Verification:
From Static to Runtime and Back
(Track Summary)

Wolfgang Ahrendt[1], Marieke Huisman[2(✉)], Giles Reger[3],
and Kristin Yvonne Rozier[4]

[1] Chalmers University of Technology, Gothenburg, Sweden
[2] University of Twente, Enschede, The Netherlands
m.huisman@utwente.nl
[3] University of Manchester, Manchester, UK
[4] Iowa State University, Ames, IA, USA

Abstract. When seeking to verify a computational system one can
either view the system as a *static* description of possible behaviours or a
dynamic collection of observed or actual behaviours. Historically, there
have been clear differences between the two approaches in terms of their
level of completeness, the associated costs, the kinds of specifications
considered, how and when they are applied, and so on. Recently there
has been a concentrated interest in the combination of static and runtime (dynamic) techniques and this track (taking place as part of ISoLA
2018) aims to explore this combination further.

1 Motivation and Goals

Traditionally, program verification has been *static* in nature, e.g. it has sought
to verify that a program, given as a piece of code in a programming language,
satisfies a specification for all possible inputs to that program. This approach can
be traced back to the seminal work of Floyd and Hoare, which has grown into
the mature field of *Deduction Software Verification* [2,15]. Another successful
static approach is that of *(Software) Model Checking* [12] where the state space
of the program is searched looking for bad states (and trying to establish their
absence). Many other static analysis techniques make use of the source code of
a program to extract information or establish properties of interest. Conversely,
the fields of *Runtime Verification* [5] and *Runtime Assertion Checking* [11,13]
abstract a program as a set of behaviours observed at *runtime*, which significantly
restricts the coverage of verification whilst improving efficiency by focusing on
"real" behaviours.

Recently, there have been multiple proposals to combine static with runtime
verification techniques [1,17,18]. Results from static verification can be exploited
to reduce the overhead of runtime verification [3,4,7], while results from runtime
verification can be is used to fill "holes" left by static verification, where static
results are too costly, or impossible, to establish. Static results can moreover

© Springer Nature Switzerland AG 2018
T. Margaria and B. Steffen (Eds.): ISoLA 2018, LNCS 11245, pp. 3–7, 2018.
https://doi.org/10.1007/978-3-030-03420-4_1

increase confidence over what runtime verification can achieve alone. And runtime analysis can learn information that can be used later for static analysis (e.g., mining invariants, and detecting data structures) [21]. Finally, it has been observed that the two approaches (static and runtime) tend to focus on different kinds of specifications with static techniques often focussing on simpler state-based properties and runtime techniques focussing on richer temporal properties. This leads to a simple benefit from combination – a wider range of properties can be checked. Significant progress has been made in these directions, but it is also evident that the communities, targets, methods, and discussions in static and runtime verification research are still too unrelated. There is even less of a connection between early design-time verification techniques (e.g., model checking), the intermediate (e.g., code analysis), and execution-time (e.g., runtime monitoring) verification techniques in the system development cycle.

Within this track, we investigate what can be achieved in joint efforts of the communities of verification techniques for different design stages, including static and dynamic analyses, model checking, deductive verification, and runtime verification. This track is a follow-up of the track *Static and Runtime Verification: Competitors or Friends?*, organised during ISoLA 2016 [18]. That track investigated the different ways in which static and runtime verification could be combined, addressed questions such as which application areas could benefit from combinations of static and dynamic analysis, which program properties can be established using which technique, what artefacts can be carried forward through different verification technologies, what is a good balance of guarantees and user efforts in various application areas, and how we can integrate the various techniques into the software, and hybrid/cyber-physical system development process. We believe that the track in 2016 was a very good catalyst for the connection of the different communities, and the formation of common agendas. At the same time, it is clear that a one-time event would not be enough to fully achieve and sustain the set goals.

The current track *A Broader View on Verification: From Static to Runtime and Back*, at ISoLA 2018, continues and further develops the cross-community endeavour for an integrated interplay of static and runtime techniques, with the overall aim of building systems that are evidently well-functioning. The track features eight contributions, by 24 authors in total, on three different topics: application areas; classes of properties; and practical issues of combining static and runtime techniques. We would like to thank all the authors for their contributions to this track, in the form of the papers written, and in the form of on-site discussions. We would also like to thank everyone who visited this track at ISoLA, showed interest in the overall topic and the individual talks, and participated in the discussions.

Finally, we would like to express our deep gratitude to the ISoLA organisers, in particular Tiziana Margaria and Bernhard Steffen, for working so hard to provide such a wonderful platform for our and other tracks, enabling lively and creative interaction between individuals and communities, helping us all to not forget the bigger picture of working for the development of systems that people can rely on.

2 Contributions

2.1 Topic 1: Application Areas for Combining Static and Runtime Verification

This topic is dedicated to different application areas of system development exploiting static and dynamic techniques.

In *Programming Safe Robotics Systems: Challenges, Advances, and Opportunities* [14], Ankush Desai, Sanjit Seshia, and Shaz Qadeer present a programming framework for building a safe robotics system. It consists of a high-level programming language for implementing, specifying, and systematically testing the reactive robotics software, as well as a runtime enforcement system ensuring that assumptions made in the testing phase actually hold at runtime.

In *Generating Component Interfaces by Integrating Static and Symbolic Analysis, Learning, and Runtime Monitoring* [19], Falk Howar, Dimitra Giannakopoulou, Malte Mues, and Jorge Navas present extensions to a tool for interface generation that integrates interpolation and symbolic search. Also, they discuss how to use information from runtime monitoring to validate the generated interfaces.

2.2 Topic 2: What are the Relevant Program Properties?

This topic is dedicated to the specific classes of program properties that deserve particular attention when combining static and runtime verification.

In *Monitoring Hyperproperties by Combining Static Analysis and Runtime Verification* [8], Borzoo Bonakdarpour, César Sánchez, and Gerardo Schneider study the problem of runtime verifying temporal hyperproperties, in particular those that involve quantifier alternation. Starting from the observation that virtually no $\forall\exists$ property can be fully monitored at runtime, they propose a combination of static analysis and runtime verification to manage the checking of such formulas. In addition, they also discuss how the notion of hyperproperties should be extended to also consider properties that relate three or more traces.

In *Temporal Reasoning on Incomplete Paths* [16], Dana Fisman and Hillel Kugler explore semantics for temporal logics on paths that are incomplete in different ways. They study incomplete ultimately periodic paths, segmentally broken paths, and combinations thereof, and discuss whether systems biology can benefit from the suggested extensions.

In *A Framework for Quantitative Assessment of Partial Program Correctness Proofs* [6], Bernhard Beckert, Mihai Herda, Stefan Kobischke, and Mattias Ulbrich introduce the concept of state-space coverage for partial proofs, which estimates to what degree the proof covers the state space and the possible inputs of a program. This concept brings together deductive verification techniques with runtime techniques used to empirically estimate the coverage.

2.3   Topic 3: Putting Combinations of Static and Runtime Verification into Practice

This topic is dedicated to practical (current and future) combinations of static and runtime verification.

In *Generating Inductive Shape Predicates for Runtime Checking and Formal Verification* [9], Jan H. Boockmann, Gerald Lüttgen, and Jan Tobias Mühlberg show how memory safety predicates, statically inferred by a program comprehension tool, can be employed to generate runtime checks for securely communicating dynamic data structures across trust boundaries. They also explore to what extent these predicates can be used within static program verifiers.

In *Runtime Assertion Checking and Static Verification: Collaborative Partners* [20], Fonenantsoa Maurica, David Cok, and Julien Signoles discuss how to achieve, on the architectural level, static and dynamic analysis systems featuring a narrow semantic gap as well as similar levels of sound and complete checking. They also describe designs and implementations that add new capabilities to runtime assertion checking, bringing it closer to the feature coverage of static verification.

In *A Language-Independent Program Verification Framework* [10], Chen and Rosu describe an approach to language-independent deductive verification, using the $\mathbb{K}$ semantics framework. They show how a program verifier as well as other, also dynamic, language tools are generated automatically, from the semantics description, correct-by-construction.

2.4   Panel Discussion

Inspired by the different talks and discussions, the final panel discussion aimed for convergence on matters that lead the way forward, and concrete next steps for the community to achieve the set goals.

References

1. Aceto, L., Francalanza, A., Ingolfsdottir, A.: Proceedings First Workshop on Pre- and Post-Deployment Verification Techniques. ArXiv e-prints, May 2016
2. Ahrendt, W., Beckert, B., Bubel, R., Hähnle, R., Schmitt, P.H., Ulbrich, M.: Deductive Software Verification-The KeY Book: From Theory to Practice. LNCS, vol. 10001. Springer, Cham (2016). https://doi.org/10.1007/978-3-319-49812-6
3. Ahrendt, W., Chimento, J.M., Pace, G.J., Schneider, G.: Verifying data- and control-oriented properties combining static and runtime verification: theory and tools. Form. Methods Syst. Des. **51**(1), 200–265 (2017). https://doi.org/10.1007/s10703-017-0274-y
4. Ahrendt, W., Pace, G.J., Schneider, G.: StaRVOOrS — episode II - strengthen and distribute the force. In: Margaria, T., Steffen, B. (eds.) ISoLA 2016. LNCS, vol. 9952, pp. 402–415. Springer, Cham (2016). https://doi.org/10.1007/978-3-319-47166-2_28
5. Bartocci, E., Falcone, Y., Francalanza, A., Reger, G.: Introduction to runtime verification. In: Bartocci, E., Falcone, Y. (eds.) Lectures on Runtime Verification. LNCS, vol. 10457, pp. 1–33. Springer, Cham (2018). https://doi.org/10.1007/978-3-319-75632-5_1

6. Beckert, B., Herda, M., Kobischke, S., Ulbrich, M.: Towards a notion of coverage for incomplete program-correctness proofs. In: Margaria, T., Steffen, B. (eds.) ISoLA 2018. LNCS, vol. 11245, pp. 53–63. Springer, Cham (2018)

7. Bodden, E., Lam, P., Hendren, L.J.: Partially evaluating finite-state runtime monitors ahead of time. ACM Trans. Program. Lang. Syst. **34**(2), 7:1–7:52 (2012). https://doi.org/10.1145/2220365.2220366

8. Bonakdarpour, B., Sánchez, C., Schneider, G.: Monitoring hyperproperties by combining static analysis and runtime verification. In: Margaria, T., Steffen, B. (eds.) ISoLA 2018. LNCS, vol. 11245, pp. 8–27. Springer, Cham (2018)

9. Boockmann, J.H., Lüttgen, G., Mühlberg, J.T.: Generating inductive shape predicates for runtime checking and formal verification. In: Margaria, T., Steffen, B. (eds.) ISoLA 2018. LNCS, vol. 11245, pp. 64–74. Springer, Cham (2018)

10. Chen, X., Rosu, G.: A language-independent program verification framework. In: Margaria, T., Steffen, B. (eds.) ISoLA 2018. LNCS, vol. 11245, pp. 92–102. Springer, Cham (2018)

11. Cheon, Y., Leavens, G.T.: A Runtime Assertion Checker for the Java Modeling Language (JML) (2002)

12. Clarke, E.M., Henzinger, T.A., Veith, H., Bloem, R.P.: Handbook of Model Checking. Springer, Cham (2016). https://doi.org/10.1007/978-3-319-10575-8

13. Clarke, L.A., Rosenblum, D.S.: A historical perspective on runtime assertion checking in software development. ACM SIGSOFT Softw. Eng. Notes **31**(3), 25–37 (2006)

14. Desai, A., Seshia, S., Qadeer, S.: Programming safe robotics systems: challenges, advances, and opportunities. In: Margaria, T., Steffen, B. (eds.) ISoLA 2018. LNCS, vol. 11245, pp. 103–119. Springer, Cham (2018)

15. Filliâtre, J.C.: Deductive software verification. Int. J. Softw. Tools Technol. Transf. **13**(5), 397 (2011). https://doi.org/10.1007/s10009-011-0211-0

16. Fisman, D., Kugler, H.: Temporal reasoning on incomplete paths. In: Margaria, T., Steffen, B. (eds.) ISoLA 2018. LNCS, vol. 11245, pp. 28–52. Springer, Cham (2018)

17. Francalanza, A., Pace, G.J.: Proceedings Second International Workshop on Pre- and Post-Deployment Verification Techniques. ArXiv e-prints, August 2017

18. Gurov, D., Havelund, K., Huisman, M., Monahan, R.: Static and runtime verification, competitors or friends? (Track Summary). In: Margaria, T., Steffen, B. (eds.) ISoLA 2016. LNCS, vol. 9952, pp. 397–401. Springer, Cham (2016). https://doi.org/10.1007/978-3-319-47166-2_27

19. Howar, F., Giannakopoulou, D., Mues, M., Navas, J.: Generating component interfaces by integrating static and symbolic analysis, learning, and runtime monitoring. In: Margaria, T., Steffen, B. (eds.) ISoLA 2018. LNCS, vol. 11245, pp. 120–136. Springer, Cham (2018)

20. Maurica, F., Cok, D., Signoles, J.: Runtime assertion checking and static verification: collaborative partners. In: Margaria, T., Steffen, B. (eds.) ISoLA 2018. LNCS, vol. 11245, pp. 75–91. Springer, Cham (2018)

21. Rupprecht, T., Chen, X., White, D.H., Boockmann, J.H., Lüttgen, G., Bos, H.: DSIbin: identifying dynamic data structures in C/C++ binaries. In: Rosu, G., Penta, M.D., Nguyen, T.N. (eds.) Proceedings of the 32nd IEEE/ACM International Conference on Automated Software Engineering, ASE 2017, Urbana, IL, USA, 30 October–3 November 2017, pp. 331–341. IEEE Computer Society (2017)

Monitoring Hyperproperties
by Combining Static Analysis
and Runtime Verification

Borzoo Bonakdarpour[1]([⊠]), Cesar Sanchez[2], and Gerardo Schneider[3]

[1] Iowa State University, Ames, USA
borzoo@iastate.edu
[2] IMDEA Software Institute, Madrid, Spain
cesar.sanchez@imdea.org
[3] University of Gothenburg, Gothenburg, Sweden
gerardo@cse.gu.se

Abstract. Hyperproperties are properties whose reasoning involve sets
of traces. Examples of hyperproperties include information-flow security
properties, properties of coding/decoding systems, linearizability and
other consistency criteria, as well as privacy properties like data minimality. We study the problem of runtime verification of hyperproperties
expressed as HyperLTL formulas that involve quantifier alternation. We
first show that even for a simple class of temporal formulas, virtually no
$\forall\exists$ property can be monitored, independently of the observations performed. To manage this problem, we propose to use a combination of
static analysis with runtime verification. By using static analysis/verifi-
cation, one typically obtains a model of the system that allows to limit
the source of "hypothetical" traces to a sound over-approximation of the
traces of the system. This idea allows to extend the effective monitorability of hyperproperties to a larger class of systems and properties. We
exhibit some examples where instances of this idea have been exploited,
and discuss preliminary work towards a general method. A second contribution of this paper is the idea of departing from the convention that
all traces come from executions of a single system. We show cases where
traces are extracted from the observed traces of agents, from projections
of a single global trace, or from executions of different (but related)
programs.

1 Introduction

In this paper, we study how to monitor hyperproperties [19], in particular $\forall\exists$
and $\exists\forall$ fragments of the temporal logic HyperLTL [18]. A *monitor* is a piece of
software that observes and analyzes execution traces of a system under analysis
(called the *monitored system*). In particular, we are concerned with *runtime verification*, that aims to determine whether the given monitored program satisfies a
pre-defined property expressed in a behavioral specification language. Monitors

© Springer Nature Switzerland AG 2018
T. Margaria and B. Steffen (Eds.): ISoLA 2018, LNCS 11245, pp. 8–27, 2018.
https://doi.org/10.1007/978-3-030-03421-4_2

may analyze the executions of the program *online* (while the program is running) or *offline* (the execution traces of the program are collected and analyzed a-posteriori)[1]. In runtime verification, the monitor is generated automatically from the property, written in a formal language, usually as a logical formula or as an automaton. As in testing, runtime verification may be *black box* or *white box*, depending on whether the monitor can only observe the behavior of the system (the input-output events or states), or whether the monitor has additionally access to the internals of the monitored program.

In the context of trace logics (where properties can be evaluated independently on each individual trace) it is known that not all properties are *monitorable*, because the monitors can only observe finite prefixes of executions. Monitorability means that there exists a monitor that can declare correctly whether the property is permanently satisfied or violated in all future extensions of the observed prefix traces. Previous results in trace logics show how to build monitors for some combinations of *safety* and *co-safety* properties. Formalisms proposed for generating monitors include, among others, LTL adapted for finite paths [9,23,29], regular expressions [43], rule based languages [7], rewriting [40], streams [21] and automata [20].

In this paper, we study a richer class of properties called *hyperproperties* [19], that is, properties of sets of traces instead of over individual traces. Many security properties, like *information-flow* properties such as *non-interference*, are hyperproperties. In particular, many of the common and interesting security properties are *2-safety* hyperproperties [19], meaning that it can be expressed using universal quantification over pairs of finite traces. Monitoring hyperproperties requires to collect and reason about multiple finite runs, and not only to collect and reason about a single run. As with trace logics, there is a source of uncertainty because the traces under observation are finite and correspond to a prefix of execution. However, in monitoring hyperproperties there is an additional source of imperfect observability because if the collection of traces is approximated dynamically by the traces executed, it is possible that the set also contains traces that have not been observed.

It has been shown that it is possible to construct monitors for $\forall\forall$ hyperproperties if the temporal formula is restricted to safety [1,12,26], where some limitations of monitorability are also explored. In particular, one cannot—in general—determine at runtime whether a $\forall\forall$ property is satisfied because this may require to obtain all possible executions of the system. However, one can monitor $\forall\forall$ safety properties for violations.

In this paper, we show that $\forall\exists$ (and $\exists\forall$) are not monitorable in general. Then, we explore new ideas on how to monitor properties of the form $\forall\exists$ by using a *grey box* approach, that is by exploiting *certain* information we have about the system to perform the monitoring task. This additional information

---

[1] The definition of offline monitoring also includes when traces are obtained from other sources than the program running in its real environment (e.g., in a simulation environment, or traces not coming from the real program but from a model, for instance).

can be represented as a model or specification of the system under analysis, which soundly approximates the set of runs of the actual system. We identify at least two different cases for how to use such models depending on their nature: (i) when the model is the formal specification of the ideal (expected) behavior of the program; (ii) when the model is extracted statically from the given program. These models can be used as a kind of *oracle* to instantiate one of the quantifiers of the specified property. Consider, for example, the goal of detecting violations of a $\forall\exists$ property. The first step is to complement the property and detect satisfactions of the $\exists\forall$ dual property. Then, at runtime, one can use the observed trace as a prefix of a witness for the outermost quantifier (the $\exists$ quantifier), and use the model to then safely check whether all traces satisfy the temporal relational formula. If the model indeed over-approximates the actual set of traces of the system, this approach can monitor violations of the $\forall\exists$ property. Then, the approach we propose reduces the monitoring activity to efficiently check the model at runtime. We exhibit in this paper examples where bounded model checking could be used, and others where symbolic execution and SAT solvers may be used. We also discuss directions for developing solutions with general applicability.

Finally, we depart from the standard view of hyperproperties, where traces that can instantiate the quantifiers are traditionally taken from the set of executions of the very same program (that is, from the program being monitored). Some other works on "relational verification" have also considered traces coming from different programs (see [10]). Here, we generalize this view allowing different quantifiers to be instantiated with traces from different "trace sets". One particular case is the monitoring approach sketched above where one set of traces is taken from the execution of the system under observation, while the other set of traces are runs of the model. Other instances are possible, and we discuss some in this paper. For example, if different quantifiers can be instantiated with the observations of different processes, threads, nodes, or agents, many properties of concurrent and distributed systems (e.g., mutual exclusion) can be viewed as hyperproperties. We argue that this interpretation makes sense in practice, as the traces coming from the different (distributed or concurrent) processes are not always available at the same time to compute a global trace view, or they are simply not available because we only have access to the local information of a given process.

The rest of the paper is organized as follows. Section 2 presents the challenges faced when monitoring hyperproperties, particularly when $\forall\exists$ properties are considered. Section 3 presents examples of hyperproperties and how the approach of instantiating quantifiers with different trace sets can lead to hyperproperties. Section 4 elaborates on the idea of combining static and dynamic analysis for monitoring two concrete hyperproperties, namely, linearizability and data minimization. Section 5 outlines potential techniques to monitor more general fragments of HyperLTL formulas. Finally, Sect. 6 presents related work and Sect. 7 concludes.

2   The Challenge of Monitoring Hyperproperties

In this section, we discuss the notion of monitorability in runtime verification of trace properties and of hyperproperties.

2.1   Monitoring Trace Properties

We first revisit monitorability of trace properties. We focus on LTL [31,37] as a representative language. Let u be a finite execution trace and φ be an LTL formula. If all infinite traces extending u satisfy φ, then we say that u *permanently* or *inevitably satisfies* φ. Similarly, if all infinite extensions of u violate φ, then we say that u *permanently violates* φ. Monitoring consists of declaring, whether u permanently satisfies or permanently violates φ, or neither. The latter occurs when there exists a future extension to u that satisfies φ and another future extension of u that violates φ. For instance, consider the LTL formula $\varphi = a \, \mathbf{U} \, b$ and the finite trace $u = aaa$. This trace can be extended to trace $u' = aaab$, which permanently satisfies φ, or can be extended to $u'' = aaa(\neg a \wedge \neg b)$, which permanently violates φ.

Pnueli and Zaks [38] characterize an LTL formula φ as *monitorable* for a finite trace u, if u can be extended to another finite trace that either permanently satisfies or permanently violates φ. We call the extension $u\sigma$ of an observation u a *trace extension*. For example, the LTL formula $\Diamond p$ is monitorable, since every finite trace u can be extended to one of the form $u \cdots p \cdots$, i.e., a finite trace in which p has become true. Conversely, formula $\Box\Diamond p$ is not monitorable, because there is no way to tell at run time whether or not in the future p will be visited infinitely often.

The above discussion clarifies the challenges in RV for LTL formulas: monitoring an LTL formula boils down to determining the verdict of the formula for a finite trace with an eye on the possible future extensions. Consequently, a system can be monitored in a *black box* manner with respect to a rich class of LTL formulas. In LTL monitoring, the monitor only needs to observe a single evolving trace of the system without having access to the code. In the next subsection, we show that this is not the case for hyperproperties.

2.2   Monitoring Hyperproperties

We focus now on HyperLTL [18] as a representative language for hyperproperties. Consider the HyperLTL formula:

$$\varphi_1 = \forall \pi. \forall \pi'. \Box(a_\pi \leftrightarrow a_{\pi'})$$

Intuitively, this formula requires that for any instantiation of trace variables π and π', say to concrete traces u and u', the value of proposition a in the i-th position of u should agree with the value of a in the i-th position of u'. For example, let $u = (\neg a)(\neg a)(a)(\neg a)(a)$ and $u' = (\neg a)(a)(a)(\neg a)(a)$. This pair of finite traces permanently violates φ because u and u' do not agree on *a* in the second position of the traces. Thus, if a HyperLTL formula φ is only universally quantified and its inner LTL formula is monitorable for violations (for traces of pairs of states), then φ can be monitored for violations. Declaring satisfaction for such a formula requires, in principle, examining *all* traces, which essentially becomes infeasible at run time. Even if the monitor could decide that for all trace extensions of pairs of traces seen, the inner property holds, it cannot know whether offending pairs of traces can be potentially emitted by the system. Dually, for an existential HyperLTL formula only satisfaction (but not violation) can be detected, and only if the inner formula is monitorable for satisfaction.

Consider now the following HyperLTL formula with one quantifier alternation

$$\varphi_2 = \forall \pi . \exists \pi' . \square(a_\pi \leftrightarrow \neg a_{\pi'})$$

and consider the same traces $u = (\neg a)(\neg a)(a)(\neg a)(a)$ and $u' = (\neg a)(a)(a)(\neg a)(a)$. These traces do not satisfy the inner temporal formula, that is (u, u') permanently violates $\square(a_\pi \leftrightarrow \neg a_{\pi'})$. However, this fact alone is not a witness for a violation of φ_2. For instance, a trace $u'' = (a)(a)(\neg a)(a)(\neg a)$ is (at least as a prefix) a perfect witness for $\exists \pi'$. A formula like φ_2 can never be declared permanently satisfied or violated, simply because at run time, it is not possible to tell whether for *all* traces, there exists another trace that satisfies the inner LTL formula. Thus, in addition to challenges of LTL monitoring, Hyper-LTL monitoring involves reasoning about quantified traces and future extensions not just in length, but also in the observed set of traces. Agrawal and Bonakdarpour [1] defined monitorability of HyperLTL as follows:

> A HyperLTL formula φ is *monitorable* for violation if every finite set U of finite traces can be extended to another finite set of finite traces U' (both by extending traces in U and by adding new traces) that guarantees that every extension of U' violates φ.

The definition for monitorability for satisfaction is analogous. An important limitation of this definition (and the work in [1]) is that the technique is restricted to the *alternation-free* fragment, that is, to formulas of the form $\forall\forall$ or formulas of the form $\exists\exists$. When considering hyperproperties with alternating quantifiers, this notion of monitorability is no longer useful: even the simplest temporal properties in the $\forall\exists$ fragment turn out to be non-monitorable.

We sketch now a very general result about the impossibility of monitoring $\forall\exists$ hyperproperties. Consider a (relational) state predicate $P(x, x')$ on two copies of variables. The intuition of such a predicate P is to represent a relational invariant between the corresponding states in two traces. Without loss of generality, assume that P is such that for every valuation v there is a valuation v' that makes $P(v, v')$ true. Also, assume that if one plugs the same valuation v to x and x', then the predicate $P(v, v)$ is false (we call such P an irreflexive relational predicate). Irreflexivity is not a restriction because every predicate P can be extended into $(P \wedge (b \leftrightarrow \neg b'))$ by introducing a fresh Boolean variable b, so if the same valuation is introduced to all variables (including b) the extended predicate evaluates to false.

We claim that the following formula is not monitorable

$$\psi = \forall \pi \exists \pi'. \Box P(x_\pi, x_{\pi'})$$

Consider an arbitrary finite set of finite traces U collected by the monitor. We show that U has a model U_{good} (set of infinite traces) that violates ψ and an extension U_{bad} that satisfies ψ. Since the monitor cannot distinguish which of the two the system can generate, the monitor cannot declare a conclusive verdict.

- We first show that U can be extended to a set of traces U_{bad} that violates ψ. Assume that all traces in U have the same length (otherwise simply add arbitrary padding states to the shorter traces). Then, create U' by adding the same state a extending every observed trace in U. Since $P(a, a)$ is false, every pair of traces in U falsifies $\Box P(x_\pi, x_{\pi'})$. The set U_{bad} is obtained by extending U' to infinite traces arbitrarily. This shows that ψ cannot be monitored for satisfaction because every observation U can be extended to a counterexample.
- We show now that U can be extended to a model U_{good} that satisfies ψ, by taking the set of all executions. It is easy to see the set of all executions satisfies ψ as every trace σ has a corresponding trace σ' that satisfies $\Box P(x_\pi, x_{\pi'})$. One can simply make, for all positions i in the trace, $\sigma'(i)$ the assignment to the state variables that make $P(\sigma(i), \sigma'(i))$ true. This shows that ψ cannot be monitored for violations because every observation U can be extended to a model.

Since ψ cannot be monitored for violation or for satisfaction, ψ is not monitorable.

The above discussion illustrates a challenge in RV for HyperLTL formulas: monitoring a HyperLTL formula boils down to determining the verdict of the formula (either satisfaction of violation) for a finite set of finite traces with an eye on the future extensions in both size and length. Consequently, HyperLTL monitoring cannot be implemented as a *black box* technique for virtually any formulas with quantifier alternations. Thus, we advocate for the development of *grey box* techniques, where the monitor observes a set of traces at run time, and can use some static information about the system under observation to narrow down the class of plausible systems (in order to be able to determine the verdict). In this paper, we argue that such an approximation is possible by using static analysis/verification techniques.

3   Examples of Hyperproperties

We show here examples of hyperproperties, some of which are $\forall\forall$, others are $\forall\exists$, and one $\forall\forall\exists$. Some of these hyperproperties follow the "standard" viewpoint in which traces are alternative executions of a single system under observation

(Sect. 3.1). Others, however, are obtained by taking a different point of view (Sect. 3.2): different quantifiers can be instantiated with traces from different systems, or from different components of a running system (e.g., the traces of execution of two threads).

3.1   Classic Examples

In this subsection, we present requirements that are inherently hyperproperties regardless of how execution traces are collected.

Information-Flow Security. Information-flow security properties stipulate how information may propagate from inputs to outputs. Such policies may belong to alternation-free as well as alternating HyperLTL formulas. For example, let the observable input to a system be the atomic proposition i and the output the atomic proposition o. Then, *observational determinism* can be expressed as the following alternation-free HyperLTL formula:

$$\varphi_{\text{obs}} = \forall \pi. \, \forall \pi'. \, \Box \, (i_\pi \leftrightarrow i_{\pi'}) \, \rightarrow \, \Box \, (o_\pi \leftrightarrow o_{\pi'}),$$

This formula establishes that if two traces π and π' agree globally on i, then they must also globally agree on o. Following the discussion in Sect. 2, the formula φ_{obs} can be monitored to detect violations, but not satisfaction. On the other hand, Goguen and Meseguer's *noninterference* [28] (GMNI) stipulates that, for all traces, the low-observable output must not change when all high inputs are removed:

$$\varphi_{\text{gmni}} = \forall \pi. \exists \pi'. (\Box \lambda_{\pi'}) \wedge \Box (o_\pi \leftrightarrow o_{\pi'})$$

where $\lambda_{\pi'}$ expresses that all of the secret inputs in the current state of π' have dummy value λ, and o denotes publicly observable output propositions. GMNI is clearly an alternating formula and following the discussion in Sect. 2 cannot be monitored using a blackbox technique. We refer the reader to [11] for examples of security properties that result in HyperLTL formulas with more quantifier alternations.

Linearizability. Informally, linearizability is a consistency model for concurrent data structures and distributed transactions and establishes that every concurrent execution of a given datatype is *observationally equivalent* to a *sequential execution* of the same datatype (or of a specified datatype like a list, set, stack, etc.). Here, observationally equivalent means that all values returned by methods of the datatype when executed concurrently are the same values returned by some sequential execution of the same client behavior. Similarly, sequential execution means that each method invocation is run to completion atomically and uninterruptedly once the internal execution of the method starts. Formally, linearizability is a hyperproperty of the form:

$$\varphi_{\text{lz}} = \forall \pi. \exists \pi'. Seq(\pi') \wedge Obs(\pi, \pi') \tag{1}$$

The first observation in (1) is that for trace variables π and π' to be observationally equivalent (as denoted by $Obs(\pi, \pi')$) the instructions that threads execute outside an invocation to the datatype or internally within the body of the datatype are not visible. Only the execution of calls and returns are visible, and $Obs(\pi, \pi')$ claim that these events are identical in both traces.

3.2   Hyperproperties Obtained by Different Source of Traces

Properties of Concurrent and Distributed Systems. Consider the well-known *mutual exclusion* requirement, where two processes cannot be in the critical section at the same time. This requirement is a safety trace property and can be expressed in LTL by the following formula:

$$\Box(\neg cs_1 \vee \neg cs_2),$$

where cs_i for $i \in \{1, 2\}$ indicates that process i is in the critical section. This formula expresses mutual exclusion over the global states of the system. However, in many concurrent and distributed systems, traces are collected from individual processes or computing cores because in some circumstances it is not easy or even possible to construct interleaved traces. This way, it is more convenient to express a requirement such as mutual exclusion as a hyperproperty where traces correspond to local executions. Thus, mutual exclusion can be expressed in HyperLTL by formula

$$\varphi_{\mathsf{me}} = \forall \pi.\forall \pi'.\Box(\neg cs_\pi \vee \neg cs_{\pi'}),$$

where π and π' are traces collected from two different processes, cores, or threads.

A similar example is *data races*. A data race happens when there are two memory accesses (at least one being a write) performed concurrently by two threads, to the same location and that are not protected by synchronization operations. For a given memory location, this property can be expressed as a $\forall\forall$ property where traces are the local executions of the threads.

Some examples of $\forall\exists$ properties in the setting of concurrent and distributed systems include the following:

- *Egalitarian schedulers.* Some problems in distributed systems can only be solved by breaking symmetries, like for example to exploit in a predictable way that process identifiers are ordered. However, one may wish that the system does not penalize a process unnecessarily (which for example could cause starvation). One way to express that a scheduler or resource manager does not unnecessarily favor a process over another is to express that for all excutions (of the system) there is an alternative execution (of the same system), where the actions taken by the scheduler to break symmetries are reversed.
- *Reads preceded by writes.* For any trace with a read on a given register, there must exist a trace with a write on that register performed in a previous moment.

– *Resource waiting.* If a process is blocked waiting for a resource, then there must exist another process that acquired that resource in the past and still holds the resource at the time the first process is waiting for it.

Data Minimization. We present now another instance of alternating hyper-properties from a different context, namely privacy. According to the Article 5 of the *General Data Protection Regulation* proposal (GDPR) "Personal data must be [...] limited to what is necessary in relation to the purposes for which they are processed" [25].[2] The above is usually called the *data minimization* princi-ple. Though data minimization is about both the collection and the processing of data, we are here only concerned with the former. In particular, we are taking the point of view of Antignac et al. [3,4], where the concept of a *data minimizer* has been defined as a pre-processor that filters the input of the given program in such a way that the functionality of the program does not change but the program only receives data that is necessary and sufficient for the intended com-putation. From there they derived the concept of data minimization and they showed how to obtain data minimizers for both the *monolithic* case (only one source of input) and the *distributed* case (more than one, independent, source of inputs). Note that the setting is for deterministic (functional) programs, and the different definitions are based only on the observable behavior relating inputs and outputs.

Results concerning the monitoring of violations of data minimization (i.e., *non-minimality*) for the monolithic case and the so-called *strong* distributed minimality has been studied in [35,36], so we will only focus here on the case of ("weak") distributed minimality as this is a $\forall\forall\exists\exists$ hyperproperty.

We now give a formal definition of distributed minimality as a hyperproperty. The definition is essentially equivalent to the one in [35] but rephrased to be consistent with the temporal style of HyperLTL.[3] We compare (terminating) functions with n parameters. We view a run of the funcion as a sequence of states, where the state predicate *end* denotes that the trace reaches the function final state and halts. In order to extend terminating executions to infinite traces, we repeat the halting state ad infinitum. We consider the state variables $in_1, \ldots, in_n$ to represent the inputs to the function, and the variable o, which represents the output, assigned once the function has been computed. We introduce the following auxiliary predicates

$$output(\pi, \pi') : \Diamond \Big(end(\pi) \wedge end(\pi') \wedge o(\pi) = o(\pi') \Big)$$

---

[2] The *General Data Protection Regulation* (EU—2016/679) was adopted on 27 April 2016, and it will enter into application 25 May 2018.

[3] A stronger version of distributed minimality, which is a $\forall\forall$ hyperproperty, is given in [36].

The predicate *output* establishes that the functions represented by the two traces terminate, and that the computed output is the same. Similarly, we define

$$differ_j(\pi, \pi') \; : \; in_j(\pi) \neq in_j(\pi') \qquad\qquad almost_j(\pi, \pi') \; : \; \bigwedge_{k \neq j} in_k(\pi) = in_k(\pi')$$

The predicate *differ$_j$* establishes that the inputs to the function are different in the parameter j, and *almost$_j$* that the input to the function agree on all parameters except possibly on j. Now we can define distributed minimality for input j as:

$$\phi_{dm}^j = \forall \pi. \forall \pi'. \exists \pi''. \exists \pi'''. differ_j(\pi, \pi') \rightarrow \begin{pmatrix} same_j(\pi, \pi'') \\ \wedge \\ same_j(\pi', \pi''') \end{pmatrix} \wedge \begin{pmatrix} almost_j(\pi'', \pi''') \\ \wedge \\ \neg output(\pi'', \pi''') \end{pmatrix}$$

where $same_j(\pi, \pi') = \neg differ_j(\pi, \pi')$. So, distributed minimality is defined as:

$$\varphi_{dm} \; : \; \bigwedge_{j=1..n} \varphi_{dm}^j.$$

Example 1 (From [35]). Consider the function $OR : \mathbb{B} \times \mathbb{B} \rightarrow \mathbb{B}$ function, which was shown not to be monolithic minimal [3,4]. This function is distributed-minimal. We have two input sources I_1 and I_2 both of sort $\mathbb{B}$. For the first input source, for each possible pair of distinct values in that position (that is $(0, \_)$ and $(1, \_)$), we can find satisfactory input tuples yielding different results (e.g., $((0,0),(1,0))$ since $OR(0,0) \neq OR(1,0))$.[4] Similarly, for input source 2, for each possible pair of distinct values in that position $((\_, 0)$ and $(\_, 1))$, we have that the tuples $(0,0)$ and $(0,1)$ satisfy the definition $(OR(0,0) \neq OR(1,0))$. □

Distributed non-minimality is simply the negation of the above formula, and thus a ∃∃∀∀ formula. As previously discussed, none of these properties (distributed minimality and its negation) are monitorable in a black-box fashion.

4   Examples of Monitoring with the Aid of Static Verification

We present two practical case studies that exploit static information to perform monitoring of specific hyperproperties.

4.1   Monitoring Linearizability

We propose the following combination of static and runtime verification to monitor linearizability violations:

---

[4] Note that the pair $((0,1),(1,1))$ would not satisfy the definition, but this is fine as the definition only requires that at least one such tuple exists.

```
                                              Item pop () {
                                                Node * hd;
                                                Node * new_hd;
void push (Item e) {                            do {
  Node * new_hd = new Node(e);                      hd = top.get();
  Node * hd;                                        if (hd == null) {
  do {                                                  return null;
      hd = top.get();                               }
      new_hd->next = hd;                            new_hd = hd.next;
  }                                               }
  while (!CAS(top, hd, new_hd));                 while (!CAS(top, hd, new_hd));
}                                                return hd.item;

                                              }
```

Fig. 1. Treiber stack implementation

1. First, the code of the concurrent datatype is *statically verified* to satisfy the pre-post specification of the programming abstraction that the datatype is meant to implement, under the assumption of sequential invocations. This activity can be performed with mature deductive verification techniques for sequential programs, using for example the KeY infrastructure for Java programs [2].
2. Then, at *run time*, a *monitor* receives events about calls and returns from concurrent clients that exercise the concurrent datatype. This monitor exhaustively explores the set of possible sequences of atomic executions (*using the specification*) that are observationally equivalent to the visible events in the observed concurrent trace.

We illustrate this approach with a concrete example, the Treiber stack [44]. It is easy to prove using state-of-the-art deductive verification that the code in Fig. 1—when executed sequentially—implements a stack. Then, at runtime, the monitor we propose works as follows.

1. The monitor maintains a set of possible states that the datatype may be into. In our example, the state will be concrete stacks. Additionally, the state of the monitor also contains two sets:
   - Pending operations of the form $(t, f, args)$, where t is a thread identifier, f the name of the method that t is executing and $args$ is the arguments to the method;
   - Operations effectively executed but not yet returned, stored as (t, f, val) where t and f are as above, and val is the returned value.
   Each tuple $(State, Pending, Executed)$ is a *plausible state* of the monitor, where *State* represents the state of the stack, *Pending* represents the pending operations, and *Executed* the operations that were performed effectively on the object but whose return have not been observed yet.
2. The initial state of the monitor is the empty stack with no pending or executed operations. This is the only plausible initial state.

3. When an operation invocation occurs in the observed trace, denoted by the execution of the instruction that calls the method from the calling thread, *every* plausible state maintained by the monitor is extended by adding the invoked operation to its pending set.
4. When an operation finishes in the observed trace, as observed by the return instruction being executed, the monitor computes—for each plausible state— the following possible successors. A successor consists on executing, in some order, a subset of the pending operations followed by the observed operation. The output of the observed operation must be equal to the observed value, otherwise the successor does not correspond to the observed outcome and it is removed from the plausible set.

If, at some point the set of plausible states is empty, then there is a violation of linearizability. For example, consider the following execution:

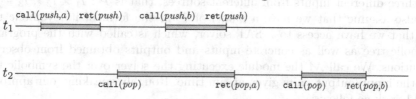

The state of the monitor after the event "call($push,b$)" executed by thread t_1 will be $\langle(a), \{(t_2, pop), (t_1, push, b)\}, \emptyset\rangle$. This state reflects that the stack contains only a and that there are two pending operations. After the observable event "ret($push$)" is executed, the monitor computes the following plausible states: $\langle(b : a), (t_2, pop), \emptyset\rangle$ and $\langle(b), \emptyset, (t_2, pop, a)\rangle$ Only later, when the pending pop operation is observed to return an a, the first plausible state is discarded by the monitor because executing the pop from state $(b : a)$ would return b and not a.

Consider now an incorrect implementation of the CAS (compare-and-swap) operation that is non-atomic. In this case, the following execution could be generated (hint: thread t_2 is preempted in the middle of the CAS operation):

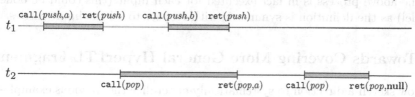

In this case, the monitor would raise a violation of linearizability. as none of the two plausible states can lead to the event "ret(pop,**null**)" by t_2. The fact that the previous *pop* returned a means that the *pop* happened "logically" before the push b and therefore the subsequent *pop* must return b and not **null**.

4.2   Monitoring Data Minimization

We now present a second example based on detecting violations of data minimization. In [3,4] Antignac et al. provided a white-box approach to statically synthesize a minimizer for the different notions of data minimization. The problem of finding a minimizer is undecidable in general, and thus the approach only works for very specific cases. In a nutshell, the approach consists in extracting the symbolic execution tree of the program under consideration and applying a SAT solver to the constraints given by such a symbolic tree by making a conjunction with the different possible outputs. Unfortunately, the approach does not scale. First, the symbolic execution is in general a coarse over-approximation of the real behavior unless the user provides more precise annotations in the form of pre- and post-conditions and invariants. Second, if the output domain is infinite or it is too big, it is not feasible to expect the SAT solver to terminate in a reasonable time.

We now sketch how this approach, apart from being interesting from a theoretical perspective can be integrated into a runtime environment in order to increase the possibility of detecting violations to minimality via monitoring. Let us assume a program $\mathcal{P}$ which for the sake of simplicity of presentation we assume has three different inputs from different sources, that is $\mathcal{P} : I_1 \times I_2 \times I_3 \to O$. We also assume that we have a model of $\mathcal{P}$ in the form of its symbolic tree and that we have access to a SAT solver, which is called with the program's symbolic tree as well as concrete inputs and outputs obtained from observed executions. We call $\mathcal{M}$ the module executing the solver over the symbolic tree and the input/output pairs given at run time. Roughly speaking, our approach would work as follows:

1. After each execution of $\mathcal{P}$, $\mathcal{M}$ gets the input/output pair $\langle (i_1, i_2, i_3), o \rangle$.
2. $\mathcal{M}$ (symbolically) executes such a pair and puts it as belonging to a given partition characterizing the inputs for the first input giving the same output.
3. Whenever an execution with a different value for the first input parameter is found but with the same output as a previous execution, then $\mathcal{M}$ is called in order to find out whether there are values for the other two input parameters giving a different output. If this is the case, then nothing can be said yet. If such values cannot be found, then distributed minimization is violated.

The above process is in fact executed for each input (this could be done in parallel) as the definition is symmetric with respect to all the input entries.

5   Towards Covering More General HyperLTL Fragments

We now sketch a direction to systematically generalize the previous examples to a wider range of properties and systems.

5.1   Predictive Semantics for LTL

Employing static analysis and verification techniques in order to enhance RV has been investigated before. For example, in [46], static analysis is introduced to allow *predictive semantics* to the 3-valued LTL, where LTL formulas are evaluated not only with respect to a runtime finite trace, but also by assistance from an abstract model of the system under inspection. The predictive semantics aims at anticipating whether the satisfaction or violation of the specification is inevitable in all continuations of the trace for the given abstract model, even when the observed execution by itself does not imply the inevitable verdict for all trace extensions. More specifically, let u be a finite trace and P be a program under inspection with respect to an LTL formula φ. Recall that the 3-valued semantics of LTL prescribes that if any future extension of u satisfies (respectively, violates) φ, then u *permanently* satisfies (respectively, violates) φ. Realistically, the future extensions of interest should only be the possible continuations of u that P can generate. One efficient way to reason about all future extensions of u in P is to compute an over-approximate abstract model of P (denoted $\widehat{P}$) and then check, given u, whether or not for all infinite extensions σ of u in the trace set of $\widehat{P}$, $u\sigma \models \varphi$ holds. If it is indeed the case that $u\sigma \models \varphi$, then we are guaranteed that u permanently satisfies φ, as the trace set of $\widehat{P}$ subsumes the trace set of P. Similarly, if for all extensions σ, we have $u\sigma \not\models \varphi$, then we can conclude that u permanently violates φ.

5.2   The $\exists\forall$ and $\forall\exists$ Fragments

As discussed in Sect. 2, most non-trivial alternating HyperLTL formulas are non-monitorable, unless we are able to have additional information about the sytem (white- or grey-box approach). We now sketch a potential grey-box approach inspired by the predictive semantics of LTL to monitor HyperLTL formulas. Let P be a program, $\varphi = \exists\pi.\forall\pi'.\psi$ be a HyperLTL formula, and u be a finite execution trace obtained at run time. In order to monitor P with respect to φ, it is sufficient to answer the following decision problem:

> *Is there an extension σ of u, such that*
> *for all executions τ of P, $(u\sigma, \tau) \models \psi$?* $(*)$

One possibility is to use a model checker to perform the necessary state exploration. Intuitively, the model to be verified is the cross product of u with an over-approximate abstract model $\widehat{P}$ in a way similar to self-composition [8][5]. Let us denote this new model by P'. We also have to modify ψ to reflect what really needs to be verified in P'. Let us denote this formula by ψ'. In summary, this approach would require algorithms that generate P' and ψ', such that $P' \models \psi'$ if and only if u is permanently satisfied (or permanently violated).

We sketch here an alternative approach using bounded model checking [17] to decide $(*)$, for a given u for a class of HyperLTL formulas. Consider a property $\varphi = \exists\pi.\forall\pi'.\psi(\pi, \pi')$, where ψ is a *co-safety* formula, for example

$$\varphi = \exists\pi.\forall\pi'.\Diamond(a_\pi \land a_{\pi'}).$$

First, observe that since ψ is a co-safety property, if a prefix (u, v) satisfies ψ, then all extensions of (u, v) will satisfy ψ as well. Then, given an over-approximation $\widehat{P}$ of P, bounded model checking (BMC) can be used to unroll $\widehat{P}$ and compute a product of u with all the traces of $\widehat{P}$ of length $|u|$. If the BMC instance declares

---

[5] We speculate that the abstract model $\widehat{P}$ may be computed using different techniques, e.g., predicate abstraction, symbolic execution, etc.

that there is no counterexample of length $|u|$, then there will be no extension that becomes a counterexample of ψ. Hence, the formula φ will be permanently satisfied and u is indeed a witness of the outermost existential quantifier. If, on the other hand, BMC produces a counterexample there are three scenarios:

1. The observation u is too short to serve as a witness for the existential quantifier. In particular, there may be extensions of u that satisfy the property φ and can be checked by the method described above.
2. The model $\widehat{P}$ has not been explored to sufficent depth to prove a satisfaction of the co-safety property ψ.
3. The approximated model $\widehat{P}$ is too coarse and includes spurious traces.

One research challenge for this approach is to explore to detect spurious counterexamples and how to refine $\widehat{P}$ to continue the exploration. Another challenge is to refine the BMC procedure to effectively compute the set of offending traces of length $|u|$ and design efficient methods to exploit this information to successive BMC queries (for lengths $|u| + 1$, etc.), thus creating an incremental approach.

Note that if the HyperLTL formula is of the form $\forall\pi.\exists\pi'.\psi(\pi, \pi')$, where ψ is a *safety* formula, then the same procedure can be used to detect violations. One such formula is $\forall\pi.\exists\pi'.\square(p_\pi \leftrightarrow p_{\pi'})$. To monitor this formula, we can compute the negation $\neg\varphi = \exists\pi.\forall\pi'.\neg\psi$. This formula is now covered by the previous case, as $\neg\psi$ is a co-safety formula. Given a runtime finite trace u, if BMC reports satisfaction, then we can conclude that φ is permanently violated by any extension of the observed trace.

5.3   More Efficient Monitoring of the ∃∃ and ∀∀ Fragments

Finally, our suggested grey-box approach can also be applied to improve the monitoring procedure for the alternation-free fragments of HyperLTL considered in [1,12,26]. Consider formula $\varphi = \exists\pi.\exists\pi'.\psi$, where ψ is a co-safety formula. Similar to the ∃∀ fragment explained above, given a runtime finite trace u, one can (1) instantiate π with u, and (2) obtain a model P' by composing u with $\widehat{P}$. The difference with the ∃∀ procedure before is in handling $\exists\pi'.\psi'$. Unlike in the ∃∀ case, here, we verify whether $P' \models \neg\psi'$. If this results in a counterexample, this counterexample is a positive witness to π' and, hence, the formula φ is permanently satisfied. Analogously, we can monitor for violation of formulas of the form $\forall\pi.\forall\pi'.\psi$, where ψ' is a safety formula.

6   Related Work

Monitoring Hyperproperties. The notion of hyperproperties was introduced by Clarkson and Schneider [19]. HyperLTL [18] is a temporal logic for hyperproperties. Model checking algorithms for HyperLTL were introduced in [27]. Runtime verification algorithms for HyperLTL include both automata-based algorithms [1,26] and rewriting-based algorithms [12]. These RV approaches either work for alternation-free formulas or for alternating formulas only if the size of the trace set for monitoring does not grow. Also, the monitoring technique only considers the traces seen, whereas in our grey-box approach, the monitor may detect errors by exploring traces of the model that have not been seen.

Static Analysis. Sabelfeld et al. [42] survey the literature focusing on static program analysis for enforcement of security policies. In some cases, for example just-in-time compilation techniques and dynamic inclusion of code at runtime in web browsers, static analysis does not guarantee secure execution at runtime. Type systems, frameworks for JavaScript [15] and ML [39] are some approaches to monitor information flow. Several tools [24,32,33] add extensions such as statically checked information flow annotations to the Java language. Clark et al. [16] present verification of information flow for deterministic interactive programs. In [5], Assaf and Naumann propose a technique for designing runtime monitors based on an abstract interpretation of the system under inspection.

Dynamic Analysis. Russo et al. [41] concentrate on permissive techniques for the enforcement of information flow under flow-sensitivity. It has been shown that in the flow-insensitive case, a sound purely dynamic monitor is more permissive than static analysis. However, they show the impossibility of such a monitor in the flow-sensitive case. A framework for inlining dynamic information flow monitors has been presented by Magazinius et al. [30]. The approach by Chudnov et al. [14] uses hybrid analysis instead and argues that due to JIT compilation processes, it is no longer possible to mediate every data and control flow event of the native code. They leverage the results of Russo et al. [41] by inlining the security monitors. Chudnov et al. [13] again use hybrid analysis of 2-safety hyperproperties in relational logic. Austin and Flanagan [6] implement a purely dynamic monitor, however, restrictions such as "no-sensitive upgrade" were placed. Some techniques deploy taint tracking and labelling of data variables dynamically [34,47]. Zdancewic et al. [45] verify information flow for concurrent programs.

SME. Secure multi-execution [22] is a technique to enforce non-interference. In SME, one executes a program multiple times, once for each security level, using special rules for I/O operations. Outputs are only produced in the execution linked to their security level. Inputs are replaced by default inputs except in executions linked to their security level or higher. Input side effects are supported by making higher-security-level executions reuse inputs obtained in lower-security-level threads. This approach is sound only for deterministic languages.

7 Conclusion

We presented in this paper preliminary work on how to monitor hyperproperties that are not monitorable in general when considering a black-box approach. In particular, we considered hyperproperties with one quantifier alternation ($\forall\exists$ and

∀∀∃∃) for which we give an informal argument about their non-monitorability. We provided initial ideas on how to monitor a large class of formulas in the fragment for violation, by monitoring the negation of such a fragment for satisfaction. Our proposal is based on a suitable combination of static analysis/verification techniques with runtime verification, thus taking a grey-box approach. Additionally, our techniques consider traces coming not only from the monitored system but also from other sources. In particular, we have explored the use of a specification of the system as a trace generator for the inner universal quantifier, as well as a model obtained from the system via symbolic execution and predicate abstraction.

The main idea behind our approach is that the current real execution of the system accounts for the outermost quantifier, while a static analysis/verification is applied to explore "runs" of the model accounting for the innermost quantifier. Note that we do not claim anticipation as we might need more traces or more observations before we could get a final verdict.

Besides the above, we have departed from the view of considering global traces of concurrent and distributed systems, and consider local traces instead. In this way, many of the traditional properties of such systems can be casted as hyperproperties (e.g., mutual exclusion and data races). Some of such properties are in the fragment ∀∀ while others are of the form ∀∃.

Our main research agenda now is to generalize the approach and apply it to all the cases presented in this paper while identifying other interesting hyperproperties fitting in the fragment under consideration.

Acknowledgment. We would like to thank Sandro Stucki for his useful comments on early drafts of the paper, and in particular in formulation of the data minimisation property. This research has been partially supported by: the NSF SaTC-1813388, a grant from Iowa State University, EU H2020 project Elastest (nr. 731535), the Spanish MINECO Project "RISCO (TIN2015-71819-P)", the Swedish Research Council (*Vetenskapsrådet*) under grant Nr. 2015-04154 (*PolUser: Rich User-Controlled Privacy Policies*), and by the EU ICT COST Action IC1402 ARVI (*Runtime Verification beyond Monitoring*).

References

1. Agrawal, S., Bonakdarpour, B.: Runtime verification of k-safety hyperproperties in HyperLTL. In: CSF 2016, pp. 239–252 (2016)
2. Ahrendt, W., Beckert, B., Bubel, R., Hähnle, R., Schmitt, P.H., Ulbrich, M. (eds.) Deductive Software Verification - The KeY Book. From Theory to Practice. LNCS, vol. 10001. Springer, Cham (2016). https://doi.org/10.1007/978-3-319-49812-6
3. Antignac, T., Sands, D., Schneider, G.: Data minimisation: a language-based approach (long version). Technical report abs/1611.05642, CoRR-arXiv.org (2016)
4. Antignac, T., Sands, D., Schneider, G.: Data minimisation: a language-based approach. In: De Capitani di Vimercati, S., Martinelli, F. (eds.) SEC 2017. IAICT, vol. 502, pp. 442–456. Springer, Cham (2017). https://doi.org/10.1007/978-3-319-58469-0_30

5. Assaf, M., Naumann, D.A.: Calculational design of information flow monitors. In: CSF 2016, pp. 210–224 (2016)
6. Austin, T.H., Flanagan, C.: Efficient purely-dynamic information flow analysis. In: ACM Transaction on Programming Languages and Systems, pp. 113–124 (2009)
7. Barringer, H., Goldberg, A., Havelund, K., Sen, K.: Rule-based runtime verification. In: Steffen, B., Levi, G. (eds.) VMCAI 2004. LNCS, vol. 2937, pp. 44–57. Springer, Heidelberg (2004). https://doi.org/10.1007/978-3-540-24622-0_5
8. Barthe, G., D'Argenio, P.R., Rezk, T.: Secure information flow by self-composition. In: CSFW 2004, pp. 100–114. IEEE Computer Society Press (2004)
9. Bauer, A., Leucker, M., Schallhart, C.: Runtime verification for LTL and TLTL. ACM Trans. Softw. Eng. Methodol. **20**(4), 14 (2011)
10. Beckert, B., Klebanov, V., Ulbrich, M.: Regression verification for Java using a secure information flow calculus. In: Proceedings of the 17th Workshop on Formal Techniques for Java-Like Programs (FTfJP 2015), pp. 6:1–6:6. ACM (2015)
11. Bonakdarpour, B., Finkbeiner, B.: The complexity of monitoring hyperproperties. In: CSF 2018 (2018, to appear)
12. Brett, N., Siddique, U., Bonakdarpour, B.: Rewriting-based runtime verification for alternation-free HyperLTL. In: Legay, A., Margaria, T. (eds.) TACAS 2017. LNCS, vol. 10206, pp. 77–93. Springer, Heidelberg (2017). https://doi.org/10.1007/978-3-662-54580-5_5
13. Chudnov, A., Kuan, G., Naumann, D.A.: Information flow monitoring as abstract interpretation for relational logic. In: CSF 2014, pp. 48–62 (2014)
14. Chudnov, A., Naumann, D.A.: Information flow monitor inlining. In: Proceedings of CSF, pp. 200–214 (2010)
15. Chugh, R., Meister, J.A., Jhala, R., Lerner, S.: Staged information flow for JavaScript. In: Proceedings of PLDI, pp. 50–62 (2009)
16. Clark, D., Hunt, S.: Non-interference for deterministic interactive programs. In: Degano, P., Guttman, J., Martinelli, F. (eds.) FAST 2008. LNCS, vol. 5491, pp. 50–66. Springer, Heidelberg (2009). https://doi.org/10.1007/978-3-642-01465-9_4
17. Clarke, E.M., Biere, A., Raimi, R., Zhu, Y.: Bounded model checking using satisfiability solving. Form. Methods Syst. Des. **19**(1), 7–34 (2001)
18. Clarkson, M.R., Finkbeiner, B., Koleini, M., Micinski, K.K., Rabe, M.N., Sánchez, C.: Temporal logics for hyperproperties. In: Abadi, M., Kremer, S. (eds.) POST 2014. LNCS, vol. 8414, pp. 265–284. Springer, Heidelberg (2014). https://doi.org/10.1007/978-3-642-54792-8_15
19. Clarkson, M.R., Schneider, F.B.: Hyperproperties. J. Comput. Secur. **18**(6), 1157–1210 (2010)
20. Colombo, C., Pace, G.J., Schneider, G.: LARVA – safer monitoring of real-time Java programs (Tool Paper). In: SEFM 2009, pp. 33–37. IEEE Computer Society (2009)
21. D'Angelo, B., et al.: LOLA: runtime monitoring of synchronous systems. In: TIME 2005, pp. 166–174. IEEE CS Press (2005)
22. Devriese, D., Piessens, F.: Noninterference through secure multi-execution. In: 31st IEEE Symposium on Security and Privacy, S&P, pp. 109–124 (2010)
23. Eisner, C., Fisman, D., Havlicek, J., Lustig, Y., McIsaac, A., Van Campenhout, D.: Reasoning with temporal logic on truncated paths. In: Hunt, W.A., Somenzi, F. (eds.) CAV 2003. LNCS, vol. 2725, pp. 27–39. Springer, Heidelberg (2003). https://doi.org/10.1007/978-3-540-45069-6_3
24. Enck, W.: Taintdroid: an information-flow tracking system for realtime privacy monitoring on smartphones. ACM Trans. Comput. Syst. **32**, 5 (2014)

25. European Commission: Proposal for a Regulation of the European Parliament and of the Council on the protection of individuals with regard to the processing of personal data and on the free movement of such data (GDPR). Technical report 2012/0011 (COD). European Commission, January 2012
26. Finkbeiner, B., Hahn, C., Stenger, M., Tentrup, L.: Monitoring hyperproperties. In: Lahiri, S., Reger, G. (eds.) RV 2017. LNCS, vol. 10548, pp. 190–207. Springer, Cham (2017). https://doi.org/10.1007/978-3-319-67531-2_12
27. Finkbeiner, B., Rabe, M.N., Sánchez, C.: Algorithms for model checking Hyper-LTL and HyperCTL*. In: Kroening, D., Păsăreanu, C.S. (eds.) CAV 2015. LNCS, vol. 9206, pp. 30–48. Springer, Cham (2015). https://doi.org/10.1007/978-3-319-21690-4_3
28. Goguen, J.A., Meseguer, J.: Security policies and security models. In: Proceedings of IEEE Symposium on Security and Privacy, pp. 11–20 (1982)
29. Havelund, K., Roşu, G.: Synthesizing monitors for safety properties. In: Katoen, J.-P., Stevens, P. (eds.) TACAS 2002. LNCS, vol. 2280, pp. 342–356. Springer, Heidelberg (2002). https://doi.org/10.1007/3-540-46002-0_24
30. Magazinius, J., Russo, A., Sabelfeld, A.: On-the-fly inlining of dynamic security monitors. Comput. Secur. **31**(7), 827–843 (2012)
31. Manna, Z., Pnueli, A.: Temporal Verification of Reactive Systems. Springer, New York (1995). https://doi.org/10.1007/978-1-4612-4222-2
32. Myers, A.C.: JFlow: practical mostly-static information flow control. In: POPL 1999, pp. 228–241 (1999)
33. Myers, A.C., Liskov, B.: Complete, safe information flow with decentralized labels (1998)
34. Nair, S., Simpson, P.N.D., Crispo, B., Tanenbaum, A.S.: A virtual machine based information flow control system for policy enforcement. ENTCS **197**(1), 3–16 (2008)
35. Pinisetty, S., Antignac, T., Sands, D., Schneider, G.: Monitoring data minimisation. Technical report abs/1801.02484, CoRR-arXiv.org (2018)
36. Pinisetty, S., Sands, D., Schneider, G.: Runtime verification of hyperproperties for deterministic programs. In: FormaliSE@ICSE 2018, pp. 20–29. ACM (2018)
37. Pnueli, A.: The temporal logic of programs. In: FOCS 1977, pp. 46–67. IEEE Computer Society Press (1977)
38. Pnueli, A., Zaks, A.: PSL model checking and run-time verification via testers. In: Misra, J., Nipkow, T., Sekerinski, E. (eds.) FM 2006. LNCS, vol. 4085, pp. 573–586. Springer, Heidelberg (2006). https://doi.org/10.1007/11813040_38
39. Pottier, F., Simonet, V.: Information flow inference for ML. In: POPL 2002, pp. 319–330 (2002)
40. Roşu, G., Havelund, K.: Rewriting-based techniques for runtime verification. Autom. Softw. Eng. **12**(2), 151–197 (2005)
41. Russo, A., Sabelfeld, A.: Dynamic vs. static flow-sensitive security analysis. In: CSF 2010, pp. 186–199 (2010)
42. Sabelfeld, A., Myers, A.C.: Language-based information-flow security. IEEE J. Sel. Areas Commun. **21**(1), 5–19 (2003)
43. Sen, K., Roşu, G.: Generating optimal monitors for extended regular expressions. ENTCS **89**(2), 226–245 (2003)
44. Treiber, R.K.: Systems programming: coping with parallelism. Technical report RJ 5118, IBM Almaden Research Center, April 1986
45. Zdancewic, S., Myers, A.C.: Observational determinism for concurrent program security. In: Computer Security Foundations Workshop, pp. 29–43 (2003)

46. Zhang, X., Leucker, M., Dong, W.: Runtime verification with predictive semantics. In: Goodloe, A.E., Person, S. (eds.) NFM 2012. LNCS, vol. 7226, pp. 418–432. Springer, Heidelberg (2012). https://doi.org/10.1007/978-3-642-28891-3_37
47. Zhu, Y., Jung, J., Song, D., Kohno, T., Wetherall, D.: Privacy scope: a precise information flow tracking system for finding application leaks. Technical report, EECS Department, University of California, Berkeley, October 2009

Temporal Reasoning on Incomplete Paths

Dana Fisman[1($\boxtimes$)] and Hillel Kugler[2($\boxtimes$)]

[1] Ben-Gurion University, Be'er-Sheva, Israel
dana@cs.bgu.ac.il
[2] Bar-Ilan University, Ramat-Gan, Israel
hillelk@biu.ac.il

Abstract. Semantics of temporal logic over truncated paths (i.e. finite paths that correspond to prefixes of computations of the system at hand) have been found useful in incomplete verification methods (such as bounded model checking and dynamic verification), in modeling hardware resets, and clock shifts and in online and offline monitoring of cyber-physical systems. In this paper we explore providing semantics for temporal logics on other types of incomplete paths, namely incomplete ultimately periodic paths, segmentally broken paths and combinations thereof. We review usages of temporal logic reasoning in systems biology, and explore whether systems biology can benefit from the suggested extensions.

1 Introduction

In 1977, in his seminal paper [47], Pnueli suggested to use temporal logic for reasoning about programs or systems. The term *reactive systems* [35,48] was later coined for the variety of systems considered. A reactive system is a system interacting with an environment in an ongoing manner. The resulting computation can thus be captured by an infinite path, and hence temporal logic formulas were originally defined over infinite paths.

To cope with systems that may exhibit terminating behaviors, semantics of temporal logic over finite *maximal* paths was proposed [44]. The extension of the semantics of infinite paths to finite paths concentrates on the temporal operator *next*. On an infinite path there is always a next time point while the same does not hold on a finite path. Thus, two versions of the *next* operator were suggested, the strong version $\underline{X}\,\varphi$ demands that there exists a next time point and that φ holds on that point, while the weak version $\overline{X}\,\varphi$ stipulates that if there exists a next time point that φ holds on that point. The *until* operator already comes with a strong ($\underline{U}$) and a weak ($\overline{W}$) version, and as expected $p\,\underline{U}\,q$ holds on a finite path if at some point on the path (before it ended) q holds and up until then p holds.

In 2003, it was observed that in many cases it is required to evaluate temporal logic formulas over finite truncated paths [22]. For instance, in incomplete methods of verification, such as bounded model checking and dynamic verification the considered paths are prefixes of computations of the system at hand.

© Springer Nature Switzerland AG 2018
T. Margaria and B. Steffen (Eds.): ISoLA 2018, LNCS 11245, pp. 28–52, 2018.
https://doi.org/10.1007/978-3-030-03421-4_3

Thus, they are not *maximal*, but *truncated*. Other early motivations for reasoning over truncated paths are operators such as hardware resets and clock shifts, that on an abstract level may be seen as truncating a path. On a truncated path not only we may not have a next time point, we may also not have a current time point, since the path can be empty (e.g. if truncated by a reset occurring on the very first cycle). This can easily be solved by introducing also weak and strong versions of atomic propositions or more generally [31], by introducing the operators $\underline{X}^i\varphi$ and $\underline{X}^i\varphi$ for $i \geq 0$. It is less obvious how to handle, or what semantics to give the *until* operator on a truncated path. Consider the formula $\varphi = (p\,\underline{U}\,q)$ and a truncated path w where p holds all along and q never does. In some cases, e.g. on a test w that was designed to be long enough for q to hold, we would like to say that φ does not hold, but in other cases. e.g. when we have no knowledge on the truncation point, we would like to say that φ holds (supporting the intuition that the fault of dis-satisfaction of q is in the test, not the system).

The approach advocated in [22] was to interpret a formula not just with regard to a path but also with regard to a *view*. The semantics considers three possible views: *weak, neutral* and *strong*. The views differ in their evaluation in cases where there is *doubt* regarding the satisfaction of the formula on an extension of the path. The *weak view* interprets the formula under the assumption that the test *is not* long enough to exhibit all the requested eventualities, and "forgives" unsatisfied eventualities, thus taking an *optimistic* view regarding the possible extension of the path to a complete infinite path of the system. The *strong view* interprets the formula under the assumption that the test *is* long enough to exhibit all the requested eventualities, thus taking a *pessimistic* view regarding the suffix. The *neutral* view interprets the truncated path as if it is a maximal computation path, thus, it will require q to occur before the path ends in order for φ above to hold. The three views approach enables the system specifier to use a single set of temporal logic formulas regardless of the verification approach/tool that will be used and altering only the view (if needed) when switching between verification approaches/tools. The three views approach is part of the IEEE standards PSL [23,37] and SVA [12,38], and it is implemented in supporting verification tools (c.f. IBM, RuleBase SixthSense Edition [36] and Synopsys, VC Formal Tools [49]).

One of the properties of the truncated semantics is the *strength relation theorem* stating that if a formula holds on a given path under the strong view then it also holds under the neutral view, and that if it holds under the neutral view, then it also holds under the weak view. This theorem allows one to interpret satisfaction in a multi-valued fashion and some tools provide satisfaction answers as one of the four possibilities: *holds strongly, holds neutrally, holds weakly* also called *pending*, and *fails*.

The truncated semantics also enjoys the *prefix-extension theorem* on which we elaborate later on, topological relations reminiscent to the safety-liveness dichotomy [24,25], and relation to classification of safety formulas [22,41].

In this paper we explore extending the semantics of temporal logic to other types of incomplete paths. For instance, since most considered systems are finite state, their computation paths are ultimately periodic. That is, their paths are of the form uv^ω for some finite paths u and v. It is conceivable that one may know a prefix u' of such an ultimately periodic path, and a prefix v' of its periodic part. In Sect. 4 we provide semantics for such *incomplete ultimately periodic paths*. Another conceivable incomplete path is a path obtained by composing several finite paths, where the time elapsing from one part to another, and the behavior of the system in the unspecified times is unknown. We refer to such paths as *segmentally broken paths* and in Sect. 5 provide semantics of temporal logic on segmentally broken paths. More generally, given segments of an observed path we might want to consider the case where the complete path is ultimately periodic and the first segments correspond to fragments of the transient part and the rest of the segments correspond to fragments of the periodic part. We provide semantics for such *segmentally broken ultimately periodic paths* in Sect. 6 and show that it generalizes the semantics on truncated paths, on incomplete ultimately periodic paths, and on segmentally broken paths. The truncated semantics was studied extensively in offline and online monitoring of cyber-physical systems [19]. Cyber-physical systems exhibit continuous (as opposed to discrete) computation paths, and a prominent logic for reasoning about CPS is Signal Temporal Logic (STL) [19,43]. In Sect. 3 we provide a semantics of STL on truncated paths, and in the sections on incomplete ultimately periodic paths, segmentally broken paths and their combination we consider both LTL and STL. Finally, in Sect. 7 we review applications of temporal logic reasoning in system biology, and identify cases in which the basic truncated semantics can be considered, and other cases where the extensions for handling ultimately periodic paths and segmentally broken paths may be useful.

2   LTL over Truncated Paths (ELTL)

Let AP be a set of atomic propositions and $\Sigma = 2^{AP}$. We use Σ^∞ for $\Sigma^* \cup \Sigma^\omega$. We use $|w|$ for the number of letters in w. For $1 \leq i \leq |w|$ we use $w[i]$ for the i-th letter of w. For overflow cases, i.e. when $i < 1$ or $i > |w|$ we regard $w[i]$ as ϵ, where ϵ is the empty word. We use $w[..i]$ for the prefix of w ending in $w[i]$, $w[i..]$ for the suffix of w starting with $w[i]$ and $w[i..j]$ for the infix of w starting in $w[i]$ and ending in $w[j]$, for $1 \leq i \leq j \leq |w|$. We use $u \preceq v$ (resp. $w \succeq v$) to denote that u is a prefix of v (resp. w is an extension of v, i.e. that there exists v' such that $w = vv'$).

The logic ELTL, the LTL core of PSL, extends the syntax of LTL by (i) having two versions of the next operator: $\underline{X}\,\varphi$ (strong next) and $\underset{\sim}{X}\,\varphi$ (weak next) and (ii) adding a truncation operator $[\varphi \,\underline{T}\, b]$ that is used to evaluate φ on a path truncated on the first satisfaction of b. All the temporal operators of ELTL have weak and strong versions, and the syntax conveniently decorates an operator op by its strength so that $\underline{\text{op}}$ is a strong operator and $\underset{\sim}{\text{op}}$ is a weak operator.

Formulas of ELTL are defined as follows

$$\varphi ::= \underline{X}^i\, p \mid \neg\varphi \mid \varphi_1 \vee \varphi_2 \mid [\varphi_1\,\underline{U}\,\varphi_2] \mid [\varphi\,\underline{T}\,b]$$

for $p \in AP$, b a Boolean expression over AP and $i \in \mathbb{N}$ (we regard $\mathbb{N}$ as the set of non-negative integers, so that $0 \in \mathbb{N}$).

Additional derived operators are defined as follows:

$$\underline{X}^i\,\varphi \overset{\text{def}}{=} \neg\underline{X}^i\,\neg\varphi \qquad \varphi! \overset{\text{def}}{=} \underline{X}^0\,\varphi \qquad \underline{F}_{[i..k]}\,\varphi \overset{\text{def}}{=} \vee_{i\le j\le k}\underline{X}^i$$

$$\underline{X}\,\varphi \overset{\text{def}}{=} \underline{X}^1\,\varphi \qquad \varphi_1 \wedge \varphi_2 \overset{\text{def}}{=} \neg(\neg\varphi_1 \vee \neg\varphi_2) \qquad \underline{G}_{[i..k]}\,\varphi \overset{\text{def}}{=} \wedge_{i\le j\le k}\underline{X}^i$$

$$\underline{X}\,\varphi \overset{\text{def}}{=} \underline{X}^1\,\varphi \qquad \underline{G}\,\varphi \overset{\text{def}}{=} \neg\underline{F}\,\neg\varphi \qquad [\varphi_1\,W\,\varphi_2] \overset{\text{def}}{=} [\varphi_1\,\underline{U}\,\varphi_2] \vee \underline{G}\,\varphi_1$$

$$\varphi \overset{\text{def}}{=} \underline{X}^0\,\varphi \qquad \underline{F}\,\varphi \overset{\text{def}}{=} [true\,\underline{U}\,\varphi] \qquad [\varphi\,\underline{T}\,b] \overset{\text{def}}{=} \neg[\neg\varphi\,\underline{T}\,b]$$

2.1 Semantics Under the Three Views

The semantics of ELTL over truncated paths is given with respect to a path, a word $w \in \Sigma^\infty$ and a view $\mathsf{v} \in \{-, \cdot, +\}$, where $-$ denote the *weak view*, $\cdot$ denotes the *the neutral view* and $+$ denotes the *strong view*. For a letter $\sigma \in \Sigma$ and a proposition $p \in AP$ we define $\sigma \models p$ iff $\sigma \in 2^{AP}$ and $p \in \sigma$. We use $\langle w, \mathsf{v}\rangle \models \varphi$ to denote that φ is satisfied on the finite or infinite word w under the view v. If $\langle w, -\rangle \models \varphi$ we say that φ *holds weakly* on w, if $\langle w, \cdot\rangle \models \varphi$ we say that φ *holds neutrally* on w, and if $\langle w, +\rangle \models \varphi$ we say that φ *holds strongly* on w. For a view $\mathsf{v} \in \{-, \cdot, +\}$ we define $\overline{\mathsf{v}}$ as follows:

$$\overline{\mathsf{v}} = \begin{cases} + & \text{if } \mathsf{v} = - \\ \cdot & \text{if } \mathsf{v} = \cdot \\ - & \text{if } \mathsf{v} = + \end{cases}$$

The truncated semantics of ELTL is defined as follows [22]:

$$\langle w, \mathsf{v}\rangle \models \underline{X}^i\, p \iff \text{either } |w| > i \text{ and } w[i+1] \models p$$
$$\text{or } \mathsf{v} = - \text{ and if } |w| > i \text{ then } w[i+1] \models p$$
$$\langle w, \mathsf{v}\rangle \models \neg\varphi \iff \langle w, \overline{\mathsf{v}}\rangle \not\models \varphi$$
$$\langle w, \mathsf{v}\rangle \models \varphi_1 \vee \varphi_2 \iff \langle w, \mathsf{v}\rangle \models \varphi_1 \text{ or } \langle w, \mathsf{v}\rangle \models \varphi_2$$
$$\langle w, \mathsf{v}\rangle \models [\varphi_1\,\underline{U}\,\varphi_2] \iff \exists k.\ \langle w[k..], \mathsf{v}\rangle \models \varphi_2 \text{ and } \forall j < k.\ \langle w[j..], \mathsf{v}\rangle \models \varphi_1$$
$$\langle w, \mathsf{v}\rangle \models [\varphi\,\underline{T}\,b] \iff \text{either } \langle w, \mathsf{v}\rangle \models \varphi$$
$$\text{or } \exists j.\ \langle w[j], \mathsf{v}\rangle \models b \text{ and } \langle w[..j-1], -\rangle \models \varphi$$

Note that in the statement $\exists k$ used in the semantics of $\underline{U}$, it may be that $k > |w|$ in which case $w[k..] = \epsilon$. To see that the semantics captures the intuition consider the formula $\underline{X}^5 p$. It holds weakly on any path of length 4 or less, but it doesn't hold strongly or neutrally on such paths. The formula $\underline{X}^5 p$, on the other hand, holds on such paths under all views. But clearly $\underline{X}^5 p$ does not hold, not even weakly, on a path of length 6 where p does not hold on the sixth letter. The formula $\underline{G}\,p$ holds weakly and neutrally on every finite path where p holds all along, but it does not hold strongly on any finite path. The formula $\underline{F}\,p$ holds weakly on all finite paths, and it holds neutrally and strongly on every path where p holds at some point. The formula $[p \underline{U} q]$ holds weakly on a finite path where p holds all along and q never holds, but it does not hold neutrally or strongly on such paths, whereas the formula $[p \underline{W} q]$ holds on such paths under all views.

The $\underline{T}$ operator gives the ability to truncate a path, and evaluate the given formula under the weak view (its less often used dual $\overline{T}$ gives the ability to truncate a path and evaluate the formula under the strong view). The formula $[\varphi \underline{T} b]$ stipulates that either φ holds on the given path or b is satisfied somewhere along the path and φ holds weakly on the path truncated at the point where b first holds.

2.2 The $\top, \bot$ Approach to Defining the Three Views Semantics

There are various ways to define the semantics of temporal logic over truncated paths under the *weak*, *neutral*, and *strong* views. The definition in Sect. 2.1 follows the original formulation in [22] and provides a direct definition for each of the views. It was shown in [26] that an equivalent definition can be given by augmenting the alphabet $\Sigma = 2^{AP}$ with two special symbols $\top$ and $\bot$ such that $\top$ satisfies everything, even *false*, and $\bot$ satisfies nothing, not even *true*. We now present this definition and follow it for the rest of the paper since it provides the basis for the extensions suggested herein.

Recall that we define $\Sigma = 2^{AP}$ for a given set of atomic propositions AP. Let $\hat{\Sigma} = \Sigma \cup \{\top, \bot\}$. Let $w = a_1 a_2 a_3 \ldots$ be a word in Σ^∞. We use $\overline{w}$ for the word obtained from w by switching $\top$ with $\bot$ and vice versa. For a letter $\sigma \in \hat{\Sigma}$ and a proposition $p \in AP$ we define $\sigma \models p$ iff $\sigma = \top$ or $\sigma \in 2^{AP}$ and $p \in \sigma$.

The concatenation of two words $u, v \in \Sigma^\infty$ is denoted $u \cdot v$ or simply uv. If $u \in \Sigma^*$ then the first $|u|$ letters of uv are u and the following $|v|$ letters are v. If $u \in \Sigma^\omega$ then uv is simply u. Given two sets $U, V \subseteq \Sigma^\infty$, their concatenation is denoted $U \cdot V$ or simply UV and it is the set $\{uv \mid u \in U \text{ and } v \in V\}$. For $k > 1$ we use U^k to denote $U \cdot U^{k-1}$, where U^1 and U^0 denote U and $\{\epsilon\}$, respectively. We use U^* for $\cup_{k \geq 0} U^k$ and U^+ for $\cup_{k \geq 1} U^k$. For a set U we use U^ω for the set $\{w \in \Sigma^\omega \mid \exists u_1, u_2, u_3, u_4, \ldots \in U \text{ s.t. } w = u_1 u_2 u_3 u_4 \cdots\}$.

Under the $\top, \bot$ approach we first provide the neutral view semantics, which we denote $\models$. It is defined very similar to the direct semantics, with the exception of using $\models$ for evaluating propositions, thus taking into account the special letters $\top$ and $\bot$. The weak and strong views are then defined using concatenations with $\top^\omega$ and $\bot^\omega$ and reverting to the neutral view. The formal definition follows.

$$
\begin{aligned}
w &\models \underline{X}^i p && \Longleftrightarrow |w| > i \text{ and } w[i+1] \models p \\
w &\models \neg\varphi && \Longleftrightarrow \overline{w} \not\models \varphi \\
w &\models \varphi_1 \vee \varphi_2 && \Longleftrightarrow w \models \varphi_1 \text{ or } w \models \varphi_2 \\
w &\models [\varphi_1 \underline{U} \varphi_2] && \Longleftrightarrow \exists k. \, w[k..] \models \varphi_2 \text{ and } \forall j < k. \, w[j..] \models \varphi_1 \\
w &\models [\varphi \underline{T} b] && \Longleftrightarrow \text{ either } w \models \varphi \\
& && \qquad \text{ or } \exists j. \, w[j] \models b \text{ and } w[..j-1] \models \varphi \\
w &\models \varphi && \Longleftrightarrow w\top^\omega \models \varphi \\
w &\models \varphi && \Longleftrightarrow w\bot^\omega \models \varphi
\end{aligned}
$$

Note that we still have three views and only one semantics—the notation $w \models \varphi$ abbreviates $\langle w, - \rangle \models \varphi$, the notation $w \models^\pm \varphi$ abbreviates $\langle w, + \rangle \models \varphi$ and the notation $w \models \varphi$ abbreviates $\langle w, \cdot \rangle \models \varphi$.

Since $\top$ satisfies every Boolean expression, including *false*, the induction definition gives us that $\top^\omega$ satisfies every formula. Likewise, since $\bot$ satisfies no Boolean expression, including *true*, the induction definition gives us that $\bot^\omega$ satisfies no formula. In particular, as shown in [26] we get the exact same semantics as the one defined in Sect. 2.1.

In general the following relations hold:

Theorem 1 (The strength relation theorem [22]). *Let φ be a formula in ELTL, and w a finite or infinite word.*

$$w \models^\pm \varphi \implies w \models \varphi \implies w \models \varphi$$

Theorem 2 (The prefix/extension theorem [22]). *Let φ be a formula in ELTL, and w a finite or infinite word.*

- $w \models \varphi \iff \forall w' \preceq w. \ w' \models \varphi$
- $w \models^\pm \varphi \iff \forall w'' \succeq w. \ w'' \models^\pm \varphi$

3   Signal Temporal Logic on Truncated Paths

Signal Temporal Logic (STL). [19,43] is a logic extending LTL to reason over continuous time that is being used for online and offline monitoring of cyber-physical systems [19]. The considered models (signals) build on the idea of timed state sequences, as proposed in [3] in order to obtain a temporal logic for reasoning over real time system, that carries with it decidable verification algorithms.

3.1   Signal Temporal Logic (STL)

STL is defined over a set of variable $\mathbf{x} = \{x_1, x_2, \ldots, x_k\}$ ranging over $\mathbb{R}$. Predicates over these variables, i.e. functions from $\mathbf{x}$ to $\{\mathtt{tt}, \mathtt{ff}\}$, act as the set of atomic propositions. For instance, linear predicates are of the form $p ::= d_1 x_1 + \ldots + d_k x_k \bowtie d$ where $\bowtie \in \{<, \leq\}$, $d_1, \ldots, d_k, d \in \mathbb{R}$ and $x \in \mathbf{x}$. The syntax of STL is defined as follows:

$$\varphi ::= p(\mathbf{x}) \mid \neg \varphi \mid \varphi_1 \vee \varphi_2 \mid \varphi_1 \underline{\mathsf{U}}_I \varphi_2$$

where $p(\mathbf{x})$ is a predicate and I is an interval of $\mathbb{R}_{\geq 0}$. Given a vector $\mathbf{c} = (c_1, \ldots, c_k) \in \mathbb{R}^k$ we use $\mathbf{c} \models p(\mathbf{x})$ if the predicate p holds when the variables $x_1, \ldots, x_k$ are assigned with the real values $c_1, \ldots, c_k$.

Formulas of STL are defined over signals, which are a mapping $\alpha : \mathbb{R}_{\geq 0} \to \mathbb{R}^k$ so that, $\alpha(t)$ provides the values of all variables $x_1, \ldots, x_k$ at any time point $t \in \mathbb{R}_{\geq 0}$. It is assumed signals are non-Zeno [34], that is they cannot change infinitely many times in any bounded interval (this property is also referred to as *finite variability*).[1] The semantics of STL is defined as follows:[2]

$$\alpha, t \models p(\mathbf{x}) \qquad\qquad \Longleftrightarrow \quad \alpha(t) \models p(\mathbf{x})$$
$$\alpha, t \models \neg\varphi \qquad\qquad \Longleftrightarrow \quad \alpha, t \not\models \varphi$$
$$\alpha, t \models \varphi_1 \vee \varphi_2 \qquad\quad \Longleftrightarrow \quad \alpha, t \models \varphi_1 \text{ or } \alpha, t \models \varphi_2$$
$$\alpha, t \models [\varphi_1 \underline{\mathsf{U}}_I \varphi_2] \quad\Longleftrightarrow \quad \exists t'' \in t + I.\; \alpha, t'' \models \varphi_2 \text{ and } \forall t' \in [t, t'').\; \alpha, t' \models \varphi_1$$

The notation $\alpha \models \varphi$ abbreviates $\alpha, 0 \models \varphi$. The operator $\underline{\mathsf{U}}$ abbreviates $\underline{\mathsf{U}}_{[0,\infty)}$. Derived operators $\underline{\mathsf{F}}_I$ and $\underline{\mathsf{G}}_I$ are defined similarly to LTL. That is, $\underline{\mathsf{F}}_I \varphi$ abbreviate $[true\ \underline{\mathsf{U}}_I \varphi]$ and $\underline{\mathsf{G}}_I \varphi$ abbreviates $\neg\,\underline{\mathsf{F}}_I \neg\varphi$. Note that when $0 \in I$ then $\underline{\mathsf{U}}_I$ satisfies the following equivalence $[\varphi_1 \underline{\mathsf{U}}_I \varphi_2] \equiv \varphi_2 \vee (\varphi_1 \wedge [\varphi_1 \underline{\mathsf{U}}_I \varphi_2])$, which resembles the until fix-point characterization in LTL.

3.2 Defining STL on Truncated Paths

To define the semantics of STL over finite paths, we consider *finite signals*—these are signals which are mappings from an interval of $\mathbb{R}$ of the form $[0, t)$ to $\mathbb{R}^k$ (recall that k is the number of variables). We call the domain interval $[0, t)$ the *time duration* of α. The value $\alpha(t')$ for $t' \geq t$ is undefined. Note that the empty signal, denoted ε is the signal with time duration $[0, 0)$ which is undefined for every t. The semantics works as is and will give, for instance, that $[p\ \underline{\mathsf{U}}_{[0,7]}\ q]$ does not hold on a signal α with time duration $[0, 6)$ where $p(\alpha(t)) = true$ and $q(\alpha(t)) = false$ for all $t \in [0, 6)$.

To extend the semantics of STL to truncated paths, we need to be able to extend a given signal α with time duration $[0, t)$ to a signal with time duration $[0, \infty)$ so that all predicates p, even *false* evaluate to $\mathbf{tt}$ on any time point $t' > t$ to get the weak view, and likewise that any predicate, even *true*, evaluates to $\mathbf{ff}$ under the strong view.

We thus extend the definitions of signals to be a mapping from $\mathbb{R}_{\geq 0}$ to $\mathbb{R}^k \cup \{\top, \bot\}$, and extend the definition of $\models$ to take elements in $\mathbb{R}^k \cup \{\top, \bot\}$ as the left hand side, so that $\top \models p(\mathbf{x})$, $\bot \not\models p(\mathbf{x})$ for any predicate p and for $\mathbf{c} \in \mathbb{R}^k$ the semantics is as before, i.e. $\mathbf{c} \models p(\mathbf{x})$ if the predicate p holds when the variables $x_1, \ldots, x_k$ are assigned with the real values $c_1, \ldots, c_k$.

Next, given a finite signal $\alpha : [0, t) \to \mathbb{R}^k$ we use $\alpha^\top : \mathbb{R}_{\geq 0} \to \mathbb{R}^k \cup \{\top, \bot\}$ to denote its extensions to the signal returning $\alpha(t')$ for every $t' \in [0, t)$ and $\top$ for every $t' \geq t$. Likewise $\alpha^\bot : \mathbb{R}_{\geq 0} \to \mathbb{R}^k \cup \{\top, \bot\}$ denotes the extension of α to the signal returning $\alpha(t')$ for every $t' \in [0, t)$ and $\bot$ for every $t' \geq t$.

---

[1] See [4] for a discussion on the difference between time-event sequences and signals, and for their algebraic representation.

[2] There are various ways to define the semantics of the until operator in STL or MTL [39], differing in the type of closedness of the interval in which φ_1 is required to hold. We follow the so called *non-strict* and *non-matching* variant since it is closest to the semantics of LTL. It is shown in [32,33] that this variant is as expressive as the strict variant.

The semantics of STL over truncated semantics follows the semantics given in Sect. 3 but using $\overline{\models}$ instead of $\models$ and switching evaluations to $\bot$ with evaluations to $\top$ and vice versa when negation is evaluated. Formally, given a signal $\alpha : D \to \mathbb{R}^k \cup \{\top, \bot\}$ we use $\overline{\alpha}$ to denote the signal that returns $\alpha(t)$ for every $t \in D$ such that $\alpha(t) \in \mathbb{R}^k$, returns $\top$ for every $t \in D$ such that $\alpha(t) = \bot$ and returns $\bot$ otherwise. The truncated semantics for STL is defined as follows.

$$\alpha, t \overline{\models} p(\mathbf{x}) \iff \alpha(t) \overline{\models} p(\mathbf{x})$$
$$\alpha, t \overline{\models} \neg \varphi \iff \overline{\alpha}, t \overline{\not\models} \varphi$$
$$\alpha, t \overline{\models} \varphi_1 \vee \varphi_2 \iff \alpha, t \overline{\models} \varphi_1 \text{ or } \alpha, t \overline{\models} \varphi_2$$
$$\alpha, t \overline{\models} [\varphi_2 \underline{\mathsf{U}}_I \varphi_2] \iff \exists t'' \in t + I. \ \alpha, t'' \overline{\models} \varphi_2 \text{ and } \forall t' \in [t, t''). \ \alpha, t' \overline{\models} \varphi_1$$
$$\alpha, t \overline{\models} \varphi \iff \alpha^\top, t \overline{\models} \varphi$$
$$\alpha, t \overline{\not\models} \varphi \iff \alpha^\bot, t \overline{\models} \varphi$$

The notations $\alpha \overline{\models} \varphi$ and $\alpha \overline{\not\models} \varphi$ abbreviate $\alpha, 0 \overline{\models} \varphi$ and $\alpha, 0 \overline{\not\models} \varphi$, respectively.

We show that the strength relation theorem (Theorem 1) holds also on STL extended to reason over truncated paths.

Theorem 3 (The strength relation theorem for STL). *Let α be a finite or infinite signal, and φ an STL formula.*

$$\alpha \overline{\not\models} \varphi \implies \alpha \models \varphi \implies \alpha \overline{\models} \varphi$$

Proof (Sketch). When φ is a predicate the claim holds by the semantics of $\overline{\models}$. The complete proof follows by induction on the structure of the formula. $\square$

Given two finite signals $\alpha_1 : [0, t_1) \to \mathbb{R}^k \cup \{\top, \bot\}$ and $\alpha_2 : [0, t_2) \to \mathbb{R}^k \cup \{\top, \bot\}$ we say that α_1 is a prefix of α_2 denoted $\alpha_1 \preceq \alpha_2$ iff $t_1 \leq t_2$ and for every $t \in [0, t_1)$ it holds that $\alpha_1(t) = \alpha_2(t)$. When $\alpha_1 \preceq \alpha_2$ we also say that α_2 is an extension of α_1 and denote it $\alpha_2 \succeq \alpha_1$.

Theorem 4 (The prefix/extension theorem for STL)

- $\alpha \overline{\models} \varphi \iff \forall \alpha' \preceq \alpha. \ \alpha' \overline{\models} \varphi$
- $\alpha \overline{\not\models} \varphi \iff \forall \alpha'' \succeq \alpha. \ \alpha'' \overline{\not\models} \varphi$

Proof (Sketch). The $\Leftarrow$ directions follow trivially since $\alpha \preceq \alpha$ (for the first item) and $\alpha \succeq \alpha$ (for the second item). The proof of the $\Rightarrow$ directions is based on Proposition 10 intuitively saying that replacing a sub-interval with $\top$ helps satisfaction, and vice versa for replacing a $\bot$ sub-interval. $\square$

4 Reasoning over Incomplete Ultimately Periodic Paths

A *truncated path* is a special case of an *incomplete path* where only a prefix of the real path is observed. One can argue that other types of incomplete paths are to be considered. For instance, most systems we reason about are finite state and deterministic. As such their paths are ultimately periodic, that is they are of the form uv^ω for some finite paths u and v. It is conceivable that one may know a prefix of such a path and a prefix of the periodic part of the path. How can we reason about such incomplete paths?

4.1   Extending ELTL to Reason over Incomplete Ultimately Periodic Paths

We suggest extending the weak and strong views to such incomplete paths as well. Assume we are given two finite words u and v such that u is a prefix of the real path and v a prefix of the periodic part. In the weak view we would like to allow some unbounded number of $\top$'s between u and v and some unbounded number of $\top$'s between v and the next time v repeats. We can define the weak view semantics of such path as satisfaction of some path in $(u\top^*)(v\top^*)^\omega$ and the strong view semantics of such a path as satisfaction of all paths in $(u\bot^*)(v\bot^*)^\omega$.

Formally, given $u, v \in \Sigma^*$ we define

$$(u, v) \models_{\overline{0}} \varphi \iff \exists w \in (u\top^*)(v\top^*)^\omega.\ w \models \varphi$$

$$(u, v) \models_{\overline{0}} \varphi \iff uv^\omega \models \varphi$$

$$(u, v) \models_{\overline{0}} \varphi \iff \forall w \in (u\bot^*)(v\bot^*)^\omega.\ w \models \varphi$$

We claim that the strength relation theorem holds for the extension to incomplete ultimately periodic paths as well.

Theorem 5 (The strength relation theorem for incomplete ultimately periodic paths)

$$(u, v) \models_{\overline{0}} \varphi \implies (u, v) \models_{\overline{0}} \varphi \implies (u, v) \models_{\overline{0}} \varphi$$

Proof. Assume $(u, v) \models_{\overline{0}} \varphi$. Then by definition $\forall w \in (u\bot^*)(v\bot^*)^\omega.\ w \models \varphi$. This is true in particular for $w = uv^\omega$. Thus $(u, v) \models_{\overline{0}} \varphi$.

Assume $(u, v) \models_{\overline{0}} \varphi$. Then since $uv^\omega \in (u\top^*)(v\top^*)^\omega$ by definition of $\models_{\overline{0}}$, we get that $(u, v) \models_{\overline{0}} \varphi$. □

For pairs of words (u, v) and (u', v') in $\Sigma^* \times \Sigma^*$ we use $(u', v') \preceq (u, v)$ if $u' \preceq u$ and $v' \preceq v$. Likewise we use $(u'', v'') \succeq (u, v)$ if $u'' \succeq u$ and $v'' \succeq v$. The proof of the prefix/extension theorem for incomplete ultimately periodic paths makes use of the following claim.

Proposition 6. *Let $w \in \hat{\Sigma}^\infty$ and $\varphi \in ELTL$.*

- *Let w' be the word obtained from w by replacing one or more letters with $\top$. Then $w \models \varphi$ implies $w' \models \varphi$.*
- *Let w'' be the word obtained from w by replacing one or more letters with $\bot$. Then $w'' \models \varphi$ implies $w \models \varphi$.*

The proposition clearly holds when w consists of a single letter. The complete proof follows the inductive definition of $\models$ for ELTL.

Note that this doesn't contradict that sometime a formula may not hold on a given path but it may hold after inserting some $\bot$'s in between. For instance $X p$ doesn't hold on a path u of length one where p holds on the first cycle, but it does hold on the path $\bot u$.

Theorem 7 (The prefix/extension theorem for incomplete ultimately periodic paths)

- $(u,v) \models_{\bigcirc} \varphi \iff \forall (u',v') \preceq (u,v).\ (u',v') \models_{\bigcirc} \varphi$
- $(u,v) \models_{\bigcirc} \varphi \iff \forall (u'',v'') \succeq (u,v).\ (u'',v'') \models_{\bigcirc} \varphi$

Proof. The $\Leftarrow$ directions follow trivially since $(u,v) \preceq (u,v)$ (for the first item) and $(u,v) \succeq (u,v)$ for the second item.

For the $\Rightarrow$ directions, assume $(u,v) \models_{\bigcirc} \varphi$. Then by definition $\exists w \in (u\top^*)(v\top^*)^\omega.\ w \models \varphi$. Assume $w = (u\top^i)(v\top^j)^\omega$. Let $w' = (u'\top^{i+|u|-|u'|})(v'\top^{j+|v|-|v'|})^\omega$. It follows from Proposition 6 that $w \models \varphi$ implies $w' \models \varphi$ for any φ. Since $w' \in (u'\top^*)(v'\top^*)^\omega$ if follows that $(u',v') \models_{\bigcirc} \varphi$.

Assume $(u,v) \models_{\bigcirc} \varphi$. We have to show that $(u'',v'') \models_{\bigcirc} \varphi$ for any $(u'',v'') \succeq (u,v)$. That is we have to show that $w'' \models \varphi$ for any $w'' \in (u''\bot^*)(v''\bot^*)^\omega$. Let $w'' = (u''\bot^i)(v''\bot^j)^\omega$. Let $w = (u\bot^{i+|u''|-|u|})(v\bot^{j+|v''|-|v|})$. From $(u,v) \models_{\bigcirc} \varphi$ we get that $w \models \varphi$. It follows from Proposition 6 that $w'' \models \varphi$. $\square$

We note that the semantics over incomplete ultimately periodic paths generalizes the semantics over truncated paths, in the following sense.

Proposition 8. *Let φ be an ELTL formula, and $u \in \Sigma^*$.*

- $u \models \varphi \iff (u,\epsilon) \models_{\bigcirc} \varphi$
- $u \models \varphi \iff (u,\epsilon) \models_{\bigcirc} \varphi$
- $u \not\models \varphi \iff (u,\epsilon) \models_{\bigcirc} \varphi$

The proof is quite immediate, noting that there is a single word in $(u\top^*)(\epsilon\top)^\omega$, which is $u\top^\omega$ (and likewise for $\bot$), and that $\epsilon^\omega = \epsilon$.

4.2   Extending STL to Reason over Incomplete Ultimately Periodic Signals

To extend STL to reason over incomplete ultimately periodic signals we define for an interval D of the reals of the form $[0,t)$ the signals $D^\top$ and $D^\bot$ as follows $D^\top(t) = \top$ for any $t \in D$ and $D^\bot(t) = \bot$ for any $t \in D$. Given two signals α and β with time durations $[0,t_\alpha)$ and $[0,t_\beta)$ we define their concatenation, denoted $\alpha\beta$, to be the signal satisfying $\alpha\beta(t) = \alpha(t)$ if $t < t_\alpha$ and $\alpha\beta(t) = \beta(t - t_\alpha)$ otherwise. We extend the notion of concatenation to sets of signals Γ and Δ, so that $\Gamma\Delta = \{\gamma\delta \mid \gamma \in \Gamma \text{ and } \delta \in \Delta\}$.

We use $\mathbb{D}^\top$ and $\mathbb{D}^\bot$ to denote the set of all signals of the form $D^\top$ and $D^\bot$ respectively. For a finite signal α with time duration $[0,t_\alpha)$ we use α^ω for the infinite concatenation of α to itself. That is, $\alpha^\omega(t) = \alpha(t \bmod t_\alpha)$.

Given two signals α and β, the *weak, neutral,* and *strong* semantics for ultimately periodic signals is defined as follows:

$$(\alpha,\beta) \models_{\bigcirc} \varphi \iff \exists\gamma \in \alpha\mathbb{D}^\top(\beta\mathbb{D}^\top)^\omega.\ \gamma \models \varphi$$
$$(\alpha,\beta) \models_{\bigcirc} \varphi \iff \alpha\beta^\omega \models \varphi$$
$$(\alpha,\beta) \models_{\bigcirc} \varphi \iff \forall\gamma \in \alpha\mathbb{D}^\bot(\beta\mathbb{D}^\bot)^\omega.\ \gamma \models \varphi$$

Theorem 9 (The strength relation theorem for incomplete ultimately periodic signals)

$$(\alpha, \beta) \models^{\pm}_{\circlearrowleft} \varphi \implies (\alpha, \beta) \models^{-}_{\circlearrowleft} \varphi \implies (\alpha, \beta) \models^{+}_{\circlearrowleft} \varphi$$

Proof. Assume $(\alpha, \beta) \models^{\pm}_{\circlearrowleft} \varphi$ then $\forall \gamma \in \alpha \mathbb{D}^{\perp}(\beta \mathbb{D}^{\perp})^{\omega}$ we have that $\gamma \models \varphi$. In particular it holds for $\gamma = \alpha[0, 0)^{\perp}(\beta[0, 0)^{\perp})^{\omega} = \alpha \beta^{\omega}$. Thus $(\alpha, \beta) \models^{-}_{\circlearrowleft} \varphi$.

Assume $(\alpha, \beta) \models^{-}_{\circlearrowleft} \varphi$ then $\alpha \beta^{\omega} = \alpha[0, 0)^{\top}(\beta[0, 0)^{\top})^{\omega} \models \varphi$. Thus, there exists $\gamma \in \alpha \mathbb{D}^{\top}(\beta \mathbb{D}^{\top})^{\omega}$ such that $\gamma \models \varphi$. Hence $(\alpha, \beta) \models^{+}_{\circlearrowleft} \varphi$. $\square$

For pairs of finite signals (α, β) and (α', β') we use $(\alpha', \beta') \preceq (\alpha, \beta)$ if $\alpha' \preceq \alpha$ and $\beta' \preceq \beta$. Recall the definition of $\preceq$ between signals as given in Sect. 3.2. Likewise we use $(\alpha'', \beta'') \succeq (\alpha, \beta)$ if $\alpha'' \succeq \alpha$ and $\beta'' \succeq \beta$.

Proposition 10. *Let α be a signal over $\mathbb{R}^k \cup \{\top, \perp\}$ and $\varphi \in STL$. Assume $\alpha = \beta \gamma \delta$ for some signals β, γ, δ.*

- *Let $\alpha' = \beta D^{\top}_{\gamma} \delta$ be the signal obtained from α by replacing the middle signal γ with the signal $D^{\top}_{\gamma}$ which has the same time duration $[0, t_{\gamma})$ as γ. Then $\alpha \models \varphi$ implies $\alpha' \models \varphi$.*
- *Let $\alpha'' = \beta D^{\perp}_{\gamma} \delta$ be the signal obtained from α by replacing the middle signal γ with the signal $D^{\perp}_{\gamma}$ which has the same time duration $[0, t_{\gamma})$ as γ. Then $\alpha'' \models \varphi$ implies $\alpha \models \varphi$.*

A corollary of Proposition 10 is that $\alpha \models \varphi$ implies that $\alpha' \models \varphi$ for any α' obtained from α by replacing any number of sub-intervals of α with $\top$ intervals of the same duration, and similarly $\alpha'' \models \varphi$ implies $\alpha \models \varphi$ for any α obtained from α'' by replacing any number of $\perp$ sub-intervals of α with arbitrary signals of the same duration.

Theorem 11 (The prefix/extension theorem for incomplete ultimately periodic signals)

- $(\alpha, \beta) \models^{-}_{\circlearrowleft} \varphi \iff \forall (\alpha', \beta') \preceq (\alpha, \beta).\ (\alpha', \beta') \models^{-}_{\circlearrowleft} \varphi$
- $(\alpha, \beta) \models^{+}_{\circlearrowleft} \varphi \iff \forall (\alpha'', \beta'') \succeq (\alpha, \beta).\ (\alpha'', \beta'') \models^{+}_{\circlearrowleft} \varphi$

Proof. The $\Leftarrow$ direction follows trivially. We prove the $\Rightarrow$ direction. We assume here that the time duration of a signal γ is $[0, t_{\gamma})$.

Assume $(\alpha, \beta) \models^{-}_{\circlearrowleft} \varphi$. And let α' and β' be such that $\alpha' \preceq \alpha$ and $\beta' \preceq \beta$. Then by definition $\exists \gamma \in \alpha \mathbb{D}^{\top}(\beta \mathbb{D}^{\top})^{\omega}.\ \gamma \models \varphi$. Assume $\gamma = (\alpha[0, t_i)^{\top})$ $(\beta[0, t_i)^{\top})^{\omega}$. Let $\gamma' = (\alpha'[0, t'_i)^{\top})(\beta'[0, t'_j)^{\top})^{\omega}$ where $t'_i = t_i + (t_{\alpha} - t_{\alpha'})$ and $t'_j = t_j + (t_{\beta} - t_{\beta'})$. It follows from Proposition 10 that $\gamma \models \varphi$ implies $\gamma' \models \varphi$ for any φ. Since $\gamma' \in \alpha' \mathbb{D}^{\top}(\beta' \mathbb{D}^{\top})^{\omega}$ if follows that $(\alpha', \beta') \models^{-}_{\circlearrowleft} \varphi$.

Assume $(\alpha, \beta) \models^{+}_{\circlearrowleft} \varphi$. We have to show that $(\alpha'', \beta'') \models^{+}_{\circlearrowleft} \varphi$ for any $(\alpha'', \beta'') \succeq (\alpha, \beta)$. That is, we have to show that $\gamma'' \models \varphi$ for any $\gamma'' \in \alpha \mathbb{D}^{\perp}(\beta \mathbb{D}^{\perp})^{\omega}$. Let $\gamma'' = (\alpha''[0, t_i)^{\perp})(\beta''[0, t_j)^{\perp})^{\omega}$. Let $\gamma = (\alpha[0, t_i + t_{\alpha''} - t_{\alpha})^{\perp})(\beta[t_j + t_{\beta''} - t_{\beta})^{\perp})$. From $(\alpha, \beta) \models^{+}_{\circlearrowleft} \varphi$ we get that $\gamma \models \varphi$. It follows from Proposition 10 that $\gamma'' \models \varphi$. $\square$

We note that the semantics over incomplete ultimately periodic signals generalizes the semantics over truncated signals, in the following sense.

Proposition 12. *Let φ be an STL formula, and α a finite signal.*

$$- \ \alpha \models \varphi \iff (\alpha, \varepsilon) \models_{\overline{\circ}} \varphi$$
$$- \ \alpha \models \varphi \iff (\alpha, \varepsilon) \models_{\overline{\circ}} \varphi$$
$$- \ \alpha \not\models \varphi \iff (\alpha, \varepsilon) \models_{\overline{\circ}} \varphi$$

The proof here is also quite immediate, noting that there is a single signal in $(\alpha \mathbb{D}^\top)(\varepsilon \mathbb{D}\top)^\omega$, which is $\alpha^\top$ (and likewise for $\bot$), and that $\varepsilon^\omega = \varepsilon$.

5 Reasoning over Segmentally Broken Paths

5.1 Discrete Time

The idea of reasoning over incomplete paths can be extended also for the case that one knows segments of the paths $u_1, u_2, \ldots, u_k$, such that the complete path is of the form $u_1 \cdot x_1 \cdot u_2 \cdot x_2 \cdots u_k \cdot x_k$ for some $x_k \in \Sigma^\omega$ and some x_i's in Σ^* for $1 \le i < k$. This might be the case in the setting where the trace is obtained by sampling or when the trace collection method is not totally reliable. In such cases we would say that the segmentally broken path holds weakly iff it holds on some replacements of the missing parts with $\top$'s and similarly that it holds strongly iff it holds on all replacement of the missing parts with $\bot$'s. Formally,

$$\langle u_1, u_2, \ldots, u_k \rangle \models_{\overline{\text{ill}}} \varphi \iff \exists \gamma \in u_1 \top^* u_2 \top^* \ldots \top^* u_k \top^\omega. \ \gamma \models \varphi$$
$$\langle u_1, u_2, \ldots, u_k \rangle \models_{\overline{\text{ill}}} \varphi \iff u_1 u_2 \ldots u_k \models \varphi$$
$$\langle u_1, u_2, \ldots, u_k \rangle \models_{\overline{\text{ill}}} \varphi \iff \forall \gamma \subset u_1 \bot^* u_2 \bot^* \ldots \bot^* u_k \bot^\omega. \ \gamma \models \varphi$$

It is immediate from the definition that the semantics over segmentally broken paths generalizes the semantics over truncated paths:

Proposition 13. *Let φ be an ELTL formula, and u a finite word.*

$$- \ u \models \varphi \iff \langle u \rangle \models_{\overline{\text{ill}}} \varphi$$
$$- \ u \models \varphi \iff \langle u \rangle \models_{\overline{\text{ill}}} \varphi$$
$$- \ u \not\models \varphi \iff \langle u \rangle \models_{\overline{\text{ill}}} \varphi$$

It is not hard to see that the extension of the strength relation theorem and the prefix relation theorem hold as well.

Theorem 14 (The strength relation theorem for segmentally broken paths)

$$\langle u_1, u_2, \ldots, u_k \rangle \models_{\overline{\text{ill}}} \varphi \implies \langle u_1, u_2, \ldots, u_k \rangle \models_{\overline{\text{ill}}} \varphi \implies \langle u_1, u_2, \ldots, u_k \rangle \models_{\overline{\text{ill}}} \varphi$$

For tuples of words $\langle u_1, \ldots, u_k \rangle$ and $\langle u'_1, \ldots, u'_k \rangle$ in $(\Sigma^*)^k$ we use $\langle u'_1, \ldots, u'_k \rangle \preceq \langle u_1, \ldots, u_k \rangle$ if $u'_i \preceq u_i$.

Theorem 15 (The prefix/extension theorem for segmentally broken paths)

- $\langle u_1, \ldots, u_k \rangle \models_{\overline{\text{ill}}} \varphi \iff \forall \langle u'_1, \ldots, u'_k \rangle \preceq \langle u_1, \ldots, u_k \rangle. \ \langle u'_1, \ldots, u'_k \rangle \models_{\overline{\text{ill}}} \varphi$
- $\langle u_1, \ldots, u_k \rangle \models_{\overline{\text{ill}}} \varphi \iff \forall \langle u''_1, \ldots, u''_k \rangle \succeq \langle u_1, \ldots, u_k \rangle. \ \langle u''_1, \ldots, u''_k \rangle \models_{\overline{\text{ill}}} \varphi$

5.2   Continuous Time

Similarly we can define STL over segmentally broken signals. Let $\langle \alpha_1, \ldots, \alpha_k \rangle$ be a tuple of finite signals. We define

$$\langle \alpha_1, \ldots, \alpha_k \rangle \models_{\text{iii}} \varphi \quad \Longleftrightarrow \quad \exists \gamma \in \alpha_1 \mathbb{D}^\top \alpha_2 \mathbb{D}^\top \ldots \alpha_k [0, \infty)^\top. \ \gamma \models \varphi$$

$$\langle \alpha_1, \ldots, \alpha_k \rangle \models_{\text{iii}} \varphi \quad \Longleftrightarrow \quad \alpha_1 \ldots \alpha_k \models \varphi$$

$$\langle \alpha_1, \ldots, \alpha_k \rangle \models_{\text{iii}}^\pm \varphi \quad \Longleftrightarrow \quad \forall \gamma \in \alpha_1 \mathbb{D}^\perp \alpha_2 \mathbb{D}^\perp \ldots \alpha_k [0, \infty)^\perp. \ \gamma \models \varphi$$

It is immediate from the definition that the semantics over segmentally broken paths generalizes the semantics over truncated paths:

Proposition 16. *Let φ be an STL formula, and α a finite signal.*

$- \ \alpha \models \varphi \Longleftrightarrow \langle \alpha \rangle \models_{\text{iii}} \varphi$

$- \ \alpha \models \varphi \Longleftrightarrow \langle \alpha \rangle \models_{\text{iii}} \varphi$

$- \ \alpha \models^\pm \varphi \Longleftrightarrow \langle \alpha \rangle \models_{\text{iii}}^\pm \varphi$

It is not hard to see that the extension of the strength relation theorem and the prefix relation theorem hold as well.

Theorem 17 (The strength relation theorem for segmentally broken paths)

$$\langle \alpha_1, \ldots, \alpha_k \rangle \models_{\text{iii}}^\pm \varphi \quad \Longrightarrow \quad \langle \alpha_1, \ldots, \alpha_k \rangle \models_{\text{iii}} \varphi \quad \Longrightarrow \quad \langle \alpha_1, \ldots, \alpha_k \rangle \models_{\text{iii}} \varphi$$

For tuples of finite signals $\langle \alpha_1, \ldots, \alpha_k \rangle$ and $\langle \alpha_1', \ldots, \alpha_k' \rangle$ we use $\langle \alpha_1', \ldots, \alpha_k' \rangle \preceq \langle \alpha_1, \ldots, \alpha_k \rangle$ if $\alpha_i' \preceq \alpha_i$.

Theorem 18 (The prefix/extension theorem for segmentally broken paths)

- $\langle \alpha_1, \ldots, \alpha_k \rangle \models_{\text{iii}} \varphi \quad \Longleftrightarrow \quad \forall \langle \alpha_1', \ldots, \alpha_k' \rangle \preceq \langle \alpha_1, \ldots, \alpha_k \rangle. \ \langle \alpha_1', \ldots, \alpha_k' \rangle \models_{\text{iii}} \varphi$
- $\langle \alpha_1, \ldots, \alpha_k \rangle \models_{\text{iii}}^\pm \varphi \quad \Longleftrightarrow \quad \forall \langle \alpha_1'', \ldots, \alpha_k'' \rangle \succeq \langle \alpha_1, \ldots, \alpha_k \rangle. \ \langle \alpha_1'', \ldots, \alpha_k'' \rangle \models_{\text{iii}} \varphi$

6   Reasoning over Segmentally Broken Ultimately Periodic Paths

It could be that we are observing segments of an ultimately periodic path where both the transient part and the periodic part are broken into segments with uncertainties on the time elapsing between them and the value of the propositions in these segments. We can combine the semantics of Sects. 4 and 5 to reason about such incomplete paths as follows.

6.1   Discrete Time

Let $u_1, u_2, \ldots, u_k \in \Sigma^*$ and $v_1, v_2, \ldots, v_\ell \in \Sigma^*$.

$$(\langle u_1, \ldots, u_k \rangle, \langle v_1, \ldots, v_\ell \rangle) \models_{\ominus}^{\underline{\ }} \varphi \iff \exists \gamma \in (u_1 \top^* \ldots u_k \top^*)(v_1 \top^* \ldots v_\ell \top^*)^\omega . \gamma \models \varphi$$

$$(\langle u_1, \ldots, u_k \rangle, \langle v_1, \ldots, v_\ell \rangle) \models_{\ominus}^{\underline{\ }} \varphi \iff (u_1 u_2 \ldots u_k)(v_1 v_2 \ldots v_\ell)^\omega \models \varphi$$

$$(\langle u_1, \ldots, u_k \rangle, \langle v_1, \ldots, v_\ell \rangle) \models_{\ominus}^{\pm} \varphi \iff \forall \gamma \in (u_1 \perp^* \ldots u_k \perp^*)(v_1 \perp^* \ldots v_\ell \perp^*)^\omega . \ \gamma \models \varphi$$

It is immediate from the definition that this semantics generalizes the semantics over (i) truncated paths, (ii) ultimately periodic paths, and (iii) segmentally broken paths.

Proposition 19. *Let φ be an ELTL formula, $u, v, u_1, \ldots, u_k$ be finite or infinite words.*

(I) $- \ u \models \varphi \iff (\langle u \rangle, \langle \epsilon \rangle) \models_{\ominus}^{\underline{\ }} \varphi$

      $- \ u \models \varphi \iff (\langle u \rangle, \langle \epsilon \rangle) \models_{\ominus}^{\underline{\ }} \varphi$

      $- \ u \not\models \varphi \iff (\langle u \rangle, \langle \epsilon \rangle) \models_{\ominus}^{\pm} \varphi$

(II) $- \ (u, v) \models_{\ominus}^{\underline{\ }} \varphi \iff (\langle u \rangle, \langle v \rangle) \models_{\ominus}^{\underline{\ }} \varphi$

      $- \ (u, v) \models_{\ominus}^{\underline{\ }} \varphi \iff (\langle u \rangle, \langle v \rangle) \models_{\ominus}^{\underline{\ }} \varphi$

      $- \ (u, v) \models_{\ominus}^{\pm} \varphi \iff (\langle u \rangle, \langle v \rangle) \models_{\ominus}^{\pm} \varphi$

(III) $- \ \langle u_1, \ldots, u_k \rangle \models_{\text{\tiny III}}^{\underline{\ }} \varphi \iff (\langle u_1, \ldots, u_k \rangle, \langle \epsilon \rangle) \models_{\ominus}^{\underline{\ }} \varphi$

      $- \ \langle u_1, \ldots, u_k \rangle \models_{\text{\tiny III}}^{\underline{\ }} \varphi \iff (\langle u_1, \ldots, u_k \rangle, \langle \epsilon \rangle) \models_{\ominus}^{\underline{\ }} \varphi$

      $- \ \langle u_1, \ldots, u_k \rangle \models_{\text{\tiny III}}^{\pm} \varphi \iff (\langle u_1, \ldots, u_k \rangle, \langle \epsilon \rangle) \models_{\ominus}^{\pm} \varphi$

It is not hard to see that the extension of the strength relation theorem and the prefix relation theorem hold as well.

Theorem 20 (The strength relation theorem for segmentally broken ultimately periodic paths)

$$(\langle u_1, \ldots, u_k \rangle, \langle v_1, \ldots, v_\ell \rangle) \models_{\ominus}^{\pm} \varphi \implies (\langle u_1, \ldots, u_k \rangle, \langle v_1, \ldots, v_\ell \rangle) \models_{\ominus}^{\underline{\ }} \varphi$$

$$\implies (\langle u_1, \ldots, u_k \rangle, \langle v_1, \ldots, v_\ell \rangle) \models_{\ominus}^{\underline{\ }} \varphi$$

Let $\mathbf{u} = \langle u_1, \ldots, u_k \rangle$, $\mathbf{u}' = \langle u_1', \ldots, u_k' \rangle$, $\mathbf{v} = \langle v_1, \ldots, v_\ell \rangle$ and $\mathbf{v}' = \langle v_1', \ldots, v_\ell' \rangle$ be tuples of words. We say that $(\mathbf{u}, \mathbf{v}) \preceq (\mathbf{u}', \mathbf{v}')$ if $\mathbf{u} \preceq \mathbf{u}'$ and $\mathbf{v} \preceq \mathbf{v}'$.

Theorem 21 (The prefix/extension theorem for segmentally broken ultimately periodic paths)

- $(\mathbf{u}, \mathbf{v}) \models_{\ominus}^{\underline{\ }} \varphi \iff \forall (\mathbf{u}', \mathbf{v}') \preceq (\mathbf{u}, \mathbf{v}). \ (\mathbf{u}', \mathbf{v}') \models_{\ominus}^{\underline{\ }} \varphi$

- $(\mathbf{u}, \mathbf{v}) \models_{\ominus}^{\pm} \varphi \iff \forall (\mathbf{u}'', \mathbf{v}'') \succeq (\mathbf{u}, \mathbf{v}). \ (\mathbf{u}'', \mathbf{v}'') \models_{\ominus}^{\pm} \varphi$

6.2   Continuous Time

Similarly we can define STL over segmentally broken ultimately periodic signals. Let $\langle \alpha_1, \ldots, \alpha_k \rangle$ and $\langle \beta_1, \ldots, \beta_\ell \rangle$ be tuples of finite signals. We define

$$(\langle \alpha_1, \ldots, \alpha_k \rangle, \langle \beta_1, \ldots, \beta_k \rangle) \models_{\overset{\equiv}{\circ}} \varphi \iff \exists \gamma \in (\alpha_1 D^\top \ldots \alpha_k D^\top)(\beta_1 D^\top \ldots \beta_\ell D^\top)^\omega. \; \gamma \models \varphi$$

$$(\langle \alpha_1, \ldots, \alpha_k \rangle, \langle \beta_1, \ldots, \beta_k \rangle) \models_{\overset{-}{\circ}} \varphi \iff (\alpha_1 \ldots \alpha_k)(\beta_1 \ldots \beta_\ell)^\omega \models \varphi$$

$$(\langle \alpha_1, \ldots, \alpha_k \rangle, \langle \beta_1, \ldots, \beta_k \rangle) \models_{\overset{\pm}{\circ}} \varphi \iff \forall \gamma \in (\alpha_1 D^\perp \ldots \alpha_k D^\perp)(\beta_1 D^\perp \ldots \beta_\ell D^\perp)^\omega \; \gamma \models \varphi$$

It is immediate from the definition that the semantics over segmentally broken ultimately periodic paths generalizes the semantics over (i) truncated signals, (ii) incomplete ultimately periodic signals, and (iii) segmentally broken signals.

Proposition 22. *Let φ be an STL formula, and $\alpha, \alpha_1, \ldots, \alpha_k, \beta, \beta_1, \ldots, \beta_\ell$ finite signals.*

(I) $- \; \alpha \models \varphi \iff (\langle \alpha \rangle, \langle \varepsilon \rangle) \models_{\overset{\equiv}{\circ}} \varphi$

$- \; \alpha \models \varphi \iff (\langle \alpha \rangle, \langle \varepsilon \rangle) \models_{\overset{-}{\circ}} \varphi$

$- \; \alpha \models \varphi \iff (\langle \alpha \rangle, \langle \varepsilon \rangle) \models_{\overset{\pm}{\circ}} \varphi$

(II) $- \; (\alpha, \beta) \models_{\overset{\equiv}{\circ}} \varphi \iff (\langle \alpha \rangle, \langle \beta \rangle) \models_{\overset{\equiv}{\circ}} \varphi$

$- \; (\alpha, \beta) \models_{\overset{-}{\circ}} \varphi \iff (\langle \alpha \rangle, \langle \beta \rangle) \models_{\overset{-}{\circ}} \varphi$

$- \; (\alpha, \beta) \models_{\overset{\pm}{\circ}} \varphi \iff (\langle \alpha \rangle, \langle \beta \rangle) \models_{\overset{\pm}{\circ}} \varphi$

(III) $- \; \langle \alpha_1, \ldots, \alpha_k \rangle \models_{\overset{\equiv}{\text{\tiny III}}} \varphi \iff (\langle \alpha_1, \ldots, \alpha_k \rangle, \langle \varepsilon \rangle) \models_{\overset{\equiv}{\circ}} \varphi$

$- \; \langle \alpha_1, \ldots, \alpha_k \rangle \models_{\overset{-}{\text{\tiny III}}} \varphi \iff (\langle \alpha_1, \ldots, \alpha_k \rangle, \langle \varepsilon \rangle) \models_{\overset{-}{\circ}} \varphi$

$- \; \langle \alpha_1, \ldots, \alpha_k \rangle \models_{\overset{\pm}{\text{\tiny III}}} \varphi \iff (\langle \alpha_1, \ldots, \alpha_k \rangle, \langle \varepsilon \rangle) \models_{\overset{\pm}{\circ}} \varphi$

It is not hard to see that the extension of the strength relation theorem and the prefix relation theorem hold as well. Let $\alpha = \langle \alpha_1, \ldots, \alpha_k \rangle$ and $\beta = \langle \beta_1, \ldots, \beta_\ell \rangle$ be tuples of finite signals.

Theorem 23 (The strength relation theorem for segmentally broken ultimately periodic paths)

$$(\alpha, \beta) \models_{\overset{\pm}{\circ}} \varphi \implies (\alpha, \beta) \models_{\overset{-}{\circ}} \varphi \implies (\alpha, \beta) \models_{\overset{\equiv}{\circ}} \varphi$$

Let $\alpha = \langle \alpha_1, \ldots, \alpha_k \rangle, \alpha' = \langle \alpha'_1, \ldots, \alpha'_k \rangle, \; \beta = \langle \beta_1, \ldots, \beta_\ell \rangle$ and $\beta' = \langle \beta'_1, \ldots, \beta'_\ell \rangle$ be tuples of finite signals. We say that $(\alpha, \beta) \preceq (\alpha', \beta')$ if $\alpha \preceq \alpha'$ and $\beta \preceq \beta'$.

Theorem 24 (The prefix/extension theorem for segmentally broken ultimately periodic paths)

- $(\alpha, \beta) \models_{\overset{\equiv}{\text{\tiny III}}} \varphi \iff \forall (\alpha', \beta') \preceq (\alpha, \beta). \; (\alpha', \beta') \models_{\overset{\equiv}{\circ}} \varphi$

- $(\alpha, \beta) \models_{\overset{\pm}{\text{\tiny III}}} \varphi \iff \forall (\alpha'', \beta'') \succeq (\alpha, \beta). \; (\alpha'', \beta'') \models_{\overset{\pm}{\circ}} \varphi$

7   Temporal Reasoning in Systems Biology

Systems Biology takes an integrated and *holistic* view to study the complexity of biological systems and emphasizes the value of computational models and methods as a complementary approach to experimental work [2,11,42,46]. A key aspect is building computational models of the biological system studied, that can typically integrate several aspects of the system behavior which according to the classical *reductionist* approach are studied in isolation. There are several advantages that can be gained by constructing computational models: (1) The process of model construction helps identify gaps in our understanding of the system; (2) Complex behavior can arise due to the interaction between different components in the system, and as the scope of the studied systems expands, it becomes hard to reason about the system behavior without computational models and supporting tools; (3) A model should in principle be able to reproduce all known experimental results. Keeping track of the relevant experiments and ensuring a mechanistic model can indeed reproduce them may become challenging as the size of the model and number of experiments grow. Using formal specification languages, in particular temporal logic, can enable a clear and accurate specification of experimental results, and the application of automated formal verification approaches to ensure the model indeed satisfies the specification; (4) The most exciting aspect of modeling is the ability to use the derived models to make new predictions that can then be tested experimentally and lead to new biological insights. Temporal logic can be used gainfully to formulate queries that form the basis for making new predictions.

While temporal logic is now being actively used in the biological context (see e.g. [7,8,13,14,20,27,50] and references therein), important open questions remain regarding the appropriate type of temporal logic needed, how to provide intuitive interfaces and tools that can facilitate use by biologists, and the complexity of key verification and synthesis algorithms in the biological context. We next provide an overview of the use of temporal logic in biological modeling, emphasizing the subsets of temporal logic that have been identified as particularly useful and are currently applied in biological modeling. We suggest that considering truncated semantics for temporal logic is of relevance for biological applications, and identify cases in which the basic truncated semantics can be considered, and other cases where the extensions for handling ultimately periodic paths and segmentally broken paths may be useful.

7.1   Truncated Path Semantics

Early work on using temporal logic in systems biology was based on the observation that specifying experiments and hypotheses in temporal logic can open the way to applying powerful model checking algorithms and tools that have been originally developed for verification of engineered systems. In [27,28] the Pathway Logic tool is presented, which allows to use rewrite logic systems and the Maude toolset [16,29] to describe how biological signalling pathways operate in cells. Such signalling pathways are composed of molecular components that regulate each others activity and allow a cell to interact with its environment and identify required nutrients or harmful toxins, and receive signals from neighbouring cells. Properties describing biological questions of interest were specified using linear temporal logic (LTL), an example of such an LTL property described in [27] is:[3]

$$\underline{\mathsf{G}}\,(\,\underline{\mathsf{G}}\,(p1 \wedge \neg p2) \rightarrow \neg\,\underline{\mathsf{F}}\,p3)$$

An additional question studied in [28] is concerned with the necessity of eventually reaching a state in which two signals $p1$ and $p2$ are activated from some initial state $q1$.

$$q1 \rightarrow \underline{\mathsf{F}}\,(p1 \wedge p2)$$

Instantiations of this formula are then studied in which certain signals are removed from state $q1$, to obtain a different initial state $q1'$. The Maude tool also provides powerful simulation capabilities, which were used to study simpler queries related to forward or backward reachability. We propose that using the truncated semantics presented in this paper could allow a unified view between the verification and simulation capabilities of the Maude tool. For large models in which verification becomes more challenging, using truncated semantics could potentially allow to use the Maude simulation capabilities to refute LTL properties or increase the confidence that they hold. More generally, for biological modeling tools that utilize temporal logic or equivalent specification languages, we suggest that the dynamic properties are specified once in a uniform manner, and the appropriate view is configured according to the tool and methods used to analyze the properties.

One of the challenges in using temporal logic for specifying biological models is making the process easy and intuitive for experimental biologists. In [45] the use of *patterns* for frequently used types of biological specification is suggested, and a set of patterns based on a survey of previous biological modeling efforts is proposed. The underlying temporal logic used is CTL. While some patterns lie in the common fragment of LTL and CTL, this does not hold for all. For instance one type of *sequence patterns* is given by the CTL formula $\mathsf{AG}\,(p \rightarrow \underline{\mathsf{EF}}\,q)$ which does not have an equivalent in LTL. *Stabilization properties*, stating a system is stabilizing if there exists a unique state that is eventually reached in all executions may be expressed using the CTL formula $\varphi = \mathsf{A}\underline{\mathsf{F}}\,(\mathsf{A}\underline{\mathsf{G}}\,(s))$. Such formulas appear in the works [14] for modeling regulatory networks and are supported by the BMA tool [17].[4] The formula φ is different than the LTL formula $\varphi' = \underline{\mathsf{F}}\,\underline{\mathsf{G}}\,(s)$. These two formulas represent a well-known example for properties that are not at the intersection of LTL and CTL, where φ' cannot be expressed in CTL, and φ cannot be expressed in LTL. It will be of interest

---

[3] These works use the traditional box and diamond notations for LTL.

[4] Formulas supported by the tool [17] use also quantification on variables and value domains. While this is not part of LTL it is part of PSL and its support is orthogonal to the use of truncated views.

to gain a better understanding of which property may be more appropriate in various biological contexts.

The models developed in [1,17] are logical models (finite state variables with deterministic logical conditions determining the transition relation) and their temporal logic semantics are described over infinite runs. A special graphic interface allows to compose the above operators into more complex formulas, ensuring that there are no problems with mismatched parenthesis, and aiming to support users that have less experience in logic or programming. While specifying temporal logic properties the users also supply an integer value that is used as a *bound* while applying bounded model checking to verify or refute the property. The supported view is the neutral view. Extending the tool to support the weak and strong views will allow the user to indicate whether unsatisfied eventualities should be forgiven or not. It would be of interest to explore support for the three views and gain experience on how they may be utilized in the process of developing biological models.

7.2   Ultimately Periodic Paths

In [51] a computational model of the mammalian cell cycle is studied using model-checking methods. The cell cycle can be viewed as a periodic mechanistic behavior that controls the process of cell division and is governed by molecular and genetic interactions, leading to the next cell division and the repetition of the cycle in the daughter cells. A logical model of some of the main genetic components is constructed in [51], extending an earlier Boolean model [30]. A translation of the model into NuSMV [15] allows using formal verification to study the dynamics of the model. One type of property that has been used is a formula of the form $[S_1, S_2 ... S_n]$ stating that there is no sequence of states that starts from an initial state satisfying some assertion S_1 and visiting a path that goes through $S_2, S_3 \cdots$ until reaching S_n. If this property does not hold, then a counterexample gives us the desired behavior of a path through states satisfying $S_1, S_2 \cdots S_n$. This property can be stated using the following LTL formula:

$$\neg(S_1 \wedge \underline{F}(S_2 \wedge \underline{F}(S_3 \wedge \cdots (S_{n-1} \wedge \underline{F} S_n)\cdots)$$

To ensure the periodic behavior of the cell cycle, the sequence can be required to form a loop or a lasso, where $S_n = S_i$ for some $i < n$. We suggest that explicitly considering the ultimately periodic paths extension is of interest, allowing to decide for given $u, v \in \Sigma^*$ if $(u, v) \models_{\circlearrowleft} \varphi$. Understanding what is the transient behavior (the word u) and what is the periodic behavior (the word v) may be of particular interest in biological modeling. Note that stabilizing dynamics ([14,17] described above) is a special case of ultimately periodic behavior with the periodic part consisting of the stable state $v \in \Sigma$.

Other properties that may benefit the extension to incomplete ultimately periodic paths are oscillation properties (c.f. [14]), e.g. stating that a molecular product p oscillates ($\underline{G}((p \rightarrow \underline{F}\neg p) \wedge (\neg p \rightarrow \underline{F}p))$ in LTL).

7.3   Segmentally Broken Paths

We have shown that when reasoning about the periodic behavior of the cell cycle it is useful to identify sequences of the form $[S_1, S_2, \ldots, S_n]$ where the sequence specifies the periodic behavior. Similar sequences are also useful for time course measurements of the system that are not periodic. In particular, sometimes it is important to specify that the events occur in a sequence as above, but each S_i should not occur before its place or after its place, which also eliminates the periodic behavior. This can be specified by the formula:

$$(S_1 \wedge \underline{X}(N\,\underline{U}\,(S_2 \wedge \underline{X}(N\,\underline{U}\,(S_3 \wedge \cdots (N\,\underline{U}\,(S_{n-1} \wedge \underline{X}(N\,\underline{U}\,S_n)\cdots)$$

Where $N = \neg S_1 \wedge \neg S_2 \wedge \cdots \neg S_n$ specifies the requirement that none of the propositions $S_1, S_2, \ldots, S_n$ hold. Such patterns are naturally specified in live sequence charts using existential charts [18,40]. We suggest that the segmentally broken paths semantics presented here could allow to use the different views to reason in a uniform way about such types of formulas, where for $S_1, S_2, \ldots, S_k$ $\models_{\overline{\text{III}}} \varphi$ for the weak view, and similarly for the neutral and strong views.

In [21,52] formal reasoning and verification methods are used to synthesize Boolean Network models satisfying a set of experimental observations. The language for specifying observations currently supports constraints on bounded paths. For each experiment, a logical proposition on the value of the components of the network can be specified, where a component can be either 1 (active) or 0 (inactive). Assuming a discrete time model, the language allows specifying the timepoint at which an assertion should hold. Abstract Boolean Networks (ABNs) are introduced as a modeling formalism that incorporates uncertainty about the precise network topology and regulation mechanisms of a biological system. ABNs can be made concrete by selecting a subset of the possible interactions and making a precise choice of the regulation condition (logical template determining the transition relation give choice of possible and definite interactions) of each component.

The specification language considers reachability properties over the states of various components at different steps during executions of the system. The goal is to formalize observations obtained from different *experiments*, denoted by the set E, where each experiment $e \in E$ represents a different execution of the system. Observations are constructed using the terms (e, n, c, v), where

– $e \in E$ is the experiment label,
– $n \in 0 \ldots K$ denotes a specific time step, and
– $c \in C$ denotes a component of the ABN,
– $v \in \mathbb{B}$ represents the observed state of component c.

Let $t = q_0, \ldots, q_K$ denote a trajectory of the transition system $\mathcal{T}$ for one of the concrete models represented by an ABN $\mathcal{A}$. Trajectory t satisfies the term (e, n, c, v) if and only if $q_n(c) = v$ and we require that, for all experiments $e \in E$, there exists a trajectory t_e that satisfies all the terms labeled by e.

This can be formalized in LTL as follows:

$$\underline{X}^{i_1}(S_1 \wedge \underline{X}^{i_2-i_1}(S_2 \wedge \underline{X}^{i_3-i_2} S_3 \wedge \cdots \underline{X}^{i_n-i_{n-1}}(S_n)\cdots)$$

where we order the terms for experiment e by time step and for the i-th term (e, j, c, v) S_i is the conjunction of assertions of the form $q_j(c) = v$.

In addition, the terms $KO(e, c, v)$ and $FE(e, c, v)$ allow to define knockout and forced expression perturbations, which are assigned to a given experiment and component but are not time dependent. These perturbations modify the dynamics of the system along trajectory t_e, where component c is always active (forced expression) or inactive (knockout) when $v = \mathtt{tt}$, regardless of the regulation conditions for c or the state of each of its regulators (the update rules are applied as before when $v = \mathtt{ff}$). Finally, the constraint $Fixpoint(e, n)$ is used to indicate that the trajectory t_e, satisfying all constraints labeled by e, must reach a fixed point at step n. In other words, the only possible transition from the state q_n of t_e (reached at time step n) is a self-loop. Different terms (e, n, c, v), $KO(e, c, v)$, $FE(e, c, v)$ and $Fixpoint(e, n)$ are combined into logical expressions using the operators $\{\land, \lor, \Rightarrow, \Leftrightarrow, \neg\}$, which allows us to formalize various experimental observations. We suggest that sometimes the exact time points specifying when certain assertions are not precisely known, and then investigating the use of segmentally broken paths semantics in the framework described in [52] may be of interest.

8   Related Work

Other approaches for reasoning about truncated paths use multi-valued logics. For instance, Ref [9] suggests LTL_3, a 3-valued logics to reason with LTL on truncated path, as well as $TLTL_3$, a 3-valued logic to reason on a continuous time extension of LTL on truncated signals, and Ref [10] suggests LTL_4, a 4-valued logics to reason with LTL on truncated paths. In both the approach is that a formula φ should be evaluated to $\mathtt{tt}$ on a finite path u if all extensions of u satisfy φ and to $\mathtt{ff}$ if all extensions falsify φ. That is, a formula evaluates to $\mathtt{tt}$ under LTL_3 iff it strongly evaluates to true, and it evaluates to $\mathtt{ff}$ under LTL_3 iff its negation strongly evaluates to true. In other cases evaluation under LTL_3 results in the value $??$ and under LTL_4 it results in either $\mathtt{tt}_p$ or $\mathtt{ff}_p$ according to whether the formula neutrally evaluates to $\mathtt{tt}$ or $\mathtt{ff}$.

A disadvantages of both approaches is that their definition is not inductive. Apart from that, they do not achieve the desired intuition of providing a way for the specifier to use the same set of formulas whichever verification method she is using, and only indicate for each verification method in what way the formula should be evaluated. To illustrate this, consider the case that the formula to be verified is $[p \underline{\cup} q]$. The user would like to evaluate it neutrally when using model checking; to evaluate it weakly when using monitoring; and to evaluate it strongly on a set of test cases designed to be long enough for q to hold.

In the truncated semantics, asking to provide an answer under the weak view provides a way to *weaken the formula*, but there is no value of LTL_3 or LTL_4

that can be understood as the value of the weak view. Consider for instance the formula $\varphi = [p \, \underline{U} \, (q \wedge \neg q)]$, its weak version $\varphi' = [p \, \underline{W} \, (q \wedge \neg q)]$ holds on a finite word w where all letters satisfy p, and indeed φ itself is evaluated to tt under the weak view, however, the semantics of φ on w under LTL$_3$ or LTL$_4$ is ff.[5]

Another disadvantage of LTL$_3$ and LTL$_4$ is that their monitors are of size doubly exponential in the size of the formula [10]. However, monitors for formulas under the weak view (the view usually chosen for monitoring) are only exponential in the size of the formula, since $w \not\models \varphi$ iff w is an *informative prefix* for φ [22] and there exist an NFA recognizing all the informative prefixes of formula φ in exponential time [41]. (Loosely speaking, an *informative prefix* for the dis-satisfaction of φ on w is a prefix that can explain why φ fails on w. Some formulas, e.g. $\underline{G} \, \underline{F} \varphi \wedge \underline{F} \, \underline{G} \neg \varphi$ do not have informative prefixes. See [41] for precise definition and classification of safety formulas and [22] for the relation of the truncated semantics to the classification of safety formulas).[6]

A recent work [6] suggests adding a counting semantics for evaluating LTL on finite paths. The motivation has to do with formulas involving both the $\underline{F}$ and $\underline{G}$ operators. Consider, for instance, the formula $\underline{G} \, (req \rightarrow \underline{F} \, gnt)$ and a finite trace where req holds on cycles 3 and 10, and gnt holds on cycle 8. Under LTL$_3$ the result will be ??, under the weak view tt and under the strong view ff. In all cases the result disregards the fact that the first req was eventually followed by gnt, and the time elapsed between that req and that gnt. The semantics provided in [6] aims to take into account the occurrences of req and gnt in the observed path and the time elapsing between them, so that if the considered path ends less than 5 cycles after the second req then the result would be tt_p corresponding to *presumably true* and meeting the intuition that the next gnt is likely to occur on cycle 15 (since 5 cycles is the time elapsed between the first req and the following gnt) whereas if the considered path ends more than 5 cycles after the last req, then the result would be ff_p corresponding to *presumably false*, meeting the intuition that we should have already observed the gnt following the second req. We disagree that the result ff_p is always the expected result in the second case, and that tt_p is always the expected result in the first case. Indeed, it can be that the periodic part is longer than a single sequence involving one req and one gnt (e.g. the periodic part may involve three reqs with different times elapsing between their corresponding gnts) or it could be that we have not yet observed the periodic part. The semantics proposed in Sect. 4 (and its generalization presented in Sect. 6) lets the user determine which part of the observed path correspond to the transient behavior and which to the periodic

---

[5] Approaches that extend the set of atomic propositions with a dedicated *end* symbol, and require formulas to explicitily reason about it (e.g. the approach implemented in the tool RULER [5]) suffer similar drawbacks.

[6] Ref [10] claims some disadvantages of the three views approach to the truncated semantics, but the analysis distinguishes the weak and strong views as if they are different semantics while they are not (they are part of the same semantics with negation switching roles) and requires the *next* operator to be a dual of itself, while the semantics is designed so that the *strong next* is dual to the *weak next*, and strong propositions are dual to weak propositions.

part. And she can do that using a combination of her knowledge on the system, her intuitions and her desire for strong/weak guarantees. For instance, in the given example, she can determine that the path starting at cycle 3 and ending in cycle 8 is the periodic part, and using the neutral ultimately periodic approach get the same result as in [6]. Or, as another example, she can determine that the periodic part started at cycle 3 and still continues, thus using the weak ultimately periodic approach she will get a positive result even if the path is longer than 15. Another drawback of the semantics proposed in [6], as observed therein, is that it cannot semantically characterize tautologies and contradiction (and, for instance, the evaluation of the formula $(p \wedge \neg p)$ on the empty word results in ?? whereas it should have result in ff, since the formula is a contradiction).

We refer the reader to [6] for a discussion on other related work.

9   Discussion

We have proposed an extension of the three views approach to reason over truncated paths from LTL to STL, and generalized reasoning over truncated paths to reasoning over incomplete ultimately periodic paths, segmentally broken paths and combinations thereof. The extensions are provided in both the discrete dimension (LTL) and the continuous dimension (STL).

The standard temporal logics PSL and SVA have regular expressions based formulas, and most formulas are written using regular expressions. The regular expression-based operators increase the expressive power of the logic from star-free ω-regular languages to the full ω-regular languages. But the main reason they are popular is because they are easier to use. The ease of use consideration is important for answering the demand for the specification to be intuitive for experimental biologists. The three views approach is defined for PSL, and thus for the regular expression-based operators as well. Timed regular expressions were defined in [4]. It would be interesting to extend timed regular expressions to consider truncated paths and more generally segmentally broken ultimately periodic paths.

We have reviewed use of temporal reasoning in system biology, and conclude that it is plausible that the proposed extensions may be useful in modeling and analyzing biological systems. We foresee that it will be useful in many other applications as well.

Acknowledgment. The research was partially supported by the Horizon 2020 research and innovation programme under grant agreement number 732482 (Bio4Comp).

References

1. Ahmed, Z., et al.: Bringing LTL model checking to biologists. In: Bouajjani, A., Monniaux, D. (eds.) VMCAI 2017. LNCS, vol. 10145, pp. 1–13. Springer, Cham (2017). https://doi.org/10.1007/978-3-319-52234-0_1
2. Alon, U.: An Introduction to Systems Biology: Design Principles of Biological Circuits. CRC Press, Boca Raton (2006)
3. Alur, R., Feder, T., Henzinger, T.A.: The benefits of relaxing punctuality. J. ACM **43**(1), 116–146 (1996)
4. Asarin, E., Caspi, P., Maler, O.: Timed regular expressions. J. ACM **49**(2), 172–206 (2002)
5. Barringer, H., Rydeheard, D., Havelund, K.: Rule systems for run-time monitoring: from EAGLE to RULER. In: Sokolsky, O., Taşıran, S. (eds.) RV 2007. LNCS, vol. 4839, pp. 111–125. Springer, Heidelberg (2007). https://doi.org/10.1007/978-3-540-77395-5_10
6. Bartocci, E., Bloem, R., Nickovic, D., Roeck, F.: A Counting Semantics for Monitoring LTL Specifications over Finite Traces. In: Chockler, H., Weissenbacher, G. (eds.) CAV 2018. LNCS, vol. 10981, pp. 547–564. Springer, Cham (2018). https://doi.org/10.1007/978-3-319-96145-3_29
7. Bartocci, E., Lió, P.: Computational modeling, formal analysis, and tools for systems biology. PLoS Comput. Biol. **12**(1), e1004591 (2016)
8. Batt, G., et al.: Validation of qualitative models of genetic regulatory networks by model checking: analysis of the nutritional stress response in *Escherichia coli*. Bioinformatics **21**, 19–28 (2005)
9. Bauer, A., Leucker, M., Schallhart, C.: Monitoring of real-time properties. In: Arun-Kumar, S., Garg, N. (eds.) FSTTCS 2006. LNCS, vol. 4337, pp. 260–272. Springer, Heidelberg (2006). https://doi.org/10.1007/11944836_25
10. Bauer, A., Leucker, M., Schallhart, C.: Comparing LTL semantics for runtime verification. J. Log. Comput. **20**(3), 651–674 (2010)
11. Brenner, S.: Sequences and consequences. Philos. Trans. R. Soc. B Biol. Sci. **365**(1537), 207–212 (2010)
12. Cerny, E., Dudani, S., Havlicek, J., Korchemny, D.: SVA: The Power of Assertions in SystemVerilog. Series on Integrated Circuits and Systems. Springer, Heidelberg (2012)
13. Chabrier, N., Fages, F.: Symbolic model checking of biochemical networks. In: Priami, C. (ed.) CMSB 2003. LNCS, vol. 2602, pp. 149–162. Springer, Heidelberg (2003). https://doi.org/10.1007/3-540-36481-1_13
14. Chabrier-Rivier, N., Chiaverini, M., Danos, V., Fages, F., Schächter, V.: Modeling and querying biomolecular interaction networks. Theor. Comput. Sci. **325**(1), 25–44 (2004)
15. Cimatti, A., Clarke, E., Giunchiglia, F., Roveri, M.: NUSMV: a new symbolic model checker. Int. J. Softw. Tools Technol. Transf. **2**(4), 410–425 (2000)
16. Clavel, M., et al.: All About Maude - A High-Performance Logical Framework: How to Specify, Program and Verify Systems in Rewriting Logic. LNCS, vol. 4350. Springer, Heidelberg (2007). https://doi.org/10.1007/978-3-540-71999-1
17. Cook, B., Fisher, J., Krepska, E., Piterman, N.: Proving stabilization of biological systems. In: Jhala, R., Schmidt, D. (eds.) VMCAI 2011. LNCS, vol. 6538, pp. 134–149. Springer, Heidelberg (2011). https://doi.org/10.1007/978-3-642-18275-4_11

18. Damm, W., Harel, D.: LSCs: breathing life into message sequence charts. Form. Methods Syst. Des. **19**(1), 45–80 (2001). Preliminary version appeared in Proc. 3rd IFIP Int. Conf. on Formal Methods for Open Object-Based Distributed Systems (FMOODS'99)
19. Deshmukh, J.V., Donzé, A., Ghosh, S., Jin, X., Juniwal, G., Seshia, S.A.: Robust online monitoring of signal temporal logic. Form. Methods Syst. Des. **51**(1), 5–30 (2017)
20. Dubrova, E., Teslenko, M., Ming, L.: Finding attractors in synchronous multiple-valued networks using SAT-based bounded model checking. In: 40th IEEE International Symposium on Multiple-Valued Logic (ISMVL), pp. 144–149 (2010)
21. Dunn, S.-J., Martello, G., Yordanov, B., Emmott, S., Smith, A.G.: Defining an essential transcription factor program for naïve pluripotency. Science **344**(6188), 1156–1160 (2014)
22. Eisner, C., Fisman, D., Havlicek, J., Lustig, Y., McIsaac, A., Van Campenhout, D.: Reasoning with temporal logic on truncated paths. In: Hunt Jr., W.A., Somenzi, F. (eds.) CAV 2003. LNCS, vol. 2725, pp. 27–39. Springer, Heidelberg (2003). https://doi.org/10.1007/978-3-540-45069-6_3
23. Eisner, C., Fisman, D.: A Practical Introduction to PSL. ICIR. Springer, Boston (2006). https://doi.org/10.1007/978-0-387-36123-9
24. Eisner, C., Fisman, D., Havlicek, J.: A topological characterization of weakness. In: Proceedings of the Twenty-Fourth Annual ACM Symposium on Principles of Distributed Computing, PODC 2005, Las Vegas, NV, USA, 17–20 July 2005, pp. 1–8 (2005)
25. Eisner, C., Fisman, D., Havlicek, J.: Safety and liveness, weakness and strength, and the underlying topological relations. ACM Trans. Comput. Log. **15**(2), 13:1–13:44 (2014)
26. Eisner, C., Fisman, D., Havlicek, J., Mårtensson, J.: The ⊤, ⊥ approach for truncated semantics
27. Eker, S., Knapp, M., Laderoute, K., Lincoln, P., Meseguer, J., Sonmez, K.: Pathway logic: symbolic analysis of biological signaling. In Biocomputing 2002, pp. 400–412. World Scientific (2001)
28. Eker, S., Knapp, M., Laderoute, K., Lincoln, P., Talcott, C.: Pathway logic: executable models of biological networks. Electron. Notes Theor. Comput. Sci. **71**, 144–161 (2004)
29. Eker, S., Meseguer, J., Sridharanarayanan, A.: The maude LTL model checker. Electron. Notes Theor. Comput. Sci. **71**, 162–187 (2004)
30. Fauré, A., Naldi, A., Chaouiya, C., Thieffry, D.: Dynamical analysis of a generic Boolean model for the control of the mammalian cell cycle. Bioinformatics **22**(14), 124–131 (2006)
31. Fisman, D.: On the characterization of until as a fixed point under clocked semantics. In: Yorav, K. (ed.) HVC 2007. LNCS, vol. 4899, pp. 19–33. Springer, Heidelberg (2008). https://doi.org/10.1007/978-3-540-77966-7_6
32. Furia, C.A., Rossi, M.: No need to be strict: on the expressiveness of metric temporal logics with (non-)strict operators. Bull. EATCS **92**, 150–160 (2007)
33. Furia, C.A., Rossi, M.: On the expressiveness of MTL variants over dense time. In: Raskin, J.-F., Thiagarajan, P.S. (eds.) FORMATS 2007. LNCS, vol. 4763, pp. 163–178. Springer, Heidelberg (2007). https://doi.org/10.1007/978-3-540-75454-1_13
34. Gargantini, A., Morzenti, A.: Automated deductive requirements analysis of critical systems. ACM Trans. Softw. Eng. Methodol. **10**(3), 255–307 (2001)

35. Harel, D., Lachover, H., Naamad, A., Pnueli, A., Politi, M., Sherman, R., Shtull-Trauring, A.: Statemate; a working environment for the development of complex reactive systems. In: Proceedings of the 10th International Conference on Software Engineering, Singapore, Singapore, 11–15 April 1988, pp. 396–406 (1988)
36. IBM: RuleBase SixthSense Edition. https://www.research.ibm.com/haifa/projects/verification/Formal_Methods-Home/index.shtml
37. IEEE Standard for Property Specification Language (PSL), Annex B. IEEE Std 1850^{TM}
38. IEEE Standard for SystemVerilog – Unified Hardware Design, Specification, and Verification Language, Annex F. IEEE Std 1800^{TM}
39. Koymans, R.: Specifying real-time properties with metric temporal logic. R. Time Syst. **2**(4), 255–299 (1990)
40. Kugler, H., Harel, D., Pnueli, A., Lu, Y., Bontemps, Y.: Temporal logic for scenario-based specifications. In: Halbwachs, N., Zuck, L.D. (eds.) TACAS 2005. LNCS, vol. 3440, pp. 445–460. Springer, Heidelberg (2005). https://doi.org/10.1007/978-3-540-31980-1_29
41. Kupferman, O., Vardi, M.Y.: Model checking of safety properties. In: Halbwachs, N., Peled, D. (eds.) CAV 1999. LNCS, vol. 1633, pp. 172–183. Springer, Heidelberg (1999). https://doi.org/10.1007/3-540-48683-6_17
42. Le Novère, N.: Quantitative and logic modelling of molecular and gene networks. Nat. Rev. Genet. **16**(3), 146–158 (2015)
43. Maler, O., Nickovic, D.: Monitoring properties of analog and mixed-signal circuits. STTT **15**(3), 247–268 (2013)
44. Manna, Z., Pnueli, A.: The Temporal Logic of Reactive and Concurrent Systems - Specification. Springer, New York (1992). https://doi.org/10.1007/978-1-4612-0931-7
45. Monteiro, P.T., Ropers, D., Mateescu, R., Freitas, A.T., De Jong, H.: Temporal logic patterns for querying dynamic models of cellular interaction networks. Bioinformatics **24**(16), i227–i233 (2008)
46. Palsson, B.: Systems Biology: Constraint-based Reconstruction and Analysis. Cambridge University Press, Cambridge (2015)
47. Pnueli, A.: The temporal logic of programs. In: 18th Annual Symposium on Foundations of Computer Science, Providence, Rhode Island, USA, 31 October–1 November 1977, pp. 46–57 (1977)
48. Pnueli, A.: Linear and branching structures in the semantics and logics of reactive systems. In: Brauer, W. (ed.) ICALP 1985. LNCS, vol. 194, pp. 15–32. Springer, Heidelberg (1985). https://doi.org/10.1007/BFb0015727
49. Synopsys: VC Formal Tools. https://www.synopsys.com/verification/static-and-formal-verification/vc-formal.html
50. Tiwari, A., Talcott, C., Knapp, M., Lincoln, P., Laderoute, K.: Analyzing pathways using SAT-based approaches. In: Anai, H., Horimoto, K., Kutsia, T. (eds.) AB 2007. LNCS, vol. 4545, pp. 155–169. Springer, Heidelberg (2007). https://doi.org/10.1007/978-3-540-73433-8_12
51. Traynard, P., Fauré, A., Fages, F., Thieffry, D.: Logical model specification aided by model-checking techniques: application to the mammalian cell cycle regulation. Bioinformatics **32**(17), i772–i780 (2016)
52. Yordanov, B., Dunn, S.-J., Kugler, H., Smith, A., Martello, G., Emmott, S.: A method to identify and analyze biological programs through automated reasoning. NPJ Syst. Biol. Appl. **2**, 16010 (2016)

Towards a Notion of Coverage
for Incomplete Program-Correctness
Proofs

Bernhard Beckert, Mihai Herda, Stefan Kobischke, and Mattias Ulbrich[✉]

Karlsruhe Institute of Technology, Karlsruhe, Germany
ulbrich@kit.edu

Abstract. Deductive program verification can give high assurances for program correctness. But incomplete partial proofs do not provide any information as to what degree or with what probability the program is correct.

In this paper, we introduce the concept of state space coverage for partial proofs, which estimates to what degree the proof covers the state space and the possible inputs of the program. Thus, similar to testing, the degree of assurance grows with the effort invested in constructing a correctness proof. The concept brings together deductive verification techniques with runtime techniques used to empirically estimate the coverage. We have implemented a prototypical tool that uses test data to estimate the coverage of partial proofs constructed with the program verification system KeY.

Keywords: Program verification · Coverage · Sequent proofs

1 Introduction

Deductive program verification can give high assurances for program correctness – if a proof can be found. An incomplete partial proof, however, does not provide any information as to what degree or with what probability the program is correct. Even if a proof is nearly complete in the sense that most proof branches (or sub-cases) have been discharged, and there are only few open branches left, then the program to be verified may be fully correct – or still fail for all inputs – or anything in between. However, a partial proof is still a correctness argument for a part of the input space, if all branches that are relevant for that part are closed. Currently no techniques are available for defining the part of the state space covered by a proof and for estimating what size or probability it has.

In this paper, we introduce the concept of *state space coverage* for partial proofs (Sect. 3), which defines to what extend a partial proof covers the state space of the program and what proportion of the possible inputs are covered by the completed part of the proof. Thus, similar to testing, the degree of assurance grows with the effort invested in constructing a correctness proof.

© Springer Nature Switzerland AG 2018
T. Margaria and B. Steffen (Eds.): ISoLA 2018, LNCS 11245, pp. 53–63, 2018.
https://doi.org/10.1007/978-3-030-03421-4_4

We evaluate our concept using (partial) proofs constructed using the KeY system [1] (Sect. 4). KeY is a deductive program verification tool with which Java programs can be verified w.r.t. contracts written in the Java Modeling Language [9]. The deductive component of KeY uses a sequent calculus for JavaDL, a program logic for Java. We have implemented a prototypical tool that estimates the coverage of partial KeY proofs using test data, thus combining static and runtime verification techniques.

The notions introduced in this paper are not restricted to the KeY system, but can easily be adapted to any deductive program verification system based on a program logic and calculus.

There has already been work on extracting useful information from incomplete proofs. Particularly helpful are counterexamples; however, they are only available if the proof is known to have failed and not if it is just incomplete, and it is unknown whether it could be completed. Another type of useful information are test cases constructed from (partial) proofs (e.g. [3]). Such tests can then be used to assess program correctness, but they do not provide information on how big the coverage of the proof is. An incomplete proof can also be used to generate a simplified software monitor [2], thus reducing the execution overhead of the monitored software. In [10], an approach for estimating the reliability of software based on statistical testing is presented. Partial proofs are used to obtain a precise reliability estimate from fewer tests.

2   Preliminaries

The ideas for evaluating a partial proof that are outlined in this paper do not heavily depend on details of the underlying logical framework. They (only) require that properties of programs are proved using a program logic, i.e., a logic in which the program syntactically occurs as part of the proof obligation. Hoare logics, predicate logic over weakest precondition predicate transformers, and dynamic logic are examples of such program logics. The framework can be applied to proof scenarios in which the calculus produces a proof in form of a proof *tree*, in which the nodes contain proof goals and the rule applications extend the tree.

In the following, we present our framework using a sequent calculus for a first-order dynamic logic, JavaDL, but the concepts can be adapted to other program logics easily.

We assume that formulas are evaluated in *states*. The set of states $\mathcal{S}$ contains all possible assignments of values to program variables. To keep the presentation simple, we assume that, in case the programming language supports sophisticated memory structures (like a heap), memory is encoded as one particular program variable. We refer to input states as the initial states of a program execution.

Dynamic logic [7] is a program logic adding modal operators like $[\pi]\varphi$ to first-order logic, where π is a program and φ a formula. This formula is true in an input state $s \in S$ if and only if φ holds in all states in which the program π can terminate if started in s.[1]

When using a sequent calculus [1,5], every node in the proof tree is a *sequent*, a tuple $\Gamma \vdash \Delta$ of two (possibly empty) sets of formulas (with Γ the *antecedent* and Δ the *succedent*). Semantically, a sequent is equivalent to the formula $\bigwedge \gamma \rightarrow \bigvee \delta$. The set of all sequents is denoted by Seq.

A proof for a dynamic logic formula φ is a tree with root $\vdash \varphi$, which grows bottom-to-top (with the root at the bottom) by applying (inference) *rules* to leaves of the tree. An inference rule

$$\frac{P_1 \quad \cdots \quad P_n}{C}$$

for sequents $P_1, \ldots, P_n, C \in \text{Seq}$ can be applied to a leaf if the conclusion C is the sequent in the leaf; the premisses $P_1, \ldots, P_n$ are then added as children (new leaves) to this node. If an axiom (a rule without premisses) is applied to a leaf, this closes the branch of the proof tree. A proof is complete if all its branches are closed.

An inference rule is (globally) sound if the validity of $P_1, \ldots, P_n$ implies the validity of C. A rule is called locally sound if $P_1 \wedge \ldots \wedge P_n \rightarrow C$ is valid. For many – but not all – rules, the equivalence $P_1 \wedge \ldots \wedge P_n \leftrightarrow C$ is valid. In that case, a locally sound rule is called confluent; otherwise, it is called a weakening rule.

One example of a locally sound, confluent sequent calculus rule for dynamic logic is the following rule schema for the if-statement, introducing a case condition for the two possible paths that the program can follow depending on the truth value of the condition:

$$\frac{\Gamma, cond \vdash [p]\varphi, \Delta \qquad \Gamma \vdash cond, [q]\varphi, \Delta}{\Gamma \vdash [\texttt{if } cond \texttt{ then } p \texttt{ else } q]\varphi, \Delta} \tag{1}$$

3 State Space Coverage

The central notion which we introduce in the following is that of *state space coverage* of a partial proof. Intuitively, this coverage is that part of the input state space (the set of possible input states) to which a given (partial) proof applies. In the domain of verification by testing, various different notions of coverage exist. Many of them are measures on a syntactical level and describe which (or how many) statements, paths, branches, or other syntactical entities have been visited by at least one test case. Please note that state space coverage is fundamentally different from these notions of test case coverage. State space coverage is a measure on the semantic level and describes which input values are covered by closed proof branches. There also exist testing methods that are semantics notions in this respect. The coverage criteria of so-called partition testing base

---

[1] The semantics of $[\pi]\varphi$ coincides with that of the weakest-liberal-precondition predicate transformer $wlp(\pi, \varphi)$.

on a partition of the input space (e.g. equivalence partitioning, category partition, or domain testing, see the survey by Grindal et al. [6]). Testing, however, investigates individual test cases of the different subsets to cover them, whereas a formal proofs cover all elements of a set. Table 1 compares state space coverage against notions of syntactical test case coverage.

Table 1. Comparison of test case coverage and state space coverage.

	Test case coverage	State space coverage
Covering entities	Test cases	Closed proof branches
Covered entities	Statements (paths, ...)	Input states
Full coverage	All statements (paths, ...) are executed by at least one test case	The claim is proved to hold on every input
Numerical value	Ratio of covered to all statements (paths, ...)	Probability that an encountered input is covered by the proof

The first characterisation of state space coverage ("the input states to which the proof applies") is kept deliberately vague. The reason is that there are several related interesting coverage criteria which we can look at:

1. The set of states on which the claim (the formula in the root of the proof) is true (the *claim coverage*).
2. For a partial proof: The set of input states that satisfy the sequents of all open goals (the *proof coverage*).
3. The set of input states whose program run does not depend on an open goal (the *program coverage*).
4. The experimental empirical approximation of the latter (the *empirical coverage*).

To eventually cast these informal notions into a more formal shape, we first need to set the stage by defining more closely the analysed artefacts:

We assume that the investigated claim (for which the coverage is to be determined) is of the shape $pre \rightarrow [\pi]post$. Here, the claim is formulated using dynamic logic; but as mentioned earlier, this can be easily adapted to other program logics. An example for a claim is the formula

$$x > 0 \rightarrow [\text{if } odd(x) \text{ then } x = x - 1 \text{ else } x = x/2]even(x) \ . \qquad (2)$$

It states that for every non-negative integer after executing the if-statement, x contains an even integer. This claim is not valid: for an input state with, e.g., $s(x) = 6$, this formula does not hold.

Figure 1 shows a partial proof tree for claim (2). First, the rule schema (1) is applied to the if-statement, splitting the proof into one branch for the "then"-case and one for the "else"-case. We assume that the "then"-case branch on the left has already been extended to a closed sub-proof (though not all rule applications are shown here). The "else"-case on the right is more complicated. We already know that it cannot be closed because the else-part of the program is not correct. But often during program verification, it is not obvious whether an open branch indicates an invalid claim or results from an insufficiently strong (automatic) proof engine, which failed to find the right rule applications to close the sub-proof. Here, we assume that the person conducting the proof applied the cut rule (case distinction) using the cut formula $\exists k.x = 4k$ to distinguish the case where x is divisible by 4 from the case where it is not. So far, both branches arising from the cut-rule application, (A) and (B), remain open. Yet one of them is closable (A) and one is not (B).

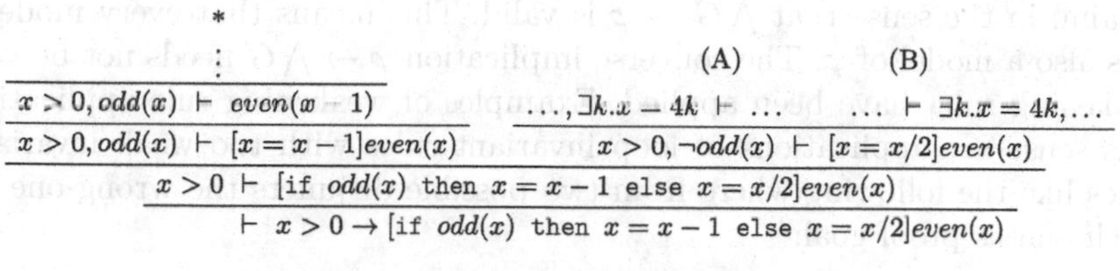

$$
\begin{array}{c}
\overline{ *} \\
\vdots \\
\hline
\dfrac{x > 0, odd(x) \vdash even(x-1) \qquad\qquad\qquad \text{(A)} \qquad\qquad \text{(B)}}{} \\
\end{array}
$$

$$
\dfrac{\dfrac{\dfrac{x > 0, odd(x) \vdash even(x-1) \qquad\qquad ..., \exists k.x = 4k \vdash ... \qquad ... \vdash \exists k.x = 4k, ...}{x > 0, odd(x) \vdash [x = x-1]even(x) \qquad\qquad x > 0, \neg odd(x) \vdash [x = x/2]even(x)}}{x > 0 \vdash [\text{if } odd(x) \text{ then } x = x-1 \text{ else } x = x/2]even(x)}}{\vdash x > 0 \to [\text{if } odd(x) \text{ then } x = x-1 \text{ else } x = x/2]even(x)}
$$

Fig. 1. Partial proof tree for (2)

3.1 Proofs and Coverage

Our first definition of state space coverage is purely semantic and fully independent of any conducted proof or the power of the applied calculus. It only depends on the models of the claim to be proved:

Definition 1 (Claim coverage). *Let* $\varphi = pre \to [\pi]post$ *be a program verification claim. Then, the claim state-space coverage* C_{claim} *is defined as*

$$
C_{claim} = \{s \in \mathcal{S} \mid s \models \varphi\} .
$$

Going a step towards analysing proofs, the next coverage notion we define will take a (partial) proof into consideration. But then, the properties of the calculus used to produce the proofs become relevant for coverage. Obviously, the calculus must be sound. Only then can closed branches be guaranteed to provide knowledge about the correctness of the claim. However, global soundness is not sufficient; rules need to be locally sound. For example, consider the following inference rule:

$$
\dfrac{\vdash x \neq 23}{\vdash x = 42}
$$

Since its premiss is not valid, any non-valid formula can be used as conclusion for the rule to be globally sound. However, the model sets of the premiss (all states with $x \neq 23$) and of the conclusion (all states with $x = 42$) are totally unrelated, which shows that it is not possible to derive knowledge about the claim at the root of the proof tree from state coverage at the leaves if this rule is applied. Thus, we require that all calculus rules must be locally sound. One exemption from that requirement is for Skolemisation rules like

$$\frac{\vdash \varphi[x \leftarrow c]}{\vdash \forall x. \varphi} \qquad \text{where } c \text{ is a constant not occurring in } \varphi \ .$$

Despite being not locally sound, such rules are admissible provided that the notion of state space coverage is restricted to the input variables of the claim (and, in particular, excludes the added constant symbol c).

Any (partial) proof for φ conducted with a calculus satisfying the above restrictions has a nice property: The conjunction of the open goals G implies the claim, in the sense that $\bigwedge G \to \varphi$ is valid. This means that every model of $\bigwedge G$ is also a model of φ. The converse implication $\varphi \to \bigwedge G$ needs not be valid if weakening rules have been applied. Examples of weakening rule applications in this sense are applications of loop invariant rules with too weak invariants or rules like the following where from two possible disjuncts the wrong one has been chosen as proof goal:[2]

$$\frac{\vdash \ even(2x + 1)}{\vdash \ even(2x) \lor even(2x + 1)}$$

The conclusion of the rule application contains a valid formula for which a closed proof could still be found. The open goal (the premiss of the rule application), however, cannot be closed anymore; it contains an unsatisfiable formula.

Definition 2 (Proof coverage). *Let* $\varphi = pre \to [\pi]post$ *be a program verification claim, let P be a (partial) proof for φ, and let $G \subseteq$ Seq be the set of open goals (leaves) of P. Then, the* proof state-space coverage $C_{proof} \subseteq S$ *for P is defined as*

$$C_{proof} = \{s \in S \mid s \models g \text{ for all } g \in G\} \ .$$

We can directly make two observations for the two definitions introduced so far:

- For a claim φ and a proof P for φ, the claim always covers at least as much as the proof: $C_{proof} \subseteq C_{claim}$. As mentioned above, the proof root is a logical consequence of the conjunction of the proof leaves, the open goals. The models of the leaves (C_{proof}) are hence a subset of the root's models (C_{claim}).
- For a proof in which every applied rule is confluent, claim and proof coverage are the same: $C_{proof} = C_{claim}$. Equivalence is also a transitive property and the proof root is equivalent to the conjunction of the proof leaves, and, therefore, has the same models.

---

[2] An instance of the rule *or-intro-2* from the natural deduction calculus.

3.2   Programs and Coverage

The problem of the two state space coverage notions introduced so far is that they are inherently semantic in the sense that they do not distinguish between a closed proof branch and one whose leaf is valid, i.e., one that *can* be closed. In practice, if a proof attempt does not lead to a closed proof, but one or more goals remain open, it *does* make a difference whether a goal *is* closed or *can* be closed. It is the purpose of the proof to establish the goal's validity, so any analysis that tries to establish whether the proof can be closed must be as complex as the proof search itself. There must be another notion of state space coverage which allows for precisely that: One in which an open goal is treated differently from a closed goal, and where the validity of the goal does not directly play into the coverage. However, a purely syntactical coverage definition is not feasible as it must be decided whether an open goal "belongs to" or "is relevant for" an input state, which is a semantic question.

In order to introduce "relevance" into our notion of coverage, we introduce a function $R : \text{Seq} \to \text{Seq}$ operating on proof nodes and assigning to each open goal $g \in G$ of a proof tree P a sequent $R(g)$ called the *relevancy* of g, which must satisfy the condition $R(g) \models g$. Technically speaking, $R(g)$ must be a strengthening[3] of g.

The relevancy decides for which part of the state space a particular goal is "responsible". Intuitively, considering a proof by repeated case distinction, a state s can satisfy an open goal for two reasons: Either because the local claim is true for s or because the goal is not relevant for s. If a case distinction rule[4] has been applied to a formula ψ, it is reasonable to assume that the relevancy of the parent node is shared amongst the two resulting branches: one is responsible for the case ψ and other for $\neg\psi$. In the context of program verification, case distinctions occur quite naturally in the form of symbolic path conditions. As can be seen in Fig. 1, any split caused by the analysis of a statement "if ψ then π else τ" adds ψ (resp. $\neg\psi$) as an assumption to the antecedent. As you can already see in Fig. 1, a proof follows the path structure of the program under investigation.

In general, during the course of the proof for a claim stating a program correctness property, several path condition assumptions $pc_1, \ldots, pc_n$ will be added to the antecedent. Typically an intermediate sequent is of the shape

$$pre, pc_1, \ldots, pc_n \vdash [\pi]post \ .$$

For a goal g of that shape, the relevancy $R(g)$ can be defined as a syntactically easily derived strengthened sequent by omitting those formulas which make up the proof obligation and concentrating on the path condition:

$$R_{path}(g) \ = \ pre, pc_1, \ldots, pc_n \vdash \ .$$

---

[3] Since, in sequent calculus, rules are applied bottom-up, i.e., from the conclusion to the premiss, strengthening a goal corresponds to applying a top-to-bottom weakening rule. This may seem paradoxical, but it is not: top-to-bottom weakening is the same as bottom-to-top strengthening.

[4] For example, the *cut*-rule in sequent calculus.

This is by no means the only possibly relevancy that one can define. Another interesting relevancy notion is first-order relevancy, in which all formulas on the sequent that are first-order formulas, i.e., do not contain a program modality, are collected.

The notion of relevancy gives us a means to define a coverage that contains those states whose *relevant* proof goals are closed:

Definition 3 (Program coverage). *Let* $\varphi = pre \rightarrow [\pi]post$ *be a program verification claim, let P be a (partial) proof for φ, and let $G \subseteq$ Seq be the set of open goals (leaves) of P. Further, let $R :$ Seq $\rightarrow$ Seq be a relevancy function. Then, the program state-space coverage $C_{program}$ for P is defined as*

$$C_{program} = \{s \in \mathcal{S} \mid s \models R(g) \text{ for all } g \in G\}$$

Intuitively, this means that $C_{program}$ contains those states for which no open proof goal in G is relevant.

3.3   Example

Let us come back to the program verification claim (2) and the partial proof tree shown in Fig. 1. Since x is the only program variable in this example, states are determined by the value of x. As the postcondition is not satisfied by all poststates that arise from states that satisfy the precondition, the claim is not universally valid and claim coverage cannot be full. Indeed, the set of models of the claim is $C_{claim} = \{v \in \mathbb{Z} \mid v \leq 0 \text{ or } v - 2 \notin 4\mathbb{Z}\}$[5].

For simplicity, let us now assume that inputs are not drawn from $\mathbb{Z}$, but that the routine can only ever be invoked with values from $\{0, 1, 2, 3\}$. Then, C_{claim} covers 75% of the state space. The probability that a program run will satisfy the claim is $\Pr(x = v, v \in C_{claim})$, which is $1 - \Pr(x = 2)$. This probability is again 75% in case the inputs are equally distributed.

The proof state space coverage cannot be greater than the claim coverage. Since the partial proof in Fig. 1 does only invoke confluent rules, a proof can still be constructed for all cases in which the claim holds: $C_{claim} = C_{proof}$ and all probabilities are the same.

The program coverage C_{path} using the path relevancy R_{path} is different, however. Non-positive numbers, including 0, are still covered because of the precondition. The odd numbers are also covered because of the closed sub-proof on the left. The open branches (A) and (B) both have the same relevancy

$$R_{path}(A) = R_{path}(B) = \qquad x > 0, \neg odd(x) \vdash$$

which is not satisfied by positive even numbers such that the program coverage is $C_{path} = \{v \in \mathbb{Z} \mid v \leq 0 \text{ or } v \notin 2\mathbb{Z}\}$. Assuming once again that the input is restricted to values between 0 and 3, this covers 50% of the state space.

If the proof was continued and case (A) was additionally closed, this number would not change since (A) and (B) share the same path relevancy. However, the

---

[5] i.e., v does not have remainder 2 when dividing by 4.

first-order coverage would increase from 50% to 75% by closing (A), since the case distinction $\exists k.x = 4k$ would be taken into account by first-order relevancy.

4   A Tool for Estimating Program Coverage

We have prototypically implemented an estimation of program coverage (using path relevance) [8] for partial proofs constructed in the KeY [1] system. KeY is a semi-interactive theorem prover for the verification of Java programs annotated with specifications in the Java Modeling Language (JML). KeY encodes the specified Java programs as a formula in JavaDL, a dynamic logic for Java. It then attempts to show the validity of this formula with a sequent calculus for JavaDL. The goal of the implementation of the presented approach is to empirically approximate the program coverage of a partial KeY proof.

In the first step of the implementation, a simple syntactical analysis of the partial proof tree finds the program statements that were symbolically executed in each proof tree branch. The sequence of executed program statements determines a program path; thus, we find the program paths that correspond to a given (open or closed) proof branch.

Using this information, in the second step, the Java code gets instrumented using counters at branching statements, allowing the counting of the number of times a path was taken when the program is executed multiple times.

In the third step, an input oracle is used producing input states according to a defined distribution. The program is executed for these inputs, and we count the number of times a path corresponding to an open goal is taken. This is done until the ratio of successful to all program runs can be estimated with sufficient confidence, by computing Wilson's Score Interval [11].

As an alternative to generating the inputs with an oracle, software monitoring could be used. Thus it can be checked at runtime how many applications of the program are covered by a proof, and how often unproved parts of the code are executed. A warning could be issued if this value drops too low.

Related approaches for the probabilistic analysis of programs have been described in a recent survey paper [4].

The example in Listing 1 consists of a Java method specified with JML [9] that, given three integers x, y, z, will return one of these three integers such that there is at least one that is greater than or equal to and one that is lower than or equal to the returned value. Proving this method with KeY results in 6 proof branches, each corresponding to one of the six paths in the program. Each of these program paths is taken for one sixth of the possible inputs. Therefore, closing each of the branches will cover one sixth of the inputs. The results of using our implementation to compute the Wilson score interval (95% confidence) for the example in Listing 1 is consistent with this observation – each closed branch increases the program coverage by one sixth.

```
/*@ public normal_behavior
 @   ensures \result <= y && \result <= z ||
 @           \result <= x && \result <= z ||
 @           \result <= x && \result <= y;
 @*/
public int middle(int x, int y, int z) {
    int mid = z;
    if (y<z) {
        if (x<y) { mid = y; }
        else if (x<z) { mid = x; }
    } else {
        if (x>y) { mid = y; }
        else if (x>z) { mid = x; }
    }
    return mid;
}
```

Listing 1. Example method

5 Conclusion and Outlook

In this paper, we introduced a new notion of coverage for incomplete correctness proofs in program calculi. State space coverage defines for which states a partial incomplete proof shows the original claim. We identified three types of state space coverage: *Claim coverage* describes the states where the claim is semantically true, *proof coverage* describes the set of states for which the claim can still at most be proved, and *program coverage* describes the set of states for which the partial proof indeed establishes that the claim is true. We described the impact of using different types of calculus rules on the coverage, and showed how different possible notions of relevant formulas can be used to define a program coverage.

A prototypical implementation on top of the theorem prover KeY allowed us to conduct first experiments to empirically estimate the program coverage of partial correctness proofs for loop-free Java methods.

It remains as future work to extend the method for estimating coverage to a notion of trace space coverage which covers more than the initial states and takes loops and (recursive) method invocations into account.

References

1. Ahrendt, W., Beckert, B., Bubel, R., Hähnle, R., Schmitt, P.H., Ulbrich, M. (eds.): Deductive Software Verification - The KeY Book: From Theory to Practice, LNCS, vol. 10001. Springer, Cham (2016). https://doi.org/10.1007/978-3-319-49812-6
2. Ahrendt, W., Chimento, J.M., Pace, G.J., Schneider, G.: Verifying data- and control-oriented properties combining static and runtime verification: theory and tools. Form. Methods Syst. Des. **51**(1), 200–265 (2017)

3. Ahrendt, W., Gladisch, C., Herda, M.: Proof-based test case generation. In: Ahrendt et al. [1], Chap. 12, pp. 415–451. https://doi.org/10.1007/978-3-319-49812-6

4. Dwyer, M.B., Filieri, A., Geldenhuys, J., Gerrard, M., Păsăreanu, C.S., Visser, W.: Probabilistic program analysis. In: Cunha, J., Fernandes, J.P., Lämmel, R., Saraiva, J., Zaytsev, V. (eds.) GTTSE 2015. LNCS, vol. 10223, pp. 1–25. Springer, Cham (2017). https://doi.org/10.1007/978-3-319-60074-1_1

5. Gentzen, G.: Untersuchungen über das logische Schließen. Mathematische Zeitschrift **39** 176–210, 405–431 (1935)

6. Grindal, M., Offutt, J., Andler, S.F.: Combination testing strategies: a survey. Softw. Test. Verif. Reliab. **15**(3), 167–199 (2005). https://doi.org/10.1002/stvr.319

7. Harel, D., Kozen, D., Tiuryn, J.: Dynamic logic. SIGACT News **32**(1), 66–69 (2001). https://doi.org/10.1145/568438.568456

8. Kobischke, S.: Sampling-based Execution Coverage Estimation for Partially Proved Java Program Specifications. Master's thesis, Karlsruhe Institute of Technology (2018)

9. Leavens, G.T., et al.: JML Reference Manual, draft Revision 2344, 31 May 2013

10. ben Nasr Omri, F.: Weighted Statistical Testing based on Active Learning and Formal Verification Techniques for Software Reliability Assessment. Ph.D. thesis, Karlsruhe Institute of Technology (2015). http://digbib.ubka.uni-karlsruhe.de/volltexte/1000050941

11. Wilson, E.B.: Probable inference, the law of succession, and statistical inference. J. Am. Stat. Assoc. **22**(158), 209–212 (1927). https://doi.org/10.1080/01621459.1927.10502953

Generating Inductive Shape Predicates for Runtime Checking and Formal Verification

Jan H. Boockmann[1], Gerald Lüttgen[1(✉)], and Jan Tobias Mühlberg[2]

[1] Software Technologies Research Group, University of Bamberg,
96045 Bamberg, Germany
{jan.boockmann,gerald.luettgen}@swt-bamberg.de
[2] imec-DistriNet, KU Leuven, Celestijnenlaan 200A, 3001 Leuven, Belgium
jantobias.muehlberg@cs.kuleuven.be

Abstract. Knowing the shapes of dynamic data structures is key when formally reasoning about pointer programs. While modern shape analysis tools employ symbolic execution and machine learning to infer shapes, they often assume well-structured C code or programs written in an idealised language. In contrast, our *Data Structure Investigator* (DSI) tool for program comprehension analyses concrete executions and handles even C programs with complex coding styles.

Our current research on memory safety develops ways for DSI to synthesise inductive shape predicates in separation logic. In the context of trusted computing, we investigate how the inferred predicates can be employed to generate runtime checks for securely communicating dynamic data structures across trust boundaries. We also explore to what extent these predicates, together with additional information extracted by DSI, can be used within general program verifiers such as *VeriFast*.

This paper accompanies a talk at the ISoLA 2018 track *"A Broader View on Verification: From Static to Runtime and Back"*. It introduces DSI, highlights the above use cases, and sketches our approach for synthesising inductive shape predicates.

1 Motivation

Formally reasoning about the memory safety and security of C code executing on processors is a serious challenge, especially when dynamic data structures are involved. The advent of separation logic [18] for modularly specifying heap operations and data structure shapes has sparked a wealth of research in the computer-aided verification of pointer programs. This has led to the development of powerful static verifiers, including shape analysis tools such as *Forester* [9] and *Infer* [6,7] and program verifiers such as *VeriFast* [17]. While the latter

---

Research supported by the German Research Foundation (DFG) under grant *"DSI2: Learning Data Structure Behaviour from Executions of Pointer Programs"* (LU 1748/4-2) and by the Research Fund KU Leuven.

© Springer Nature Switzerland AG 2018
T. Margaria and B. Steffen (Eds.): ISoLA 2018, LNCS 11245, pp. 64–74, 2018.
https://doi.org/10.1007/978-3-030-03421-4_5

requires significant manual effort in annotating programs with contracts, recent automated shape analysis techniques employ machine learning [4,25] but assume well-structured code and a well-behaved execution environment. However, these assumptions are violated by software for modern processors that include field-programmable hardware such as Intel's *Broadwell Xeon* or Xilinx' *Zync*, and on processors that provide secure enclaves such as Intel's *SGX* [13].

This motivates us to consider recent advancements in dynamic analysis tools for identifying pointer-based data structures such as linked lists and their interconnections such as parent-child nesting, from concrete execution traces of instrumented source code [1,12,24] or even binaries [5,8,10,19]. Among these, the *Data Structure Investigator* (DSI) tool [24] distinguishes itself by a novel heap representation based on so-called *strands*, which can handle even C programs employing complex and sometimes 'dirty' coding styles and pointer operations; see, e.g., the cyclic doubly-linked list (DLL) of the Linux kernel [11]. Indeed, cyclicity is a runtime property that is nontrivial to check with static analysis; the same is true when figuring out whether the two pointers in a DLL struct do indeed contribute to a DLL rather than a binary tree.

While DSI has so far aimed at program comprehension, its inferred data structure information may be useful for generating inductive shape predicates for a variety of use cases that range from runtime checking to formal verification, including the following two:

Specifying Secure Wrappers. Isolation and trust boundaries between software and hardware components play an important role when implementing security features, e.g., using trusted execution environments such as *SGX* [13] or *Sancus* [16]. Trust boundaries must be crossed to transfer data in and out of protection domains, thus rendering these transfers a potential attack vector. When linked data structures with pointers are accessed from within an enclave, these pointers may be abused to manipulate the execution flow of the enclave.

The underlying problem can be generalised as execution of trusted code in an untrusted context. It bears similarity with executing formally verified software in an unverified operating system, thereby exposing the verified code to interactions not captured during verification. In a similar way, field-programmable hardware extensions in modern computing systems may violate the assumed program semantics by modifying memory concurrent to the main processor and in a way unknown at the time of software development. It is likely that these problems can best be addressed at runtime.

Recent work [2,21] has demonstrated how shape specifications of dynamic data structures written in VeriFast's flavour of separation logic can be used to employ *secure wrappers* for copying data between trusted and untrusted system components. These wrappers execute checks of shape properties at runtime, thereby monitoring the secure communication of dynamic data structures between protection domains and helping one to prevent crashes and a range of vulnerabilities including code injection attacks. However, shape specifications are difficult to obtain in practice, not at least due to the serious cost in terms of person hours for developing them when complex, low-level C code is involved [17].

An open question is how to automatically generate shape specifications suitable for secure wrapper synthesis from source code.

Generating Verification Annotations. Our second use case concerns the challenge of formally verifying the memory safety of C programs in tools such as Veri-Fast [17]. While VeriFast has been successfully employed to verifying C source code of industrial projects, it requires a skilled engineer to annotate each C function with its contract, i.e., a pre- and post-condition specified in a separation logic dialect. Our prior work [15] employed DSI's predecessor *dsOli* [23] to support this time-consuming task, by inferring those parts of contracts that involve data structure shape only.

The tool dsOli combines machine learning and pattern matching to automatically locate and identify operations on linked-list data structures in C programs, and outputs a set of instantiated operation templates. Each such template describes a data structure operation performed by the program, e.g., list inserts and removals. Corresponding verification annotation templates for VeriFast can then be instantiated and injected into the program's source code automatically, which allows VeriFast to discharge memory safety properties either automatically or after slight manual adjustments of the annotations.

However, our approach inherited dsOli's restrictions of well-structured C code and non-nested list structures. The advancements of DSI in terms of its fine-granular strand abstraction of list structures and its robustness against different C coding styles now allows us to generate verification annotations for general list structures, i.e., without the limitation that each shape requires us to define a new template. The research questions here are (a) in how far one can also auto-generate suitable loop invariants and lemmas needed by VeriFast, and (b) to what degree memory safety proofs can be automated in VeriFast. Notably, VeriFast predicates, lemmas and invariants must not only be inferred but phrased in ways that enable VeriFast's advanced automation capabilities.

Agenda. Our current research explores to what extent the data structure information excavated by DSI can be employed to address the above uses cases. At the heart will be a novel generator that automatically synthesises inductive shape predicates of linked-list data structures, taking DSI's global strand representation as input and providing local separation logic predicates suitable for VeriFast as output. In this context, we also need to extract some additional information internally inferred by DSI, in order to obtain shape contracts for the functions contained in the C source code under study, in terms of pre- and post-conditions and accompanying lemmas.

Such shape contracts are exactly the input needed to construct secure wrapper functions for protection domains in our first use case. Our second use case of memory safety verification in VeriFast requires the synthesis of more general lemmas and verification annotations. This is significantly more challenging, e.g., due to the necessity of loop invariants, so that we expect to only be able to generate skeletons of verification annotations.

Organisation. The remainder of this paper is structured as follows. The next section briefly introduces our DSI tool and its strand abstraction of list-based dynamic data structures. We then explain how shape specifications in VeriFast's language may be inferred from DSI's output, illustrate this via a simple but non-trivial example involving a Linux-style list with nested child lists, and discuss the challenges for making our approach work for our two use cases.

2   DSI: Data Structure Investigator

DSI is a dynamic analysis for the automatic identification of pointer-based data structures [24]. It detects (cyclic) singly and doubly linked lists (SLLs/DLLs) and binary trees, as well as other structures such as skip lists that are not handled by related work [5,8,10]. Additionally, DSI allows for arbitrary parent-child nesting combinations of such data structures, which is also out of scope of related work. This section surveys DSI's technologies and sketches its representation of data structure shapes by means of an example.

Memory Abstraction. DSI operates by executing C source code that is instrumented for recording pointer writes and memory allocations and deallocations. Its dynamic analysis relies on a novel memory abstraction, *strand graphs*, for interpreting the points-to graphs constructed from such recordings. Intuitively, a strand graph represents a data structure shape at a specific time step of the program's execution. Its nodes are strands that essentially consist of singly linked lists, and its edges are strand connections that represent, e.g., nesting.

A *strand* consists of list nodes that are permitted to cover sub-regions of memory and are termed *cells*. A strand's cells must all have the same linkage condition, i.e., all pointers originate at the same linkage offset relative to the cell's start address, and must point to the start address of the following cell. This general definition allows us to deal with complex coding styles of lists in C, such as the one employed by the Linux cyclic DLL [11] whose nodes may run through types of structs that are embedded in outer structs. Thereby, different list nodes may be of different types, and a node's successor (predecessor) field may point inside the successor's (predecessor's) node.

A *strand connection* describes exactly one way out of the potentially multiple ways in which the cells of two strands may be related. Typical connections are, e.g., *indirect nesting* or *overlay nesting*, where the latter means that a child list's head node is contained in its parent node, or the *dll* connection, where two strands running through list nodes are overlaid in such a way that two neighbouring nodes are mutually linked.

Evidence Gathering. The biggest challenge for detecting linked-list data structures at runtime comes with data structure operations. These tend to temporarily break a data structure's shape, e.g., when rewriting pointers during the insertion into a linked list. To discriminate against degenerate shapes, DSI uses a unique evidence-collecting algorithm, which utilises the structural complexity of an observed shape as evidence measure and which reinforces evidence counts by exploiting structural and temporal repetition.

For structural repetition, DSI detects and folds all strands that perform the same role within one time step, e.g., the strands representing the child lists of the nodes of a parent list. Regarding temporal repetition, DSI determines which folded strands represent the same data structure building block over multiple time steps. For each entry pointer to a data structure and each time step in which the entry pointer exists, the temporal repetition is performed by extracting the folded strand graph's subgraph that is reachable from the entry pointer. All extracted subgraphs are then merged over the lifetime of the entry pointer, resulting in an aggregate strand graph.

All evidence counts of strand connections are accumulated when folding strands and aggregating strand graphs. The identified data structure shape then manifests itself by the aggregate strand graph when ignoring strand connections with low evidence counts. Evidence counts for the correct shape of a data structure accumulate quickly, because the majority of stable shapes within a program execution overrides the minority of degenerate shapes. Experimental evaluations with our DSI tool have shown that a significant variety and quantity of complex C source code can be handled and that, in each case, our evidence-based approach leads to the correct identification of data structure shape [24] and reveals sufficient contextual data to inform static verification [15].

Example. Figure 1 contains a simple example of a 'Linux-style' cyclic SLL with overlay-nested non-cyclic child SLLs. A snippet of the C source code is depicted on the left, showing the data structure definition via nested structs and a node insert operation into the child list. DSI's interpretation of the data structure – from a given entry pointer, here ep – is displayed on the right in terms of the points-to graphs, the strand graphs and the folded strand graphs across two consecutive time steps t and $t+1$, as well as the resulting aggregate strand graph, each decorated with evidence counts for the detected strand connections.

The time steps are selected such that the data structure is in a degenerate shape at time step t, as it is in the middle of an insert operation at the head of the second child list, whereas it is in a stable shape at time step $t+1$, i.e., at the end of the insertion operation. DSI's evidence counts for the strand connection types occurring in this example are as follows: 1 for two nested strands where the head cell of the child strand is located in the same node as the parent strand's cell (*overlay nesting*), and k for two strands that intersect in k nodes (*overlay intersection*). Evidences of corresponding strand connections are simply summed up when folding and again when aggregating strand graphs. Observe that, when aggregating the folded strand graphs, strand $\{S_4\}$ is not considered as the full strand is not reachable from the entry pointer ep.

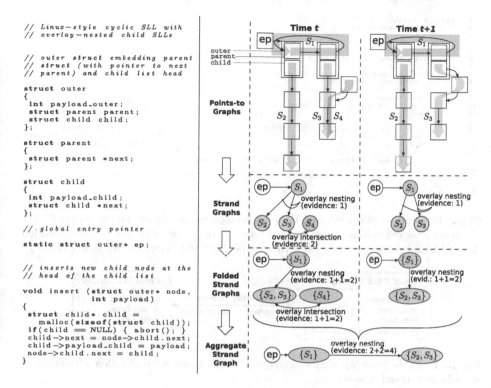

```
// Linux-style cyclic SLL with
// overlay-nested child SLLs

// outer struct embedding parent
// struct (with pointer to next
// parent) and child list head

struct outer
{
  int payload_outer;
  struct parent parent;
  struct child child;
};

struct parent
{
  struct parent *next;
};

struct child
{
  int payload_child;
  struct child *next;
};

// global entry pointer

static struct outer* ep;

// inserts new child node at the
// head of the child list

void insert (struct outer* node,
             int payload)
{
  struct child* child =
    malloc(sizeof(struct child));
  if(child == NULL) { abort(); }
  child->next = node->child.next;
  child->payload_child = payload;
  node->child.next = child;
}
```

Fig. 1. Example: C source code (left) and DSI's strand representation (right).

3   Inferring Shape Information for VeriFast

To enable the two use cases for DSI envisaged in Sect. 1, a tool that infers shape information for VeriFast on the basis of DSI's analysis results is required. This section first sketches the synthesis of inductive shape predicates by means of our example. We then discuss the concrete challenges for generating secure wrapper specifications and, resp., more general verification annotations.

Constructing Shape Predicates from Aggregate Strand Graphs. Shape predicates are constructed via a two step approach: first, the rich type information available in the program's source code is statically analysed to build a predicate skeleton, and second, the runtime information provided by DSI in form of an aggregate strand graph is employed to refine these skeletons.

The first step creates a predicate skeleton for each struct 'touched' by a strand, using an approach similar to [14] and exploiting the structural similarity between C struct definitions and VeriFast predicate definitions. The skeleton generated for **struct parent** of our example of Fig. 1 consists of the black coloured parts of **predicate NodesCSLL** shown in Fig. 2: parameter **node** is the entry pointer to the list, while **count** is the number of nodes contained in the list. The

```
1    struct parent {
2      struct parent *next;
3      //@ struct outer *ghost_outer;
4    };
5
6    predicate NodesCSLL(struct parent *node, struct outer *outer,
7      struct parent *head, int count;) =
8      node == NULL ? count == 0 && head == NULL
9      : count >= 1 && head != NULL
10        && [1/2]node->ghost_outer |-> outer
11        && node->next |-> ?tail
12        && outer->payload_outer |-> _              // payload of outer
13        && outer->child.next |-> ?child            // entry pointer to child
14        && SLL(child, outer, _)                    // child list predicate
15        && outer->child.payload_child |-> _        // payload of child
16        && malloc_block_outer(outer)               // allocated memory chunk
17        && count == 1 ? tail == head :             // tail points to head
18            [1/2]tail->ghost_outer |-> ?tail_outer  &&
19            NodesCSLL(tail, tail_outer, head, count-1);  // continued tail
20
21   predicate CSLL(struct parent *list, struct outer *outer, int count;) =
22     [1/2]list->ghost_outer |-> outer
23     && NodesCSLL(list, outer, list, count);
```

Fig. 2. Example (cont'd): Inferred VeriFast predicates (*simplified*) for the parent CSSL. Elements coloured in blue, green and red relate to the cyclicity property, the embedded child SLL and the Linux-style list structure of this CSLL, resp. (Color figure online)

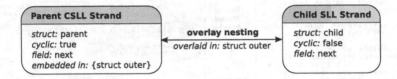

Fig. 3. Example (cont'd): DSI's aggregate strand graph with detailed attributes of strands and strand connections.

predicate is inductive, with the empty list being handled as base case in l. 8 and the induction step's recursive call wrt. the tail list in l. 19.

Observe that the skeleton still lacks information regarding the parent list's cyclicity, the nesting of the child list, and the fact that the parent is a Linux-style list. This information cannot be determined statically from the struct definitions, but is inferred by DSI's analysis. Indeed, when looking at the details of the aggregate strand graph output by DSI as shown in Fig. 3, one can see that the parent strand has property *cyclic*, contains an overlaid-nested child strand of struct child nodes, and the parent nodes of type struct parent are embedded in struct outer. These pieces of information are successively implanted into predicate NodesCSLL as follows.

Firstly, the predicate is refined regarding the list's cyclicity property by adding the parts coloured in blue. In particular, NodesCSLL gains a third parameter (l. 7), namely the head pointer referring to the node in which the cycle is expected to be closed (l. 17). The wrapper predicate CSLL invariantly sets the head to the list's original entry pointer list (l. 21-23). Secondly, the green coloured parts are added to predicate NodesCSLL so as to reflect nesting. Predicate SLL (l. 14) describing the child list is simpler than CSLL and thus not shown in Fig. 2. However, note that parameter outer is required due to the nesting not being indirect nesting but overlay nesting. Thirdly, the parent's Linux-style list is modelled in VeriFast by the red coloured parts in predicate NodesCSLL. We first add a new pointer `outer` as parameter to `NodesCSLL` (l. 6) and extend `struct parent` with a *ghost field* `ghost_outer` to express the link between `struct parent` and `struct outer` (l. 3, and similarly in `struct child`). This field is set via *ghost statements* placed into the source code at locations that can be determined automatically. The connection between a `parent` struct referenced by `node->next` and the corresponding `outer` struct (i.e., `&(outer.parent) == node->next`) is then maintained by consuming a fractional permission [1/2] of the heap chunk associated with this reference in `NodesCSLL(node, ...)`, while the other [1/2] of that chunk is consumed in `NodesCSLL(tail, ...)` where `tail` is `node->next`. This way, each element of the recursive list definition maintains a partial and unmodifiable reference to its successor, while 'opening' the predicates for both the current `node` and the successor `tail` yields a complete reference that allows for list manipulations at that location. To the best of our knowledge, a Linux-style list has not been verified in VeriFast so far.

To conclude, the predicates obtained for our example constructively represent a fairly intricate data structure and are sufficient to generate or verify code that iterates over the list or modifies it by inserting and removing elements at arbitrary positions. Also note that our approach is not compositional: simply defining an inductive VeriFast predicate for each strand of DSI's inferred strand graph and then gluing the predicates together according to the strand connections does, in general, not result in a shape predicate suitable for VeriFast.

Generating Secure Wrapper Specifications. Our first use case employs our approach to synthesising inductive shape predicates for generating secure wrapper specifications for a variant of VeriFast [2,21]. Essentially, secure wrapper specifications are shape contracts between trusted and untrusted program functions, so that the actual shapes of dynamic data structures passed across trust boundaries can be checked against expected shapes by inspecting or deep-copying the data structures at runtime. This poses an exciting application for DSI at the intersection of formal specification and run-time monitoring, in particular because no existing code needs to be verified.

For the integration with VeriFast, only *precise* predicates may be used, where the same input arguments represent the same memory region and always have the same output arguments. This enables constructive reasoning in VeriFast and, thus, allows for advanced automatic processing in verification and code generation. Because our specifications and wrappers can operate on data structures without taking the functional properties of a program's context into account, e.g., we can traverse or copy a linked list from start to end rather than support insert and remove operations at arbitrary positions, we consider this synthesis to be significantly easier than actual program verification. Relying on extended features of DSI, specifically the identification of entry pointers and list types in function prototypes, we can construct shape contracts that correctly associate C-function parameters with data structures, which we believe can be transformed into wrappers for real application code.

Generating Verification Annotations. Our second use case aims at extending our previous work on inferring shape annotations [15] to support full-program verification in VeriFast. Such annotations should be derived directly from strand graphs by exploiting type and allocation information as well as strand connections, rather than relying on the instantiation of annotation templates. For each function contract in the program under analysis, DSI will collect the pair of aggregate strand graphs wrt. the function's head and return, together with the entry pointers for any of its pointer parameters and locally declared function pointers that are relevant to the program's dynamic data structure. Overall, this will result in a fairly generic approach to annotation generation, which would be capable of providing partial annotations for programs that make use of data structures for which no annotation templates exist.

However, generating verification annotations is a much more difficult challenge than generating shape contracts for secure wrappers. Firstly, program verification requires stronger shape contracts that, e.g., express whether and how a data structure is modified, for which list length is an important information. Indeed, DSI internally stores the length of strands so that we can infer whether a strand has grown or shrunk between some function call and return, or between consecutive iterations of a loop body. This provides evidence as to whether the operation encapsulating a function is, e.g., an insert or a delete operation, and which strand is traversed in a particular loop via which entry pointer.

Secondly, we also have to provide annotations that facilitate the verification of function bodies. In particular, we aim to construct loop invariants, which typically requires additional specification elements such as supporting lemmas or even inline annotations to handle data structure manipulations that cannot be expressed as precise predicates. Early-out conditions in iterators as well as insert and delete operations at arbitrary positions within a data structure are challenges that are considered to be hard for verification tools. Here, we believe that our annotation inference approach together with extended automation in VeriFast [14,22] can alleviate verification engineers from some of the burden of writing program specifications. However, it remains to be seen how much can be done in this respect, particularly when considering that the inferred annotations must be phrased in a way that enables VeriFast's automation capabilities.

4   Outlook

Knowing the shapes of a program's dynamic data structures is essential when reasoning about pointer programs. In the context of low-level C programs that frequently employ complex coding styles, this paper argued that such shapes can be inferred automatically by the recent dynamic shape analyser DSI [24] and represented in the separation logic dialect of the VeriFast verifier [17]. This potentially enables two important use cases in the context of secure and safe computing: the automatic synthesis of secure wrappers for securing trust boundaries at runtime [21] and the formal verification of memory safety properties [17].

While our current work focuses on single-threaded C source code, it is conceivable that our applications of DSI to runtime checking and formal verification may be extended to (i) multi-threaded code by considering the *VerCors* verifier [3] and (ii) C/C++ binaries by employing the *DSIbin* front end of DSI [19]. Both extensions are worthwhile because security applications frequently involve concurrent computing architectures and untrusted components that are only available in compiled form. However, the adaptation of DSI to binaries requires either a novel instrumentation tool for modern processors with field-programmable hardware extensions, or extending DSI with memory snapshot support [20] to correlate strand graphs between non-contiguous time steps.

References

1. Aftandilian, E.E., Kelley, S., Gramazio, C., Ricci, N., Su, S.L., Guyer, S.Z.: Heapviz: interactive heap visualization for program understanding and debugging. In: Software Visualization (SOFTVIS 2010), pp. 53–62. ACM (2010)
2. Agten, P., Jacobs, B., Piessens, F.: Sound modular verification of C code executing in an unverified context. In: Principles of Programming Languages (POPL 2015), pp. 581–594. ACM (2015)
3. Blom, S., Darabi, S., Huisman, M., Oortwijn, W.: The VerCors tool set: verification of parallel and concurrent software. In: Polikarpova, N., Schneider, S. (eds.) IFM 2017. LNCS, vol. 10510, pp. 102–110. Springer, Cham (2017). https://doi.org/10.1007/978-3-319-66845-1_7
4. Brockschmidt, M., Chen, Y., Kohli, P., Krishna, S., Tarlow, D.: Learning shape analysis. In: Ranzato, F. (ed.) SAS 2017. LNCS, vol. 10422, pp. 66–87. Springer, Cham (2017). https://doi.org/10.1007/978-3-319-66706-5_4
5. Caballero, J., Grieco, G., Marron, M., Lin, Z., Urbina, D.: Artiste: automatic generation of hybrid data structure signatures from binary code executions. Technical Report TR-IMDEA-SW-2012-001, IMDEA, Spain (2012)
6. Calcagno, C., Distefano, D.: Infer: an automatic program verifier for memory safety of C programs. In: Bobaru, M., Havelund, K., Holzmann, G.J., Joshi, R. (eds.) NFM 2011. LNCS, vol. 6617, pp. 459–465. Springer, Heidelberg (2011). https://doi.org/10.1007/978-3-642-20398-5_33
7. Calcagno, C., et al.: Moving fast with software verification. In: Havelund, K., Holzmann, G., Joshi, R. (eds.) NFM 2015. LNCS, vol. 9058, pp. 3–11. Springer, Cham (2015). https://doi.org/10.1007/978-3-319-17524-9_1
8. Haller, I., Slowinska, A., Bos, H.: Scalable data structure detection and classification for C/C++ binaries. Emp. Softw. Eng. **21**(3), 778–810 (2016)
9. Holík, L., Lengál, O., Rogalewicz, A., Šimáček, J., Vojnar, T.: Fully automated shape analysis based on forest automata. In: Sharygina, N., Veith, H. (eds.) CAV 2013. LNCS, vol. 8044, pp. 740–755. Springer, Heidelberg (2013). https://doi.org/10.1007/978-3-642-39799-8_52
10. Jung, C., Clark, N.: DDT: design and evaluation of a dynamic program analysis for optimizing data structure usage. In: Microarchitecture Symposium (MICRO 2009), pp. 56–66. ACM (2009)
11. Linux kernel 4.1 Cyclic DLL (`include/linux/list.h`). http://www.kernel.org/. Accessed 31 Jan 2017
12. Marron, M., Sanchez, C., Su, Z., Fähndrich, M.: Abstracting runtime heaps for program understanding. IEEE Trans. Softw. Eng. **39**(6), 774–786 (2013)

13. McKeen, F., et al.: Innovative instructions and software model for isolated execution. In: Hardware and Architectural Support for Security and Privacy (HASP 2013), p. 10. ACM (2013)
14. Mohsen, M., Jacobs, B.: One step towards automatic inference of formal specifications using automated VeriFast. In: ter Beek, M.H., Gnesi, S., Knapp, A. (eds.) FMICS/AVoCS -2016. LNCS, vol. 9933, pp. 56–64. Springer, Cham (2016). https://doi.org/10.1007/978-3-319-45943-1_4
15. Mühlberg, J.T., White, D.H., Dodds, M., Lüttgen, G., Piessens, F.: Learning assertions to verify linked-list programs. In: Calinescu, R., Rumpe, B. (eds.) SEFM 2015. LNCS, vol. 9276, pp. 37–52. Springer, Cham (2015). https://doi.org/10.1007/978-3-319-22969-0_3
16. Noorman, J., et al.: Sancus 2.0: a low-cost security architecture for IoT devices. ACM Trans. Priv. Secur. **20**(3), 7:1–7:33 (2017)
17. Philippaerts, P., Mühlberg, J.T., Penninckx, W., Smans, J., Jacobs, B., Piessens, F.: Software verification with VeriFast: industrial case studies. Sci. Comput. Programm. **82**, 77–97 (2014)
18. Reynolds, J.C.: Separation logic: a logic for shared mutable data structures. In: Logic in Computer Science (LICS 2002), pp. 55–74. IEEE (2002)
19. Rupprecht, T., Chen, X., White, D.H., Boockmann, J.H., Lüttgen, G., Bos, H.: DSIbin: identifying dynamic data structures in C/C++ binaries. In: Automated Software Engineering (ASE 2017), pp. 331–341. IEEE/ACM (2017)
20. Urbina, D., Gu, Y., Caballero, J., Lin, Z.: SigPath: a memory graph based approach for program data introspection and modification. In: Kutyłowski, M., Vaidya, J. (eds.) ESORICS 2014. LNCS, vol. 8713, pp. 237–256. Springer, Cham (2014). https://doi.org/10.1007/978-3-319-11212-1_14
21. van Ginkel, N., Strackx, R., Piessens, F.: Automatically generating secure wrappers for SGX enclaves from separation logic specifications. In: Chang, B.-Y.E. (ed.) APLAS 2017. LNCS, vol. 10695, pp. 105–123. Springer, Cham (2017). https://doi.org/10.1007/978-3-319-71237-6_6
22. Vogels, F., Jacobs, B., Piessens, F., Smans, J.: Annotation inference for separation logic based verifiers. In: Bruni, R., Dingel, J. (eds.) FMOODS/FORTE -2011. LNCS, vol. 6722, pp. 319–333. Springer, Heidelberg (2011). https://doi.org/10.1007/978-3-642-21461-5_21
23. White, D.H., Lüttgen, G.: Identifying dynamic data structures by learning evolving patterns in memory. In: Piterman, N., Smolka, S.A. (eds.) TACAS 2013. LNCS, vol. 7795, pp. 354–369. Springer, Heidelberg (2013). https://doi.org/10.1007/978-3-642-36742-7_25
24. White, D.H., Rupprecht, T., Lüttgen, G.: DSI: an evidence-based approach to identify dynamic data structures in C programs. In: Software Testing and Analysis (ISSTA 2016), pp. 259–269. ACM (2016)
25. Zhu, H., Petri, G., Jagannathan, S.: Automatically learning shape specifications. In: Programming Language Design and Implementation (PLDI 2016), pp. 491–507. ACM (2016)

Runtime Assertion Checking and Static Verification: Collaborative Partners

Fonenantsoa Maurica, David R. Cok[✉], and Julien Signoles

CEA, LIST, Software Safety and Security Laboratory,
PC 174, 91191 Gif-sur-Yvette, France
david.cok@cea.fr

Abstract. Runtime assertion checking aspires to a similar level of sound and complete checking of software as does static deductive verification. Furthermore, for the same source language and specification language, runtime and static checking should implement as closely as possible the same semantics. We describe here the architecture used by two different systems to achieve this goal. We accompany that with descriptions of novel designs and implementations that add new capabilities to runtime assertion checking, bringing it closer to the feature coverage of static verification.

1 Introduction

Automated deductive, static verification of software has been increasing in capability over the past decade.[1] This trend was initially fueled by performance and feature improvements in SMT solvers and has now reached the point that software verifications of industrial software in practical use are being executed [9]. Similarly, runtime assertion checking is improving in capability. Runtime checking requires creative and efficient implementations to be able to execute programs instrumented with runtime checks effectively.

In addition, runtime and static checkers are increasingly part of suites of tools, with the assertions being checked coming from some common specification language. Other related tools might perform tasks like specification inference, white box testing, and abstract interpretation. As parts of tool suites, acting on common programming and specification languages, these tools should all adopt a common semantics for both the programming and specification languages. Ideally they accomplish this using a common software infrastructure.

This paper has two goals. First we describe how two different tool suites — OpenJML [13–16] for Java and the Java Modeling Language [10] and Frama-C [26] for ANSI C and the ANSI-C specification language [7] — have each architected common infrastructures in order to achieve both common semantics for their respective languages and common software implementations. Secondly, we describe advances in runtime assertion checking that are closing the gap between

---

[1] As has abstract-interpretation-based static analysis, but in this paper we focus on proof-based verification.

© Springer Nature Switzerland AG 2018
T. Margaria and B. Steffen (Eds.): ISoLA 2018, LNCS 11245, pp. 75–91, 2018.
https://doi.org/10.1007/978-3-030-03421-4_6

the kinds of assertions that can be checked by runtime checkers and those provable by static deductive program verification.

2   Tool Suites for Specification Languages

In response to the ubiquitous presence of non-robust software, and in particular, software that contains safety or security risks, there is active research and tool development whose goal is to ensure that software does what it is supposed to do. However, defining what a software system is supposed to do is not simple. One aspect, called implicit specifications, is that a program should not violate any of the rules of its underlying programming language, such as executing undefined operations. This is important, since such undefined operations, like out of bounds memory accesses, are an important contributor to security vulnerabilities. However, this aspect alone does not enable checking that a program's actions are correct. For that we need a means to express the functional requirements for the program, using explicit specifications, in a precise enough way that those requirements can be checked against the implementation by (largely) automated tools. That is we need languages to express formal specifications.

A number of such specification languages are in active use, each paired with a programming language:

- Eiffel [29], a programming language, has a built-in specification language;
- JML [10], the Java Modeling Language, expresses specifications for Java programs;
- ACSL [7], the ANSI/ISO-C Specification Language, expresses specifications for ANSI-C programs, and the in-development ACSL++ specification language for C++;
- SPARK [3] expresses specifications for the Ada programming language;
- Spec# [4] expresses specifications for C#, with the following CodeContracts [20] system working for .NET environments;
- Dafny [28] is a specification and programming language purpose-built for verification.

These are all examples of *Behavioral Interface Specification Languages* [24] (BISLs), in that the specification language syntax and semantics are closely aligned with the associated programming language, with modifications to accommodate logical specification and reasoning. Alternative examples are the Z specification language [37] and the B-method [1] whose designs are more mathematical and programming-language independent. The rationale for BISLs is that the similarity to programming languages makes learning easier. All of these languages use similar designs and follow the pioneering work of Larch [22].

Each of these specification/programming languages has associated tool suites. In this paper we will focus on two such tool suites: the OpenJML [13–16] tool for Java and JML, and the Frama-C [26] platform for C and ACSL. We will also limit discussion to two applications: automated static deductive verification (DV) and runtime assertion checking (RAC).

DV follows the following paradigm: the intent of the software under study (the 'target software') is expressed in machine-readable specifications, with the implicit specifications being generated by tools based on the programming language semantics; the specifications and the target software are together translated into a logical form; a logical proof tool then determines, if possible, whether the logical representations of the specifications and the implementation are consistent. If so, then the implementation is considered *verified*, that is, to be consistent with the specifications; if not, then either the implementation or the specifications (or both) have some fault to be found and corrected. Automation is critically important for the technique to become widespread and for efficiency in application, though some elements of the proof in some tools are delegated to interactive provers. Also, human interaction takes the form of writing and debugging the specifications so that they are amenable to machine proof. Specifications for programs that are affected by the external system or physical environment must include models of those aspects as well. For example, software for cyber-physical systems will include models of the physics of the physical world, including the possibility of inaccuracies or outright failures in sensors and effectors.

Runtime assertion checking[2] also takes explicit and (possibly tool-generated) implicit specifications as input. The specifications are converted into boolean assertions that are then compiled into the target software as instrumentation. The target software is then run as usual, perhaps on a suite of dynamic test cases. If any instrumented assertion is found to be false during these executions, the RAC platform will alert the user to the assertion violation. If no such alert is given, then the target software meets the specifications for the given set of test inputs. Software that interacts with the environment is a particular challenge for RAC (and dynamic testing in general), because it is difficult to arrange for all the unusual situations and error conditions that the environment might display.

DV can prove correct behavior for any input, if the required proof is not beyond the capability of the underlying tools. RAC always succeeds but only checks assertions that are executable and only for those inputs tested. In each case, "correctness" is measured by conformance to the specifications, which themselves must be reviewed for fidelity to the system's actual requirements. Both tools are useful together, and all the more so when the target software is safety- or security-critical.

3   Software Architecture

With similar goals and similar reliance on a common specification language, it is good design that static and runtime checking would use a common architecture. In the following subsections we describe how that is achieved by two different systems.

---

[2] Here we are distinguishing runtime assertion checking from runtime verification [6], which typically deals with temporal properties, e.g. LTL properties.

3.1   OpenJML for Java and JML

The Java Modeling Language is a specification language for Java programs. An example of JML is given in Fig. 1. Syntactically, JML specifications are written as structured Java comments (beginning with //@ or /*@). A method's specification is expressed as a sequence of *clauses*. The **requires** clause is a pre-condition, stating what must be true at the time a method is called, and then equivalently, what may be assumed when checking the implementation of a method. The **assignable** clause denotes a frame-condition, which must list any memory locations that are possibly modified by a method. An **ensures** clause is a post-condition, stating conditions the method implementation must guarantee and thus what may be assumed by callers after the method executes. A **signals** clause is a post-condition that must hold when the method exits by throwing an exception. **Invariant** clauses are part of a class's specification and state data structure consistency properties that must be maintained by all methods. Tools such as OpenJML [13–16] and KeY [2] are able to read and check the consistency of the Java implementation and the associated specifications.

OpenJML is a tool built on the OpenJDK [42] Java compiler. The architecture of OpenJDK and OpenJML is shown in Fig. 2. As is common for compilers, OpenJDK has multiple phases: the input source code is scanned, parsed, names resolved, and type-checked, producing a forest of Abstract Syntax Trees (ASTs) representing the program. This AST is then subject to various optimizations and transformations and then emitted as Java byte code. The OpenJDK compiler phases are Java classes that are readily extended by JML versions, which scan, parse, resolve, and type-check the text contained in the JML annotations along with the Java code. The JML annotations are converted into assumptions and assertions that are inserted into the AST. This translation step embodies the semantics of the JML specifications. Furthermore, the AST serves as an intermediate representation and the focal point for other tools and program analyses. It can be pretty-printed, subjected to other programmer-initiated transformations, and the like. In this case, the modified ASTs can be sent to the (unmodified) code-generation phase to produce output byte-code with embedded JML assertions. Or the ASTs can be sent to the Java and JML logical encoding phase, which produces an SMT-LIB [5] equivalent of the AST (embodying the semantics of Java). SMT solvers can then determine whether all assertions in the SMT-LIB encoding are valid. A central point of this architecture is that the JML semantics are embodied in the JML-enhanced AST, which is used by both runtime and static checking. Thus by design the two modes of checking rely on a common semantics and a common implementation of AST transformations

```
1 //@ requires i != Integer.MIN_VALUE;
2 //@ assignable \nothing;
3 //@ ensures \result >= 0 && (\result == i || \result == -i);
4 //@ signals (Exception e) false;
5 int abs(int i);
```

Fig. 1. Example JML specification of an absolute-value method.

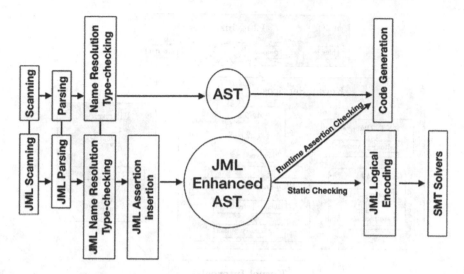

Fig. 2. Architecture of OpenJDK and OpenJML

and optimizations. The Java semantics is still implemented separately, since for runtime checking the Java semantics is embodied in the code generator and for static checking it is embodied in the logical encoding.

3.2   Frama-C for C Code and (E-)ACSL Specifications

Frama-C [26] is an open source platform that provides a collection of interoperable sound software analysis tools for C source code (more precisely, ISO C99 code). The analyzed C source code may be annotated with formal specifications written in the ACSL specification language [7]. ACSL formal annotations may also be generated by Frama-C analyzers in order to be verified by others. ACSL shares many features with JML for Java, but relies on the C syntax, as shown in Fig. 3, which is a translation of the JML example of Fig. 1 to ACSL. Note that there is no **signals** clause in ACSL since there is no exception mechanism in C.

The Frama-C platform is based on a common kernel that provides a uniform setting and common services to analyzers seen as plug-ins, as depicted by its architecture shown in Fig. 4. The most important service shared by the Frama-C analyzers is a common normalized typed AST for ACSL-annotated C code. It

```
1 #include <limits.h>
2
3 //@ requires i != INT_MIN;
4 //@ assigns \nothing;
5 //@ ensures \result >= 0 && (\result == i || \result == -i);
6 int abs(int i);
```

Fig. 3. Example ACSL specification of an absolute-value function.

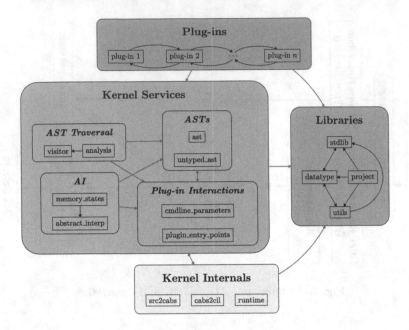

Fig. 4. Frama-C software architecture

ensures that every Frama-C tool has the very same abstract view of the analyzed code and the same pieces of information about implementation-defined behaviors (e.g., the size of C types and endianness are provided by a kernel parameter controlling machine-dependent information: they are shared by every analyzer).

However, the Frama-C kernel only provides a small amount of semantic information about the code: the Frama-C plug-ins must analyze the AST in a consistent and sound way with respect to the ISO C99 standard and the ACSL reference manual. Only a few kernel checks prevent introducing inconsistency and unsoundness. Among them, the kernel checks (1) that most AST internal invariants are preserved by program transformation and (2) that the validity statuses of properties are consistently emitted by Frama-C analyzers (that is, no analyzer A indicates that property p is valid, while analyzer B indicates that property p is invalid) [17].

Among many others, Frama-C plug-ins include three principal plugins: the abstract-interpretation based value analysis Eva [8], the deductive verification tool Wp, and the runtime assertion checker E-ACSL [36].

Eva computes a sound over-approximation of the set of values for each program memory location at each program point. It also checks each potential undefined behavior and raises an alarm for any of them as soon as it might happen. These alarms are also expressed by ACSL annotations: if proven valid (resp. invalid) (possibly, by another Frama-C analyzer), it ensures that the undefined behavior never happens (resp. does happen in at least one concrete execution).

In addition, to checking for undefined behaviors, Eva also tries to evaluate ACSL annotations, but it usually succeeds for the simplest ones only.

Indeed, verifying statically that the analyzed code satisfies its ACSL annotations is the goal of Wp, by means of deductive verification. For that purpose, Wp generates proof obligations to be proven by external provers (e.g., Alt-Ergo, Z3, CVC4) or proof assistants (e.g., Coq, PVS) through Why3 [21].

Compliance of the code to ACSL annotations may also be checked at runtime through the E-ACSL tool, which converts each annotation to an equivalent C expression. However, even if close to JML, the ACSL specification language was designed with deductive verification in mind. Thus, some of its constructs cannot be checked in finite time at runtime, typically (unbounded) quantifications over all mathematical integers or reals. Consequently, the E-ACSL tool only deals with a (large) subset of the ACSL specification language, named the E-ACSL specification language [19,35].[3] It is worth noting that, while being consistent, the semantics of the ACSL and E-ACSL specification languages differ. The former is a (total) mathematical semantics such that the predicate 1/0 == 1/0 is well defined and trivially holds by reflexivity of equality. However, this semantics is not suitable at runtime because terms such as 1/0 cannot be evaluated. To solve this issue, the E-ACSL specification language follows Chalin's strong validity principle [12]: such terms and the predicates that use them are undefined. Consequently, the E-ACSL tool reports a runtime error when trying to evaluate them. JML also uses a semantics requiring well-defined specification expressions for both static and runtime checking.

4   Recent Improvements in Runtime Assertion Checking

In some arenas, RAC has been the poor cousin to DV. One of the reasons for this opinion is that static verification, when successful, can prove the absence of errors and property violations for all permitted inputs, whereas RAC only demonstrates this for the test inputs with which the program is run. On the other hand, DV attempts can fail because of lack of capability in the logical solvers used to determine validity of assertions.[4] RAC can always run a program, albeit with some performance degradation caused by assertion checking instrumented into the program. A second problem with RAC, however, is that not all of

---

[3] Similarly, runtime checking of JML does not encode unbounded or even very large ranges of quantification, though the language subset supported by RAC in OpenJML is not as precisely defined as E-ACSL is for Frama-C.

[4] This is not just a theoretical concern. The state-of-the-art in SMT technology is rapidly evolving, but still does not efficiently handle all the concepts natural to software. Proofs using bit-vector operations on 64-bit numbers and floating-point operations can routinely take tens of minutes if they complete at all; quantified expressions require heuristic algorithms to decide when to instantiate the expressions; recursion is not natural to ground solvers such as SMT tools; dynamic allocations and heterogeneous casts between integers and pointers (in C) require low-level memory models that make proof intractable.

the assertions contained in a specification are executable. Although DV may encounter assertions that are not provable, the set of such assertions is smaller than the current limitations of RAC.

Accordingly it is a research area for RAC to find well-performing algorithms to check what have been to date non-executable assertions. The following subsections describe some in-progress advances in this area. Most of these advances are too recent to have a full assessment of their performance and general applicability; such studies are planned for future publications. Here we will describe the overall motivation, present the current state of practice and outline the in-progress advances. This discussion focuses on the work on Frama-C using E-ACSL for C programs, though most considerations apply also to RAC in OpenJML.

4.1   Memory-Related Properties

As already explained, E-ACSL for C is close to JML for Java. However, since the C programming language contains low-level constructs to access to the program memory, in particular pointers, E-ACSL must be able to express memory-related properties. Consequently, it contains a set of built-in logic functions and predicates that are absent from JML (and from the other behavioral specification languages designed for high-level programming languages).

One such construct is \valid(p), which means that pointer p can safely be dereferenced in order to access the pointed-to value. Another construct is \initialized(&x), stating that variable x has been initialized. Checking these kinds of properties at runtime is usually the role of dynamic memory analyzers such as AddressSanitizer [33] or MemCheck [34] that rely on efficient implementations of memory shadowing. Such tools are able to access in constant time the necessary information (such as its validity or its initialization status) about a particular memory address to detect memory violations at runtime.

However, not only is E-ACSL able to express properties about some particular address, but it may also refer to allocated memory blocks. For instance, \block_length(p) is the size (in bytes) of the memory block containing p, \base_address(p) is the first address of the memory block containing p, and \offset(p) is the byte-offset from this first address to p. Unfortunately, traditional memory shadowing techniques are not able to express such block-level properties. Consequently, the E-ACSL tool relies on a custom shadow memory model [41] with a compact representation of block-level properties to support these operations.

Evaluations over standard benchmarks demonstrated that this memory model is able to express more properties than classical models [40], while being as efficient as MemCheck (but still slower than AddressSanitizer) and consuming *less* memory than these tools [41].

Note that in DV, memory models are based on abstractions: such memory models allow proof to be done automatically but can only express properties about high-level data structures such as arrays, records and objects, while low-level models may express additional operations (such as dynamic allocations and heterogeneous casts between integers and pointers), but usually require the help of a proof assistant (e.g. Coq) to prove the expected program properties. RAC can deal with any programming language construct, but cannot accurately check finest properties that may be expressed by DV memory models.

4.2 Efficient Integer Computations

Computations over integers are ubiquitous in software. Most programming languages provide various precisions of integers for different needs. Specifications, however, are most naturally expressed in unbounded, mathematical integers ($\mathbb{Z}$). Indeed, Chalin's research [11] showed that specifications using mathematical integers not subject to over- or under-flow were the expected semantics and best understood by readers of specifications. Accordingly E-ACSL and JML allow specifications to be written using unbounded integers.

It is possible, using a dedicated arithmetic library (e.g., GMPZ for C code), to perform all numeric calculations using unbounded precision. However, this is not at all efficient compared to using machine integers. For example there is no need to rely on unbounded precision when handling the term `1 + 2`: addition over the C type `int` is sufficient. Similarly, if c is a C `char` variable, the `int` expression `c+1` will not overflow. The idea, introduced through a dedicated type system in [25] and implemented in E-ACSL, consists in tracking the range of possible values for each E-ACSL arithmetic term to determine what precision is needed to perform the computation. In practice, almost all integer arithmetic operations are computed with machine bounded integers thanks to this type system. It is worth noting that Adacore has adapted this idea to Spark2014.

This type system has recently been extended to logic functions and predicates in E-ACSL. For instance, the user can now define, say, the sum function `integer sum(integer a, integer b) = a + b`. If the only call to sum is done through `sum(1, 2)` then the prototype of the corresponding generated C function is `long __gen_e_acsl_sum(int a, int b)` (on a standard 64 bit architecture) and so only relies on bounded machine integers. We present in the following a few points on that work that are worth mentioning.

Recursive Functions. Recursive functions need special attention. For example, consider the function f presented in Fig. 5. We need to generate multiple prototypes for f. Indeed if it is called with an argument that fits into `int` (resp. `long`, `mpz`) then we will generate the C function of prototype `int __gen_e_acsl_f1(int n)` (resp. `int __gen_e_acsl_f2(long n)`, `int __gen_e_acsl_f3(mpz n)`). The return type of the different prototypes is `int` since f always returns 1 for any possible value of its argument.

Now, *automatically* computing the most precise range of E-ACSL's recursive functions *in the general case* is extremely hard, if not impossible, considering the expressiveness of the language. For example, even for the very restricted subset of E-ACSL where we only consider linear expressions, the problem is already NP. Fortunately, our concern is not to perform the utmost precise interval inference, but rather to perform an interval inference that is only precise enough so that we do not call bignum libraries.

```
1  /*@ logic integer f(integer n) =
2        n < 0 ? 1 : f(n - 1) * f(n - 2) / f(n - 3); */
3  int __gen_e_acsl_f1(int __gen_e_acsl_n);
4  int __gen_e_acsl_f2(long __gen_e_acsl_n);
5  int __gen_e_acsl_f3(mpz __gen_e_acsl_n);
```

Fig. 5. A logic function f defined in ACSL and declarations of three corresponding C functions depending on the value of n. The most precise interval within which f ranges is $I = [1; 1]$. Thus f will be typed into int in the best scenario.

To achieve that, we consider an over-approximation of the problem, that we express in a system of interval equations. For example, the system we build for the above presented f is $X_1 = [1; 1] \cup X_2 \cdot X_2/X_2 \bigwedge X_2 = [1; 1] \cup X_3 \cdot X_3/X_3 \bigwedge X_3 = [1; 1] \cup X_3 \cdot X_3/X_3$ where X_1 (resp. X_2, X_3) denotes the interval over which ranges __gen_e_acsl_f1 (resp. __gen_e_acsl_f2, __gen_e_acsl_f3). Our current way of solving those systems is such that we can infer that f ranges over $[-10^3; 10^3]$. Though $[-10^3; 10^3]$ is much wider than the optimal range $[1; 1]$, it still lies within int: E-ACSL is able to determine that int is sufficient as return type of f.

Termination. We point out that the interval inference process is independent of the function's termination. Indeed we always obtain an interval, $[-\infty; +\infty]$ in the worst case, in a finite amount of time whether the function terminates or not. This raises the following question: how should we treat non-terminating recursive functions? The user will most likely not appreciate having his analysis stuck in some infinite recursion. Unfortunately, it is impossible to check termination of E-ACSL logic functions in the general case. This is, once again, due to its expressiveness.

We could perform (incomplete) termination analysis before translating and emit a warning every time termination is not guaranteed. However there is a solution that completely ensures that no non-terminating function is defined. This solution requires the user to provide a ranking function for each recursive function definition. This can be achieved by syntactically forcing each E-ACSL recursive function definition to have an attached **decreases** clause. Such clauses already exist for specifying termination of (recursive) C functions.

A **decreases** clause takes some quantity Q that is *supposed* to strictly decrease at *each* function call until reaching a minimum value, thus guaranteeing termination. During RAC, if Q is indeed decreasing then the function runs normally. Otherwise the execution is aborted with the indication that Q failed to decrease: the user needs to provide another ranking function candidate and/or check whether the function is actually non-terminating. Support for **decreases** clauses is a future work for E-ACSL and is complicated by the possibility of defining arbitrarily large groups of mutually recursive functions.

4.3 On Support for Real Numbers

RAC is especially well-suited for verifying programs that manipulate Floating-Point (FP) numbers. FP computations are affected by tricky rounding behaviors. For example the Java equality `0.2f == 0.199999999254941940307617187875f` counter-intuitively evaluates to `true`. These behaviors render verification extremely hard. The father of modern FP computation himself, Kahan, called out for "desperately needed remedies for the undebuggability of large floating-point computations in science and engineering" in 2011[5]. Still, industrial programs that deal with FP numbers, including those from critical industries, perform very complex numeric computations.

For the time being, DV still needs maturation before being able to handle large FP computations. This is mainly due to the fact that SMT solvers do not scale for large FP formulas. Until then, we propose RAC to come to the rescue. For verifying numeric programs written in C, we propose to write the specifications in standard mathematics and let E-ACSL, coupled with a few other tools, check them at runtime. By standard mathematics we mean real semantics for which operations are error-free. One advantage of our approach is that it can be used by users that are not familiar with FP computations, which is the case for "95% of folks out there" as jokingly said by the father of Java, Gosling[6], as long as they remember their high school mathematics.

The role of E-ACSL is to generate the sequence of calls to the real-arithmetic functions for all the real operations found in the specifications. In particular, special care needs to be taken to make sure that support for reals is well integrated with the interval inference and the type system for integers discussed in the previous section. Moreover, we can minimize calls to specialized libraries for real arithmetic in the same way as is accomplished for integers, as illustrated in Fig. 6. However, such optimizations are not yet implemented. Plus, we have only implemented support for rationals for the time being. Indeed, we only use FP numbers and the operations $+ - */$ in our current test cases. Thus, though we can have complex use cases within such a setting, such as inversions by LU decomposition, computations can still be done with rational numbers.

```
1 //@ assert \let real r = (float)(0.1f + 0.2f); ...
2 __e_acsl_real __gen_e_acsl_1 = __e_acsl_real_of(0.1f);
3 __e_acsl_real __gen_e_acsl_2 = __e_acsl_real_of(0.2f);
4 __e_acsl_real __gen_e_acsl_add = __e_acsl_real_add(__gen_e_acsl_1,
5                                                    __gen_e_acsl_2);
6 float __gen_e_acsl_r = __e_acsl_real_to_float(__gen_e_acsl_add);
7 ...
```

Fig. 6. An unoptimized translation. However, by taking advantage of the fact that correct rounding is guaranteed for FP addition, as required by IEEE-754, we could simply generate `float __gen_e_acsl_r = 0.1f + 0.2f;`

---

[5] https://people.eecs.berkeley.edu/~wkahan/Boulder.pdf.
[6] https://people.eecs.berkeley.edu/~wkahan/JAVAhurt.pdf, p. 4.

Superset of $\mathbb{Q}$. Now what if we go beyond rational numbers? As a motivating example, positioning systems use trigonometric functions ubiquitously, say for computing distances and angles in polar coordinates[7]. First, we point out that any sound and fully automatic runtime checking of numeric properties expressed in a specification language as rich as E-ACSL is doomed to be incomplete in the general case. This is because of the undecidability of equality between computable numbers [39][8]. Since we want neither to sacrifice soundness nor to resort to non-automatic solutions, there are only two remaining options:

1. restrict the supported constructs in a way such that decidability is preserved. Unfortunately, the obtained restriction would be too limited to be of interest. Indeed Richardson's theorem [32] prevents us from going beyond the set $\mathbb{Q} \cup \{\pi\}$ and the operations $+, *, -, /, sin$.
2. be incomplete, that is allow the emission of I DON'T KNOW at runtime.

In practice, libraries for exact real arithmetic already exist [23][9]. In particular, we could use iRRAM [30], which provides support for algebraic functions such as square root, transcendentals such as exponential and logarithm, and an extensive set of trigonometric functions. Unfortunately iRRAM may not terminate when comparing two reals that are equal. The simplest solution to that would be to stop iRRAM when it takes too much time, in which case we should return I DON'T KNOW. We expect that simple stopping criterion to give relatively satisfying performance since comparison between two equal reals does not happen often. However this is yet to be supported by experimental evidence which we leave as future work.

5 Related Work

There are large bodies of related work on both deductive verification and runtime assertion checking, which we will not enumerate here. Our principal concern is systems that seek to integrate these tools with others in a common architecture and with well-defined specification semantics. Some of the systems we have already referenced are in this category.

- The Eiffel language [29] pioneered specifications integrated with programs. Its first intent was RAC, with specifications limited to being executable, and later has been adding proof capability.
- Ada has a well-supported commercial companion tool, SPARK, which also supports both DV and RAC using an integrated architecture. Like ACSL, many contracts are executable, but non-executable assertions can be written.

---

[7] For example at NASA, some containment algorithms are verified at runtime [38].

[8] This theoretical limitation says that there is no *terminating* algorithm that can decide, statically through DV or at runtime through RAC, the equality relation between any pair of numbers that can be computed by Turing machines.

[9] See also sections "Software Using MPFR" and "Other Related Free Software" on MPFR's webpage, https://www.mpfr.org/.

– Spec# [4] was built as an extension of C# with non-null types as well as contracts, enforced by Eiffel-like run-time checks and by a static program verifier. En route to market, it became CodeContracts [20], a simplified and language-agnostic specification language for .NET with a tool to insert run-time checks and with a static analyzer to check certain properties statically.

Dafny [28], mentioned above, is designed to ensure that all assertions are statically verified as part of compilation, so no assertions are compiled into the code. It has mechanisms for adding detailed proof steps if necessary to verify difficult assertions.

Regarding the verification of numeric properties, as discussed in Sect. 4 for the particular case of RAC, the authors of [18] present a sound way of compiling specifications written in real semantics into programs that can be executed on machines with finite amount of memory (Scala programs). From a conceptual point of view, the main difference with our work is that they require a tolerance as well as the target precision to be explicitly stated. In contrast to that, we want our compiled programs to be 100% accurate, no less. Moreover, we let our tool decide the precision (the types) within which the different computations must be done.

6   Combining DV and RAC

DV and RAC tools working against a common target software and its specifications can be usefully used together. One helpful workflow is the following. When the target software is partially written, not yet provable, but executable and has some specifications, RAC can be run to check that the specifications are valid for the set of unit test cases. It takes more effort to actually prove (including to debug) the software and specifications with DV, so RAC is used to perform quick initial checks of the specifications. Once RAC has shown the software and specifications to be largely correct, then DV can be used more efficiently to verify that the combination of software and specifications is indeed consistent for all possible program inputs.

Similarly, suppose DV is not able to prove a set of specifications and produces a counterexample, which is a set of program inputs that DV cannot prove to obey the specifications. Then the engineer (or tools) can create an executable version of the counterexample to be run with RAC; RAC will then pinpoint which assertions are failing, identifying the incorrect software or the misconceptions in the specifications [31].

Furthermore, when combining DV and testing with RAC, it may be hard to know whether all the pieces of code and all the specifications are covered by the verification campaign. Here the combination of RAC+runtime coverage measurements and DV+ tools that check specification coverage can be enhanced by new tools [27] that provide unified coverage criteria for both runtime testing and static proof. The cited paper also provides means to avoid verifying the same functions redundantly with both DV and RAC.

7   Future Work

While the architectures we described are fairly well implemented, the principal areas for improvement are these:

- Improvements in both the usability of specification languages and the clarity of their semantics
- Reducing the gap between what can be checked at runtime and what can be checked deductively. The biggest challenges for RAC are checking memory properties, complex properties over real numbers and checking axiomatically-stated specifications. The challenges for DV are specification in the presence of abstraction and refinement, information hiding, and effective performance of solvers with quantified expressions.
- Reducing the time- and memory-overhead of runtime checking, extending the areas discussed in this paper.

One of the gaps to be filled for both static and runtime checking is modeling the semantics of concurrency. Concurrency is a challenge for runtime checking because the runtime assertion instrumentation can change the timing of portions of the program and so change what races or deadlocks might occur. Even worse, concurrent accesses to E-ACSL's shadow memory model may lead to incorrectness. Concurrency is a challenge for static verification because of its complexity: one must model and check all possible interleavings of concurrent threads, along with the appropriate memory model. Neither ACSL nor JML currently models concurrency. However, the closed-source prototype plug-in Mthread at CEA relies on Eva to automatically detect unsafe concurrent accesses to shared variables. Another Frama-C plug-in[10], developed by Adelard on a quite old version of Frama-C, shares the same goal.

This paper has discussed two tools: Frama-C for C/ACSL and OpenJML for Java/JML. At present these are independent tools, sharing common history, specification language concepts and implementation techniques, but no common software or intermediate representations. It is, of course, possible for this situation to be different. Indeed, Frama-C is already evolving to support C++. One can envision a Frama-X framework whose internal representation of software and specifications is general enough to accommodate multiple modern programming languages. Each programming language would have a front-end and a specialized specification language as similar as possible to specification languages for other supported programming languages. All the languages would then use a common back-end that created the logical encoding of the software+specifications and managed the proof environment.

8   Conclusion

Practical, sound runtime assertion checking depends on two characteristics. First, the translation of programming language source code and specification

---

[10] https://bitbucket.org/adelard/simple-concurrency.

language assertions must be correct, according to a well-understood semantics. This correctness is best achieved when the RAC tool shares an intermediate form with other tools also needing correct semantic translations. Here we have presented static deductive verification as one such tool, but a few other possibilities are model checkers, test generation, and specification inference. A shared infrastructure reduces the implementation work and increases the semantic conformance among tools.

The second needed characteristic is practicality: the RAC tool must be able to check as many kinds of assertions as possible and do so as efficiently as possible. In this paper we presented advances in three areas—memory properties and integer and real computations—demonstrating that implementations of RAC are continuously improving and that RAC is a viable and useful element in a suite of program analysis tools, at times in ways that cannot yet be achieved by deductive verification.

Acknowledgements. This work is done in the context of project VESSEDIA, which has received funding from the European Union's 2020 Research and Innovation Program under grant agreement No. 731453.

References

1. Abrial, J.-R., Hoare, A., Chapron, P.: The B-Book: Assigning Programs to Meanings. Cambridge University Press, Cambridge (1996)
2. Ahrendt, W., Beckert, B., Bubel, R., Hähnle, R., Schmitt, P.H., Ulbrich, M. (eds.): Deductive Software Verification – The KeY Book. LNCS, vol. 10001. Springer, Cham (2016). https://doi.org/10.1007/978-3-319-49812-6
3. Barnes, J.: Spark: The Proven Approach to High Integrity Software. Altran Praxis, UK (2012). http://www.altran.co.uk
4. Barnett, M., Fähndrich, M., Leino, K.R.M., Müller, P., Schulte, W., Venter, H.: Specification and verification: the Spec# experience. Commun. ACM **54**(6), 81–91 (2011)
5. Barrett, C., Stump, A., Tinelli, C.: The SMT-LIB standard: version 2.0. In: Gupta, A., Kroening, D. (eds.) Proceedings of the 8th International Workshop on Satisfiability Modulo Theories (Edinburgh, England) (2010)
6. Bartocci, E., Falcone, Y., Francalanza, A., Reger, G.: Introduction to runtime verification. In: Bartocci, E., Falcone, Y. (eds.) Lectures on Runtime Verification. LNCS, vol. 10457, pp. 1–33. Springer, Cham (2018). https://doi.org/10.1007/978-3-319-75632-5_1
7. Baudin, P., et al.: ACSL: ANSI/ISO C Specification Language
8. Blazy, S., Bühler, D., Yakobowski, B.: Structuring abstract interpreters through state and value abstractions. In: Bouajjani, A., Monniaux, D. (eds.) VMCAI 2017. LNCS, vol. 10145, pp. 112–130. Springer, Cham (2017). https://doi.org/10.1007/978-3-319-52234-0_7
9. Brahmi, A., Delmas, D., Essoussi, M.H., Randimbivololona, F., Atki, A., Marie, T.: Formalise to automate: deployment of a safe and cost-efficient process for avionics software. In: Embedded Real-Time Software and Systems (ERTS^2 2018), January 2018

10. Burdy, L., et al.: An overview of JML tools and applications. In: Arts, T., Fokkink, W. (eds.) Eighth International Workshop on Formal Methods for Industrial Critical Systems (FMICS 2003). Electronic Notes in Theoretical Computer Science (ENTCS), vol. 80, pp. 73–89. Elsevier, June 2003

11. Chalin, P.: Logical foundations of program assertions: what do practitioners want? In: Third IEEE International Conference on Software Engineering and Formal Methods (SEFM 2005), pp. 383–393 (2005)

12. Chalin, P.: A sound assertion semantics for the dependable systems evolution verifying compiler. In: International Conference on Software Engineering (ICSE 2007), pp. 23–33, May 2007

13. Cok, D.R.: Improved usability and performance of SMT solvers for debugging specifications. STTT **12**, 467–481 (2010)

14. Cok, D.R.: OpenJML: JML for Java 7 by extending OpenJDK. In: Bobaru, M., Havelund, K., Holzmann, G.J., Joshi, R. (eds.) NFM 2011. LNCS, vol. 6617, pp. 472–479. Springer, Heidelberg (2011). https://doi.org/10.1007/978-3-642-20398-5_35

15. Cok, D.R.: OpenJML: software verification for Java 7 using JML, OpenJDK, and Eclipse. In: Workshop on Formal Integrated Development Environment (F-IDE 2014). EPTCS, vol. 149, pp. 79–92, 06 April 2014, Grenoble, France (2014)

16. Cok, D.R., Kiniry, J.R.: ESC/Java2: uniting ESC/Java and JML. In: Barthe, G., Burdy, L., Huisman, M., Lanet, J.-L., Muntean, T. (eds.) CASSIS 2004. LNCS, vol. 3362, pp. 108–128. Springer, Heidelberg (2005). https://doi.org/10.1007/978-3-540-30569-9_6

17. Correnson, L., Signoles, J.: Combining analyses for C program verification. In: Stoelinga, M., Pinger, R. (eds.) FMICS 2012. LNCS, vol. 7437, pp. 108–130. Springer, Heidelberg (2012). https://doi.org/10.1007/978-3-642-32469-7_8

18. Darulova, E., Kuncak, V.: Sound compilation of reals. In: The 41st Annual ACM SIGPLAN-SIGACT Symposium on Principles of Programming Languages, POPL 2014, San Diego, CA, USA, 20–21 January 2014, pp. 235–248 (2014)

19. Delahaye, M., Kosmatov, N., Signoles, J.: Common specification language for static and dynamic analysis of C programs. In: Symposium on Applied Computing (SAC 2013), March 2013

20. Fähndrich, M., Barnett, M., Leijen, D., Logozzo, F.: Integrating a set of contract checking tools into visual studio. In: TOPI@ICSE (2012)

21. Filliâtre, J.-C., Paskevich, A.: Why3 — where programs meet provers. In: Felleisen, M., Gardner, P. (eds.) ESOP 2013. LNCS, vol. 7792, pp. 125–128. Springer, Heidelberg (2013). https://doi.org/10.1007/978-3-642-37036-6_8

22. Garland, S.J., Guttag, J.V.: A guide to LP, the larch prover. Technical report 82, Digital Equipment Corporation, Systems Research Center, 130 Lytton Avenue, Palo Alto, CA 94301, December 1991. Order from src-report@src.dec.com

23. Gowland, P., Lester, D.: A survey of exact arithmetic implementations. In: Blanck, J., Brattka, V., Hertling, P. (eds.) CCA 2000. LNCS, vol. 2064, pp. 30–47. Springer, Heidelberg (2001). https://doi.org/10.1007/3-540-45335-0_3

24. Hatcliff, J., Leavens, G.T., Leino, K.R.M., Müller, P., Parkinson, M.: Behavioral interface specification languages. Technical report CS-TR-09-01, University of Central Florida, School of EECS, Orlando, FL, March 2009

25. Jakobsson, A., Kosmatov, N., Signoles, J.: Rester statique pour devenir plus rapide, plus précis et plus mince (French). In: Journées Francophones des Langages Applicatifs, JFLA 2015, January 2015. In French

26. Kirchner, F., Kosmatov, N., Prevosto, V., Signoles, J., Yakobowski, B.: Frama-C: a software analysis perspective. Formal Aspects Comput. **27**(3), 573–609 (2015)

27. Le, V.H., Correnson, L., Signoles, J., Wiels, V.: Verification coverage for combining test and proof. In: Dubois, C., Wolff, B. (eds.) TAP 2018. LNCS, vol. 10889, pp. 120–138. Springer, Cham (2018). https://doi.org/10.1007/978-3-319-92994-1_7
28. Leino, K.R.M.: Dafny: an automatic program verifier for functional correctness. In: Clarke, E.M., Voronkov, A. (eds.) LPAR 2010. LNCS (LNAI), vol. 6355, pp. 348–370. Springer, Heidelberg (2010). https://doi.org/10.1007/978-3-642-17511-4_20
29. Meyer, B.: Object-oriented Software Construction. Prentice Hall, New York (1988)
30. Müller, N.T.: The iRRAM: exact arithmetic in C++. In: Blanck, J., Brattka, V., Hertling, P. (eds.) CCA 2000. LNCS, vol. 2064, pp. 222–252. Springer, Heidelberg (2001). https://doi.org/10.1007/3-540-45335-0_14
31. Petiot, G., Kosmatov, N., Botella, B., Giorgetti, A., Julliand, J.: Your proof fails? testing helps to find the reason. In: Aichernig, B.K.K., Furia, C.A.A. (eds.) TAP 2016. LNCS, vol. 9762, pp. 130–150. Springer, Cham (2016). https://doi.org/10.1007/978-3-319-41135-4_8
32. Richardson, D.: Some undecidable problems involving elementary functions of a real variable. J. Symbolic Logic **33**(4), 514–520 (1968)
33. Serebryany, K., Bruening, D., Potapenko, A., Vyukov, D.: AddressSanitizer: a fast address sanity checker. In: Annual Technical Conference (ATC 2012), June 2012
34. Seward, J., Nethercote, N.: Using valgrind to detect undefined value errors with bit-precision. In: Annual Technical Conference (ATC 2005), April 2005
35. Signoles, J.: E-ACSL: Executable ANSI/ISO C Specification Language. http://frama-c.com/download/e-acsl/e-acsl.pdf
36. Signoles, J., Kosmatov, N., Vorobyov, K.: E-ACSL, a runtime verification tool for safety and security of C programs. Tool paper. In: International Workshop on Competitions, Usability, Benchmarks, Evaluation, and Standardisation for Runtime Verification Tools (RV-CuBES 2017), September 2017
37. Spivey, J.M.: The Z notation: A Reference Manual. Prentice Hall International (UK) Ltd. (1992)
38. Titolo, L., Muñoz, C.A., Feliu, M.A., Moscato, M.M.: Eliminating Unstable Tests in Floating-Point Programs. ArXiv e-prints, August 2018. To appear in the proceedings of LOPSTR 2018
39. Alan Mathison Turing: On computable numbers, with an application to the entscheidungsproblem. Proc. Lond. Math. Soc. **2**(1), 230–265 (1937)
40. Vorobyov, K., Kosmatov, N., Signoles, J.: Detection of security vulnerabilities in C code using runtime verification: an experience report. In: Dubois, C., Wolff, B. (eds.) TAP 2018. LNCS, vol. 10889, pp. 139–156. Springer, Cham (2018). https://doi.org/10.1007/978-3-319-92994-1_8
41. Vorobyov, K., Signoles, J., Kosmatov, N.: Shadow state encoding for efficient monitoring of block-level properties. In: International Symposium on Memory Management (ISMM 2017), pp. 47–58, June 2017
42. OpenJDK. http://www.openjdk.org

A Language-Independent Program Verification Framework

Xiaohong Chen[1(✉)] and Grigore Roşu[1,2]

[1] University of Illinois at Urbana-Champaign, Champaign, USA
xc3@illinois.edu
[2] Runtime Verification Inc., Champaign, USA

Abstract. This invited paper describes an approach to language-independent deductive verification using the $\mathbb{K}$ semantics framework, in which an operational semantics of a language is defined and a program verifier together with other language tools are generated automatically, correct-by-construction.

1 Introduction and Motivation

Given a program and a specification of the program, the *deductive verification problem* asks if the program satisfies the specification. If the answer is positive, a collection of proof obligations is expected to be generated as evidence, while counterexamples, often of the form of concrete program execution traces, witness the negative answer. Many program verification approaches are associated with a *program logic* and a *proof system* of that logic that allows to derive new facts about programs from axioms and established facts. The *proof rules* of the proof system define the semantics of the target language. Hoare logic [12], for example, is a program logic proposed in 1969 for a simple imperative language which we refer to as IMP. The syntax of IMP is defined in Fig. 1, where *Id* is the category for program variables and *Exp* is the category for arithmetic expressions. If-statements and while-statements use *Exp* as conditions, where zero means false and nonzero values mean true. The specification of an IMP program is written as a *Hoare triple*, consisting of the program and its precondition and postcondition (e.g., Fig. 2). A set of Hoare logic proof rules can then be used to rigorously reason about the correctness of IMP programs (Fig. 3). Notice how every IMP language construct has a corresponding Hoare logic proof rule.

$$Exp \ ::= \ Id \mid Int \mid Exp + Exp \mid Exp - Exp$$
$$Stmt ::= Id = Exp; \mid Stmt \ Stmt \mid \{ \ Stmt \ \} \mid \{\}$$
$$\mid \ \texttt{if} \ (\ Exp \ ) \ Stmt \ Stmt \mid \texttt{while} \ (\ Exp \ ) \ Stmt$$

Fig. 1. The syntax of the language IMP.

© Springer Nature Switzerland AG 2018
T. Margaria and B. Steffen (Eds.): ISoLA 2018, LNCS 11245, pp. 92–102, 2018.
https://doi.org/10.1007/978-3-030-03421-4_7

$$\{n = n \wedge n \geq 0\}$$
$$\texttt{s = 0; while(n)\{s = s + n; n = n - 1;\}}$$
$$\{s = n(n+1)/2\}$$

Fig. 2. An IMP program sum that calculates the sum from 1 to n, together with its formal specification given as a pair of precondition (the first line) and postcondition (the last line). We use `teletype` font to write program variables (e.g. `n` and `s`) and *italic* font to write mathematical variables (e.g. n).

$$\frac{}{\{\varphi[E/X]\}\ X = E;\ \{\varphi\}}\ \text{HL-Asgn}$$

$$\frac{\{\varphi_1\}\ P\ \{\varphi_2\}\quad \{\varphi_2\}\ Q\ \{\varphi_3\}}{\{\varphi_1\}\ P\ Q\ \{\varphi_3\}}\ \text{HL-Seq}$$

$$\frac{\{\varphi_1 \wedge B \neq 0\}\ P\ \{\varphi_2\}\quad \{\varphi_1 \wedge B = 0\}\ Q\ \{\varphi_2\}}{\{\varphi_1\}\ \texttt{if}(B)\ P\ Q\ \{\varphi_2\}}\ \text{HL-If}$$

$$\frac{\{\varphi_{inv} \wedge B \neq 0\}\ P\ \{\varphi_{inv}\}}{\{\varphi_{inv}\}\ \texttt{while}(B)\ P\ \{\varphi_{inv} \wedge B = 0\}}\ \text{HL-While}$$

$$\frac{\vDash \varphi_1' \rightarrow \varphi_1 \quad \{\varphi_1\}\ P\ \{\varphi_2\}\quad \vDash \varphi_2 \rightarrow \varphi_2'}{\{\varphi_1'\}\ P\ \{\varphi_2'\}}\ \text{HL-Cnsq}$$

Fig. 3. The Hoare logic proof system of the language IMP.

Hoare logic remains one of the most popular program logics since the day it was born, and researchers have proposed many variants of Hoare logic for more complicated languages and programs [3,14,17,18,21,22]. In the following, we will use the term "Hoare logic" to refer to all Hoare-style program logics, where the semantics of the target language is defined/axiomatized by the proof rules of that logic. Obviously, this makes Hoare logic *language-dependent*, as every language construct is associated with one or even more proof rules. When the language changes, the Hoare logic proof system for that language has to change accordingly, and thus all verification tools based on Hoare logic and its variants are language-dependent: a Java verifier cannot be used to verify C programs. Another notable characteristic of Hoare logic is that it is not directly executable. Therefore, in practice, language semanticists may need to define a separate trusted operational semantics that is executable, and carry out complex proofs of equivalence between the two semantics, which can take years to complete. All these facts make language design a highly expensive task, and *changing* the language rather inconvenient and demotivating, as it requires a thorough change of the Hoare logic proof system for that language and thus of all the related verification tools. If a trusted operational semantics is given, it needs to change, too, and a new proof of equivalence between the new Hoare logic and the new operational semantics should be carried out. This high cost brings us poor *reusability* of verification tools. Considering the fact that these tools often need several man-years to develop, the lack of reusability leads to a remarkable waste of resources and talent, as well as to duplicate work.

A common practice is then to develop verification tools for *intermediate verification languages* (IVL) such as Boogie [2] and Why [9], and translate the target languages to IVL. This brings some reusability, as verification tools are designed and implemented for IVL, in isolation from the target languages. However, correct program translation can be hard to develop. The proof of its correctness (called *soundness proof*) often involves the usage of higher-order theorem provers such as Coq [16] and Isabelle [20], not to mention that many real languages such as Java do not even have an official formal specification of the semantics. Thus, research about language-specific program logics and IVL tools sometimes have to compromise and claim "no intention of formally proving the soundness result" [1] (Fig. 5).

Fig. 4. The 𝕂 framework approach to language design and verification.

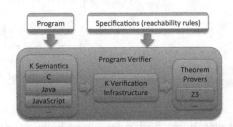

Fig. 5. A language-independent program verifier takes a program and its specification, and verifies it with respect to its formal semantics.

This motivated us to look for a verification methodology that is *language-independent*, which allows us to build verification tools that can verify *any property* of *any program* written in *any programming language*. The 𝕂 framework (www.kframework.org) is our attempt towards such a verification methodology, based on the firm belief that every language should have a formal semantics, and all related language tools should be automatically generated from the semantics in a correct-by-construction manner (Fig. 4). 𝕂 provides a meta-programming language to design programming languages. The formal semantics of a language, written as a 𝕂 definition, serves as the *only* canonical reference to *all* language tools, and no other formal or informal semantics is needed. Case studies with a variety of real languages demonstrates that this ideal scenario is indeed feasible and practical.

The rest of the paper is organized as follows. Section 2 briefly introduces the $\mathbb{K}$ framework, and Sect. 3 shows how program verification is carried out with $\mathbb{K}$. We conclude in Sect. 5.

2 $\mathbb{K}$ Framework

$\mathbb{K}$ is a rewrite-based executable semantics framework for programming language design. We use the language IMP in Fig. 1 as our running example (with minor modification on its syntax) to illustrate how to define programming languages and verify programs in $\mathbb{K}$.

The complete $\mathbb{K}$ definition for IMP is shown in Fig. 6, consisting of two $\mathbb{K}$ modules IMP-SYNTAX and IMP. The module IMP-SYNTAX defines the syntax of the language using the conventional BNF grammar, where terminals are in quotes. Syntax productions are separated by the "|" and ">", where "|" means the two productions have the same precedence while ">" means the previous production has higher precedence (binds tighter) than the one that follows. In other words, in the language IMP, all language constructs bind tighter than the sequential operator. Int and Id are two built-in categories of integers and identifiers (program variables), respectively. Exp is the category of expressions, which subsumes Int and Id, and contains two other productions for plus and minus. Pgm is the category of IMP programs. A wellformed IMP program declares a list of program variables in the beginning, followed by a statement. Ids is the category for lists of program variables, and it is defined using $\mathbb{K}$'s built-in template List. The first argument is the base category Id, and second argument is the separating character ",".

Attributes are wrapped with braces "[" and "]". Some attributes are only for parsing purpose while others may carry additional semantic meaning and affect how $\mathbb{K}$ executes programs. The attribute left means that "+" and "-" are left-associative, so 1 - 2 + 3 should be parsed as (1 - 2) + 3. The attribute strict defines evaluation contexts. When $\mathbb{K}$ sees the expression e_1 + e_2 (and similarly e_1 - e_2), it first evaluates e_1 to an integer i_1 and e_2 to an integer i_2 in a *fully nondeterministic* way, and then evaluates $i_1 + i_2$. For example, there are in total 3! = 6 different orders to evaluate the expression ((1 + 2) + (3 + 4)) + (5 + 6), because the most inner three parentheses must be evaluated first, and they can be evaluated in any order. The attribute strict(1) defines evaluation contexts only for the first argument. Therefore, when $\mathbb{K}$ sees an if-statement if (b) P Q, it only evaluates the condition b and keeps the branches P and Q untouched. In other words, the two branches of if-statements are *frozen* and will not be evaluated until the condition becomes a value. The attribute bracket tells $\mathbb{K}$ that certain productions are only used for grouping, and $\mathbb{K}$ will not generate nodes in its internal abstract syntax trees for those productions. Here, parentheses "( )" are used to group arithmetics expressions while curly brackets "{ }" are used to group program statements. The empty curly bracket "{}" represents the empty statement.

```
module IMP-SYNTAX
  imports DOMAINS-SYNTAX
  syntax Exp  ::= Int | Id
              | Exp "+" Exp                              [left, strict]
              | Exp "-" Exp                              [left, strict]
              | "(" Exp ")"                              [bracket]
  syntax Stmt ::= Id "=" Exp ";"                         [strict(2)]
              | "if" "(" Exp ")" Stmt Stmt              [strict(1)]
              | "while" "(" Exp ")" Stmt
              | "{" Stmt "}"                             [bracket]
              | "{" "}"
              > Stmt Stmt                                [left]
  syntax Pgm  ::= "int" Ids ";" Stmt
  syntax Ids  ::= List{Id, ","}
endmodule
module IMP
  imports IMP-SYNTAX
  imports DOMAINS
  syntax KResult ::= Int
  configuration  <T> <k> $PGM:Pgm </k> <state> .Map </state> </T>
  rule <k> X:Id => I ...</k> <state>... X |-> I ...</state>
  rule I1 + I2 => I1 +Int I2
  rule I1 - I2 => I1 -Int I2
  rule <k> X = I:Int; => . ...</k> <state>... X |-> (_ => I) ...</state>
  rule S1:Stmt S2:Stmt => S1 ~> S2                       [structural]
  rule if (I) S _ => S requires I =/=Int 0
  rule if (0) _ S => S
  rule while(B) S => if(B) {S while(B) S} {}            [structural]
  rule {} => .                                          [structural]
  rule <k> int (X, Xs => Xs); S </k> <state>... (. => X |-> 0) </state> [structural]
  rule int .Ids; S => S                                 [structural]
endmodule
```

Fig. 6. The complete $\mathbb{K}$ definition for the language IMP.

The module IMP defines the operational semantics of IMP in terms of a set of human-readable rewrite rules (followed by the keyword **rule**). The category KResult tells $\mathbb{K}$ which categories contain non-reducible values. It helps $\mathbb{K}$ perform efficiently with evaluation contexts. The only category of values here is Int. Configuration is a core concept in the $\mathbb{K}$ framework. A *configuration* represents a *program execution state*, holding all information that is needed for program execution. Configurations are organized into *cells*, which are labeled and can be nested. Simple languages such as IMP have only a few cells, while complex real languages such as C may have a lot more. Configurations are written in XML format.

The configurations of IMP have two cells: a k cell and a state cell. For clarity, we gather both cells and put them in a top-level cell called the T cell, but it is not mandatory. The k cell holds the rest computation (program fragments) that needs to execute and the state cell holds a map from program variables to their values in the memory. Initially, the state cell holds the empty map, denoted as .Map. In $\mathbb{K}$, we write "." for "nothing", and .Map means that nothing has type Map.

Initially, the k cell contains an IMP program $PGM:Pgm, where $PGM is a special $\mathbb{K}$ variable name that tells $\mathbb{K}$ the program is saved in a source file, and the name of the file is passed as argument in the command line when $\mathbb{K}$ is invoked. $\mathbb{K}$ will then read the source file and parse it as a Pgm, and put the result in the k cell.

$\mathbb{K}$ defines the language semantics in terms of a set of rewrite rules. A rewrite rule has the form *lhs* => *rhs*, saying that any configuration γ that matches *lhs* rewrites to *rhs*, but as we will see later, $\mathbb{K}$ offers a more flexible and succinct way to define rewrite rules. All rewrite rules in a language definition specify a transition system on *configurations*, giving an operational semantics of the language. Notice that rewrites rules are inherently nondeterministic and concurrent, which makes it easy and naturally to define semantics for nondeterministic/concurrent languages in $\mathbb{K}$.

We emphasize two important characteristics of rewrites rules in $\mathbb{K}$. The first is *local rewrites*, i.e., the rewrite symbol "=>" does not need to appear in the top level, but can appear locally in which the rewrite happens. Take as an example the rule that looks up the value of a program variable in the state. Instead of writing

```
rule <k> X:Id ...</k> <state>... X |-> I ...</state>
  => <k> I ...</k> <state>... X |-> I ...</state>
```

one writes

```
rule <k> X:Id => I ...</k> <state>... X |-> I ...</state>
```

to not only reduce space but also avoid duplicates. The "..." has a special meaning in $\mathbb{K}$. It stands for things "that exist but do not change in the rewrite". The rule, therefore, says that if a program variable X:Id is in the top of the computation in the k cell, and X binds to the integer I somewhere in the state cell, then rewrite X:Id to its value I, and do not change anything else.

The second characteristic of rewrite rules in $\mathbb{K}$ is *configuration inference and completion*. The rewrite rules may not explicitly mention all cells in the configuration, but only mention related ones. $\mathbb{K}$ will infer the implicit cells and compete the configuration automatically. For example, instead of writing

```
rule <T> <k> I1 + I2 => I1 +Int I2 ... </k> <state> M </state> </T>
```

one writes

```
rule I1 + I2 => I1 +Int I2
```

which is simpler. It is also more modular: if in the future we need to add a new cell to the configuration, then we do not need to modify the rules above, as the new cells can be inferred and completed by $\mathbb{K}$ automatically. In fact, configuration inference and completion is one of the most important features that make $\mathbb{K}$ definitions extensible and easy to adapt to language changes.

The rest of the semantics are self-explained. The rule for assignment X = I:Int;. updates the value that is bound to X in the state cell, as specified in the local rewrite X |-> (_ => I). Here the underscore "_" is an anonymous $\mathbb{K}$ variable. After the update, the assignment statement X = I:Int; is removed from the k cell, as specified by the local rewrite X = I:Int; => .. Recall that the dot "." means nothing, and rewriting something to a dot means removing it. Attribute `structural` means the associated rewrite rule is not counted as an explicit step by $\mathbb{K}$, but an implicit one. It should not affect how $\mathbb{K}$ executes the programs. The empty statement {} simply reduces to nothing. The last two rules process the declaration list of program variables and initialize their values to zero.

3   Program Execution and Verification in $\mathbb{K}$

Given the semantics of a programming language, $\mathbb{K}$ provides a variety of language tools, among which the most useful ones include a *parser*, an *interpreter* and a *verifier* for that language. In this section, we use the language IMP as a running example and show how to use these language tools that $\mathbb{K}$ offers, once we feed it the formal semantics (as in Fig. 6). For a more comprehensive introduction about $\mathbb{K}$ and $\mathbb{K}$ tools, we refer to the $\mathbb{K}$ framework website (https://runtimeverification. com/blog/k-framework-an-overview/).

3.1   Program Execution

The most basic tool that is automatically generated by $\mathbb{K}$ is a parser for IMP, based on the formal syntax definition. For example, the parser can parse IMP programs like the one in Fig. 7. Suppose that the $\mathbb{K}$ definition for IMP (Fig. 6) is saved in a file `imp.k`, the command `kompile imp.k` generates an *interpreter* for IMP which is invoked with the `krun` command. Suppose the IMP program sum is saved in a file `sum.imp`, then `krun sum.imp` executes the program and yields the final configuration as in Fig. 8. Notice that the k cell is empty, meaning that the program was completely executed, or consumed. In the end of its execution, n has the value 0 and s has the value 5050, which is the total of numbers up to 100, as expected. This execution capability of $\mathbb{K}$ is crucial for testing language semantics, and thus for increasing confidence in the adequacy of a language semantics. The above also illustrates another useful $\mathbb{K}$ tool, which like the parser generator, is used by almost any other tool, the $\mathbb{K}$ *unparser*. Indeed, the above configuration result uses concrete syntax to display the cells and their contents, although internally these are all represented as abstract data types. $\mathbb{K}$ also has the capability to display its results using abstract instead of concrete syntax, which helps users disambiguate in case the concrete syntax is ambiguous.

```
int s, n; n = 100; while(n) { s = s + n; n = n - 1; }
```

Fig. 7. The IMP program sum where n is initialized to 100.

We should point out that the interpreters automatically generated by $\mathbb{K}$ can be *very efficient*. For example, the formal semantics of the Ethereum Virtual

```
<T> <k> . </k> <state> n |-> 0 s |-> 5050 </state> </T>
```

Fig. 8. The final configuration after executing the IMP program sum in Fig. 7.

Machine (EVM) bytecode language, one of the most popular virtual machine languages for the blockchain, yields an EVM interpreter that is only one order of magnitude slower than the reference C++ implementation of the EVM [11,13].

3.2 Program Verification

K aims to naturally support not only execution, but also full program verification, in an ideal, mathematically grounded manner. Therefore, we require a *fixed* logic with a *fixed* sound and (relatively) complete proof system, where all languages become theories in the logic, about which we can reason using the fixed proof system. In this scenario, program execution is just one particular proof for a certain reachability property (the initial configuration reaches the final configuration). The logic is fixed, so it does not depend on any particular programming language, very much unlike Hoare logic and its variants.

The logical foundation of K's verification infrastructure is reachability logic [5,6] for dynamic properties, which uses matching logic [19] for static properties. We refer interested readers to the mentioned references for more technical details. Here, we use the sum program as an example, showing how verification can be easily done in K. The first step, of course, is to specify what properties about the program we want to prove. In Hoare logic, such specifications are given in terms of Hoare triples. In reachability logic and K, specifications are written using the already existing K rule syntax.

```
module SUM_SPEC
  imports IMP

  rule      // invariant spec
     <k> while(n){ s = s + n; n = n - 1; } => .K ... </k>
     <state>
       n |-> (N:Int => 0)
       s |-> (S:Int => S +Int ((N +Int 1) *Int N /Int 2))
     </state>
  requires N >=Int 0

  rule      // main spec
     <k> int n, s; n = N:Int; while(n){ s = s + n; n = n - 1; } => .K </k>
     <state> .Map =>
       n |-> 0
       s |-> ((N +Int 1) *Int N /Int 2)
     </state>
  requires N >=Int 0
endmodule
```

Fig. 9. A functional specification of sum, consisting of two rules: a main one capturing the desired property, and an "invariant" one to be used as a lemma.

Figure 9 shows a specification of the sum program. The specification consists of two reachability claims, which follows the keyword `rule`. The second claim is the main specification, which says that the sum program (where n is now initialized to a symbolic value n, written as a $\mathbb{K}$ variable `N:Int`) will terminate (and thus reaches .K in the k cell), and when it terminates, the value of s equals $n(n+1)/2$. The condition after the keyword `requires` has the similar meaning of a pre-condition in Hoare logic. It asks $\mathbb{K}$ to prove the mentioned reachability claim given that $n \geq 0$. The first claim is provided as a *lemma*, known as the *invariant* of the while-loop, in order for $\mathbb{K}$ to prove the main claim. The invariant claim says that when $n \geq 0$, the while-loop will terminate, and the value of s will increased by $n(n+1)/2$.

What is interesting is how $\mathbb{K}$ establishes the invariant claim via a *circular proof*, based on reachability logic proof system. $\mathbb{K}$ starts with the configuration with a while-loop in the k cell and n mapping to n and s mapping to s, as required by the left-hand side of the claim. Then, $\mathbb{K}$ rewrites the configuration *symbolically*, following the semantics rules we defined in Fig. 6, so the while-loop will be de-sugared to an if-statement, and the two assignments are resolved accordingly, too. After that, $\mathbb{K}$ reaches a configuration which contains exactly the same while-loop in the k cell, but in the state cell n maps to $n-1$ and s maps to $s+n$. For clarity, let us denote *that* configuration as γ and let $n' = n-1$ and $s' = s+n$. At this point, the (Circularity) proof rule of the reachability logic proof system (see, e.g., [6]) takes effect, and the invariant claim itself becomes a regular *axiom* which can be used in further proofs. Therefore, we can *instantiate* the variables n and s in the invariant claim by n' and s', yielding exactly the configuration γ, and the invariant claim immediately tells us that γ will terminate at a state where n maps to 0 and s maps to $s' + n'(n'+1)/s$. And this tells us that the initial configuration, with n mapping to n and s mapping to s, can reach γ and then terminate at the same state. Finally, $\mathbb{K}$ calls SMT solvers (such as Z3 [8]) to prove that $s' + n'(n'+1)/2$ equals $s + n(n+1)/2$, and concludes the proof successfully.

4   Towards Language-Independent Runtime Verification

Runtime verification is a system analysis technique that extracts execution information from a running system and uses it to detect and react to observed behaviors satisfying or violating certain properties [7]. As it avoids complex traditional formal verification techniques and analyzes only a few system execution traces, runtime verification tools have good scalability on real-world projects and practical codebase, and thus has gained significant interest from the research community.

Typically speaking, runtime verification tools take a target system as input together with event specifications and desired properties, and yield as output a modified "monitored" system which checks the desired properties during execution and reacts in case of property violation. At present, a suite of runtime verification tools are available for many real-world languages, including RV-MATCH that checks undefined behavior of C programs [10], RV-PREDICT that checks data race for Java and C/C++ programs [4], and RV-MONITOR that checks and enforces properties of Java and C programs [15], just to name a few.

Given the existing positive results that we have achieved in language-independent program execution and verification with the $\mathbb{K}$ framework, we propose a new promising direction towards *language-independent runtime verification*, where event specifications and desired properties are formally defined in the semantics and programs, and monitors are automatically generated in a correct-by-construction manner.

5 Conclusion

The $\mathbb{K}$ Framework was born from our firm belief that an ideal language framework is possible, where programming languages must have formal semantics, and that language tools such as parsers, interpreters, and deductive program verifiers are derived from just one reference formal definition of the language, at no additional cost specific to that language. $\mathbb{K}$ provides a user-friendly frontend (the meta-programming language) with which a variety of programming languages can be defined, while in its backend, a fixed language-independent logic powers $\mathbb{K}$'s deductive program verification. $\mathbb{K}$ may not be the final answer to this quest, but it proves that it is possible to have a language-independent program verification framework.

References

1. Ahrendt, W., Beckert, B., Bubel, R., Hahnle, R., Schmitt, P.H., Ulbrich, M.: Deductive Software Verification-The KeY Book. Springer, Heidelberg (2016). https://doi.org/10.1007/978-3-319-49812-6
2. Barnett, M., Chang, B.-Y.E., DeLine, R., Jacobs, B., Leino, K.R.M.: Boogie: a modular reusable verifier for object-oriented programs. In: de Boer, F.S., Bonsangue, M.M., Graf, S., de Roever, W.-P. (eds.) FMCO 2005. LNCS, vol. 4111, pp. 364–387. Springer, Heidelberg (2006). https://doi.org/10.1007/11804192_17
3. Bornat, R.: Proving pointer programs in Hoare logic. In: Backhouse, R., Oliveira, J.N. (eds.) MPC 2000. LNCS, vol. 1837, pp. 102–126. Springer, Heidelberg (2000). https://doi.org/10.1007/10722010_8
4. Şerbănuţă, T.F., Chen, F., Roşu, G.: Maximal causal models for sequentially consistent systems. In: Qadeer, S., Tasiran, S. (eds.) RV 2012. LNCS, vol. 7687, pp. 136–150. Springer, Heidelberg (2013). https://doi.org/10.1007/978-3-642-35632-2_16
5. Ştefănescu, A., Ciobâcă, Ş., Mereuţă, R., Moore, B.M., Şerbănuţă, T.F., Roşu, G.: All-path reachability logic. In: Dowek, G. (ed.) RTA 2014. LNCS, vol. 8560, pp. 425–440. Springer, Cham (2014). https://doi.org/10.1007/978-3-319-08918-8_29
6. Ştefănescu, A., Park, D., Yuwen, S., Li, Y., Roşu, G.: Semantics based program verifers for all languages. In: Proceedings of the 2016 ACM SIGPLAN International Conference on Object Oriented Programming, Systems, Languages and Applications (OOPSLA 2016), pp. 74–91. ACM, November 2016

7. Daian, P., et al.: Runtime verification at work: a tutorial. In: Falcone, Y., Sánchez, C. (eds.) RV 2016. LNCS, vol. 10012, pp. 46–67. Springer, Cham (2016). https://doi.org/10.1007/978-3-319-46982-9_5

8. de Moura, L., Bjørner, N.: Z3: an efficient SMT solver. In: Ramakrishnan, C.R., Rehof, J. (eds.) TACAS 2008. LNCS, vol. 4963, pp. 337–340. Springer, Heidelberg (2008). https://doi.org/10.1007/978-3-540-78800-3_24

9. Filliâtre, J.-C., Marché, C.: The Why/Krakatoa/Caduceus platform for deductive program verification. In: Damm, W., Hermanns, H. (eds.) CAV 2007. LNCS, vol. 4590, pp. 173–177. Springer, Heidelberg (2007). https://doi.org/10.1007/978-3-540-73368-3_21

10. Guth, D., Hathhorn, C., Saxena, M., Roşu, G.: RV-Match: practical semantics-based program analysis. In: Chaudhuri, S., Farzan, A. (eds.) CAV 2016. LNCS, vol. 9779, pp. 447–453. Springer, Cham (2016). https://doi.org/10.1007/978-3-319-41528-4_24

11. Hildenbrandt, E., et al.: KEVM: a complete semantics of the Ethereum virtual machine. In: Proceedings of the 2018 IEEE Computer Security Foundations Symposium (CSF 2018). IEEE (2018). http://jellopaper.org

12. Hoare, C.A.R.: An axiomatic basis for computer programming. Commun. ACM **12**(10), 576–580 (1969)

13. KEVM Team: KEVM: Semantics of EVM in K (2017). https://github.com/kframework/evm-semantics

14. Lamport, L.: The 'Hoare logic' of concurrent programs. Acta Inform. **14**(1), 21–37 (1980)

15. Luo, Q., et al.: RV-Monitor: efficient parametric runtime verification with simultaneous properties. In: Bonakdarpour, B., Smolka, S.A. (eds.) RV 2014. LNCS, vol. 8734, pp. 285–300. Springer, Cham (2014). https://doi.org/10.1007/978-3-319-11164-3_24

16. The Coq development team. The Coq proof assistant reference manual. LogiCal Project (2004)

17. Régis-Gianas, Y., Pottier, F.: A Hoare logic for call-by-value functional programs. In: Audebaud, P., Paulin-Mohring, C. (eds.) MPC 2008. LNCS, vol. 5133, pp. 305–335. Springer, Heidelberg (2008). https://doi.org/10.1007/978-3-540-70594-9_17

18. Reynolds, J.C.: Separation logic: a logic for shared mutable data structures. In: Proceedings of the 17th Annual IEEE Symposium on Logic in Computer Science (LICS 2002), pp. 55–74. IEEE (2002)

19. Roşu, G.: Matching logic. Log. Meth. Comput. Sci. **13**(4), 1–61 (2017)

20. The Isabelle development team: Isabelle (2018). https://isabelle.in.tum.de/

21. von Oheimb, D.: Hoare logic for Java in Isabelle/HOL. In: Concurrency and Computation: Practice and Experience, pp. 1173–1214 (2001)

22. Zhao, L., Wang, S., Liu, Z.: Graph-based object-oriented Hoare logic. In: Liu, Z., Woodcock, J., Zhu, H. (eds.) Theories of Programming and Formal Methods. LNCS, vol. 8051, pp. 374–393. Springer, Heidelberg (2013). https://doi.org/10.1007/978-3-642-39698-4_23

Programming Safe Robotics Systems: Challenges and Advances

Ankush Desai[1]([✉]), Shaz Qadeer[2], and Sanjit A. Seshia[1]

[1] University of California, Berkeley, USA
ankush@eecs.berkeley.edu
[2] Microsoft, Redmond, USA

Abstract. A significant challenge for large-scale deployment of autonomous mobile robots is to program them with formal guarantees and high assurance of correct operation. Our approach towards enabling safe programming of robotics system consists of two parts: (1) a programming language for implementing, specifying, and compositionally (assume-guarantee) testing the high-level reactive robotics software; (2) a runtime assurance system to ensure that the assumptions used during design-time testing of high-level software hold at runtime. Combining high-level programming language and its systematic testing with runtime enforcement helps us bridge the gap between software testing that makes assumptions about the low-level controllers and the physical world, and the actual execution of the software on a real robotic platform in the physical world. We implement our approach in DRONA, a programming framework for building safe robotics systems. This paper introduces the DRONA toolchain and describes how it addresses the unique challenges involved in programming safety-critical robots.

1 Introduction

Autonomous robotics systems have diverse and safety-critical roles in society today, including delivery systems, surveillance, and personal transportation. This drive towards autonomy is leading to increasing levels of software complexity. To tame this complexity and ensure safe and reliable operation of robotics systems, we have developed tools and techniques for programming and reasoning about them. In this paper, we present an overview of our work.

At the heart of an autonomous robot is the specialized onboard software that must ensure safe operation without any human intervention. The robotics software stack usually consists of several interacting modules grouped into two categories: *high-level* controllers, taking discrete decisions and planning to ensure that the robot safely achieves complex tasks, and *low-level* controllers, usually consisting of closed-loop controllers and actuators that determine the robot's continuous dynamics.

The high-level controllers must react to events (inputs) from the physical world as well as other components in the software stack (Fig. 2). These controllers are therefore implemented as concurrent event-driven software. However,

© Springer Nature Switzerland AG 2018
T. Margaria and B. Steffen (Eds.): ISoLA 2018, LNCS 11245, pp. 103–119, 2018.
https://doi.org/10.1007/978-3-030-03421-4_8

such software can be notoriously tricky to test and debug due to nondeterministic interactions with the environment and interleaving of the event handlers. We advocate writing the high-level controller in our domain-specific language P [1] which is suitable for expressing not only the asynchronous event-driven computation in the controllers but also models of other software components and the physical world (used for analysis/testing). By expressing both the controller and its environment in a single programming language, we bring advanced specification and testing techniques incorporated in P to the domain of robotics software.

Real-world robotics systems are rarely built as a monolithic system. Instead, they are a composition of multiple interacting components that together ensure the desired system specification (e.g., our case study in Fig. 2). P supports a module-system for the compositional reasoning of such complex event-driven software [2,3]. The P module-system enables implementing each component of the robotics software stack as a separate module and perform scalable compositional testing based on principles of assume-guarantee reasoning [4–6]. Compositional testing provides orders of magnitude more test-coverage compared to the traditional monolithic systematic testing approaches [2], uncovering several critical bugs in our implementation that could have caused safety violations.

Since the physical world often exhibits non-linear behavior, discrete-state models of the physical world used when testing the high-level controllers are necessarily approximate. Similarly, discrete-state models of the low-level controllers, which often use machine learning techniques, are also approximate. Verification of a high-level controller against such approximate models, although useful for finding and fixing errors quickly, cannot give us full assurance over the runtime behaviors of the controller. Therefore, we propose performing runtime monitoring of the assumptions (i.e., a discrete-state model of the environment and low-level controllers) used during design-time testing; and on detecting a divergence from the model at runtime, automatically triggering a fault recovery procedure to bring the system into a safe state. Thus, our approach combines modeling, specification, and testing with runtime monitoring and fault recovery to ensure safe execution of robotics software.

In this paper, we present DRONA, a programming language framework for building safe robotics systems. We implement the software components that must satisfy critical properties using a high-level programming language called P [1]. P supports scalable compositional testing backend for analysis of the asynchronous reactive programs. DRONA extends P with runtime assurance [7,8] capabilities to ensure that the assumptions made during testing about the low-level controllers and the environment hold at runtime. DRONA provides features for specifying the robot workspace and also runtime libraries for deploying the generated code from P compiler on ROS [9]. The DRONA toolchain is publicly available on GitHub (https://drona-org.github.io/Drona/).

1.1   Related Work

There are three popular approaches for building robotics systems with high-assurance of correctness:

(1) *Reactive synthesis*. There is increasing interest towards synthesizing reactive robotics controllers from temporal logic [10–13]. The programmer describes the system requirements in a high-level specification language and uses automated synthesis techniques for generating correct-by-construction high-level controllers. Tools like TuLip [14] and LTLMoP [15] construct a finite transition system that serves as an abstract model of the physical system and synthesizes a strategy, represented by a finite state automaton, satisfying the given high-level specification based on this model. Though this generated strategy is guaranteed to be safe in the abstract model of the environment, this approach has following limitations: (1) there is gap between the abstract models of the system and its actual behavior in the physical world; (2) there is gap between the generated strategy state-machine and its actual software implementation that interacts with the low-level controllers; and finally (3) the synthesis approach scale poorly both with the complexity of the mission and the size of the workspace. Other tools such as ComPlan [12] and SMC [13] generate both high-level and low-level plans, but still need additional work to translate these plans into reliable software on top of robotics platforms. Our approach is to provide a high-level language to (1) enable programmers to implement and specify the complex reactive system, (2) leverage advances in scalable systematic-testing techniques for validation of the actual implementation of the software, and (3) provide a safety envelope for operation in the real physical world via runtime assurance.

(2) *Reachability analysis*. Reachability analysis tools [16–18] have been used to verify robotics systems modeled as hybrid systems. If the tool successfully explores all possible reachable states of the system, then it provides a formal guarantee of correctness for the system model. Differently, from our work, reachability methods require an explicit representation of the robot dynamics and often suffer from scalability issues when the system has a large number of discrete states. Also, the analysis is performed using the models of the system, and hence, there is a gap between the models being verified and their implementation.

(3) *Simulation-based falsification*. Simulation-based tools for the falsification of CPS models (e.g., [19]) are more scalable than reachability methods, but generally, they do not provide any formal guarantees. In this approach, the entire robotics software stack is tested by simulating it in a loop with a high-fidelity model of the robot. The high-level controllers, the low-level controllers, and the robot dynamics are all executed together when exploring a behavior of the system and hence, this approach does not suffer from the gap between model and implementation described in the previous approaches. However, a challenge to achieving scalable coverage comes from the considerable time it can take for simulations.

In DRONA, we decompose the validation problem into two parts: (1) we propose using systematic testing methods (known to scale for complex software systems) for high-level software and use discrete models of the low-level software (ignoring dynamics), and (2) we combine it with runtime assurance [7,8] to tackle the challenges associated with low-level controllers that involve dynamics and other uncertainties of the robotics system. Runtime verification has been applied to robotics [20–23] where online monitors are used to check the status of the system. In this paper, we use runtime assurance to address the limitations of design-time analysis.

2   Overview

We use the case study of an autonomous drone surveillance system to present our approach for programming safe robotics systems. We consider an application where a drone must autonomously patrol a set of locations in a city. Figure 1(a) shows a snapshot of the workspace in the Gazebo simulator [24]. Figure 1(b) presents the obstacle map for the workspace with the surveillance points (blue dots) and a possible path that the autonomous drone can take when performing the surveillance task (black trajectory). We consider a simplified setting where the obstacles in the workspace are always static (e.g., houses and parked cars).

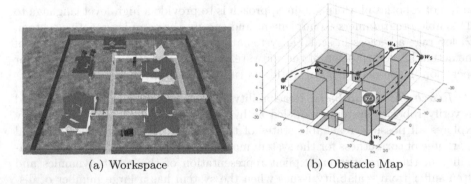

(a) Workspace   (b) Obstacle Map

Fig. 1. Case study: drone surveillance system (Color figure online)

The software stack for the drone surveillance system, even in such a simplified setting, consists of multiple complex components (Fig. 2). At the top, there is the implementation of the surveillance protocol that ensures the application specific properties (e.g., repeatedly visit the surveillance points in some priority order). The rest of the components are generic components such as the motion planner, the motion primitives and the perception module that together ensure safe movement of the drone in the workspace. The surveillance protocol generates the next target location for the drone. The motion planner computes a motion plan which is a sequence of waypoints from the current location to the target location. The waypoints $w_1 \ldots w_6$ in Fig. 1(b) represent one such motion plan generated by the planner and the dotted lines represent the reference trajectory for the drone.

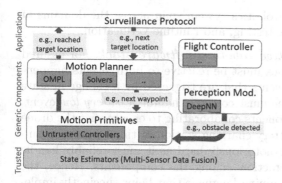

Fig. 2. Robotics software stack (Color figure online)

The motion primitives on receiving the next waypoint generate the required low-level controls necessary to follow the reference trajectory. The trajectory in Fig. 1(b) represents the actual path of the drone, which deviates from the reference trajectory because of the underlying dynamics and disturbances. The flight controller module maintains information about the mode of operation of the system and ensures that the critical events are prioritized correctly in all the modes. The perception module is used for detection obstacles and passing the information to the planner and controller to avoid a collision.

Programming the robotics software stack (Fig. 2) is challenging as it consists of multiple components, each implementing a complicated protocol, and continuously interacting with each other for accomplishing the mission safely. These components may, in turn, use third-party or machine-learning components that are hard to verify or test for correctness at design time. Hence, providing end-to-end correctness guarantees for robotics system is challenging and requires advances in both design time (static) and runtime analysis research.

2.1 Drona: Programming Framework for Safe Robotics

Figure 3 provides an overview of the DRONA toolchain, a unified framework for modeling, implementing and testing safe robotics systems.

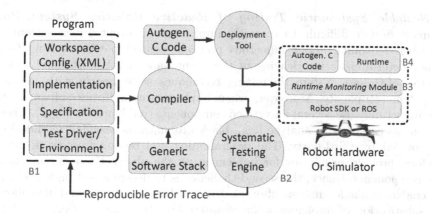

Fig. 3. DRONA tool chain

The challenges in building safe robotics system span across the domains of programming languages, systematic testing, and runtime verification.

(1) *Safe programming of reactive robotics software stack.* For assured autonomy, the robotics software stack must be reactive to both, events happening in the environment as well as events that are triggered by a change in state of the robot. For example, the drone must correctly handle a *battery low* event, which might involve multiple components collaborating to ensure that the drone lands safely or navigates to the battery charging station in time. Safe programming of such a reactive behavior is notoriously hard as it must reliably handle concurrency and event-driven interaction among the components. Hence, the first challenge is to design a programming language that helps succinctly implement the event-driven software stack at a higher level of abstraction. Moreover, the programming language must also support modular design and implementation as the robotics software is in general built as a composition of several components.

For addressing this challenge, DRONA uses the P programming language framework (Fig. 3B1). The P module system allows modular implementation of software stack where each component (protocol) is implemented as a separate module and modules are assembled (composed) together to build the complex system (Sect. 3). Further details about the P programming language is provided in Sect. 3 and in [2,3].

A DRONA application consists of four blocks—*implementation, specification, workspace configuration,* and *test-driver.* The *implementation* block is a collection of P modules implementing the high-level controllers. *Specification* block capture the application specific correctness properties. The *workspace configuration* XML file provides details about the workspace, like the size of the workspace grid, location of static obstacles, location of battery charging points, and the starting position of each robot. The *test-driver* block implements the *finite* environment state machines (models) and abstractions of untrusted components to close the system for systematic testing.

(2) *Scalable Systematic Testing of Reactive Robotics System.* Programmers find it difficult to correctly implement an event-driven system as it involves reasoning about numerous program control paths resulting from the non-deterministic interleaving of the event handlers. Unfortunately, even the state-of-the-art systematic testing techniques scale poorly with increasing system complexity. Moreover, when implementing robotics software, the programmer may use several uncertified components (red blocks in Fig. 2). These components are hard to analyze (e.g., black box machine-learning modules) or are provided by third-party. The programming and testing framework must, therefore, provide primitives for implementing the abstractions or models of these components. Hence, the second challenge is to design a testing framework that enables scalable analysis of event-driven robotics software and also allows easy substitution of implementation modules with their abstractions (models) during testing.

One can scale systematic testing to large, industrial-scale implementations by decomposing the system-level testing problem into a collection of component-level testing problems. Moreover, the results of component-level testing can be lifted to the whole system level by leveraging the theory of assume-guarantee (AG) reasoning. DRONA leverages the *compositional testing* [2,3] backend of P (Fig. 3B2) for addressing this challenge. The compiler generates a translation of the system implementation into a decomposed component-level testing problems. For each decomposed test instance the systematic testing tool enumerates executions resulting from scheduling and explicit nondeterministic choices. A programmer typically spends the initial part of development in the iterative edit-compile-test-debug loop enabled by our systematic testing tool. The feedback from the tool is an error trace that picks a particular sequence of nondeterministic choices leading to the error. Compositional testing provides orders of magnitude more test-coverage compared to the traditional monolithic systematic testing approaches [2], uncovering several critical bugs in our implementation that could have caused safety violations.

(3) *Guaranteeing safety when using untrusted components.* In practice, when building a robotics software stack, the programmer may use several uncertified components (red blocks in Fig. 2). For example, implementing an on-the-fly motion planner may involve solving an optimization problem or using an efficient search technique that relies on a solver or a third-party library (e.g., OMPL). Similarly, motion primitives are either designed using machine-learning techniques or optimized for specific tasks without considering safety or are off-the-shelf controllers provided by third parties. Ultimately, in the presence of such uncertified or hard-to-verify components, no formal guarantees can be provided using design-time testing or verification techniques. The final challenge, therefore, is to design a runtime assurance framework that guarantees the safety of the system at runtime even when the untrusted components violate the assumptions made during design time.

DRONA extends the P programming framework with capabilities for runtime assurance, it supports efficient online monitoring of design time assumptions and allows the programmer to specify recovery mechanism in case the assumptions can be violated (Fig. 3B3). The idea is to wrap each untrusted component inside a runtime assurance module that monitors the assumptions made for that component during the design-time analysis and triggers a recovery procedure to guarantee that the assumptions are not violated at runtime.

The DRONA compiler also generates C code that is compiled by a standard C compiler and linked against the runtime to create the executable that can be deployed on the target platform, a collection of machines, or robotics system. Runtime ensures that the behavior of a DRONA program matches the semantics validated by the systematic testing. Further details about DRONA toolchain and the case-study of programming distributed mobile robotics is available in [25].

3   P: Modular and Safe Event-Driven Programming

A significant challenge in building reactive robotics software is safe asynchronous event-driven programming. Asynchrony and reactivity are challenging to get right because it inevitably leads to the concurrency with its notorious pitfalls of race conditions and Heisenbugs. To address the challenges of asynchronous computation, we have developed P [1] (https://github.com/p-org/P), a (domain-specific) programming language for modeling, specifying and compositionally testing protocols in asynchronous event-driven applications.

The P programmer writes the protocol and its specification at a high-level. P provides first-class support for modeling concurrency, specifying safety and liveness properties, and checking that the program satisfies its specification [26,27]. In these capabilities, it is similar to TLA+ [28] and SPIN [29]. Unlike TLA+ and SPIN, a P program can also be compiled into executable C code. This capability bridges the gap between high-level model and low-level implementation and eliminates a massive hurdle to the acceptance of formal modeling and specification among programmers.

P got its start in Microsoft software development when it was used to ship the USB 3.0 drivers in Windows 8.1 and Windows Phone. P enabled the detection and debugging of hundreds of race conditions and Heisenbugs early on in the design of the drivers. Since then, P has been used to ship many more drivers in subsequent versions of Windows. More recently, we have used P to build fault-tolerant distributed systems [2,3] and distributed robotics systems [25].

3.1   Basic Programming Constructs

P [1] is an actor-oriented [30] programming language where actors are implemented as state machines. A P program comprises state machines communicating asynchronously with each other using events accompanied by typed data values. Each machine has an input buffer, event handlers, and a local store. The machines run concurrently, receiving and sending events, creating new machines, and updating the local store.

We introduce the key constructs of P through a simple client-server application (see Fig. 4) implemented as a collection of P state machines. In this example, the client sends a request to the server and waits for a response; on receiving a response from the server, it computes the next request to send and repeats this in a loop. The server waits for a request from the client; on receiving a request, it interacts with a helper protocol to compute the response for the client.

Events and Interfaces. An event declaration has a name and a payload type associated with it. Figure 4(a) (line 2) declares an event eRequest that must be accompanied by a tuple of type RequestType. Figure 4(a) (line 6) declares the named tuple type RequestType. P supports primitive types like int, bool, float, and complex types like tuples, sequences and maps. Each interface declaration has an interface name and a set of events that the interface can receive. For example, the interface ClientIT declared at Fig. 4(b) (line 3) is willing to receive

```
1  /* Events */
2  event eRequest : RequestType;
3  event eResponse: ResponseType;
4  ...
5  /* Types */
6  type RequestType =
7  (source: ClientIT, reqId:int, val: int);
8  type ResponseType = (resId: int, success: bool);
9
10 machine ClientImpl receives eResponse;
11 sends eRequest; creates ServerToClientIT;
12 {
13     var server : ServerToClientIT;
14     var nextId, nextVal : int;
15     start state Init {
16         entry {
17             server = new ServerToClientIT;
18             goto StartPumpingRequests;
19         }
20     }
21     state StartPumpingRequests {
22         entry {
23             if(nextId < 5) //send 5 requests
24             {
25                 send server, eRequest, (source = this,
26                     reqId = nextId, val = nextVal);
27                 nextId++;
28             }
29         }
30         on eResponse do (payload: ResponseType) {
31             /* compute nextVal */
32             goto StartPumpingRequests;
33         }
34     }
35 }
```

```
1  /* Interfaces */
2  interface ServerToClientIT receives eRequest;
3  interface ClientIT receives eResponse;
4  interface HelperIT receives eProcessReq;
5
6  machine ServerImpl
7  sends eResponse, eProcessReq;
8  receives eRequest, eReqSuccess, eReqFail;
9  creates HelperIT;
10 {
11     var helper: HelperIT;
12     start state Init {
13         entry {
14             helper = new HelperIT;
15             goto WaitForRequests;
16         }
17     }
18
19     state WaitForRequests {
20         on eRequest do (payload: RequestType) {
21             var client: ClientIT;
22             var result: bool;
23             client = payload.source;
24             /* interacts with the helper machine */
25             send helper, eProcessReq,
26                 (payload.reqId, payload.val);
27             ...
28             /* outcome: result = true or false*/
29             send client, eResponse,
30                 (resId = payload.reqId, success = result);
31         }
32     }
33 }
34 machine HelperImpl receives eProcessReq;
35 sends eReqSuccess, eReqFail, ..; creates .. ;
36 { /* body */ }
```

(a) Client State Machine   (b) Server State Machine

Fig. 4. A client-server application using P state machines

only event **eResponse**. Interfaces are like symbolic names for machines. In P, unlike in the actor model where an instance of an actor is created using its name, an instance of a machine is created indirectly by performing **new** of an interface and linking the interface to the machine separately. For example, execution of the statement **server = new ServerToClientIT** at Fig. 4(a) (line 17) creates a fresh instance of machine **ServerImpl** and stores a unique reference to the new machine instance in **server**. The link between **ServerToClientIT** and **ServerImpl** is provided separately by the programmer using the **bind** operation (details in Sect. 3.2).

Machines. Figure 4(a) (line 10) declares a machine **ClientImpl** that is willing to receive event **eResponse**, guarantees to send no event other than **eRequest**, and guarantees to create (by executing **new**) no interface other than **ServerToClientIT**. The body of a state machine contains variables and states. Each state can have an entry function and a set of event handlers. The machine executes the entry function each time it enters that state. After executing the entry function, the machine tries to dequeue an event from the input buffer or blocks if the buffer is empty. Upon dequeuing an event from the input queue of the machine, the attached handler is executed. Figure 4(a) (line 30) declares an event-handler in the **StartPumpingRequests** state for the **eResponse** event, the **payload** argument stores the payload value associated with the dequeued **eResponse** event. The machine transitions from one state to another on executing the goto statement. Executing the statement send t,e,v adds event e with payload value v into the buffer of the target machine t. Sends are buffered, non-blocking, and directed. For example, the send statement Fig. 4(a) (line 25) sends eRequest event to the machine referenced by the server identifier. In P, the type of a machine-reference variable is the name of an interface.

Next, we walk through the implementation of the client (ClientImpl) and the server (ServerImpl) machines in Fig. 4. Let us assume that the interfaces ServerToClientIT, ClientIT, and HelperIT are programmatically linked to the machines ServerImpl, ClientImpl, and HelperImpl respectively (we explain these bindings in Sect. 3.2). A fresh instance of a ClientImpl machine starts in the Init state and executes its entry function; it first creates the interface ServerToClientIT that leads to the creation of an instance of the ServerImpl machine, and then transitions to the StartPumpingRequests state. In the StartPumpingRequests state, it sends a eRequest event to the server with a payload value and then blocks for a eResponse event. On receiving the eResponse event, it computes the next value to be sent to the server and transitions back to the StartPumpingRequests state. The this keyword is the "self" identifier that references the machine itself. The ServerImpl machine starts by creating the HelperImpl machine and moves to the WaitForRequests state. On receiving a eResponse event, the server interacts with the helper machine to compute the result that it sends back to the client.

3.2 Compositional Programming

P allows the programmer to decompose a complex system into simple components where each component is a P module. Figure 5 presents a modular implementation of the client-server application. A primitive module in P is a set of bindings from interfaces to state machines.

```
1  module ClientModule = {
2    ClientIT -> ClientImpl
3  };
4  module ServerModule = {
5    ServerToClientIT -> ServerImpl,
6    HelperIT -> HelperImpl
7  };
8  //C code generation for the implementation.
9  implementation app: ClientModule || ServerModule;
10
11 module ServerModule' = {
12   ServerToClientIT -> ServerImpl',
13   HelperIT -> HelperImpl
14 };
15 implementation app': ClientModule || ServerModule';
```

Fig. 5. Modular client-server implementation

ServerModule is a primitive module consisting of machines ServerImpl and HelperImpl where the ServerImpl machine is bound to the ServerToClientIT interface and the HelperImpl machine is bound to the HelperIT interface. The compiler ensures that the creation of an interface leads to the creation of a machine to which it binds. For example, creation of the ServerToClientIT interface (executing new ServerToClientIT) by any machine inside the module or by any machine in the environment (i.e., outside ServerModule) would lead to the creation of an instance of ServerImpl machine.

The client-server application (Fig. 4) can be implemented modularly as two separate modules ClientModule and ServerModule; these modules can be implemented and tested in isolation. Modules in P are *open systems*, i.e., machines inside the module may create interfaces that are not bound in the module; similarly, machines may send events to or receive events from machines that are not in the module. For example, the ClientImpl machine in ClientModule creates an interface ServerToClientIT that is not bound to any machine in ClientModule, it sends eRequest and receives eResponse from machines that are not in ClientModule.

Composition in P (denoted ||) is supported by type checking. If the composition type checks (typing rules for module constructors are defined in [2,3]) then the composition of modules behaves like language intersection over the traces of the modules. The compiler ensures that the joint actions in the composed module (ClientModule || ServerModule) are linked appropriately, e.g., the creation of the interface ServerToClientIT (Fig. 4(a) line 18) in ClientModule is linked to ServerImpl in ServerModule and all the sends of eRequest events are enqueued in the corresponding ServerImpl machine. The compiler generates C code for the module in the implementation declaration.

Note that the indirection enabled by the use of interfaces is critical for implementing the key feature of *substitution* required for modular programming, i.e., the ability to seamlessly replace one implementation module with another. For example, ServerModule' (Fig. 5 line 11) represents a module where the server protocol is implemented by a different machine ServerImpl'. In module ClientModule || ServerModule', the creation of an interface ServerToClientIT in the client machine is linked to machine ServerImpl'. The *substitution* feature is also critical for compositional reasoning, in which case, an implementation module is replaced by its abstraction.

3.3 Compositional Testing

Monolithic testing of large systems is prohibitively expensive due to an explosion of behaviors caused by concurrency and failures. The P approach to this problem is to use the principle of assume-guarantee reasoning for decomposing the monolithic system-level testing problem into component-level testing problems; testing each component in isolation using abstractions of the other components.

Spec Machines. In P, a programmer can specify temporal properties via specification machines (monitors). spec s observes E1, E2 { .. } declares a specification machine s that observes events E1 and E2. If the programmer chooses to attach s to a module M, the code in M is instrumented automatically to forward any event-payload pair (e, v) to s if e is in the observes list of s; the handler for event e inside s executes synchronously with the delivery of e. The specification machines observe only the output events of a module. Thus, specification machines introduce a publish-subscribe mechanism for monitoring events to check temporal specifications while testing a P module. The module constructor assert s in P attaches specification machine s to module P. In Fig. 6(a),

```
 1  machine AbstractServerImpl receives eRequest;
 2  sends eResponse;
 3  {
 4    start state Init {
 5      on eRequest do (payload: RequestType) {
 6      send payload.source, eResponse,
 7      (resId = payload.reqId,success = choose());
 8      }
 9    }
10  }
11  spec ReqIdsAreMonoInc observes eRequest {
12    var prevId : int;
13    start state Init {
14      on eRequest do (payload: RequestType) {
15        assert(payload.reqId == prevId + 1);
16        prevId = payload.reqId;
17      }
18    }
19  }
20  spec ResIdsAreMonoInc observes eResponse
21  {
22    var prevId : int;
23    start state Init {
24      on eResponse do (payload: ResponseType) {
25        assert(payload.resId == prevId + 1);
26        prevId = payload.resId;
27      }
28    }
29  }
30
```

```
 1  module AbstractServerModule = {
 2    ServerToClientIT -> AbstractServerImpl
 3  };
 4
 5  module AbstractClientModule = {
 6    ClientIT -> AbstractClientImpl
 7  };
 8
 9  /* Compositional Safety Checking */
10  //Test: ClientModule.
11  test test0: (assert ReqIdsAreMonoInc in ClientModule)
12                || AbstractServerModule;
13  //Test: ServerModule.
14  test test1: (assert ResIdsAreMonoInc in ServerModule)
15                || AbstractClientModule;
16
17  /* Circular Assume-Guarantee */
18  //Check that client abstraction is correct.
19  test test2: ClientModule || AbstractServerModule
20              refines
21              AbstractClientModule || AbstractServerModule;
22  //Check that server abstraction is correct.
23  test test3: AbstractServerModule || ServerModule
24              refines
25              AbstractClientModule || AbstractServerModule;
26
27  // Create abstract module using Hide
28  module hideModule = hide X in AbstractServerModule;
29
30  test test4: ClientModule || ServerModule
31              refines
32              AbstractClientModule || hideModule;
```

(a) Abstraction and Specifications   (b) Test Declarations for Compositional Testing

Fig. 6. Compositional testing of the client-server application using P modules

ReqIdsAreMonoInc and ResIdsAreMonoInc are specification machines observing events eRequest and eResponse to assert the safety property that the reqId and resId in the payload of these events are always monotonically increasing. Note that ReqIdsAreMonoInc is a property of the client machine and ResIdsAreMonoInc is a property of the server machine.

In P, abstractions used for assume-guarantee reasoning are also implemented as modules. For example, AbstractServerModule is an abstraction of the ServerModule where the AbstractServerImpl machine implements an abstraction of the interaction between ServerImpl and HelperImpl. The AbstractServerImpl machine on receiving a request sends back a random response.

P enables decomposing the monolithic problem of checking: (assert ReqIdsAreMonoInc, ResIdsAreMonoInc in ClientModule || ServerModule) into four simple proof obligations. P allows the programmer to write each obligation as a test-declaration. The declaration test tname: P introduces a safety test obligation that the executions of module P do not result in a failure/error. The declaration test tname: P refines Q introduces a test obligation that module P refines module Q. The notion of refinement in P is trace-containment based only on externally visible actions, i.e., P refines Q, if every trace of P projected onto the visible actions of Q is also a trace of Q. P automatically discharges these test obligations using systematic testing. Using the theory of compositional safety [2,3], we decompose the monolithic safety checking problem into two obligations (tests) test0 and test1 (Fig. 6(b)). These tests use abstractions to check that each module satisfies its safety specification. Note that interfaces and the programmable bindings together enable substitution during compositional reasoning. For example, `ServerToClientIT` gets linked to `ServerImpl` in implementation but to its abstraction `AbstractServerImpl` during testing.

Meaningful testing requires that these abstractions used for decomposition be sound. To this end, P module system supports circular assume-guarantee reasoning [2,3] to validate the abstractions. Tests `test2` and `test3` perform the necessary refinement checking to ensure the soundness of the decomposition (`test0,test1`). The challenge addressed by our module system is to provide the theorems of compositional safety and circular assume-guarantee for a dynamic programming model of P state machines.

P module system also provides module constructors like `hide` for hiding events (interfaces) and `rename` for renaming of conflicting actions for more flexible composition. Hide operation introduces privates events (interface) into a module, it can be used to converts some of the visible actions of a module into private actions that are no longer part of its visible trace. For example, assume that modules `AbstractServerModule` and `ServerModule` use event X internally for completely different purposes. In that case, the refinement check between them is more likely to hold if X is not part of the visible trace of the abstract module. Figure 6(b) (line 28–33) show how hide can be used in such cases.

P enables modular programming of the complex robotics software stack where each component can be implemented as a separate module and compositionally tested in isolation using the principles of assume-guarantee reasoning. We have used P to implement robotics software stack for drones and found several critical bugs during the development process that could have potentially lead to a drone crash. More details along with demonstration videos are available at https://drona-org.github.io/Drona/.

4   Safe Robotics Using Runtime Assurance

When performing the compositional testing of the high-level controller, we use abstractions or models of the low-level controllers. For carrying over the analysis of high-level controllers performed at design time to runtime, one must ensure that the assumptions about the low-level controllers made during testing hold at runtime. Hence the need for a framework that supports runtime monitoring of design time assumptions and provides safety assurance if these assumptions can be violated.

Let us consider the example of guaranteeing safety in the presence of an untrusted motion primitive component. A drone navigates in the 3D space by tracking trajectories between waypoints computed by the motion planner (Fig. 2). Given the next waypoint, an appropriate motion primitive is used to track the reference trajectory. Informally, a motion primitive consists of a pre-computed control law (sequence of control actions) that regulates the state of the drone as a function of time. A motion primitive take as input the next waypoint and generates the low-level control to traverse the reference trajectory from the current position to the target waypoint. When testing the high-level controllers in the software stack, we assume that the motion primitives safely takes the drone from its current position to the target position by remaining inside the green tube and use the corresponding discrete abstraction. Since the control is optimized for performance rather than safety and also approximates the drone dynamics, it can be potentially unsafe.

To demonstrate this, we experimented with the motion primitives provided by the drone manufacturers. The drone was tasked to repeatedly visit locations g_1 to g_4 in that order,i.e., the sequence of waypoints $g_1, \ldots g_4$. The blue lines represent the trajectories of the drone. Given the complex dynamics of a drone and noisy sensors, ensuring that it precisely follows a fixed trajectory (ideally a straight line joining the waypoints) is tough.

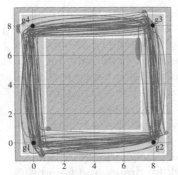

The low-level controller (untrusted third party controller) optimizes for time and, hence, during high-speed maneuvers, the reduced control on the drone leads to overshoot and trajectories that collide with obstacles (represented by the red regions). Note that the controller can be used during the majority of this mission except for a few instances of unsafe maneuvers. Hence, there is a need for runtime verification techniques that ensure the safety of the system when the design-time assumptions can be violated.

We use runtime verification to monitor at runtime the assumptions and abstractions used during systematic testing. An online monitor is useful as it can determine if any of the assumptions (specifications) can be violated and notify the operator about the unexpected behavior or trigger some correcting input actions to fix the problem. In our recent work [31], we use runtime verification to monitor the assumptions about low-level controllers and drone dynamics; we show that violations of these assumptions can be predicted in time to make corrective measure and ensure overall correctness of the mission implemented by the high-level controller. We have used runtime assurance to build end-to-end correct robotics software stack, more details about the framework and experiments is available in [32].

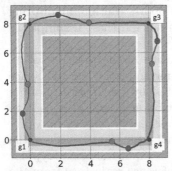

Fig. 7. Experiment using runtime assurance (Color figure online)

Let us revisit the experiment described earlier. We monitor the assumption that the drone under the influence of the motion primitive will remain inside the yellow tube.

This assumption may get violated at runtime because of various reasons, runtime assurance guarantees that it can be predicted in time and recovery operation can be triggered to bring the drone back to the safe (green) tube. Figure 7 presents one of the interesting trajectories where the recovery module takes control multiple times and ensures the overall correctness of the mission.

The red dots represent the points where the runtime monitoring system switches control to recovery, and the green dots represent the locations where it returns control to the untrusted controller for mission completion.

5   Conclusion

DRONA is a novel programming framework that makes it easier to implement, specify, and compositionally test robotics software. It uses a mechanism based on runtime assurance to ensure that the assumptions about the untrusted components in the software stack hold at runtime. We firmly believe that this combination of design time techniques like programming languages and testing with runtime assurance is the right step towards solving the problem of building robust robotics systems. P enables modular implementation of the software stack and is effective in finding critical software bugs in our implementation; the runtime assurance extension helps ensure safety if there are bugs in the untrusted software components. We have evaluated DRONA by deploying the generated code both on real drone platforms and running rigorous simulations in high-fidelity drone simulators. Both DRONA (https://drona-org.github.io/Drona/) and P (https://github.com/p-org/P) are publicly available. For future work, we are investigating the role a system like DRONA can play in the design and implementation of verified learning-based robotics, and more generally for verified artificial intelligence [33], where we believe runtime assurance will play a central role.

Acknowledgments. The work of the first and third authors was supported in part by the TerraSwarm Research Center, one of six centers supported by the STARnet phase of the Focus Center Research Program (FCRP) a Semiconductor Research Corporation program sponsored by MARCO and DARPA, by the DARPA BRASS and Assured Autonomy programs, and by Toyota under the iCyPhy center.

References

1. Desai, A., Gupta, V., Jackson, E., Qadeer, S., Rajamani, S., Zufferey, D.: P: safe asynchronous event-driven programming. In: Programming Language Design and Implementation (PLDI) (2013)
2. Desai, A., Phanishayee, A., Qadeer, S., Seshia, S.A.: Compositional programming and testing of dynamic distributed systems. Technical report UCB/EECS-2018-95, EECS Department, University of California, Berkeley, July 2018
3. Desai, A., Phanishayee, A., Qadeer, S., Seshia, S.A.: Compositional programming and testing of dynamic distributed systems. In: Proceedings of the ACM on Programming Languages (PACMPL) (OOPSLA) (2018)
4. Alur, R., Henzinger, T.A.: Reactive modules. Form. Methods Syst. Des. **15**, 7–48 (1999)
5. Abadi, M., Lamport, L.: Composing specifications. ACM Trans. Program. Lang. Syst. (TOPLAS) **15**, 73–132 (1993)
6. Abadi, M., Lamport, L.: Conjoining specifications. ACM Trans. Program. Lang. Syst. (TOPLAS) **17**, 507–535 (1995)

7. Sha, L.: Using simplicity to control complexity. IEEE Softw. **18**, 20–28 (2001)
8. Schierman, J.D., et al.: Runtime assurance framework development for highly adaptive flight control systems. Technical report AD1010277, Barron Associates, Inc., Charlottesville (2015)
9. Quigley, M., et al.: ROS: an open-source robot operating system. In: ICRA Workshop on Open Source Software (2009)
10. Kress-Gazit, H., Fainekos, G.E., Pappas, G.J.: Temporal logic based reactive mission and motion planning. IEEE Trans. Robot. **25**, 1370–1381 (2009)
11. Fainekos, G.E., Girard, A., Kress-Gazit, H., Pappas, G.J.: Temporal logic motion planning for dynamic robots. Automatica **45**, 343–352 (2009)
12. Saha, I., Ramaithitima, R., Kumar, V., Pappas, G.J., Seshia, S.A.: Automated composition of motion primitives for multi-robot systems from safe LTL specifications. In: Intelligent Robots and Systems, IROS, pp. 1525–1532. IEEE (2014)
13. Shoukry, Y., et al.: Linear temporal logic motion planning for teams of underactuated robots using satisfiability modulo convex programming. In: 56th IEEE Annual Conference on Decision and Control (CDC), pp. 1132–1137 (2017)
14. Wongpiromsarn, T., Topcu, U., Ozay, N., Xu, H., Murray, R.M.: TuLiP: a software toolbox for receding horizon temporal logic planning. In: International Conference on Hybrid Systems: Computation and Control (HSCC) (2011)
15. Finucane, C., Jing, G., Kress-Gazit, G.: LTLMoP: experimenting with language, temporal logic and robot control. In: IEEE/RSJ International Conference on Intelligent Robots and Systems (2010)
16. Frehse, G., et al.: SpaceEx: scalable verification of hybrid systems. In: Gopalakrishnan, G., Qadeer, S. (eds.) CAV 2011. LNCS, vol. 6806, pp. 379–395. Springer, Heidelberg (2011). https://doi.org/10.1007/978-3-642-22110-1_30
17. Chen, X., Ábrahám, E., Sankaranarayanan, S.: Flow*: an analyzer for non-linear hybrid systems. In: Sharygina, N., Veith, H. (eds.) CAV 2013. LNCS, vol. 8044, pp. 258–263. Springer, Heidelberg (2013). https://doi.org/10.1007/978-3-642-39799-8_18
18. Duggirala, P.S., Mitra, S., Viswanathan, M., Potok, M.: C2E2: a verification tool for stateflow models. In: Baier, C., Tinelli, C. (eds.) TACAS 2015. LNCS, vol. 9035, pp. 68–82. Springer, Heidelberg (2015). https://doi.org/10.1007/978-3-662-46681-0_5
19. Dreossi, T., Donzé, A., Seshia, S.A.: Compositional falsification of cyber-physical systems with machine learning components. In: Barrett, C., Davies, M., Kahsai, T. (eds.) NFM 2017. LNCS, vol. 10227, pp. 357–372. Springer, Cham (2017). https://doi.org/10.1007/978-3-319-57288-8_26
20. Gat, E., Slack, M.G., Miller, D.P., Firby, R.J.: Path planning and execution monitoring for a planetary rover. In: Robotics and Automation. IEEE (1990)
21. Pettersson, O.: Execution monitoring in robotics: a survey. Robot. Auton. Syst. **53**, 73–88 (2005)
22. Lotz, A., Steck, A., Schlegel, C.: Runtime monitoring of robotics software components: increasing robustness of service robotic systems. In: International Conference on Advanced Robotics (ICAR) (2011)
23. Lee, I., Ben-Abdallah, H., Kannan, S., Kim, M., Sokolsky, O., Viswanathan, M.: A monitoring and checking framework for run-time correctness assurance (1998)
24. Koenig, N., Howard, A.: Design and use paradigms for gazebo, an open-source multi-robot simulator. In: International Conference on Intelligent Robots and Systems (IROS) (2004)

25. Desai, A., Saha, I., Yang, J., Qadeer, S., Seshia, S.A.: DRONA: a framework for safe distributed mobile robotics. In: International Conference on Cyber-Physical Systems (ICCPS) (2017)
26. Desai, A., Qadeer, S., Seshia, S.A.: Systematic testing of asynchronous reactive systems. In: Foundations of Software Engineering (FSE) (2015)
27. Mudduluru, R., Deligiannis, P., Desai, A., Lal, A., Qadeer, S.: Lasso detection using partial-state caching. In: Conference on Formal Methods in Computer-Aided Design (FMCAD) (2017)
28. Lamport, L.: Specifying Systems: The TLA+ Language and Tools for Hardware and Software Engineers. Addison-Wesley Longman, Boston (2002)
29. Holzmann, G.: The Spin Model Checker: Primer and Reference Manual, 1st edn. Addison-Wesley Professional, Boston (2003)
30. Agha, G.: Actors: A Model of Concurrent Computation in Distributed Systems. MIT Press, Cambridge (1986)
31. Desai, A., Dreossi, T., Seshia, S.A.: Combining model checking and runtime verification for safe robotics. In: Lahiri, S., Reger, G. (eds.) RV 2017. LNCS, vol. 10548, pp. 172–189. Springer, Cham (2017). https://doi.org/10.1007/978-3-319-67531-2_11
32. Desai, A., Ghosh, S., Seshia, S.A., Shankar, N., Tiwari, A.: SOTER: programming safe robotics system using runtime assurance. Technical report UCB/EECS-2018-127, EECS Department, University of California, Berkeley, August 2018
33. Seshia, S.A., Sadigh, D., Sastry, S.S.: Towards verified artificial intelligence. CoRR, vol. abs/1606.08514 (2016)

Generating Component Interfaces by Integrating Static and Symbolic Analysis, Learning, and Runtime Monitoring

Falk Howar[1]([⊠]), Dimitra Giannakopoulou[2], Malte Mues[3], and Jorge A. Navas[4]

[1] Dortmund University of Technology and Fraunhofer ISST, Dortmund, Germany
falk.howar@tu-dortmund.de
[2] NASA Ames Research Center, Moffett Field, CA, USA
[3] Dortmund University of Technology, Dortmund, Germany
[4] Computer Science Laboratory, SRI International, Menlo Park, USA

Abstract. Behavioral interfaces describe the safe interactions with a component without exposing its internal variables and computation. As such, they can serve as documentation or formal contracts for black-box components in safety-critical systems. Learning-based generation of interaces relies on learning algorithms for inferring behavioral interfaces from observations, which are in turn checked for correctness by formal analysis techniques. Learning-based interface generation is therefore an interesting target when studying integration and combination of different formal analysis methods. In this paper, which accompanies an invited talk at the ISoLA 2018 track "A Broader View on Verification: From Static to Runtime and Back", we introduce interpolation and symbolic search for validating inferred interfaces. We discuss briefly how interface validation may utilize information from runtime monitoring.

1 Introduction

In the automotive and aeronautic industries, it is customary for original equipment manufacturers (OEMs) to contract the design and implementation of system components to external companies [18]. In such a scenario, the OEM specifies a set of requirements on the component that is to be developed. The contractor develops the component as a black-box: the delivered product does not typically include intermediate artifacts such as design models or source code. As a consequence, the only means of verifying external components is black-box testing, which provides no formal guarantees.

This situation can be mitigated to some extent if contractors produce high-level behavioral models which, while suitable for verification, do not expose details of the component implementation. For example, behavioral component interfaces describe the safe interactions with a component without exposing its internal variables and computation. Such interfaces can serve as assume-guarantee-style formal contracts for black-box components of flight-critical systems [18]. In general, substituting component models with abstract component

© Springer Nature Switzerland AG 2018
T. Margaria and B. Steffen (Eds.): ISoLA 2018, LNCS 11245, pp. 120–136, 2018.
https://doi.org/10.1007/978-3-030-03421-4_9

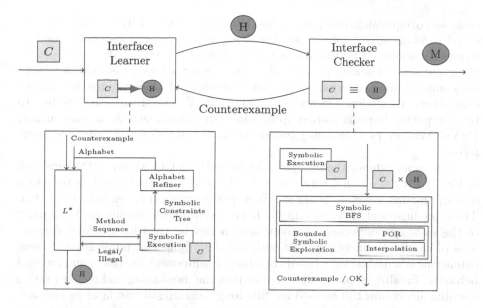

Fig. 1. Architecture of the PSYCO tool for interface generation.

interfaces can significantly increase the scalability of formal analysis techniques for component-based safety-critical systems.

In order to generate such component interfaces for component implementations, the internal details of the component have to be abstracted and relevant observable behavior has to be projected to the interface. Learning-based interface-generation frameworks use learning algorithms to infer behavioral interfaces from observations; by design, the generated interfaces do not include structural or internal component information. On the other hand, learning from observations needs to be complemented by methods that check the quality (i.e., accuracy) of an inferred model, and that trigger model refinement, if necessary. The variety of formal techniques involved in learning-based interface generation makes interface learning frameworks great platforms for studying the integration and combination of different formal analysis methods.

This work uses the Java Pathfinder extension PSYCO [14,17] for learning-based computation of behavioral interfaces of Java components. As discussed above, and as shown in Fig. 1, PSYCO iterates between two modes of operation when generating interfaces: *interface learning*, the part that learns a model from observations, and *interface checking*, the part that checks the quality of the produced interfaces.

To generate candidate interfaces, PSYCO uses a combination of (1) active automata learning [2,21] with alphabet abstraction refinement [19] and (2) dynamic symbolic execution [15]. Active automata learning algorithms infer finite state models by generating sequences of invocations to component methods and observing the resulting output of components. Alphabet abstraction represents sets of equivalent concrete method invocations (especially with data parameters) symbolically. Symbolic predicates are recorded when executing method sequences generated by the learning algorithm with symbolic data parameters. Since automata learning infers models from observations, it is neither correct nor complete unless inferred models can be discharged against component implementations. To validate a candidate interface, PSYCO compares the interface to the component implementation up to a user-specified depth. As a consequence, PSYCO cannot provide strong guarantees on the correctness of generated interfaces.

This paper extends the *Interface Checker* of PSYCO (shown in the right half of Fig. 1) with additional approaches. First, we use interpolation [10] to obtain over-approximating state predicates from paths explored in symbolic execution. These predicates allow us to skip symbolic execution for already explored parts of the state space. Second, symbolic search can be used for checking correctness of candidate interfaces. The basis for describing and implementing these extensions is a unified logic-based encoding of component interfaces and internal behavior. Finally, we briefly discuss how runtime monitoring and modern active learning algorithms can be used for "life-long" learning of interfaces at runtime. We evaluate the presented extensions on a set of Java components that have served as benchmarks in previous works on PSYCO.

The contribution of the presented work is two-fold: On the one hand, our extensions enable PSYCO to actually compute correct component interfaces—as opposed to interfaces with bounded guarantees. On the other hand, we show how quite different formal methods (at design time as well as at runtime) can be integrated and exchange information to solve the interface generation problem.

Related Work. Interface generation for white-box components has been studied extensively in the literature (e.g., [1,6,13,14,16,29]). To the best of our knowledge, PSYCO [14,17] is unique in that it generates interfaces that combine constraints over sequences of method invocations with constraints over values of method parameters and integrates static, dynamic, and symbolic analysis.

In this paper, we focus on the problem of checking equivalence of a conjectured interface model and a component implementation. We show that this problem can be formulated as a reachability analysis on the product of component and interface, which is a classic model-checking problem. Coudert et al. [9] present the idea of building the cross product of a component interface and its specification using Boolean formulas for verifying implementation correctness of electronic circuits. Our symbolic search is similar to this approach. We provide a state-of-the-art implementation of the search algorithm that allows solving of cross products in quantified bitvector logic.

Binary decision diagrams have been successfully used in the past as encoding for model checking algorithms to increase verifiable system size (e.g. [5]). These works are not directly applicable to our scenario as methods have data parameters which appear as quantified variables in state predicates. Another class of approaches relies on logic-based encoding and SAT- or SMT-solvers: Biere et. al. [4] developed a logic-based Bounded Model Checker for LTL properties. McMillan [26] has shown that model checking can verify CTL properties using a SAT-solver able to solve universally quantified Boolean formulas. These works have shown that a symbolic encoding based on Boolean formulas is more space-efficient than BDDs but depends on deciding quantified formulas for reaching completeness. More recent works replaced SAT-solvers by SMT-solvers [3,8]. Ge et al. [12] implemented complete instantiation for quantified formulas in Z3 allowing to solve quantified formulas in SMT. Wintersteiger et al. [30] extended this for the theory of quantified bitvector formulas (QBVF) and introduced symbolic quantifier instantiation to avoid complete instantiations whenever possible. Unfortunately, no effective interpolation techniques are available for bitvector formulas with or without quantifiers.

Jaffar et al. [24] were the first to tackle the path-explosion problem of symbolic execution by annotating symbolic states with learned facts (i.e., interpolants) after a search backtracks, and pruning future searches. This work was presented in the context of Constraint Logic Programming and it was extended to deal with C programs by [22,23], but limited to intra-procedural programs over linear arithmetic and arrays. McMillan [27] generalized further Jaffar and colleagues' ideas to deal with richer SMT theories and recursive functions, naming also the idea with the term *Lazy Annotation*. Our work applies the ideas presented in these works to symbolic execution of reactive components. The main difference between our use case and symbolic execution of sequential programs is that for components there is no sensible notion of program location. The environment can call arbitrary sequences of methods. As a consequence, we can use state predicates only for component states at the same depth of exploration.

Outline. The remainder of the paper is structured as follows: We start by providing some intuition on the problem we are addressing in the next section before providing some formal preliminaries in Sect. 3. In Sect. 4, we present the technical details on the new extensions to PSYCO. Results from an evaluation can be found in Sect. 5. We conclude in Sect. 6 by discussing future research directions with a particular focus on combining analysis steps at design time and at runtime.

2   Motivating Example

We are interested in generating behavioral interfaces for components. In our context, a component comprises a finite set of primitive state variables and one or more methods with data parameters that operate on the state variables. Recursion and loops without constant bounds are not allowed in methods. This is a common restriction for embedded systems that must guarantee safety critical constraints. A formal definition of components can be found in [14,17].

For the remainder of the paper we assume JAVA implementations for components. An example of a component is shown in Fig. 2a. The Explorer Component exposes methods move(int p) and check(). Method move adds the value of parameter p to internal state variable x if x and p are within certain bounds. Method check asserts that state variable x is not zero.

```
class Explorer {
    int x = 0;
    void move( int p ) {
        if ( x < 200 &&
            0 < p && p < 20 )
            x = x + p;
    }
    void check() {
        assert x != 0;
    }
}
```

(a)

$\mathcal{I} = (x = 0)$

$\varphi_{m,1} = (x \geq 200) \wedge (x' = x)$

$\varphi_{m,2} = (x < 200) \wedge (0 \geq p) \wedge (x' = x)$

$\varphi_{m,3} = (x < 200) \wedge (0 < p) \wedge (p \geq 20) \wedge (x' = x)$

$\varphi_{m,4} = (x < 200) \wedge (0 < p) \wedge (p < 20) \wedge (x' = x + p)$

$\varphi_{c,1} = (x \neq 0) \wedge (x' = x)$

$\varphi_{c,2} = (x = 0) \wedge (x' = x)$ // assertion failure.

(b)

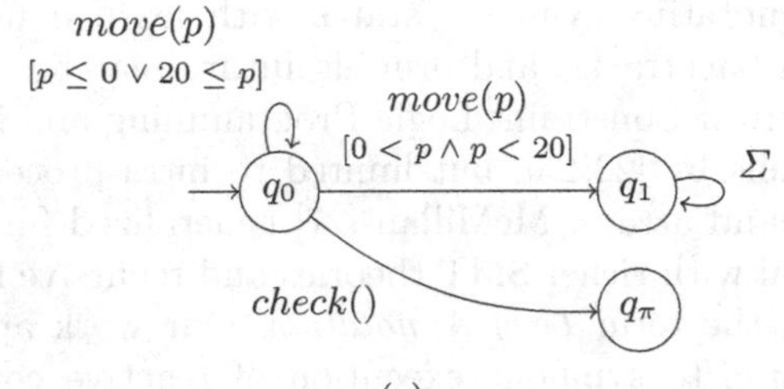

(c)

Fig. 2. JAVA component (a), corresponding symbolic method paths (b), and behavioral interface (c).

Behavioral interfaces are formal models of components that describe all sequences of method invocations on a component that are safe, i.e., will not lead to errors. For the Explorer component shown in the figure, the sequence of method invocations $\tau_1 = \text{move}(1)\text{check}()$ will not lead to an error while sequence $\tau_2 = \text{move}(0)\text{check}()$ leads to an assertion violation. The interfaces generated by PSYCO are finite-state automata whose transitions are labeled with method names and guarded with constraints on the corresponding method parameters, as shown in Fig. 2c. Initially, it is not safe to call check (the automaton enters the error state q_π). The guards partition the input spaces of parameters: Invocations of move with values of p in the interval $[1, 19]$ put the component into a state (q_1 in the model) from which all method invocations are safe. Calling move after instantiation with value of p outside $[1, 19]$ has no effect on the state of the component.

As shown in Fig. 1 and detailed in [17], PSYCO generates interfaces by iterating two modes of operation: The *interface learner* generates conjectured interfaces using a combination of active automata learning, automated alphabet abstraction, and dynamic symbolic execution. As learning is neither sound nor complete, learned interfaces have to be validated against the component implementation. The *interface checker* of PSYCO does this by executing the interface and the component in parallel, and checking agreement of their error states. For the remainder of the paper, we focus on two extensions of the interface checker that compute correctness of interfaces on symbolic representations of component and interface.

Figure 2b shows fully symbolic execution paths (including symbolic state variables) of methods of the Explorer component. PSYCO uses the JDART dynamic symbolic execution engine for computing these paths. These fully symbolic method summaries can be understood as a logic-based encoding of the component's behavior as a transition system. We can represent the interface as a symbolic transition system, too. In the next section, we explain how candidate interfaces are validated against components where symbolic representations are used for both components and interfaces.

3   Symbolic Representation of Components and Interfaces

We are interested in reactive components that manipulate a set of internal state variables. Components expose methods with data parameters that can be invoked from the outside. We abstract from output since we are only interested in safe interactions with a component, i.e., ones that do not trigger an error. For the sake of presentation we assume that all methods have the same number of parameters. We use logic-based symbolic transition systems for specifying the behavior of components and their interfaces.

Let $\mathbb{L}$ be a logic with decidable entailment $\models_\mathbb{L}$, and a set V of values allowed in $\mathbb{L}$. For the sake of readability we abstract from types in the presentation. For a formula φ in $\mathbb{L}$ with free variables $\mathbf{x}$, we write $\varphi[\mathbf{x}]$ when we want to emphasize that φ has free variables $\mathbf{x}$ and $\mathbb{F}_\mathbf{x}$ for the set of formulas with free variables $\mathbf{x}$. We write $\varphi[y/x]$ for the formula that results from replacing x by y in φ. For variables $\mathbf{x} = \langle x_1, \ldots, x_n \rangle$, a valuation is a mapping $\sigma : \mathbf{x} \mapsto V$ and $V_\mathbf{x}$ is the set of all valuations of $\mathbf{x}$. For a formula $\varphi[\mathbf{x}]$ and a valuation $\sigma \in V_\mathbf{x}$, let $\varphi[\sigma]$ denote the instantiation of $\mathbf{x}$ by σ in φ, i.e., $\varphi[\sigma(x_1)/x_1][\ldots][\sigma(x_n)/x_n]$. A valuation σ satisfies φ if $\varphi[\sigma]$ is true. A formula φ is satisfiable if there exists a valuation σ that satisfies φ. When a formula $\varphi[\mathbf{x}]$ entails a formula $\psi[\mathbf{x}]$, denoted by $\varphi \models_\mathbb{L} \psi$, then $\varphi[\sigma]$ being true implies that $\psi[\sigma]$ is true for any valuation σ in $V_\mathbf{x}$. We can test entailment by checking if $\varphi \wedge \neg\psi$ is satisfiable. If this formula is satisfiable then φ does not entail ψ. Entailment is more complex to check for formulas $\varphi[\mathbf{x}]$ and $\psi[\mathbf{y}]$, where $\mathbf{y}$ contains variables that do not belong to $\mathbf{x}$. Let $\mathbf{z} = \mathbf{y} \setminus \mathbf{x}$. In such a case, the formula testing for entailment becomes $(\varphi \wedge \forall \mathbf{z}. \neg\psi)$, where $\forall \mathbf{z}. \neg\psi$ denotes the formula in which all variables in $\mathbf{z}$ are bound by universal quantifiers for $\neg\psi$. Finally, if we have two inconsistent formulas $\varphi[\mathbf{x}]$ and $\psi[\mathbf{y}]$ (i.e., $\varphi \wedge \psi$ is not satisfiable), an interpolant [10] is a formula $i[\mathbf{x} \cap \mathbf{y}]$ over the common variables in φ and ψ that is implied by φ (i.e., $\varphi \implies i$) and inconsistent with ψ (i.e., $i \wedge \psi$ is unsatisfiable).

Definition 1 (Symbolic Transition System). *A symbolic transition system is a tuple $\mathcal{STS} = \langle M, \mathbf{x}, \mathcal{I}, \mathcal{T}, \mathcal{T}_\pi \rangle$, where M is a finite set of methods with method parameters $\mathbf{p}$, $\mathbf{x}$ is a set of state variables, $\mathcal{I}[\mathbf{x}]$ is a logic formula describing a* set of initial states, and $T \subseteq M \times \mathbb{F}_{x \cup p \cup x'}$ is a set of guarded method executions (i.e., transitions) with guards over state variables $\mathbf{x}$ and method parameters $\mathbf{p}$, and effects on updated state variables $\mathbf{x}'$. Finally, $T_\pi \subseteq T$ is a subset of guarded method executions that lead to errors.

For the remainder of this paper, we focus on deterministic and input-complete symbolic transition systems, where for every method $m \in M$, every valuation $v_\mathbf{x} \in V_\mathbf{x}$ of state variables and every valuation $v_\mathbf{p} \in V_\mathbf{p}$ of method parameters, there exists exactly one transition $(m, \varphi) \in T$ for which $\varphi[v_\mathbf{x}][v_\mathbf{p}]$ is satisfiable.

We define the semantics of a symbolic transition system $T = \langle M, \mathbf{x}, \mathcal{I}, T, T_\pi \rangle$ in terms of feasible sequences of transitions. For a sequence $(m_1, \varphi_1), \ldots, (m_k, \varphi_k)$ of transitions, we define the strongest postcondition, denoted by $spc(\mathcal{I} \cdot \varphi_1 \cdot \ldots \cdot \varphi_k)$, as the conjunction

$$\mathcal{I}[\mathbf{y}_1/\mathbf{x}] \ \wedge \ \varphi_1[\mathbf{y}_1/\mathbf{x}][\mathbf{p}_1/\mathbf{p}][\mathbf{y}_2/\mathbf{x}'] \ \wedge \ \ldots \ \wedge \ \varphi_k[\mathbf{y}_k/\mathbf{x}][\mathbf{p}_k/\mathbf{p}][\mathbf{x}/\mathbf{x}'],$$

where we assume sets $\mathbf{y}_i$ and $\mathbf{p}_i$ to contain uniquely named variables (especially when working with multiple post conditions). Analogously, the weakest precondition of a sequence of transitions and a state predicate $\psi[\mathbf{x}]$, denoted by $wpc(\varphi_1 \cdot \ldots \cdot \varphi_k \cdot \psi)$, is the conjunction

$$\varphi_1[\mathbf{x}/\mathbf{x}][\mathbf{p}_1/\mathbf{p}][\mathbf{y}_1/\mathbf{x}'] \ \wedge \ \ldots \ \wedge \ \varphi_k[\mathbf{y}_k/\mathbf{x}][\mathbf{p}_k/\mathbf{p}][\mathbf{y}_{k+1}/\mathbf{x}'] \ \wedge \ \psi[\mathbf{y}_{k+1}/\mathbf{x}].$$

Please note, that wpc and spc are formulas over $\mathbf{x}$ and sets of uniquely named variables.

A sequence $(m_1, \varphi_1), \ldots, (m_k, \varphi_k)$ of transitions is a (symbolic) *trace* of STS if the first $k - 1$ transitions are from $(T \setminus T_\pi)$ and $spc(\mathcal{I} \cdot \varphi_1 \cdot \ldots \cdot \varphi_k)$ is satisfiable. It is a *safe trace* if it ends with a transition from $T \setminus T_\pi$. A trace that ends with a transition from T_π is an *error trace* of STS.

Example. Figure 2b shows path conditions for the JAVA component from Fig. 2a. These paths are the basis for $STS_{Ex} = \langle M, \mathbf{x}, \mathcal{I}, T, T_\pi \rangle$ with methods $M = \{move(p), check()\}$, variables $\mathbf{x} = \{x\}$, initial condition $\mathcal{I} = (x = 0)$, as well as transitions $T = \{(move(p), \varphi_{m,1}), \ldots, (check(), \varphi_{c,2})\}$ and $T_\pi = \{(check(), \varphi_{c,2})\}$. The strongest post-condition of the sequence of transitions $(move(p), \varphi_{m,2}), (check(), \varphi_{c,2})$ is

$$(y_1 = 0) \ \wedge \ (y_1 < 200) \ \wedge \ (0 \geq y_2) \ \wedge \ (y_3 = y_1) \ \wedge \ (y_3 = 0) \ \wedge \ (x = y_3).$$

The condition is satisfiable, which makes the transition sequence an error trace of STS_{Ex}. Also, the condition describes the strongest post-condition on x after executing these method paths in sequence.

Behavioral Interfaces. We fix a component with set of methods M and method parameters $\mathbf{p}$. A behavioral interface is a finite automaton that describes the safe traces of the component.

Definition 2 (Behavioral Interface). *A behavioral interface is a tuple* $\mathcal{A} = \langle \Sigma, Q, q_0, q_\pi, \Gamma \rangle$, *where* $\Sigma \subseteq M \times \mathbb{F}_\mathbf{p}$ *is finite set of guarded methods (and guards are only over* $\mathbf{p}$*),* Q *is a finite set of states,* $q_0 \in Q$ *is the initial state,* $q_\pi \in Q$ *is the error state, and* $\Gamma : (Q \setminus \{q_\pi\}) \times \Sigma \mapsto Q$ *is the transition function.*

As for symbolic transition systems, we assume deterministic automata where for every method $m \in M$, and every $v_\mathbf{p} \in V_\mathbf{p}$ there exists exactly one transition $(m, \varphi) \in \Gamma$ for which $\varphi[v_\mathbf{p}]$ is satisfiable.

For some fixed mapping $\kappa : Q \mapsto \mathbb{N}_0$, we define the semantics of an interface automaton $\mathcal{A} = \langle \Sigma, Q, q_0, q_\pi, \Gamma \rangle$ by means of the symbolic transition system $\mathcal{STS}_\mathcal{A} = \langle M, \mathbf{x}, \mathcal{I}, \mathcal{T}, \mathcal{T}_\pi \rangle$ where M has been fixed above, $\mathbf{x} = \{x_q\}$ contains a single variable for maintaining the current state, the initial condition q_0 is $(x_q = \kappa(q_0))$, and for every transition $(q, (m, \varphi), q') \in \Gamma$, we define transition $t = (m, \psi)$ in $\mathcal{T}$ with $\psi = (x_q = \kappa(q) \wedge \varphi \wedge x'_q = \kappa(q'))$. We add t to $\mathcal{T}_\pi$ if $q' = q_\pi$. A sequence of method invocations is safe in $\mathcal{A}$ if it is a safe trace of $\mathcal{STS}_\mathcal{A}$ and erroneous if it is an error trace of $\mathcal{STS}_\mathcal{A}$.

Example. Figure 2c shows the behavioral interface for the component from Fig. 2. Formally, the interface is defined by the tuple $\mathcal{A}_{Ex} = \langle \Sigma, Q, q_0, q_\pi, \Gamma \rangle$ with $\Sigma = \{(move(p), (0 < p \wedge p < 20)), \ldots, (check(), true)\}$, states $Q = \{q_0, q_1, q_\pi\}$ and transitions as in the figure. When generating a symbolic transition system from $\mathcal{A}_{Ex}$, the $(check(), true)$ transition from q_0 to q_π will be the basis for the only error transition.

Checking Components against Interfaces. Since we are interested in precise interfaces, correctness means behavioral equivalence between the interface and the component, i.e., equality of sets of safe and error traces. Behavioral equivalence is checked on the composition of the corresponding transition systems, as described below.

For symbolic transition systems $\mathcal{STS}^1 = \langle M, \mathbf{x}^1, \mathcal{I}^1, \mathcal{T}^1, \mathcal{T}_\pi^1 \rangle$ and $\mathcal{STS}^2 = \langle M, \mathbf{x}^2, \mathcal{I}^2, \mathcal{T}^2, \mathcal{T}_\pi^2 \rangle$ over identical methods M and over disjoint sets of variables $(\mathbf{x}^1 \cap \mathbf{x}^2 = \emptyset)$, we define the product as

$$\mathcal{STS}^{1 \times 2} = \langle M, \mathbf{x}^1 \cup \mathbf{x}^2, \mathcal{I}^1 \wedge \mathcal{I}^2, \mathcal{T}^{1 \times 2}, \mathcal{T}_\pi^{1 \times 2} \rangle$$

with

- $\mathcal{T}^{1 \times 2} = \{(m, \varphi_1 \wedge \varphi_2) : ((m, \varphi_1), (m, \varphi_2)) \in \mathcal{T}^1 \times \mathcal{T}^2\}$, and
- $\mathcal{T}_\pi^{1 \times 2} = \{(m, \varphi_1 \wedge \varphi_2) : ((m, \varphi_1), (m, \varphi_2)) \in$
$$((\mathcal{T}^1 \setminus \mathcal{T}_\pi^1) \times \mathcal{T}_\pi^2) \cup (\mathcal{T}_\pi^1 \times (\mathcal{T}^2 \setminus \mathcal{T}_\pi^2))\}.$$

The composition $\mathcal{STS}^{1 \times 2}$ has error traces if and only if symbolic transition systems $\mathcal{STS}^1$ and $\mathcal{STS}^2$ are not behaviorally equivalent.

4   Checking Component Interfaces

As discussed in the previous section, we check correctness of a candidate interface against a component implementation by searching for reachable error transitions

---

Algorithm 1. Bounded Exploration

Global: $\mathcal{STS} = \langle M, \mathbf{x}, \mathcal{I}, \mathcal{T}, \mathcal{T}_\pi \rangle$, depth bound k
```
 1: procedure EXPAND( ((m_1, φ_1), . . . , (m_i, φ_i)) )
 2:     if i < k then
 3:         for (m, φ) ∈ T do
 4:             if spc(I · φ_1 · . . . · φ_i · φ) satisfiable then
 5:                 if (m, φ) ∈ T_π then
 6:                     stop with error trace ((m_1, φ_1), . . . , (m_i, φ_i), (m, φ))
 7:                 else
 8:                     EXPAND( ((m_1, φ_1), . . . , (m_i, φ_i), (m, φ)) )
 9:                 end if
10:             end if
11:         end for
12:     end if
13: end procedure
```

---

on the product of the component and the interface. For the remainder of this section, we fix $\mathcal{STS} = \langle M, \mathbf{x}, \mathcal{I}, \mathcal{T}, \mathcal{T}_\pi \rangle$ as this product. The baseline approach for validating interfaces that is implemented in PSYCO is exhaustive, depth- or time-bound symbolic exploration of $\mathcal{STS}$. In this mode, symbolic candidate traces from $\mathcal{T}^i$ are generated for growing i (up to some bound k) and checked for feasibility as shown in Algorithm 1. Exploration stops as soon as it finds a symbolic error trace. In [17], it is shown how information from a static analysis about reading and writing of state variables in methods can be used for a partial order reduction. This optimization is still available in PSYCO. In the remainder of this section, we present two newer extensions that optimize discharging conjectures.

4.1 Optimized Exploration Through Interpolation

In order to expand fewer states during exploration, we over-approximate states reached by symbolic execution of method path sequences and under-approximate safe states with the help of interpolation. We give an example before presenting the modified exploration of $\mathcal{STS}$: On the component from Fig. 2, after $\varphi_{m,4}$, path $\varphi_{c,2}$ of method check (which would lead to an error) is not executable and correspondingly $spc(\mathcal{I} \cdot \varphi_{m,1} \cdot \varphi_{c,2})$ is unsatisfiable. We can feed the pair

$$\left[\ (spc(\mathcal{I} \cdot \varphi_{m,1}), \quad wpc(\varphi_{c,2} \cdot true) \ \right]$$

to an interpolation constraint solver and will receive an interpolant that is implied by the left formula but is inconsistent with $\varphi_{c,2}$, and is only over variables shared by both formulas, e.g., $(0 < x \wedge x < 20)$. The interpolant over-approximates the states reached after $\varphi_{m,4}$ and under-approximates the safe states from which no immediate error can be triggered.

Figure 3 and Algorithm 2 show how we collect and propagate interpolants during symbolic exploration in order to stop expanding after transitions that

---

Algorithm 2. Optimized Exploration

Global: $STS = \langle M, \mathbf{x}, \mathcal{I}, \mathcal{T}, \mathcal{T}_\pi \rangle$, bound k, safe states $\psi_0 = \ldots = \psi_{k-1} = false$

```
 1: procedure EXPANDITP( ((m_1, φ_1), ..., (m_i, φ_i)) )
 2:     if i < k then
 3:         if ( spc(I · φ_1 · ... · φ_i) ∧ ¬ψ_i) satisfiable then            ▷ Not in Cache?
 4:             for (m, φ) ∈ T do
 5:                 if spc(I · φ_1 · ... · φ_i · φ) satisfiable then
 6:                     if (m, φ) ∈ T_π then
 7:                         stop with error ((m_1, φ_1), ..., (m_i, φ_i), (m, φ))
 8:                     else
 9:                         EXPANDITP( ((m_1, φ_1), ..., (m_i, φ_i), (m, φ)) )
10:                     end if
11:                 end if
12:             end for                                                     ▷ Update Cache
13:             if i < k − 1 then
14:                 ψ_i ← ψ_i ∨ itp[ spc(I · φ_1 · ... · φ_i), ⋁_(m,φ)∈(T∖T_π) wpc(φ · ¬ψ_{i+1})]
15:             else
16:                 ψ_i ← ψ_i ∨ itp[ spc(I · φ_1 · ... · φ_i), ⋁_(m,φ)∈T_π (φ) ]
17:             end if
18:         end if
19:     end if
20: end procedure
```

---

lead to known safe states: After exploring to depth k after sequence of transitions $((m_1, \varphi_1), \ldots, (m_i, \varphi_{k-1}))$ without finding error traces, we use the conditions of the error transitions for computing an interpolant $I[\mathbf{x}]$ that over-approximates $spc(\mathcal{I} \cdot \varphi_1 \cdot \ldots \cdot \varphi_{k-1})$ (cf. bottom left of Fig. 3). We propagate interpolants upwards in the tree by computing weakest preconditions for transitions and negated interpolants as indicated in the the figure: if $spc(\mathcal{I} \cdot \varphi_1 \cdot \ldots \cdot \varphi_{k-1})$ and φ_k are inconsistent with interpolant I, then $spc(\mathcal{I} \cdot \varphi_1 \cdot \ldots \cdot \varphi_{k-2})$ is guaranteed to be inconsistent with $wpc(\varphi_{k-1} \cdot \neg I)$. Please note that, on one hand, negating I does not introduce universal quantification since I only has free variables $\mathbf{x}$. On the other hand, exploration still has to be depth-bounded since safe states are only computed w.r.t. some remaining depth of exploration.

4.2   Symbolic Search

In order to move from (bounded) exploration to search, we need to check if some sequence of paths reaches states that another sequence cannot reach. In our motivational example, e.g., in order to test if $spc(\varphi_{m,2}) \models_L spc(\varphi_{m,4})$ as a basis for deciding if exploration can stop or if it has to expand $\varphi_{m,2}$. This can be done by checking if a model for $spc(\varphi_{m,2})$ exists that is not a model for $spc(\varphi_{m,4})$ and corresponds to checking the satisfiability of formula $spc(\varphi_{m,2}) \wedge \neg spc(\varphi_{m,4})$. Negation of $spc(\varphi_{m,4})$ requires universal quantification of variables private to $spc(\varphi_{m,4})$, resulting in test

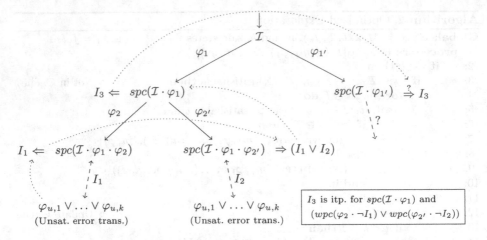

Fig. 3. Optimizing Symbolic Exploration in PSYCO based on Interpolation. Simplified schematic propagation of interpolants through symbolic exploration tree. In general, unsatisfiable error transitions occur on every level.

$$\left(\forall y_1 \forall p_1 \, . \, \neg(y_1 = 0 \, \wedge \, y_1 < 200 \, \wedge \, 0 < p_1 \, \wedge \, p_1 < 20 \, \wedge \, x = y_1 + p)\right) \wedge$$
$$\left(y_{10} = 0 \, \wedge \, y_{10} < 200 \, \wedge \, 0 \geq p_{11} \, \wedge \, x = y_{10}\right)$$

In this particular case, it is necessary to explore after $spc(\varphi_{m,2})$: all models of $spc(\varphi_{m,2})$ imply $x = y_{10} = 0$ while there is no model for $spc(\varphi_{m,4})$ in which $x = 0$. Our symbolic search algorithm is based on checking entailment in this fashion. Algorithm 3 shows the resulting simple symbolic depth-first search algorithm. We used symbolic search for analyzing the depth of a component's state space in previous work [28]. On the product of component and interface, the algorithm enables PSYCO to discharge interfaces on component implementations.

5   Implementation and Evaluation

This section highlights some details of our implementation and presents results from an evaluation on a small set of benchmark components.

Implementation. The complete PSYCO[1] tool is implemented in Java and available as open source software on github. As pointed out in the introduction, PSYCO integrates different analysis methods with the aim of generating behavioral component interfaces. For active automata learning, PSYCO uses LEARNLIB [21] and AUTOMATALIB[2], which also provides basic support for different automata transformations and visualization tasks. Internally, PSYCO

---

[1] https://github.com/psycopaths/psyco.
[2] https://github.com/Learnlib/automatalib.

Algorithm 3. Symbolic Search

Global: $\mathcal{STS} = \langle M, \mathbf{x}, \mathcal{I}, \mathcal{T}, \mathcal{T}_\pi \rangle$, reached states $\psi_{Reach} \leftarrow \mathcal{I}$

```
 1:  procedure SEARCH( ((m₁, φ₁), ..., (mᵢ, φᵢ)) )
 2:      for (m, φ) ∈ T do
 3:          ψ_Next ← spc(I · φ₁ · ... · φᵢ · φ)
 4:          if ψ_Next satisfiable then
 5:              if (m, φ) ∈ T_π then
 6:                  stop with error ((m₁, φ₁), ..., (mᵢ, φᵢ), (m, φ))
 7:              else
 8:                  if (ψ_Next ∧ ∀y∀p.¬ψ_Reach) satisfiable then
 9:                      ψ_Reach ← (ψ_Reach ∨ ψ_Next)
10:                      SEARCH( ((m₁, φ₁), ..., (mᵢ, φᵢ), (m, φ)) )
11:                  end if
12:              end if
13:          end if
14:      end for
15:  end procedure
```

1: **procedure** SEARCH($((m_1, \varphi_1), \ldots, (m_i, \varphi_i))$)
2:     **for** $(m, \varphi) \in \mathcal{T}$ **do**
3:         $\psi_{Next} \leftarrow spc(\mathcal{I} \cdot \varphi_1 \cdot \ldots \cdot \varphi_i \cdot \varphi)$
4:         **if** ψ_{Next} satisfiable **then**
5:             **if** $(m, \varphi) \in \mathcal{T}_\pi$ **then**
6:                 stop with error $((m_1, \varphi_1), \ldots, (m_i, \varphi_i), (m, \varphi))$
7:             **else**
8:                 **if** $(\psi_{Next} \wedge \forall\mathbf{y}\forall\mathbf{p}.\neg\psi_{Reach})$ satisfiable **then**
9:                     $\psi_{Reach} \leftarrow (\psi_{Reach} \vee \psi_{Next})$
10:                     SEARCH($((m_1, \varphi_1), \ldots, (m_i, \varphi_i), (m, \varphi))$)
11:                 **end if**
12:             **end if**
13:         **end if**
14:     **end for**
15: **end procedure**

---

works on a logic encoding of analyzed components, for which JCONSTRAINTS[3] is used. The Z3 constraint solver [11] is used in most cases for deciding satisfiability of such encodings. The single exemption is construction of interpolants over linear integer arithmetic for state abstraction, which is done by SMTINTERPOL [7]. The symbolic search algorithm described in Sect. 4.2 is implemented in the JSTATEEXPLORER library.

Finally, PSYCO currently uses JDART [25] for symbolic execution. JDART allows conversion of execution paths through java methods into symbolic transition systems. However since verification and learning is completely language independent in PSYCO, it could be used for components in other languages than JAVA by replacing JDART with another tool for producing symbolic method summaries.

Evaluation. We evaluate four configurations of PSYCO. As a baseline, we use exhaustive depth-limited exploration as presented in [14]. We compare partial order reduction, as presented in [17], interpolation-based caching, and symbolic search, against the baseline. Our experiments have been conducted on a native 64 bit Linux host. The CPU is an i9-7960X combined with 128 GB RAM. The JVM was provided with 32 GB RAM. We run each experiment three times. We limit PSYCO runs regarding time and memory resources and execute different exhaustive depth checks during the run.

Results are summarized in Table 1. For all approaches, we report limits on runtime, sizes of final alphabet and model, $|\alpha M|$ and $|Q_I|$ respectively, and depth k_{max} up to which a configuration was able to explore the product of component and model. For symbolic search we additionally report actual runtimes. Since symbolic search is the only method that terminates once the state space

---

[3] https://github.com/psycopaths/jconstraints.

Table 1. Comparison between the existing PSYCO model checks and the newly introduces ones based on interpolation and symbolic search. n/a: no interpolants due to unsupported language features. $*_1$ This experiment hits the memory limit after 44 min. $*_2$ This experiment hits the memory limit after 23 min. $*_3$ This experiment hits the memory limit after 5 min.

Example		Baseline (runtime: 1 h)			Baseline + POR (runtime: 1 h)			Interpolation (runtime: 1 h)			Symbolic search			
Name	$|\mathcal{M}|$	$|\alpha M|$	$|Q_I|$	k_{max}	$|\alpha M|$	$|Q_I|$	k_{max}	$|\alpha M|$	$|Q_I|$	k_{max}	$|\alpha M|$	$|Q_I|$	k_{max}	Time
ALTBIT	3	7	6	160	7	6	162	-	-	n/a	8	6	256	63 min
STREAM	5	6	4	11	6	4	14	6	4	>272,000	6	4	2	1 min
SIGNATURE	6	6	5	11	6	5	12	6	5	>451,000	6	5	2	1 min
INTMATH	8	11	3	10	11	3	13	-	-	n/a	11	3	1	1 min
ACCMETER	9	9	5	5	9	5	5	9	5	>9,200	-	-	-	dnf
CEV	19	27	34	6	27	34	6	27	34	17^{*1}	-	-	-	dnf
CEV V2	20	21	8	4	21	8	4	21	20	18^{*2}	21	20	7	13 min
SOCKET	49	57	42	5	57	42	5	57	42	7^{*3}	57	42	8	19 min
KMAX1	3	4	8	11	4	8	11	4	9	109,821	4	9	12	1 min
KMAX2	4	9	7	5	9	7	5	-	-	n/a	9	8	6	1 min

is explored completely, we do not impose a time limit - we let it complete or run out of resources. We report the smallest k_{max} and (for symbolic search) the maximum runtime from the three runs of an experiment.

The experiments show that interpolation and symbolic search clearly outperform the baseline and partial order reduction: symbolic search terminates within minutes in most cases and interpolation increases k_{max} by several orders of magnitude in some cases. However, it is not possible to apply both approaches to all benchmarks. One challenge for search are deep state spaces: The ALTBIT example, e.g., is implemented using a counter internally that is incremented with each call to this component. $k_{max} = 256$ represents a byte counter, that overflows exactly after 256 increments. While symbolic search runs to completion in this case, it requires 63 min. Cycling through deep state spaces becomes intractable on the bigger examples: The CEV experiment, e.g., has a bug that traverses the complete integer domain. When the bug is fixed (in CEV V2), both interpolation and search outperform the baseline approach: while bounded exploration with interpolation is able to explore up to to 2.5 times the depth of the baseline (and size of explored space grows exponentially with depth), symbolic search terminates after 13 min with a definitive verdict. We can observe something similar for the SOCKET example. Interpolation reaches one depth less than the k_{max} of the search before running out of memory but does this in half the time. Relaxing the memory limit to 64 GB, interpolation outperforms the search in depth for this example in less than 9 min.

Validation. In order to also have an external reference for assessing the efficiency of the implemented extensions, we submitted some of the smaller products of hypothesis model and component to SV-COMP[4]. Most of the SV-COMP participants in 2017 and 2018 were not able to solve these tasks, which provides some confidence that discharging interfaces on component implementations is not trivial.

6 Conclusions and Future Work

PSYCO is a tool for computing interfaces of components and to this end integrates multiple dynamic and static analysis methods. In this paper, we have presented two methods for discharging conjectured interfaces on component implementations (or vice versa). Bounded checking through symbolic exploration and optimized by interpolation-based caching of explored states is able to reach much greater depth than ordinary bounded exploration. Symbolic search terminates with a definitive verdict in most of our benchmarks. The basis for developing both extensions is a generic logic encoding of component behavior and interface. The main benefits of such an encoding are that (1) it allows to separate development of analysis techniques from generating formal representations, and (2) that it provides a lingua franca in which different analysis methods can exchange information.

The presented work brings us one step closer to the ultimate goals of using interfaces in compositional verification of properties on component-based systems and as contracts for third-party components. There are multiple intriguing directions for future research that are motivated by the work on PSYCO but also pertain to the challenge of integrating different program analysis paradigms in general:

Support for More Languages. Exchanging JDART by a symbolic execution engine for another programming language would allow to use the complete PSYCO approach without any modification on other languages as well. In theory, JDART might be replaced by a symbolic execution engine analyzing assembly or byte code of a virtual machine, enabling formal analysis of binary component realizations in domains that typically do not disclose their source code.

Adequate Representation. We have made the interesting observation when analyzing the main reason for the slow symbolic search performance on the AccMeter example: The logic encoding of states contains many math-heavy constraints. These constraints originate from parts of complex guards, but do not taint state variables. Based on this observation, we suspect that performance of symbolic search can be improved by pruning irrelevant parts of constraints. Moreover, alphabet refinement during learning and product generation before checking interfaces currently produce fairly complex logic constraints. Constraint simplification likely has a potential for improving performance and it will lead to models that are better comprehensible to human experts. While simplifying

---

[4] https://sv-comp.sosy-lab.org/2018/results.

constraints may not be solvable efficiently in general, complex constraints arise in specific situations in PSYCO and have well-defined patterns, which may make the problem tractable.

Integration of More Analysis Paradigms. For application domains in which discharging interfaces against implementations is not possible (e.g., for thrid-party services in Web-applications) we plan to integrate runtime monitoring of interface-conformance on integrated services. This will require, among other things, the integration of a modern learning algorithm (e.g. TTT [20]) that perform well on potentially long sequences observed by a monitor. While LEARN-LIB offers very efficient algorithms, PSYCO currently is based on the classic L^* algorithm. Integrating TTT is also expected to have a positive impact on performance in cases where interfaces can be discharged: Currently, PSYCO spends about 50% of runtime on automata learning and TTT has been demonstrated to achieve substantial savings in runtime over L^* [21].

References

1. Alur, R., Cerný, P., Madhusudan, P., Nam, W.: Synthesis of interface specifications for Java classes. In: ACM SIGPLAN-SIGACT Symposium on Principles of Programming Languages (POPL), pp. 98–109 (2005)
2. Angluin, D.: Learning regular sets from queries and counterexamples. Inf. Comput. **75**(2), 87–106 (1987)
3. Armando, A., Mantovani, J., Platania, L.: Bounded model checking of software using SMT solvers instead of SAT solvers. In: Valmari, A. (ed.) SPIN 2006. LNCS, vol. 3925, pp. 146–162. Springer, Heidelberg (2006). https://doi.org/10.1007/11691617_9
4. Biere, A., Cimatti, A., Clarke, E., Zhu, Y.: Symbolic model checking without BDDs. In: Cleaveland, W.R. (ed.) TACAS 1999. LNCS, vol. 1579, pp. 193–207. Springer, Heidelberg (1999). https://doi.org/10.1007/3-540-49059-0_14
5. Burch, J.R., Clarke, E.M., McMillan, K.L., Dill, D.L., Hwang, L.-J.: Symbolic model checking: 10^{20} states and beyond. Inf. Comput. **98**(2), 142–170 (1992)
6. Caso, G.D., Braberman, V., Garbervetsky, D., Uchitel, S.: Enabledness-based program abstractions for behavior validation. ACM Trans. Softw. Eng. Methodol. **22**(3), 25:1–25:46 (2013)
7. Christ, J., Hoenicke, J., Nutz, A.: SMTInterpol: an interpolating SMT solver. In: Donaldson, A., Parker, D. (eds.) SPIN 2012. LNCS, vol. 7385, pp. 248–254. Springer, Heidelberg (2012). https://doi.org/10.1007/978-3-642-31759-0_19
8. Clarke, E., Kroening, D., Lerda, F.: A tool for checking ANSI-C programs. In: Jensen, K., Podelski, A. (eds.) TACAS 2004. LNCS, vol. 2988, pp. 168–176. Springer, Heidelberg (2004). https://doi.org/10.1007/978-3-540-24730-2_15
9. Coudert, O., Berthet, C., Madre, J.C.: Verification of synchronous sequential machines based on symbolic execution. In: Sifakis, J. (ed.) CAV 1989. LNCS, vol. 407, pp. 365–373. Springer, Heidelberg (1990). https://doi.org/10.1007/3-540-52148-8_30
10. Craig, W.: Three uses of Herbrand-Gentzen theorem in relating model theory and proof theory. J. Symb. Comput. **22**, 269–285 (1955)

11. de Moura, L., Bjørner, N.: Z3: an efficient SMT solver. In: Ramakrishnan, C.R., Rehof, J. (eds.) TACAS 2008. LNCS, vol. 4963, pp. 337–340. Springer, Heidelberg (2008). https://doi.org/10.1007/978-3-540-78800-3_24
12. Ge, Y., de Moura, L.: Complete instantiation for quantified formulas in satisfiabiliby modulo theories. In: Bouajjani, A., Maler, O. (eds.) CAV 2009. LNCS, vol. 5643, pp. 306–320. Springer, Heidelberg (2009). https://doi.org/10.1007/978-3-642-02658-4_25
13. Giannakopoulou, D., Păsăreanu, C.S.: Interface generation and compositional verification in JavaPathfinder. In: Chechik, M., Wirsing, M. (eds.) FASE 2009. LNCS, vol. 5503, pp. 94–108. Springer, Heidelberg (2009). https://doi.org/10.1007/978-3-642-00593-0_7
14. Giannakopoulou, D., Rakamarić, Z., Raman, V.: Symbolic learning of component interfaces. In: Miné, A., Schmidt, D. (eds.) SAS 2012. LNCS, vol. 7460, pp. 248–264. Springer, Heidelberg (2012). https://doi.org/10.1007/978-3-642-33125-1_18
15. Godefroid, P., Klarlund, N., Sen, K.: Dart: directed automated random testing. In: Proceedings of the 2005 ACM SIGPLAN Conference on Programming Language Design and Implementation, PLDI 2005, pp. 213–223. ACM (2005)
16. Henzinger, T.A., Jhala, R., Majumdar, R.: Permissive interfaces. In: European Software Engineering Conference (ESEC) Held Jointly with ACM SIGSOFT International Symposium on Foundations of Software Engineering (FSE), pp. 31–40 (2005)
17. Howar, F., Giannakopoulou, D., Rakamaric, Z.: Hybrid learning: interface generation through static, dynamic, and symbolic analysis. In: ISSTA 2013, pp. 268–279 (2013)
18. Howar, F., Kahsai, T., Gurfinkel, A., Tinelli, C.: Trusting outsourced components in flight critical systems. In: AIAA Infotech@ Aerospace. AIAA (2015)
19. Howar, F., Steffen, B., Merten, M.: Automata learning with automated alphabet abstraction refinement. In: Jhala, R., Schmidt, D. (eds.) VMCAI 2011. LNCS, vol. 6538, pp. 263–277. Springer, Heidelberg (2011). https://doi.org/10.1007/978-3-642-18275-4_19
20. Isberner, M., Howar, F., Steffen, B.: The TTT algorithm: a redundancy-free approach to active automata learning. In: Bonakdarpour, B., Smolka, S.A. (eds.) RV 2014. LNCS, vol. 8734, pp. 307–322. Springer, Cham (2014). https://doi.org/10.1007/978-3-319-11164-3_26
21. Isberner, M., Howar, F., Steffen, B.: The open-source LearnLib - a framework for active automata learning. In: Kroening, D., Păsăreanu, C.S. (eds.) CAV 2015, Part I. LNCS, vol. 9206, pp. 487–495. Springer, Cham (2015). https://doi.org/10.1007/978-3-319-21690-4_32
22. Jaffar, J., Murali, V., Navas, J.A., Santosa, A.E.: TRACER: a symbolic execution tool for verification. In: Madhusudan, P., Seshia, S.A. (eds.) CAV 2012. LNCS, vol. 7358, pp. 758–766. Springer, Heidelberg (2012). https://doi.org/10.1007/978-3-642-31424-7_61
23. Jaffar, J., Navas, J.A., Santosa, A.E.: Unbounded symbolic execution for program verification. In: Khurshid, S., Sen, K. (eds.) RV 2011. LNCS, vol. 7186, pp. 396–411. Springer, Heidelberg (2012). https://doi.org/10.1007/978-3-642-29860-8_32
24. Jaffar, J., Santosa, A.E., Voicu, R.: An interpolation method for CLP traversal. In: Gent, I.P. (ed.) CP 2009. LNCS, vol. 5732, pp. 454–469. Springer, Heidelberg (2009). https://doi.org/10.1007/978-3-642-04244-7_37
25. Luckow, K., et al.: JDART: a dynamic symbolic analysis framework. In: Chechik, M., Raskin, J.-F. (eds.) TACAS 2016. LNCS, vol. 9636, pp. 442–459. Springer, Heidelberg (2016). https://doi.org/10.1007/978-3-662-49674-9_26

26. McMillan, K.L.: Applying SAT methods in unbounded symbolic model checking. In: Brinksma, E., Larsen, K.G. (eds.) CAV 2002. LNCS, vol. 2404, pp. 250–264. Springer, Heidelberg (2002). https://doi.org/10.1007/3-540-45657-0_19
27. McMillan, K.L.: Lazy annotation for program testing and verification. In: Touili, T., Cook, B., Jackson, P. (eds.) CAV 2010. LNCS, vol. 6174, pp. 104–118. Springer, Heidelberg (2010). https://doi.org/10.1007/978-3-642-14295-6_10
28. Mues, M., Howar, F., Luckow, K.S., Kahsai, T., Rakamaric, Z.: Releasing the PSYCO: using symbolic search in interface generation for Java. ACM SIGSOFT Softw. Eng. Notes 41(6), 1–5 (2016)
29. Singh, R., Giannakopoulou, D., Păsăreanu, C.: Learning component interfaces with may and must abstractions. In: Touili, T., Cook, B., Jackson, P. (eds.) CAV 2010. LNCS, vol. 6174, pp. 527–542. Springer, Heidelberg (2010). https://doi.org/10.1007/978-3-642-14295-6_45
30. Wintersteiger, C.M., Hamadi, Y., De Moura, L.: Efficiently solving quantified bit-vector formulas. Form. Methods Syst. Des. 42(1), 3–23 (2013)

Evaluating Tools for Software Verification

Evaluating Tools for Software Verification
(Track Introduction)

Markus Schordan[1], Dirk Beyer[2], and Stephen F. Siegel[3]

[1] Lawrence Livermore National Laboratory, Livermore, CA, USA
[2] LMU Munich, Munich, Germany
[3] University of Delaware, Newark, DE, USA

Abstract. Over the last several years, tools for program analysis and verification have became much more mature. There are now a number of competitions that evaluate and compare the implemented analyses for a given set of benchmarks. The comparison of the analyses either focuses on the analysis results themselves (verification of specified properties) or on the impact on a client analysis. This track is concerned with methods of evaluation for comparing analysis and verification techniques and how verified program properties can be represented such that they remain reproducible and reusable as intermediate results in the overall verification process (i.e., for other verification tools or verification steps).

1 Contributions with Published Papers in the Track

Six papers dealing with different aspects of evaluating, comparing, and combining software-verification tools were accepted for this track.

Over the last few years, competitions and challenges have played an increasingly important role in the verification community. The annual RERS Challenge [7,10] exemplifies this trend. Each RERS problem presents a reactive system and a set of properties of that system, and asks the participants to determine whether each property holds. The system may be expressed in various ways, including in Java or C, or as a set of communicating labeled transition systems. The answers are known only to the organizers. Participants can use any tools or approaches they like, and have a long time—on the order of months—to solve the challenges. For the competition to be meaningful, the problems must be extremely hard—they must require clever techniques and should not be amenable to straightforward brute-force approaches. Generating appropriate problems is a challenge in itself.

In *Synthesizing Subtle Bugs with Known Witnesses* [11], Jasper and Steffen introduce a new method for generating such problems using automata-theoretic techniques. Their approach is able to guarantee that a problem will be sufficiently "hard" according to quantifiable metrics, such as the length of a minimal counterexample. It can also guarantee that counterexamples to different properties are not "clustered" together—so that solving one problem will probably not automatically yield solutions to others. The authors intend to deploy their approach to generate problems for future instances of RERS.

T. Margaria and B. Steffen (Eds.): ISoLA 2018, LNCS 11245, pp. 139–143, 2018.
https://doi.org/10.1007/978-3-030-03421-4_10

In contrast to RERS, the VerifyThis competition [8,9] takes place in real time in the course of one day. Participants are presented with 3 challenges and given 90 min to solve each. A typical challenge describes an algorithm informally, perhaps with a code snippet or pseudocode, along with desired properties of the algorithm. Participants are asked to implement the algorithm and verify the properties in any language and using any tools they choose. Results are presented to a panel of judges, who evaluate solutions on a number of criteria.

In *Symbolic Execution and Deductive Verification Approaches to VerifyThis 2017 Challenges* [14], Luo and Siegel present solutions to the VerifyThis 2017 challenges using the CIVL verifier [15]. Whereas most of the verification tools used at VerifyThis take deductive approaches to prove properties of programs, CIVL uses finite-state symbolic execution techniques to check that properties hold for bounded instances of C programs. The authors compare the CIVL solutions to existing solutions using deductive tools, notably Why3 [6], in order to illuminate the advantages and disadvantages of each approach. They conclude by presenting a new hybrid technique which aims to capture the best features of both approaches.

Whereas VerifyThis invites participants to implement algorithms so that they are easy to verify, Efremov, Mandrykin, and Khoroshilov are interested in the problem of verifying unmodified "real-world" code that presents extreme challenges to formal methods. In *Deductive Verification of Unmodified Linux Kernel Library Functions* [5], they focus on some of the most widely-used, critical, and complex software: the Linux kernel. The paper makes several important contributions. First, it presents a new suite of 26 Linux kernel functions, together with formal ACSL specifications of intended behavior. Determining the intended behavior is tricky, given the lack of correct and sufficiently detailed documentation. This suite itself is a valuable contribution, and will be useful for evaluating other verification tools that target systems-level C code. The authors have also applied the Jessie Frama-C plugin to this suite, and have identified several limitations of that approach—e.g., regarding the memory model—as well as ideas for overcoming those limitations. The authors have also realized these ideas in their AstraVer toolset, which they have applied to the suite.

The International Competition on Software Verification (SV-COMP) [1] differs from both RERS and VerifyThis in that it is fully automated. The competition publishes a large benchmark suite, comprising thousands of C programs divided into various categories. A number of correctness properties are specified for each program. The properties include the absence of assertion violations, memory errors, and the ability to reach specified program locations. The programs, properties, and expected results are all made known to the participants before-hand. One participates by submitting an automated verification tool to the organizers, who run all the tools in a controlled environment and compute scores based on the number of correct and incorrect results.

Several of the tools that have competed successfully at SV-COMP combine different techniques and strategies within a single tool. These tools typically provide a number of tunable parameters and alternative strategy options. Usually, the user is responsible for choosing the strategy, and the difference between a good choice and a bad one can be significant. In *Strategy Selection for Verification Based on Boolean Features* [3], Beyer and Dangl explore simple automated techniques for selecting one of the many available analysis strategies in the CPAchecker tool [2]. The selection is based on a small set of program features such as whether the program has a loop, floating-point numbers, arrays, or composite types (e.g., structs and unions in C). The strategy selection is performed automatically and can outperform the winning strategy that was used at SV-COMP'17.

Another interesting aspect of verification is how to decompose a verification problem into separate tasks and avoid repeated exploration of reusable parts of the analysis. One approach to this problem is block summarization, which is investigated in *In-place vs. Copy-on-write CEGAR Refinement for Block Summarization with Caching* [4], by Beyer and Friedberger. In order to benefit also from abstraction, block summarization is combined with counterexample-guided abstraction refinement (CEGAR). The problem that arises is that whenever CEGAR instructs the model checker to refine the abstraction along a path, several block summaries are affected and need to be updated. In the paper, two different refinement strategies are compared and evaluated.

In *Runtime and Memory Evaluation of Data Race Detection Tools* [13], Lin, Liao, Schordan, and Karlin evaluate four dynamic data race detection tools. The tools are evaluated with the DataRaceBench suite [12] regarding the overhead in runtime and memory consumption that is introduced in comparison to the original program. Dynamic tools instrument the code of the program to be analyzed and analyze the data collected on the execution trace. The benchmarks use the OpenMP parallel programming model and one challenging problem for data race detection tools is the number of different thread schedules that a program might use. Consequently, a data race might not happen in every run of a program even when using the exact same input data. Furthermore, cases exist where a data race occurs only with a certain number of threads. In some cases, a tool must be run multiple times (as is also shown in [12]) to detect a certain data race, because only some thread schedules exhibit the race at runtime. Such multiple runs of a tool add to the total time required to do a thorough analysis of the program. Memory is not limited in the evaluation and the maximum memory consumption is recorded to allow the dynamic tools to produce the best possible analysis results.

2   Discussion Topics in the Track

– **Dynamic vs. static verification tools for the verification of parallel programs:** the runtime overhead that is introduced by dynamic analysis tools is usually considered to be small in comparison with the time that a static analysis might require. For parallel programs, dynamic tools face the additional problem of different thread schedules, and thus, multiple executions of the same application can produce different results in the presence of data races. Thus, for parallel programs dynamic tools face additional problems, which can make static verification tools more competitive even when the goal is just to find bugs.

– **Cooperative verification:** The goal of *cooperative* verification is to combine verification approaches in such a way that they work together to verify a system model. In particular, cooperative verifiers *provide* exchangeable information *to* other verifiers or *consume* information *from* other verifiers with the goal of increasing the overall effectiveness and efficiency. In the track, we discuss an overview over different approaches for leveraging benefits from different approaches, algorithms, and tools in order to increase the power and abilities of the state of the art in software verification.
– **Deductive vs. finite-state verification:** all other things being equal, proving a program correct is more desirable than showing it to be correct on some bounded region of its parameter space. However, the additional assurance comes at the cost of greater human effort and skill. What are the precise trade-offs and how can they be measured in a meaningful way?
– **Verification competitions:** this introduction mentions three popular verification competitions/challenges—RERS, VerifyThis, and SV-COMP—and there are others. Each takes a different approach and focuses on a different aspect of the problem. How successful have these competitions been at moving the field forward? What are the advantages and disadvantages of each, and how can they be improved?

3   Conclusion

The evaluation and comparison of software verification tools has become an increasingly important topic. In this track we discuss six contributions in this area, ranging from the competitions themselves to specific tools, and their combination. We discuss tools and contributions from the VerifyThis, RERS, and SV-COMP competitions. The presented tools are static as well as dynamic tools, and the codes range from parallel benchmarks to Linux kernel drivers. Together, the presented publications provide an important contribution to the response of the research community to the increasing importance of program correctness in the design and development of evolving software.

Acknowledgments. This work was partially performed under the auspices of the U.S. Department of Energy by Lawrence Livermore National Laboratory under Contract DE-AC52-07NA27344, Lawrence Livermore National Security, LLC. IM release number LLNL-CONF-757485.

References

1. Beyer, D.: Software verification with validation of results (Report on SV-COMP 2017). In: Proc. TACAS. LNCS, vol. 10206, pp. 331–349. Springer (2017). https://doi.org/10.1007/978-3-662-54580-5_20
2. Beyer, D., Keremoglu, M.E.: CPAchecker: A tool for configurable software verification. In: Proc. CAV. LNCS, vol. 6806, pp. 184–190. Springer (2011). https://doi.org/10.1007/978-3-642-22110-1_16

3. Beyer, D., Dangl, M.: Strategy selection for software verification based on Boolean features: A simple but effective approach. In: Proc. ISoLA. LNCS, vol. 11245, pp. 144–159. Springer (2018). https://doi.org/10.1007/978-3-030-03421-4_11

4. Beyer, D., Friedberger, K.: In-place vs. copy-on-write CEGAR refinement for block summarization with caching. In: Proc. ISoLA. LNCS, vol. 11245, pp. 197–215. Springer (2018). https://doi.org/10.1007/978-3-030-03421-4_14

5. Efremov, D., Mandrykin, M., Khoroshilov, A.: Deductive verification of unmodified Linux kernel library functions. In: Proc. ISoLA. LNCS, vol. 11245, pp. 216–234. Springer (2018). https://doi.org/10.1007/978-3-030-03421-4_15

6. Filliâtre, J.C., Paskevich, A.: Why3: Where programs meet provers. In: Proc ESOP. LNCS, vol. 7792, pp. 125–128. Springer, Berlin (2013). https://doi.org/10.1007/978-3-642-37036-6_8

7. Howar, F., Isberner, M., Merten, M., Steffen, B., Beyer, D., Păsăreanu, C.S.: Rigorous examination of reactive systems. Int. J. Softw. Tools Technol. Transf. **16**(5), 457–464 (2014). https://doi.org/10.1007/s10009-014-0337-y

8. Huisman, M., Klebanov, V., Monahan, R., Tautschnig, M.: VerifyThis 2015. Int. J. Softw. Tools Technol. Transf. **19**(6), 763–771 (2017). https://doi.org/10.1007/s10009-016-0438-x

9. Huisman, M., Monahan, R., Müller, P., Mostowski, W., Ulbrich, M.: VerifyThis 2017: A Program Verification Competition. Technical report, Karlsruhe Reports in Informatics, number 2017-10, Karlsruhe Institute of Technology, Faculty of Informatics (2017). https://www.ethz.ch/content/dam/ethz/special-interest/infk/chair-program-method/pm/documents/Verify%20This/Solutions%202017/CompetitionReportVerifyThis2017.pdf

10. Jasper, M., Fecke, M., Steffen, B., Schordan, M., Meijer, J., Pol, J.v.d., Howar, F., Siegel, S.F.: The RERS 2017 challenge and workshop (invited paper). In: Proc. SPIN, pp. 11–20. ACM, New York (2017). https://doi.org/10.1145/3092282.3098206

11. Jasper, M., Steffen, B.: Synthesizing subtle bugs with known witnesses. In: Proc. ISoLA. LNCS, vol. 11245, pp. 235–257. Springer (2018). https://doi.org/10.1007/978-3-030-03421-4_16

12. Liao, C., Lin, P.H., Asplund, J., Schordan, M., Karlin, I.: DataRaceBench: A benchmark suite for systematic evaluation of data race detection tools. In: Proc. SC, pp. 11:1–11:14. ACM, New York (2017). https://doi.org/10.1145/3126908.3126958

13. Lin, P.H., Schordan, M., Liao, C., Karlin, I.: Runtime and memory evaluation of data race detection tools. In: Proc. ISoLA. LNCS, vol. 11245, pp. 179–196. Springer (2018). https://doi.org/10.1007/978-3-030-03421-4_13

14. Luo, Z., Siegel, S.F.: Symbolic execution and deductive verification approaches to VerifyThis 2017 challenges. In: Proc. ISoLA. LNCS, vol. 11245, pp. 160–178. Springer (2018). https://doi.org/10.1007/978-3-030-03421-4_12

15. Siegel, S.F., Zheng, M., Luo, Z., Zirkel, T.K., Marianiello, A.V., Edenhofner, J.G., Dwyer, M.B., Rogers, M.S.: CIVL: The Concurrency Intermediate Verification Language. In: Proc. SC, pp. 61:1–61:12. ACM, New York (2015). https://doi.org/10.1145/2807591.2807635

Strategy Selection for Software Verification Based on Boolean Features
A Simple but Effective Approach

Dirk Beyer and Matthias Dangl

LMU Munich, Germany

Abstract. Software verification is the concept of determining, given an input program and a specification, whether the input program satisfies the specification or not. There are different strategies that can be used to approach the problem of software verification, but, according to comparative evaluations, none of the known strategies is superior over the others. Therefore, many tools for software verification leave the choice of which strategy to use up to the user, which is problematic because the user might not be an expert on strategy selection. In the past, several learning-based approaches were proposed in order to perform the strategy selection automatically. This automatic choice can be formalized by a strategy selector, which is a function that takes as input a model of the given program, and assigns a verification strategy. The goal of this paper is to identify a small set of program features that (1) can be statically determined for each input program in an efficient way and (2) sufficiently distinguishes the input programs such that a strategy selector for picking a particular verification strategy can be defined that outperforms every constant strategy selector. Our results can be used as a baseline for future comparisons, because our strategy selector is simple and easy to understand, while still powerful enough to outperform the individual strategies. We evaluate our feature set and strategy selector on a large set of 5 687 verification tasks and provide a replication package for comparative evaluation.

Keywords: Strategy selection · Software verification
Algorithm selection · Program analysis · Model checking

1 Introduction

The area of automatic software verification is a mature research area, with a large potential for adoption in industrial development practice. However, there are many usability issues that hinder the widespread use of the technology that is developed by researchers. One of the usability problems is that it is not explainable, for a given input program, which verification strategy to use. Different verification tools, algorithms, abstract domains, configurations, coexist with their different strengths in terms of approaching a verification problem.

© Springer Nature Switzerland AG 2018
T. Margaria and B. Steffen (Eds.): ISoLA 2018, LNCS 11245, pp. 144–159, 2018.
https://doi.org/10.1007/978-3-030-03421-4_11

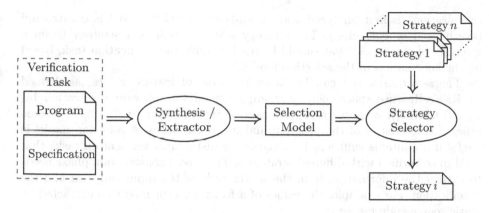

Fig. 1. Architecture of strategy selection (compare with Fig. 3 by Rice [28])

The insight that different verification techniques have different strengths was emphasized several times in the literature already. Most intensively, this can be derived from the results of the competition on software verification [4].[1] A recent survey on SMT-based algorithms [6] (including bounded model checking, k-induction, predicate abstraction, and IMPACT) explains this insight concretely on specific example programs (from different categories of a well-known benchmark repository[2]): For each of the four considered algorithms, one example program is given that only this algorithm can efficiently verify and all other algorithms fail or timeout on this program. While there are powerful basic techniques, combinations or a selection are often a valuable strategy to further improve.

The problem has been understood for a long time in the research community, and there are several methods to approach the problem [24]. The standard techniques are sequential and parallel combinations [2,7,23,26,35]. These techniques are mostly based on statically assembling the combinations, and, by trying out one technique after the other (sequential) or by trying all at the same time (parallel), the problem is often solved by the approach that works best. However, there might be a considerable amount of resources wasted on unsuccessful computation work. For example, it might happen that one approach could solve the problem if all available resources were given to it, but since the resource is shared and assigned to several approaches, the overall verification does not succeed.

In order to solve this problem, a few techniques were proposed in the last few years that automatically select a potentially good verification strategy based on machine learning [18,19,20,28,32]. All those proposals share the common idea of strategy selection.

Strategy selection can be illustrated by the flow diagram in Fig. 1: The verification task (consisting of the source code of the input program and the

---

[1] https://sv-comp.sosy-lab.org/2018/results/results-verified/
[2] https://github.com/sosy-lab/sv-benchmarks

specification) is first analyzed and an abstract selection model is constructed (synthesized or extracted). The strategy selector predicts a strategy (from a given set of strategies) that should be used to solve the verification task, based on the information in the selection model.

The *selection model* can be either a vector of feature values, as defined by Rice's 'feature space' [28] (and implemented for software verification by, e.g., [19,20,32]), a graph representation of the program (e.g., [18]), or some other characteristics of the program and its specification. A selection model is *useful* if it contains sufficient information to distinguish verification tasks that need to be verified with different strategies. The model construction phase needs to extract the information from the source code of the input program and the specification. For example, the values of a feature vector might be extracted by static source-code measures.

The *set of strategies* (also called 'algorithm space' [28]) is either a set of algorithms, verification tools, different configurations of a configurable verification framework, or just a mere set of different parameter specifications for a single verifier.

The *strategy selector* is a function that takes as input a set of strategies and the selection model that represents some information about the program and its specification, and returns as output the strategy that is predicted to be useful to solve the verification task that is represented by the selection model.

Contributions. This paper makes the following contributions:

- We define a minimalist selection model, which (1) consists of an extremely small set of features that define the selection model and (2) a minimal range of values: all features are of type Boolean.
- We define an extremely simple strategy selector, which is based on insights from verification researchers.
- We implemented our feature measures and strategy selection in CPACHECKER; the replication package contains all data for replicating the results.
- We perform a thorough experimental evaluation on a large benchmark set.

Related Work. We categorize the related work into the three areas of combinations, models, and machine learning.

Sequential and Parallel Combinations (Portfolios). While it seems obvious that combinations of strategies have a large potential, the topic was not yet systematically investigated in the area of software verification, while it has been used in other areas for many years [24,28]. One of the first ideas to combine different tools was for eliminating false alarms: after the core verifier has found an error path, this error path is not immediately reported to the user, but first converted into a program again which is then verified by an external verifier, and only if that external tool reports an error path as well, then the alarm is shown as a result to the user. [3]

---

[3] An early version of CPACHECKER [9] had constructed a path program [8], dumped it to a file in C syntax, and then called CBMC [17] as external verifier for validation. Meanwhile, such an error-path check is a standard component in many verifiers.

Other examples for sequential combinations are CPACHECKER and SDV. CPACHECKER [9] won the competition on software verification 2013 (SV-COMP'13, [3]) using a sequential combination [35] that started with explicit-state model checking for up to 100 s and then switched to a predicate analysis [10]. The static driver verification (SDV) [2] tool chain at Microsoft used a sequential combination (described in [32]) which first runs Corral [25] for up to 1 400 s and then Yogi [27].

Examples of parallel combinations are the verifiers UFO [23] and PREDATORHP [26], which start several different strategies simultaneously and take the result from the approach that terminates first.

Conditional model checking [7] is a technique to construct combinations with passing information from one verifier to the other. This technique can also be used to split programs into parts that can be independently verified [30].

Selection Models. A strategy selector needs a selection model of the program, in order to be able to classify the program and select a strategy. The classic way of abstracting is to define a set of features and the resulting vector of feature values is the selection model, which is in turn given to the strategy selector as input. There are various works on identifying features that are useful for classifying programs using its source code. Domain types [1] refine the integer types of C programs into more fine-grained integer types, in order to estimate what kind of abstract domain should be used to verify the program, for example, whether a BDD-based analysis or an SMT-based analysis is preferable. Variable roles [15,29,33,34] were used to analyze and understand programs, but also to classify program variables [22] according to how they are used in the program, i.e., what their role is. It has been shown that variable roles can help to determine which predicates should be used for predicate abstraction [21]. More sophisticated selection models can be used for machine-learning-based approaches. For example, one approach is based on graph representations of the program [18].

Machine-Learning-Based Approaches. The technique MUX [32] can be used to synthesize a strategy selector for a set of features of the input program and a given number of strategies. The strategies are verification tools in this case, and the feature values are statically extracted from the source code of the input program. Unfortunately, this technique is not reproducible, as reported by others [20]. Later, a technique that uses more sophisticated features was proposed [19,20]. While the above techniques use explicit features (defined by measures on the source code), a more recently developed technique [18] leaves it up to the machine learning to obtain insights from the input program. The advantage is that there is no need to define the features: the learner is given the control-flow graph, the data-dependency graph, and the abstract syntax tree, and automatically derives internally the characteristics that it needs. Also, the technique predicts a ranking, that is, the strategy selector is a function that maps verification tasks not to a single strategy, but to a sequence of strategies.

2 An Approach Based on Simple Boolean Features

Our goal is to define a strategy-selection approach that is simple and easy to understand but still effectively improves the overall performance.

2.1 Selection Model

We identify the following criteria from which we define our selection model:

- The model is based on features of the input program that are efficiently extractable from the program's source code using a simple static analysis.
- The model consists of a small set of features.
- The features have a small set of values.

Based on sets of program characteristics that were reported in the literature [1,22], we selected a few extremely coarse features. We will later evaluate whether our choice of features can instantiate a model that contains sufficient information to distinguish programs that should be verified by different strategies. Let $V = P \times S$ be the set of all verification tasks, each of which consists of a program from the set P and a specification from the set S, and let $\mathbb{B}$ be the set of Boolean values. We define the following four features for our selection model:

hasLoop : $V \rightarrow \mathbb{B}$ with
  hasLoop$((p, \cdot)) = true$ if program p has a loop, and *false* otherwise
hasFloat : $V \rightarrow \mathbb{B}$ with
  hasFloat$((p, \cdot)) = true$ if program p has a variable of a floating-point type
  (`float`, `double`, and `long double` in C), and *false* otherwise
hasArray : $V \rightarrow \mathbb{B}$ with
  hasArray$((p, \cdot)) = true$ if program p has a variable of an array type, and *false* otherwise
hasComposite : $V \rightarrow \mathbb{B}$ with
  hasComposite$((p, \cdot)) = true$ if program p has a variable of a composite type
  (`struct` and `union` in C), and *false* otherwise

For example, consider a program with a loop and only variables of integer type; the selection model would be the feature vector $(true, false, false, false)$.

2.2 Strategies

For our example instantiation of a strategy-selection approach, we use different strategies from one verification framework. [4] We choose the software-verification framework CPACHECKER as framework to configure our strategies, because it

---

[4] This has the advantage that the performance difference is not caused by the use of different programming languages, parser frontends, SMT solvers, libraries, but by the conceptual difference of the strategy (better internal validity). While it would be technically easy to extend the set of available strategies to other software verifiers, we already obtain promising results by just using different CPACHECKER strategies.

consistently yielded good results in the competition on software verification (SV-COMP) [4], and we can actually also compare against CPA-Seq, the winning strategy that CPACHECKER used in SV-COMP 2018.[5] Also, CPACHECKER is highly configurable and provides a comprehensive set of algorithms and components to choose from (e.g., [6,11]) as well as a simple mechanism for sequential [35] and parallel composition [31]. The description of our three verification strategies will refer to the following components:[6]

VA-NoCEGAR: value analysis without CEGAR[7] [11]
VA-CEGAR: value analysis with CEGAR [11]
PA: predicate analysis with CEGAR [10]
KI: k-induction with continuously refined invariant generation [5]
BAM$_R$: block-abstraction memoization (BAM) [36] for a composite abstract domain of predicate analysis and value analysis
BMC: bounded model checking (BMC) [13]

The set of three verification strategies that we use in our strategy selector are the above mentioned strategy CPA-Seq that won the last competition and two more strategies that are based on components from the above list:

CPA-Seq is a sequential combination of VA-NoCEGAR, VA-CEGAR, PA, KI, and BAM$_R$ as depicted in Fig. 2a: VA-NoCEGAR runs for up to 90 s, then VA-CEGAR runs for up to 60 s, then PA for up to 200 s, followed by KI for the remaining time. Any of the components may terminate early if it detects that it cannot handle the task. If none of the aforementioned components can handle the task and the last one (KI) fails because the task requires handling of recursion, the BAM$_R$ component runs, which in our implementation is the only one that is able to handle recursion but lacks support for handling pointer aliasing and is therefore only desirable as a fallback for recursive tasks. If either VA-NoCEGAR or VA-CEGAR find a bug in the verification task, the error path is checked for feasibility with a PA-based error-path check; if the check passes, the bug is reported, otherwise, the component result is ignored and the next component runs.

BMC-BAM$_R$-PA is a sequential combination of BMC, BAM$_R$, and PA as depicted in Fig. 2b. As above, any of the components may terminate early if it detects that it cannot handle the task; otherwise there are no individual time limits for components in this strategy: As a result the first component of this strategy, BMC, runs until it solves the task or fails. If it fails because the task requires handling of recursion, the BAM$_R$ component runs, with the same reasoning as for CPA-Seq; if the reason why bounded model checking failed was not recursion or if BAM$_R$ also fails to solve the task, PA runs. This means that BAM$_R$ and PA are only used as fallback components if the BMC component fails due to recursion or some other unsupported feature, whereas in all other cases, BMC would be the only component that runs.

---

[5] https://sv-comp.sosy-lab.org/2018/
[6] KI is, strictly speaking, already a composition, because it uses bounded model checking (BMC) [14] as a component.
[7] CEGAR is the abbreviation for counterexample-guided abstraction refinement [16].

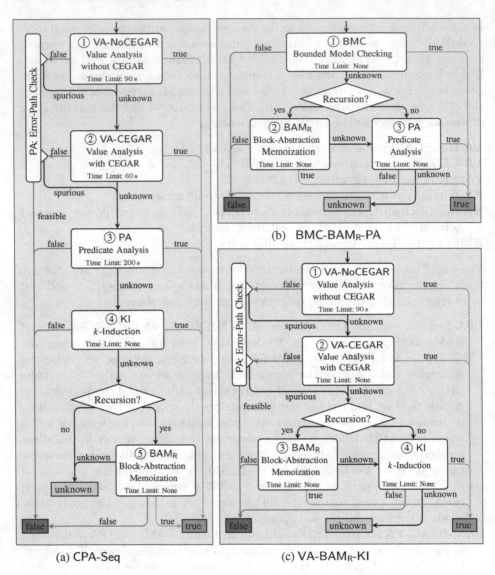

Fig. 2. Sequential combinations of strategies

VA-BAM$_R$-KI is a sequential combination of VA-NoCEGAR, VA-CEGAR, BAM$_R$, and KI, as depicted in Fig. 2c. As above, any of the components may terminate early if it detects that it cannot handle the task; only the first component, VA-NoCEGAR, has an individual time limit and runs for up to 90 s. Afterwards, VA-CEGAR runs until it exceeds its time limit, fails, or solves the task. As in CPA-Seq, if either VA-NoCEGAR or VA-CEGAR find a bug in the verification task, the error path is checked for feasibility with a

PA-based error-path check; if the check passes, the bug is reported, otherwise, the component result is ignored and the next component runs. If VA-CEGAR fails because the task requires handling of recursion, the BAM_R component runs, with the same reasoning as for CPA-Seq; if the reason why VA-CEGAR failed was not recursion or if BAM_R also fails to solve the task, KI runs. This means that BAM_R and KI are only used as fallback components if VA-NoCEGAR and VA-CEGAR both fail due to recursion or some other unsupported feature, whereas in all other cases, either VA-NoCEGAR would solve the task within at most 90 s, or VA-CEGAR would attempt to solve it in the remaining time without switching to any further components.

2.3 Strategy Selector

Based on the three strategies and the selection model described above, we define our strategy selector Model-Based. Our strategy selector chooses the strategy based on the selection model as follows: It is defined to always choose the strategy $BMC-BAM_R$-PA if hasLoop is *false*, because if there is no loop, we do not need any potentially expensive invariant-generating algorithm. If hasLoop is *true*, and either of hasArray, hasFloat, or hasComposite is *true*, it chooses the strategy VA-BAM_R-KI. If hasLoop is *true* and all of hasArray, hasFloat, and hasComposite are *false*, it chooses the strategy CPA-Seq:

$$strategy = \begin{cases} BMC\text{-}BAM_R\text{-}PA & \text{if } \neg hasLoop \\ VA\text{-}BAM_R\text{-}KI & \text{if } hasLoop \wedge (hasFloat \vee hasArray \vee hasComposite) \\ CPA\text{-}Seq & \text{otherwise} \end{cases}$$

While CPA-Seq consists of a wider variety of components that should in theory be more accurate for these complex features, VA-BAM_R-KI, which consists mainly of value analysis, does not require expensive SMT solving and therefore often solves tasks where CPA-Seq exceeds the resource limitations.

3 Evaluation

In this section, we present an experimental study to compare the effectiveness of our approach to strategy selection to various fixed strategies (i.e., constant strategy selectors) and to serve as a baseline for future comparisons of potentially more elaborate approaches.

3.1 Evaluation Goals

The goal of our experimental evaluation is to confirm the following claims:

Claim 1: We claim that combining different strategies sequentially is more effective than each individual strategy by itself. To confirm this claim, we evaluate the composite strategy CPA-Seq as well as each of its individual components, and compare their results. For a successful confirmation, CPA-Seq must yield a higher score than each of its component strategies. If confirmed, this claim supports the insight that combinations should be used in practice.

Claim 2: We claim that by classifying a verification task using a small set of features and selecting a strategy to solve a task from a small set of verification strategies based on this classification, we can further improve effectiveness significantly. To confirm this claim, we evaluate three verification strategies individually, as well as two strategy selectors that can choose from the three sequential strategies: One of the strategy selectors will choose randomly, while the other one will base its choice on the selection model that we extracted from the task. To successfully show that strategy selection can improve effectiveness, the model-based strategy selector must yield a higher score than each of the individual strategies that it chooses from, and to show that the selection model is useful for the strategy selection, the model-based strategy selector must yield a higher score than the random strategy selector.

The random strategy selector Random that we need for Claim 2 chooses randomly with uniform distribution from the set of strategies, ignoring the selection model.

3.2   Benchmark Set

The set of verification tasks that we use in our experiments is taken from the benchmark collection that is also used in SV-COMP. In particular, we use all benchmark categories from SV-COMP 2018 [8] for which we have identified different strategies.

This means that we exclude the category *ConcurrencySafety* as well as the categories for verifying the properties for overflows, memory safety, and termination, for each of which there is only one known suitable strategy in CPACHECKER. The remaining set of categories consists of 5 687 verification tasks from the subcategory *DeviceDriversLinux64_ReachSafety* of the category *SoftwareSystems* and from the following subcategories of the category *ReachSafety*: *Arrays, Bitvectors, ControlFlow, ECA, Floats, Heap, Loops, ProductLines, Recursive*, and *Sequentialized*. A total of 1 501 of these tasks are known to contain a specification violation, and we expect the other 4 186 to satisfy their specification.

3.3   Experimental Setup

For our experiments, we executed version `1.7.6-isola18` of CPACHECKER on machines with one 3.4 GHz CPU (Intel Xeon E3-1230 v5) with 8 processing units and 33 GB of RAM each. The operating system was Ubuntu 16.04 (64 bit), using Linux 4.4 and OpenJDK 1.8. We limited each verification run to two CPU cores, a CPU run time of 15 min, and a memory usage of 15 GB. We used the benchmarking framework BENCHEXEC [9] [12] to conduct our experiments, to ensure reliable and accurate measuremenfts.

---

[8] https://sv-comp.sosy-lab.org/2018/benchmarks.php
[9] https://github.com/sosy-lab/benchexec

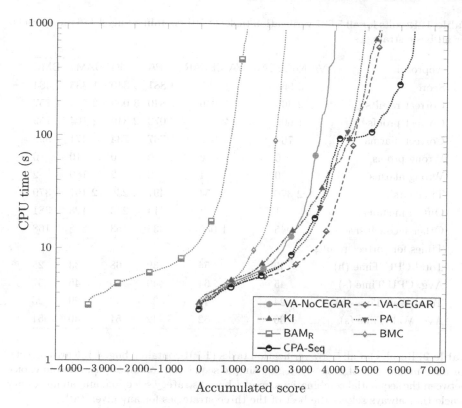

Fig. 3. Quantile functions of different individual strategies and one sequential combination of those strategies (CPA-Seq), as well as one further individual strategy (BMC), for their accumulated scores showing the CPU time for the successful results, offset to the left by the total penalty for incorrect results of each corresponding strategy

3.4   Presentation

The full results of our evaluation are available on a supplementary web page. [10] All reported times are rounded to two significant digits. To evaluate the choices of our strategy selector, we use the community-agreed scoring schema of SV-COMP, which assigns quality values to each verification result, i.e., we calculate a score that quantifies the quality of the results for a verification strategy. For every correct safety proof, 2 points are assigned and for every real bug found, 1 point is assigned. A score of 32 points is subtracted for every wrong proof of safety (false negative) and 16 points are subtracted for every wrong alarm (false positive) reported by the strategy, This scoring follows a community consensus [4] on the difficulty of verification versus falsification and the importance of correct results, and is designed to value safety higher than finding bugs, and to punish wrong answers severely.

---

[10] https://www.sosy-lab.org/research/strategy-selection/

Table 1. Results for all 5 687 verification tasks (1 501 contain a bug, 4 186 are correct), for all basic strategies

Approach	VA-NoCEGAR	VA-CEGAR	PA	KI	BAM$_R$	BMC
Score	3 966	5 397	4 881	5 340	1 335	2 484
Correct results	2 365	3 046	2 840	3 053	2 575	1 757
Correct proofs	1 601	2 367	2 073	2 319	2 104	759
Correct alarms	764	679	767	734	471	998
Wrong proofs	0	0	0	0	10	0
Wrong alarms	0	1	2	2	189	2
Timeouts	2 376	1 554	2 497	2 236	2 167	3 379
Out of memory	1	1	14	243	128	381
Other inconclusive	945	1 085	334	153	618	168
Times for correct results						
Total CPU Time (h)	30	54	39	68	33	28
Avg. CPU Time (s)	45	64	49	80	46	57
Total Wall Time (h)	24	44	33	43	29	25
Avg. Wall Time (s)	36	52	42	51	40	51

Table 2. Results for all 5 687 verification tasks (1 501 contain a bug, 4 186 are correct), for all combinations of basic strategies: simple sequential combinations, random choice between the sequential combinations, model-based strategy selection, and an imaginary oracle that always selects the best of the three strategies for any given task.

Approach	Sequential Combinations			Random	Model-Based	Oracle
	CPA-Seq	BMC-BAM$_R$-PA	VA-BAM$_R$-KI			
Score	6 399	2 612	6 442	5 174	6 790	7 036
% of Oracle Score	91	37	92	74	97	100
Correct results	3 740	1 840	3 740	3 122	3 932	4 111
Correct proofs	2 691	804	2 734	2 084	2 922	2 957
Correct alarms	1 049	1 036	1 006	1 038	1 010	1 154
Wrong proofs	0	0	0	0	0	0
Wrong alarms	2	2	2	2	4	2
Timeouts	1 715	3 385	1 879	2 317	1 486	1 347
Out of memory	194	406	26	202	224	185
Other inconclusive	36	54	40	44	41	42
Times for correct results						
Total CPU Time (h)	79	28	87	66	99	96
Avg. CPU Time (s)	76	54	83	76	90	84
Total Wall Time (h)	65	25	70	55	80	79
Avg. Wall Time (s)	63	48	67	63	73	69

3.5   Claim 1: Combining Strategies is Effective

In our first experiment we confirm the common knowledge that a sequential combination of several basic strategies can be more effective than either of its components. For this experiment, we compare the verification results of the winning strategy of the 7th Intl. Competition on Software Verification "CPA-Seq", to the results obtained by the basic strategies that it is composed of. Figure 3 shows the quantile functions for these strategies and Table 1 displays the detailed verification results and times for all basic strategies, whereas Table 2 contains the corresponding data for CPA-Seq and other combinations of strategies. We observe that CPA-Seq clearly outperforms the other strategies used in this experiment, even though it is only a sequential combination of the other strategies and contains no added features. We make the same observation for VA-BAM$_R$-KI, which is better than each of VA-NoCEGAR, VA-CEGAR, BAM$_R$, and KI. While BMC-BAM$_R$-PA is better than its main component BMC and its fallback component for recursion, BAM$_R$, it has a lower score than its other fallback component PA. The large amount of incorrect results produced by BAM$_R$ and the resulting low score is caused by the lack of support for pointer-alias handling of this component mentioned in the description of strategies in Sect. 2.2, but while it is obviously unsuitable as a standalone strategy, it does add value as a fallback solution for CPA-Seq.

3.6   Claim 2: Strategy Selection is Effective

In our second experiment, we show that (1) using a strategy selector can be more effective than always choosing the same strategy. This is shown by the model-based strategy selector Model-Based, which achieves a higher score than each of the three strategies that it chooses from (compare column Model-Based with the columns CPA-Seq, BMC-BAM$_R$-PA, and VA-BAM$_R$-KI). Even the strategy selector Random performs better than one of the strategies that it chooses from (compare column BMC-BAM$_R$-PA with column Random).

We also show that (2) using our proposed selection model (consisting of a few simple Boolean features) is effective, because the strategy selector based on that model is more effective than a random choice between the three strategies, and also, for all three available choices, more effective than any constant strategy selector (always choosing the same strategy).

As we can see in Fig. 4, this model-based strategy selection pays off and yields a significantly higher score than each of its competitors. Table 2 shows that while this model-based strategy selection still offers room for improvement because it causes two more wrong alarms than the next-best strategy, this drawback is outweighed by the large amount of correct proofs it produces. This shows that even with a very simple set of Boolean features and a very small set of choices, we can already obtain very promising results. Due to the nature of this approach, adding more features to improve the granularity of the classification and adding more strategy choices to take advantage of the ability to complement this fine-grained classification with a better strategy for each class of tasks, can further improve upon our results. Table 2 also contains the column Oracle that

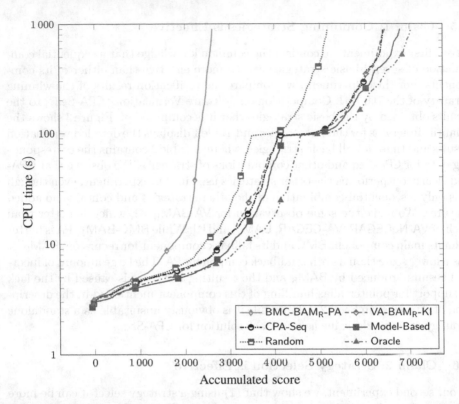

Fig. 4. Quantile functions of three different constant strategy selectors, one model-based strategy selector, one random strategy selector, and one selector based on a hypothetical all-knowing oracle, for their accumulated scores showing the CPU time for the successful results, offset to the left by the total penalty for incorrect results of each corresponding strategy

shows the best results obtainable by an (imaginary) ideal strategy selector based on an oracle that is able to determine the best of the three strategies CPA-Seq, BMC-BAM$_R$-PA, and VA-BAM$_R$-KI for each task, which achieves only 246 more points than our model-based selector. This means that our model-based selector reaches 97 % of the maximum score achievable by selecting between CPA-Seq, BMC-BAM$_R$-PA, and VA-BAM$_R$-KI on tasks of our benchmark set.

3.7   Threats to Validity

External Validity. Approaches for strategy selection that are not based on unsupervised learning are dependent on the strategies in the image range that the selector maps to. Therefore, our concrete instantiation of the selector is limited to the chosen strategies and does not consider other strategies of CPACHECKER or other software verifiers.

We only showed that our selection model is useful for the given benchmark set. The benchmark set is taken from the largest and most diverse set of verification tasks that is publicly available, but the selection model might not sufficiently well distinguish verification tasks that are different from those in the benchmark set.

Note also that we considered only one verification property in the selection of the benchmark set and in the strategy selector. For benchmark sets with more than one verification property, it may be beneficial to define a strategy selector that considers the verification property as an additional feature to distinguish between tasks.

While the scoring schema from SV-COMP, which we used to model quality, is community agreed and quite stable in its design, a different scoring schema might favor a different strategy-selection function.

Internal Validity. While we used one of the best available benchmarking frameworks, namely BENCHEXEC [11] [12], which is used by several international competitions, to conduct our experiments and ensure reliable and accurate measurements, there still might be measurement errors.

4   Conclusion

This paper explains an approach for strategy selection that is based on a simple selection model —a small set of Boolean features— that is easy to extract statically from the program source code. As strategies to choose from we use the winner of the last competition on software verification (SV-COMP'18) and two more strategies that we constructed from the same verification framework. We evaluated our approach to strategy selection on a benchmark set consisting of 5 687 verification tasks and show that our strategy selector outperforms the winner of the last competition. We hope that this result can be taken as a baseline for comparison of more sophisticated approaches to strategy selection.

References

1. Apel, S., Beyer, D., Friedberger, K., Raimondi, F., Rhein, A.v.: Domain types: Abstract-domain selection based on variable usage. In: Proc. HVC. LNCS, vol. 8244, pp. 262–278. Springer (2013)
2. Ball, T., Bounimova, E., Kumar, R., Levin, V.: SLAM2: Static driver verification with under 4% false alarms. In: Proc. FMCAD, pp. 35–42. IEEE (2010)
3. Beyer, D.: Second competition on software verification (Summary of SV-COMP 2013). In: Proc. TACAS. LNCS, vol. 7795, pp. 594–609. Springer (2013)
4. Beyer, D.: Software verification with validation of results (Report on SV-COMP 2017). In: Proc. TACAS. LNCS, vol. 10206, pp. 331–349. Springer (2017)
5. Beyer, D., Dangl, M., Wendler, P.: Boosting k-induction with continuously-refined invariants. In: Proc. CAV. LNCS, vol. 9206, pp. 622–640. Springer (2015)
6. Beyer, D., Dangl, M., Wendler, P.: A unifying view on SMT-based software verification. J. Autom. Reasoning 60(3), 299–335 (2018)

---

[11] https://github.com/sosy-lab/benchexec

7. Beyer, D., Henzinger, T.A., Keremoglu, M.E., Wendler, P.: Conditional model checking: A technique to pass information between verifiers. In: Proc. FSE, pp. 57:1–57:11. ACM (2012)
8. Beyer, D., Henzinger, T.A., Majumdar, R., Rybalchenko, A.: Path invariants. In: Proc. PLDI, pp. 300–309. ACM (2007)
9. Beyer, D., Keremoglu, M.E.: CPACHECKER: A tool for configurable software verification. In: Proc. CAV. LNCS, vol. 6806, pp. 184–190. Springer (2011)
10. Beyer, D., Keremoglu, M.E., Wendler, P.: Predicate abstraction with adjustable-block encoding. In: Proc. FMCAD, pp. 189–197. FMCAD (2010)
11. Beyer, D., Löwe, S.: Explicit-state software model checking based on CEGAR and interpolation. In: Proc. FASE. LNCS, vol. 7793, pp. 146–162. Springer (2013)
12. Beyer, D., Löwe, S., Wendler, P.: Reliable benchmarking: Requirements and solutions. Int. J. Softw. Tools Technol. Transfer (2017)
13. Biere, A., Cimatti, A., Clarke, E.M., Strichman, O., Zhu, Y.: Bounded model checking. Adv. Comput. **58**, 117–148 (2003)
14. Biere, A., Cimatti, A., Clarke, E.M., Zhu, Y.: Symbolic model checking without BDDs. In: Proc. TACAS. LNCS, vol. 1579, pp. 193–207. Springer (1999)
15. Bishop, C., Johnson, C.G.: Assessing roles of variables by program analysis. In: Proc. CSEIT, pp. 131–136. TUCS (2005)
16. Clarke, E.M., Grumberg, O., Jha, S., Lu, Y., Veith, H.: Counterexample-guided abstraction refinement for symbolic model checking. J. ACM **50**(5), 752–794 (2003)
17. Clarke, E.M., Kröning, D., Lerda, F.: A tool for checking ANSI-C programs. In: Proc. TACAS. LNCS, vol. 2988, pp. 168–176. Springer (2004)
18. Czech, M., Hüllermeier, E., Jakobs, M., Wehrheim, H.: Predicting rankings of software verification tools. In: Proc. SWAN, pp. 23–26. ACM (2017)
19. Demyanova, Y., Pani, T., Veith, H., Zuleger, F.: Empirical software metrics for benchmarking of verification tools. In: Proc. CAV. LNCS, vol. 9206, pp. 561–579. Springer (2015)
20. Demyanova, Y., Pani, T., Veith, H., Zuleger, F.: Empirical software metrics for benchmarking of verification tools. Form. Methods Syst. Des. **50**(2-3), 289–316 (2017)
21. Demyanova, Y., Rümmer, P., Zuleger, F.: Systematic predicate abstraction using variable roles. In: Proc. NFM. LNCS, vol. 10227, pp. 265–281 (2017)
22. Demyanova, Y., Veith, H., Zuleger, F.: On the concept of variable roles and its use in software analysis. In: Proc. FMCAD, pp. 226–230. IEEE (2013)
23. Gurfinkel, A., Albarghouthi, A., Chaki, S., Li, Y., Chechik, M.: UFO: Verification with interpolants and abstract interpretation (competition contribution). In: Proc. TACAS. LNCS, vol. 7795, pp. 637–640. Springer (2013)
24. Huberman, B.A., Lukose, R.M., Hogg, T.: An economics approach to hard computational problems. Science **275**(7), 51–54 (1997)
25. Lal, A., Qadeer, S., Lahiri, S.K.: A solver for reachability modulo theories. In: Proc. CAV. LNCS, vol. 7358, pp. 427–443. Springer (2012)
26. Müller, P., Peringer, P., Vojnar, T.: Predator hunting party (competition contribution). In: Proc. TACAS. LNCS, vol. 9035, pp. 443–446. Springer (2015)
27. Nori, A.V., Rajamani, S.K., Tetali, S., Thakur, A.V.: The yogiproject: Software property checking via static analysis and testing. In: Proc. TACAS. LNCS, vol. 5505, pp. 178–181. Springer (2009)

28. Rice, J.R.: The algorithm selection problem. Adv. Comput. **15**, 65–118 (1976)
29. Sajaniemi, J.: An empirical analysis of roles of variables in novice-level procedural programs. In: Proc. HCC, pp. 37–39. IEEE (2002)
30. Sherman, E., Dwyer, M.B.: Structurally defined conditional data-flow static analysis. In: Beyer, D., Huisman, M. (eds.) Proc. TACAS, Part II. LNCS, vol. 10806, pp. 249–265. Springer (2018)
31. Stieglmaier, T.: Augmenting predicate analysis with auxiliary invariants. Master's Thesis, University of Passau, Software Systems Lab (2016)
32. Tulsian, V., Kanade, A., Kumar, R., Lal, A., Nori, A.V.: MUX: Algorithm selection for software model checkers. In: Proc. MSR. ACM (2014)
33. van Deursen, A., Moonen, L.: Type inference for COBOL systems. In: Proc. WCRE, pp. 220–230. IEEE (1998)
34. van Deursen, A., Moonen, L.: Understanding COBOL systems using inferred types. In: Proc. IWPC, pp. 74–81. IEEE (1999)
35. Wendler, P.: CPACHECKER with sequential combination of explicit-state analysis and predicate analysis (competition contribution). In: Proc. TACAS. LNCS, vol. 7795, pp. 613–615. Springer (2013)
36. Wonisch, D., Wehrheim, H.: Predicate analysis with block-abstraction memoization. In: Proc. ICFEM. LNCS, vol. 7635, pp. 332–347. Springer (2012)

Symbolic Execution and Deductive Verification Approaches to VerifyThis 2017 Challenges

Ziqing Luo and Stephen F. Siegel[✉]

Verified Software Laboratory, Department of Computer and Information Sciences,
University of Delaware, Newark, DE 19716, USA
{ziqing,siegel}@udel.edu

Abstract. We present solutions to the VerifyThis 2017 program verification challenges using the symbolic execution tool CIVL. Comparing these to existing solutions using deductive verification tools such as Why3 and KeY, we analyze the advantages and disadvantages of the two approaches. The issues include scalability; the ability to handle challenging programming language constructs, such as expressions with side-effects, pointers, and concurrency; the ability to specify complex properties; and usability and automation. We conclude with a presentation of a new CIVL feature that attempts to bridge the gap between the two approaches by allowing a user to incorporate loop invariants incrementally into a symbolic execution framework.

Keywords: VerifyThis · Symbolic execution · Deductive verification
Loop invariants · CIVL

1 Introduction

The 2017 VerifyThis program verification competition [6,9] took place April 22–23, 2017, in Uppsala, Sweden. The competition consisted of three programming/verification challenges. For each, an informal description of one or more algorithms was given, together with properties expected to hold. Participants were allowed to use any languages and tools to implement the algorithms and verify the properties. Teams of one or two members are given 90 min to complete each challenge.

A panel of judges evaluated each solution based on criteria such as correctness, completeness, readability, automation, and novelty. Given the variety of languages, verification approaches, and tools used, the judging is necessarily subjective, and reflects the skill of the team members as well as the quality of the verification tools and techniques used. This contrasts with other competitions, such as SV-COMP [3], which are fully automated and use algorithmic judging.

The second author of this paper participated in VerifyThis 2017 using the CIVL verification tool [12], and won the Distinguished Tool Feature award for

© Springer Nature Switzerland AG 2018
T. Margaria and B. Steffen (Eds.): ISoLA 2018, LNCS 11245, pp. 160–178, 2018.
https://doi.org/10.1007/978-3-030-03421-4_12

the ability to automatically verify functional equivalence of two programs. Jean-Christophe Filliâtre won the Best Team award using Why3 [7]. After the competition, participants and others are welcome to publish cleaned up solutions on the competition web site [6]. VerifyThis challenges are often used in other projects and papers to demonstrate new verification approaches or tool features.

CIVL uses symbolic execution to enumerate a finite state space of a sequential or concurrent C program. It checks assertions in the user code, as well as a number of generic safety properties, including absence of deadlocks, illegal pointer dereferences, divisions by zero, and memory leaks. As a finite state symbolic executor, CIVL requires the user to specify (typically small) bounds on program parameters, such as the sizes of input arrays or the number of processes in a concurrent system, and can only prove the program correct within those bounds. On the other hand, the C code requires very little modification and the tool is highly automated, making it relatively easy to use. This contrasts with the majority of the tools used at VerifyThis, which use deductive verification approaches. These require more in the way of annotations and skill on the part of the user, but are able to prove properties without such bounds.

In this paper, we present CIVL solutions to the 2017 VerifyThis challenges. These solutions are based on those submitted at the competition, but have been improved and extended. We also compare the CIVL solutions with some of those from deductive tools, including Why3, KeY [1] and Frama-C [5], with the goal of illuminating the advantages and disadvantages of each approach. Finally, we introduce a new feature which enables CIVL to use loop invariants to verify some programs without bounds—a symbolic execution analog to the standard use of loop invariants in verification condition generation.

All the CIVL solutions were evaluated using CIVL v1.17.1[1] on a Linux machine with a 3.70 GHz Intel Xeon W-2145 CPU. We set the initial and maximum Java heap size to 32 GB and the Java thread stack size to 32 GB. Experimental materials are available at http://vsl.cis.udel.edu/civl/isola18/. Performance statistics for all CIVL solutions are given in Fig. 1.

This paper makes the following contributions:

- an exploration of the limits—e.g., scalability, expressive power of the specification language, ability to deal with the complexities of a real programming languages—of a state-of-the-art symbolic execution tool on a challenging set of problems,
- an analysis of the trade-offs—including the need for manual code manipulation, the annotation burden, and the ability to deal with challenging programming language concepts such as pointers and parallelism—inherent in finite-state symbolic execution vs. deductive verification approaches, and
- an exploration of the possibilities of a hybrid approach that combines the best aspects of symbolic execution and deductive techniques.

---

[1] Download from http://vsl.cis.udel.edu/lib/sw/civl/1.17.1. The SHA1 checksum for `civl-1.17.1_4987.jar` is 65006c21fd77cc5ed6791a9ed33283b95965121d.

Challenge	Scale	States	Prover Calls	Time (seconds)
Pair-Insertion	$1 \leq n \leq 5$	13,918	826	19
Pair-Insertion	$1 \leq n \leq 6$	115,269	6,036	159
Pair-Insertion^l	$1 \leq n$	1,136	226	15
Odd-Even Sort^s	$1 \leq n \leq 4$	11,909	493	11
Odd-Even Sort^s	$1 \leq n \leq 5$	103,606	3,892	87
Odd-Even Sort^s	$1 \leq n \leq 6$	1,041,917	37,001	1,231
Odd-Even Sort^p	$1 \leq n \leq 4$	61,116	499	26
Odd-Even Sort^p	$1 \leq n \leq 5$	476,776	3,952	173
Odd-Even Sort^p	$1 \leq n \leq 6$	4,491,620	37,006	2,000
Tree Buffers^{nc}	$1 \leq n \leq 6$	1,795,270	1,945	102
Tree Buffers^{nc}	$n = 7$	15,805,485	10,819	1,009
Tree Buffers^{nr}	$1 \leq n \leq 6$	3,476,924	1,945	199
Tree Buffers^{nr}	$n = 7$	30,543,383	10,819	2,190
Tree Buffers^c	$1 \leq n \leq 6$	696,133	2,912	85
Tree Buffers^c	$n = 7$	6,020,981	18,035	707
Tree Buffers^r	$1 \leq n \leq 6$	1,579,100	3,809	169
Tree Buffers^r	$n = 7$	13,392,054	22,970	1,380

Fig. 1. Results of CIVL verification of challenges. The solution marked with l uses loop invariants; s indicates the sequential version; p the parallel version; nc checks the functional equivalence between the naive and caterpillar versions; nr the functional equivalence between the naive and real-time versions; c (resp. r) verifies absence of memory leaks and other run-time errors for the caterpillar (resp. real-time) versions.

2 Challenge 1: Pair Insertion Sort

The *pair insertion sort* is a variant of the standard insertion sort which handles two elements at a time. This algorithm occurs in Oracle's Java Development Kit (JDK) version 8, class DualPivotQuicksort.java, lines 245–274[2]. The challenge description provided that exact Java code snippet, which is also valid C code, and which is identical (except for some white space and unnecessary braces, which we have removed for brevity) to lines 22–32 of Fig. 2. The description further stated that "left and right are valid indices into a that set the range to be sorted" and the "implementation is an optimised algorithm which uses the borders a[left] and a[right] as sentinels." The task is to verify the usual sort properties: the resulting array is sorted and is a permutation of the original.

Our CIVL solution is given in Fig. 2. Lines 1–4 specify the inputs and pre-conditions. The CIVL-C type qualifier $input specifies an *input variable*—a read-only variable that represents an input to the program. A concrete value can be specified on the command line, otherwise CIVL uses the value specified in the initializer, and if that is not present the variable is assumed to have an arbitrary value of its type. In symbolic execution, this last case is modeled by assigning a fresh symbolic constant to the variable. In this case there are five

---

[2] http://hg.openjdk.java.net/jdk8/jdk8/jdk/file/687fd7c7986d/src/share/classes/
java/util/DualPivotQuicksort.java.

```
1  typedef int T;
2  $input int n, N = 5, LEFT, RIGHT; // n is array size with upper bound N
3  $assume(1<=n && n<=N && 1<=LEFT && LEFT<=RIGHT && RIGHT<n);
4  $input T A[n];
5  int count(int n, T *p, int val) {
6    int result = 0;
7    for (int i=0; i < n; i++) if (p[i] == val) result++;
8    return result;
9  }
10 /* Asserts the sequence starting at p2 is the permutation of that
11  * starting at p1 with elements occurring in nondecreasing order */
12 void assertSortOf(int n, T *p1, T *p2) {
13   $assert($forall (int i : 0..n-2) p2[i]<=p2[i+1]);
14   $assert($forall (int i : 0..n-1) $exists (int j : 0..n-1) p1[i]==p2[j]);
15   for (int i=0; i<n; i++) $assert(count(n, p1, p2[i]) == count(n, p2, p2[i]));
16 }
17 int main() {
18   for (int i=LEFT; i<=RIGHT; i++) $assume(A[LEFT-1]<=A[i]);
19   int a[n];
20   for (int i=0; i<n; i++) a[i]=A[i];
21   int left = LEFT, right = RIGHT;
22   for (int k = left; ++left <= right; k = ++left) {
23     int a1 = a[k], a2 = a[left];
24     if (a1 < a2) { a2 = a1; a1 = a[left]; }
25     while (a1 < a[--k]) a[k + 2] = a[k];
26     a[++k + 1] = a1;
27     while (a2 < a[--k]) a[k + 1] = a[k];
28     a[k + 1] = a2;
29   }
30   int last = a[right];
31   while (last < a[--right]) a[right + 1] = a[right];
32   a[right + 1] = last;
33   $assert($forall (int i:0..LEFT-1) a[i]==A[i]);
34   $assert($forall (int i:RIGHT+1..n-1) a[i]==A[i]);
35   assertSortOf(RIGHT-LEFT+1, A+LEFT, a+LEFT);
36 }
```

Fig. 2. Solution for Challenge 1: pair insertion sort

inputs: an integer n which is the length of the array, an upper bound N (given default value 5) for n, the original array A, and the start and end indexes LEFT and RIGHT.

Using CIVL, we were able to discover the correct preconditions for the code, though these were not explicit in the challenge description or the final report. First, LEFT cannot be *any* valid index; it must be positive. Originally, we had only assumed $0 \leq$ LEFT, but CIVL reported an out-of-bound array index at line 25:

```
Violation 0 encountered at depth 29:
CIVL execution violation in p0 (kind: OUT_OF_BOUNDS, certainty: PROVEABLE)
at challenge1-short.cvl:25.16-21
    while (a1 < a[--k]) a[k + 2] = a[k];
                 ~~~~~~
possible negative array index: -1
```

After changing the assumption to $1 \leq$ LEFT, this error went away. Second, it is actually the element at position LEFT $- 1$ that acts as the "sentinel", and the correctness of the algorithm depends on the fact that every element in the range LEFT..RIGHT is greater than or equal to that sentinel (line 18). Again, that assumption was deduced easily after CIVL reported an error message without it.

Finally, no sentinel is required on the right border: originally we had assumptions on the right which were the mirror image of those on the left, but after removing them the program still verified successfully. We found this incremental, inter-active process, in which assumptions were repeatedly added or modified, CIVL was run, and the output examined to understand a problem, to be very useful in determining the precise assumptions necessary for correctness.

The function `isSortOf` is used to specify the correctness of the post-state. Given two sequences p_1 and p_2 of length n, it asserts that p_2 is nondecreasing; every element of p_1 occurs in p_2; and every element of p_2 occurs in p_1 and with the same multiplicity as in p_2. Since CIVL does not provide any built-in primitive for `count`, this function was defined in ordinary C code. Finally, we also check that the array segments outside of the region `LEFT..RIGHT` are unchanged (lines 33–34).

CIVL verifies this program in 19 seconds (19 s) with an upper bound $N = 5$, and in 159 s with $N = 6$.

Discussion. The code snippet contains programming constructs which allow the code to be very concise, but also make it difficult to understand and reason about. In particular, it has expressions with side-effects, namely the pre/post-increment and decrement operators. Furthermore, these are used within loop conditions of `while` loops and in both the incrementer and condition expressions of `for` loops. CIVL deals with these by first transforming the program into a normal form which has no side-effect expressions. This involves introducing auxiliary variables and restructuring certain loops. This internal transformation is usually invisible to the user, though there is an option that will cause CIVL to print the transformed program.

Verification tools for languages that do not have such constructs do not have to deal with these issues. But to apply those tools to code such as the pair-insertion snippet, one must either transform the code manually (which can be error-prone) or use another tool as a front end. In the case of this Challenge, the competition organizers also provided pseudocode for a simplified version of the algorithm. The simplified version uses only `while` loops, has no side-effect expressions, and does not have `left` and `right`, but instead just sorts the entire array. The sentinel assumptions described above do not arise in the simplified version. While the ultimate goal was to verify the original code, most teams used the simplified code; the winning Why3 team fully verified the simplified version for arbitrary inputs.

Like CIVL, Frama-C operates on C code, though the Frama-C solution[3] is based on the simplified version of the code. That solution adds approximately 50 lines of ACSL[4] annotations to the code. The annotations specify loop invariants, function contracts, and an inductive predicate for specifying that an array at one state is a permutation of the same array at another state. The deductive verification was carried out by the Frama-C WP plug-in. This solution verifies the sortedness of the resulting array, but it fails to prove that the result is a

---

[3] https://www.ethz.ch/content/dam/ethz/special-interest/infk/chair-program-method/pm/documents/Verify%20This/Solutions%202017/program.c.

[4] ANSI/ISO C Specification Language. http://frama-c.com/acsl.html.

```
1 let pair_insertion_sort (a: array int)
2 = let i = ref 0 in (* i is running index (inc by 2 every iteration)*)
3   while !i < length a - 1 do
4     let x = ref a[!i] let y = ref a[!i + 1] in
5     if !x < !y then (* ensure that x is not smaller than y *)
6       begin let tmp = !x in x := !y; y := tmp end (* swap x and y *)
7     end;
8     let j = ref (!i - 1) in while !j >= 0 && a[!j] > !x do
9         j := !j - 1
10    done;
11    a[!j + 2] <- !x; (* store x at its insertion place *)
12    while !j >= 0 && a[!j] > !y do (* #ind the insertion point for y *)
13        j := !j - 1
14    done;
15    a[!j + 1] <- !y; i := !i + 2
16 done;
17 if !i = length a  - 1 then begin (* if length(A) is odd, an extra  *)
18   let y = a[!i] in let j = ref (!i - 1) in
19   while !j >= 0 && a[!j] > y do
20       j := !j - 1
21   done;
22   a[!j + 1] <- y
23 end
```

Fig. 3. Executable portion of WhyML model of simplified pair insertion sort (excerpt)[5]

permutation of the initial array. In addition, Frama-C verified that the program is free of runtime errors such as division by zero or integer overflow.

CIVL also checks for certain runtime errors, such as division by zero, out-of-bound array indexes, and null pointer dereferences —all of which are checked by Frama-C+WP as well. Unlike Frama-C, CIVL does not currently check for integer overflows, because numerical values are modeled with the mathematical integers or reals in CIVL. CIVL does have a precise model of memory heaps and `malloc/free`, and verifies absence of double-frees, memory leaks, use-after-free, and similar properties. In contrast, reasoning about programs with dynamic memory allocation is currently very difficult with Frama-C+WP.

The Why3 solution[5] is a WhyML model of the simplified algorithm (Fig. 3) with function contracts, loop invariants, and some intermediate assertions; it consists of approximately 90 lines. The target properties are expressed as postconditions:

```
ensures { forall k l. 0 <= k <= l < length a -> a[k] <= a[l] }
ensures { permut_all (old a) a }
```

The WhyML program generates 113 proof obligations (after splitting), which can be proved in parallel.

WhyML is a language designed for verification—it includes high-level abstractions that make it easy to specify properties and algorithms, and avoids many of the tricky programming language constructs in languages such as C (e.g., pointers and pointer arithmetic, memory management, side-effect expressions, preprocessing, linking, and I/O functions). However, it is possible to generate OCaml code from the verified WhyML program, and in this sense Why3 is also

---

[5] http://toccata.lri.fr/gallery/verifythis_2017_pair_insertion_sort.en.html.

able to verify correctness of programs in a "real" programming language. This solution fully verifies that the resulting array is a sorted permutation of the initial array. It uses existing array permutation theories in the Why3 library, which reduces the specification burden.

We were able to find only one other successful verification of the original Java code. This solution uses KeY, and adds approximately 60 annotation lines to the code[6]. It verifies the final array is ordered, but does not verify that it is a permutation of the original.

For all of these solutions, the loop invariants are non-trivial and are discussed further in Sect. 5.

3   Challenge 3: Odd-Even Transposition Sort

Challenge 3[7] presented another sorting algorithm. The odd-even transposition sort,

> "...developed originally for use on parallel processors, compares all odd-indexed list elements with their immediate successors in the list and, if a pair is in the wrong order...swaps the elements. The next step repeats this for even-indexed list elements.... The algorithm iterates between these two steps until the list is sorted." [9]

```
1 #include <stdbool.h>
2 typedef double T;
3 $input int n, N = 5; // N is upper bound on array size n
4 $assume(1<=n && n<=N);
5 $input T A[n]; // input array: constant, fixed forever
6 void swap(T *p, int i, int j) { T temp = p[i]; p[i] = p[j]; p[j] = temp; }
7 void oddEvenSort(int n, T *list) {
8   _Bool sorted = false;
9   while (!sorted) {
10     sorted = true;
11     for (int i = 1; i < n-1; i += 2)
12       if (list[i] > list[i+1]) { swap(list, i, i+1); sorted = false; }
13     for (int i = 0; i < n-1; i += 2)
14       if (list[i] > list[i+1]) { swap(list, i, i+1); sorted = false; }
15   }
16 }
17 int main() {
18   T a[n];
19   for (int i=0; i<n; i++) a[i] = A[i];
20   oddEvenSort(n, a);
21   assertSortOf(n, A, a); // see definition in Figure 2
22 }
```

Fig. 4. Sequential solution for Challenge 3: odd-even transposition sort

---

[6] https://www.key-project.org/wp-content/uploads/2017/08/PairInsertionSort.java.

[7] Challenge 2 was replaced by another challenge shortly before the competition began, hence the gap in the numbering.

```
 1 #include <mpi.h>
 2 #define T double
 3 #define MPI_T MPI_DOUBLE
 4 $input int n, N = 4;
 5 $assume(0 < n && n <= N);
 6 $input T A[n];
 7 T myvalue; // this is a local variable for each process in MPI
 8 void oddEvenPar(int n, int id) {
 9   T othervalue;
10   for (int i=0; i<n; i++) {
11     if ((i+id)%2 == 0) {
12       if (id < n-1) {
13         MPI_Send(&myvalue, 1, MPI_T, id+1, 0, MPI_COMM_WORLD);
14         MPI_Recv(&othervalue, 1, MPI_T, id+1, 0, MPI_COMM_WORLD, MPI_STATUS_IGNORE);
15         if (othervalue < myvalue) myvalue = othervalue;
16       }
17     } else {
18       if (id > 0) {
19         MPI_Send(&myvalue, 1, MPI_T, id-1, 0, MPI_COMM_WORLD);
20         MPI_Recv(&othervalue, 1, MPI_T, id-1, 0, MPI_COMM_WORLD, MPI_STATUS_IGNORE);
21         if (othervalue > myvalue) myvalue = othervalue;
22       }
23     }
24   }
25 }
26 int main() {
27   int nprocs, rank;
28   MPI_Init(NULL, NULL); // initialize MPI
29   MPI_Comm_size(MPI_COMM_WORLD, &nprocs); // get the number of procs
30   MPI_Comm_rank(MPI_COMM_WORLD, &rank); // get my "rank" (id)
31   $assume(nprocs == n); // number of procs must equal n, prune other cases
32   myvalue = A[rank]; // get my value from the global input array A
33   oddEvenPar(nprocs, rank); // call the function that does the work
34   if (rank == 0) { // proc 0 will gather all data and check it is correct
35     T a[n]; // used for verification---gather all elements into one array on proc 0
36     MPI_Gather(&myvalue, 1, MPI_T, a, 1, MPI_T, 0, MPI_COMM_WORLD);
37     assertSortOf(n, A, a); // see definition in Figure 2
38   } else
39     MPI_Gather(&myvalue, 1, MPI_T, NULL, 0, MPI_T, 0, MPI_COMM_WORLD);
40   MPI_Finalize();
41 }
```

Fig. 5. Parallel solution for Challenge 3: odd-even transposition sort

Pseudocode for a sequential and a parallel version was given. Application of CIVL to the sequential version is straightforward; see Fig. 4. We have re-used the `assertSortOf` function from Challenge 1. The definition of function `oddEvenSort` is almost identical to the given pseudocode; we have added only the definition of `swap`. CIVL verifies the program with the upper bound $N = 4$ in 11 s; $N = 5$ in 87 s; and $N = 6$ in 1,231 s.

The pseudocode for the parallel version is expressed using the message-passing style. Each process maintains one element in its local memory and performs exchanges with its left and right neighbors. CIVL supports MPI[8], the standard message-passing API, and the pseudocode maps directly to the C/MPI code in function `oddEvenPar` of Fig. 5. We have added a driver in the `main` function which (1) includes standard MPI boilerplate, (2) initializes the

---

[8] A Message-Passing Interface Standard, Version 3.1. http://www.mpi-forum.org/docs/.

local variable `myvalue` on each process by reading from the `$input` array A, (3) invokes `oddEvenPar`, and then (4) gathers the final result into a single array a on process 0, which (5) checks the result using the same function `assertSortOf` we used in the other sorting routines. The input variable n is the exact size of the array, which is also the number of processes, and N is an upper bound on n. CIVL verifies the case $N = 4$ in 26 s; $N = 5$ in 173 s; and $N = 6$ in 2,000 s.

Discussion. The MPI functions used in the code are defined using lower-level CIVL concurrency primitives in CIVL's implementation of `mpi.h`. The MPI API is quite large, comprising hundreds of functions, types, and constants, and the CIVL implementation is not complete. However, it does support the most commonly-used MPI primitives, including the blocking, standard-mode send, receive, and send-receive operations, the primitive datatypes, multiple communicators, wildcard sources and tags, and the blocking collective operations (such as `MPI_Gather`). These suffice for this problem, and for many real-world applications. Support for more advanced MPI constructs is in progress.

There is a minor limitation: it is not possible to use a typedef name as the type of an input variable when using MPI, due to code transformations performed by CIVL which re-order certain declarations, so we used a preprocessor macro definition for T instead. This will be addressed in a future release of CIVL.

The Why3 solution fully verifies the sequential version of this challenge.[9] The solution uses standard theories, e.g., for array permutations, array swaps, and integer division. It also defines a predicate `odd_sorted` which states that each odd-indexed element of an array is less than or equal to the next (even-indexed) element in the array. A predicate `even_sorted` is defined similarly for the even-indexed elements. A lemma claims that if an array is `odd_sorted` and `even_sorted` then it is sorted. The lemma includes a few "hints" for its proof in the form of by directives:

```
let lemma odd_even_sorted (a: array int) (n: int)
    requires { 0 <= n <= length a }
    requires { odd_sorted a n }
    requires { even_sorted a n }
    ensures  { sorted_sub a 0 n }
  = if n > 0 && length a > 0 then
    for i = 1 to n - 1 do
      invariant { sorted_sub a 0 i }
      assert { forall j. 0 <= j < i -> a[j] <= a[i]
                by a[i-1] <= a[i]
                by i-1 = 2 * div (i-1) 2 \/
                   i-1 = 2 * div (i-1) 2 + 1 }
    done
```

The lemma is proved independently and used as an axiom while proving the algorithm. This kind of proof decomposition is common in deductive verification, but is unnecessary in bounded symbolic execution. This WhyML program generates 57 proof obligations.

---

[9] http://toccata.lri.fr/gallery/verifythis_2017_odd_even_transposition_sort.en.html.

The Why3 team did not attempt to verify the parallel version because WhyML has no model of concurrency. As far as we know, VerCors [4] is the only other team that has attempted to verify the concurrent algorithm [6]. The VerCors team wrote the parallel algorithm as a GPU kernel function and attempted to verify it against a specification, but the global invariant remains unproved.

4   Challenge 4: Tree Buffers

Challenge 4 describes an abstract data structure called a *tree buffer*. It is essentially an immutable list which only needs to "remember" the h most recent elements added, for a specified constant integer h ("history"). It supports three operations: *empty* takes h and returns an empty tree buffer with parameter h associated to it; *add* consumes an element x and a tree buffer t, and returns a new tree buffer (with the same h as that associated to t) obtained by adding x to the front of t; *get* consumes a tree buffer and returns its first h elements, or all of its elements if it has fewer than h elements. Because it is observably immutable, sharing is allowed, e.g.,

```
e = empty(3);     /* e is a root, with h=3 */
t1 = add(1,e);    /* t1 has parent e */
t2 = add(2,t1);   /* t2 has parent t1 */
t3 = add(3,t1);   /* t3 has parent t1 */
```

```
1  struct Node {
2    Node * parent;
3    int data;
4  };
5  struct Tree {
6    int history;
7    Node * last; // reference to the last added node
8  };
9  Node * make_node(int data) {
10   Node * node = (Node*)malloc(sizeof(Node));
11   node->parent = NULL; node->data = data; return node;
12 }
13 int get_data(Node * node) { return node->data; }
14 Tree * empty(int history) {
15   Tree * tree = (Tree*)malloc(sizeof(Tree));
16   tree->history = history; tree->last = NULL; return tree;
17 }
18 Tree * add(int data, Tree * tree) {
19   Node * child = make_node(data);
20   Tree * new_tree = empty(tree->history);
21   if (tree->last == NULL) new_tree->last = child;
22   else { child->parent = tree->last; new_tree->last = child; }
23   return new_tree;
24 }
25 void get(Tree * tree, Node * ancestors[]) {
26   int i = 0, history = tree->history;
27   Node * ancestor = tree->last; // "ancestors" is a NULL-terminated array
28   while (i < history && ancestor != NULL) {
29     ancestors[i++] = ancestor; ancestor = ancestor->parent;
30   }
31   ancestors[i] = NULL;
32 }
33 void delete(Tree * tree) {}
```

Fig. 6. The naive implementation of the tree buffer

defines four distinct tree buffers, but each may be contained in a single tree of 4 nodes. The interface and a simple naive implementation are given in OCaml. We have translated the naive implementation to C in Fig. 6.

The naive implementation is memory inefficient: nodes are never removed, yet it is only required to remember at most h nodes for each tree buffer. The description then provides a *caterpillar* implementation in OCaml which offers a solution to this problem. The first task is to show the naive and caterpillar implementations are functionally equivalent, using any imperative language for the caterpillar implementation. Our C implementation of the caterpillar is given in Fig. 7.

To establish functional equivalence, we first created a common interface for tree buffers, in the form of the header file `treebuffer.h`, shown in Fig. 8. We then created a driver that can be linked to any tree buffer implementation, as it uses only the header file; see Fig. 9. The idea is to show that any sequence of *get* and *add* operations will result in the same output from the two implementations. We take it as clear that *get* does not modify any tree buffer, so any two *get* operations commute. It therefore suffices to consider an arbitrary sequence of *add* operations followed by a single arbitrary *get* operation, and show the result must be the same across implementations.

The driver works by first creating an empty node, then repeatedly choosing an existing node and adding a child to it. In the end, it chooses a node to which to apply *get*, and records the result in an *output* variable. The choices in the driver are controlled by input variables, e.g., the input array `PICKS` determines which node will be chosen at each step to be the parent of the new node. Hence the program comprising the driver and a tree buffer implementation is a deterministic function of its input.

CIVL has the ability to verify that two programs with compatible input-output signatures are functionally equivalent. In keeping with the general CIVL philosophy, this is accomplished primarily by code transformation: the new programs are merged into a single program that invokes each constituent program sequentially, on the same inputs, and then asserts that the outputs agree. This merged program is verified as usual. In this case, CIVL is able to verify the equivalence of the naive and caterpillar implementations, with an upper bound of 6 on the number of nodes, in 102 s. For exactly 7 nodes, the time is 1,009 s. When using CIVL in `compare` mode, the standard runtime properties are also checked, but in this case we turned off the check for memory leaks because the naive version (intentionally) does not free any of the memory it allocates. The command used looks like:

```
civl compare -checkMemoryLeak=false -inputN=6 -spec treebuffer-driver.cvl
    treebuffer-naive.c -impl treebuffer-driver.cvl treebuffer-realtime.c
```

The caterpillar implementation depends on a garbage collector, which we modeled in our C implementation with function `gc`. The next task involves an even more complex "real-time" implementation that manually manages memory in a time and space-efficient way. The description presents untested C++ pseudocode, and references a git repository with a well-tested but much more

```
1 struct Node {
2   Node * parent;
3   int data, ref_count; // reference counter
4   int num_ancest; // number of ancestors
5 };
6 struct Tree {
7   int history;
8   Node * xs, * ys; // xs: reference to the last added node, ys: caterpillar
9 };
10 void gc(Node * node) { // garbage collection
11   if (node == NULL || node->ref_count > 0) return;
12   Node * next = node->parent;
13   free(node);
14   if (next != NULL) {next->ref_count--; gc(next);}
15 }
16 Node * make_node(int data) {
17   Node * node = (Node*)malloc(sizeof(Node));
18   node->parent = NULL;  node->data = data; node->ref_count = 0;  node->num_ancest = 0;
19   return node;
20 }
21 int get_data(Node * node) { return node->data; }
22 Tree * empty(int history) {
23   Tree * tree = (Tree*)malloc(sizeof(Tree));
24   tree->history = history; tree->xs = NULL; tree->ys = NULL; return tree;
25 }
26 Tree * add(int data, Tree * tree) {
27   Node * node = make_node(data);
28   Tree * new_tree = empty(tree->history);
29   if (tree->xs == NULL) {
30     new_tree->xs = node; new_tree->xs->ref_count++; new_tree->ys = tree->ys;
31     if (tree->ys!=NULL)    tree->ys->ref_count++;
32     else if (tree->xs->num_ancest < tree->history - 2) {
33       node->parent = tree->xs;  node->parent->ref_count++;
34       node->num_ancest = node->parent->num_ancest + 1;
35       new_tree->xs = node;  new_tree->xs->ref_count++; new_tree->ys = tree->ys;
36       if (tree->ys != NULL) new_tree->ys->ref_count++;
37       else {
38         node->parent = tree->xs; node->parent->ref_count++;
39         node->num_ancest = node->parent->num_ancest + 1;
40         new_tree->ys = node; new_tree->ys->ref_count++;
41       }
42     }
43   }
44   return new_tree;
45 }
46 void get(Tree * tree, Node * ancestors[]) {
47   int i = 0, history = tree->history;
48   Node * ancestor = tree->xs; // "ancestors" is a NULL-terminated array
49   while (i < history && ancestor != NULL) {
50     ancestors[i++] = ancestor; ancestor = ancestor->parent;
51   }
52   ancestor = tree->ys;
53   while (i < history && ancestor != NULL) {
54     ancestors[i++] = ancestor; ancestor = ancestor->parent;
55   }
56   ancestors[i] = 0;
57 }
58 void delete(Tree * tree) {
59   if (tree->ys != NULL) { // take ys off and collect garbage:
60     Node * ys = tree->ys; tree->ys = NULL; ys->ref_count--; gc(ys);
61   }
62   if (tree->xs != NULL) {
63     Node * xs = tree->xs;  tree->xs = NULL;  xs->ref_count--; gc(xs);
64   }
65   free(tree);
66 }
```

Fig. 7. The caterpillar implementation of the tree buffer

```
 1 #ifndef TREEBUFFER_H
 2 #define TREEBUFFER_H
 3 typedef struct Node Node;
 4 typedef struct Tree Tree;
 5 void delete(Tree * tree);
 6 void get(Tree * tree, Node * ancestors[]);
 7 Tree * add(int data, Tree * tree); /* returns new tree with a new node added to given tree */
 8 Tree * empty(int history); /* Creates a new tree */
 9 int get_data(Node * node); /* Gets the data in a node */
10 #endif
```

Fig. 8. The common header `treebuffer.h` for all tree buffer implementations

```
 1 #include "treebuffer.h"
 2 $input int n, H, NODE_TO_READ, N = 5;
 3 $assume(0 < n && n <= N && 0 < H && H < n && 0 <= NODE_TO_READ && NODE_TO_READ < n);
 4 $input int DATA[n-1], PICKS[n];
 5 $assume($forall (int i : 0 .. n-1) 0 <= PICKS[i] && PICKS[i] <= i);
 6 $output int out[H]; // output
 7 int main() {
 8   Tree * node = empty(H), * nodes[n]; // n new refs to node + empty()
 9   int num_nodes = 0;
10   nodes[num_nodes++] = node; $elaborate(n);
11   while (num_nodes < n) {
12     int idx = PICKS[num_nodes-1];
13     node = nodes[idx]; $elaborate(idx);
14     Tree * new_node = add(DATA[num_nodes-1], node);
15     nodes[num_nodes++] = new_node; node = new_node;
16   }
17   Node * history[H + 1];
18   int i;
19   $elaborate(NODE_TO_READ); get(nodes[NODE_TO_READ], history);
20   for (i = 0; i < H; i++)
21     if (history[i] != NULL) out[i] = get_data(history[i]); else break;
22   for (; i < H; i++) out[i] = -1;
23   for (int i = 0; i < num_nodes; i++) delete(nodes[i]);
24 }
```

Fig. 9. The CIVL-C driver for tree buffer implementations. The driver performs an arbitrary sequence of `add` operations and finally a single arbitrary `get` operation to yield the output. All choices are controlled by the input variables.

verbose C implementation[10], which is 329 lines long. The second task is to show that one of these real-time implementations is also functionally equivalent to the naive implementation.

We downloaded the C implementation, and made very minor modifications to it so that it implements the interface in our header file. (We renamed the `Tree` structure `TBTree` and added a shell structure `Tree` to wrap a `TBTree`.) Using the same driver, CIVL verified equivalence with the naive implementation, taking 199 s for the number of nodes $n \leq 6$; and 2,190 s for $n = 7$.

---

[10] https://github.com/rgrig/treebuffers/blob/master/treebuffer.c.

CIVL is also able to verify that neither the caterpillar nor the real-time implementation has a memory-leak: every malloc-ed object is eventually freed. This is accomplished by verifying each program normally (without comparing to the naive version); results are shown in Fig. 1.

A final task is to verify the space efficiency property of the real-time implementation, i.e., to show that the memory usage is bounded by a constant factor of the live-heap size of the caterpillar version. We have constructed a solution to this challenge as well, but space does not permit us to discuss it here. The solution can be found in the online archive.

Discussion. The Why3 team implemented all three versions in WhyML.[11] The functional equivalence of the naive version with the advanced versions is expressed by adding a ghost field to the data structures in the advanced versions. The ghost field has the type of the structure used in the naive implementation and each advanced operation also updates the ghost field using the corresponding naive operation. A postcondition captures this behavior by stating that the resulting value of the ghost field equals the value obtained by invoking the naive version. Finally, an invariant states that the data in the ghost field always corresponds to the data in the non-ghost part of the structure.

The real-time version is based on the given C++ code. The entire Why3 solution comprises less than 160 lines of code and generates 33 proof obligations.

Neither the KeY nor the Frama-C solutions deal directly with functional equivalence of different implementations. Unlike WhyML, the languages of those tools do not permit function calls in specifications. The KeY team did implement both the naive and caterpillar versions and verified them separately against contract specifications.[12]

We are not aware of any application of verification tools to the C implementation of the real-time tree buffer algorithm, other than the CIVL one described above.

5   Conclusion and Future Directions

Of the two verification approaches—symbolic execution and deductive reasoning—there is no "better", but each has different advantages and disadvantages. Our examination of solutions to VerifyThis 2017 challenges confirms earlier impressions that symbolic execution is easier to use: it is easier to automate, it requires less in the way of code annotation and modification, it is better able to support complexities such as concurrency (including for C/MPI programs), it provides useful error traces when properties are violated, and it requires less sophistication in logic and specification [11].

To compare execution times, we verified the Why3 solutions on the same platform used for the CIVL runs. The Why3 verification process is not always

---

[11] http://toccata.lri.fr/gallery/verifythis_2017_tree_buffer.en.html.
[12] https://www.ethz.ch/content/dam/ethz/special-interest/infk/chair-program-method/pm/documents/Verify%20This/Solutions%202017/Kirsten_TreeBuffer.java.

fully automatic, even when using only automated provers in the back end, as it can require user interaction to select provers and strategies. Using Why3 1.0.0, we specified a custom strategy that first applies the *split_goal_right* transform; then applies provers in the following order, until a conclusive result is obtained: Alt-Ergo 1.30, Z3 4.4.1, E theorem prover 1.8, and CVC3 2.4.1, each with 1 s timeout and 1 GB memory; then CVC4 1.5 with 3 s timeout and 1 GB memory. With this strategy, all programs were proved without further interaction. It took approximately 5 s and 162 prover calls to verify Challenge 1, 2 s and 90 calls for Challenge 3 (sequential part), and 10 s and 60 calls for Challenge 4.

The Why3 solutions are quite different programs from the C programs verified by CIVL (especially in Challenge 4), so one cannot conclude much from this comparison. Nevertheless, these results indicate that symbolic execution is generally more computationally intensive than deductive verification, except possibly when using very small bounds. The same conclusion can be drawn by comparing the number of theorem prover calls. This is not surprising: finite-state symbolic execution is essentially a "brute-force" approach in which nondeterministic choices are explored exhaustively. This is also the main reason execution time blows up as parameter n increases in the CIVL solutions.

We also see some advantages in the rich logical theories provided by deductive tools such as Why3, e.g., support for a theory of permutation, which simplify the specification task.

The primary drawback of symbolic execution is that it requires some way to bound the number of iterations of each loop. Earlier work, e.g., [2,8,10,13], has explored ways to incorporate loop invariants into the basic symbolic execution algorithm in order to overcome this limitation. We have recently added a similar capability to CIVL.

Our approach has two advantages.

First, it is incremental. This means a user can start by developing a simple bounded program, as in the preceding examples of this paper. Once that is working, the user can add loop invariants for a single loop, and (possibly) get some advantage, such as the ability to remove the bounds on a parameter. Once that is working, the user can move on to a second loop, and so on. At any point in this process, one has a useful model that is at least as good as the preceding one. Once every loop is annotated, the program can be verified without any bounds, exactly as in deductive verification.

Second, our approach is language-based. Instead of implementing extensive changes in the verification kernel, we have added a small number of new, general-purpose language primitives. Code with loop invariants is transformed by the CIVL front end to one without invariants, but with uses of these new primitives. This is in keeping with the general philosophy of CIVL, which is to support a small number of general primitives well, and do the rest of the work by source code transformation. This keeps the symbolic execution engine simple and easy to optimize and maintain. The new primitives are as follows:

1. $assuming(*expr*) *stmt* adds the assumption *expr* to the current path condition, but only for the duration of the execution of *stmt*. The path condition is actually represented as a stack of conditions; *expr* is pushed onto the stack at the beginning, and popped after *stmt* completes;
2. $mem is a type representing a set of memory locations;
3. $mem_contains(*m1,m2*) is a boolean function that return true iff the set of memory locations represented by *m1* contains all of those represented by *m2*;
4. $mem_havoc(*m*) "havocs" (assigns arbitrary values to) all the memory locations in the $mem *m*;
5. $capture *stmt* is an expression that is evaluated by executing *stmt* and returning a $mem consisting of all memory locations that were modified in the course of executing *stmt*.

A loop annotated with an invariant and a frame condition has the form
```
/*@ loop invariant θ;
  @ loop assigns Δ; */
  while (b) C
```
and is transformed to

```
$assert(θ); // check loop invariant establishment
while ($choose_bool()) {  // nondeterministic choice: stay or exit
  $assuming(b && θ) {
    $mem ws = $capture C // execute body, capturing the write set
    $assert($mem_contains(Δ, ws)); // check the frame condition
    $assert(θ); // check loop invariant preservation
    $mem_havoc(Δ);
  }
}
$assume(¬b && θ);
```

It is not hard to see this transformation is sound: if $θ$ is not a loop invariant or C can write to a memory location not in $Δ$, an assertion will be violated. Otherwise, all of the executions in the original program correspond to executions in the transformed program. The transformation is effective because the symbolic constants used in the havoc operation are renamed in a canonical way at each step, which enables the loop to eventually return to a state that has been seen before. In our experience, most loops converge after two or three iterations. The result is a finite symbolic state space that can be explored in the usual way.

Loop invariants are expressed in ACSL. Support is still partial; limitations include (1) there are some cases where the loop does not converge, and (2) in some cases, the original code has to be modified by hand to remove side-effects.

We have successfully applied this new CIVL capability to verify the sorted property of the pair insertion sort, without any bounds on the input size. The CIVL input is given in Fig. 10. This program was verified by CIVL in 15 s. Support for the permutation property is in progress.

While there are similarities between this approach and that of verification generation tools such as Why3, there are significant differences. Symbolic execution may explore many paths through the loop, each with a different path

```
1 #pragma CIVL ACSL
2 $input int n, LEFT, RIGHT;
3 $assume(1<=n && 1<=LEFT && LEFT <= RIGHT && RIGHT<n);
4 $input int A[n];
5 int main() {
6   $assume($forall (int j : LEFT .. RIGHT) A[j] >= A[LEFT-1]);
7   int a[n], left = LEFT, right = RIGHT, k = left;
8   memcpy(a, A, n * sizeof(int)); left++;
9   /*@ loop invariant 2 <= left <= right + 2 && (k == left - 1);
10   @ loop invariant LEFT <= k <= RIGHT+1 && k == left - 1;
11   @ loop invariant \forall int t; LEFT <= t < k ==> a[t - 1] <= a[t];
12   @ loop invariant \forall int t; LEFT <= t <= RIGHT ==> a[LEFT-1] <= a[t];
13   @ loop assigns k, left, a[LEFT .. n-1]; @*/
14   for (; left <= right; k = left++) {
15     int a1 = a[k], a2 = a[left];
16     if (a1 < a2) { a2 = a1; a1 = a[left]; }
17     k--;
18     /*@ loop invariant LEFT - 1 <= k && k < left - 1;
19     @ loop invariant a1 < a[k] ==> k >= LEFT;
20     @ loop invariant \forall int t; LEFT <= t <= k ==> a[t - 1] <= a[t];
21     @ loop invariant \forall int t; k + 3 < t <= left ==> a[t - 1] <= a[t];
22     @ loop invariant \forall int t; LEFT <= t <= RIGHT ==> a[LEFT-1] <= a[t];
23     @ loop invariant k + 3 <= left ==> a[k + 3] >= a1 && a[k+3] >= a[k];
24     @ loop assigns k, a[LEFT .. n-1]; @*/
25     while (a1 < a[k]) { a[k + 2] = a[k]; k--; }
26     a[++k + 1] = a1; k--;
27     /*@ loop invariant LEFT - 1 <= k < left - 1 && (a2 < a[k] ==> k >= LEFT);
28     @ loop invariant \forall int t; LEFT <= t <= k ==> a[t - 1] <= a[t];
29     @ loop invariant \forall int t; k + 2 < t <= left ==> a[t - 1] <= a[t];
30     @ loop invariant \forall int t; LEFT <= t <= RIGHT ==> a[LEFT-1] <= a[t];
31     @ loop invariant k + 2 <= left ==> a[k + 2] >= a2 && a[k + 2] >= a[k];
32     @ loop assigns k, a[LEFT .. n-1]; @*/
33     while (a2 < a[k]) { a[k + 1] = a[k]; k--;}
34     a[k + 1] = a2; left++;
35   }
36   int last = a[right--];
37   /*@ loop invariant LEFT-1 <= right <= RIGHT-1 && (right < RIGHT-1 ==> last < a[right+1]);
38   @ loop invariant right < RIGHT-1 ==> (\forall int i; LEFT <= i <= RIGHT ==>
39   @                   a[i-1] <= a[i]);
40   @ loop invariant right == RIGHT-1 ==> (\forall int i; LEFT <= i <= RIGHT-1 ==>
41   @                   a[i-1] <= a[i]);
42   @ loop assigns right, a[LEFT .. RIGHT]; @*/
43   while (last < a[right]) { a[right + 1] = a[right]; right--;}
44   a[right + 1] = last;
45   $assert( $forall (int i : LEFT .. RIGHT-1) a[i] <= a[i+1] );
46 }
```

Fig. 10. The loop invariant solution for Challenge 1: pair insertion sort

condition. This has the potential to generate more, but simpler, theorem prover queries. For this problem, Why3 verifies all properties of its solution with 162 prover calls, while CIVL takes 226 prover calls to verify only sortedness. It will take further investigation to understand the differences and trade-offs in the two approaches.

Acknowledgments. This research was supported by the U.S. National Science Foundation under Award CCF-1319571, and by the U.S. Department of Energy, Office of Science, Office of Advanced Scientific Computing Research, under Award Number DE-SC0012566. This report was prepared as an account of work sponsored by an agency of the United States Government. Neither the United States Government nor any agency thereof, nor any of their employees, makes any warranty, express or implied, or assumes any legal liability or responsibility for the accuracy, completeness, or usefulness of any information, apparatus, product, or process disclosed, or represents that its use would not infringe privately owned rights. Reference herein to any specific commercial product, process, or service by trade name, trademark, manufacturer, or otherwise does not necessarily constitute or imply its endorsement, recommendation, or favoring by the United States Government or any agency thereof. The views and opinions of authors expressed herein do not necessarily state or reflect those of the United States Government or any agency thereof.

References

1. Ahrendt, W., Beckert, B., Bubel, R., Hähnle, R., Schmitt, P.H., Ulbrich, M. (eds.): Deductive Software Verification - The KeY Book - From Theory to Practice. LNCS, vol. 10001. Springer, Cham (2016). https://doi.org/10.1007/978-3-319-49812-6
2. Barnett, M., Leino, K.R.M.: Weakest-precondition of unstructured programs. In: Ernst, M.D., Jensen, T.P. (eds.) Proceedings of the 2005 ACM SIGPLAN-SIGSOFT Workshop on Program Analysis For Software Tools and Engineering, PASTE'05, Lisbon, Portugal, 5–6 September 2005, pp. 82–87. ACM (2005). https://doi.org/10.1145/1108792.1108813
3. Beyer, D.: Software verification with validation of results. In: Legay, A., Margaria, T. (eds.) TACAS 2017, Part II. LNCS, vol. 10206, pp. 331–349. Springer, Heidelberg (2017). https://doi.org/10.1007/978-3-662-54580-5_20
4. Blom, S., Huisman, M.: The VerCors tool for verification of concurrent programs. In: Jones, C., Pihlajasaari, P., Sun, J. (eds.) FM 2014. LNCS, vol. 8442, pp. 127–131. Springer, Cham (2014). https://doi.org/10.1007/978-3-319-06410-9_9
5. Cuoq, P., Kirchner, F., Kosmatov, N., Prevosto, V., Signoles, J., Yakobowski, B.: Frama-C: a software analysis perspective. Form. Asp. Comput. **27**, 573–609 (2012). https://doi.org/10.1007/s00165-014-0326-7
6. Eidgenössische Technische Hochschule Zürich: Chair of Programming Methodology (2017). http://www.pm.inf.ethz.ch/research/verifythis/Archive/2017.html
7. Filliâtre, J.-C., Paskevich, A.: Why3 — where programs meet provers. In: Felleisen, M., Gardner, P. (eds.) ESOP 2013. LNCS, vol. 7792, pp. 125–128. Springer, Heidelberg (2013). https://doi.org/10.1007/978-3-642-37036-6_8
8. Hentschel, M., Bubel, R., Hähnle, R.: The Symbolic Execution Debugger (SED): a platform for interactive symbolic execution, debugging, verification and more. Int. J. Softw. Tools Technol. Transf. (2018). https://doi.org/10.1007/s10009-018-0490-9
9. Huisman, M., Monahan, R., Müller, P., Mostowski, W., Ulbrich, M.: VerifyThis 2017: a program verification competition. Technical report, Karlsruhe Reports in Informatics 2017, 10, Karlsruhe Institute of Technology, Faculty of Informatics (2017). https://doi.org/10.5445/IR/1000077160
10. Păsăreanu, C.S., Visser, W.: Verification of Java programs using symbolic execution and invariant generation. In: Graf, S., Mounier, L. (eds.) SPIN 2004. LNCS, vol. 2989, pp. 164–181. Springer, Heidelberg (2004). https://doi.org/10.1007/978-3-540-24732-6_13
11. Siegel, S.F.: CIVL solutions to VerifyThis 2016 challenges. ACM SIGLOG News **4**(2), 55–75 (2017). https://doi.acm.org/10.1145/3090064.3090070

12. Siegel, S.F., et al.: CIVL: the concurrency intermediate verification language. In: Proceedings of the International Conference for High Performance Computing, Networking, Storage and Analysis, SC 2015, pp. 61:1–61:12. ACM, New York (2015). https://doi.org/10.1145/2807591.2807635
13. Siegel, S.F., Zirkel, T.K.: Loop invariant symbolic execution for parallel programs. In: Kuncak, V., Rybalchenko, A. (eds.) VMCAI 2012. LNCS, vol. 7148, pp. 412–427. Springer, Heidelberg (2012). https://doi.org/10.1007/978-3-642-27940-9_27

Runtime and Memory Evaluation
of Data Race Detection Tools

Pei-Hung Lin[✉], Chunhua Liao, Markus Schordan, and Ian Karlin

Lawrence Livermore National Laboratory, Livermore, CA 94550, USA
lin32@llnl.gov

Abstract. An analysis tool's usefulness depends on whether its runtime and memory consumption remain within reasonable bounds for a given program. In this paper we present an evaluation of the memory consumption and runtime of four data race detection tools: Archer, Thread-Sanitizer, Helgrind, and Intel Inspector, using DataRaceBench version 1.1.1 using 79 microbenchmarks. Our evaluation consists of four different analyses: (1) runtime and memory consumption of the four data race detection tools using all DataRaceBench microbenchmarks, (2) comparison of the analysis techniques implemented in the evaluated tools, (3) for selected benchmarks an in-depth analysis of runtime behavior with CPU profiler and the identified differences, (4) data analysis to investigate correlations within collected data. We also show the effectiveness of the tools using three quantitative metrics: precision, recall, and accuracy.

Keywords: Data race detection · DataRaceBench · Evaluation Benchmark

1   Introduction

The widespread use of threaded programming models and the increasing on-node parallelism necessitate effective and efficient tools to detect and fix data races within limited time and system resources. A data race occurs when two or more threads perform simultaneous conflicting data accesses to the same memory location without proper synchronization and at least one access is a write. Data race bugs may lead to unpredictable results of a parallel program even with the exact same input. Due to this behavior, the difficulties in detecting and fixing data race bugs can greatly reduce programming productivity. Therefore there is an increasing demand for data race detection tools and many industrial and research efforts are providing tools with data race detection capabilities. An effective data race detection tool needs to have high accuracy in detecting and reporting the data race instances. In the ideal case, the tool is efficient in exploiting shared system resources and detects data races in the short time.

Prepared by LLNL under Contract DE-AC52-07NA27344. LDRD 17-ERD-023. LLNL-CONF-750746.

© Springer Nature Switzerland AG 2018
T. Margaria and B. Steffen (Eds.): ISoLA 2018, LNCS 11245, pp. 179–196, 2018.
https://doi.org/10.1007/978-3-030-03421-4_13

The DataRaceBench benchmark suite [12] was specifically designed for systematic evaluation of data race detection tools with focus on the OpenMP parallel programming model. The development team of DataRaceBench has presented initial evaluation results using quantitative metrics for four selected data race detection tools: Archer, ThreadSanitizer, Helgrind and Intel Inspector.

The evaluation with DataRaceBench lead to the following discoveries:

- OpenMP awareness is a necessity for detecting data races in programs using the OpenMP programming model. Even if an OpenMP runtime library is implemented using Pthreads, a tool that only considers pthread semantics will miss certain details of the OpenMP semantics, leading to false alarms (false positives) in the analysis.
- There is no existing dynamic tool supporting data race detection for SIMD directives.
- With all four of the evaluated dynamic data race detection tools, it is necessary to run the tool multiple times (with the exact same input) because some data races only occur with certain thread schedules. Note that this adds to the overall runtime of dynamic analysis tools in practice.
- Dynamic testing tools can be sensitive to the number of threads used in testing. DataRaceBench includes microbenchmarks that are specifically designed to only have data races with a certain number of threads.

DataRaceBench is useful in evaluating the effectiveness of data race detection tools, but it remains difficult to predict how fast a tool can detect a race and how many system resources it requires.

This paper continues the experiments from [12] to include more details about the runtime and memory consumption of the selected data race detection tools. We use these metrics as basis to determine the most efficient race detection tools.

We present results for four kinds of evaluations. First, we analyze the differences among microbenchmarks in DataRaceBench and show characteristics in microbenchmarks. Second, we compare the selected tools to understand their different runtime behaviors. Third, we use additional evaluation tools to investigate the differences between two selected data race detection tools: ThreadSanitizer and Archer. For Intel Inspector we also show the differences between the default configuration and the max-resource configuration. Finally, we apply a data analysis tool to investigate correlations within the collected experimental results.

The following contributions are be presented in this paper:

- We present an updated evaluation of the tools accuracy extended with memory consumption results for DataRaceBench version 1.1.1 with additional microbenchmarks.
- We collect the runtime overheads of the selected tools when run on DataRaceBench microbenchmarks.
- We show three different evaluations with analysis using DataRaceBench. We provide a tool comparison using quatifiable metrics, detailed analysis to understand the behaviors of specific tools, and analysis of our collected data with a data analysis tool to show what features of the benchmarks impact our metrics the most.

The rest of the paper is organized as follows: in Sect. 2 we present the DataRaceBench suite. In Sect. 3 we describe the selected data race detection tools and the analysis techniques they use. In Sect. 4 we present the experimental results and analyses. In Sect. 5 we discuss the related work and in Sect. 6 we conclude.

2   DataRaceBench Suite

DataRaceBench was designed to capture possible data race patterns in OpenMP programs and serve as a measurement suite to evaluate the accuracy and overhead of data race detection tools. The development of the DataRaceBench suite followed specific design guidelines to achieve its design goals:

- Each microbenchmark should be compact and representative.
- Each program should be self-contained so they can be easily used as part of regression tests for developing data race detection tools.
- Each microbenchmark has a main function to support dynamic data race detection.
- The benchmark suite contains microbenchmarks that allow arbitrary problem sizes to probe static data race detection tools.
- The benchmark suite categorizes code patterns (or properties) of data races in OpenMP programs in its microbenchmark collection.
- The microbenchmarks are divided into two categories: microbenchmarks with known data races and those which are known to be data race free.
- If possible, a program in the category with known data races (race-yes set) should only contain a single pair of source locations that cause data races.
- All microbenchmark programs have built-in input data. A subset of microbenchmarks comes with one additional variant using C99 variable-length arrays to allow probing the impact of changing input data sizes.

The collected microbenchmarks we selected from four major sources: (1) regression test cases from the auto-parallelization tool AutoPar [13]; (2) parallel optimization variants, generated by polyhedral optimizations; (3) data access patterns found in development branches of real scientific applications; and (4) microbenchmarks built by the DataRaceBench developers.

In order to represent different patterns found in OpenMP programs with and without data races, a list of property labels are assigned to the collected microbenchmarks in the DataRaceBench, as shown in Table 1.

The DataRaceBench suite is available at https://github.com/LLNL/dataracebench. The version 1.1.1 used in this paper, uses 79 microbenchmarks to represent all the property labels shown in Table 1.

Table 1. Property labels of microbenchmarks

Property labels for race-yes set	Property labels for race-no set
Y1: Unresolvable dependencies	N1: Embarrassingly parallel
Y2: Missing data sharing clauses	N2: Use of data sharing clauses
Y3: Missing synchronization	N3: Use of synchronization
Y4: SIMD data races	N4: Use of SIMD directives
Y5: Accelerator data races	N5: Use of accelerator directives
Y6: Undefined behaviors	N6: Use of special language features
Y7: Numerical kernel data races	N7: Numerical kernels

3   Data Race Detection Tools

In this paper, we use the same race detection tools used in [12]: Helgrind, Thread-Sanitizer, Archer and Intel Inspector. All these tools use dynamic analysis to find data races during the runtime. Helgrind and ThreadSanitizer are recommended for applications using the POSIX thread API. The versions of the selected data race detection tools we used are listed in Table 2, with the respective compilers used (either to build the tools, compile the microbenchmarks, or both).

Table 2. Data race detection tools: versions and compilers

Tool	Version	Compiler
Helgrind	3.12.0	GCC 4.9.3
ThreadSanitizer	4.0.1	Clang/LLVM 4.0.1
Archer	towards_tr4 branch	Clang/LLVM 4.0.1
Intel Inspector	2017 (build 475470)	Intel Compiler 17.0.2

Helgrind. Helgrind[1] is a Valgrind-based error detection tool for C, C++ and Fortran programs with POSIX threads. It targets three classes of errors: (a) Misuses of the Pthreads API: Helgrind intercepts POSIX thread function calls to detect errors and provides stack trace information for the detected error. (b) Potential deadlock from lock ordering problems: The order in which threads acquire locks is monitored by Helgrind to detect potential deadlocks. (c) Data races: Helgrind follows the "happen-before" tracking and intercepts a selected list of events. It monitors all memory access and builds a directed acyclic graph that represents the collective happens-before dependencies. Analysis with Helgrind can have slowdowns on the order of 100:1, as noted in the documentation. In [15] a slowdown of 20× to 30× is reported. We use Valgrind version 3.12.0 (built with GCC 4.9.3) and GCC version 4.9.3 to compile the microbenchmarks.

---

[1] http://valgrind.org/docs/manual/hg-manual.html.

ThreadSanitizer. ThreadSanitizer (Tsan)[2] is a runtime data race detector developed by Google. ThreadSanitizer is now part of the LLVM and GCC compilers to enable data race detection for C++ and Go code. Every memory access is instrumented by ThreadSanitizer and every aligned 8-byte word of application memory is mapped to N shadow words through direct address mapping (N is configurable to 2, 4 and 8). A state machine that updates the shadow state at every memory address iterates over all stored shadow words. A warning message is printed when one shadow word constitutes a data race with the other shadow word. The memory overhead of ThreadSanitizer comes from four main sources [23]: (1) a constant size buffer that stores segments (a segment has a sequence of events of one thread that contains only memory access events), including stack traces, (2) vector time clocks attached to each segment, (3) Per-ID state, and (4) segment sets and locksets. The segment sets and locksets may potentially consume arbitrary large amount of memory. On an average Google unit test the memory overhead is within a factor of 3 to 4 (compared to a native run).

Archer. Archer is an OpenMP data race detector that exploits ThreadSanitizer to achieve scalable happen-before tracking. It takes the LLVM-based tooling approach to develop LLVM passes within the LLVM package. In addition to the dynamic analysis performed by ThreadSanitizer, Archer adopts static analysis to categorize OpenMP regions into *guaranteed race-free* and *potentially racy*. LLVM passes are designed to identify guaranteed sequential regions within OpenMP code. Memory accesses within OpenMP parallelizable loops, detected by LLVM's Polly[3], are black-listed for the dynamic analysis checking. The unmodified ThreadSanitizer reports a high number of false positives in OpenMP code caused by potential confusion in OpenMP runtime actions. To avoid the confusion for better OpenMP race detection, Archer includes a customized ThreadSanitizer and employs ThreadSanitizer's annotation API to identify the synchronization points within OpenMP runtime.

In this paper, we use the development branch of Archer built based on LLVM version 4.0.1[4]. The OpenMP runtime support for Archer is from the OMPT[5].

Intel Inspector. Intel Inspector[6] is a dynamic analysis tool that detects threading and memory errors in C, C++ and Fortran codes. It supersedes Intel's Thread Checker tool [18,21], with added memory error checking. Supported thread errors include race conditions and deadlocks.

We used a commercial version of Intel Inspector. This tool provides three different levels of analysis. The widest scope maximizes the load on the system

---

[2] https://github.com/google/sanitizers.
[3] https://polly.llvm.org.
[4] https://github.com/PRUNERS/archer 5ad2f47bc8ca8aad006a82a567179d2e0ce1ba75.
[5] https://github.com/OpenMPToolsInterface/LLVM-openmp.git
6e7140bf94d178f719200a6543558d7ae079183b
[6] https://software.intel.com/en-us/intel-inspector-xe.

for more thorough analysis but has higher analysis overhead. Intel Inspector also allows customized configuration in the data race analysis, e.g. byte granularity, stack frame depth and resources used. By default, Intel uses four bytes for monitoring memory accesses, a stack frame depth of 1, without exploiting maximum resources. Setting the access granularity to be a single byte and increasing the stack frame depth to 16 leads to exploiting the maximum resources and increases precision. One limitation is that this version does not support GCC's OpenMP runtime and may report false positives for OpenMP codes compiled by GCC. Therefore, we used Intel C/C++ compilers (with the supported Intel OpenMP runtime) to compile our microbenchmark programs. We also turned off optimizations to keep the best possible debugging information available for dynamic analysis. The graphic user interface of Intel Inspector can provide analysis time overhead and memory overhead to help quickly estimate the time and memory required for the data race analysis. The Livermore computing center reports that slowdowns in the order of 2x to 160x from Intel Inspector can be expected. It is suggested that users choose a small, representative workload, when running Intel Inspector rather than a full production workload.

4   Evaluation

The evaluation in this paper is based on DataRaceBench, version 1.1.1, with seven new microbenchmarks compared to version 1.0.1 used in [12]. Several microbenchmarks in DataRaceBench are designed to have data races only when running with a specific number of OpenMP threads. To allow tools to detect such data races, the experiments were run with different number of OpenMP threads from a selected list of numbers: $(3, 36, 45, 72, 90, 180, 256)$. Different array sizes $(32, 64, 128, 256, 512, 1024)$ are provided on the command line to allocate arrays of different sizes in the microbenchmarks (var-length set). There are 79 microbenchmarks in total and 16 of them are in the var-length set, a set of benchmarks that allow users to define the length of arrays used in the benchmark as parameter on the command line.

Each tool is run five times for every microbenchmark with the exact same input and independent of any other run. The reason why we run the tools several times is that the analysis results can differ dependent on the thread schedule. A total of $(5 \times 7 \times 6 \times 16) + (5 \times 7 \times 1 \times 63) = 5565$ tests were performed by each tool. The evaluation collects the detected number of data races, testing time, and memory consumption, and computes the quantitative metrics for all microbenchmarks using the selected data race detection tools.

Our testing platform is the Quartz cluster hosted at the Livermore Computing Center. Each computation node of the cluster has two Intel 18-core Xeon E5-2695 v4 processors with hyper threading support (18 cores$\times$2 sockets$\times$2 = 72 threads in total). The details of each data race detection tool and the used compilers are shown in Table 2.

The test script provided as part of the DataRaceBench distribution, collects the execution time as wall time (millisecond precision). The memory is not limited and we measure the maximum amount of memory that is used by the tool when analyzing the execution of the microbenchmark. None of the benchmarks fork processes. The computation nodes are configured to use no swap space. We use the Linux command /usr/bin/time -f "%M" to record the maximum resident set size (RSS), the portion of memory occupied by a process that is held in main memory, of the data race detection process during its lifetime. All the collected information is recorded in csv file format for further post processing and analysis.

4.1   Data Race Detection Report

Table 3 reports the data race detection results for the seven new microbenchmarks in DataRaceBench version 1.1.1 following the same format as in [12]. The results include the range of minimum and maximum number of races (min race–max race) and the type of result in true positive (TP), false negative (FN), true negative (TN) or false positive (FP).

Table 3. Data race detection report for the seven new microbenchmarks. See [12] for the microbenchmarks 1–72. Column R shows whether a program contains a data race.

ID	Microbenchmark Program	R	Data Race Detection Tools							
			Helgrind		ThreadSanitizer		Archer		Intel Inspector	
			min-max race race	type	min-max race race	type	min-max race race	type	min-max race race	type
73	doall2-orig-yes.c	Y	13 - 18	TP	3 -120	TP	2 -126	TP	1 - 1	TP
74	flush-orig-yes.c	Y	9 - 13	TP	9 - 9	TP	1 - 3	TP	1 - 1	TP
75	getthreadnum-orig-yes.c	Y	6 - 13	TP	3 -124	TP	2 -255	TP	0 - 1	TP/ FN
76	flush-orig-no.c	N	10 - 11	FP	5 - 8	FP	0 - 0	TN	0 - 0	TN
77	single-orig-no.c	N	6 - 12	FP	2 - 11	FP	0 - 0	TN	0 - 0	TN
78	taskdep2-orig-no.c	N	26 -123	FP	2 - 11	FP	0 - 0	TN	0 - 0	TN
79	taskdep3-orig-no.c	N	21 -134	FP	1 - 14	FP	0 - 0	TN	0 - 0	TN

Table 4 summarizes the numbers of true/false positive and true/false negative results for all 79 microbenchmarks. In Table 5 we show the usual evaluation metrics for precision, recall and accuracy for the selected data race detection tools. The results show that the OpenMP-aware tools Archer and Intel Inspector have higher accuracy than Helgrind and ThreadSanitizer. Archer has the smallest range in the accuracy. Intel Inspector with max resources configuration has both higher value and smaller range in recall and accuracy, but a slightly larger range in precision compared to the default configuration.

4.2   Runtime Behavior Analysis

For analyzing the runtime behavior of the analysis tools, we determine a baseline by collecting measurements from running the DataRaceBench microbenchmarks using GCC, Clang and the Intel compiler. This gives us measurements for all microbenchmarks without any interference with the data race detection tools. We also collect runtime and memory consumption results for all microbenchmarks with the data race detection tools.

Table 4. Positive and negative results of the tools

Tool	Race: Yes			Race: No		
	TP	TP/FN	FN	TN	TN/FP	FP
Helgrind	41	0	2	1	0	35
ThreadSanitizer	41	0	2	1	0	35
Archer	36	5	2	33	3	0
Intel Inspector default	12	24	7	35	1	0
Intel Inspector max resources	32	9	2	33	3	0

Table 5. Metrics for the tools

Tool	Precision		Recall		Accuracy	
	min	max	min	max	min	max
Helgrind	0.539	0.539	0.953	0.953	0.532	0.532
ThreadSanitizer	0.539	0.539	0.953	0.953	0.532	0.532
Archer	0.923	1.000	0.837	0.953	0.873	0.975
Intel Inspector default	0.923	1.000	0.279	0.837	0.595	0.911
Intel Inspector max resource	0.914	1.000	0.744	0.953	0.823	0.975

We run each evaluation five times for every microbenchmark with the exact same input and independent of any other run. This is necessary because analysis results can differ dependent on the thread schedule and as reported in [12] this is necessary to get good analysis results.

The average values of runtime and memory consumption from the 5 independent runs are also used in the runtime behavior analysis. To simplify the analysis, we select only a data size of 1024 for microbenchmarks in the var-length set.

We conduct an empirical analysis using the collected data and focus on the following four tasks:

1. Analyzing the differences between microbenchmarks in DataRaceBench
2. Comparing selected data race detection tools
3. Investigating differences between specific tools
4. Correlation study using data analysis tool

Differences Within DataRaceBench. DataRaceBench was designed to represent OpenMP programs used for data race detection. There are 70 microbenchmarks with a single OpenMP parallel region, 6 microbenchmarks with multiple OpenMP parallel regions (#41–#44, #55, #56), and 3 microbenchmarks with no OpenMP parallel region (#25, #26, #70). In the results we discovered that the number of OpenMP threads used in the test has no impact on the execution time and memory consumption for microbenchmarks #25, #26, #70, #74, and #76. The microbenchmarks #25, #26, and #70 have the SIMD property

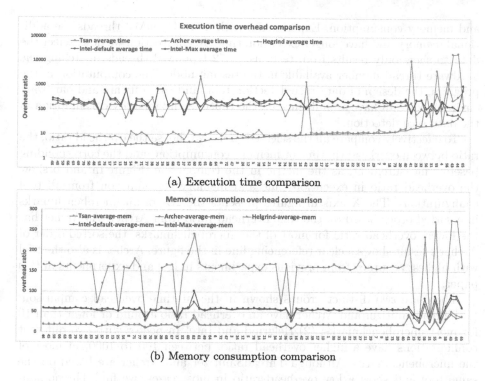

(a) Execution time comparison

(b) Memory consumption comparison

Fig. 1. Tool comparison

label and have only a `OMP SIMD` pragma in the microbenchmark. Without `omp parallel` used in test codes, these tests will be run by only a single thread. The microbenchmarks #74 and #76 have the `num_threads(10)` clause to enforce having 10 OpenMP threads during the execution. The microbenchmarks #25, #26, and #70 also show the lowest execution time and memory consumption, with and without tools involved, in the sorted experiment results, and are run with a single thread and therefore have no OpenMP runtime overhead involved. The selected tools can perform data race detection only in multi-threaded programs (with OpenMP or Pthread). Therefore, the tools cannot detect data races existent in SIMD loops.

Microbenchmarks consuming high testing time are mainly from the Polyhedral microbenchmarks (#41–#44, #55, #56), programs with nested loops and an OpenMP loop as their innermost loop (#37, #38, #62), programs with multidimensional arrays (#23, #31, #32, #37, #38, #58), and a program with high loop iterations (#65). Based on the results we find that microbenchmarks with large arrays (#4, #15, #31, #32, #37, #38) all have higher memory consumption in the experiments with all data race detection tools.

Comparing Data Race Detection Tools. We observe the number of OpenMP threads used in experiments has a strong impact on both runtime and memory consumption. Experiments with more OpenMP threads use additional memory and have longer execution time. In this section we downselect the data to show only results from tests using 72 OpenMP threads, matching the hardware thread number available in the testing node. The computation in the program, the design of data race detection tool, and the software and hardware environment - all have an influence on the runtime and memory consumption in the data race detection.

To effectively compare all the selected tools, we choose the overhead ratio, the ratio between overhead (in time or memory consumption) and the corresponding baseline measurement, as the metric in the comparison. Figure 1a and b show the overhead ratio in execution time and memory consumption from all tool configurations. The X axis in figures presents the IDs of all microbenchmarks in a sorted order based on the time overhead ratio from Archer. As Archer has the lowest overhead ratio for most of the microbenchmarks, the sorted order of Archer's result shows a clear referencing line in the figure. Archer is also the tool with highest accuracy from previous experiments in [12] and experiments in this paper.

There are two distinct groups shown in the runtime overhead comparison: (1) ThreadSanitizer and Archer have an overhead ratio around or lower than 10 for most microbenchmarks; (2) Helgrind and Intel Inspector with two different configurations have a higher overhead ratio, between 100 to 1000, in most of the microbenchmarks. Although ThreadSanitizer and Archer are based on the same tool and show a low overhead ratio in most cases, we find ThreadSanitizer has the highest overhead ratio among all selected tools for the six Polyhedral microbenchmarks (#41–#44, #55, #56). The figure shows a high similarity between the results from two configurations of Intel Inspector. The max-resource configuration shows a higher overhead ratio in 4 Polyhedral microbenchmarks (#43, #44 #55, #56), a microbenchmark with Jacobi kernel (#58), and a microbenchmark with a high OpenMP loop iteration count (#65).

The memory consumption comparison shows 3 different groups in Fig. 1b. Archer and ThreadSanitizer have a very similar overhead ratio (around 20) for all microbenchmarks. Intel Inspector also has a high similarity in the overhead ratio (between 55 to 60) with two different configurations. Helgrind has the highest memory overhead ratio, most microbenchmarks around 160, but for 6 microbenchmarks higher than 220.

Comparing all results regardless of the OpenMP thread number used in the experiments, ThreadSanitizer and Archer have a time overhead ratio lower than 100, Helgrind has a range between 50 and 500, Inspector has a range at 200 to 2000. Regarding the memory consumption overhead: ThreadSanitizer and Archer have a range between 10 to 20, Helgrind has the highest number with a range between 50 and 250, Intel Inspector has a range at 20 to 80. From our collected data, we find that using a higher number of OpenMP threads results in a higher execution time, but does not always result in a higher time overhead ratio. On the other hand, having more OpenMP threads, always leads to a high memory consumption and a higher memory consumption ratio. The time overhead is less sensitive to the OpenMP thread number used in the experiments. Comparing the highest time overhead ratio to the lowest time overhead ratio for each microbenchmark using different number of OpenMP threads, we see ThreadSanitizer has an average of $1.84\times$, Archer has $1.99\times$, Helgrind has $4.68\times$, Intel has $1.77\times$ and $1.65\times$ for default and max-resource configuration. Doing the same comparison for the memory consumption overhead ratio, ThreadSanitizer has an average of $4.62\times$, Archers has $2.94\times$, Helgrind has $7.77\times$, Intel has $7.96\times$ and $5.96\times$ for default and max-resource configuration.

Comparing ThreadSanitizer and Archer. We further investigate the differences between ThreadSanitizer and Archer, especially for those microbenchmarks with a high difference in execution time between these two tools. Archer adopts static polyhedral analysis to detect data dependencies within a test code. A detected OpenMP parallelizable loop (i.e. a loop that is found to have no conflicting dependencies, such that it can be run in parallel) will be blacklisted in Archer for dynamic analysis checking. This can reduce the testing time for Archer. For comparison we also use modified Archer command line arguments to perform data race detection without static analysis provided from LLVM's Polly. For all 79 microbenchmarks, using Archer with static analysis has a range between $0.66\times$ to $1.09\times$, or an average of $0.97\times$, of execution time using Archer without static analysis. As Archer does not report the parallelizable loops detected by its static analysis, we do not have information whether loops are detected and blacklisted for the dynamic analysis. Microbenchmarks in DataRaceBench that were generated using polyhedral transformations are the candidates to be detected by the polyhedral analysis in LLVM's Polly. We exam the results from Polyhedral microbenchmarks in the DataRaceBench and the execution time using Archer with static analysis is $0.83\times$, on average, of the execution time from experiments using Archer without static analysis. We can conclude that the static analysis in Archer can help reduce the runtime of the data race detection if parallelizable loops are detected.

ThreadSanitizer has an extremely high time overhead ratio for polyhedral microbenchmarks (#43–#44 #55, #56) and microbenchmark with the Jacobi kernel (#58). We use the CPU profiler tool from gperftools (originally Google Performance Tools)[7] to inspect two selected microbenchmarks, adi-tile-no.c (#44) and jacobikernel-orig-no.c (#58). CPU profiler uses a default frequency of 100 interrupts per second to profile active CPU usage. The profiler does not consider idle time (sleeping, blocked on locks, waiting for IO, waiting for work etc.) in its report. The profile report can generate an annotated call graph with timing information and top N functions sorted by the execution time. Tables 6 and 7 list the top 3 functions and total sample counts from the profile reports. For adi-tile-no.c (#44), ThreadSanitizer and Archer have 1518 and 1067 total sample counts respectively. This implies that ThreadSanitizer has $1.42\times$ more active CPU usage than Archer. However, the execution time report shows that ThreadSanitizer (1474.2 s) and Archer (3.4 s) has a $432.9\times$ difference in execution

---

[7] https://github.com/gperftools/gperftools.

time. For jacobikernel-orig-no.c (#58), ThreadSanitizer has 7.17× more active CPU usage than Archer. The execution times are 121.3 s for ThreadSanitizer and 7.8 s for Archer (15.51× difference).

The function call `kmp_flag_64::wait` is found in the top 3 functions for both microbenchmarks using both tools. It contains spin wait loop that does pause, then yield, and sleep in OpenMP runtime and it is likely to appear at a synchronization point. A `_kmp_release` from another thread has to appear to wake up this function from sleep. As idle time is not profiled by CPU profiler, this `kmp_flag_64::wait` could contribute a significant amount of sleeping time in the execution. We observe that ThreadSanitizer finishes reporting detected data races to stdout in the very beginning of the testing and then goes into an idle mode till the end of execution. The OpenMP standard specifies several high-level synchronization points: barrier, critical, atomic, taskwait, single, task, and reduction. ThreadSanitizer lacks information about these OpenMP synchronization points. In contrast, Archer with its OpenMP-awareness, has the advantage to use the annotation API of ThreadSanitizer to mark synchronization points within the OpenMP runtime and potentially save testing time for in the synchronization points. Our analysis concludes that ThreadSanitizer can require more time than Archer at the OpenMP synchronization points in the data race detection.

Table 6. Profile report for adi-tile-no.c

Functions	ThreadSanitizer			Archer		
	Name	Count	%	Name	Count	%
#1	kmp_flag_64::wait	457	30.1	kmp_flag_64::wait	334	31.3
#2	_GI__sched_yield	222	14.6	_GI__sched_yield	291	27.3
#3	_kmp_hardware_timestamp	208	13.7	_kmp_hardware_timestamp	162	15.2
Total count	1518			1067		

Table 7. Profile report for jacobikernel-orig-no.c

Functions	ThreadSanitizer			Archer		
	Name	Count	%	Name	Count	%
#1	kmp_flag_64::wait	15218	28.1	_tsan_read8	2337	30.9
#2	_GI__sched_yield	10410	19.2	kmp_flag_64::wait	1430	18.9
#3	_tsan::ReportRace	9499	17.5	_tsan_read4	1017	13.5
Total count	54173			7554		

Comparing Default Option and Max-Resource Option in Intel Inspector. The default data race detection configuration in Intel Inspector, ti2 analysis, aims to find out if a data race exists. In the configuration with maximum resources, we use the ti3 analysis which tries to answer where are the data races in the program. We setup the analysis knob to use an extreme scope to detect data races on the stack with a 1-byte data race detection granularity and cross-thread stack access detection. An additional analysis knob, use-maximum-resources, is set to allow Intel Inspector to exploit maximum system resources in data race detection. The collected data does not show significant difference between the results of the two configurations. There are higher variations in time overhead ratio and memory consumption overhead ratio for microbench-marks with more computation involved, i.e. polyhedral microbenchmarks and Jacobi kernels. Many microbenchmarks in DataRaceBench were designed to be compact and representative for OpenMP programs, but might not have enough complexity in the computation. Therefore, we do not see a significant difference between the runtime behaviors from Intel with default and maximum resource configurations. We do expect to see the configuration with maximum resources consuming more memory and execution time for real-world applications.

Table 8. Correlation report with following attribute ID and correlation value. Attribute list: (1) tool, (2) filename, (3) haverace, (4) threads, (5) dataset, (6) races, (7) elapsed-time, (8) used-mem.

ThreadSanitizer		Archer		Helgrind		Intel-default		Intel-Max	
Time	Memory	Time	Memory	Time	Memory	Time	Memory	Time	Memory
6 (0.48)	4 (0.85)	8 (0.27)	4 (0.86)	6 (0.25)	4 (0.92)	8 (0.24)	4 (0.91)	8 (0.35)	4 (0.88)
8 (0.30)	6 (0.58)	3 (0.16)	6 (0.50)	3 (0.20)	6 (0.15)	4 (0.22)	7 (0.24)	4 (0.31)	7 (0.35)
3 (0.27)	7 (0.30)	4 (0.10)	7 (0.27)	5 (0.08)	7 (0.07)	6 (0.05)	6 (0.13)	3 (0.15)	6 (0.08)

Comparing Data Race Detection Tools. We use the data analysis tool, Weka [7], to investigate the correlations within the collected data. There are eight attributes used by the data analysis tool representing the eight columns of data recorded in the csv files. We can calculate the correlation between each attribute using Weka and rank the attributes with the strongest correlation. Table 8 shows the top three attributes with strong correlation to the execution time and memory consumption using the selected data race detection tools. Each cell in the table shows the attribute ID with its correlation value. Higher correlation values represent stronger correlation between attributes. The data analysis report shows that the thread number (attribute #4) has a strong correlation to memory consumption for every tool. The number of races detected has a moderate correlation to the memory consumption for Archer and ThreadSanitizer. The report shows no attribute with a strong correlation to the execution time for all tools. Only the number of races detected also has a moderate correlation, 0.48, to the execution time for ThreadSanitizer.

5   Related Work

All of the tools evaluated in this paper are dynamic; they run the target program under instrumentation and analyze the execution trace [28]. Many dynamic analyses use a happens-before approach. Reads and writes to shared memory are modeled by a partial order over events within the system [11]. This technique is heavily dependent on the application scheduler, and may miss many latent races. Many advances have been made in this area over the years by using more specialized concepts than traditional vector clocks in order to reduce overhead [4,5], expanding it to single-threaded event-driven programs [14], and defining additional relations such as casually-precedes [24].

Lockset analyses such as Eraser [22] present an alternative to happens-before techniques; they infer the set of mutually-exclusive locks that protect each shared location. If a variable's lockset is empty then accesses to that location may trigger races. These analyses can find races that happens-before techniques cannot, but they incur steep performance costs.

Hybrid approaches combining both methods have also been developed [8,16, 19,23,28]. These methods leverage information about local control flow, recent access, and common race patterns in order to dynamically adjust the analysis. This leads to greater flexibility when balancing accuracy and performance, as well as enabling long-term [28] and large-scale [23] analyses that might not be possible with other techniques.

Static data race detection techniques do not require the program to be executed in order to identify data-races. Static tools do not rely on instrumented schedulers, and therefore may find races that dynamic tools could not. Locksmith [20] is one such tool that seeks to correlate locks with the shared memory locations they guard. It over-approximates the set of data races, possibly returning some false positives. Another analysis seeks to improve the detection of shared variables [9] by performing pointer analysis in order to find global variables that are locally aliased. The RELAY analysis [26] modularizes each source of unsoundness in its analysis so that more accurate methods can be substituted when they are developed. OmpVerify [2] is a static race detector that targets OpenMP exclusively. It uses a polyhedral model to determine data dependencies in shared data.

An analysis of Intel Thread Checker was performed in 2008 [10], evaluating its performance in detecting races during loop parallel and section parallel codes. The benchmark suite used for the evaluation was not released along with the paper. Another work evaluated three data race detection tools: Sun's Thread Analyzer, Intel's Thread Checker and GNU's RaceStand [6]. With the EPCC OpenMP benchmark, Thread Analyzer was about five times faster than Thread Checker and two times slower than RaceStand.

Similar multi-tool analyses have been performed with other languages. Two targeting the Java language [1,27] analyzed several data race detection tools and compared the accuracy and performance of each. The first [1] compared Race-Fuzzer, RacerAJ, JCHORD, Race Condition Checker, and Java RaceFinder. The authors compared the compilation time, accuracy, precision, along with several other metrics. Java RaceFinder performed the best on their tests, although it only reported the first race found even if there were others in the program.

The second [27] focused on detection methods rather than tools, and compared five different algorithms: FastTrack, Acculock, Multilock-HB, SimpleLock+, and casually precedes (CP) detection. The report used FastTrack as a baseline to compare detection accuracy and performance against. Multilock-HB reported the most races without any false-positives, but generated significant overhead; SimpleLock+ was had the lowest overhead, but missed at least one race that MultiLock found.

There exist several frameworks that can simplify the evaluation of large sets of programs: DataMill deals with the problem of varying hardware [17], EMP addresses the problem of varying runtimes on repeated executions of the same program [25], and BenchExec [3] provides a framework for execution (measurement and control), collecting data from large benchmark sets, and results representation (tables, graphs). As the complexity of the DataRaceBench benchmarks grows and their tested environments become more complicated we consider using one of those frameworks in future.

6   Conclusion

In this paper, we present a runtime and memory evaluation for four data race detection tools using the DataRaceBench suite. Regardless of the effectiveness in finding data races, ThreadSanitizer and Archer (based on ThreadSanitizer), have the lowest overheads in time and memory consumption among the four tools. These two tools have high similarity in the overhead of memory consumption but differ more in the time overhead for several microbenchmarks. We conclude the differences in runtime are from two factors: (1) the static analysis available in Archer blacklists serial execution and uses polyhedral analysis to determine whether affine loops nests have a data race to reduce dynamic analysis testing. (2) ThreadSanitizer can have a higher idling time for spin-wait at the synchronization points compared to Archer. The OpenMP-awareness in Archer provides higher accuracy in performing data race detection in OpenMP programs. The time overhead ratio from Helgrind in data race detection is between the overheads from Intel Inspector and ThreadSanitizer-based tools. Helgrind has the highest memory consumption overhead ratio among the selected tools. The reason is that Helgrind lacks knowledge about OpenMP semantics and reports many false positive data races from microbenchmarks in DataRaceBench. Intel Inspector offers many configurable parameters to increase the accuracy and provides detailed information about detected data races. The two configurations used in our evaluation, default and maximum resources, show only a small difference in many microbenchmarks in DataRaceBench. A few microbenchmarks, those with multiple OpenMP parallel regions and more computation involved in the parallel loops, show higher memory consumption for the configuration with maximum resources. Intel Inspector also stores the tracing information to disk and it allows users to use an interface to review and inspect the detected races with references to the source code. Intel Inspector delivers higher accuracy in data race detection when configured with maximum resources verse its default configuration. Through data analysis, we find a strong correlation between the number of OpenMP threads and memory consumption. There are weak correlations between the runtime and other data collected in the experiments.

In conclusion, Archer and Intel Inspector with OpenMP awareness provide higher accuracy in finding data races. Intel Inspector, with two configurations, has a roughly 4 times higher overhead in memory consumption and a much higher overhead in execution time compared to Archer. Intel Inspector requires additional disk storage to store tracing information and writing data to disk could have an impact on the overall runtime.

References

1. Alowibdi, J.S., Stenneth, L.: An empirical study of data race detector tools. In: 2013 25th Chinese Control and Decision Conference (CCDC), May 2013, pp. 3951–3955 (2013). https://doi.org/10.1109/CCDC.2013.6561640
2. Basupalli, V., et al.: ompVerify: polyhedral analysis for the OpenMP programmer. In: Chapman, B.M., Gropp, W.D., Kumaran, K., Müller, M.S. (eds.) IWOMP 2011. LNCS, vol. 6665, pp. 37–53. Springer, Heidelberg (2011). https://doi.org/10.1007/978-3-642-21487-5_4
3. Beyer, D., Löwe, S., Wendler, P.: Reliable benchmarking: requirements and solutions. Int. J. Softw. Tools Technol. Transf. 1–29 (2017). https://doi.org/10.1007/s10009-017-0469-y
4. Effinger-Dean, L., Lucia, B., Ceze, L., Grossman, D., Boehm, H.: IFRit: interference-free regions for dynamic data-race detection. In: Leavens, G.T., Dwyer, M.B. (eds.) Proceedings of the 27th Annual ACM SIGPLAN Conference on Object-Oriented Programming, Systems, Languages, and Applications, OOPSLA 2012, part of SPLASH 2012, Tucson, AZ, USA, 21–25 October 2012, pp. 467–484. ACM (2012). https://doi.org/10.1145/2384616.2384650
5. Flanagan, C., Freund, S.N.: FastTrack: efficient and precise dynamic race detection. In: Hind, M., Diwan, A. (eds.) Proceedings of the 2009 ACM SIGPLAN Conference on Programming Language Design and Implementation, PLDI 2009, Dublin, Ireland, 15–21 June 2009, pp. 121–133. ACM (2009). https://doi.org/10.1145/1542476.1542490
6. Ha, O.-K., Kim, Y.-J., Kang, M.-H., Jun, Y.-K.: Empirical comparison of race detection tools for OpenMP programs. In: Ślęzak, D., Kim, T., Yau, S.S., Gervasi, O., Kang, B.-H. (eds.) GDC 2009. CCIS, vol. 63, pp. 108–116. Springer, Heidelberg (2009). https://doi.org/10.1007/978-3-642-10549-4_13
7. Hall, M., Frank, E., Holmes, G., Pfahringer, B., Reutemann, P., Witten, I.H.: The Weka data mining software: an update. SIGKDD Explor. Newsl. 11(1), 10–18 (2009)
8. Huang, J., Meredith, P.O., Rosu, G.: Maximal sound predictive race detection with control flow abstraction. In: O'Boyle, M.F.P., Pingali, K. (eds.) ACM SIGPLAN Conference on Programming Language Design and Implementation, PLDI 2014, Edinburgh, UK, 09–11 June 2014, pp. 337–348. ACM (2014). https://doi.org/10.1145/2594291.2594315
9. Kahlon, V., Yang, Y., Sankaranarayanan, S., Gupta, A.: Fast and accurate static data-race detection for concurrent programs. In: Damm, W., Hermanns, H. (eds.) CAV 2007. LNCS, vol. 4590, pp. 226–239. Springer, Heidelberg (2007). https://doi.org/10.1007/978-3-540-73368-3_26

10. Kim, Y., Kim, D., Jun, Y.: An empirical analysis of Intel thread checker for detecting races in OpenMP programs. In: Lee, R.Y. (ed.) 7th IEEE/ACIS International Conference on Computer and Information Science, IEEE/ACIS ICIS 2008, Portland, Oregon, USA, 14–16 May 2008, pp. 409–414. IEEE Computer Society (2008). https://doi.org/10.1109/ICIS.2008.79

11. Lamport, L.: Time, clocks, and the ordering of events in a distributed system. Commun. ACM **21**(7), 558–565 (1978). https://doi.org/10.1145/359545.359563

12. Liao, C., Lin, P.H., Asplund, J., Schordan, M., Karlin, I.: DataRaceBench: a benchmark suite for systematic evaluation of data race detection tools. In: Proceedings of the International Conference for High Performance Computing, Networking, Storage and Analysis, SC 2017, pp. 11:1–11:14. ACM, New York (2017). https://doi.org/10.1145/3126908.3126958

13. Liao, C., Quinlan, D.J., Willcock, J.J., Panas, T.: Semantic-aware automatic parallelization of modern applications using high-level abstractions. Int. J. Parallel Program. **38**(5), 361–378 (2010)

14. Maiya, P., Kanade, A., Majumdar, R.: Race detection for android applications. In: O'Boyle, M.F.P., Pingali, K. (eds.) ACM SIGPLAN Conference on Programming Language Design and Implementation, PLDI 2014, Edinburgh, UK, 09–11 June 2014, pp. 316–325. ACM (2014). https://doi.org/10.1145/2594291.2594311

15. Müehlenfeld, A., Wotawa, F.: Fault detection in multi-threaded C++ server applications. In: Proceedings of the 12th ACM SIGPLAN Symposium on Principles and Practice of Parallel Programming, PPoPP 2007, pp. 142–143. ACM, New York (2007)

16. O'Callahan, R., Choi, J.: Hybrid dynamic data race detection. In: Eigenmann, R., Rinard, M.C. (eds.) Proceedings of the ACM SIGPLAN Symposium on Principles and Practice of Parallel Programming, PPOPP 2003, San Diego, CA, USA, 11–13 June 2003, pp. 167–178. ACM (2003). https://doi.org/10.1145/781498.781528

17. de Oliveira, A.B., Petkovich, J.C., Reidemeister, T., Fischmeister, S.: DataMill: rigorous performance evaluation made easy. In: Proceedings of the 4th ACM/SPEC International Conference on Performance Engineering, ICPE 2013, pp. 137–148. ACM, New York (2013). https://doi.org/10.1145/2479871.2479892

18. Petersen, P., Shah, S.: OpenMP support in the Intel® thread checker. In: Voss, M.J. (ed.) WOMPAT 2003. LNCS, vol. 2716, pp. 1–12. Springer, Heidelberg (2003). https://doi.org/10.1007/3-540-45009-2_1

19. Poznianski, E., Schuster, A.: Efficient on-the-fly data race detection in multithreaded C++ programs. In: 17th International Parallel and Distributed Processing Symposium (IPDPS 2003), Nice, France, 22–26 April 2003. CD-ROM/Abstracts Proceedings, p. 287. IEEE Computer Society (2003). https://doi.org/10.1109/IPDPS.2003.1213513

20. Pratikakis, P., Foster, J.S., Hicks, M.W.: LOCKSMITH: context-sensitive correlation analysis for race detection. In: Schwartzbach, M.I., Ball, T. (eds.) Proceedings of the ACM SIGPLAN 2006 Conference on Programming Language Design and Implementation, Ottawa, Ontario, Canada, 11–14 June 2006, pp. 320–331. ACM (2006). https://doi.org/10.1145/1133981.1134019

21. Sack, P., Bliss, B.E., Ma, Z., Petersen, P., Torrellas, J.: Accurate and efficient filtering for the Intel thread checker race detector. In: Proceedings of the 1st Workshop on Architectural and System Support for Improving Software Dependability, pp. 34–41. ACM (2006)

22. Savage, S., Burrows, M., Nelson, G., Sobalvarro, P., Anderson, T.E.: Eraser: a dynamic data race detector for multithreaded programs. ACM Trans. Comput. Syst. **15**(4), 391–411 (1997). https://doi.org/10.1145/265924.265927

23. Serebryany, K., Iskhodzhanov, T.: ThreadSanitizer: data race detection in practice. In: Proceedings of the Workshop on Binary Instrumentation and Applications, WBIA 2009, pp. 62–71. ACM, New York (2009)
24. Smaragdakis, Y., Evans, J., Sadowski, C., Yi, J., Flanagan, C.: Sound predictive race detection in polynomial time. In: Field, J., Hicks, M. (eds.) Proceedings of the 39th ACM SIGPLAN-SIGACT Symposium on Principles of Programming Languages, POPL 2012, Philadelphia, Pennsylvania, USA, 22–28 January 2012, pp. 387–400. ACM (2012). https://doi.org/10.1145/2103656.2103702
25. Suh, Y., Snodgrass, R.T., Kececioglu, J.D., Downey, P.J., Maier, R.S., Yi, C.: EMP: execution time measurement protocol for compute-bound programs. Softw. Pract. Exper. **47**(4), 559–597 (2017). https://doi.org/10.1002/spe.2476
26. Voung, J.W., Jhala, R., Lerner, S.: RELAY: static race detection on millions of lines of code. In: Crnkovic, I., Bertolino, A. (eds.) Proceedings of the 6th Joint Meeting of the European Software Engineering Conference and the ACM SIGSOFT International Symposium on Foundations of Software Engineering, Dubrovnik, Croatia, 3–7 September 2007, pp. 205–214. ACM (2007). https://doi.org/10.1145/1287624.1287654
27. Yu, M., Park, S.M., Chun, I., Bae, D.H.: Experimental performance comparison of dynamic data race detection techniques. ETRI J. **39**(1), 124–134 (2017). https://doi.org/10.4218/etrij.17.0115.1027
28. Yu, Y., Rodeheffer, T., Chen, W.: RaceTrack: efficient detection of data race conditions via adaptive tracking. In: Herbert, A., Birman, K.P. (eds.) Proceedings of the 20th ACM Symposium on Operating Systems Principles 2005, SOSP 2005, Brighton, UK, 23–26 October 2005, pp. 221–234. ACM (2005). https://doi.org/10.1145/1095810.1095832

In-Place vs. Copy-on-Write CEGAR Refinement for Block Summarization with Caching

Dirk Beyer and Karlheinz Friedberger

LMU Munich, Germany

Abstract. Block summarization is an efficient technique in software verification to decompose a verification problem into separate tasks and to avoid repeated exploration of reusable parts of a program. In order to benefit from abstraction at the same time, block summarization can be combined with counterexample-guided abstraction refinement (CEGAR). This causes the following problem: whenever CEGAR instructs the model checker to refine the abstraction along a path, several block summaries are affected and need to be updated. There exist two different refinement strategies: a destructive *in-place* approach that modifies the existing block abstractions and a constructive *copy-on-write* approach that does not change existing data. While the *in-place* approach is used in the field for several years, our new approach of *copy-on-write* refinement has the following important advantage: A complete exportable proof of the program is available after the analysis has finished. Due to the benefit from avoiding recomputations of missing information as necessary for *in-place* updates, the new approach causes almost no computational overhead overall. We perform a large experimental evaluation to compare the new approach with the previous one to show that full proofs can be achieved without overhead.

Keywords: Software model checking · Block summarization
Copy-on-write · CEGAR · Abstraction refinement · CPAchecker
Program analysis

1 Introduction

Software model checking is a powerful technique for proving programs correct as well as for finding errors in programs. Given a program and a specification, a model checker either finds an error path through the program that exposes the specification violation or proves that the specification is satisfied by the program. In this paper, we take a look at the combination of two orthogonal approaches, *block summaries* and *abstraction refinement*.

The technique of constructing summaries of program blocks [18] is effective to reduce the overhead that an exploration without summaries would otherwise

© Springer Nature Switzerland AG 2018
T. Margaria and B. Steffen (Eds.): ISoLA 2018, LNCS 11245, pp. 197–215, 2018.
https://doi.org/10.1007/978-3-030-03421-4_14

cause. Block-abstraction memoization (BAM) [27] is based on a standard state-space exploration using a given control-flow automaton (CFA) that represents the program. The CFA is partitioned into blocks, which are analyzed separately by BAM. Block abstractions (e.g., the results of a block's analysis) represent summaries of blocks. Block abstraction is a generalization of function summaries, if the block size is chosen according to function bodies. In general, block abstraction also works for loop bodies and other block definitions. Block abstractions are stored in a cache, such that they can be reused whenever the same block is explored again. The exact behavior of the analysis and the precision of BAM is determined by a wrapped underlying analysis, such as predicate analysis or explicit-value analysis.

Abstraction, i.e., verifying an overapproximating abstract model of the program instead of its concrete state space, is an idea for scaling model checking to large programs orthogonal to summaries. The verification of the abstract model is often less complex and more resource-efficient. Counterexample-guided abstraction refinement (CEGAR) [15] is a property-directed approach for the automatic construction of an abstract model for a given system: it automatically determines a level of abstraction for program verification that is coarse enough to omit unnecessary information from the abstract model and precise enough to refute spurious counterexamples. The basic idea is to iteratively identify relevant facts from infeasible program paths and use them for the further and more precise state-space exploration. Many existing software model-checking algorithms are based on this approach, such as predicate analysis [8], IMPACT [23], and explicit-value analysis [12].

Our combination of block abstraction with CEGAR needs a special refinement strategy such that only the necessary parts of the (cached) state space are touched. However, block abstractions are cached and can be used at different locations during the analysis and even several times on the same error path. The problem is how to correctly refine the block abstractions in the context of BAM based on a the underlying refinement strategy. The original definition of refinement in BAM [27] describes a destructive *in-place* update of block abstractions and explains that *holes* occur in the state space which are caused by modifications on existing block abstractions. Those holes need to be recomputed on demand. However, this is not possible in general, e.g., after the analysis has finished, because the information which block abstraction was computed for which block is no longer accessible. Succeeding analysis steps are not able to recompute the missing information, as not only the block abstractions themselves, but also their dependencies are deleted in the destructive approach. A recomputation would imply to rerun a large part of the complete analysis. Due to the unforeseeable appearance of cache accesses, the recomputation might even produce a completely different counterexample or proof than the previous analysis.

The user usually wants the model checker to terminate with a proof, which in this setting might be an abstract reachability graph (ARG). The ARG is expected to include all initial abstract states and all abstract states that are reachable from the initial abstract states. This guarantee does not hold if the ARG contains holes. Succeeding analysis steps that are executed after the termination of the block-abstraction-based analysis and depend on the full abstract state space (without holes) have no possibility to recompute the missing parts. For example, correctness witnesses [6,22] can not be reliably produced with block-abstraction-based analyses [1]: the exported correctness witness is either invalid because no graph from root to all reached abstract states could be written, or a missing part in the correctness witness (branch in the graph) is responsible for incorrectly guiding the witness validator.

The main contribution of this paper is a new refinement approach based on a constructive *copy-on-write* strategy. Our work includes a comparative evaluation of the new *copy-on-write* approach with the previous *in-place* refinement, showing that the new approach has only a small computational overhead for run time and memory usage. Because BAM is independent of (and orthogonal to) other analyses in a full program analysis, it can be combined with analyses based on different abstract domains like predicate, value, or interval analysis [11,12], or combinations thereof [1,17]. Our new refinement strategy is fully integrated into BAM in CPACHECKER and does not depend on the underlying analysis. Thus, there is no change in the behavior of the sub-analyses.

Contributions. We make the following contributions:

- We design a *copy-on-write* approach that solves two open problems: (i) strictly monotonic refinement for summary-based approaches in combination with CEGAR and (ii) abstract reachability graphs without holes that cause problems in later steps of the analysis.
- We implement the approach of *copy-on-write* refinement in the verification framework CPACHECKER and make the source code available to others.[1]
- We experimentally evaluate the new approach on a large number of verification tasks to show that the *copy-on-write* approach is about as efficient and effective as the *in-place* approach, although the approach produces *complete* abstract reachability graphs.
- We make all experimental results, including raw data, tables, experiment setup, etc., available on a supplementary web site.[2]

Related Work. There are several techniques based on block-based summarization, as this idea dates back to Hoare [20]. The special case of *function summaries* aims at scalability for interprocedural analyses and is integrated in several algorithms and tools.

FUNFROG [25,26] uses an SMT solver and Craig interpolation to compute function summaries in the context of bounded model checking. Starting from an initially empty set of function summaries, the tool explores the problem's traces and computes interpolants from path formulas for all missing procedure calls. The interpolants are then directly used as summaries. This strategy is applied in a CEGAR loop until the specified property can be proven or is definitely violated.

---

[1] https://cpachecker.sosy-lab.org
[2] https://www.sosy-lab.org/research/bam-cow-refinement

FUNFROG uses a cache for function summaries, but does never modify existing function summaries.

BEBOP [3] and SATURN [28] use binary decision diagrams (BDDs) and SMT to encode the program's semantics. The function summary is build by renaming variables in formulas, such that the direct encoding of a procedure call can be reused several times within the same encoding of the program behavior. Both tools work on a very precise abstraction level and do not refine their summarizations.

BAM is a domain-independent approach for caching and reusing block abstractions. It is independent of functions and can be used with an arbitrary block size. Instead of being limited to a special domain like BDDs, SMT, or intervals, BAM works on an abstract level and can be applied to any abstract domain or even combinations of several domains, including predicate analysis and explicit value analysis [1]. The integration of CEGAR refinement in BAM was already described in the context of predicate analysis [27]. Our new approach of *copy-on-write* refinement for BAM makes the approach really lazy (matching the principles of *lazy abstraction refinement* [19]).

2   Background on Block Summarization

The following section provides an overview of some basic concepts and definitions that we use for our approach. We describe the program representation and the most important details of block-abstraction memoization that are used for state-space exploration (cf. other literature on block-abstraction memoization for more detailed descriptions [2,7,27]).

2.1   Program and State-Space Representation

A program is represented by a *control-flow automaton* (CFA) $A = (L, l_0, G)$, which consists of a set L of program locations (modeling the program counter), a set $G \subseteq L \times Ops \times L$ (modeling the control flow), and an initial program location l_0 (entry point; initial call of the main function). The set Ops contains the operations of the program, i.e., assignment and assume operations, function calls, and function returns. Let V be the set of variables in the program. A *concrete data state* assigns a value to each variable from the set V; the set C contains all concrete data states. For every edge $g \in G$, the transition relation is defined by $\overset{g}{\rightarrow} \subseteq C \times \{g\} \times C$. If there exists a sequence of concrete data states $\langle c_0, c_1, ..., c_n \rangle$ with $\forall i \in [1, n] : \exists g : c_{i-1} \overset{g}{\rightarrow} c_i \wedge (l_{i-1}, g, l_i) \in G$, then state c_n is called *reachable* from c_0 for l_0, i.e., there exists a syntactic walk through the CFA.

We perform a reachability analysis that unrolls the program lazily [19] into an *abstract reachability graph* (ARG) [8]. An ARG $S = (N, E)$ is a directed acyclic graph, consisting of a set N of ARG nodes (representing the abstract program states, e.g., including program location and variable assignments) and a set $E \subseteq N \times N$ of edges modeling the transfer that leads from one abstract state to the next one. We define a *subgraph* $S_s = (s, N_s, E_s)$ as a connected component of an ARG $S = (N, E)$, starting at a given abstract state $s \in N_s$ (denoted as root), such that $N_s \subseteq N, E_s \subseteq E$, and $\forall s' \in N_s : (s', s'') \in E \Rightarrow (s'' \in N_s \wedge (s', s'') \in E_s)$.

```
1   void main() {
2       int x = 0;
3       while (x<10) {
4           x = f(x);
5       }
6       assert(x>=10);
7   }
8
9   int f(int n) {
10      return n+1;
11  }
```

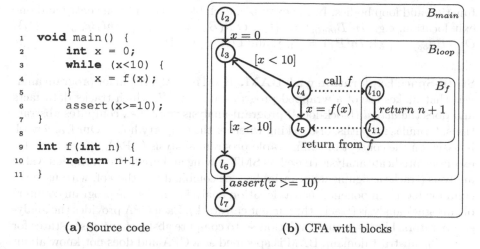

(a) Source code   (b) CFA with blocks

Fig. 1. Example program and its control-flow automaton with 3 blocks

2.2 Block Summarization

Block-abstraction memoization (BAM) [27] is a generalization of several block-based summarization approaches [18,24,25]. BAM divides an input program into smaller parts, named *blocks*, to analyze them separately by summary construction. It uses an arbitrary block size and is not limited to function boundaries. In addition, BAM uses a cache to reuse block abstractions. The blocks allow us to abstract from the surrounding context, reducing computational overhead, and improving the performance of an analysis. The analysis of each block corresponds to an abstract initial state at the block-entry location and a set of abstract exit states at the block-exit locations (both described later). Block abstractions (e.g., the combination of initial states and exit states of a block's analysis) are stored in a cache, such that they can be reused whenever the same block is visited again.

Blocks. The basic components of BAM are *blocks*, which are formally defined as parts of a program: A block $B = (L', G')$ of a CFA $A = (L, l_0, G)$ consists of a set $L' \subseteq L$ of connected program locations and a set $G' = \{(l_1, op, l_2) \in G \mid l_1, l_2 \in L'\}$ of control-flow edges. Two different blocks $B_1 = (L'_1, G'_1)$ and $B_2 = (L'_2, G'_2)$ are either disjoint ($L'_1 \cap L'_2 = \emptyset$) or one block is completely nested in the other block ($L'_1 \subset L'_2$). Each block $B = (L', G')$ has *entry* and *exit locations*, which are defined as $In(B) = \{l \in L' \mid (\exists(l', op, l) \in G \wedge l' \notin L') \vee \nexists(l', op, l) \in G\}$ and $Out(B) = \{l \in L' \mid (\exists(l, op, l') \in G \wedge l' \notin L') \vee \nexists(l, op, l') \in G\}$, respectively. In general, the block size can be freely chosen in BAM. In most cases, function and loop bodies are taken as blocks, because they represent logical structures of the program and seem to be a good choice for block abstraction.

Figure 1 shows the CFA (b) for an example program (a). The CFA is structured into three nested blocks B_{main}, B_{loop}, and B_f, such that their sizes align with the function and loop bodies. In the example, each block has only one entry and one exit location, e.g., $In(B_{main}) = \{l_2\}$, $Out(B_{main}) = \{l_7\}$, $In(B_{loop}) = \{l_3\}$, $Out(B_{loop}) = \{l_6\}$, $In(B_f) = \{l_{10}\}$, and $Out(B_f) = \{l_{11}\}$.

State-Space Exploration with BAM. BAM is an algorithm for program analysis that makes use of a wrapped program analysis $\mathbb{W}$, which tracks data facts and does the *actual* (block-local) program-analysis work, i.e., computes abstractions, formulas for paths, or checking whether the property holds. Our framework is based on the concept of configurable program analysis (CPA) [9] and uses, for example, predicate analysis (based on SMT solving and predicates), explicit-value analysis (tracks assignments of variables), or combinations thereof, with usage of common basic components such as location analysis (tracks the program counter) or call-stack analysis (tracks the current call stack). Each CPA provides the analysis operators, like the transfer relation $\rightsquigarrow$ to compute abstract successor states for a specific abstract domain. BAM is specified as a CPA and does not know about the internals of the wrapped analysis $\mathbb{W}$, which is also a CPA. The approach of BAM just operates on abstract states of a (possibly combined) abstract domain to generate block abstractions.

The state-space exploration with BAM is defined recursively for blocks. The successor computation for abstract states chooses between two possible steps, depending on the currently analyzed program location: At an entry location of a block B, the successor computation $\overset{B}{\rightsquigarrow}_B$ of the containing block executes a separate *nested sub-analysis* of the block B (starting with the initial abstract state for the block-entry location). This step produces a separate ARG that is later integrated as block abstraction into the surrounding analysis context. The block abstraction can either be computed or taken from a cache, if the block has been analyzed before. For block-exit locations of blocks, there is no succeeding abstract state (in the nested sub-analysis). For other program locations, the successor computation $\rightsquigarrow_\mathbb{W}$ is applied, which acts according to the abstract domain of the wrapped analysis $\mathbb{W}$ (e.g., tracks variables or computes abstractions for abstract states). Abstract states where a specification violation occurs are handled as if those abstract states are at block-exit locations of the current block, i.e., the nested sub-analysis terminates and returns the violating abstract states directly for the block abstraction.

Note that an ARG can contain edges representing block abstractions. The block of the block abstraction is inlined whenever a concrete program path without block abstractions is needed. This overhead is the necessary price for having a block-modular analysis. When CEGAR modifies the ARGs during the refinement, a problem occurs, which we will describe later.

2.3   CEGAR

Counterexample-guided abstraction refinement (CEGAR) is an approach to automatically adjust the granularity of an analysis by learning from infeasible error paths the relevant analysis facts that are needed to verify a program. We use

CEGAR as a wrapper algorithm around the state-space exploration algorithm, which is implemented as CPA algorithm [10]. The granularity of the analysis is defined as a *precision* that is refined in each iteration of the CEGAR algorithm. Each abstract state in an ARG has a precision. The precision of an abstract state can be changed during the refinement step. A too coarse precision would lead to an imprecise analysis that reports false alarms, a too fine precision would lead to an expensive state-space exploration; CEGAR tries to find the "right" level of abstraction in between.

CEGAR consists of two steps, an exploration step and a refinement step, which are executed alternatingly until a feasible error path is found (and a bug is reported) or all error paths are proven to be infeasible (and a proof can be reported): The exploration step computes new successor abstract states and builds the abstract state space in form of an ARG $G = (N, E)$, using the level of abstraction determined by CEGAR. When finding a possible specification violation, a feasibility check is applied, which examines the error path to the violation. A feasible error path is reported and the analysis terminates. An infeasible error path is used for a refinement step to gain more relevant facts from the program, e.g., by applying interpolation, and refine the precision. If the exploration step does not find any property violation and all abstract states are explored, the algorithm terminates and the program is proven correct.

The refinement step determines a *cut point* $s_{cut} \in N$ and a new precision for this position, such that the new level of abstraction is sufficient to exclude the infeasible error path from further exploration of the state space. The level of abstraction depends on the abstract domain of the analysis and might consist of, e.g., predicates (for predicate analysis) or a set of variables to be tracked (for value analysis). The outdated (too imprecise) subgraph $S_{s_{cut}} = (s_{cut}, N', E')$ of the already explored state space is removed from the ARG G and the subgraph's root state s_{cut} alone is re-added to G, such that the next exploration step of CEGAR recomputes this part of the state space with a higher precision. There are several approaches to determine the cut point s_{cut} along the error path [13]:

- **cut point at root:** full eager refinement is applied, where the whole explored state space is withdrawn and re-exploration starts from the initial root state of the ARG (e.g. [4, 14, 16]),
- **cut point as deep as possible:** only a (minimal) part of the explored state space is removed (lazy refinement [19]), such that a large part of the explored state space remains intact and can be reused in the further analysis (e.g. [8, 10]), or
- **cut point in between:** trade-off between reuse and reexploration is somewhere in between the above two choices [13].

The second approach performs best in most cases and is currently used in the field. As shown in Alg. 1, the refinement procedure first determines an abstract state s_{cut} where the infeasible subgraph is to be cut off and new facts are applied to the precision of the analysis. Lazy refinement is based on the idea that some parts of a program are analyzed with a coarse abstraction level and only some

---

Algorithm 1. Default refinement procedure of CEGAR

Input: an infeasible error path σ, an ARG G of the analysis

$s_{cut}, newFacts := \mathsf{refine_W}(\sigma)$

$\mathsf{refinePrecision}(G, s_{cut}, newFacts)$

$\mathsf{removeSubgraph}(G, s_{cut})$

---

other parts of a program use a more fine-grained precision. Cutting off only a part of the ARG in each refinement fulfills this requirement.

2.4   Requirement for Refinement Approaches: New Precision Strictly More Precise

We use a (partial) order on precisions, such that a precision is considered as *more precise* compared to another precision, if it causes the analysis to track more information. For example, if an analysis uses a precision to track a set of variables or predicates (as predicate analysis and value analysis do), this relation is implicitly given by the subset relation. If a precision p is a superset of another precision p', then p is *more precise* than p'. Let an infeasible error path be a sequence of abstract states $\langle s_0, s_1, ...s_n \rangle$ with their precisions $\langle p_0, p_1, ...p_n \rangle$, such that s_0 is the root of the program and s_n violates the specification. The sequence $\langle p_0, p_1, ...p_n \rangle$ of precisions is *more precise* then a sequence $\langle p'_0, p'_1, ...p'_n \rangle$ of precisions if either p_0 is more precise than p'_0, or $p_0 = p'_0$ and the remaining sequence $\langle p_1, ...p_n \rangle$ of precisions is *more precise* than the sequence $\langle p'_1, ...p'_n \rangle$. We require a *refined* precision to be strictly more precise than its original, in order to guarantee *progress* in CEGAR (monotonic refinement).

Since CEGAR is a fixed-point algorithm that starts with a coarse precision and refines it until it is sufficiently precise to prove or refute the program, the termination criterion for the CEGAR loop depends on a refinement approach that monotonically increases the precision. To ensure progress of the analysis, the refinement requirement needs to hold for each single refinement step in a program analysis with CEGAR.

Removing a subgraph $S_{s_{cut}} = (s_{cut}, N', E')$ from an ARG and applying a refined precision at its cut point s_{cut} fulfills the property, because the precision itself is more precise for the cut point, the predecessors are not touched, and the successors are deleted (and implicitly inherit the refined precision). Even if the removed subgraph $S_{s_{cut}}$ contained a more precise precision for some abstract state, the refinement requirement holds: Because the refined precision is represented as mapping from locations to precisions, and assigned as precision of the root abstract state s_{cut} of the subgraph, an ancestor of any removed state will be seeded with the new, refined precision. During re-exploration of the deleted subgraph, the analysis will re-explore prefixes of previously encountered error paths in this part of the state space and perform refinements of other error paths with cut points that also satisfy the refinement requirement. Strengthening the precision by additional information (like invariants from an external tool) before applying the update during the refinement also fulfills the property.

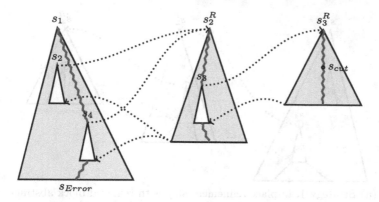

Fig. 2. State-space exploration with BAM and cut points for refinement

The refinement requirement is not fulfilled by the *in-place* approach, because the *in-place* refinement potentially deletes block abstractions for already analyzed parts of the state space and causes additional overhead if recomputation is needed for those missing block abstractions. The *copy-on-write* approach does not suffer from this problem.

After defining all necessary parts, we will now go on with a motivating example, before giving the detailed description of the refinement approaches in BAM. Our goal is to replace an implementation that *in-place* modifies the ARG by a new *copy-on-write*-based approach for modifying the ARG. This allows us to efficiently keep the original as well as the copy for further processing. In the later evaluation we show that keeping the original data improves our analysis in several cases, and in particular, leaves the ARG complete (without holes).

3   Motivating Example

The following example illustrates the differences of the two strategies that could be used as refinement step in a CEGAR approach. In BAM, the analysis explores the state space and computes block abstractions for blocks. An example for such a state-space exploration is given in Fig. 2 (gray triangles represent ARGs, rooted at the top corner; white triangles represent block abstractions). We use block abstractions for nested blocks at the entry abstract states s_2, s_3, and s_4 with the corresponding initial abstract states s_2^R, s_3^R, and s_4^R in the nested analysis for the blocks at those program locations. In the example, let s_4^R be equal to s_2^R, such that we can reuse the existing block abstraction here. Block abstractions are shown as white triangles and are connected with their ARG via dotted lines. When finding the property violation s_{Error}, the analysis stops and performs a refinement for the found counterexample. The lazy refinement approach determines a possible cut-state, i.e., an abstract state s_{cut} along the error path, from where the found property violation is no longer reachable if a refined precision is applied.

At this point, the two refinement strategies differ:

Figure 3a shows the *in-place* refinement, removing parts of the explored state space, i.e., everything after the cut point s_{cut} and after the block abstractions (for

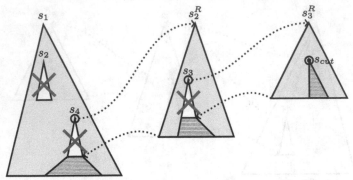

(a) Strategy 1: In-place refinement step with removed block abstractions and subgraphs

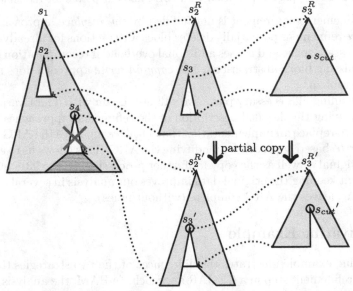

(b) Strategy 2: Copy-on-write refinement step with copied ARGs and changes only in the most outer ARG

Fig. 3. In-place and copy-on-write refinement approach for BAM

abstract states s_3 and s_4). At the abstract state s_2 the *in-place* approach implicitly invalidates the ARG for the block abstraction and causes a *hole* in the surrounding ARG. Here, the applied block abstraction itself remains valid, because those abstract states were computed before the refinement.

Figure 3b shows the *copy-on-write* approach, updating the abstract states. All inner (nested) ARGs are updated *copy-on-write*. The red horizontal lines represent the removed abstract successor states after the block abstraction for abstract state s_4. The ARGs rooted at s_2^R and s_3^R are copied into new ARGs with roots at $s_2^{R'}$ and $s_3^{R'}$, leaving out the parts that are invalid after updating the precision. The references to or from block abstractions are also updated.

The difference in the refinement strategies is visible in Figs. 3a and 3b. While the first approach deletes and recomputes parts of the ARGs, the second approach works on fresh copies of the ARGs and uses them along with the old ARGs. In the following we explain both refinement strategies in more detail and discuss benefits of the second approach.

4   *In-Place* Refinement for BAM

The existing approach for refinement in BAM (as described earlier [27]) is sound, simple, and efficient, but has problems when abstract states need to be accessible afterwards. Briefly worded, the existing approach modifies cached block abstractions *in-place* and deletes important information that is not available after the refinement and needs to be recomputed for further steps of the analysis.

4.1   *In-Place* Refinement Algorithm for BAM

Algorithm 2 gives an overview of the *in-place* refinement of CEGAR for BAM, without going into detail for the further operation of BAM itself (cache management). The *in-place* refinement tries to mimic lazy abstraction refinement and CEGAR, i.e., it touches only a small number of abstract states and aims to update only those states where a precision update will avoid the re-exploration of the currently found infeasible error path. In contrast to Alg. 1, there is no single ARG G to work on, but with BAM there are several ARGs and the refinement must be applied to several of them. Algorithm 2 applies the following steps of the refinement:

After the refinement procedure of the underlying analysis has computed new facts for the analysis and determined an abstract state s_{cut} along the error path, the refinement approach determines the subgraph $S = (N, E)$ where the cut point s_{cut} is located. BAM might have used the block abstraction for S several times along the error path, and thus, we need to find out which outer subgraphs we need to remove (see Fig. 3a). Thus, we start from the correct block abstraction, and apply the removal operations for *in-place* refinement: The cut point s_{cut}

Algorithm 2. In-place refinement procedure of CEGAR with BAM

Input: an infeasible error path σ

  $s_{cut}, newFacts := \mathsf{refine}_W(\sigma)$
  $S := \mathsf{getARG}(s_{cut}, \sigma)$
  $\mathsf{refinePrecision}(S, s_{cut}, newFacts)$
  $\mathsf{removeSubgraph}(S, s_{cut})$
  while S is nested in another ARG S^* along σ **do**
    $s^* := \mathsf{getInitState}(S, S^*, \sigma)$
    $\mathsf{removeSubgraph}(S^*, s^*)$
    $S := S^*$

---

and its subgraph $S_s(s_{cut}, N_s, E_s)$ get removed from S (with $s_{cut} \in N_s \subseteq N$ and $E_s \subseteq E$).

If the ARG S represents a block abstraction for a block B, i.e., S is nested within another ARG $S^* = (N^*, E^*)$, with the ARG S rooted at the initial abstract state $s^* \in N^*$, the subgraph S_{s^*} starting at the abstract state s^* of the nested-block abstraction is removed from the surrounding ARG S^*. This strategy is applied transitively up to the most outer ARG. The most outer block is not used as a block abstraction (it represents the whole program) and thus never referred to elsewhere in the state space.

The succeeding exploration step of CEGAR will re-explore the removed parts, use or recompute block abstractions and reach the abstract state with the refined precision, from where the state space is analyzed without exploring the previously encountered infeasible error path. Every ARG modification happens *in-place* and directly modifies the existing block abstractions. This approach does not consider whether a block abstraction was already used in another part of the state space, e.g., as part of another another ARG.

4.2   Problem of Cached Block Abstractions with *In-Place* Updates

The *in-place* refinement approach suffers from the *in-place* update of block abstractions in the following way: Whenever an missing abstract state belonging to a *hole* (missing block abstraction) in the state space is needed to be accessed, e.g., as part of a new error path, the block-entry state of the *hole*'s block abstraction is determined (depending on the context) and a possible valid block abstraction is recomputed. The previously updated ARG can not be used to fill the *hole*, because its precision might have been refined and updated *in-place*, such that it is more precise than before and leads to different block-exit abstract states. In order to not loose this refined precision for further exploration, all abstract states following the recomputed block abstraction need to be replaced by their recomputed counterparts (which also happens *in-place*).

In Fig. 3a this case happens when a property violation is found with an error path going through the removed block abstraction of s_2. Then the subgraph of s_2 needs to be removed and recomputed with a new block abstraction.

After BAM terminates (with or without finding a property violation) we often generate statistics or collect some data from the reached abstract state space. However, with *holes* there also comes the problem of missing data. This is only a minor problem, however might also irritate and mislead the user. Numeral statistics like the *number of abstract states* or the *number of predicates* are potentially misleading. Missing parts in non-numerical output, such as proofs and correctness witnesses, cause problems for later processing of the verification results. For example, we have identified several tasks in SV-COMP'17, for which CPACHECKER (competition contribution BAM-BnB [1]) computed the correct result during the analysis, but did not write a correctness witness for the validation, or a witness was written, but the graph of the witness was missing some parts, such that the witness validator was not correctly guided to some branches and could not successfully validate the result.

The new *copy-on-write* approach does not suffer from these problems, because the necessary data are kept until it is no longer needed, and we obtain correct statistics and valid (and complete) correctness witnesses.

5   *Copy-on-Write* Refinement for BAM

This section describes our new approach for *copy-on-write* refinement in BAM and considers the computational difference to *in-place* refinement.

5.1   *Copy-on-Write* Algorithm for BAM

We define a *copy* of an ARG $S = (N, E)$ as a second graph $S' = (N', E')$, where each ARG abstract state from N and transition from E is copied into N' and E'. Technically, a copy is just a new instance of the same ARG. Instead of changing an existing ARG S, whenever we would need to remove a subgraph S_θ from it, the *copy-on-write* algorithm (Alg. 3) copies the ARG S into a new ARG S', omitting the corresponding subgraph. Then, we update the precision only for abstract states in the new instance S'. The new ARG S' is then registered in the cache as new block abstraction for one position where previously S was used, such that further explorations use the new instance S'. The old ARG S remains untouched, is still valid, and can be accessed when revisiting existing block abstractions.

When copying an ARG S that contains an embedded ARG S^{nested} from a nested sub-analysis, Alg. 3 only references the existing instance S^{nested} in the new ARG S' and does not copy it, except S^{nested} itself has to be modified. In this case, a copy $S^{nested'}$ is inserted instead of the original S^{nested}.

Computational Overhead for *Copy-on-Write* Refinement. The run time of the *copy-on-write* refinement is similar to the *in-place* approach, because every affected ARG is exactly traversed once in each of the approaches. Thus, the run time of both refinement strategies is linear in the number of reached states. The conceptional difference comes with the operation performed on the affected abstract states: Instead of removing a subgraph of abstract states from an ARG, we create a flat copy of all other abstract states, i.e., those abstract states that are not part of the subgraph.

Algorithm 3. Copy-on-write refinement procedure of CEGAR with BAM

Input: an infeasible error path σ

$s_{cut}, newFacts := \mathsf{refine}_W(\sigma)$
$S := \mathsf{getARG}(s_{cut}, \sigma)$
$S', s'_{cut} := \mathsf{copyWithoutSubgraph}(S, s_{cut})$
$\mathsf{registerARG}(S')$
$\mathsf{refinePrecision}(S', s'_{cut}, newFacts)$
while S' is nested in another ARG S^* along σ **do**
    $S^* := \mathsf{getInitState}(S', S*, \sigma)$
    $S^{*'}, s^{*'} := \mathsf{copyWithoutSubgraph}(S^{*'}, s^*)$
    $\mathsf{registerARG}(S^{*'})$
    $S' := S^{*'}$

To reduce the run time of the copy operation and the memory footprint for the copied abstract states, the *flat copy* keeps all internal data of abstract states untouched (e.g., information about program location, call stack, data state, etc.) and just references them from the new abstract states. This perfectly matches the *copy-on-write* idea and also the internal data structure of our framework, where abstract states consist of separate components for separate domains. Only those components where data needs to be changed are effectively constructed again, the rest is just referenced. This approach has two benefits:

- There is no need to implement and execute methods for copying internal data of abstract states (predicates, variable assignments, program counter, call-stack information, ...). Thus our new approach can easily be applied to all existing analyses.
- The *copy-on-write* approach has only a small memory overhead, because only new ARG states are constructed, the internal data of abstract states are shared and do not require additional memory.

6   Evaluation

Next we give evidence that the improvements in our refinement approach (no holes in the ARG) do not lead to significant performance drawbacks.

Benchmark Set. We evaluate our new *copy-on-write* refinement approach on a large subset of the SV-benchmark suite[3] containing over 5 500 verification tasks and compare it with the existing *in-place* approach.

Setup. We run all our experiments on computers with Intel Xeon E3-1230 v5 CPUs with 3.40 GHz, and limit the CPU time to 15 min and the memory to 15 GB. We use our implementation in CPACHECKER[4] in revision r29066. The time needed for parsing the input program and exporting data is rather small compared to the analysis time, thus we measure the complete CPU time for the verification run of CPACHECKER (i.e., including parsing, analysis, and witness export).

Analysis Configuration. BAM can be combined with several analyses and for our experiments, we choose two combinations that are used in practice: BAM with predicate analysis (PA) and BAM with value analysis (VA) [2]. We configure BAM to use function and loop bodies as blocks, and predicate analysis computes abstractions, just as in the original work [27]. The expressive power of the program analysis depends only on the expressiveness of the predicate analysis or value analysis, and is not influenced by BAM. Except for the refinement approach itself, we do not change any configuration for each of the analyses. Thus, each of analyses should give the same verification answer in both cases.

---

[3] https://github.com/sosy-lab/sv-benchmarks
[4] https://cpachecker.sosy-lab.org

Results and Discussion. The experiments show nearly no difference in CPU time and also no significant difference in memory consumption between the two refinement approaches for each analysis. The reason for this result in terms of run time is that *copy-on-write* is extremely efficient and the light overhead is compensated by savings for recomputing missing parts of the state space. The reason for the same memory footprint is that the memory overhead for the additional ARGs is very small compared to the shared data (e.g., formulas for tracking variables). Note that memory usage is not fully predictable in general, as the Java garbage collection is applied non-deterministically.

The quantile plots in Fig. 4 show how many tasks are solved correctly with each of the approaches and each of the analyses. Figure 4a presents the results for all correctly solved verification tasks with low number of refinements (≤ 1): no difference in the results is visible for the two approaches per underlying analysis. For a low number of refinements, the equality of the results for different refinement approaches was expected, because the effect of missing block abstractions depends on a sufficiently large number of refinements. With only zero or one refinement the new approach behaves exactly as the *in-place* approach. With a growing number of refinements, the analysis could in principle perform differently. Figure 4b shows the CPU time for all correctly solved verification tasks where more than one refinement was needed. Both refinement approaches perform very similar, e.g., keeping block abstractions using *copy-on-write* is as good as recomputing missing block abstractions for both underlying analyses. (The similar performance of predicate analysis and value analysis is a coincidence, because both analyses use completely different techniques to track variables, assignments, and relations.)

Table 1 shows statistics about all verification results, for both approaches. There are some cases (for both predicate analysis and value analysis), where the analysis with one refinement approach delivers a result while the other does not. Sometimes eager application of a refined precision is beneficial, sometimes the overhead for recomputation of a missing block abstraction is too expensive. While the difference for value analysis is negligible, predicate analysis performs better with the *in-place* refinement, but needs more refinements than with *copy-on-write*. It seems that predicate analysis reacts much more fragile to changes in the refinement strategy and application of refined precisions than value analysis.

Figures 5a and 5b compare the number of needed refinements for each solved task using scatter plots. The number of refinements includes also cases where a missing block abstraction has to be recomputed (recomputation is lazy and only applied if an error path with a *hole* was found; thus it counts as refinement, too). For predicate analysis with the *copy-on-write* approach, the majority of results is computed with a smaller number of refinements than with the *in-place* refinement: on average the new approach needs only a third of the refinements. For value analysis there is no clear difference in the number of refinements and the average number of refinements is also similar.

Threats to Validity. Our evaluation uses a large publicly available benchmark suite of C verification tasks in order to optimize the diversity in size and type of

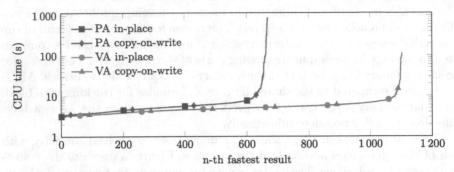

(a) CPU time of refinement approaches of BAM, ≤ 1 refinements only (plots are identical, because the changed approach does not affect the analysis)

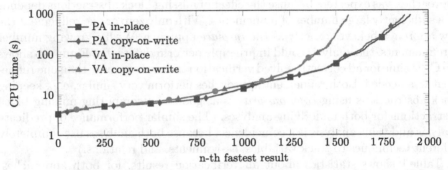

(b) CPU time of refinement approaches of BAM, ≥ 2 refinements only (plots only differ for predicate analysis with a larger run time, e.g., over 200 s, because the changed approach only affects the analysis if several blocks are analyzed repeatedly and the cache is accessed)

Fig. 4. Quantile plots for CPU time of refinement approaches

Table 1. Statistics of refinement approaches of BAM

	Predicate Analysis		Value Analysis	
	In-place	Copy-on-write	In-place	Copy-on-write
Found proofs	2149	2121	2352	2352
Found bugs	425	422	322	322
Incorrectly found proofs	2	2	0	0
Incorrectly found bugs	0	0	2	2
Solved by only one approach	40	9	4	4
Avg. no. of refinements	53.7	19.4	8.21	8.35

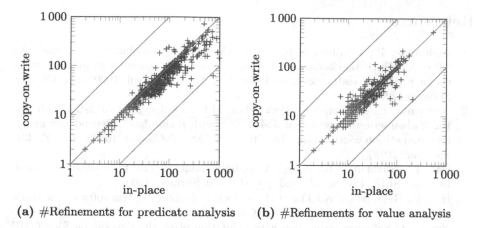

(a) #Refinements for predicate analysis   (b) #Refinements for value analysis

Fig. 5. Comparison of *in-place* and *copy-on-write* refinement approach for predicate analysis and value analysis

programs. While it seems clear that the concepts and results can be transferred to other verification tasks, such a claim is not backed up by our experiments. Besides the internal structure of a verification task, there are other factors that influence the behavior of an analysis. Thus, the external validity of the experiments regarding the application of refinements and precision updates is increased by the large number of experiments on different tasks. The chosen time limit of 15 min and memory limit of 15 GB for verifying a given task is inspired by the research community on software verification (cf. one of the reports on the International Competition on Software Verification [5]). Of course, the evaluation of our approach depends on the tool where it is implemented. To our knowledge, there is no other tool directly implementing the approach of BAM.

7   Conclusion

We developed a new approach for CEGAR-based refinement of block summaries that is based on *copy-on-write*. The new approach makes it possible to construct an abstract reachability graph without holes, such that at the end of the program analysis, a complete proof is available to the user. The proof can be dumped for inspection, or a correctness witness can be extracted from the proof. We designed and implemented the *copy-on-write* refinement and provide a ready-to-use implementation in the framework CPACHECKER. Re-using existing underlying analyses is possible without any further development overhead. The experimental comparison showed that there is almost no performance overhead for copy-on-write. Furthermore, the experimental comparison of the existing *in-place* with the new *copy-on-write* refinement strategy revealed interesting insights into some aspects of block summarization. In the future, we plan to design a parallel version of BAM to utilize a network of computers for our domain-independent analysis technique (cf. SWARM [21]): The new immutable block abstractions might also be beneficial in the context of resource-intensive communication between nodes of a computer network.

References

1. Andrianov, P., Friedberger, K., Mandrykin, M.U., Mutilin, V.S., Volkov, A.: CPABAM-BnB: Block-abstraction memoization and region-based memory models for predicate abstractions. In: Proc. TACAS. LNCS, vol. 10206, pp. 355–359. Springer (2017)
2. Andrianov, P., Mutilin, V.S., Mandrykin, M.U., Vasilyev, A.: CPA-BAM-Slicing: Block-abstraction memoization and slicing with region-based dependency analysis (competition contribution). In: Proc. TACAS. LNCS, vol. 10806, pp. 427–431. Springer (2018)
3. Ball, T., Rajamani, S.K.: Bebop: A symbolic model checker for boolean programs. In: Proc. SPIN. LNCS, vol. 1885, pp. 113–130. Springer (2000)
4. Ball, T., Rajamani, S.K.: The SLAM project: Debugging system software via static analysis. In: Proc. POPL, pp. 1–3. ACM (2002)
5. Beyer, D.: Software verification with validation of results (Report on SV-COMP 2017). In: Proc. TACAS. LNCS, vol. 10206, pp. 331–349. Springer (2017)
6. Beyer, D., Dangl, M., Dietsch, D., Heizmann, M.: Correctness witnesses: Exchanging verification results between verifiers. In: Proc. FSE, pp. 326–337. ACM (2016)
7. Beyer, D., Friedberger, K.: Domain-independent multi-threaded software model checking. In: Proc. ASE, pp. 634–644. ACM (2018)
8. Beyer, D., Henzinger, T.A., Jhala, R., Majumdar, R.: The software model checker BLAST. Int. J. Softw. Tools Technol. Transfer 9(5–6), 505–525 (2007)
9. Beyer, D., Henzinger, T.A., Théoduloz, G.: Program analysis with dynamic precision adjustment. In: Proc. ASE, pp. 29–38. IEEE (2008)
10. Beyer, D., Keremoglu, M.E.: CPACHECKER: A tool for configurable software verification. In: Proc. CAV. LNCS, vol. 6806, pp. 184–190. Springer (2011)
11. Beyer, D., Keremoglu, M.E., Wendler, P.: Predicate abstraction with adjustable-block encoding. In: Proc. FMCAD, pp. 189–197. FMCAD (2010)
12. Beyer, D., Löwe, S.: Explicit-state software model checking based on CEGAR and interpolation. In: Proc. FASE. LNCS, vol. 7793, pp. 146–162. Springer (2013)
13. Beyer, D., Löwe, S., Wendler, P.: Refinement selection. In: Proc. SPIN. LNCS, vol. 9232, pp. 20–38. Springer (2015)
14. Chaki, S., Clarke, E.M., Groce, A., Jha, S., Veith, H.: Modular verification of software components in C. IEEE Trans. Softw. Eng. 30(6), 388–402 (2004)
15. Clarke, E.M., Grumberg, O., Jha, S., Lu, Y., Veith, H.: Counterexample-guided abstraction refinement for symbolic model checking. J. ACM 50(5), 752–794 (2003)
16. Clarke, E.M., Kröning, D., Sharygina, N., Yorav, K.: SATABS: SAT-based predicate abstraction for ANSI-C. In: Proc. TACAS. LNCS, vol. 3440, pp. 570–574. Springer (2005)
17. Friedberger, K.: CPA-BAM: Block-abstraction memoization with value analysis and predicate analysis. In: Proc. TACAS. LNCS, vol. 9636, pp. 912–915. Springer (2016)
18. Henzinger, T.A., Jhala, R., Majumdar, R.: Race checking by context inference. In: Proc. PLDI, pp. 1–13. ACM (2004)
19. Henzinger, T.A., Jhala, R., Majumdar, R., Sutre, G.: Lazy abstraction. In: Proc. POPL, pp. 58–70. ACM (2002)
20. Hoare, C.A.R.: Procedures and parameters: An axiomatic approach. In: Symposium on Semantics of Algorithmic Languages, pp. 102–116. Springer (1971)
21. Holzmann, G.J., Joshi, R., Groce, A.: Tackling large verification problems with the SWARM tool. In: Proc. SPIN 2008. LNCS, vol. 5156, pp. 134–143. Springer (2008)

22. McConnell, R.M., Mehlhorn, K., Näher, S., Schweitzer, P.: Certifying algorithms. Comput. Sci. Rev. **5**(2), 119–161 (2011)

23. McMillan, K.L.: Lazy abstraction with interpolants. In: Proc. CAV. LNCS, vol. 4144, pp. 123–136. Springer (2006)

24. Reps, T.W.: Program analysis via graph reachability. In: Proc. ILPS, pp. 5–19. MIT (1997)

25. Sery, O., Fedyukovich, G., Sharygina, N.: Funfrog: Bounded model checking with interpolation-based function summarization. In: Proc. ATVA. LNCS, vol. 7561, pp. 203 207. Springer (2012)

26. Sery, O., Fedyukovich, G., Sharygina, N.: Interpolation-based function summaries in bounded model checking. In: Proc. HVC. LNCS, vol. 7261, pp. 160–175. Springer (2012)

27. Wonisch, D., Wehrheim, H.: Predicate analysis with block-abstraction memoization. In: Proc. ICFEM. LNCS, vol. 7635, pp. 332–347. Springer (2012)

28. Xie, Y., Aiken, A.: Saturn: A scalable framework for error detection using boolean satisfiability. TOPLAS **29**(3), 16 (2007)

Deductive Verification of Unmodified Linux Kernel Library Functions

Denis Efremov[1,2(✉)], Mikhail Mandrykin[2], and Alexey Khoroshilov[1,2,3,4]

[1] National Research University Higher School of Economics, Moscow, Russia
defremov@hse.ru
[2] Ivannikov Institute for System Programming of the RAS, Moscow, Russia
{mandrykin,khoroshilov}@ispras.ru
[3] Moscow Institute of Physics and Technology, Moscow, Russia
[4] Lomonosov Moscow State University, Moscow, Russia

Abstract. This paper presents results from the development and evaluation of a deductive verification benchmark consisting of 26 unmodified Linux kernel library functions implementing conventional memory and string operations. The formal contract of the functions was extracted from their source code and was represented in the form of preconditions and postconditions. The correctness of 23 functions was completely proved using AstraVer toolset, although success for 11 functions was achieved using 2 new specification language constructs. Another 2 functions were proved after a minor modification of their source code, while the final one cannot be completely proved using the existing memory model. The benchmark can be used for the testing and evaluation of deductive verification tools and as a starting point for verifying other parts of the Linux kernel.

Keywords: Formal verification · Deductive verification · Linux kernel

1 Introduction

Deductive verification is one of the most rigorous techniques to ensure software satisfies its requirements. In spite of significant advances in tool support, it still requires deep user involvement in the verification process to provide manual guidance (e. g., to specify the contract of each function and to identify loop invariants). As a result deductive verification is used mainly to analyze the most critical pieces of software.

Under such conditions, it is more cost-effective to rewrite code to make it easier to verify than to implement support for all the complex corner cases in the semantics of the target programming platform, most notably in low-level platforms based on C which lack well-defined semantics for many cases widely used in practice.

Nevertheless, there are situations where changing the code under verification is undesirable or even impossible. For example, components to be integrated

T. Margaria and B. Steffen (Eds.): ISoLA 2018, LNCS 11245, pp. 216–234, 2018.
https://doi.org/10.1007/978-3-030-03421-4_15

into a predefined framework have to follow the coding style, interfaces and data structures of that framework. We have met such limitations with Linux kernel modules where a lot of implementation details are imposed by Linux kernel core infrastructure.

One of the well-established approaches to specifying the behavioral contract of functions written in C is ANSI/ISO C Specification Language (ACSL) [1]. FRAMA-C [2] provides a framework for an analysis of C programs with optional ACSL specification annotations. FRAMA-C integrates specifications and code into a single intermediate representation and allows plugins to work with it. There are two plugins for deductive verification built on top of FRAMA-C: WP [2] and JESSIE [3].

Because existing plugins were not able to correctly handle many constructs widely used in the Linux kernel (e. g., `container_of`, pointer type reinterpretation between integer types of different size), we started developing a new deductive verification ASTRAVER plugin based on JESSIE. We implemented and proposed many improvements for the toolchain, including a new memory model [4], but there is no representative benchmark to evaluate the progress. The primary purpose of this work is to fill this gap.

Following previous efforts [5,6], we have chosen for the first step Linux kernel library functions implementing conventional memory and string operations. The benchmark built from such functions helped us to detect a number of local tool issues and several fundamental problems discussed below.

The main contributions of the paper include:

- a benchmark of unmodified Linux kernel library functions extended with annotations formalizing their contracts in the form of preconditions and postconditions [7];
- a new approach to annotate modulo arithmetic operations on values of integral C types;
- evaluation of ASTRAVER deductive verification toolchain on the benchmark.

The paper is organized as follows. Section 2 discusses similar efforts aimed at the specification and deductive verification of C library functions. Section 3 provides background on ACSL basic concepts. Section 5 presents improvements in the toolchain made during the development of the benchmark. Sections 6 describes specification techniques designed and applied for specification of library functions. Section 7 defines a set of open problems. Section 8 presents the evaluation of the solvers. Section 9 summarizes the results of the work.

2   Related Work

Since the deductive verification tools, WP and JESSIE are mature enough there are many examples where these tools were applied for verification of real-life software. In [6] 12 string functions from OpenBSD were examined, using JESSIE as a deductive verification plug-in. The correctness of 7 functions was fully proved (all verification conditions, or VCs, were successfully discharged). For the other 5 functions, some VCs were left unproved. The author did three iterations on the development of a specification contract for each function. First, one was developed based on the standard and the author's experience. The second one was developed based on informal documentation (man pages) exclusively. The final one was written based on the implementation (source code) and the man pages. The final revision in most cases has significant differences from previous versions. Thus it shows that it is difficult to develop a formal specification in ACSL language for already developed source code without taking the implementation into account. However, such an iterative approach allowed the author to find inaccuracies in the documentation for several functions, and a lack of documentation completeness in many cases.

To prove some functions, the author changed the source code. Changes were performed in two specific situations. In the first case `char *` type in `strcmp` and `strncmp` functions were cast to `unsigned char *`. In the second case, the unsigned loop iterator in `strlcat` underflowed at the last iteration step due to the postfix decrement. The loop termination, in this case, occurs when the variable equals zero, but after comparison, the value of the variable is still decreasing by one. This results in the unsigned integer underflow (which is not an undefined behavior). However, the unsigned underflow does not lead to an error in the code: after the loop, the variable is not used anywhere. But in this situation, it is not possible to prove the VC demanding the absence of an integer overflow (more generally, over- or underflow). The VC is necessary due to the use of the `defensive` integer model (see section Sect. 5.2) when the bounded integers are modeled using mathematical unbounded integers assuming the absence of integer overflows. To prove the VCs, ALT-ERGO (0.7.3), SIMPLIFY (1.5.4) and Z3 (2.0) solvers were used.

In [5] authors used FRAMA-C with the WP deductive verification plugin to verify the functions of the KLIBC library. The authors were able to fully prove 14 string functions. For 12 functions some VCs were not discharged. Four more functions failed to analyze due to errors in the verification tools. In addition to the string functions (from `string.h`), functions from the `stdio.h` were also analyzed. As noted by the authors, almost all functions from this header file use system calls, which in most cases results in a weak specification. To overcome the limitations of the verification tools and to simplify the generated VCs the authors made changes to the source code.

The authors analyzed in advance the problems with type casts modeling (for example, `unsigned char *` to `char *`) and modified the code to exclude such operations. The authors also faced the code pattern with the postfix decrement in a while loop. To prove the VCs, ALT-ERGO (0.95.1), CVC3 (2.4.1) and Z3 (4.3.1) solvers were used.

The most comprehensive document on ACSL specifications development is ACSL by Example [8]. It contains ACSL specifications for functions from the C++ standard library (Standard Template Library). Initial implementation converted from C++ function templates to C functions that work on arrays of type `int`. The authors regularly update the document with new specifications and functions, bug-fixes, etc. This project started in 2009. The document contains a number of fully verified functions. They were proved with ALT-ERGO, CVC3, CVC4, Z3, and EPROVER solvers. Authors use the WP deductive verification plugin.

GrammaTech report [9] describes typical problems the authors encountered when developing specifications for the GTLIBC library. FRAMA-C with WP was used. Among other points, the authors report memory model problems with pointers type casts and pointers comparison.

3   ACSL

ACSL is designed to be suitable for specifying safety properties of C programs, including contract specifications (pre- and postconditions) and assertions with arbitrary predicates on one or several memory states. The language also supports the specification of function frame conditions, axiomatic theories and additional annotations required by particular verification tools to check the specified properties (examples of additional specifications are loop invariants and pragmas). ACSL includes specification constructs for expressing C-specific attributes related to explicit low-level memory management such as start addresses and lengths of allocated memory blocks, pointers with support for arbitrary pointer type conversions and accessibility predicates for read-only and read-write access.

```
1  /*@ requires valid_strn(s, count);
2      assigns \nothing;
3      behavior exists:
4      assumes ∃ char *p; s ≤ p < s+strnlen(s,count) ∧ *p ≡ (char %)c;
5      ensures s ≤ \result ≤ s+strnlen(s, count);
6      ensures *\result ≡ (char %) c;
7      ensures ∀ char *p; s ≤ p < \result ⇒ *p ≢ (char %)c;
8      behavior not_exists:
9      assumes ∀ char *p; s ≤ p < s+strnlen(s,count) ⇒ *p ≢ (char %)c;
10      ensures \result ≡ \null;
11      complete behaviors;
12      disjoint behaviors;*/
13  char *strnchr(const char *s, size_t count, int c) {
14  //@ ghost char *os = s;
15  //@ ghost size_t ocount = count;
16  /*@ loop invariant 0 ≤ count ≤ ocount;
17      loop invariant os ≤ s ≤ os+strnlen(os, ocount);
18      loop invariant s−os ≡ ocount−count;
19      loop invariant valid_strn(s, count);
20      loop invariant strnlen(os,ocount) ≡ s−os+strnlen(s, count);
21      loop invariant ∀ char *p; os ≤ p < s ⇒ *p ≢ (char %) c;
22      loop variant count;
23  */
24  for (; count--/*@%*/ && *s != '\0'; ++s)
25    if (*s ≡ (char)/*@%*/c)
26      return (char *)s;
27  return NULL;
28  }
```

Listing 1. From Linux 4.12, lib/string.c

Let's consider an example of a simple C function with an appropriate ACSL specification. Listing 1 presents one of the implementations for function strnchr from the Linux kernel. The function searches for the first occurrence of character c in a string s of length bounded by the parameter cnt. The precondition in line 1 requires the string s to address a valid memory area of length min(strlen(s), cnt) + 1. strnchr is a pure function, the absence of effects on memory state is specified in line 2. The further specification is split into two cases: The first one when the string includes the searched character and the second one when it does not. ACSL includes a special construct for such composite specifications, which is called *behaviors*. In ACSL behaviors are not treated as syntactic sugar (unlike, e. g., JML), but fully integrated into the language such that nearly all specification constructs both in contracts and in function bodies are attributed to one or several behaviors and thus different behaviors of a function are intended to be checked separately. To verify the function strnchr against its contract specification with a deductive verification tool, the loop invariant and a ranking function (loop variant) are specified in lines 16–22.

The implementation of strnchr contains an intentional type cast (char)c in line 25 and a postfix decrement of a loop iterator count in line 24. In both of those cases, the corresponding operation (type cast or decrement) discards some parts of the bitwise representation of the argument (higher bits of the int value and the sign bit correspondingly), which corresponds to the intention of the programmer. To distinguish those intentionally overflowing operations, whose semantics is described in terms of bitwise interpretation of bounded integers, we introduced a special annotation construct /*@%*/.

4   Region Separation in Jessie

Since there are two deductive verification plugins for the FRAMA-C platform, we had to make a choice between JESSIE and WP. While there may be many arguments for choosing a more up-to-date and actively maintained WP plugin, which, among others, has capabilities for bitwise modelling of in-memory data representation and support for interactive proofs, here we emphasize that our initial justification for choosing JESSIE over WP was due to its more flexible architecture that enabled easier experimentation with custom ACSL extensions (including the composite integer model described in section Sect. 5.2) and also its support for region-based modelling of the heap.

In particular, the heap in JESSIE is separated into disjoint regions according to the results of a preliminary conservative static analysis presented in [10]. While the separation analysis is coarse (so that its soundness is easy to establish), it is still useful in many cases arising during verification of imperative code. For example, consider the following loop invariant:

```
1 /*@ loop invariant \at(src ,Pre) ≤ src ≤
2                        \at(src ,Pre)+strlen(\at(src ,Pre));
3      loop invariant \at(dest ,Pre) ≤ dest ≤
4                        \at(dest ,Pre)+strlen(\at(src , Pre));
5      //...
6 */
7 while ((*dest++ = *src++) != '\0')
8   ;
```

Listing 2. From Linux 4.12, lib/string.c

Here, in general, proof of the fact that `strlen{LoopCurrent}`
`(\at(src, Pre))` == `strlen{Here}(\at(src, Pre))` holds at the end of every
iteration requires inductive reasoning since the definition of `strlen` is recursive
and the side effect of the assignment `*dest++` = `*src++` can generally interfere
with the memory footprint of the function `strlen`. But the static separation
analysis implemented in JESSIE assigns disjoint memory regions to the pointers
`dest` and `src` and so both applications of `strlen` to src before and after the
loop iteration are encoded using a heap variable separate from that of `dst` and
therefore literally coincide. So in JESSIE the non-interference trivially holds and
does not require any additional proof effort. In general, the separation analysis is
imprecise and may require explicit weakening, e. g., if the surrounding function
can be called in context with more aliasing (e. g., when `src` may intersect with
`dest`), but it can still considerably simplify the verification by eliminating the
need in inductive framing lemmas.

5 Limitations of the Current Implementation

5.1 Jessie Byte-Level Block Memory Model

There are a number of ways to logically represent pointers and memory blocks
in the generated VCs. JESSIE implements the *byte-level block memory model* [3],
where pointers are logically represented as pairs of the form (l, o) and memory
blocks are represented as triples of the form (l, a, s). Here l is a label uniquely
identifying a memory block, o is the offset of the pointer from the starting
address a of the block l, and s is the size of the block. The introduction of
unique block labels allows us to ensure that no memory access occurs beyond
the bounds of the pointed memory block even if the corresponding memory
area is also allocated. Although such access cannot break segmentation checks,
it is forbidden by C standard [11] (subsection 6.5.6, paragraph 8 classifies out-
of-bounds pointers, except for pointers to the one past the last element of an
array, as undefined). As explained in [3] describing the design choices behind
the JESSIE tool, byte-level block memory model in principle allows us to express
common but non-standard C code fragments, such an implementation of the
function `memmove`, while retaining the ability to detect use-after-free memory
safety errors and potential pointer overflows.

The actual implementation of the memory model in the tool, however, diverges from its simple theoretical description in several ways and imposes a number of additional restrictions on the supported subset of C.

First, pointers are implemented in the corresponding JESSIE theory (in WhyML) as values of an abstract type `pointer` with four corresponding abstract operations:

$$\texttt{sub\_pointer} \ : \ \texttt{pointer} \times \texttt{pointer} \rightarrow \texttt{int},$$
$$\texttt{shift} \ : \ \texttt{pointer} \times \texttt{int} \rightarrow \texttt{pointer},$$
$$\texttt{same\_block} \ : \ \texttt{pointer} \times \texttt{pointer} \rightarrow \texttt{bool}, \text{ and}$$
$$\texttt{address} \ : \ \texttt{pointer} \rightarrow \texttt{int}.$$

Block sizes are represented implicitly by so-called *allocation tables*, mutable values of an abstract type with two axiomatically defined functions

$$\texttt{offset\_min} \ : \ \texttt{alloc\_table} \times \texttt{pointer} \rightarrow \texttt{int and}$$
$$\texttt{offset\_max} \ : \ \texttt{alloc\_table} \times \texttt{pointer} \rightarrow \texttt{int}.$$

The functions represent the minimal and maximal allowed offset of a pointer in its corresponding allocated memory block i. e., for a pointer $p = (l, o)$ and its corresponding memory block (l, a, s) which has size s in the state represented by allocation table t, $\texttt{offset\_min}(t, p) = -o$, $\texttt{offset\_max}(t, p) = s - o - 1$. Thus a pointer p can be safely dereferenced iff $0 \leq o \leq s - 1$ i. e., $\texttt{offset\_min}(t, p) \leq 0 \wedge \texttt{offset\_max}(t, p) \geq 0$. We denote this condition as $\texttt{valid}(t, p)$. There is no direct representation for block labels (l) or starting addresses (a) of the memory blocks. The VCs generated for dynamic memory allocations and deallocations (function calls to `kmalloc` and `kfree` are treated specially in JESSIE[1]) involve only allocation tables and functions `sub_pointer`, `shift` and `same_block`. This makes the corresponding axiomatization inherently incomplete. In particular, the function `address` is not only left entirely uninterpreted in the current implementation, but cannot be even theoretically given a complete axiomatization. Consider the following property of this function: *two valid pointers from different blocks cannot have the same address*. It cannot be expressed as a logical proposition using the current JESSIE theory since this would involve bounded existential quantification over all possible *reachable* states of the corresponding allocation table:

$$\forall p_1, p_2. \ (\exists t. \ Reachable(t) \wedge \texttt{valid}(t, p_1) \wedge \texttt{valid}(t, p_2)) \wedge \neg\texttt{same\_block}(p_1, p_2)$$
$$\implies \texttt{address}(p_1) \neq \texttt{address}(p_2).$$

Since the problem of inferring an explicit representation of the predicate $Reachable(t)$ is undecidable, the tool should implement an implicit encoding of the pointer address properties at every allocation point:

---

[1] The special treatment is necessary because JESSIE does not support arbitrary pointer type casts, in particular, reinterpretation casts such as `char *→int*`, so the return type of memory allocating functions should be specialized at each call site, which can not be directly expressed in ACSL.

$\forall p.\ \mathtt{valid}(t, p)$
$\implies \mathtt{address}(p) < \mathtt{address}(p^*) \lor \mathtt{address}(p) \geq \mathtt{address}(p^*) + sizeof(*p^*) \times s,$

where p^* points to the start of a freshly allocated memory block of size $s \times sizeof(*p^*)$ and t is the state of the allocation table just before the allocation. The unavailability of a precise formalization for the function $\mathtt{address}$ prevents the generation of the appropriate VCs for potential pointer overflows and a more flexible formalization of pointer comparison and difference operations (allowing the verification of functions such as $\mathtt{memmove}$).

Moreover, the pointer offset and difference, as formalized by the functions $\mathtt{shift}$ and $\mathtt{sub\_pointer}$, are measured in units equal to the sizes of the addressed values, according to the pointer indexing semantics of C, rather than in bytes or words. In particular, an expression $\mathtt{p\ +\ 1}$, where p has type $\mathtt{int\ *}$, is translated roughly as $p+1$ rather than as $p+s$, where s is the size of the integer type (usually equal to 4). Such translation immediately prevents many common combinations of pointer casts and arithmetic, including the uses of the $\mathtt{container\_of}$ macro. To see this, it is enough to consider two pointers: $\mathtt{p\ +\ 1}$ and $\mathtt{((char\ *)p)\ +\ 1}$, where p has type $\mathtt{int\ *}$ and points to the beginning of an allocated memory block. In the byte-level block memory model with size-proportional offsets, these pointers would have the same representation $(l, 1)$, while their actual addresses cannot be equal (they should differ at least by 1, usually by 3). This contradicts the functional consistency of the function $\mathtt{address}$. To circumvent this contradiction (and for other reasons, see [10, 12]) current JESSIE implementation makes use of two separate techniques. First, it introduces *tag tables* tracking the precise dynamic types of the objects in the allocated memory. These tag tables allow us to introduce the necessary checks for pointer shift operations in the generated safety VCs (more on this in [12, 13]). Second, it implements a number of *normalizing* code transformations that rewrite nested structures and addressed fields of simple types into pointers to separately allocated structures or values of the corresponding type (the transformations are described in [10]). This allows us to express the addresses of nested objects in the JESSIE memory model. However, a combination of these two approaches results in a number of significant restrictions. In particular, unions containing nested structures as their members cannot be soundly represented by the model. This is because that it is impossible to approximate statically whether a pointer to a structure obtained, say, as a function parameter is actually a pointer to a structure nested in some union and so writing to a field of this structure should be translated into a *strong coercion* [12] of the corresponding outer union possibly invalidating other representations of the underlying memory and updating the tag table.

To address these and some other limitations of the current JESSIE memory model, a new model was proposed in [4]. This model, though, suggests simple byte-level modeling of pointers. Since we usually assume an arbitrary memory allocation strategy, this should not lead to missed C standard violations due to the dereferencing of valid pointers in different memory blocks in practice. This is because usually in such cases at least one of the possible arbitrary allocation strategies leads to the dereference of an invalid pointer and thus it is impossible to spuriously prove that such a dereference is safe. However, the memory model suggested in [4] is not yet implemented in the tool. So in this study, we used the current implementation of the JESSIE memory model as-is.

The only change we made to the tool concerns the translation of pointer inequalities. Since the current implementation does not provide enough support for arbitrary pointer comparisons, we restricted pointer inequalities to support only pointers in the same memory block by generating the corresponding VCs and changing the translation of the corresponding predicates of the form $p_1 \Diamond p_2$ into $\mathtt{sub\_pointer}(p_1, p_2) \Diamond 0 \land \mathtt{same\_block}(p_1, p_2)$ (here $\Diamond \in \{>, <, =, \leq, \geq, \neq\}$). This made many specifications slightly shorter as the pervasive condition $\mathtt{same\_block}(p_1, p_2)$ was made implicit.

5.2 Jessie Integer Models, Composite Integer Model and Modulo Arithmetic Annotations

JESSIE originally implements three logical models for machine integer types of different size and signedness. The simplest model called `math` (or *unbounded*) unconditionally encodes values of all integer types as mathematical integers. It does not support overflow checks and does not model the wrap-around behavior of machine integers. It in principle allows the modelling of some bitwise operations on unbounded integers with an appropriate axiomatization, but in practice such modeling is usually very inefficient. Another, most commonly used integer model is called `defensive` (or *bounded*) and differs from the `math` model in two ways:

- for integer operations in code it generates appropriate VCs preventing arithmetic overflows;
- bounded integral types in *logic* (i. e., in specifications) are modeled by abstract types with special injection/projection functions (e. g., `int32_of_-integer`/`integer_of_int32`), thus only allowing the injection of values fitting the destination type.

The `defensive` model is simple and efficient and is suitable for most cases except when precise modeling of machine arithmetic or bitwise operations is needed. For these purposes JESSIE implements `modulo` integer model, which precisely models values of integral types as bitvectors.

Unfortunately, the integer model in JESSIE can only be chosen once for the entire program analyzed using the corresponding pragma. In practice, however, it is desirable to be able to choose the appropriate integer model on a very fine-grained basis, down to every arithmetic operation. Consider the following example:

```
 1 int strncasecmp(const char *s1, const char *s2, size_t len) {
 2   unsigned char c1, c2;
 3   if (!len) return 0;
 4   do {
 5     c1 = *s1++;
 6     c2 = *s2++;
 7     if (!c1 || !c2) break;
 8     if (c1 == c2) continue;
 9     c1 = tolower(c1);
10     c2 = tolower(c2);
11     if (c1 != c2) break;
12   } while (--len);
13   return (int)c1 - (int)c2;
14 }
```

Listing 3. From Linux 4.12, `lib/string.c`

Here in lines 5 and 6 the `modulo` integer model would be suitable as the cast from `char` to `unsigned char` may overflow and this is in line with the intention of the programmer. However we would also like a potential overflow to be detected if we accidentally change the return type of the function to `char`. So the `defensive` integer model is suitable to model the subtraction in line 13.

To support such fine-grained integer model selection, we implemented an extension to the ACSL specification language with *modulo arithmetic annotations*. The following new modulo arithmetic annotations were introduced:

- for arithmetic operations: `+/*@%*/`, `-/*@%*/`, `*/*@%*/`, ...
- for compound assignments: `+=/*@%*/`, `-=/*@%*/`, `/=/*@%*/`, ...
- for prefix and postfix operators: `++/*@%*/`, `--/*@%*/`
- for explicit casts: `(unsigned char)/*@%*/`, ...
- for modulo arithmetic in logic: `+%`, `-%`, `*%`, ...

The integer model used to model both `defensive` (the default) and `modulo` arithmetic operations is a combined one. In this model, bounded integers are modeled as bitvectors with two injection/projection functions to/from the mathematical unbounded integers.

Let's illustrate the encoding employed by the model on a sample arithmetic operation +, a bitwise operation &, a relation <, and a sample bounded integer type `bint` (with injection function `to_int`). The operation + *in logic* is encoded simply as integer addition and has type $int \times int \rightarrow int$. The operation +% *in logic* is encoded as bitvector addition and has type $bint \times bint \rightarrow bint$. It is also augmented with axioms relating the operation to +, e.g., $\forall a, b : bint.$ `in_bounds`$\big($`to_int`$(a) +$ `to_int`$(b)\big) \implies$ `to_int`$(a +\% b) =$ `to_int`$(a) +$ `to_int`(b). The operation & *in logic* is encoded as bitwise conjunction with the same type as +%. The relation < *in logic* is encoded as either bitwise or integer relation depending on the type of arguments. The bitwise relations is augmented with an axiom relating it to the integer one. The operation $a + b$ *in code* is encoded as an abstract operation (`val` in WHY3ML) on bitvectors with precondition requiring `in_bounds`$($`to_int`$(a) +$ `to_int`$(b))$ end ensuring two postconditions: `result` $= a +\% b$ and `to_int`$($`result`$) =$ `to_int`$(a) +$ `to_int`(b). The operation $a +/*@%*/ b$ *in code* is also encoded as an abstract operation with no precondition and two postconditions: `result` $= a +\% b$ and `to_int`$($`result`$) =$

norm(to_int(a) + to_int(b)), where norm stands for an expression for range normalization involving axiomatization of modulo arithmetic. The operation & *in code* is an abstract operation with a straightforward postcondition `result = a & b`. Finally, the predicate < *in code* is an abstract operation with two postconditions `result` $\iff$ $a < b$ and `result` $\iff$ to_int(a) < to_int(b). Other operations are represented similarly.

This encoding enables construction of more expressive and predictable models while avoiding direct use of any interpretation for function to_int, which usually can't be efficiently handled by the solvers. On the other hand, the use of quantified axioms significantly reduces both predictability and performance of the solvers. This can be potentially addressed by either adding some preliminary instantiation step or implementing similar support for the necessary operations as an SMT theory directly in the solver (by converting axioms into inference rules of the theory).

Lastly, let's demonstrate some practical capabilities of this integer model, even in the naive implementation, with an example proof of a bit-twiddling trick for computing average of two unsigned integers:

```
1 //@ ensures \result ≡ (a + b) / 2;
2 unsigned average(unsigned a, unsigned b)
3 {
4    /*@ ghost unsigned long long result1 =
5       (a ^ b) + ((unsigned long long) (a & b) << 1ULL); */
6    /*@ ghost unsigned long long result2 =
7       (unsigned long long) a + b; */
8    //@ assert result1 ≡ result2;
9    return (a & b) + ((a ^ b) >> 1U);
10 }
```

Here the expressions in the ghost code trigger succinct instantiation of necessary lemmas relating bitwise and integer interpretations of bounded integers (through the double post-conditions of the corresponding WHY3 operations).

The use of such a combined model and the introduction of new fine-grained modulo arithmetic annotations allowed us to significantly simplify the specification and verification of many functions included in this study.

6   Formal Specifications

We were guided by several techniques in the development of specifications: the use of excessive specifications (explicit specifications and specifications that establish the correspondence with a logical function), the development of specifications based on source code, and the context of function calls.

The results described in [6] show that the development of a function contract, based exclusively on documentation is difficult: almost always, at the proof stage we have to rewrite the specification based on the source code. This approach is also explained by the fact that in this work we develop specifications on the complete code. Linux code is not written in accordance with a certain set of formal specifications. Also, the kernel does not have documentation for a lot of functions. We intentionally did not follow the standard documentation (man pages) for such functions, since their implementation in the kernel can differ from the others (for example, from implementation in the standard library), and the documentation is incomplete and may contain inaccuracies [6].

```
1 /*@ predicate valid_strn(char *s, size_t cnt) =
2     ( ∃size_t n; n<cnt ∧ s[n] ≡ '\0' ∧ \valid(s+(0..n)) ) ∨
3       \valid(s+(0..cnt));
4     requires valid_strn(s, cnt);
5     assigns \nothing;
6     ensures \result ≡ strnlen(s, cnt);
7     behavior null_byte:
8       assumes ∃Z i; 0≤i≤cnt ∧ s[i] ≡ '\0';
9       ensures s[\result] ≡ '\0';
10      ensures ∀Z i; 0≤i<\result ⇒ s[i] ≢ '\0';
11    behavior cnt_len:
12      assumes ∀Z i; 0≤i≤cnt ⇒ s[i] ≢ '\0';
13      ensures \result ≡ cnt;
14    complete behaviors; disjoint behaviors;*/
15 size_t strnlen(const char *s, size_t cnt);
```

Listing 4. strnlen contract

Following this approach, the specifications for some functions have a slightly more detailed view. For example, for strn* functions (see Listings 4 and 5) we do not require the presence of the string's end marker. In the strnlen's precondition (see Listing 4), it is assumed that the string should be valid until the minimum of the string's length (if there is one) and the second argument of the function strnlen. The return value is explicitly specified in the postcondition. In the strncmp case (see Listing 5), there are also no restrictions on the fact that the input strings must contain a zero byte. This leads to the point where it is necessary to explicitly describe the behavior of the function when the input strings with end markers differ in length. We tried to maximally weaken the preconditions and strengthen the postcondition in order to test the instruments of deductive verification, the expressiveness of the ACSL language, and the capabilities of solvers.

```
1 /*@ requires valid_strn(cs, cnt) ∧ valid_strn(ct, cnt);
2      assigns \nothing;
3      ensures \result ≡ −1 ∨ \result ≡ 0 ∨ \result ≡ 1;
4      behavior equal:
5        assumes cnt ≡ 0 ∨ (cnt > 0 ∧
6          ( ∀Z i; 0≤i<strnlen(cs,cnt) ⇒ (cs[i] ≡ ct[i])) ∧
7          strnlen(cs, cnt) ≡ strnlen(ct, cnt));
8        ensures \result ≡ 0;
9      behavior len_diff:
10       assumes cnt > 0;
11       assumes ∀Z i; 0≤i<min(strnlen(cs,cnt),strnlen(ct,cnt))
12                 ⇒ cs[i] ≡ ct[i];
13       assumes strnlen(cs, cnt) ≢ strnlen(ct, cnt);
14       ensures strnlen(cs,cnt)<strnlen(ct,cnt) ⇒ \result ≡ −1;
15       ensures strnlen(cs,cnt)>strnlen(ct,cnt) ⇒ \result ≡ 1;
16     behavior not_equal:
17       assumes cnt > 0;
18       assumes ∃Z i; 0≤i<strnlen(cs, cnt) ∧ cs[i] != ct[i];
19       ensures ∃Z i; 0≤i<strnlen(cs, cnt) ∧
20         ( ∀Z j; 0≤j<i ⇒ cs[j] ≡ ct[j] ) ∧
21         cs[i] ≢ ct[i] ∧
22         ((u8 %)cs[i]<(u8 %)ct[i]? \result ≡ −1: \result ≡ 1);
23     complete behaviors; disjoint behaviors;*/
24 int strncmp(const char *cs, const char *ct, size_t cnt);
```

Listing 5. strncmp contract

6.1   Logic Functions

The specifications are redundant for some functions. In fact, they describe a function's behavior in two different ways. For example, strlen specification consists of the usual functional requirements and the requirement for the correspondence between the returned value and the logical function. This approach is motivated by the fact that the logic function strlen is convenient to use in specifications of other functions, e. g., strcmp (and a logical function that describes the behavior of the function strcmp—when describing the functional requirements for strcpy). All the basic properties of logic functions are specified by means of axioms and lemmas. The lemmas were not proved at the first stage presented in this paper only contradiction checks were performed[2]. However, such specifications do not suit all situations. For example, in the general case, they cannot be translated by E-ACSL [18] as executable specifications. Therefore, for functions with an associated logical function, the "usual" specifications were also developed.

A logical function can be associated with a C function (one-to-one) only if the last one is "pure". A logical function is useful for developing specifications of other C-functions. For example, in postconditions of memcpy, you can express the equality of src and dest by calling the memcmp logical function.

---

[2] Since then we proved all the lemmas using techniques of auto-active verification [14, 15], in particular, *lemma functions* [16]. This work is available at [17].

7   Open Issues

At the specification level, the authors faced many problems related to significant inaccuracies in the modeling of pointer operations, as well as the insufficient level of ACSL language support by the tools.

Thus, for the `memmove` function, there is the VC, which states that the `dest` and `src` pointers should lie in the same allocated memory block. This is necessary in order for the result of their comparison to be determined by the standard [11]. Recall how the `memmove` function works: it copies a memory area of n bytes from the `src` address to `dst`, provided that the two memory regions can either overlap or be disjoint. To implement the latter condition, the function performs an ordinal comparison of the `dest` and `src`. In that case, if `dest` is located before `src` the byte-by-byte copy from the beginning of `src` is performed (thus, if the regions overlap, already copied part will be overwritten); if `dest` is located after `src`, then copying is performed starting at the end of the `src` memory region.

The memory model implemented in AstraVer plugin allows arithmetic operations on pointers (in `memmove` this is a comparison implemented through the difference between pointers) only when the pointers belong to the same allocated memory block. For `memmove`, this is not necessarily the case. If we state in the specification contract that `src` and `dest` may belong to different allocated memory blocks, then it is impossible to prove the VC that states that they should belong to the same memory block. The unproved VC is reflected in the results (Table 1). Although comparison of pointers to different memory blocks is the undefined behavior in ACSI C, the comparison can be made defined by casting the pointers to the corresponding underlying integral type. Yet adding such casts is in odds with the goal of the presented work (verifying the functions without modifications) and also not currently supported by the AstraVer plugin.

The `strcat` function concatenates two strings by appending the `src` to the `dest`. To do this, the end of the `dest` string is determined first. Then the `src` string is copied in the same way as in `strcpy`. In order to prove the VCs that state the safety of memory operations in this function, it was enough to require the validity of the strings `src` and `dest` and sufficient memory behind the end of `dest` to accommodate the contents of `src`. However, proving the functional correctness of the implementation, it was revealed that it is necessary to formulate an additional requirement stating that the sum of the string's lengths fits the `size_t` type. The function is implemented through the pointers iteration. Therefore, the ability to prove the memory operation safety without the last requirement in the function means that the `AstraVer` memory model does not take into account the possibility of pointer overflow.

It was required to change the code of two functions to prove their correctness. Despite the fact that we want to minimize code changes, in two cases we cannot fully prove correctness without code modification. The functions `memset` and `strcmp` use the implicit type cast with overflow. `memset` casts `int` to `char`, and `strcmp` casts implicitly `char` to `unsigned char`. To mark these overflows as intentional it was required to make the casts explicit. Our ACSL extension with modulo arithmetic annotations still lacks the corresponding construction (e.g., `/*@(unsigned int %)*/`) for implicit casts.

At the specification level, tools do not support the use of predicates in definitions of logical functions or predicates as first arguments of the ternary operator in lemmas and axioms. Because of this, it is sometimes difficult to give an explicit definition of a logical function, and we have to use an axiomatic (implicit) definition. This drawback prevents the explicit definition of the logical functions for `skip_spaces`, `strcspn`, `strpbrk`, and `strspn`.

Functions from the file `ctype.h` (`isspace`, `isdigit`, `isalnum`, `isgraph`, `islower`, ...) are defined as macros that operate on the array `_ctype` of 256 bytes, which specifies the belonging of each character to a particular class. To simplify the verification task, these macros have been replaced by inline functions: verification tools do not allow the writing of specifications for macros, only for functions. The `_ctype` array was redefined as a string (string initialization is translated into model axioms) because the global array initialization is not translated into the WhyML model. However, it was not possible to prove the correspondence of functions from the `ctype.h` file to their specifications even after the described transformations: solvers cannot cope with the proof when the model has an axiomatic definition of the `_ctype` array 256 characters long.

8   Evaluation of Solvers

ASTRAVER translates FRAMA-C's internal representation into the program model in WhyML [19], based on the memory model and semantics of operations with integers. The WHY3 tool generates VCs for a WhyML program and converts them into an input for solvers. WHY3 supports a number of solvers, such as ALT-ERGO, CVC3, CVC4, Z3, SPASS, EPROVER, SIMPLIFY and others. WHY3 also supports transformations of VCs, for example, splitting conjunctions into separate conditions.

ALT-ERGO (1.30) and CVC4 (1.4) SMT solvers are able to discharge all VCs generated (except for the one for `memmove`). However, it is interesting to evaluate other solvers on the given benchmark. For that purpose we conduct an experiment using the following system configuration: CPU—AMD FX-8120 (Eight-Core Processor), RAM—16 GB, time limit—60 s, memory limit—6000 MB, OS—GNU/Linux (kernel: 4.12.12 (smp preempt) x86_64), software (from ASTRAVER repository): WHY3 (0.87.3+git), FRAMA-C (Silicon-20161101), JESSIE2 (alpha3).

8.1   VC Transformation Strategy

To put all solvers in similar conditions all VCs were transformed by WHY3 using the following strategy:

1. Split goal by conjuncts (`split_goal_wp`) repeatedly until fixed point.
2. Inline definition of all logical symbols (`inline_all`).
3. Split goal by conjuncts (`split_goal_wp`) repeatedly until fixed point.
4. Skolemize goal (`introduce_premises`).

If there are many predicates with long dependency chains, the `inline_all` transformation makes the work of the solvers more difficult. This is not the case for the given benchmark and experiments have shown the positive impact of this transformation. The addition of `introduce_premises` transformation also comes from preliminary experiments demonstrating that solvers work better with formulas of the form $f(x) \wedge \neg g(x)$ than with ones of the form $\neg \forall x.\ f(x) \implies g(x)$. Otherwise, the strategy tries to split the VC into the smallest possible conjuncts.

During the development of specifications, the strategy is not applied by default. Only some of the transformations are applied if solvers fail to discharge VCs by themselves.

8.2   Statistics

Table 1 presents the results of the evaluation. The first column contains the target function name the second one includes the number of VCs generated (safety and behavioral) after application of the transformation strategy. The rest of the table presents solver statistics: the amount of discharged VCs and the average time for successful runs.

The symbol ✓ marks cases when a solver proved all VCs for the corresponding function. Maximal numbers of discharged VCs are highlighted in green . Minimal VC counts are highlighted by red . The minimal average time is highlighted in cyan , the maximal average time is highlighted in brown .

8.3   Discussion

All VCs except one for `memmove` are successfully discharged by at least one of the solvers. The best result was achieved by ALT-ERGO and CVC4. This is expected as those solvers were most extensively used during the development and testing of the toolset.

CVC4 1.5 discharged the greatest number of VCs, while Z3 required the smallest amount of time. This can be partially explained by the fact that we counted only successful proof attempts. Z3 was able to prove fewer VCs than ALT-ERGO or CVC4.

Table 2 presents maximal solving times for successful proof attempts and counts of unique proofs, i.e., VCs that were only discharged by one of the solvers.

Table 1. Solvers. Proofs statistics (times are given in seconds)

Function	VC	Alt-Ergo 1.30		CVC3 2.4.1		CVC4 1.4		CVC4 1.5		Eprover 1.9.1-001		Spass 3.9		Z3 4.5.0	
	total	vc	atime	vc	atime	vc	atime	vc	atime	vc	atime	vc	atime	vc	atime
_parse_integ.	282	276	0.10	280	0.83	✓	0.18	✓	0.10	212	0.24	197	1.69	279	0.06
check_bytes8	50	49	0.55	49	0.09	49	0.09	✓	0.11	38	1.76	31	8.38	36	1.52
kstrtobool	1096	✓	0.05	✓	0.08	✓	0.10	✓	0.09	1006	0.13	937	0.38	1065	0.15
memchr	39	✓	6.05	11	0.22	✓	0.37	✓	0.15	31	2.58	11	5.73	29	0.12
memcmp	60	58	0.13	✓	0.15	58	0.10	✓	0.10	49	0.51	36	4.45	55	0.15
memcpy	43	✓	4.18	✓	0.35	✓	0.16	✓	0.14	30	1.05	16	6.85	30	0.06
memmove	93*(92)	90	3.94	✓	0.88	87	0.16	✓	0.18	63	0.95	43	11.87	68	0.30
memscan	47	46	0.07	✓	0.10	✓	0.09	✓	0.09	41	0.59	34	4.55	42	0.06
memset	27	26	5.02	14	0.19	✓	0.19	✓	0.16	19	3.82	12	11.12	18	0.08
skip_spaces	34	30	0.76	32	1.96	✓	0.51	33	0.14	27	0.70	24	0.34	30	0.09
strcasecmp	58	50	0.43	52	1.65	57	0.79	✓	0.53	43	0.28	35	2.85	49	0.49
strcat	73	68	0.58	66	2.16	✓	1.13	71	0.17	54	2.56	39	0.67	60	0.94
strchr	43	35	4.57	23	0.17	✓	0.23	✓	0.22	31	1.03	24	3.65	32	0.11
strchrnul	46	42	2.07	37	0.26	✓	0.19	✓	0.16	40	1.91	31	2.27	39	0.31
strcmp	60	51	1.76	16	0.60	✓	1.75	59	1.08	47	1.05	36	1.65	47	0.10
strcpy	46	43	1.33	45	0.66	✓	0.48	✓	0.17	33	1.13	26	0.65	39	1.43
strcspn	78	68	0.38	69	0.37	74	2.95	75	1.82	58	1.85	46	1.68	61	0.11
strlcpy	84	82	0.15	82	0.14	✓	1.08	✓	0.24	67	1.20	52	1.74	78	0.42
strlen	26	✓	1.12	24	0.12	✓	0.16	✓	0.23	19	3.36	14	2.96	21	0.08
strnchr	49	38	4.44	19	0.23	46	3.34	✓	0.72	35	2.57	24	1.56	27	0.09
strncmp	102	81	2.57	25	0.25	94	2.39	99	2.32	76	1.06	55	2.56	76	0.57
strnlen	44	39	1.91	42	1.04	39	1.23	✓	1.31	31	2.40	26	5.52	32	0.08
strpbrk	70	57	0.64	58	1.54	62	3.18	67	1.57	48	1.89	39	0.75	53	0.09
strrchr	62	53	4.57	12	0.17	✓	1.09	60	0.85	46	2.33	31	4.67	46	0.11
strsep	62	60	0.25	60	0.09	✓	0.19	✓	0.15	55	0.12	51	1.48	58	0.06
strspn	107	99	0.84	100	0.69	104	1.32	103	0.61	89	1.37	75	1.59	91	0.13
TOTAL	2781	2645	0.90	2454	0.42	2740	0.61	2761	0.37	2288	0.76	1945	1.72	2461	0.22

Table 2. Solvers. Max time and number of uniq proofs

Alt-Ergo 1.30		CVC3 2.4.1		CVC4 1.4		CVC4 1.5		Eprover 1.9.1-001		Spass 3.9		Z3 4.5.0	
mtime	uniq	mtime	uniq	mtime	uniq	mtime	uniq	mtime	uniq	mtime	uniq	mtime	uniq
58.75	1	56.68	0	57.97	7	52.27	20	47.80	0	59.74	0	26.74	0

9   Conclusion

This paper presents results from the development and evaluation of a deductive verification benchmark consisting of 26 unmodified Linux kernel library functions implementing conventional memory and string operations. Formal contracts of the functions were extracted from their source code and were represented in the form of preconditions and postconditions. The benchmark detected a number of problems with existing deductive verification toolchains. Some of the issues required only fixes in the tools, some of them led to the design of proposals to extend ACSL language, others were left open.

For example, two newly proposed ACSL constructs allowed us to successfully proof 11 more functions without modification of their source code. With these extensions, the authors have successfully and fully proved the correctness of 23 functions. Another 2 functions were proved after a minor modification of their source code, while the final one cannot be completely proved using existing memory model. Specifications of the benchmark contain $\approx$2.6 times as many lines as the source code of the library functions.

The source code of the benchmark and proof protocols are publicly available together with instructions describing how to reproduce the results [7]. The benchmark can be used for the testing and evaluation of deductive verification tools and the starting point for verifying other parts of Linux kernel. A possible next step is to extend the benchmark with other library functions (e. g., bitwise operations).

References

1. Baudin, P., et al.: ACSL: ANSI/ISO C specification language. Technical report 1.12, CEALIST and INRIA, March 2017
2. Kirchner, F., Kosmatov, N., Prevosto, V., Signoles, J., Yakobowski, B.: Frama-C: a software analysis perspective. Formal Aspects Comput. **27**(3), 573–609 (2015). https://doi.org/10.1007/s00165-014-0326-7
3. Moy, Y.: Automatic Modular Static Safety Checking for C Programs. Ph.D. thesis, Université Paris-Sud, January 2009. http://www.lri.fr/~marche/moy09phd.pdf
4. Mandrykin, M.U., Khoroshilov, A.V.: Region analysis for deductive verification of c programs. Program. Comput. Softw. **42**(5), 257–278 (2016). https://doi.org/10.1134/S0361768816050042
5. Carvalho, N., da Silva Sousa, C., Pinto, J.S., Tomb, A.: Formal verification of kLIBC with the WP frama-C Plug-in. In: Badger, J.M., Rozier, K.Y. (eds.) NFM 2014. LNCS, vol. 8430, pp. 343–358. Springer, Cham (2014). https://doi.org/10.1007/978-3-319-06200-6_29
6. Torlakcik, M.: Contracts in OpenBSD. M.sc. dissertation report, University College Dublin (2010)
7. Verker: Verification of linux kernel library functions (2017). https://forge.ispras.ru/projects/verker
8. Burghardt, J., Clausecker, R., Gerlach, J., Pohl, H.: ACSL by example. Technical report, Fraunhofer Institute for Open Communication Systems (2017)
9. Cok, D.R., Blissard, I., Robbins, J.: C library annotations in ACSL for frama-C: experience report. GrammaTech, Inc, Technical report, March 2017
10. Hubert, T., Marché, C.: Separation analysis for deductive verification. In: Heap Analysis and Verification (HAV 2007), Braga, Portugal, pp. 81–93, March 2007. http://www.lri.fr/~marche/hubert07hav.pdf
11. ISO/IEC 9899: 2011: C11 standard for C programming language. Standard, JTC and ISO (2011). http://www.open-std.org/jtc1/sc22/wg14/www/docs/n1570.pdf
12. Moy, Y.: Union and cast in deductive verification. In: Proceedings of the C/C++ Verification Workshop. Technical report ICIS-R07015, pp. 1–16. Radboud University Nijmegen, July 2007. http://www.lri.fr/~moy/Publis/moy07ccpp.pdf
13. Mandrykin, M.U., Khoroshilov, A.V.: High-level memory model with low-level pointer cast support for jessie intermediate language. Program. Comput. Softw. **41**(4), 197–207 (2015). https://doi.org/10.1134/S0361768815040040
14. Leino, K.R.M., Moskal, M.: Usable auto-active verification (2010)

15. Dross, C., Moy, Y.: Auto-active proof of red-black trees in SPARK. In: Barrett, C., Davies, M., Kahsai, T. (eds.) NFM 2017. LNCS, vol. 10227, pp. 68–83. Springer, Cham (2017). https://doi.org/10.1007/978-3-319-57288-8_5

16. Jacobs, B., Smans, J., Piessens, F.: A quick tour of the verifast program verifier. In: Ueda, K. (ed.) APLAS 2010. LNCS, vol. 6461, pp. 304–311. Springer, Heidelberg (2010). https://doi.org/10.1007/978-3-642-17164-2_21

17. Verker: Verification of linux kernel library functions, lemma functions branch (2017). https://forge.ispras.ru/projects/verker/repository?rev=lemma_functions

18. Delahaye, M., Kosmatov, N., Signoles, J.: Common specification language for static and dynamic analysis of C programs. In: Proceedings of the 28th Annual ACM Symposium on Applied Computing, SAC 2013, pp. 1230–1235. ACM, New York (2013). http://doi.acm.org/10.1145/2480362.2480593

19. Filliâtre, J.-C., Paskevich, A.: Why3—where programs meet provers. In: Felleisen, M., Gardner, P. (eds.) ESOP 2013. LNCS, vol. 7792, pp. 125–128. Springer, Heidelberg (2013). https://doi.org/10.1007/978-3-642-37036-6_8

Synthesizing Subtle Bugs
with Known Witnesses

Marc Jasper[✉] and Bernhard Steffen

TU Dortmund University, Dortmund, Germany
{marc.jasper,steffen}@cs.tu-dortmund.de

Abstract. This paper presents a new technique for the generation of verification benchmarks that are automatically guaranteed to be hard, or as we say, to contain *subtle bugs/property violations*: (i) Identifying a bug requires to match many computation steps and (ii) corresponding counterexamples are sparse among all feasible executions. Key idea is to iteratively synthesize Büchi automata for variations of a set of LTL properties and to combine these automata in a fashion that each property can be individually controlled in the resulting model: Based on our notion of a *counterexample handle*, it is possible to switch the satisfaction of a given property on and off without affecting that of the other considered properties. This *orthogonality* of our treatment of counterexamples is vital for the subsequent parts of the benchmark generation process. Together with the mentioned hardness, it helps to overcome the undesired clustering of counterexamples observed during previous iterations of the RERS Challenge. Even more importantly, these handles and associated counterexamples are sufficient to automatically generate the modal contracts required for the parallel decomposition process that allows us to generate parallel verification benchmarks of arbitrary size, for example in form of a Petri net or in Promela.

Keywords: Benchmark generation · Program verification
Model checking · Error witnesses · Temporal logic · LTL synthesis
Büchi automata · Modal transition systems · Modal contracts

1 Introduction

Formal program verification and other systematic validation techniques are crucial for the development of safety-critical systems [20,30]. However, finding the best fitting tools for a given applications scenario is quite a challenge, in particular when it comes to validating validation tools themselves. Numerous verification competitions and challenges have been established to advance the field, classify corresponding tools, and validate the application profile of these tools.

Popular events include the Software Verification Competition (SV-COMP) [4], the Rigorous Examination of Reactive Systems (RERS) Challenge [11], the Model Checking Contest (MCC) [17], VerifyThis [12], and the Runtime Verification Competition (RV) [2]. The tasks and rules vary

© Springer Nature Switzerland AG 2018
T. Margaria and B. Steffen (Eds.): ISoLA 2018, LNCS 11245, pp. 235–257, 2018.
https://doi.org/10.1007/978-3-030-03421-4_16

among these events, in particular concerning the considered input data, in this case benchmark programs/problems to be analyzed or verified: SV-COMP for instance is mostly concerned with C programs whereas MCC covers Petri nets [22]. For both competitions, a committee selects the used benchmark scenarios (verification tasks) and many of them are reused during successive competitions. Within MCC, not all solutions are known by the challenge organizers and an evaluation is then based on a majority voting.

In contrast, the RERS Challenge features automatically generated benchmark scenarios such that the solutions are always known to the challenge organizer based on property-preserving transformations [28]. RERS covers (reactive) transition systems that strongly resemble PLC controllers, a type of program that is frequently used in industry [7] and for which verification approaches have been widely studied [10,14,21,25]. RERS provides reactive systems in various languages such as C, Java, Promela, and Petri nets. Since 2016, RERS also features benchmark scenarios concerned with parallel programs [9]. Multiple approaches to automatically generate such parallel scenarios have been conceived and some applied in practice [9,27]. Only recently, a new approach to this generation was introduced which uses modal contracts in order to guarantee formal hardness properties [29]. This hardness was empirically evaluated [26] and the approach successfully used for RERS 2017 [13].

This paper presents a new technique for benchmark generation that automatically guarantees benchmark hardness in the sense that minimal counterexamples explaining property violations are extremely rare, deep[1], and maintained throughout the benchmark generation process. Some bugs in real-world systems are subtle in this manner—especially when considering parallel programs—as shown by the August 2003 blackout in the northeastern US that was in part triggered by a race condition and cost several billion US dollars [32].[2] Being able to synthesize verification benchmarks with subtle property violations promotes the development of tools that can detect such subtle yet often severe bugs.

In addition, the fact that we maintain counterexamples during our generation technique allows us to (i) check whether or not a witness that was reported by a tool is an actual counterexample and (ii) output exemplary traces that violate a given property. Checking proposed counterexamples allows to validate tools even further [5] and gives tool developers valuable feedback in case spurious error traces are reported. Generating witnesses for a property violation also fosters the development of tools by providing information on critical parts of a program that were not examined in sufficient detail. The remainder of this paper shows how one witness for a violated property can be maintained.

Our approach elaborates on the technique presented in [28] by iteratively synthesizing[3] and combining Büchi automata [3] for variations of a set of properties

---

[1] An execution is *deep* if it requires the observation of many computation steps.

[2] According to a news article (https://www.securityfocus.com/news/8016), a spokesman of an involved company said: "This fault was so deeply embedded, it took them weeks of poring through millions of lines of code and data to find it".

[3] We are using LTL2BA [8] and SPOT [6] for this part of the generation process.

in a fashion that each property can be individually controlled in the final Büchi automaton, as well as in all subsequently considered model types (modal transition systems [18], labeled transition systems [23], and Mealy machines [19]): Based on our notion of a *counterexample handle*, it is possible to switch the satisfaction of a given property on and off without affecting that of the other considered properties.

This *orthogonality* of our treatment of counterexamples is vital for the subsequent parts of the benchmark generation process where the models are refined and put in context. For example, our technique helps to overcome a problem observed within the sequential programs of recent RERS iterations: Counterexamples arose typically in big clusters—sometimes a single trace was sufficient to show the violation of multiple properties that were used for the benchmark scenario. Even stronger is the impact of orthogonality on the generation of parallel benchmarks: The handles and associated counterexamples are sufficient to automatically transform the generated modal transition systems into corresponding modal contracts, which are themselves sufficient to start the parallel decomposition process presented in [29].

2   Preliminaries

This section covers Büchi automata, linear temporal logic, and the relationship between the two. We start by defining a Büchi automaton [3] with a unique start state:

Definition 1 (Büchi Automaton). *Let* $B = (S, \Sigma, \Delta, s_0, F)$ *be a finite automaton with a set S of states and an alphabet Σ. $s_0 \in S$ is an initial state and $F \subseteq S$ a set of accepting states. The relation $\Delta \subseteq (S \times \Sigma \times S)$ represents transitions between states in S. We also write $p \xrightarrow{\sigma} q$ to denote $(p, \sigma, q) \in \Delta$.*

*A **path** p in B is a sequence of transitions $u_i \xrightarrow{\sigma_i} u_{i+1}$ with i ranging from 1 to either a fixed integer n or infinity. Path p **spells** the word $w = \sigma_1 \sigma_2 \ldots$.*

*Then B is called a **Büchi automaton (BA)** if it adheres to Büchi acceptance, meaning that it accepts infinite words $w \in \Sigma^\omega$ based on the following criteria:*

1. *There exists a path p in B that starts in s_0 and that spells w*
2. *This path p visits a state in F infinitely often*

*The set $\mathcal{L}(B) := \{w \in \Sigma^\omega \mid B \text{ accepts } w\}$ defines the **language** of B.*

A finite path p is written as $p = (s_1 \xrightarrow{\sigma_1} s_2 \xrightarrow{\sigma_2} \ldots \xrightarrow{\sigma_n} s_{n+1})$. Considering infinite paths, we are only interested in eventually periodic paths that we denote as $p = (s_1 \xrightarrow{\sigma_1} \ldots \xrightarrow{\sigma_{i-1}} s_i (\xrightarrow{\sigma_i} \ldots \xrightarrow{\sigma_n} s_{n+1})^\omega)$.

The following definitions specify (propositional) linear temporal logic (LTL). In essence, LTL is an extension of propositional logic that includes additional temporal operators. Its syntax is defined as follows [1]:

Definition 2 (Syntax of Propositional Linear Temporal Logic (LTL)).
*Let AP be a set of atomic propositions and $a \in AP$. The **syntax of propositional LTL** is defined using the following Backus-Naur form:*

$$\phi ::= \top \mid a \mid \phi \wedge \phi \mid \neg\phi \mid \mathbf{X}\, \phi \mid (\phi\, \mathbf{U}\, \phi)$$

***LTL** is the set of formulas ϕ that can be constructed this way.*

The operator $\mathbf{X}$ (or "next") describes behavior that has to hold at the next
time step. A formula $(\phi_1\, \mathbf{U}\, \phi_2)$ describes that ϕ_2 has to occur eventually and
that ϕ_1 has to hold until ϕ_2 occurs in a sequence. The semantics of LTL is based
on a satisfaction relation between infinite words and LTL formulas [1]:

Definition 3 (Satisfaction Relation Between Words and LTL). *Let AP
be an alphabet of atomic propositions and let $(2^{AP})^\omega$ denote infinite sequences
over sets $A \in 2^{AP}$. For any sequence $w = (A_1, A_2, ...) \in (2^{AP})^\omega$ and any $i \in \mathbb{N}$,
let $w_i = A_i$ be the i-th element of w and $w^i = (A_i, A_{i+1}, ...)$ be the suffix of w
starting at index i.*
*The **satisfaction relation** $\models\, \subseteq ((2^{AP})^\omega \times LTL)$ is defined as the minimal
relation that adheres to the following rules for any $w \in (2^{AP})^\omega$ and any $\phi, \psi \in
LTL$:*

1. $w \models \top$
2. $w \models a$ *iff* $a \in w_1$
3. $w \models (\phi \wedge \psi)$ *iff* $w \models \phi$ *and* $w \models \psi$
4. $w \models \neg\phi$ *iff* $w \not\models \phi$
5. $w \models \mathbf{X}\, \phi$ *iff* $w^1 \models \phi$
6. $w \models (\phi\, \mathbf{U}\, \psi)$ *iff* $\exists k \in \mathbb{N} : w^k \models \psi$ *and* $\forall i \in \mathbb{N}_{<k} : w^i \models \phi$

Definition 4 (Semantics of LTL). *Let ϕ be an LTL property over AP. The
semantics of ϕ is denoted as $[\![\phi]\!]$ and defined as follows:*

$$[\![\phi]\!] := \{w \in (2^{AP})^\omega \mid w \models \phi\}$$

Using the basic set of operators in Definition 2, abbreviations for commonly
described constraints can be introduced. Popular ones include $\mathbf{F}(\phi) := (\top\, \mathbf{U}\, \phi)$
which expresses that ϕ will eventually become true and its dual operator
$\mathbf{G}(\phi) := \neg\mathbf{F}(\neg\phi)$ which claims that ϕ is always true. A later example also utilizes the release operator $(\phi\, \mathbf{R}\, \psi) := \neg(\neg\phi\, \mathbf{U}\, \neg\psi)$ which is the dual of the until
operator and states that ψ has to be true until and including the point where ϕ
first becomes true, or that ψ remains true indefinitely.
We can now define a satisfaction relation between Büchi automata and LTL:

Definition 5 (Satisfaction Relation Between BAs and LTL). *Let AP be an alphabet of atomic propositions and $B = (S, 2^{AP}, \Delta, s_0, F)$ a Büchi automaton. Let ϕ be any LTL formula over AP. Then the following holds:*

$$B \models \phi \text{ iff } \forall w \in \mathcal{L}(B) : w \models \phi$$

Büchi automata are strictly more expressive than LTL [31]. One can synthesize a Büchi automaton B from an LTL property ϕ such that $\mathcal{L}(B) = \llbracket \phi \rrbracket$ holds [24].

3   Synthesizing Büchi Automata with Subtle and Controllable LTL Counterexamples

Within this section, we present the main synthesis procedure that our approach is based on. Our aim is to generate a Büchi automaton (BA) B based on a set of LTL properties Φ with subtle and controllable counterexamples for properties in $\{\phi \in \Phi \mid B \not\models \phi\}$.

3.1   General Definitions

In order to simplify the presentation within this paper, we introduce the following three definitions that help to constrain BAs.

Definition 6 (Junk-Free Büchi Automata). *A BA B is called a **junk-free BA** iff every state in B lies on an accepted path.*

Any BA can be transformed into a junk-free BA based on a simple pruning procedure. The following definition will be relevant in Sect. 4:

Definition 7 (Reducibility of Non-accepting Simple Cycles). *A simple cycle[4] that solely consists of non-accepting states is called a **non-accepting simple cycle.***

*Let B be a BA. Let O be any simple cycle in B. Then O is called **reducible** iff there exists only one transition $t = (p \xrightarrow{\sigma} q)$ in B with p not being a state in O and q being a state in O. A simple cycle is called **irreducible** if it is not reducible.*

Note that any irreducible simple cycle within a BA B can be altered to be reducible without changing the language of B: Such a transformation is based on a duplication of that simple cycle. This will be employed in our main algorithm.

In general, paths in a BA B that results from an LTL synthesis spell words over 2^{AP} (see Definitions 1 and 4). In order to later transform a BA into an action-based transition system, we prefer BAs where transitions are labeled with individual atomic propositions $a \in AP$ that correspond to the underlying LTL properties. We therefore define the following language filter:

---

[4] Also called elementary circuit [16]: A simple cycle is a path $s_1 \xrightarrow{\sigma_1} \dots \xrightarrow{\sigma_{n-1}} s_n \xrightarrow{\sigma_n} s_1$ such that $s_i \neq s_j$ for any $i, j \in 1..n$ with $i \neq j$.

Definition 8 (Singleton Filter). *Let AP be a set of atomic propositions and* $\mathcal{L} \subseteq 2^{(2^{AP})^{\omega}}$ *a corresponding language of infinite word. Then the **singleton filter** $\Xi : 2^{(2^{AP})^{\omega}} \to 2^{(2^{AP})^{\omega}}$ is defined as follows:*

$$\Xi(\mathcal{L}) = \{w \in \mathcal{L} \mid \forall A \in w : |A| = 1\}$$

For LTL properties, this filter can be implemented by adding an invariant Ω:

Proposition 1. *Let ϕ be any LTL property over AP. Furthermore, let*

$$\Omega = \mathbf{G} \left(\bigvee_{\sigma \in AP} \left(\sigma \wedge \left(\bigwedge_{\gamma \in AP \backslash \{\sigma\}} (\neg \gamma) \right) \right) \right).$$

Then the following holds:

$$\Xi(\llbracket \phi \rrbracket) = \llbracket \phi \wedge \Omega \rrbracket$$

As a result, we can apply a standard synthesis approach based on $\phi \wedge \Omega$ in order to generate a BA with $\mathcal{L}(B) = \Xi(\llbracket \phi \rrbracket)$ for any LTL property ϕ. Within this paper, we implicitly cast a language $\Xi(\mathcal{L}) \subseteq 2^{(2^{AP})^{\omega}}$ to the domain $2^{(AP)^{\omega}}$ because only singletons remain. We consistently apply our filter Ξ throughout this paper. Set notation within illustrations of a BA therefore represents multiple transitions with the same source and target, and *not* transitions where multiple atomic propositions are true. Note that we cannot lift this filter to a constraint on LTL properties because the technique that is presented in Sect. 3 negates those properties: For most LTL properties ϕ with $\Xi(\llbracket \phi \rrbracket) = \llbracket \phi \rrbracket$, we have that $\Xi(\llbracket \neg \phi \rrbracket) \neq \llbracket \neg \phi \rrbracket$.

3.2   Goals

Given the above definitions, we now present our synthesis approach. Given a set Φ of LTL properties, we intend to synthesize a BA B with the following features regarding each property $\phi \in \Phi$ with $B \not\models \phi$:

1. <u>Controllable:</u> All counterexamples for ϕ in B can be disabled by removing a single transition from B (*counterexample handle*) without affecting other properties of interest (*orthogonality*).
2. <u>Deep:</u> A long trace of transition symbols has to be observed in order to determine that a path in B cannot satisfy ϕ anymore.[5]
3. <u>Rare:</u> Counterexamples for ϕ are sparse among all accepted paths in B.

The second and third goal aim at hardness of the corresponding refutation task. We first introduce how we realize controllable counterexamples (first goal) before discussing the other two goals.

---

[5] This refers to the matching of computation steps in our introduction. Here, we talk about transition symbols because the BA has not been transformed to a final code model yet.

3.3   Controllable Counterexamples

The first of our three goals allows us to later toggle all counterexamples for a property ϕ based on a single transition in the BA B. This feature makes it possible to generate almost identical systems that differ regarding property ϕ and therefore to generate benchmark scenarios for model checking that contain subtle "bugs". Furthermore, this feature will be used in Sect. 5.2 by enforcing that such a counterexample handle has to synchronize with a parallel context, thus letting the satisfaction of ϕ be solely controlled by that context.

We now specify a counterexample handle formally:

Definition 9 (CE-handle). *Let B be a BA and ϕ an LTL formula such that $B \not\models \phi$. Let t be a transition in B. Then t is called a **counterexample handle** (**CE-handle**) for ϕ in B iff the removal of t in B results in $B \models \phi$.*

As stated in our first goal, we would like our CE-handles to be free of side effects, meaning that the removal of a CE-handle does not change whether or not B satisfies another LTL property that is part of the generated benchmark scenario:

Definition 10 (OCEH-map). *Let B be a BA and Φ a set of LTL formulas. Let H map each property $\phi \in \Phi$ with $B \not\models \phi$ to a CE-handle for ϕ in B.*

*Then H is called a **Φ-orthogonal-CE-handle-map** (**Φ-OCEH-map**) for B iff for any $\Psi \subseteq \{\psi \in \Phi \mid B \not\models \psi\}$, the removal of transitions $T = \{H[\psi] \mid \psi \in \Psi\}$ from B does <u>not</u> influence whether or not $B \models \phi$ holds for any $\phi \in (\Phi \setminus \Psi)$.*

In summary, our first goal is to automatically generate a BA B based on LTL properties Φ together with a Φ-OCEH map. We would further like to maintain counterexample witnesses. In order to store all corresponding information, we introduce the following data structure:

Definition 11 (OCEBA). *Let B be a BA with $\mathcal{L}(B) = \Xi(\mathcal{L}(B))$ (Definition 8). Let Φ be a set of LTL properties. Let H be a Φ-OCEH map for B. Let $\Phi_\perp := \{\phi \in \Phi \mid B \not\models \phi\}$ and let W be a map that stores a counterexample path in B for every property in $\Phi_\perp$. Then the quadruple $C = (B, \Phi, H, W)$ is called an **orthogonal counterexample Büchi automaton** (**OCEBA**).*

In the following, we describe how to generate an OCEBA $C = (B, \Phi, H, W)$ given just the set Φ of LTL properties. Our approach uses so called OCE-extensions that we introduce next. Intuitively speaking, a ϕ-OCE-extension of an OCEBA $C = (B, \Phi, H, W)$ inserts an accepting "lasso" (path that leads back to itself) into B such that the first transition of this lasso becomes a CE-handle for ϕ. In order to formally specify an OCE-extension, we first define certain prefix languages, both based on a suffix of infinite words and on a state in a BA:

Definition 12 (Prefix Languages). *Let $\mathcal{L} \subseteq \Sigma^\omega$ be a language of infinite words over Σ. Given any word $\beta \in \Sigma^\omega$, we define:*

$$pre(\beta, \mathcal{L}) := \{\alpha \in \Sigma^* \mid \alpha\beta \in \mathcal{L}\}$$

Let $B = (S, \Sigma, \Delta, s_0, F)$ be a BA. Given any state $s \in S$, we define:

$$pre(s, B) := \{\alpha \in \Sigma^* \mid \exists \text{ path } p \text{ in } B \text{ from } s_0 \text{ to } s \text{ that spells } \alpha\}$$

Additionally, we define:[6]

$$pre_s(s, B) := \{\alpha \in \Sigma^* \mid \exists \underline{\text{simple}} \text{ path } p \text{ in } B \text{ from } s_0 \text{ to } s \text{ that spells } \alpha\}$$

Using these prefix definitions, we can now specify our iterable and orthogonal extension that inserts a counterexample for property ϕ. Examples can be found in Sect. 3.5.

Definition 13 (OCE-Extension). *Let $C = (B, \Phi, H, W)$ be an OCEBA. Let AP be the alphabet of atomic propositions that occur in Φ. Let $\phi \in \Phi$ be any property with $B \models \phi$. Let $\mathcal{L}_\Phi^{\neg\phi} := \Xi([\![(\bigwedge_{\psi \in \Phi \setminus \{\phi\}} \psi) \wedge (\neg\phi)]\!])$.*

*Then the quadruple (B', Φ, H', W') is called a ϕ-**OCE-extension** of C if it can be generated as follows:*

1. *Choose any word $\alpha\sigma\beta \in \mathcal{L}_\Phi^{\neg\phi}$ with $\alpha \in (AP)^*, \sigma \in AP, \beta \in (AP)^\omega$ and any state u_0 in B such that the following hold:*
   (a) $\alpha \in pre_s(u_0, B)$
   (b) $pre(u_0, B) \subseteq pre(\sigma\beta, \mathcal{L}_\Phi^{\neg\phi})$
   (c) The reachability of u_0 does not depend on transitions in H[7]
2. *Generate B' based on B by adding a path $l = (u_0 \xrightarrow{\sigma} u_1 \xrightarrow{\beta_1} \ldots \xrightarrow{\beta_{n-1}} u_n \xrightarrow{\beta_n} u_i)$ such that*
   (a) $0 \le i \le n$ ("lasso")
   (b) At least one u_j with $max(i, 1) \le j \le n$ is accepting ("accepting lasso")
   (c) The infinite path that starts in u_0 and traverses l spells the word $\sigma\beta$
   (d) All states u_j with $j \in 1..n$ and all transitions of l did not exist in B
3. *Let h' be the first transition $(u_0 \xrightarrow{\sigma} u_1)$ in l. Let $H' = H \uplus \{(\phi, h')\}$.*
4. *Choose a simple path p' from the start state of B' to u_0. Let c' be the concatenation of paths p' and l. Let $W' = W \uplus \{(\phi, c')\}$.*

We now state the correctness of a ϕ-OCE-extension in the sense that it again results in an OCEBA and such that the satisfaction/violation of all other considered properties remains unchanged:[8]

Theorem 1 (Correctness of OCE-Extensions). *Let $C = (B, \Phi, H, W)$ be an OCEBA and let $C' = (B', \Phi, H', W')$ be a ϕ-OCE-extension of C. Then the following hold:*

1. *C' is an OCEBA*
2. *$B' \not\models \phi$*
3. *$\forall\psi \in \Phi \setminus \{\phi\} : B \models \psi \iff B' \models \psi$*

---

[6] A simple path visits each state at most once.
[7] Let B' be a modified version of BA B where all transitions $t \in \{t \mid (\psi, t) \in H\}$ have been removed. Then state u_0 is still reachable in B'.
[8] Details can be found in [15].

Algorithmically, one can synthesize a BA $B_\perp$ with $\mathcal{L}(B_\perp) = [\![\mathcal{L}_\Phi^{-\phi}]\!]$ and then identify a candidate word $\alpha\sigma\beta$ and a state u_0 by traversing B and $B_\perp$ in parallel. Those details are omitted within this paper. Note that a ϕ-OCE-extension does not always exist: Combinations of an OCEBA $C = (B, \Phi, H, W)$ and a property $\phi \in \Phi$ with $B \models \phi$ are possible such that no ϕ-OCE-extension of C exists.[9] However, we do not require such an existence because our goal is to generate verification benchmarks: We can simply choose a different set of properties for our synthesis or alter the solution of the benchmark.

The following algorithm presents a high-level description of our synthesis:

Algorithm 1. OCEBA Synthesis

Input: $\Phi_\top$: Set of LTL properties that shall be satisfied
Input: $\Phi_\perp$: Set of LTL properties that shall be violated
Output: $C = (B, (\Phi_\top \uplus \Phi_\perp), H, W)$: Resulting OCEBA

1   $\Phi \leftarrow \Phi_\top \uplus \Phi_\perp$;
2   $B \leftarrow$ any BA with $\mathcal{L}(B) = \Xi([\![\bigwedge_{\phi \in \Phi} \phi]\!])$ (Definition 8) ;
3   Remove junk in B (Definition 6) ;
4   $C \leftarrow (B, \Phi, \emptyset, \emptyset)$;
5   **foreach** $\psi \in \Phi_\perp$ **do**
6   **if** *a ψ-OCE-extension of C exists* **then**
7       $C \leftarrow \psi$-OCE-extension of C ;
8   **foreach** *irreducible non-accepting simple cycle O (Definition 7) in B that the newly added counterexample witness traverses* **do**
9   Transform O to be reducible while maintaining the language of B (based on duplications of O) ;
10   **end**
11   **else**
12   **return** "No insertable counterexample exists for property ψ." ;
13   **end**
14   **end**
15   **return** C ;

The transformation within lines 8 and 9 of Algorithm 1 is applied in order to later remove the Büchi acceptance condition from B (see Sect. 4). This transformation is implemented using simple node splitting. Given our generation of OCEBAs and therefore controllable counterexamples (Algorithm 1), we now briefly discuss our other two goals.

---

[9] For example, semantic interference between properties in Φ can be the reason why no ϕ-OCE-extension exists: If ϕ is implied by the formula $\bigwedge_{\psi \in \Psi} \psi$ with $\Psi \subseteq \{\psi \in \Phi \mid B \models \psi \wedge \psi \neq \phi\}$, then the language $\mathcal{L}_\Phi^{-\phi}$ has to be empty.

3.4 Deep and Rare Counterexamples

As mentioned earlier, our second goal is to construct deep counterexamples that require the observation of a long trace of symbols in order to be detected.[10] We achieve this goal by choosing a state u_0 for a ϕ-OCE-extension (Definition 13) that has a certain minimum depth from the start state of the corresponding BA B. Because $B \models \phi$ holds and because of Definition 6, we know that $B' \not\models \phi$ will remain a possibility when state u_0 is reached during an exploration from the source of the extended BA B'. As a result, the transition handle stored as part of the ϕ-OCE-extension is the first transition that could reveal a path which can no longer satisfy ϕ.

If controllable and deep counterexamples (goals 1 and 2) are achieved, then our third goal, a certain rarity of counterexamples, follows by construction: If a CE-handle for a property ϕ exists, then all counterexamples have to traverse this handle. Only a single path is traversable starting from that handle if it was inserted using a ϕ-OCE-extension. If this handle has a certain minimum depth from the start state of the corresponding BA B, then—assuming a certain degree of branching within B—the ratio of counterexample paths for ϕ to all accepted paths in B will be low. This effect towards a rarity of counterexamples is more striking the larger the initially synthesized BA is and therefore not necessarily visible in the following small example.

3.5 Examples

Example 1. We are now going to begin with a small running example. It starts with a call of Algorithm 1 and thus first describes the generation of an OCEBA C. Consider the following three LTL formulas:

$$\phi := (c \; \mathbf{R} \; \neg a)$$
$$\psi_1 := \mathbf{G}(a \implies ((\neg b \; \mathbf{U} \; c) \vee \mathbf{G}(\neg c)))$$
$$\psi_2 := ((\neg b \; \mathbf{U} \; c) \vee \mathbf{G}(\neg c))$$

Let $\Phi_\top := \{\phi\}$, $\Phi_\bot := \{\psi_1, \psi_2\}$, and $\Phi := \{\phi, \psi_1, \psi_2\}$. Then Fig. 1 illustrates a BA B that is the result of line 2 of Algorithm 1: B accepts exactly those words in $\Xi([\![\phi \wedge \psi_1 \wedge \psi_2]\!])$ (see Definition 8).[11] As a result, $C = (B, \Phi, \emptyset, \emptyset)$ is an OCEBA.

Example 2. We now enter the loop within Algorithm 1 and therefore generate a second OCEBA $C' = (B', \Phi, H', W')$ based on OCEBA C (Example 1) using a ψ_1-OCE-extension (Definition 13). In order to choose a word $\alpha\sigma\beta \in \mathcal{L}_\Phi^{\neg\psi_1}$ according to Definition 13, we synthesize a BA $B_\bot^1$ that represents this language (Fig. 2a). We then choose $\alpha := ca, \sigma := b$, and $\beta := c(a)^\omega$ based on the accepted path $w = (0 \xrightarrow{c} 1 \xrightarrow{a} 2 \xrightarrow{b} 3 \xrightarrow{c} 4(\xrightarrow{a} 4)^\omega)$ in $B_\bot^1$.

---

[10] Here, we say that a counterexample for ϕ is detected once the corresponding path can no longer satisfy ϕ. Due to Definition 6, this implies an existing counterexample.

[11] The synthesized Büchi automata illustrated within this paper were generated using SPOT [6] and modified regarding their visualization.

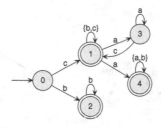

Fig. 1. Initially synthesized automaton B of our running example with $\mathcal{L}(B) = \Xi(\llbracket \phi \wedge \psi_1 \wedge \psi_2 \rrbracket)$. This automaton does therefore not contain counterexamples yet.

We choose state $u_0 := 3$ in B (Fig. 1). This is a valid choice according to Definition 13 because:

(1.a) $\alpha = ca \subset prc_s(3, B)$ because of the simple path $0 \xrightarrow{c} 1 \xrightarrow{a} 3$ in B

(1.b) $pre(3, B) \subseteq pre(bc(a)^\omega, \mathcal{L}_\Phi^{\neg\psi_1})$ because every path from 0 to 3 in B spells a word w' for which a path in $B_\perp^1$ exists that
- begins in the start state 0 of $B_\perp^1$,
- also spells w', and
- can be continued by traversing an accepted path that spells $bc(a)^\omega$

(1.c) As H is still empty, its handles cannot affect the reachability of u_0

In step 2. of Definition 13, we now generate BA B' (Fig. 2b) based on B and the new path ("lasso") $l = (3 \xrightarrow{b} 5 \xrightarrow{c} 6 \xrightarrow{a} 6)$. This satisfies:

(2.a) Because source and target of the last transition in l are identical

(2.b) Because we mark the new state 6 as accepting

(2.c) Because $3 \xrightarrow{b} 5 \xrightarrow{c} 6(\xrightarrow{a} 6)^\omega$ spells $\sigma\beta - bc(a)^\omega$

(2.d) Because regarding transitions and states in l, only state 3 exists in B

In step 3 of Definition 13, we let H' map ψ_1 to transition $t_1 = (3 \xrightarrow{b} 5)$ in B' (and therefore assign $H' := \emptyset \uplus \{(\psi_1, t_1)\}$). In step 4., we let W' map ψ_1 to a counterexample path $c' = (0 \xrightarrow{c} 1 \xrightarrow{a} 3 \xrightarrow{b} 5 \xrightarrow{c} 6(\xrightarrow{a} 6)^\omega)$ in B' (bold arrows in Fig. 2b).

Example 3. Using a ψ_2-OCE-extension, we now generate a third OCEBA $C'' = (B'', \Phi, H'', W'')$ based on C' (Example 2). The reasoning is similar to Example 2. We first synthesize BA $B_\perp^2$ with $\mathcal{L}(B_\perp^2) = \mathcal{L}_\Phi^{\neg\psi_2}$ (Fig. 2c) in order to choose word $\alpha\sigma\beta$ with $\alpha = b$, $\sigma = c$, and $\beta = (ac)^\omega$. Furthermore, we choose state $u_0 = 2$ in B' (Fig. 2b).

Afterwards, we add a lasso $l = (2 \xrightarrow{c} 7 \xrightarrow{a} 8 \xrightarrow{c} 7)$ in order to generate BA B'' (Fig. 2d). OCEBA C' contains a CE-handle and witness path for ψ_1, and such information related to ψ_2 is now added in order to generate H''. The result for the CE-handles is $H'' = \{(\psi_1, t_1), (\psi_2, t_2)\}$ (see Fig. 2d). Map W'' stores counterexample paths for ψ_1 and ψ_2 (bold arrows in Fig. 2d).

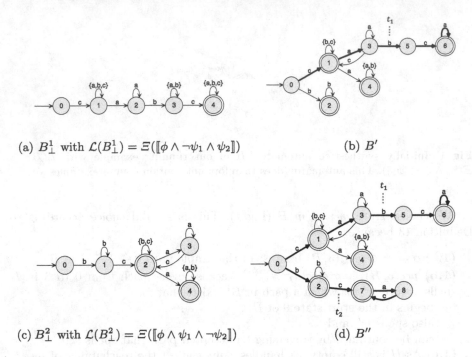

(a) $B_{\perp}^1$ with $\mathcal{L}(B_{\perp}^1) = \Xi([\![\phi \wedge \neg\psi_1 \wedge \psi_2]\!])$ (b) B'

(c) $B_{\perp}^2$ with $\mathcal{L}(B_{\perp}^2) = \Xi([\![\phi \wedge \psi_1 \wedge \neg\psi_2]\!])$ (d) B''

Fig. 2. BAs involved in two consecutive OCE-extensions (see Examples 2 and 3).

The following Sect. 4 describes how we transform the BA in an OCEBA C into a modal transition system (MTS) while maintaining the counterexample information in C.

4 Transformation to an MTS with Witness Data

This section is dedicated to transforming an OCEBA $C = (B, \Phi, H, W)$ (see Sect. 3) to a so called OCEMTS by transforming B to a modal transition system (MTS) M. Due to the modalities within M, model checking LTL properties on M is an instance of three-valued model checking where the result may be indecisive. This cannot be the case when model checking LTL properties on B. Our transformation however is property-preserving, meaning that $M \models \phi \vee M \not\models \phi$ (decisive result) and $M \models \phi \Longleftrightarrow B \models \phi$ hold for each $\phi \in \Phi$. We begin by introducing MTSs and their relation to LTL formally.

4.1 Modal Transition Systems and LTL

An MTS extends a traditional labeled transition system (LTS) with modalities and is formally defined as follows [18]:

Definition 14 (Modal Transition System). *Let S be a set of states and Σ an alphabet of action symbols. $M = (S, s_0, \Sigma, \diamond, \Box)$ is called a **(rooted) modal transition system (MTS)** with root $s_0 \in S$ if the following condition holds:*

$$\Box \subseteq \diamond \subseteq (S \times \Sigma \times S)$$

Elements of $\diamond$ are called may transitions, those of $\Box$ must transitions, and those of $(\diamond \setminus \Box)$ may-only transitions.

Intuitively speaking, a may transition in an MTS stands for an underspecification and indicates a transition that may or may not be present in an actual implementation. Because MTSs generalize LTSs, we can simply derive an LTS as follows:

Definition 15 (Labeled Transition System). *A **labeled transition system (LTS)** is an MTS $M = (S, s_0, \Sigma, \diamond, \Box)$ with $\diamond = \Box$. We omit the duplicate entry and retrieve a quadruple.*

*The **language** $\mathcal{L}(M)$ of M is defined as the language of the related prefix-closed non-deterministic finite automaton (NFA) that results from marking all states in S as accepting.*

For the model checking of LTL properties, the maximal and minimal languages defined by an MTS M are important. These can be derived from the may and must LTS of M, respectively:

Definition 16 (May and Must LTS of an MTS). *Let $M = (S, s_0, \Sigma, \diamond, \Box)$ be an MTS. The LTSs $M_\top := (S, s_0, \Sigma, \diamond)$ and $M_\bot := (S, s_0, \Sigma, \Box)$ are called **may and must LTS of M**, respectively.*

Analogously to Definition 5 but with added modalities, we define (three-valued) model checking based on an MTS and an LTL property as follows:

Definition 17 (Satisfaction/Violation Between MTSs and LTL). *Let M be an MTS. Let ϕ be an LTL formula. For any language $\mathcal{L}$, let $\mathcal{L}^\omega$ denote the sub-language of infinite words in $\mathcal{L}$.*

*Then M **satisfies** ϕ (also denoted as $(M \models \phi) = \top$ or just $M \models \phi$) iff:*

$$\forall w \in \mathcal{L}^\omega(M_\top) : w \models \phi$$

*Similarly, M **violates** ϕ (also denoted as $(M \models \phi) = \bot$ or just $M \not\models \phi$) iff:*

$$\exists w \in \mathcal{L}^\omega(M_\bot) : w \not\models \phi$$

*Furthermore, M **is indecisive concerning** ϕ (also denoted as $(M \models \phi) = ?$) iff M neither satisfies nor violates ϕ.*

4.2   OCEMTS

Input to the transformation described in this section is an OCEBA C (Definition 11).[12] We now define the output of this transformation: It is called OCEMTS and—intuitively speaking—represents an OCEBA where the BA has been replaced with an MTS. We first rephrase required definitions that were introduced for BAs in Sect. 3.

Definition 18 (CE-handle). *Let M be an MTS and ϕ an LTL formula such that $M \not\models \phi$. Let t be a transition in M. Then t is called a **counterexample handle (CE-handle)** for ϕ in M iff the removal of t in M results in $M \models \phi$.*

As a consequence of the above definition, a CE-handle in an MTS has to be a must transition.

Definition 19 (OCEH-map). *Let M be an MTS and Φ a set of LTL formulas. Let H map each property $\phi \in \Phi$ with $M \not\models \phi$ to a CE-handle for ϕ in M.*
  *Then H is called a **Φ-orthogonal-CE-handle-map (Φ-OCEH-map)** for M iff for any $\Psi \subseteq \{\psi \in \Phi \mid M \not\models \psi\}$, the removal of transitions $T = \{H[\psi] \mid \psi \in \Psi\}$ from B does <u>not</u> influence the result of $M \models \phi$ for any $\phi \in (\Phi \setminus \Psi)$.*

Note that in contrast to Definition 10, Definition 19 makes a statement on the *result* of $M \models \psi$ because we now work with three-valued as opposed to two-valued model checking.

Definition 20 (OCEMTS). *Let M be an MTS and Φ be a set of LTL properties. Let H be a Φ-OCEH map for M. Let $\Phi_\perp := \{\phi \in \Phi \mid M \not\models \phi\}$ and let W be a map that stores a counterexample path in M for every property in $\Phi_\perp$. Then the quadruple $C = (M, \Phi, H, W)$ is called an **orthogonal counterexample modal transition system (OCEMTS)**.*

4.3   Transformation

In the following, we first state one important property of OCEBAs generated by Algorithm 1 that is vital for our transformation. This property is based on allowed cut-points in the corresponding BA:

Definition 21 (Allowed Cut-Point). *Let $C = (B, \Phi, H, W)$ be an OCEBA (Definition 11). Let O be a simple cycle in B (see Definition 7).*
  *Then a transition t in O is an **allowed cut-point** for O iff t is not part of any counterexample trace in W, meaning $t \notin \{t' \in W[\phi] \mid \phi \in \Phi \wedge B \not\models \phi\}$.*

We can now specify the required characteristic:

Definition 22 (Cut-Point-OCEBA). *Let $C = (B, \Phi, H, W)$ be an OCEBA (Definition 11). Then C is called a **cut-point-OCEBA** iff there exists an allowed cut-point for each non-accepting simple cycle (Definition 7) in B.*

---

[12] An input OCEBA has to adhere to an additional constraint, however it is guaranteed to do so if it was generated using Algorithm 1. See the next sub-section for details.

Theorem 2 (Allowed Cut-Points). *Let C be an OCEBA generated by Algorithm 1. Then C is a cut-point-OCEBA (Definition 22).*

Thoerem 2 is based on lines 8–10 of Algorithm 1 and the fact that the path p' chosen in step *4.* of Definition 13 is a simple path. See [15] for details.

When transforming an OCEBA to an OCEMTS and therefore a BA B to an MTS M, the Büchi acceptance condition is lost. Intuitively speaking, every state in M is accepting (see Definitions 15 and 16). In order to achieve our goal of property preservation, we proceed as follows:

Definition 23 (Cut-Point-OCEBA-Based MTS). *Let $C = (B, \Phi, H, W)$ be a cut-point-OCEBA (Definition 22). An MTS M is a **C-based MTS** if it can be generated based on B as follows:*

1. *Remove one allowed cut-point within each non-accepting simple cycle*
2. *Remove the acceptance condition*
3. *Mark every counterexample transition $t \in \{t \in W[\phi] \mid \phi \in \Phi \wedge B \not\models \phi\}$ as a must transition and all other transitions as may-only transitions*

The just-described transformation results in an OCEMTS and is property-preserving:[13]

Theorem 3 (Cut-Point-OCEBA to OCEMTS). *Let $C = (B, \Phi, H, W)$ be a cut-point-OCEBA (Definition 22). Let M be a C-based MTS (Definition 23). Then $C' = (M, \Phi, H, W)$ is an OCEMTS and the following hold for all $\phi \in \Phi$:*

1. $M \models \phi \vee M \not\models \phi$
2. $(B \models \phi) \Longleftrightarrow (M \models \phi)$

4.4 Example

Example 4. Consider again OCEBA $C'' = (B'', \Phi, H'', W'')$ from Example 3. B'', H'', and W'' are illustrated in Fig. 2d. Because C'' was generated using Algorithm 1, it is a cut-point-OCEBA (Definition 22). The only non-accepting simple cycle in B'' is the self-loop $(3 \xrightarrow{a} 3)$ which is therefore not marked by any counterexample trace.

According to Definition 23, we now generate a C-based MTS M based on B'' by

1. removing the transition $3 \xrightarrow{a} 3$,
2. discarding the acceptance condition, and
3. marking all counterexample transitions (bold arrows in Fig. 2d) as must transitions (and all others as may-only transitions).

---

[13] Details can be found in [15].

The resulting M can be seen in Fig. 3. Theorem 3 guarantees that $C''' = (M, \Phi, H'', W''')$ is an OCEMTS and that properties in Φ have been preserved.

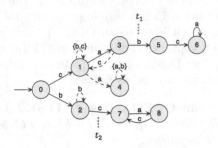

Fig. 3. MTS M that B'' from Fig. 2d was transformed into in a property-preserving manner. CE-handles (t_1 and t_2) and counterexample paths from the corresponding OCEBA have been maintained.

4.5   Modal Refinement

Given an OCEMTS $C = (M, \Phi, H, W)$, we can replace M with another MTS M' that refines[14] M and such that the following hold:

– $\forall \phi \in \Phi : M \models \phi \Longleftrightarrow M' \models \phi$
– $C' = (M', \Phi, H, W)$ is again an OCEMTS.

The first item is trivial because MTS refinement preserves all temporal properties for which M is decisive. The second aspect is true if M and M' feature the same set of states: In this section, we therefore restrict ourselves to state-preserving modal refinement.[15] In this case, CE-handles in H and counterexample paths in W will remain untouched by this refinement because intuitively speaking, refinement preserves must transitions.

MTS refinement can also be used to transform M to an LTS and thereby remove modalities. It is formally defined as follows [18]:

Definition 24 (MTS Refinement). *Let* $M_p = (S_p, s_0^p, \Sigma_p, \Diamond_p, \Box_p), M_q = (S_q, s_0^q, \Sigma_q, \Diamond_q, \Box_q)$ *be two MTSs. A relation* $\lesssim \; \subseteq (S_p \times S_q)$ *is called a **refinement** if the following hold for all* $(p, q) \in \; \lesssim:$

$$(1) \; \forall (p \xrightarrow{\sigma} p') \in \Diamond_p, \; \exists (q \xrightarrow{\sigma} q') \in \Diamond_q : (p', q') \in \; \lesssim$$
$$(2) \; \forall (q \xrightarrow{\sigma} q') \in \Box_q, \; \exists (p \xrightarrow{\sigma} p') \in \Box_p : (p', q') \in \; \lesssim$$

M_p ***refines*** M_q*, written as* $M_p \lesssim M_q$*, if there exists a refinement* $\lesssim$ *with* $(s_0^p, s_0^q) \in \; \lesssim.$

---

[14] Refinement will be formally specified in Definition 24.
[15] Note that modal refinement which expands the MTS M can also be used if the CE-handle and witness information is updated accordingly.

Example 5. Consider the MTS M illustrated in Fig. 3 (Example 4). Figure 4 depicts an MTS M' with $M' \lesssim M$ (Definition 24) such that the states in M and M' are identical. It follows that $M' \models \phi$, $M' \not\models \psi_1$, and $M' \not\models \psi_2$ hold for the properties from Example 1. Furthermore, we know that $C^{(4)} = (M', \Phi, H'', W'')$ is an OCEMTS (see Example 4).

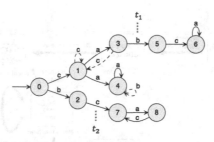

Fig. 4. MTS M' that refines M (Fig. 3). CE handles t_1 and t_2 are again maintained.

The following section discusses how the presented pipeline from LTL properties over an OCEBA to an OCEMTS can be utilized to improve the benchmark generation framework that is used for the RERS Challenge.

5   Applications

We now show how our new synthesis and transformation technique of Sects. 3 and 4 can be used to significantly improve the workflow of the RERS benchmark generation. In Sect. 5.1, we highlight the benefits of our new technique for the generation of sequential programs. Afterwards, Sect. 5.2 introduces a new workflow that allows to generate parallel programs. This latter workflow utilizes the approach of [29] and renders it possible to generate hard parallel benchmark scenarios automatically based on a chosen property profile[16].

5.1   Sequential Benchmark Scenarios of RERS

Figure 5 illustrates the workflow that was previously used in order to generate sequential benchmark scenarios for the RERS Challenge. The challenge organizer provides a benchmark profile as input to the automatic generation. Apart from parameters concerning for example the size of the resulting program, this profile describes a few LTL properties that the generated program needs to satisfy. Based on the idea of requirement-driven engineering, these properties are used for a single BA synthesis. The synthesized BA is first transformed to a Mealy machine before the property profile is completed based on model checking of additional properties. This previous approach has some drawbacks:

- The organizer cannot freely design the property profile: Only a few input properties are required to be satisfied, but violated ones cannot be specified.

---

[16] A property profile is a map from benchmark properties that need to be checked on a given program to their correct true/false valuation for that program.

- Hardness of violated properties is not guaranteed because counterexamples are not constructed explicitly.
- The intermediate Mealy machine used for the completion of the property profile needs to be small enough to be model checked efficiently.

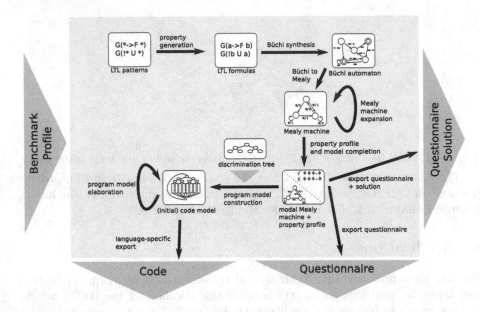

Fig. 5. Previous workflow to generate sequential benchmarks for RERS [28]. A few properties that have to be satisfied are used to construct an initial model, however the remaining property profile is chosen (randomly) based on model checking.

In contrast, our new workflow (Fig. 6) based on the technique presented in this paper overcomes these drawbacks. This time, the organizer can provide the entire property profile as input to the automatic generation process. This profile maps considered LTL properties to the correct statement of whether or not the generated program satisfies it and therefore serves as a solution to the corresponding verification tasks. As this entire property profile is known in advance, a questionnaire and corresponding solution exist already. In the following, we summarize the key benefits of our updated workflow:

- Decoupled property profile from code generation: The entire property profile (solution to the verification tasks) is used as input to the code generation process.
- Rare, deep, and orthogonal counterexamples guarantee a hardness for violated properties.
- No model checking after the initial generation process: Once an OCEMTS has been constructed, it can be expanded based on modal refinement. The entire property-preserving code generation of [28] can be reused afterwards.

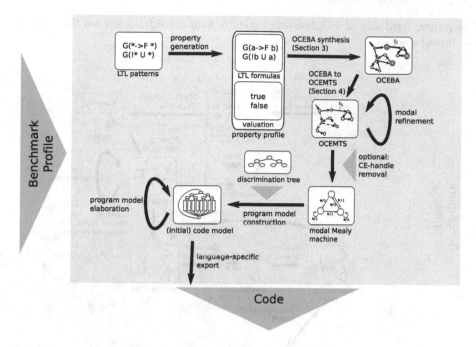

Fig. 6. Improved workflow for the generation of sequential benchmarks. The entire property profile can be chosen initially.

The orthogonality of counterexamples that this new technique guarantees ensures that each execution path in the generated program can only serve as a witness for at most one violated property. Furthermore, we can accelerate the generation of almost identical programs based on the same set of properties, but different verification solutions: Due to the orthogonal CE-handles, we can simply remove counterexamples for a subset of properties during the transformation to a modal Mealy machine.

5.2   Parallel Benchmark Scenarios of RERS

We now present a new workflow for the generation of parallel benchmark programs for the RERS Challenge (Fig. 7). It utilizes the recently conceived approach of a parallel decomposition based on modal contracts that preserves the corresponding property profile [29].[17] Until the generation of a (modally refined) OCEMTS, the process is identical to the updated workflow for sequential programs (Fig. 6, see Sect. 5.1) and therefore based on an initially selected property profile. Because the generation until this step uses the technique presented in

---

[17] In contrast to the technique presented in this paper, the approach of [29] only preserves a subset of temporal properties. This subset is very expressive as it covers many common LTL patterns.

this paper, hardness of violated properties is guaranteed already on the level of the initial system.

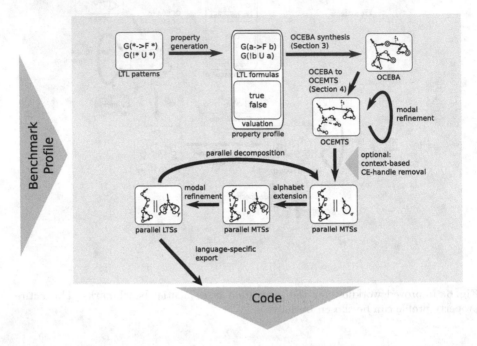

Fig. 7. Workflow for the generation of parallel RERS benchmarks. The orthogonality of counterexamples in an OCEMTS allows us to control the (in-)feasibility of counterexamples through a parallel context.

We first highlight the achievements of this workflow before explaining it:

- A fully automatic generation of parallel benchmark scenarios based on an input property profile
- The possibility to alter the solution to corresponding verification tasks solely by replacing the parallel context
- Hardness of counterexamples (rare, deep, and orthogonal) and parallel hardness according to [29]

Given the final OCEMTS $C = (M, \Phi, H, W)$, the process diverges from the generation of sequential programs. Instead of transforming C to a modal Mealy machine, we extend it to a parallel composition by pairing M with a new context MTS M_c such that properties of interest are again preserved. This step employs a modal contract [29] that allows to generate a parallel context and to optionally (de-)activate counterexample handles solely through this added context.

Once an initial parallel decomposition into $M \parallel M_c$ based on a modal contract has been applied, the iterated and property-preserving procedure of alphabet extensions, possibly modal refinement, and further decompositions can be utilized as introduced in [29] and applied in [26]. Afterwards, the parallel composition can be translated for example to Promela code [9] or a Petri net [26].

6   Conclusion and Perspective

In this paper, we have presented a new approach to synthesize benchmark scenarios from LTL properties that are hard in the sense that counterexamples are sparse and require the matching of many computation steps to detect them. It has been shown how our notion of a *counterexample handle* allows us to switch the satisfaction of a given property on and off without affecting that of the other considered properties. This *orthogonality* of our treatment of counterexamples is key for a better control of subsequent parts of the benchmark generation process where we can now freely choose whether a property should be satisfied or violated. Moreover, the handles and associated counterexamples are sufficient to automatically generate modal contracts required for the parallel decomposition process that allows us to generate parallel verification benchmarks of arbitrary size.

Currently, we are working on integrating this new technology in our benchmark generation framework in a fashion that parallel benchmarks of a given hardness profile (distribution of the depth of counterexamples, number of parallel components required for verification, size of individual components, alphabet size, patterns for considered properties, target language, etc.) can be generated fully automatically. The new technique presented in this paper will be used to generate benchmarks for future iterations of the RERS Challenge[18].

References

1. Baier, C., Katoen, J.P., Larsen, K.G.: Principles of Model Checking. MIT Press, Cambridge (2008)
2. Bartocci, E., et al.: First international competition on runtime verification: rules, benchmarks, tools, and final results of CRV 2014. STTT 1–40 (2017). https://doi.org/10.1007/s10009-017-0454-5
3. Büchi, J.R.: Symposium on decision problems: on a decision method in restricted second order arithmetic. In: Logic, Methodology and Philosophy of Science, Studies in Logic and the Foundations of Mathematics, vol. 44, pp. 1–11. Elsevier (1966)
4. Beyer, D.: Competition on software verification. In: Flanagan, C., König, B. (eds.) TACAS 2012. LNCS, vol. 7214, pp. 504–524. Springer, Heidelberg (2012). https://doi.org/10.1007/978-3-642-28756-5_38
5. Beyer, D.: Software verification and verifiable witnesses. In: Baier, C., Tinelli, C. (eds.) TACAS 2015. LNCS, vol. 9035, pp. 401–416. Springer, Heidelberg (2015). https://doi.org/10.1007/978-3-662-46681-0_31
6. Duret-Lutz, A., Poitrenaud, D.: SPOT: an extensible model checking library using transition-based generalized Büchi automata. In: 12th Annual International Symposium on Modeling, Analysis, and Simulation of Computer and Telecommunications Systems (MASCOTS 2004), pp. 76–83. IEEE (2004)

---

[18] http://www.rers-challenge.org.

7. Erickson, K.T.: Programmable logic controllers. IEEE Potentials **15**(1), 14–17 (1996). https://doi.org/10.1109/45.481370
8. Gastin, P., Oddoux, D.: Fast LTL to Büchi automata translation. In: Berry, G., Comon, H., Finkel, A. (eds.) CAV 2001. LNCS, vol. 2102, pp. 53–65. Springer, Heidelberg (2001). https://doi.org/10.1007/3-540-44585-4_6
9. Geske, M., Jasper, M., Steffen, B., Howar, F., Schordan, M., van de Pol, J.: RERS 2016: parallel and sequential benchmarks with focus on LTL verification. In: Margaria, T., Steffen, B. (eds.) ISoLA 2016. LNCS, vol. 9953, pp. 787–803. Springer, Cham (2016). https://doi.org/10.1007/978-3-319-47169-3_59
10. Gourcuff, V., Smet, O.D., Faure, J.M.: Efficient representation for formal verification of PLC programs. In: 2006 8th International Workshop on Discrete Event Systems, pp. 182–187, July 2006
11. Howar, F., Isberner, M., Merten, M., Steffen, B., Beyer, D., Păsăreanu, C.: Rigorous examination of reactive systems. The RERS challenges 2012 and 2013. STTT **16**(5), 457–464 (2014)
12. Huisman, M., Klebanov, V., Monahan, R.: VerifyThis 2012. STTT **17**(6), 647–657 (2015)
13. Jasper, M., et al.: The RERS 2017 challenge and workshop (invited paper). In: Proceedings of the 24th ACM SIGSOFT International SPIN Symposium on Model Checking of Software, SPIN 2017, pp. 11–20. ACM (2017)
14. Jasper, M., Schordan, M.: Multi-core model checking of large-scale reactive systems using different state representations. In: Margaria, T., Steffen, B. (eds.) ISoLA 2016. LNCS, vol. 9952, pp. 212–226. Springer, Cham (2016). https://doi.org/10.1007/978-3-319-47166-2_15
15. Jasper, M., Steffen, B.: Synthesizing verification benchmarks with subtle bugs for given property profiles. (To appear)
16. Johnson, D.B.: Finding all the elementary circuits of a directed graph. SIAM J. Comput. **4**(1), 77–84 (1975)
17. Kordon, F.: Report on the model checking contest at petri nets 2011. In: Jensen, K., van der Aalst, W.M., Ajmone Marsan, M., Franceschinis, G., Kleijn, J., Kristensen, L.M. (eds.) Transactions on Petri Nets and Other Models of Concurrency VI. LNCS, vol. 7400, pp. 169–196. Springer, Heidelberg (2012). https://doi.org/10.1007/978-3-642-35179-2_8
18. Larsen, K.G.: Modal specifications. In: Sifakis, J. (ed.) CAV 1989. LNCS, vol. 407, pp. 232–246. Springer, Heidelberg (1990). https://doi.org/10.1007/3-540-52148-8_19
19. Mealy, G.H.: A method for synthesizing sequential circuits. Bell Syst. Tech. J. **34**(5), 1045–1079 (1955)
20. Miller, S.P., Whalen, M.W., Cofer, D.D.: Software model checking takes off. Commun. ACM **53**(2), 58–64 (2010)
21. Moon, I.: Modeling programmable logic controllers for logic verification. IEEE Control Syst. **14**(2), 53–59 (1994)
22. Peterson, J.L.: Petri Net Theory and the Modeling of Systems. Prentice Hall PTR, Upper Saddle River (1981)
23. Plotkin, G.D.: A structural approach to operational semantics. DAIMI FN-19, Computer Science Department, Aarhus University (1981)
24. Pnueli, A., Rosner, R.: On the synthesis of a reactive module. In: Proceedings of the 16th ACM SIGPLAN-SIGACT Symposium on Principles of Programming Languages, POPL 1989, pp. 179–190. ACM, New York (1989)
25. Rausch, M., Krogh, B.H.: Formal verification of PLC programs. In: Proceedings of the 1998 American Control Conference, ACC, vol. 1, pp. 234–238, June 1998

26. Steffen, B., Jasper, M., Meijer, J., van de Pol, J.: Property-preserving generation of tailored benchmark petri nets. In: 17th International Conference on Application of Concurrency to System Design (ACSD), pp. 1–8, June 2017
27. Steffen, B., Howar, F., Isberner, M., Naujokat, S., Margaria, T.: Tailored generation of concurrent benchmarks. STTT **16**(5), 543–558 (2014)
28. Steffen, B., Isberner, M., Naujokat, S., Margaria, T., Geske, M.: Property-driven benchmark generation: synthesizing programs of realistic structure. STTT **16**(5), 465–479 (2014)
29. Steffen, B., Jasper, M.: Property-preserving parallel decomposition. In: Aceto, L., Bacci, G., Bacci, G., Ingólfsdóttir, A., Legay, A., Mardare, R. (eds.) Models, Algorithms, Logics and Tools. LNCS, vol. 10460, pp. 125–145. Springer, Cham (2017). https://doi.org/10.1007/978-3-319-63121-9_7
30. Visser, W., Mehlitz, P.: Model checking programs with Java PathFinder. In: Godefroid, P. (ed.) SPIN 2005. LNCS, vol. 3639, p. 27. Springer, Heidelberg (2005). https://doi.org/10.1007/11537328_5
31. Wolper, P.: Temporal logic can be more expressive. Inf. Control **56**(1), 72–99 (1983)
32. Zhivich, M., Cunningham, R.K.: The real cost of software errors. IEEE Secur. Priv. **7**(2), 87–90 (2009)

Statistical Model Checking

Statistical Model Checking the 2018 Edition!

Kim Guldstrand Larsen[1,2]([⊠]) and Axel Legay[1,2]

[1] Aalborg University, Aalborg, Denmark
kgl@cs.aau.dk
[2] Inria Rennes – Bretagne Atlantique, Rennes, France

Abstract. This short note introduces statistical model checking and gives a brief overview of the *Statistical Model Checking, past present and future* session at Isola 2018. This is the fourth edition of the track at Isola.

1 Context

Quantitative properties of stochastic systems are usually specified in logics that allow one to compare the measure of executions satisfying certain temporal properties with thresholds. The model checking problem for stochastic systems with respect to such logics is typically solved by a numerical approach [BHHK03, CG04] that iteratively computes (or approximates) the exact measure of paths satisfying relevant subformulas; the algorithms themselves depend on the class of systems being analysed as well as the logic used for specifying the properties.

Another approach to solve the model checking problem is to *simulate* the system for finitely many runs, and use *hypothesis testing* to infer whether the samples provide *statistical* evidence for the satisfaction or violation of the specification. This approach was first applied in [LS91], where it was shown that hypothesis testing could be used to settle probabilistic modal logic properties with arbitrary precision, leading in the limit to probabilistic bisimulation. More recently [You05a] this approach has been known as statistical model checking (SMC) and is based on the notion that since sample runs of a stochastic system are drawn according to the distribution defined by the system, they can be used to obtain estimates of the probability measure on executions. Starting from time-bounded PCTL properties [You05a], the technique has been extended to handle properties with unbounded until operators [SVA05b], as well as to black-box systems [SVA04, You05a]. Tools, based on this idea have been built [HLMP04, SVA05a, You05a, You05b, BDD+11, DLL+11, BCLS13], and have been used to analyse many systems that are intractable numerical approaches.

The SMC approach enjoys many advantages. First, the algorithms require only that the system be simulatable (or rather, sample executions be drawn according to the measure space defined by the system). Thus, it can be applied to larger class of systems than numerical model checking algorithms, including

T. Margaria and B. Steffen (Eds.): ISoLA 2018, LNCS 11245, pp. 261–270, 2018.
https://doi.org/10.1007/978-3-030-03421-4_17

black-box systems and infinite state systems. In particular, SMC avoids the 'state explosion problem' [CES09]. Second the approach can be generalized to a larger class of properties, including Fourier transform based logics. Third, SMC requires many independent simulation runs, making it easy to parallelise and scale to industrial-sized systems.

While it offers solutions to some intractable numerical model checking problems, SMC also introduces some additional problems. First, SMC only provides probabilistic guarantees about the correctness of the results. Second, the required sample size grows quadratically with respect to the required confidence of the result. This makes rare properties difficult to verify. Third, only the simulation of purely probabilistic systems is well defined. Nondeterministic systems, which are common in the field of formal verification, are especially challenging for SMC.

2   On Statistical Model Checking

Consider a stochastic system S and a logical property φ that can be checked on finite executions of the system. Statistical Model Checking (SMC) refers to a series of simulation-based techniques that can be used to answer two questions: (1) *Qualitative*: Is the probability for S to satisfy φ greater or equal to a certain threshold? and (2) *Quantitative*: What is the probability for S to satisfy φ? In contrast to numerical approaches, the answer is given up to some correctness precision.

In the sequel, we overview two SMC techniques. Let B_i be a discrete random variable with a Bernoulli distribution of parameter p. Such a variable can only take 2 values 0 and 1 with $Pr[B_i = 1] = p$ and $Pr[B_i = 0] = 1 - p$. In our context, each variable B_i is associated with one simulation of the system. The outcome for B_i, denoted b_i, is 1 if the simulation satisfies φ and 0 otherwise.

Qualitative Answer. The main approaches [You05a, SVA04] proposed to answer the qualitative question are based on *sequential hypothesis testing* [Wal45]. Let $p = Pr(\varphi)$. To determine whether $p \geq \theta$, we can test $H : p \geq \theta$ against $K : p < \theta$. A test-based solution does not guarantee a correct result but it is possible to bound the probability of error. The *strength* of a test is determined by two parameters, α and β, such that the probability of accepting K (respectively, H) when H (respectively, K) holds, called a Type-I error (respectively, a Type-II error) is less or equal to α (respectively, β). A test has *ideal performance* if the probability of the Type-I error (respectively, Type-II error) is exactly α (respectively, β). However, these requirements make it impossible to ensure a low probability for both types of errors simultaneously (see [Wal45, You05a] for details). A solution is to use an *indifference region* $[p_1, p_0]$ (given some δ, $p_1 = \theta - \delta$ and $p_0 = \theta + \delta$) and to test $H_0 : p \geq p_0$ against $H_1 : p \leq p_1$. We now sketch the Sequential Probability Ratio Test (SPRT). In this algorithm, one has to choose two values A and B ($A > B$) that ensure that the strength of the test is respected. Let m be the number of observations that have been made so far.

The test is based on the following quotient:

$$\frac{p_{1m}}{p_{0m}} = \prod_{i=1}^{m} \frac{Pr(B_i = b_i \mid p = p_1)}{Pr(B_i = b_i \mid p = p_0)} = \frac{p_1^{d_m}(1-p_1)^{m-d_m}}{p_0^{d_m}(1-p_0)^{m-d_m}},$$

where $d_m = \sum_{i=1}^{m} b_i$. The idea is to accept H_0 if $\frac{p_{1m}}{p_{0m}} \geq A$, and H_1 if $\frac{p_{1m}}{p_{0m}} \leq B$. The algorithm computes $\frac{p_{1m}}{p_{0m}}$ for successive values of m until either H_0 or H_1 is satisfied. This has the advantage of minimizing the number of simulations required to make the decision.

Quantitative Answer. In [HLMP04] Peyronnet et al. propose an estimation procedure to compute the probability p for S to satisfy φ. Given a *precision* δ, the *Chernoff bound* of [Oka59] is used to compute a value for p' such that $|p' - p| \leq \delta$ with *confidence* $1 - \alpha$. Let $B_1 \dots B_m$ be m Bernoulli random variables with parameter p, associated to m simulations of the system considering φ. Let $p' = \sum_{i=1}^{m} b_i/m$, then the Chernoff bound [Oka59] gives $Pr(|p' - p| \geq \delta) \leq 2e^{-2m\delta^2}$. As a consequence, if we take $m = \lceil \ln(2/\alpha)/(2\delta^2) \rceil$, then $Pr(|p' - p| \leq \delta) \geq 1 - \alpha$.

2.1 Rare Events

Statistical model checking avoids the exponential growth of states associated with probabilistic model checking by estimating probabilities from multiple executions of a system and by giving results within confidence bounds. Rare properties are often important but pose a particular challenge for simulation-based approaches, hence a key objective for SMC is to reduce the number and length of simulations necessary to produce a result with a given level of confidence. In the literature, one finds two techniques to cope with rare events: *importance sampling* and *importance splitting*.

In order to minimize the number of simulations, importance sampling (see e.g., [Rid10,DBNR00]) works by estimating a probability using weighted simulations that favour the rare property, then compensating for the weights. For importance sampling to be efficient, it is thus crucial to find good importance sampling distributions without considering the entire state space. In [CZ11] Zuliani and Clarke outlined the challenges for SMC and rare-events. A first theory contribution was then provided by Barbot et al. who proposed to use reduction techniques together with cross-entropy [BHP12]. In [JLS12], we presented a simple algorithm that uses the notion of cross-entropy minimisation to find an optimal importance sampling distribution. In contrast to previous work, our algorithm uses a naturally defined low dimensional vector of parameters to specify this distribution and thus avoids the intractable explicit representation of a transition matrix. We show that our parametrisation leads to a unique optimum and can produce many orders of magnitude improvement in simulation efficiency.

One of the open challenges with importance sampling is that the variance of the estimator cannot be usefully bounded with only the knowledge gained from simulation. Importance *splitting* (see e.g., [CG07]) achieves this objective by estimating a sequence of conditional probabilities, whose product is the required result. In [JLS13] motivated the use of importance splitting for statistical model checking and were the first to link this standard variance reduction technique [KM53] with temporal logical. In particular, they showed how to create *score functions* based on logical properties, and thus define a set of *levels* that delimit the conditional probabilities. In [JLS13] they also described the necessary and desirable properties of score functions and levels, and gave two importance splitting algorithms: one that uses fixed levels and one that discovers optimal levels adaptively.

2.2 Nondeterminism

Markov decision processes (MDP) and other nondeterministic models interleave nondeterministic *actions* and probabilistic transitions, possibly with rewards or costs assigned to the actions [Bel57, Put94]. These models have proved useful in many real optimisation problems (see [Whi85, Whi88, Whi93] for a survey of applications of MDPs) and are also used in a more abstract sense to represent concurrent probabilistic systems (e.g., [BDA95]). Such systems comprise probabilistic subsystems whose transitions depend on the states of the other subsystems, while the order in which concurrently enabled transitions execute is nondeterministic. This order may radically affect the expected reward or the probability that a system will satisfy a given property. Numerical model checking may be used to calculate the upper and lower bounds of these quantities, but a simulation semantics is not immediate for nondeterministic systems and SMC is therefore challenging.

SMC cannot be applied to nondeterministic systems without first resolving the nondeterminism using a *scheduler* (alternatively a *strategy* or a *policy*). Since nondeterministic and probabilistic choices are interleaved, schedulers are typically of the same order of complexity as the system as a whole and may be infinite.

In [LS14] Jegouret et al. presented the basis of the first lightweight SMC algorithms for MDPs and other nondeterministic models, using an $\mathcal{O}(1)$ representation of history-dependent schedulers. This solution is based on pseudo-random number generators and an efficient hash function, allowing schedulers to be sampled using Monte Carlo techniques. Some previous attempts to apply SMC to nondeterministic models [BFHH11, LP12, HMZ+12, HT13] have been memory-intensive (heavyweight) and incomplete in various ways. The algorithms of [BFHH11, HT13] consider only systems with 'spurious' nondeterminism that does not actually affect the probability of a property. In [LP12] the authors consider only memoryless schedulers and do not consider the standard notion of optimality used in model checking (i.e., with respect to probability). The algorithm of [HMZ+12] addresses a standard qualitative probabilistic model checking problem, but is limited to memoryless schedulers that must fit into memory and does not in general converge to the optimal scheduler. Most recently [DJL+], SMC – or reinforcement learning – has been applied to learn near-cost-optimal strategies for priced timed stochastic games subject to guaranteed worst-case time bounds. The method is implemented using a combination of UPPAAL-TIGA (for timed games) and UPPAAL SMC and provides three alternatives light-weight datastructures for representing stochastic strategies.

3   Content of the Session

SMC has been implemented in several prototypes and tools, which includes UPPAAL SMC [DLL+11], PLASMA [BCLS13], YMER [You05b], or COSMOS [BDD+11]. Those tools have been applied to several complex problems coming from a wide range of areas. This includes systems biology (see e.g., [Zul14]), automotive and avionics (see e.g., [BBB+12]), energy-centric systems (see e.g., [DDL+13]), or power grids (see e.g., [HH13]).

This isola session discusses several aspects of SMC, which includes: rare-events, application to railway and security, sampling minimization, nondeterminism, or real-time extensions. Summary of the contributions:

- In [DJS18], the authors propose schemes to reduce the number of samplings needed for SMC to converge. It is known that Bayesian and rare event techniques can be used to reduce the sample size but they can not be applied without prerequisite or knowledge about the system under scrutiny. Recently, sequential algorithms based on Monte Carlo estimations and Massart bounds have been proposed to reduce the sample size while providing guarantees on error bounds which has been shown to outperform alternative frequentist approaches. In this work, the authors discuss some features regarding the distribution and the optimisation of these algorithms.
- In [Str18], the author focuses on processor based systems with interruptible executions. Their predictability analysis becomes more difficult especially when interrupts may occur at arbitrary times, suffer from arrival and servicing jitters, are subject to priorities, or may be nested and un/masked at run-time. Such a behavior of interrupts and executions has stochastic aspects and leads to the explosion of the number of situations to be considered. To cope with such a behavior, the author proposes a simulation model that relies on a network of stochastic timed automata and involves the above-mentioned behavioral aspects related to interrupts and executions. For a system, modeled by means of the automata, the author shows that the problem of analyzing its predictability may be efficiently solved by means of the statistical model checking.
- In [ALR18], the authors study incomplete stochastic systems that are missing some parts of their design, or are lacking information about some components. For such systems, it is interesting to get early analysis results of the requirements, in order to adequately refine their design. The main contribution of the paper takes the form of a three-valued temporal logics for which authors offer SMC algorithms.

- In [ABK18], The maximum reachability probabilities in a Markov decision process can be computed using value iteration (VI). Recently, simulation-based heuristic extensions of VI have been introduced, such as bounded real-time dynamic programming (BRTDP), which often manage to avoid explicit analysis of the whole state space while preserving guarantees on the computed result. In this paper, the authors introduce a new class of such heuristics, based on Monte Carlo tree search (MCTS), a technique celebrated in various machine-learning settings. They also provide a spectrum of algorithms ranging from MCTS to BRTDP. Finally, the authors evaluate these techniques and show that for larger examples, where VI is no more applicable, our techniques are more broadly applicable than BRTDP with only a minor additional overhead.
- In [BBL18], the authors propose to synthesize defense configurations to counter sophisticated attack strategies minimizing resource usage while ensuring a high probability of success. For this, they combine Statistical Model Checking techniques with Genetic Algorithms. Experiments performed on real-life case studies show substantial improvements compared to existing techniques.
- In [FGP18], authors discuss the application of SMC on assisted/automated driving systems. For developers of assisted or automated driving systems, gaining specific feedback and quantitative figures on the safety impact of the systems under development is crucial. However, obtaining such data from simulation of their design models is a complex and often time-consuming process. Especially when data of interest hinge on extremely rare events, an estimation of potential risks is highly desirable but a non-trivial task lacking easily applicable methods. In this paper, the authors describe how a quantitative statement for a risk estimation involving extremely rare events can be obtained by guiding simulation based on reinforcement learning. The method draws on variance reduction and importance sampling, yet applies different optimization principles than related methods, like the cross-entropy methods against which they compare
- In [DHS18], authors extend their work on Lightweight scheduler sampling. It is known that this approach brings statistical model checking to nondeterministic formalisms with undiscounted properties, in constant memory. Its direct application to continuous-time models is rendered ineffective by their dense concrete state spaces and the need to consider continuous input for optimal decisions. In this paper the authors describe the challenges and state of the art in applying lightweight scheduler sampling to three continuous-time formalisms: After a review of recent work on exploiting discrete abstractions for probabilistic timed automata, they discuss scheduler sampling for Markov automata and apply it on two case studies, and offer a large discussion on potential future research and extensions.
- In [BBC18], the authors present an experience in modelling and statistical model checking a satellite-based moving block signalling scenario from the railway industry with Uppaal SMC. This demonstrates the usability and applicability of Uppaal SMC in the railway domain. The authors also propose

a promising direction for future work, in which they envision spatio-temporal analysis with Uppaal SMC.

- In [BPS18], the authors discuss the link between SMC and Randomized testing. The latter is a lightweight approach for searching for bugs. There is a tradeoff between the number of testing experiments performed and the probability to find errors. An important challenge in random testing is when the errors that we try to detect are scattered with very low probability among the different executions, forming a "rare event". In this paper, the authors suggest the use of a "biasing automaton", which observes the tested sequence and controls the distribution of the different choices of extending it. Authors also show how to find such a biasing automaton based on genetic programming techniques.

4   Conclusion

This fourth edition of the SMC track at ISOLA shows two interesting points. The first is that researchers keep on working and produce new results on SMC core topics. This includes, e.g., nondeterminism or rare events. In addition, new challenges have emerged. This includes, e.g., a study comparison with testing, or the introduction of uncertainty. This gives motivation to keep on working on the topic and get ready for the fifth edition which will take place in 2020 where we will celebrate twenty years of SMC!

References

[ABK18]   Ashok, P., Brazdil, T., Kretinsky, J., Slamecka, O.: Monte Carlo tree search for verifying reachability in Markov decision processes. In: Margaria, T., Steffen, B. (eds.) ISoLA 2018. LNCS, vol. 11245, pp. 322–335. Springer, Cham (2018)

[ALR18]   Arora, S., Traonouez, L.-M., Legay, A., Richmond, T.: Statistical model-checking of incomplete stochastic systems. In: Margaria, T., Steffen, B. (eds.) ISoLA 2018. LNCS, vol. 11245, pp. 354–371. Springer, Cham (2018)

[BBB+12]   Basu, A., Bensalem, S., Bozga, M., Delahaye, B., Legay, A.: Statistical abstraction and model-checking of large heterogeneous systems. STTT 14(1), 53–72 (2012)

[BBC18]   ter Beek, M., Basile, D., Ciancia, V.: Statistical model checking a moving block railway signalling scenario with Uppaal SMC. In: Margaria, T., Steffen, B. (eds.) ISoLA 2018. LNCS, vol. 11245, pp. 372–391. Springer, Cham (2018)

[BBL18]   Mediouni, B.L., Nouri, A., Bozga, M., Legay, A., Bensalem, S.: Mitigating security risks through attack strategies exploration. In: Margaria, T., Steffen, B. (eds.) ISoLA 2018. LNCS, vol. 11245, pp. 392–413. Springer, Cham (2018)

[BCLS13]   Boyer, B., Corre, K., Legay, A., Sedwards, S.: PLASMA-lab: a flexible, distributable statistical model checking library. In: Joshi, K., Siegle, M., Stoelinga, M., D'Argenio, P.R. (eds.) QEST 2013. LNCS, vol. 8054, pp. 160–164. Springer, Heidelberg (2013). https://doi.org/10.1007/978-3-642-40196-1_12

[BDA95]   Bianco, A., de Alfaro, L.: Model checking of probabilistic and nondetermin-
          istic systems. In: Thiagarajan, P.S. (ed.) FSTTCS 1995. LNCS, vol. 1026,
          pp. 499–513. Springer, Heidelberg (1995). https://doi.org/10.1007/3-540-
          60692-0_70
[BDD+11] Ballarini, P., Djafri, H., Duflot, M., Haddad, S., Pekergin, N.: COSMOS:
          a statistical model checker for the hybrid automata stochastic logic. In:
          QEST, pp. 143–144. IEEE Computer Society (2011)
[Bel57]   Bellman, R.: Dynamic Programming. Princeton University Press, Princeton
          (1957)
[BFHH11] Bogdoll, J., Ferrer Fioriti, L.M., Hartmanns, A., Hermanns, H.: Partial
          order methods for statistical model checking and simulation. In: Bruni, R.,
          Dingel, J. (eds.) FMOODS/FORTE -2011. LNCS, vol. 6722, pp. 59–74.
          Springer, Heidelberg (2011). https://doi.org/10.1007/978-3-642-21461-5_4
[BHHK03] Baier, C., Haverkort, B.R., Hermanns, H., Katoen, J.-P.: Model-checking
          algorithms for continuous-time Markov chains. IEEE 29(6), 524–541 (2003)
[BHP12]   Barbot, B., Haddad, S., Picaronny, C.: Coupling and importance sampling
          for statistical model checking. In: Flanagan, C., König, B. (eds.) TACAS
          2012. LNCS, vol. 7214, pp. 331–346. Springer, Heidelberg (2012). https://
          doi.org/10.1007/978-3-642-28756-5_23
[BPS18]   Peled, D., Bu, L., Shen, D., Tzirulnikov, Y.: Chasing errors using bias-
          ing automata. In: Margaria, T., Steffen, B. (eds.) ISoLA 2018. LNCS, vol.
          11245, pp. 271–286. Springer, Cham (2018)
[CES09]   Clarke, E.M., Emerson, E.A., Sifakis, J.: Model checking: algorithmic veri-
          fication and debugging. Commun. ACM 52(11), 74–84 (2009)
[CG04]   Ciesinski, F., Größer, M.: On probabilistic computation tree logic. In: Baier,
          C., Haverkort, B.R., Hermanns, H., Katoen, J.-P., Siegle, M. (eds.) Valida-
          tion of Stochastic Systems. LNCS, vol. 2925, pp. 147–188. Springer, Hei-
          delberg (2004). https://doi.org/10.1007/978-3-540-24611-4_5
[CG07]   Cérou, F., Guyader, A.: Adaptive multilevel splitting for rare event analysis.
          Stoch. Anal. Appl. 25, 417–443 (2007)
[CZ11]   Clarke, E.M., Zuliani, P.: Statistical model checking for cyber-physical sys-
          tems. In: Bultan, T., Hsiung, P.-A. (eds.) ATVA 2011. LNCS, vol. 6996,
          pp. 1–12. Springer, Heidelberg (2011). https://doi.org/10.1007/978-3-642-
          24372-1_1
[DBNR00] De Boer, P.-T., Nicola, V.F., Rubinstein, R.Y.: Adaptive importance sam-
          pling simulation of queueing networks. In: Winter Simulation Conference,
          vol. 1, pp. 646–655 (2000)
[DDL+13] David, A., Du, D., Guldstrand Larsen, K., Legay, A., Mikučionis, M.:
          Optimizing control strategy using statistical model checking. In: Brat,
          G., Rungta, N., Venet, A. (eds.) NFM 2013. LNCS, vol. 7871, pp.
          352–367. Springer, Heidelberg (2013). https://doi.org/10.1007/978-3-642-
          38088-4_24
[DHS18]   D'Argenio, P., Hartmanns, A., Sedwards, S.: Lightweight statistical model
          checking in nondeterministic continuous time. In: Margaria, T., Steffen, B.
          (eds.) ISoLA 2018. LNCS, vol. 11245, pp. 336–353. Springer, Cham (2018)
[DJL+]   David, A., Jensen, P.G., Larsen, K.G., Legay, A., Lime, D., Sorensen, M.G.,
          Taankvist, J.H
[DJS18]   Jegourel, C., Sun, J., Dong, J.-S.: On the sequential Massart algorithm for
          statistical model checking. In: Margaria, T., Steffen, B. (eds.) ISoLA 2018.
          LNCS, vol. 11245, pp. 287–304. Springer, Cham (2018)

[DLL+11] David, A., Larsen, K.G., Legay, A., Mikučionis, M., Wang, Z.: Time for statistical model checking of real-time systems. In: Gopalakrishnan, G., Qadeer, S. (eds.) CAV 2011. LNCS, vol. 6806, pp. 349–355. Springer, Heidelberg (2011). https://doi.org/10.1007/978-3-642-22110-1_27

[FGP18] Puch, S., Fraenzle, M., Gerwinn, S.: Quantitative risk assessment of safety-critical systems via guided simulation for rare events. In: Margaria, T., Steffen, B. (eds.) ISoLA 2018. LNCS, vol. 11245, pp. 305–321. Springer, Cham (2018)

[HH13] Hermanns, H., Hartmanns, A.: An internet inspired approach to power grid stability. IT Inf. Technol. **55**(2), 45–51 (2013)

[HLMP04] Hérault, T., Lassaigne, R., Magniette, F., Peyronnet, S.: Approximate probabilistic model checking. In: Steffen, B., Levi, G. (eds.) VMCAI 2004. LNCS, vol. 2937, pp. 73–84. Springer, Heidelberg (2004). https://doi.org/10.1007/978-3-540-24622-0_8

[HMZ+12] Henriques, D., Martins, J.G., Zuliani, P., Platzer, A., Clarke, E.M.: Statistical model checking for Markov decision processes. In: 2012 Ninth International Conference on Quantitative Evaluation of Systems, pp. 84–93. IEEE (2012)

[HT13] Hartmanns, A., Timmer, M.: On-the-fly confluence detection for statistical model checking. In: Brat, G., Rungta, N., Venet, A. (eds.) NFM 2013. LNCS, vol. 7871, pp. 337–351. Springer, Heidelberg (2013). https://doi.org/10.1007/978-3-642-38088-4_23

[JLS12] Jegourel, C., Legay, A., Sedwards, S.: Cross-entropy optimisation of importance sampling parameters for statistical model checking. In: Madhusudan, P., Seshia, S.A. (eds.) CAV 2012. LNCS, vol. 7358, pp. 327–342. Springer, Heidelberg (2012). https://doi.org/10.1007/978-3-642-31424-7_26

[JLS13] Jegourel, C., Legay, A., Sedwards, S.: Importance splitting for statistical model checking rare properties. In: Sharygina, N., Veith, H. (eds.) CAV 2013. LNCS, vol. 8044, pp. 576–591. Springer, Heidelberg (2013). https://doi.org/10.1007/978-3-642-39799-8_38

[KM53] Kahn, H., Marshall, A.W.: Methods of reducing sample size in Monte Carlo computations. Oper. Res. **1**(5), 263–278 (1953)

[LP12] Lassaigne, R., Peyronnet, S.: Approximate planning and verification for large Markov decision processes. In: Proceedings of the 27th Annual ACM Symposium on Applied Computing, pp. 1314–1319. ACM (2012)

[LS91] Guldstrand Larsen, K., Skou, A., Kim Guldstrand Larsen and Arne Skou: Bisimulation through probabilistic testing. Inf. Comput. **94**(1), 1–28 (1991)

[LS14] Legay, A., Sedwards, S.: Lightweight Monte Carlo verification of Markov decision processes (2014, submitted)

[Oka59] Okamoto, M.: Some inequalities relating to the partial sum of binomial probabilities. Ann. Inst. Stat. Math. **10**, 29–35 (1959)

[Put94] Puterman, M.L.: Markov Decision Processes: Discrete Stochastic Dynamic Programming. Wiley, Hoboken (1994)

[Rid10] Ridder, A.: Asymptotic optimality of the cross-entropy method for Markov chain problems. Procedia Comput. Sci. **1**(1), 1571–1578 (2010)

[Str18] Strnadel, J.: Statistical model checking of processor systems in various interrupt scenarios. In: Margaria, T., Steffen, B. (eds.) ISoLA 2018. LNCS, vol. 11245, pp. 414–429. Springer, Cham (2018)

[SVA04] Sen, K., Viswanathan, M., Agha, G.: Statistical model checking of black-box probabilistic systems. In: Alur, R., Peled, D.A. (eds.) CAV 2004. LNCS, vol.

3114, pp. 202–215. Springer, Heidelberg (2004). https://doi.org/10.1007/978-3-540-27813-9_16

[SVA05a] Sen, K., Viswanathan, M., Agha, G.A.: VESTA: a statistical model-checker and analyzer for probabilistic systems. In: QEST, pp. 251–252. IEEE Computer Society (2005)

[SVA05b] Sen, K., Viswanathan, M., Agha, G.: On statistical model checking of stochastic systems. In: Etessami, K., Rajamani, S.K. (eds.) CAV 2005. LNCS, vol. 3576, pp. 266–280. Springer, Heidelberg (2005). https://doi.org/10.1007/11513988_26

[Wal45] Wald, A.: Sequential tests of statistical hypotheses. Ann. Math. Stat. **16**(2), 117–186 (1945)

[Whi85] White, D.J.: Real applications of Markov decision processes. Interfaces **15**(6), 73–83 (1985)

[Whi88] White, D.J.: Further real applications of Markov decision processes. Interfaces **18**(5), 55–61 (1988)

[Whi93] White, D.J.: A survey of applications of Markov decision processes. J. Oper. Res. Soc. **44**(11), 1073–1096 (1993)

[You05a] Younes, H.L.S.: Verification and planning for stochastic processes with asynchronous events. Ph.D. thesis, Carnegie Mellon (2005)

[You05b] Younes, H.L.S.: Ymer: a statistical model checker. In: Etessami, K., Rajamani, S.K. (eds.) CAV 2005. LNCS, vol. 3576, pp. 429–433. Springer, Heidelberg (2005). https://doi.org/10.1007/11513988_43

[Zul14] Zuliani, P.: Statistical model checking for biological applications. CoRR, abs/1405.2705 (2014)

Chasing Errors Using Biasing Automata

Lei Bu[2], Doron Peled[1(✉)], Dashuan Shen[2], and Yael Tzirulnikov[1]

[1] Department of Computer Science, Bar Ilan University, Ramat Gan, Israel
doron.peled@gmail.com
[2] State Key Laboratory for Novel Software Technology,
Nanjing University, Nanjing, China

Abstract. Randomized testing is a lightweight approach for searching for bugs. It presents a tradeoff between the number of testing experiments performed and the probability to find errors. An important challenge in random testing is when the errors that we try to detect are scattered with very low probability among the different executions, forming a "rare event". We suggest here the use of a "biasing automaton", which observes the tested sequence and controls the distribution of the different choices of extending it. By the careful selection of a biasing automaton, we can increase the chance of errors to be found and consequently reduce the number of tests we need to perform. The biasing automaton is constructed through repeated testing of variants of the system under test. We show how to construct biasing automata based on genetic programming.

1 Introduction

Testing and model checking are complementary methods for achieving system reliability. While model checking is comprehensive, covering *all* the executions in a model of the system, testing is sometimes more affordable, allowing to *sample* the executions. The border between these techniques is becoming blurred, as new hybrid methods are developed. The choice between methods and tools is indeed not easy, with a clear tradeoff between coverage and complexity. *Statistical model checking* [13,14,17], applies repeated verification of executions against a specification (as in run-time verification), based on random sampling. The number of samples that need to be checked grows when the focus is on detecting event that contain executions that occur with low probability. As the expectation to hit an execution that belongs to such an event during random (Monte Carlo) testing is low, the potential advantage of using it over model checking diminishes.

Our goal is to provide a light-weight approach for random search for errors. It is similar to statistical model checking in that the executions are sampled

The research in this paper was partially funded by an ISF-NSFC grant "Runtime Measuring and Checking of Cyber Physical Systems" (ISF award 2239/15, NSFC No. 61561146394). The authors from Nanjing University were also partially funded by a National Natural Science Foundation of China grant No. 61572249.

© Springer Nature Switzerland AG 2018
T. Margaria and B. Steffen (Eds.): ISoLA 2018, LNCS 11245, pp. 271–286, 2018.
https://doi.org/10.1007/978-3-030-03421-4_18

and analyzed against a temporal specification. However, we do not attempt to calculate the probability of occurrence of erroneous executions, but rather to discover them. The method is based on learning a *biasing automaton*, which inspects the current execution and provides the distribution on the different choices for extending the tested execution. In this paper, we study the problem of learning effective biasing automata using genetic programming.

We are interested in constructing biasing automata that will improve the choice of tested executions for finding an error in a family of programs. Thus, we expect an effective biasing automata to be useful in the process of regression testing. The use of a collection of candidate programs, within genetic programming, helps to discover inherent structure that is important for identifying errors. We embed the learning and use of biasing automata in the process of genetic synthesis of correct-by-design code. We apply a *coevolution* process [12], where both solutions and biasing automata are constructed simultaneously, helping to improve each other.

A related technique for handling rare events, in the context of statistical model checking, is *importance splitting* [8], one uses a splitting of the test sequences into cases. Then one can zoom into checking cases where the rare events are believed to appear more frequently. The statistical result for each such case is the *conditional probability* of the rare event to occur under that case. The distribution of the different cases are assumed to be known, and the statistical results of the different cases are multiplied by the distribution of selecting the different cases in order to normalize the overall statistical result. Biasing automata can also be seen as splitting the test cases (according to their prefixes) for concentrating more on some cases. However, it is meaningless to normalize the experiment results in order to obtain a statistical measurement on the relative occurrence rate of the rare event. In a sense, a biasing automaton can be considered to be an approximation to a fault model [15], which helps detecting erroneous executions on future versions of the tested system.

2   Preliminaries

2.1   Labeled Markov Chains

A *labeled Markov Chain* is a stochastic model, describing sequences of events, in which the probability of choosing the next event depends only on the state reached so far after the previous event. We describe a labeled Markov Chain as a tuple $\mathcal{M} = (Q, q_0, A, B, T, D, L)$ where

- Q is a finite set of *states*, with $q_0 \in Q$ the initial state.
- A is a finite set of *actions*.
- B is a finite set of *propositions*.
- $T : Q \times A \mapsto Q$ is the *transition function*.
- $D : Q \times A \mapsto [0, 1]$ is the *distribution* on selecting the next action from the current state, where $\Sigma_{a \in A} P(q, a) = 1$.
- $L : Q \mapsto 2^B$ is a labeling function.

An *execution* of a Markov Chain is a finite alternating sequence of states and actions $\sigma = q^0 c^1 q^1 c^2 \ldots c^n q^n$, where $q^0 = q_0$, and $T(q^{i-1}, c^i) = q^i$, the length $|\sigma|$ of the execution is n. From each state q^{i-1} in the execution, an action c^i is selected with probability $D(q^{i-1}, c^i) > 0$ (we say that c^i is *enabled* from q^i); then the state is changed to $q^i = T(q^{i-1}, c_i)$. The probability of selecting the particular execution $\sigma = q^0 c^1 q^1 c^2 \ldots c^n q^n$ is $p(\sigma) = D(q^0, c^1) \times D(q^1, c^2) \times \ldots \times D(q^{n-1}, c^n)$.

2.2 Testing Experiments

Our testing process consists of generating random walks on a Markov Chain and checking them against a given specification. A *property* φ is a set of finite sequences over 2^B. An execution $\sigma = q^0 c^1 q^1 c^2 \ldots c^n q^n$ *satisfies* the property φ if $L(\sigma) = L(q^0)L(q^1)\ldots L(q^n) \in \varphi$. That is, the sequence of labels of the execution σ is in the set φ. We also write in this case that $\sigma \models \varphi$. The formalism used for specifying the property φ needs to be effective for checking whether a given sequence satisfies it or not. We use biasing automata only for checking violation of "safety properties" [1], where violations can be detected on finite executions that cannot be completed anymore into executions that satisfy the specification.

A *testing experiment* is an execution (random walk) σ of $\mathcal{M}$, limited to some predefined number n of actions, and terminating as soon as it first violates the checked specification φ.

2.3 Genetic Programming

During the 1970s, Holland [5] established the field known as *Genetic Algorithms* (GA). Individual candidate solutions are represented as fixed length strings of bits, corresponding to chromosomes in biological systems. Candidates are evaluated using a *fitness* function; It approximates the distance of the candidate from a desired solution. Genetic algorithms evolves a *set of candidates* into a successor set. Each such set forms a *generation*, and there is no backtracking. Candidates are usually represented as fixed length strings. They progress from one generation to the next one according to one of the following cases:

Reproduction. Part of the candidates are selected to propagate from one generation to the subsequent one. The reproduction is done at random, with probability relative to the relation between the fitness of the individual candidate and the average of fitness values in the current generation.

Crossover. Some pairs of the candidates, selected at random for reproduction, are combined using the crossover operation. This operation takes parts of bit strings from two parent solutions and combines them into new solutions, which potentially inherit useful attributes from their parents.

Mutation. This operation randomly alters the content of small number of bits from candidates selected for reproduction (this can also be done after performing crossover). One can decide on mutating each bit separately with some probability.

The different candidates in a single generation have a combined effect on the search; progress tends to promote, improve and combine candidates that are better than others in the same generation. The process of selecting candidates from the previous generation and deciding whether to apply crossover or mutation continues until we complete a new generation. All generations are of some predefined fixed size N. This can be, typically, a number between 50 and 500. Genetic algorithms perform the following steps:

1. Randomly generate N initial candidates.
2. Evaluate the fitness of the candidates.
3. If a satisfactory solution is found, or the number of generations created exceeds a predefined limit (say hundreds or a few thousands), terminate.
4. Otherwise, select candidates for reproduction using randomization, proportional to the fitness values and apply crossover or mutation on some of them, again using randomization, until N candidates are obtained.
5. Go to step 2.

If the algorithm does not terminate with a satisfying solution after a predefined limit on the number of generations, we can restart it with a new random seed, or change the way that we calculate the fitness function.

Genetic programming, suggested by Koza [12], is a direct successor of genetic algorithms. Each individual organism represents a computer program. Programs are represented by variable length structures, such as syntax trees or a sequences of instructions. Each node is classified as *code*, *Boolean*, *condition* or *expression*. Leaf nodes are variables or constants, and other nodes have successors according to their type. For example, a while node (of type *code*) has one successor of type *Boolean* and one successor of type *code* (for the loop body); the *Boolean* node "and" has two successors that can be of type *Boolean* or *condition*, and a *condition* node "<" has two successors of type *expression*. The genetic operations need to respect typing restrictions, e.g., *expressions* cannot be exchanged with *Booleans*.

Crossover is performed on a pair of trees by selecting a subtree rooted with the same node type in each tree, and then swapping between them. This results in two new programs, each having parts from both of its parents. There are several kinds of mutation transformations on syntax trees. First, a node, which roots a subtree, is selected at random. Then, one of the following mutations is performed:

Replacement. Throw away the selected subtree and replace it with a randomly generated subtree of the same type.

Insertion. Generate a new node of the same type as the selected subtree and insert it as its parent node. Then complete the other descendants of the newly inserted node, if necessary.

Reduction. The selected node is replaced with one of its descendants, and the rest of the descendant are deleted.

Deletion. Delete the selected subtree and update its ancestor nodes recursively.

The fitness is often calculated in GP by running the candidate programs on a large set of test cases and evaluating the results, but also using model checking [9–11].

3   Biasing Automata

A biasing automaton is a tool for controlling the probabilities of random walks. It observes the sequence of states of the execution selected so far, and provides the probability distribution for selecting the next action that extends the execution. Based on its current state and the (labeling on the) last observed state of the random walk, the biasing automaton can change its state and provide a different distribution.

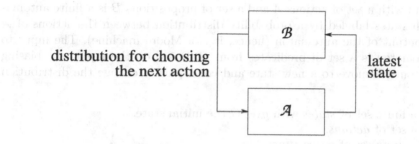

Fig. 1. Controlling random walks using a biasing automaton

A model automaton represents the state space and transition relation of the system under test (SUT). The goal of a biasing automaton is to provide probabilities for selecting the tested execution sequences, in a way that increases the chance of finding violations of the specification that appear among the executions of the model automaton with low probability. A biasing automaton provides, in our context, the probabilities for making the individual selections between possible actions during the random walk. Figure 1 describes the combination of an automaton $\mathcal{A}$, representing the state space for the random walks, and a biasing automaton $\mathcal{B}$ that *controls* the probabilities of selecting the next action of $\mathcal{A}$. The combination of $\mathcal{A}$ and $\mathcal{B}$ forms a Markov Chain.

A *model automaton* $\mathcal{A} = \{S, s_0, A, B, \Delta, M\}$ represents the system under test, where transitions are marked by actions, and states by propositions from a finite set B. It is defined as follows:

- S is a finite set of *states*, with $s_0 \in S$ the *initial state.*
- A is a finite set of *actions.*
- B is a a set of Booelan *propositions.*
- $\Delta : S \times A \mapsto S$ is the *transition relation.*
- $M : S \mapsto 2^B$ is the *labeling* on the states.

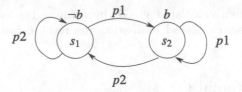

Fig. 2. A model automaton with initial state s_1

The actions of the model automaton in Fig. 2 are $p1$ and $p2$ (corresponding in our context to process names). There is a single Boolean variable b, hence $B = \{b\}$ and the nodes of the model automaton are marked either by b (corresponding to the propositions $\{b\}$ holding in the state), or $\neg b$ (corresponding to $\emptyset$).

A biasing automaton $\mathcal{B} = \{G, g_0, A, B, \Gamma, \mathcal{D}, o\}$ for a family of model automata with a set of actions A and a set of propositions B is a finite automaton with states labeled by a probability distribution between the actions of $\mathcal{A}$ as the output of the automaton (hence, it is a Moore machine). The input to the automaton is a set of predicates from B. Based on the input, the biasing automaton will move to a new state and consequently change the distribution output.

- G is a finite set of *states* with $g_0 \in G$ the initial state.
- A is a set of *actions*.
- B is a finite set of *propositions*.
- $\Gamma : G \times 2^B \mapsto G$ is the *transition function*.
- $\mathcal{D}$ is the space of a distributions over A (i.e., each $D \in \mathcal{D}$ is a *distribution function* $D : A \mapsto [0,1]$).
- $o : G \mapsto \mathcal{D}$ is the *output function* on states. It returns a distribution function on the set of actions A.

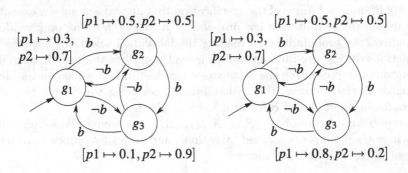

Fig. 3. Two variants of biasing automata

In Fig. 3 we have an example of two variants of biasing automata for the model in Fig. 2. The biasing automata in Fig. 3 differ from one another in the probabilities in state g_3.

The *convolution* of a model automaton $\mathcal{A}$ and a biasing automaton $\mathcal{B}$, denoted $\mathcal{A}[\mathcal{B}]$ over a common set of actions A and a set of Boolean propositions B, is a synchronization of both automata. The probability distribution on actions from the same state is given by the output on the state of the biasing automaton. The convolution produces a Markov chain, obtained as follows:

- The set of *states* is $S \times G$. The *initial state* is (s_0, g_0).
- A is the set of *actions*.
- B is the set of *propositions*.
- The *transition* function $Tr : (S \times G \times A) \mapsto (S \times G)$, where $Tr : ((s, g), a) - (s', g')$ if $\Delta(s, a) = s'$, $\Gamma(g, M(s')) = g'$.
- $D((s, g), a) = o(g)(a)$.
- $L(s, g) = M(s)$.

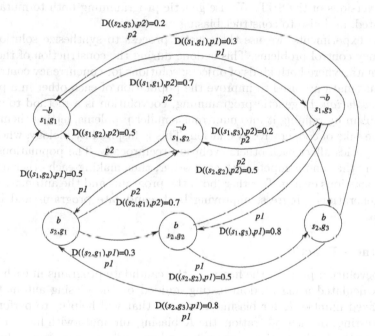

Fig. 4. The convolution automaton

The convolution automaton $\mathcal{A}[\mathcal{B}]$ is a labeled Markov Chain. The automaton in Fig. 4 is the convolution of $\mathcal{A}$, which appears in Fig. 2, and $\mathcal{B}$, which appears on the righthand side of Fig. 3.

4   Obtaining Biasing Automata Through Genetic Programming

Constructing a biasing automaton that improves the chance of finding executions that manifest an event with low probability (e.g., the event that consists

of the executions that violate the specification) involves a tradeoff between optimality and time complexity. One can perform a complete analysis (based on
model checking) of the executions of the system under test (SUT), and check
weather there are executions that demonstrate the problem we want to trace. If
such an execution exists, we can construct a biasing automaton that allows this
execution exclusively. However, the complexity of the complete analysis is high,
and this would defy using random testing as an alternative method for the complete analysis. Moreover, changes to the SUT, e.g., implementing a correction
that would eliminate this erroneous execution, and the success rate in finding
erroneous executions using this biasing automaton will be reduced to 0%. In
fact, we are interested in constructing biasing automata that are robust to such
changes, and applicable to a family of related SUTs. The process we propose
here for obtaining a useful biasing automaton is thus based on experiments with
different versions of the SUT. We use genetic programming both to mutate the
SUTs tested, and also to construct biasing automata.

In our experiments, we use the genetic process to synthesize solutions for
concurrency control problems. This is done during the construction of the biasing automata, where both kinds of objects: solutions for concurrency control and
biasing automata are used to improve the population of each other in a process
called *coevolution*. In genetic programming, coevolution is a method to solve a
large problem by refining it into numerous smaller problems, letting them interact for the sake of cooperative evaluation. This is inspired by biology, where two
or more species affect each others evolution reciprocally. The populations challenge each other and compete with each other, thus making each other improve
as the generations evolve. Together, both the programs and the automata evolve
and as generations progress, improving both candidate programs and biasing
automata.

4.1   Fitness Functions

In the coevolution process, the fitness of the candidate programs in each generation is calculated using random testing, guided by the biasing automata. We
select a fixed number K for biasing automata that will help us to perform the
random testing. In each generation, the K biasing automata with highest fitness
are used to guide the testing. For each random walk we first randomly select
which one of these automata will guide it. The biasing automata observe the
predicates on the states of the current random walk, and provide the distribution for selecting the next process to extend it. To express the fitness for the
biasing automata we define the following:

- G_1 is the set of all programs in the current generation.
- G_2 is the set of all biasing automata in the current generation.
- $s(\mathcal{A}[\mathcal{B}], \varphi, n, N)$ is the number of times we found a violation of φ when running
  N executions of the program represented by automaton $\mathcal{A}$ according to bias
  automaton B with at most n actions per execution. This is an experiment
  that could yield different results each time.
  We have that when $n, N \rightsquigarrow \infty$, then $s(\mathcal{A}[\mathcal{B}], \varphi, n, N) \rightsquigarrow p(\mathcal{A}[\mathcal{B}], \varphi)$.

- $minScore = \min\limits_{\mathcal{B} \in G_2} \Sigma_{\mathcal{A} \in G_1} s(\mathcal{A}[\mathcal{B}], \varphi, n, N)$ as the minimum fitness score on all biasing automata in the generation.
- $maxScore = \max\limits_{\mathcal{B} \in G_2} \Sigma_{\mathcal{A} \in G_1} s(\mathcal{A}[\mathcal{B}], \varphi, n, N)$ as the maximum fitness score on all biasing automata in the generation.

We use $N=300$ and $n=150$. The fitness function is defined as:

$$fitness(\mathcal{B}) = \frac{\Sigma_{\mathcal{A} \in G_1} s(\mathcal{A}[\mathcal{B}], \varphi, n, N) - minScore}{maxScore - minScore}$$

The fitness of the candidate programs are based on the randomized testing (using the co-generated biasing automata) of their correctness properties. Because the testing is based on inspecting limited length sequences, and due to the sampling nature of testing, we also make light use of model checking for providing fitness for the candidate programs: if a candidate is detected with a very high fitness value, which is above a certain threshold that we define, we run the SPIN model checker [6] on this candidate to check whether indeed it satisfies the desired properties. For more details on the fitness function used on candidate programs see [3].

4.2   Mutations

For the biasing automata, we define the following types of mutations:

Change a transition. Choose randomly a state to mutate and redirect one of its outgoing edges.

Change probabilities. Choose a state and assign new distribution on choosing the actions from it.

Add a state. Generate a new state and connect it to the other states in the automaton graph.

Delete a state. Choose randomly a state, delete it from the automaton and assign a random target state for each edge that previously led to it.

Sub-automaton. Create new sub-automaton. Choose one of the states and delete all states with index larger than it. Grow a new automaton with some number of states and merge it to the remaining states of the original automaton.

As an example, consider the automaton in Fig. 5. The labeling we use is over the set of propositions $\{p1\ in\ CS_1, p2\ in\ CS_2,\}$. Each edge is labeled with a subset of these propositions, where the lack of a label, e.g., $p2\ in\ CS_2$ is denoted by $\neg p2\ in\ CS_2$. We compact the presentation, where several edges have the same source and target, by depicting a single edge, marked by a Boolean formula that is equivalent to the disjunction of the formulas on the edges.

After a *change transitions* mutation was performed, and state q_2 is chosen as the mutation point, edges coming out of state q_2 were randomly changed. Specifically, the depicted self edge from q_2 to itself represents two edges: one labeled with $\neg(p1\ in\ CS_1) \wedge p2\ in\ CS_2$ and the other with $\neg(p1 in\ CS_1) \wedge \neg(p2\ in\ CS_2)$. The former edged was replaced with an edge from q_2 to q_0. We thus obtained from 5 the automaton in Fig. 6.

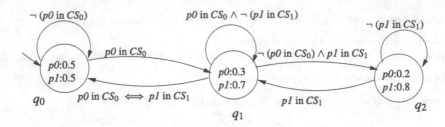

Fig. 5. Biasing automaton before mutation

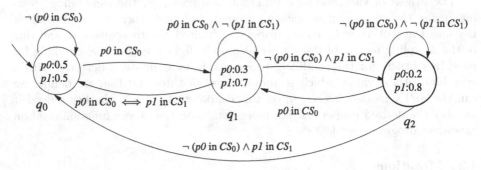

Fig. 6. Biasing automaton after a change transition mutation

Extrapolating Mutating Probabilities. The mutation and crossover operations of genetic programming allow us to jump from one candidate solution to another, while preserving part of the structure of the former candidate. Two other search heuristics allow us to make finer changes around the candidates, in order to search for local or global optima. In *simulated annealing* [16], one controls the amount of change allowed between candidates; the probability of making big changes decreases when the fitness increases. Accordingly, a small change tends to search around the candidates that look more promising, while a big change tends to avoid hill climbing. In *gradient descent*, one uses exterpolation of a multivariable function, based on the direction of its gradient (multivariable derivative), to assist in progressing to a better solution.

Inspired by these techniques, we refine the genetic programming search. In particular, we want to make the "change-probabilities" mutation more sensitive to the results of the testing experiments. $s_1, \ldots, s_n$. Define a function

$$f(\mathcal{B}, \mathcal{A}, D(s_1, p1), \ldots, D(s_n, p1)) \tag{1}$$

that returns the probability of random walks over a model automaton $\mathcal{A}$, performed according to the distributions on the nodes of $\mathcal{B}$, to satisfy the checked property φ. We assume a fixed structure for the biasing automata that are allowed for the parameter $\mathcal{B}$, in particular, they all have n states. These automata can differ only in the probability distributions attached to the states[1], which appear explicitly as parameters to this function. Since our goal is to increase the chance of observing violations of φ, we would like to select these distributions in a way that will minimize the value of that function over the family of models $\mathcal{A}$ that we consider.

It is of course pointless to try to calculate the actual value of the function f. But we can try to approximate its behavior using experiments. In addition to the above mutations, we allow selecting to change the distribution parameters using extrapolation approximation that is based on such experiments. Consider the case where there are two automata $\mathcal{B}$, and $\mathcal{B}'$, where $\mathcal{B}'$ is obtained from $\mathcal{B}$ using change probability mutation. Suppose, without loss of generality, that $\mathcal{B}'$ returns better results, i.e., more violations, when applied to various model automata that we consider. Then we can change the distributions proportional to the change between the distributions of $\mathcal{B}$ and $\mathcal{B}'$.

5   Implementation and Experiments

In [3] we presented the use of genetic programming, based on statistical model checking (SMC) and model checking [4], for synthesizing concurrent code from temporal specification. One of the goals was to replace most of the use of model checking in [9–11] by lighter reliability methods. However, we quickly realized that using the random-based sampling approaches is very sensitive to the occurrence of events with low probability, which may be missed. This required several adaptations, e.g., bringing back the use of model checking, even if in a very limited way, at the last stages of the genetic synthesis. The observations made in that work motivated the definition and use of biasing automata in the current paper, in order to better control the statistical evaluation during the genetic process. We provide here experimental results based on integrating the software reported in [3] with an implementation of a genetic coevolution process for constructing and using biasing automata.

5.1   Running Example: Mutual Exclusion

We take the synthesis of solutions for the mutual exclusion problem as a running example. Following is the template that needs to be concretized.

```
p0: While W0 do            p1: While W1 do
      NonCrit0                 NonCrit1
      preCS0                   preCS1
      CS0                      CS1
      postCS0                  postCS1
    end while                end while
```

---

[1] For the case of two processes, $D(s_i, p2) = 1 - D(s_i, p1)$, hence this is a unique function of the distributions. In case of k choices, we need to use $k - 1$ parameters for each state.

NonCSi represents the actions of process pi outside the critical section. It can actually be fixed as empty code. CSi represents the critical section, which both processes want to enter a finite or unbounded number of times. It is not part of the synthesis task, and can be represented by trivial code (which serves only to allow checking that it is eventually entered upon request). The goal of the mutual exclusion problem is to allow eventual access to the critical section each time a process wants to enter it, but to disallow both processes to enter the critical section at the same time. Entering and exiting the critical section is controlled by the code in preCSi and postCSi. These are the program segments that consist of the mutual exclusion protocol and are the focus of the synthesis.

The properties we want to satisfy here are:

- *Safety* :$\Box\neg(p0\ in\ CS_0 \wedge p1\ in\ CS_1)$
- *Liveness* :$\Box(pi\ in\ preCS_i \rightarrow \Diamond pi\ in\ CS_i)$

5.2   Experiment Setting

Our program is written in C and runs in Linux. We run the GP procedure for at most 2000 generations, with 100 candidates in each generation. For the fitness evaluation, we randomly simulate each candidate 300 times per generation. Based on coevolution, we also generate candidate biasing automata. Each generation includes 5–20 biasing automata and each biasing automaton is allowed to have at most 50 states.

Mutation is performed on 40% randomly chosen candidates among the one that are selected to propagate to the next generation. The distribution on the different mutations is according to the Table 1, where the *create sub-automaton* mutation is selected with a very low probability, due to its rather extensive effect.

Table 1. Distribution of types of mutations

	Mutation rate
Change transitions	24%
Change probabilities	24%
Add state	24%
Remove state	24%
Create sub-automaton	4%

5.3   Biasing Automata Learned

The automaton in Fig. 7 is one of the biasing automaton that the system learned. State q_1 corresponds to process $p0$ being in the critical section, while $p1$ is not in its critical section. Then, higher probability is given to process $p1$ to progress. This biasing automaton helps capturing both processes at their critical section, violating the safety property; it reduces the probability to generate an execution sequence where $p0$ enters its critical section, immediately and independently of $p1$ leaving the critical section, and only then $p1$ enters its critical section. Intuitively, it encourages $p0$, when in its critical section, to wait and give chance for $p1$ to also enter its critical section, rather than leaving immediately.

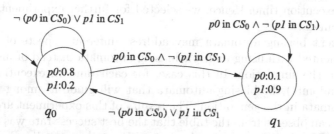

Fig. 7. A biasing automaton generated during the GP synthesis of mutual exclusion

5.4   Performance Evaluation

We conducted experiments to check whether the integration of biasing automata can help with detecting errors. We picked up a biasing automaton that was generated through a coevolution process. Then we randomly selected 20 candidates for solution for the mutual exclusion, also generated as part of the genetic process, and run each of them 300 times with both random simulation and biasing automata guided simulation respectively. With the help of biasing automata we locate 348 executions that triggered error states, while we only found 120 erroneous executions by using random simulation.

Table 2. Applying a single biasing automaton in the GP synthesis procedure

No. of biasing aut. per generation	Success rate	Average iterations until convergence	Average time per execution (minutes)
Without biasing aut.	20%	1930	20
5	28%	1890	31
10	32%	1700	40
15	31%	1720	61
20	30%	1731	83

We next evaluated whether using biasing automata can help, when integrated into the GP procedure, in generating correct solutions with greater success rate and less iterations. In this experiment, we select the best biasing automaton in each generations We change the number of biasing automata candidates generated in each generation to guide the testing. The data is reported in Table 2. From the table we can observe that the best performance, in terms of the success rate of finding correct solutions, was with 10 biasing automata per generation. Not surprisingly, the overhead of learning more biasing automata per generation affects the execution time. Hence, we selected for further experiments using 10 biasing automata.

As different biasing automata may address different aspects of errors, we also experimented with using multiple biasing automata instead of just the best one to guide the simulation. In this case, for each random execution we first selected (randomly) the biasing automata that will guide it among the k best biasing automata in the generation. The results of this experiment are shown in Table 3. We can observe from the table that the best success rate was with using 3 automata. The declined success above 3 automata can possibly be explained by adding lower fitness biasing automata to guide the random selection.

Table 3. Applying multiple biasing automata in the simulation of mutual exclusion

k: No. of best biasing automata used per generation	Fitness value of the kth automata in the last generation	Success rate	Average iterations until convergence
1	1	32%	1700
2	0.95	34%	1693
3	0.93	40%	1640
4	0.81	36%	1712
5	0.73	33%	1730
6	0.69	32.5%	1746
7	0.67	31.9%	1751

We performed further experiments, e.g., synthesizing solutions for the dinning philosophers problem, where we found also an improvement in the number of errors that could be found, when we introduced a biasing automaton to guide the random testing. However, the improvement of the success rate of the genetic search on that example was more modest than for the mutual exclusion problem, only up to 5%.

6   Conclusions

Random simulations are widely used in software testing and verification. However, the low probability ("rare event") errors which appear with very low probability may be elusive to discover. This may cause incorrect assessment of the system behavior and quality. In this paper, we presented biasing automata, which helps the randomized selection of test cases in a way that is leaned towards the sought errors.

We implemented this idea as part of a genetic programming synthesis system for concurrent code from temporal specification. Our experiments show that with the help of biasing automata, we can locate more errors during random testing. In addition, the success rate of the synthesis process was significantly improved. The experiments lead us to believe that the approach presented here is effective for enhancing the results of random testing. Of course, further experiments, and additional work on the implementation are called for.

The embedding of the generation of a biasing automaton in a genetic coevolution, as reported in this paper, was a matter of convenience, as we already experimented with the genetic synthesis separately. In addition, it turned out to improve the success of generating correct-by-design solutions. However, biasing automata can also be generated by mutating the already available system under test. In that sense, the process is related to "mutation testing" [2]. In mutation testing, one checks if a collected set of test suite is strong enough to cover the testing of a program. Here, mutation can used to find a biasing automaton that would improve the guidance for random testing, in order to increase the chance of finding errors.

Acknowledgements. The second author would like to thank Sergiy Bogomolov and Ken McMillan for interesting discussions on this subject.

References

1. Alpern, B., Schneider, F.B.: Recognizing safety and liveness. Distrib. Comput. **2**(3), 117–126 (1987)
2. Ammann, P., Offutt, J.: Introduction to Software Testing. Cambridge University Press, Cambridge (2008)
3. Bu, L., Peled, D., Shen, D., Zhuang, Y.: Genetic synthesis of concurrent code using mode checking and statistical model checking. In: SPIN 2018, pp. 275–291 (2018)
4. Clarke, E.M., Grumberg, O., Peled, D.: Model Checking. MIT Press, Cambridge (2000)
5. Holland, J.H.: Adaptation in Natural and Artificial Systems: An Introductory Analysis with Applications to Biology, Control and Artificial Intelligence. MIT Press, Cambridge (1992)
6. Holzmann, G.J.: The SPIN Model Checker - Primer and Reference Manual. Addison-Wesley, New Jersey (2004)
7. Grosu, R., Smolka, S.A.: Monte Carlo model checking. In: Halbwachs, N., Zuck, L.D. (eds.) TACAS 2005. LNCS, vol. 3440, pp. 271–286. Springer, Heidelberg (2005). https://doi.org/10.1007/978-3-540-31980-1_18
8. Jegourel, C., Legay, A., Sedwards, S.: An effective heuristic for adaptive importance splitting in statistical model checking. In: Margaria, T., Steffen, B. (eds.) ISoLA 2014. LNCS, vol. 8803, pp. 143–159. Springer, Heidelberg (2014). https://doi.org/10.1007/978-3-662-45231-8_11

9. Johnson, C.G.: Genetic programming with fitness based on model checking. In: Ebner, M., O'Neill, M., Ekárt, A., Vanneschi, L., Esparcia-Alcázar, A.I. (eds.) EuroGP 2007. LNCS, vol. 4445, pp. 114–124. Springer, Heidelberg (2007). https://doi.org/10.1007/978-3-540-71605-1_11

10. Katz, G., Peled, D.: Model checking-based genetic programming with an application to mutual exclusion. In: Ramakrishnan, C.R., Rehof, J. (eds.) TACAS 2008. LNCS, vol. 4963, pp. 141–156. Springer, Heidelberg (2008). https://doi.org/10.1007/978-3-540-78800-3_11

11. Gal Katz, D.: Peled: Synthesizing, correcting and improving code, using model checking-based genetic programming. STTT **19**(4), 449–464 (2017)

12. Koza, J.R.: Genetic Programming: On the Programming of Computers by Means of Natural Selection. MIT Press, Cambridge (1992)

13. Larsen, K.G., Legay, A.: On the power of statistical model checking. In: Margaria, T., Steffen, B. (eds.) ISoLA 2016. LNCS, vol. 9953, pp. 843–862. Springer, Cham (2016). https://doi.org/10.1007/978-3-319-47169-3_62

14. Legay, A., Delahaye, B., Bensalem, S.: Statistical model checking: an overview. In: Barringer, H., et al. (eds.) RV 2010. LNCS, vol. 6418, pp. 122–135. Springer, Heidelberg (2010). https://doi.org/10.1007/978-3-642-16612-9_11

15. Pretschner, A., Holling, D., Eschbach, R., Gemmar, M.: A generic fault model for quality assurance. In: Moreira, A., Schätz, B., Gray, J., Vallecillo, A., Clarke, P. (eds.) MODELS 2013. LNCS, vol. 8107, pp. 87–103. Springer, Heidelberg (2013). https://doi.org/10.1007/978-3-642-41533-3_6

16. Kirkpatrick, S., Gelatt Jr., C.D., Vecchi, M.P.: Optimization by simulated annealing. Science **220**(4598), 671–680 (1983)

17. Younes, H.L.S., Simmons, R.G.: Probabilistic verification of discrete event systems using acceptance sampling. In: Brinksma, E., Larsen, K.G. (eds.) CAV 2002. LNCS, vol. 2404, pp. 223–235. Springer, Heidelberg (2002). https://doi.org/10.1007/3-540-45657-0_17

On the Sequential Massart Algorithm
for Statistical Model Checking

Cyrille Jegourel[1(✉)], Jun Sun[1], and Jin Song Dong[2]

[1] Singapore University of Technology and Design, Singapore, Singapore
[2] Griffith University, Mount Gravatt, Australia
cyrille.jegourel@gmail.com, sunjunhqq@gmail.com, dongjs1@gmail.com

Abstract. Several schemes have been provided in Statistical Model Checking (SMC) for the estimation of property occurrence based on predefined confidence and *absolute* or *relative* error. Simulations might be however costly if many samples are required and the usual algorithms implemented in statistical model checkers tend to be conservative. Bayesian and rare event techniques can be used to reduce the sample size but they can not be applied without prerequisite or knowledge about the system under scrutiny. Recently, sequential algorithms based on Monte Carlo estimations and Massart bounds have been proposed to reduce the sample size while providing guarantees on error bounds which has been shown to outperform alternative frequentist approaches [15]. In this work, we discuss some features regarding the distribution and the optimisation of these algorithms.

1 Introduction

Statistical Model Checking (SMC) [22] is a formal verification method used to estimate quantitative properties of probabilistic systems by simulations sampled from an executable model of the system. Unlike other probabilistic Model Checking techniques, the results are not exact but given within predefined precision and confidence bounds that rely in general on the Monte Carlo method [5,18]. An important issue is to design algorithms that provide enough statistical evidence about the probabilistic occurrence of properties.

SMC was initially proposed to address the problem of verifying whether a property probability exceeds a threshold or not. This problem can be solved by using the sequential probability ratio test in hypothesis testing [21,22]. Other issues have been considered since, notably the estimation of the probability that a system property holds. In spite of similarities, the two problems are different and in what follows, we focus on the estimation problem. The need of rigorous sampling schemes have been addressed from the early days of SMC [10,22] to the more recent [8,9,15] just to cite a few. A key feature in designing a sampling procedure is to determine the number of simulations necessary to generate an estimation within acceptable margins of error and confidence.

© Springer Nature Switzerland AG 2018
T. Margaria and B. Steffen (Eds.): ISoLA 2018, LNCS 11245, pp. 287–304, 2018.
https://doi.org/10.1007/978-3-030-03421-4_19

In many case studies, reducing the sample size while rigorously guaranteeing the control of these error bounds is critical. For example, Secure Water Treatment (SWaT)[1] is a scaled-down but fully operational water treatment testbed at the Singapore University of Technology and Design, capable of producing five gallons of safe drinking water per minute. Probabilistic SWaT models have been designed to understand the response of SWaT to a variety of cyber attacks [4]. However, the simulations are costly and time-consuming. Then checking whether the probabilistic model is a faithful representation of this system is critical and must be done efficiently, under the constraint that the system is executed as few as possible.

Several classes of schemes such as Bayesian SMC [23], or rare event simulation techniques [12,13] have been considered to address this problem. However, in Bayesian SMC, the probability to estimate must be given by a prior random variable whose density is based on previous experiments and knowledge about the system. Rare event techniques can not be easily deployed for general problems and for arbitrary class of probabilistic systems. Also, these techniques require either the full knowledge of the probabilistic distribution of the system or the design of an accurate score function. Finally, the error bounds remain approximate in rare event simulation. These limitations motivate the recourse to sequential algorithms based on exact error bounds for frequentist estimations. This work is limited to this class of schemes.

In [10], the authors discussed the notion of *absolute* and *relative* margin of error for SMC. The absolute error is defined as the magnitude of the difference between a probability and an estimation of this probability whereas the relative error is defined as the absolute error divided by the magnitude of the probability. To guarantee that the absolute error is bounded, they introduced a procedure relying on the Okamoto bound[2] that, given fixed confidence and error parameters, determines *a priori* the number of Bernoulli samples required, which is independent of the probability to estimate. Supporting relative errors (i.e., errors which depend on the probability to quantify) is more difficult, although theoretical bounds exist. The relative error was initially handled by Dagum et al.'s algorithm [7].

In [15], new sequential sampling schemes based on Massart bounds and exact confidence intervals were proposed to handle absolute and relative error problems and were compared with other approaches, including some that have not been necessarily used in the context of SMC. We refer the readers to [15] for a comparison among these algorithms. The results were promising as they show that the Massart sequential sampling schemes outperformed the standard algorithms implemented in statistical model checkers like PRISM [16], PLASMA [11], APMC [10], COSMOS [2] and UPPAAL-SMC [8]. It is worth saying that these sequential Massart algorithms are not limited to a particular class of models and could be easily implemented in any of these statistical model checkers.

---

[1] https://itrust.sutd.edu.sg/testbeds/secure-water-treatment-swat/.

[2] The Okamoto bound is sometimes called the Chernoff bound in the literature.

In this work, we take the opportunity to discuss some features of the sequential Massart algorithms that were not initially considered and to explain with more details on how to set up the algorithms. First of all, given error and confidence parameters, ϵ and δ, it is necessary to provide a third parameter α such that $0 < \alpha < \delta$. In [15], α was set by default at $\delta/2$. In an expanded version [14], we showed empirically that α could not be optimised a priori since it is dependent on the (unknown) probability to estimate. In this work, we give guidelines about setting α up and we show that the gains in terms of sample size reduction are quite significant if α is set up closer to zero.

These algorithms also require the recursive computation of confidence intervals. For the sake of rigorousness, these confidence intervals were initially chosen to be exact confidence intervals. However, these intervals are always rather conservative. Instead, approximate confidence intervals are in general easier to compute, their precision is better in the sense that their width is narrower but their confidence is not always strictly guaranteed. In what follows, we will consider two alternative approximate confidence intervals to measure empirically the impact on the sample sizes and the reliability of our algorithms.

Finally, an important aspect of SMC is that its performance can be improved by distributing the simulations on a multi-threaded system once the sample size of the experiment has been determined. For sequential algorithms, extra work must be done since the sample size is unknown a priori. In this work, we introduce a simple procedure to handle this issue.

In Sect. 2, we formally state the absolute and relative specifications that must be fulfilled by the SMC schemes. We also recall the basics of Monte Carlo estimation and Okamoto and Massart bounds. In Sect. 3, we present the sequential Massart algorithms. We discuss the coverage parameter in Sect. 4. We show in Sect. 5 the impact of approximate confidence intervals on the sampling size reduction. In Sect. 6, we propose a simple algorithm to distribute our sequential algorithms in a multi-threaded system. Section 7 concludes the article.

2   Background

In the following, a stochastic system $\mathcal{S}$ is interpreted as a set of interacting components in which the state is determined randomly with respect to a global probability distribution. Let $(\Omega, \mathcal{F}, \mu)$ be the probability space induced by the system with Ω a set of finite paths with respect to system's property ϕ, $\mathcal{F}$ a σ-algebra of Ω and μ the probability distribution defined over $\mathcal{F}$.

2.1   Absolute and Relative Error Specifications

Given a probabilistic system $\mathcal{S}$, a property ϕ and a probability γ, we write $\mathcal{S} \models Pr(\phi) = \gamma$ if and only if the probability that a random execution of $\mathcal{S}$ satisfies ϕ is equal to γ. In principle, if γ is unknown, we can apply analytical methods to determine this value. However, due for example to numerical imprecisions, we often relax the constraints over γ and introduce the following notations:

$$\mathcal{S} \models_\epsilon^a Pr(\phi) = \gamma \quad \text{and} \quad \mathcal{S} \models_\epsilon^r Pr(\phi) = \gamma \tag{1}$$

The left formula means that a random execution of S satisfies ϕ with probability γ plus or minus an absolute error ϵ, i.e. $Pr(\phi) \in [\gamma - \epsilon, \gamma + \epsilon]$. The right formula means that a random execution of S satisfies ϕ with probability γ up to some relative error ϵ, i.e. $Pr(\phi) \in [(1 - \epsilon)\gamma, (1 + \epsilon)\gamma]$.

SMC applies to an executable system S and a property ϕ whose truth value can be determined in finite time. In SMC, the satisfaction of property ϕ is quantified by a Bernoulli random variable of unknown mean γ. This mean is then approximated using a Monte Carlo estimation scheme. The output of the scheme is thus not an exact value but an approximate one, given within certain error bounds and a confidence parameter δ that is the probability of outputting a false estimate. SMC thus requires a sampling scheme which outputs, after n samples, an estimate $\hat{\gamma}_n$ close to γ up to some absolute or relative ϵ-based error with probability greater or equal than $1 - \delta$. Formally, we write:

$$S \models_{\epsilon,\delta}^{a} Pr(\phi) = \hat{\gamma}_n \quad \text{or} \quad S \models_{\epsilon,\delta}^{r} Pr(\phi) = \hat{\gamma}_n \tag{2}$$

if and only if an algorithm outputs estimators while guaranteeing:

$$Pr(|\hat{\gamma}_n - \gamma| > \epsilon) \leq \delta \tag{3}$$

or respectively:

$$Pr(|\hat{\gamma}_n - \gamma| > \epsilon\gamma) < \delta. \tag{4}$$

We call (3) the absolute error specification and (4) the relative error specification.

2.2 Monte Carlo Estimation

Let ω be a path sampled from space Ω with respect to distribution μ; z be a function from Ω to $\{0, 1\}$ assigning 1 if ω satisfies property ϕ and 0 otherwise; and γ be the probability that an arbitrary path of the system satisfies ϕ. In SMC, the behaviour of function z is interpreted as a Bernoulli random variable Z with mean parameter γ. By definition, the average value γ is the integral of function z with respect to distribution μ over space Ω: $\gamma = E_\mu[Z] = \int_\Omega z(\omega) \, d\mu(\omega)$ and an estimator $\hat{\gamma}_n$ is given by the Monte Carlo method by drawing n independent samples $\omega_i \sim \mu$, $i \in \{1, \ldots, n\}$, as follows:

$$\hat{\gamma}_n = \frac{1}{n} \sum_{i=1}^{n} z(\omega_i) \approx E_\mu[Z] \tag{5}$$

Let $m = \sum_{i=1}^{n} z(\omega_i)$ be the number of successes and $\sigma^2 = \gamma(1 - \gamma)$ the variance of Z. In what follows, for sake of simplicity, we use both notations $\hat{\gamma}_n$ and m/n to denote the estimate.

The purpose of the algorithms presented in Sect. 3 is to fulfil Specification (3) or (4) with as few samples as possible. In other words, their goal is to improve the performance of statistical model checkers with algorithms that output reliable Monte Carlo estimates, in terms of precision and confidence. For this purpose, they make use of the bounds below.

2.3   Okamoto and Massart Bounds

In the literature, the Chernoff bounds [5] refer to exponential decreasing bounds, in the number of simulations, of the probability of deviation between a Monte Carlo estimate and its mean. Tighter bounds have been established since, notably in [17]. Note that in their original respective works, these bounds are only one-sided. In what follows, we give the two-sided versions of these bounds, for which the proofs can be found in the expanded version of [15][3].

Absolute Error Bounds. Though the seminal work is due to Chernoff [5], the following two-sided absolute error bound has been stated for binomial distributions by Okamoto in [19].

Theorem 1 (Okamoto bound). *For any ϵ, $0 < \epsilon < 1$, we have the following inequality:*

$$Pr(|\hat{\gamma}_n - \gamma| > \epsilon) \leq 2\exp(-2n\epsilon^2) \tag{6}$$

Given ϵ, δ, writing out $\delta = 2\exp(-2n\epsilon^2)$, the Okamato bound can be used to determine a minimal number n of simulations to perform a Monte Carlo plan fulfilling the absolute error specification (3). The main advantage of the Okamoto bound is that it does not depend on γ, the value to estimate. However, the bound is very conservative and in many cases, a much lower sample size would achieve the same absolute error specification.

Massart established in [17] a sharper bound that holds if the absolute error ϵ is lower than probabilities γ and $1 - \gamma$.

Theorem 2 (Absolute Error Massart bound). *For all γ such that $0 < \gamma < 1$ and any ϵ such that $0 < \epsilon < \min(\gamma, 1 - \gamma)$, we have the following inequality:*

$$Pr(|\hat{\gamma}_n - \gamma| > \epsilon) \leq 2\exp\left(-n\epsilon^2 h_a(\gamma, \epsilon)\right) \tag{7}$$

where $h_a(\gamma, \epsilon) = \begin{cases} 9/2\left((3\gamma + \epsilon)(3(1 - \gamma) - \epsilon)\right)^{-1} & if\ 0 < \gamma < 1/2 \\ 9/2\left((3(1 - \gamma) + \epsilon)(3\gamma + \epsilon)\right)^{-1} & if\ 1/2 \leq \gamma < 1 \end{cases}$

Figure 1 shows the number of samples per probability necessary to satisfy an absolute error specification defined by $\epsilon = 0.01$ and $\delta = 0.05$ according to the Okamoto and the Massart bounds. For values close to the boundaries, we can see that the Okamoto bound is very conservative in comparison of the Massart bound. However, the two bounds are similar for $\gamma = 1/2$.

---

[3] A journal version with the proofs is currently submitted [14]. The proofs are also available here: https://www.researchgate.net/publication/317823195_Sequential_Schemes_for_Frequentist_Estimation_of_Properties_in_Statistical_Model_Checking.

Relative Error Bounds. In practice, the absolute error is set independently of γ. However, it could be that the approximation is meaningless, especially if the absolute error is large with respect to γ. In this case, setting a relative error that remains 'small' with respect of γ may be adequate. The Massart bound has a two-sided relative form.

Theorem 3 (Relative Error Massart bound). *For γ, $0 < \gamma < 1$ and any ϵ, $0 < \epsilon < (1 - \gamma)/\gamma$, we have the following inequality:*

$$Pr(|\hat{\gamma}_n - \gamma| \geq \epsilon\gamma) \leq 2\exp\left(-n\epsilon^2 h_r(\gamma, \epsilon)\right) \tag{8}$$

$$with \quad h_r(\gamma, \epsilon) = \begin{cases} 9\gamma/2 \left((3 + \epsilon)(3 - \gamma(3 + \epsilon))\right)^{-1} & if\, 0 < \gamma < 1/2 \\ 9\gamma/2 \left((3 - \epsilon)(3 - \gamma(3 - \epsilon))\right)^{-1} & if\, 1/2 \leq \gamma < 1 \end{cases}$$

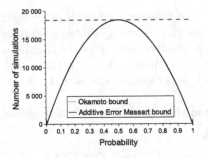

Fig. 1. Okamoto (dash) and Massart (plain) bounds with absolute error $\epsilon = 0.01$ and confidence parameter $\delta = 0.05$.

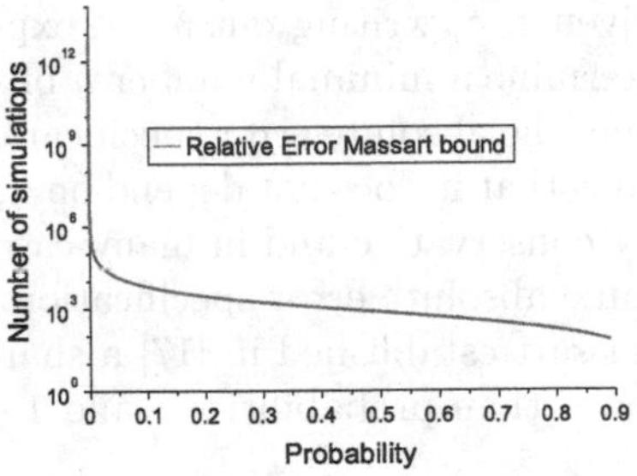

Fig. 2. Massart bounds with relative error $\epsilon = 0.1$ and confidence parameter $\delta = 0.05$.

Figure 2 shows the number of samples per probability necessary to satisfy a relative error specification defined by $\epsilon = 0.1$ and $\delta = 0.05$ according to the relative error Massart bound. As expected, the sample size explodes when γ tends to zero.

2.4   Bounds with Coverage

In contrast to the Okamoto bound, the Massart bounds depend on γ and they are thus not directly applicable since γ is the probability that we want to estimate. However, one may still exploit some information about γ. For example, depending on the problem, one may know or numerically evaluate with certainty a rough interval in which γ evolves. In what follows, we denote $C(\gamma, I)$ the notional coverage of γ by a confidence interval I, that is the probability that I contains γ.

Theorem 4 (Absolute Error Massart Bound with coverage). *Let a and b be the lower and upper bounds of a confidence interval I and I^c be the complement of I in $[0, 1]$:*

$$Pr\left(|\hat{\gamma}_n - \gamma| > \epsilon\right) \leq 2\exp\left(-n\epsilon^2 h_a(x, \epsilon)\right) + C(\gamma, I^c) \qquad (9)$$

where function h_a is defined in Theorem 2 and $x = b$ if $b < 1/2$, $x = a$ if $a > 1/2$ and $x = 1/2$ if $1/2 \in I$.

By default, $a = 0$, $b = 1$, $C(\gamma, [0, 1]^c) = 0$ and the above theorem is consistent with the Okamoto bound. We remark that even if an accurate estimation of γ is not feasible within a reasonable time, Theorem 4 can exploit coarse but exact bounds a, b, calculated analytically. In that case, we would have $C(\gamma, [a, b]^c) = 0$. Finally, a similar theorem involving relative error can be established.

Theorem 5 (Relative Error Massart Bound with coverage). *Let a be the lower bound of a confidence interval $I = [a, 1]$ and h_r defined as in Theorem 3.*

$$Pr\left(|\hat{\gamma}_n - \gamma| > \epsilon\gamma\right) \leq 2\exp\left(-n\epsilon^2 h_r(a, \epsilon)\right) + C(\gamma, [0, a[) \qquad (10)$$

Both theorems state that the probability of absolute or relative error is bounded by the respective Massart bound applied over the most pessimistic value of a confidence interval plus the probability that the interval does not contain γ. We deduce from both theorems the following sample-size result:

Theorem 6. *Let $\alpha < \delta$ such that $C(\gamma, I^c) < \alpha$. (i) Under the conditions of Theorem 4, a Monte Carlo algorithm $\mathcal{A}$ that outputs an estimate $\hat{\gamma}_n$ fulfils Specification (3) if $n > \frac{1}{h_a(x, \epsilon)\epsilon^2} \log \frac{2}{\delta - \alpha}$.*

(ii) Similarly, under the conditions of Theorem 5, a Monte Carlo algorithm $\mathcal{A}$ that outputs an estimate $\hat{\gamma}_n$ fulfils Specification (4) if $n > \frac{1}{h_r(a, \epsilon)\epsilon^2} \log \frac{2}{\delta - \alpha}$.

The bounds of Theorem 6 are more conservative than the bounds induced by Theorems 2 and 3 because the Massart bounds are evaluated using the most pessimistic value of the confidence interval $[a, b]$. In addition, our bound also takes into account the probability that γ is not in I, implying that an additional number of samples are required in the final sample size. In the absolute error case, if a confidence interval I containing $1/2$ is determined, applying the previous theorem is unnecessary because the sample size is simply bounded with respect to the Okamoto bound. Similarly, if a (or b) is lower-bounded (or respectively upper-bounded) by $1/2$ but still close to $1/2$, the Okamoto bound is likely better. However, if γ is closer to 0 or 1, the logarithmic extra number of samples is largely compensated by the evaluation of the Massart bound in a or b.

3   Sequential Massart Algorithm

In this section, we recall the sequential Massart schemes for the absolute and relative error specifications. Both of them require three inputs: an error parameter

ϵ, and two confidence parameters δ and α such that $\alpha < \delta$. To avoid confusion between δ and α, below we call α the coverage parameter.

After each sample, we update a Monte Carlo estimator and a $(1 - \alpha)$-confidence interval for γ. Then, the most pessimistic bound of the confidence interval is used in the Massart function to compute a new minimal sample size n that satisfies Theorem 6. The process is repeated until the calculated sample size is lower than or equal to the current number of runs. In the pseudo-code of Algorithms 1 and 2, keywords GENERATE corresponds to a sample path generation and function CONFINT to the evaluation of the confidence interval (two-sided in the absolute error scheme but only one-sided in the relative error scheme). Theorems 4 and 5 guarantee the correctness of our schemes since, for any couple (m, n), if we are able to compute a $(1 - \alpha)$-confidence interval I and its coverage, the deviation probability is bounded by δ defined as the sum of the coverage plus the Massart function evaluated at the most pessimistic value of I.

Absolute Error Sequential Algorithm. We initiate the algorithm with an interval I_0 in which γ belongs (by default, $I_0 = [0, 1]$) and a worst-case (ϵ, δ)-sample size $n_0 = M$ with $M = \lceil \frac{1}{2\epsilon^2} \log \frac{2}{\delta} \rceil$ determined by the Okamoto bound (where $\lceil . \rceil$ denotes the ceiling function). Once a trace $\omega^{(k)}$ is generated and monitored, the number of successes with respect to property ϕ and the total number of traces are updated. Then, a $(1 - \alpha)$-confidence interval I_k is evaluated. Iteration after iteration, the interval width tends to shorten and becomes more and more accurate. Theorem 6-(i) is applied to determine a new sample size n_k, bounded from above by M if necessary. These steps are repeated until $k \geq n_k$ at which Specification (3) is rigorously fulfilled.

Relative Error Sequential Algorithm. We first assume the existence, in a practical case study, of a threshold γ_{min}, supposedly low, corresponding to a tolerated precision error (e.g. a floating-point approximation). Estimating a value below γ_{min} is then unnecessary. The maximal number of simulations is consequently bounded by the maximal Massart bound, $M = \lceil \frac{1}{\epsilon^2 h_r(\gamma_{min}, \epsilon)} \log \frac{2}{\delta} \rceil$. The relative error scheme is similar to the absolute error scheme. Note however that it is only necessary to determine a lower bound of I_k since h_r is a decreasing function in γ. Then, we determine a one-sided $(1 - \alpha)$-interval of shape $[a_k, 1]$. Theorem 6-ii is applied to determine a new sample size n_k, upper bounded by M if $a_k < \gamma_{min}$ and the steps are repeated until $k \geq n_k$. If the final output $\hat{\gamma}_k$ is higher than γ_{min}, Specification (4) is rigorously fulfilled. Otherwise, we can still output that γ is lower than γ_{min} with probability greater that $1 - \delta$.

4   Discussion on the Coverage Parameter

Coverage parameter α must be chosen such that $0 < \alpha < \delta$. Note that the sample sizes at which Specifications (3) and (4) are fulfilled are guaranteed to be lower or equal than the Okamoto and the maximal Massart bounds.

Algorithm 1. Absolute Error Sequential Algorithm

Data:

ϵ, δ, α : the original parameters

$M = \lceil \frac{1}{2\epsilon^2} \log \frac{2}{\delta} \rceil$: the Okamoto bound

$k = 0$

$m = 0$: the number of successes

$n_k = M$

$I_k = [a_k, b_k] = [0, 1]$: the initial interval in which γ is known to belong

1   **while** $k < n_k$ **do**

2     $k \leftarrow k + 1$

3   GENERATE $\omega^{(k)}$

4     $z(\omega^{(k)}) = \mathbb{1}(\omega^{(k)} \models \phi)$

5     $m \leftarrow m + z(\omega^{(k)})$

6     $I_k \leftarrow \text{CONFINT}(m, k, \alpha)$

7   **if** $1/2 \in I_k$ **then**

8 | $n_k = M$

9   **else if** $b_k < 1/2$ **then**

10       $n_k = \lceil \frac{2}{h_a(b_k, \epsilon)\epsilon^2} \log \frac{2}{\delta - \alpha} \rceil$

11   **else**

12       $n_k = \lceil \frac{2}{h_a(a_k, \epsilon)\epsilon^2} \log \frac{2}{\delta - \alpha} \rceil$

13     $n_k \leftarrow \min(n_k, M)$

Output: $\hat{\gamma}_k = m/k$

Algorithm 2. Relative Error Sequential Algorithm

Data:

ϵ, δ, α, γ_{min} : the original parameters

$M = \lceil \frac{1}{\epsilon^2 h_r(\gamma_{min}, \epsilon)} \log \frac{2}{\delta} \rceil$

$k = 0$

$n_k = M$

$I_k = [a_k, 1] = [\gamma_{min}, 1]$: the initial interval in which γ is supposed to belong

1   **while** $k < n_k$ **do**

2     $k \leftarrow k + 1$

3   GENERATE $\omega^{(k)}$

4     $z(\omega^{(k)}) = \mathbb{1}(\omega^{(k)} \models \phi)$

5     $m \leftarrow m + z(\omega^{(k)})$

6     $I_k \leftarrow \text{CONFINT}(m, k, \alpha)$

7   **if** $\gamma_{min} \geq a_k$ **then**

8 | $n_k = M$

9   **else**

10       $n_k = \lceil \frac{1}{\epsilon^2 h_r(a_k, \epsilon)} \log \frac{2}{\delta - \alpha} \rceil$

11     $n_k \leftarrow \min(n_k, M)$

Output: $\hat{\gamma}_k = m/k$

If α tends to zero, the $(1 - \alpha)$-confidence interval converges to $[0, 1]$. In the absolute error case, since $1/2$ belongs to the confidence interval, $h_a(x, \epsilon) = h_a(1/2, \epsilon) = 2$. Then, according to Theorem 6-(i), Specification (3) is fulfilled when n is greater than $\frac{1}{2\epsilon^2} \log \frac{2}{\delta}$, that is equivalent to the Okamoto bound. In the relative error case, the sample size fulfilling Specification (4) tends to infinity because $h_r(a, \epsilon)$ tends to zero when a tends to zero. As mentioned previously, n however can be bounded in practice by $M = \lceil \frac{1}{\epsilon^2 h_r(\gamma_{min}, \epsilon)} \log \frac{2}{\delta} \rceil$. In both cases, setting α too close to zero thus does not improve the predetermined bounds. Similarly, when α tends to δ, $\log \frac{2}{\delta - \alpha}$ tends to infinity. Consequently, the sample sizes are respectively bounded by the Okamato bound and M in the absolute and relative error case.

However, determining *a priori* a value for α that would minimise the sample size on average is a conundrum. A closed-form expression would depend on ϵ and δ, but also on probability of interest γ. Given $\epsilon = 0.01$ and $\delta = 0.05$, Fig. 3 shows for different probabilities the sample size (averaged over 150 experiments) necessary to achieve Specifications (3) and (4) with various α. In the absolute error case, the minimal sample size is empirically achieved for $10^{-4} < \alpha < 10^{-3}$ given $\gamma = 0.02$ and for $0.01 < \alpha < 0.015$ given $\gamma = 0.25$. Similarly, in the relative error case, the minimal sample size is achieved for $0.0015 < \alpha < 0.003$ given $\gamma = 0.1$ and for $0.006 < \alpha < 0.0125$ given $\gamma = 0.7$.

Since γ impacts the choice of an optimal α but is unknown, it is not possible to optimise α a priori. Though the empirical observations cannot be generalised to any triples $(\epsilon, \delta, \gamma)$, it is worth remarking that all our results suggest a quicker convergence to the maximal bound when α converges to δ than when α converges to zero. This comes from the logarithmic speed of convergence in α of the confidence interval to the estimate given fixed number of samples and successes.

Figure 4 shows how the bounds of a (Wald) $(1 - \alpha)$-confidence interval evolves when α varies between 10^{-5} and 0.05, given two different estimates m/n. The figure would be similar with any other intervals described in Sect. 5. When α is low, the variations in the bounds of the confidence interval are more important. But when α tends to 0.05, variations are smoother and the width of the intervals does not vary much. So, the Massart function at the bounds of the confidence interval does not vary much as well in this case.

5   Approximate Versus Exact Confidence Intervals

At line 6 of Algorithms 1 and 2, we iteratively compute an intermediate $(1 - \alpha)$-confidence interval for γ. For the sake of rigorousness, we initially used exact Clopper-Pearson confidence intervals [6]. This confidence interval is directly derived from the binomial distribution and not from its approximation. It guarantees that the actual coverage is always equal to or above the nominal confidence level. In others words, a $(1 - \alpha)$-Clopper-Pearson confidence interval I_{CP} guarantees that $C(\gamma, I_{CP}) \geq 1 - \alpha$ and its closed-form expression can be easily computed: $I_{CP} = [\beta^{-1}(\frac{\alpha}{2}, m, n - m + 1), \beta^{-1}(1 - \frac{\alpha}{2}, m+ 1, n - m)]$ with $\beta^{-1}(\alpha, u, v)$ being the α-th quantile of a Beta distribution parametrised by u and

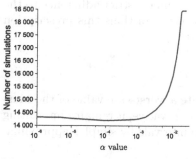

(a) Absolute error $\epsilon = 0.01$ and $\gamma = 0.25$.

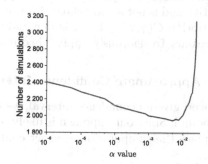

(b) Absolute error $\epsilon = 0.01$ and $\gamma = 0.02$.

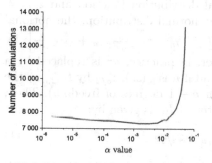

(c) Relative error $\epsilon = 0.1$ and $\gamma = 0.1$

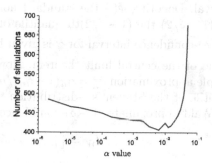

(d) Relative error $\epsilon = 0.1$ and $\gamma = 0.7$.

Fig. 3. Number of simulations for α

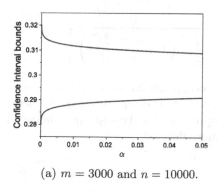

(a) $m = 3000$ and $n = 10000$.

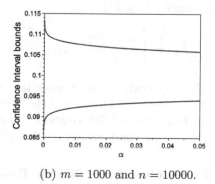

(b) $m = 1000$ and $n = 10000$.

Fig. 4. Lower and upper bounds of (Wald) $(1 - \alpha)$-confidence intervals given different number of successes m and a fixed number of samples n.

v. Unfortunately, to quote [3], "the Clopper-Pearson interval I is wastefully conservative and is not a good choice for practical use, unless strict adherence to the prescription $C(\gamma, I) \geq 1 - \alpha$ is demanded". In our algorithms this prescription is necessary to rigorously apply Theorems 4 and 5.

5.1   Approximate Confidence Intervals

However, given a confidence interval, we evaluate a worst-case value of the Massart bound. Since our approach is likely to be conservative, it remains interesting to replace the computation of exact confidence intervals by simpler approximations.

The Wald confidence interval is the most standard approximate confidence interval. Denoting $\Phi(.)$ the standard normal distribution function and $z_{\delta/2} = \Phi^{-1}(1 - \delta/2)$ the $(1 - \delta/2)$th quantile of the normal distribution, the notional $(1 - \delta)$-confidence interval for γ is given by $I = \left[\hat{\gamma}_n - z_{\delta/2}\frac{\sigma}{\sqrt{n}}, \hat{\gamma}_n + z_{\delta/2}\frac{\sigma}{\sqrt{n}}\right]$, by virtue of the central limit theorem. However, in practice, σ^2 is replaced by a sample approximation $\hat{\sigma}_n^2 = \hat{\gamma}_n(1 - \hat{\gamma}_n)/n$ (and if n is small, $z_{\delta/2}$ by $t_{\delta/2,n-1}$ the quantile of the Student's t-distribution with $n - 1$ degrees of freedom). Then, the Wald approximate $(1 - \delta)$-confidence interval $\tilde{I}_W$ is given by:

$$\tilde{I}_W = \left[\hat{\gamma}_n - z_{\delta/2}\hat{\sigma}_n, \hat{\gamma}_n + z_{\delta/2}\hat{\sigma}_n\right] \tag{11}$$

The coverage of γ by Wald interval $\tilde{I}_W$, may be significantly below the (desired) notional coverage: $C(\gamma, \tilde{I}_W) < C(\gamma, I) = 1 - \delta$. More details about this topic are available in [3].

The Agresti-Coull confidence Interval consists of replacing the number of samples n by $n + z_\delta^2$ and the number of successes m by $m + z_\delta^2/2$ in the Wald confidence interval (11):

$$\tilde{I}_{AC} = \left[\frac{m + z_\delta^2/2}{n + z_\delta^2} \pm z_{\delta/2}\sqrt{\frac{1}{n + z_\delta^2}\frac{m + z_\delta^2/2}{n + z_\delta^2}\left(1 - \frac{m + z_\delta^2/2}{n + z_\delta^2}\right)}\right] \tag{12}$$

This approximate confidence interval is recommended in several textbooks [3, 20] to overcome the flaws of the Wald interval. Its coverage remains excellent, even close to probabilities 0 and 1 and may represent a good compromise between exactness and conservativeness (see [3] for more details).

5.2   Absolute Error Scheme Results

We repeated each set of experiments 200 times with the three different confidence intervals for several values of γ, ϵ and δ. We set $\alpha = \delta/50 = 10^{-3}$ in these experiments. We estimated the empirical coverage by the number of times Specification (3) is fulfilled divided by 200 and computed the average, the standard deviation and the extrema values of the estimations $\hat{\gamma}$ and the sample size. For the sake of clarity, as our results are consistent for all ϵ, δ and are symmetric with respect to $\gamma = 1/2$, we summarize the most relevant results for $\epsilon = 0.01$, $\delta = 0.05$ and $0 < \gamma \le 1/2$ in Table 1.

Table 1. Results of the absolute error scheme with $\epsilon = 0.01$ and $\delta = 0.05$

γ	0.005	0.01	0.02	0.05	0.1	0.3	0.5
Coverage (Wald), $\alpha = \delta/50$	1	**0.925**	0.97	0.995	0.98	0.995	0.99
$\hat{\gamma}$ min (Wald)	0	0	0	0.039	0.089	0.29	0.49
$\hat{\gamma}$ max (Wald)	0.011	0.022	0.028	0.057	0.113	0.314	0.512
$\bar{N}$ (Wald)	480	835	1629	3765	6893	15687	18445
Coverage (AC), $\alpha = \delta/50$	1	0.995	0.995	1	0.99	0.995	0.98
$\hat{\gamma}$ min (AC)	0	0	0.01	0.041	0.088	0.29	0.487
$\hat{\gamma}$ max (AC)	0.011	0.018	0.029	0.058	0.111	0.31	0.511
$\bar{N}$ (AC)	710	1047	1753	3782	6874	15692	18445
Coverage (CP), $\alpha = \delta/50$	1	1	0.995	0.995	0.99	0.99	1
$\hat{\gamma}$ min (CP)	0	0.003	0.01	0.04	0.089	0.29	0.488
$\hat{\gamma}$ max (CP)	0.009	0.015	0.028	0.058	0.114	0.311	0.508
$\bar{N}$ (CP)	971	1318	2031	4095	7192	15826	18445

Replacing Clopper-Pearson intervals by Agresti-Coull intervals (respectively denoted CP and AC in Tables 1 and 2) has no negative impact on the coverage of the experiment, while the ratio of the average sample sizes obtained with the Agresti-Coull and Clopper-Pearson intervals decreases from 1 to 0.73. This illustrates the wasteful amount of samples using the Clopper-Pearson method, especially for the small probabilities. Regarding the Wald confidence interval, the results are in general even better. However, we remark that for one set of experiments ($\gamma = 0.01, \epsilon = 0.01, \delta = 0.05, \alpha = 10^{-3}$), the empirical coverage were below the theoretical level $(1 - \delta)$ (in bold red in Table 1). This illustrates one of the issues encountered when using the Wald interval: the interval is too narrow. Then, the Massart function is evaluated on a too optimistic extremal point of the Wald interval that prematurely causes the termination of Algorithm 1. In order to optimise the performance of our algorithm, we thus recommend the use of the Agresti-Coull confidence interval.

5.3 Relative Error Scheme Results

As for the absolute error algorithm, we repeated our relative error scheme 200 times per set of experiments with Wald and Clopper-Pearson intervals. We have not reported the empirical coverage since the empirical coverages were all equal to 1. This suggests that our relative error scheme remains conservative, even

Table 2. Sample size average of the relative error schemes, given ϵ and δ.

γ	0.9	0.7	0.5	0.3	0.1	0.05	0.01	0.001
$\bar{N}$ Wald, $(\epsilon, \delta, \alpha) = (0.05, 0.01, 0.001)$	573	2016	4617	10508	39927	83858	437847	4400530
$\bar{N}$ CP, $(\epsilon, \delta, \alpha) = (0.05, 0.01, 0.001)$	648	2119	4701	10686	40303	84880	438929	4438120
$\bar{N}$ Wald, $(\epsilon, \delta, \alpha) = (0.1, 0.01, 0.001)$	148	548	1220	2734	10204	21502	111522	1121966
$\bar{N}$ CP, $(\epsilon, \delta, \alpha) = (0.1, 0.01, 0.001)$	204	583	1273	2822	10484	21930	112880	1135687
$\bar{N}$ Wald, $(\epsilon, \delta, \alpha) = (0.1, 0.05, 0.001)$	94	361	828	1838	6922	14642	75644	761563
$\bar{N}$ CP, $(\epsilon, \delta, \alpha) = (0.1, 0.05, 0.001)$	156	431	905	1970	7333	15310	67511	789934
$\bar{N}$ Wald, $(\epsilon, \delta, \alpha) = (0.05, 0.05, 0.001)$	374	1366	3132	7162	27200	57368	298397	3004281
$\bar{N}$ CP, $(\epsilon, \delta, \alpha) = (0.05, 0.05, 0.001)$	471	1489	3296	7422	27951	58724	301258	3043438

if we replace the exact confidence interval by an approximation. The sample sizes are always lower with the Wald intervals. However, they tend to become similar when γ tends to zero since the lower bound of the respective intervals are alike. We have not performed our relative error scheme with the Agresti-Coull confidence intervals since the Agresti-Coull interval contains $\tilde{I}_W(\gamma)$ and is less conservative than $I_{CP}(\gamma)$. The results would have thus been similar. Given these results, we also recommend the use of an approximate confidence interval, the Agresti-Coull confidence interval being a good compromise between rigorousness and performance.

Last but not least, it is worth recalling that the coverage of the Agresti-Coull confidence interval remains conservative for probability values lower than 0.1 or greater than 0.9. In between, it is possible to find couples (n, γ) for which the coverage of the interval is below the desired $1 - \alpha$ level. But, as far we know, this remains rare and the distance between the coverage and $1 - \alpha$ never exceeds 1% in the literature (e.g. [1,3]).

6   Distributing the Algorithms

The standard absolute error Monte Carlo scheme can be easily distributed. Indeed, once the sample size has been calculated with the Okamoto bound, the simulations are executed independently of each other. In what follows, we call 'server' the root node of a network of computational devices and 'client' the leaf nodes. In a multi-thread system, the clients correspond to independent computational threads on a machine. In a multi-client network, the server globally manages the estimation and the clients perform the simulations. Each client executes a number of traces equal to the Okamoto bound divided by the number of threads used by the server (assuming for the sake of simplicity that the remainder is equal to zero). Once the client has finished its simulation task, it communicates the number of successes to the server. The server centralises the information from all the clients and the estimator is computed at the level of the server.

But for sequential algorithms, the sample size is a priori unknown and the estimator should be updated on-the-fly until Specification (3) or (4) holds. In

---

Algorithm 3. Distributed Absolute Error Sequential Algorithm

Data:

ϵ, δ, β : the original parameters

$M = \lceil \frac{1}{2\epsilon^2} \log \frac{2}{\delta} \rceil$: the Okamoto bound

$K = 0$

$m = 0$: the number of successes

$n_K = M$

$I_K = [a_K, b_K] = [0, 1]$: the initial interval to which γ is known to belong

1 $j = 0$
2 **while** $K < n_K$ **do**
3   Server sends m, K and $M^{(j)} = \frac{M-K}{r^{(j)}}$ to $r^{(j)}$ clients.
4   Each client i, $1 \le i \le r^{(j)}$, samples at most $\frac{M-K}{r^{(j)}}$ traces.
5      $m_i = 0$
6      $k_i = 0$
7   **while** $K + k_i < \frac{n_{K+k_i}}{r^{(j)}}$ *and* $k_i < \frac{M-K}{r^{(j)}}$ **do**
8          $k_i \leftarrow k_i + 1$
9   GENERATE $\omega^{(k_i)}$
10          $z(\omega^{(k_i)}) = \mathbb{1}(\omega^{(k_i)} \models \phi)$
11          $m_i \leftarrow m_i + z(\omega^{(k_i)})$
12          $I_{K+k_i} \leftarrow$ CONFIDENCE INTERVAL$(m + m_i, K + k_i, \beta)$
13   **if** $1/2 \in I_{K+k_i}$ **then**
14 | $n_{K+k_i} = M$
15   **else if** $b_{K+k_i} < 1/2$ **then**
16             $n_{K+k_i} = \lceil \frac{2}{h_a(b_{K+k_i}, \epsilon)\epsilon^2} \log \frac{2}{\delta - \beta} \rceil$
17   **else**
18             $n_{K+k_i} = \lceil \frac{2}{h_a(a_{K+k_i}, \epsilon)\epsilon^2} \log \frac{2}{\delta - \beta} \rceil$
19          $n_{K+k_i} \leftarrow \min(n_{K+k_i}, M)$
20      $m = m + \sum_{i=1}^{r^{(j)}} m_i$
21      $K = K + \sum_{i=1}^{r^{(j)}} k_i$
22      $n_K \leftarrow$ UPDATE$(m, K, \epsilon, \delta, \beta)$
23      $j = j + 1$

Output: $\hat{\gamma}_K = m/K$

---

what follows, we propose a distributed algorithm for the absolute error that reduces the amount of central processing and reduces the amount of time due to communication between the clients and the server.

6.1 A Distributed Version of the Absolute Error Scheme

The following idea can be easily adapted to the relative error scheme. For the sake of readability, we only explain how to distribute our absolute error sampling scheme. Initially the server computes the Okamato bound, divides the simulation work between $r^{(0)}$ clients and sends to the clients the parameters of the algorithm

ϵ, δ, β, the current number of successes $m = 0$ and samples $K = 0$ and the maximal number of samples $M^{(0)} = M/r^{(0)}$ that each client, indexed by i, may perform.

Each client executes simulations as in Algorithm 1 but stops as soon as its sample size k_i is greater than $n_{k_i}/r^{(0)}$. Once all the clients communicated their local number of successes and samples, the server updates $m = \sum_{i=1}^{r^{(0)}} m_i$, $K = \sum_{i=1}^{r^{(0)}} k_i$ and computes a global n_K to check whether $K < n_K$ or not. If $K \geq n_K$ holds, then the server outputs $\hat{\gamma}_K = m/K$ and Specification (3) is fulfilled. The simulations are all independent and the clients do not communicate with the other clients their local results. Then, since the server waits for all the clients' local results before updating n_K, the correctness of the algorithm is preserved. The idea behind stopping client i once $k_i > n_{k_i}/r^{(0)}$ is the following: if all the clients (roughly) communicate the same number of successes and samples, $m \approx r^{(0)} m_i$, $K \approx r^{(0)} k_i$ and consequently $K \geq n_K$. However, if the local results are very different, it could be that $K < n_K$. Then, the server divides the maximal remaining samples $M - K$ between all the available clients $r^{(1)}$ and sends them the updated values of m and K. The procedure is repeated until $K \geq n_K$. Note that the number of available clients $r^{(j)}$ may change from one step to another.

Gain in Time. This distributed version of the algorithm potentially involves several rounds of communication between a server and the clients. However, the number of rounds j likely remains small. For the sake of simplicity, we assume that the number of clients r is constant. Let c be the cost in time of the communication between a server and a client and d be the average cost of one execution trace. We can reasonably assume that the cost of the intermediate calculations is negligible in comparison of c and d and that d is significantly greater than c. Then, the amount of time taken by the whole experiment is roughly $jcr + dK/r$ instead of dK where the overhead cost jcr due to communication is largely compensated by the gain due to the division of dK by r.

7   Conclusion

In this work we discussed several optimisations and features for the sequential Massart algorithm introduced in [15]. In particular, it appears that in practice, using approximate instead of exact confidence intervals in the algorithm facilitates at least faster preliminary analysis. Moreover, the Agresti-Coull confidence interval reduces the sample size without significant impact on the coverage. Also, even if setting up optimally the coverage parameter a priori is not possible, it seems likely to set it up closer to zero than δ. Last but not least, we showed that the schemes can be efficiently distributed on high performance parallel computational architectures.

Acknowledgment. This work was supported in part by the National Research Foundation (NRF), Prime Minister's Office, Singapore, under its National Cybersecurity

R&D Programme (Award No. NRF2014NCR-NCR001-040) and administered by the National Cybersecurity R&D Directorate.

References

1. Agresti, A., Caffo, B.: Simple and effective confidence intervals for proportions and differences of proportions result from adding two successes and two failures. Am. Stat. **54**(4), 280–288 (2000)
2. Ballarini, P., Barbot, B., Duflot, M., Haddad, S., Pekergin, N.: HASL: a new approach for performance evaluation and model checking from concepts to experimentation. Perform. Eval. **90**, 53–77 (2015)
3. Brown, L., Cai, T., DasGupta, A.: Interval estimation for a binomial proportion. Stat. Sci. **16**(2), 101–133 (2001)
4. Chen, Y., Poskitt, C.M., Sun, J.: Learning from mutants: using code mutation to learn and monitor invariants of a cyber-physical system. In: SP, pp. 648–660 (2018)
5. Chernoff, H.: A measure of asymptotic efficiency for tests of a hypothesis based on the sum of observations. Ann. Math. Statist. **23**(4), 493–507 (1952)
6. Clopper, C.J., Pearson, E.S.: The use of confidence or fiducial limits illustrated in the case of the binomial. Biometrika **26**, 404–413 (1934)
7. Dagum, P., Karp, R.M., Luby, M., Ross, S.M.: An optimal algorithm for Monte Carlo estimation. SIAM J. Comput. **29**(5), 1484–1496 (2000)
8. David, A., Larsen, K.G., Legay, A., Mikucionis, M., Poulsen, D.B.: Uppaal SMC tutorial. STTT **17**(4), 397–415 (2015)
9. Grosu, R., Peled, D., Ramakrishnan, C.R., Smolka, S.A., Stoller, S.D., Yang, J.: Using statistical model checking for measuring systems. In: Margaria, T., Steffen, B. (eds.) ISoLA 2014. LNCS, vol. 8803, pp. 223–238. Springer, Heidelberg (2014). https://doi.org/10.1007/978-3-662-45231-8_16
10. Hérault, T., Lassaigne, R., Magniette, F., Peyronnet, S.: Approximate probabilistic model checking. In: Steffen, B., Levi, G. (eds.) VMCAI 2004. LNCS, vol. 2937, pp. 73–84. Springer, Heidelberg (2004). https://doi.org/10.1007/978-3-540-24622-0_8
11. Jegourel, C., Legay, A., Sedwards, S.: A platform for high performance statistical model checking – PLASMA. In: Flanagan, C., König, B. (eds.) TACAS 2012. LNCS, vol. 7214, pp. 498–503. Springer, Heidelberg (2012). https://doi.org/10.1007/978-3-642-28756-5_37
12. Jegourel, C., Legay, A., Sedwards, S.: Importance splitting for statistical model checking rare properties. In: Sharygina, N., Veith, H. (eds.) CAV 2013. LNCS, vol. 8044, pp. 576–591. Springer, Heidelberg (2013). https://doi.org/10.1007/978-3-642-39799-8_38
13. Jegourel, C., Legay, A., Sedwards, S.: Command-based importance sampling for statistical model checking. Theor. Comput. Sci. **649**, 1–24 (2016)
14. Jegourel, C., Sun, J., Dong, J.S.: Sequential schemes for frequentist estimation of properties in statistical model checking (Journal version). Currently submitted
15. Jegourel, C., Sun, J., Dong, J.S.: Sequential schemes for frequentist estimation of properties in statistical model checking. In: Bertrand, N., Bortolussi, L. (eds.) QEST 2017. LNCS, vol. 10503, pp. 333–350. Springer, Cham (2017). https://doi.org/10.1007/978-3-319-66335-7_23
16. Kwiatkowska, M.Z., Norman, G., Parker, D.: PRISM 2.0: a tool for probabilistic model checking. In: QEST, pp. 322–323. IEEE (2004)
17. Massart, P.: The tight constant in the Dvoretzky-Kiefer-Wolfowitz inequality. Ann. Probab. **18**, 1269–1283 (1990)

18. Metropolis, N., Ulam, S.: The Monte Carlo method. J. Am. Stat. Assoc. **44**(247), 335–341 (1949)
19. Okamoto, M.: Some inequalities relating to the partial sum of binomial probabilities. Ann. Inst. Stat. Math. **10**, 29–35 (1958)
20. Samuels, M.L., Witmer, J.W.: Statistics for the Life Sciences, 2nd edn. Prentice Hall, Englewood Cliffs (1999)
21. Wald, A.: Sequential tests of statistical hypotheses. Ann. Math. Stat. **16**(2), 117–186 (1945)
22. Younes, H.: Verification and planning for stochastic processes with asynchronous events. Ph.D. thesis, Carnegie Mellon University (2004)
23. Zuliani, P., Platzer, A., Clarke, E.M.: Bayesian statistical model checking with application to stateflow/simulink verification. FMSD **43**(2), 338–367 (2013)

Quantitative Risk Assessment of Safety-Critical Systems via Guided Simulation for Rare Events

Stefan Puch[2（✉)], Martin Fränzle[1（✉)], and Sebastian Gerwinn[2]

[1] Carl von Ossietzky Universität Oldenburg, 26111 Oldenburg, Germany
fraenzle@informatik.uni-oldenburg.de
[2] OFFIS e.V., Escherweg 2, 26121 Oldenburg, Germany
puch@offis.de

Abstract. For developers of assisted or automated driving systems, gaining specific feedback and quantitative figures on the safety impact of the systems under development is crucial. However, obtaining such data from simulation of their design models is a complex and often time-consuming process. Especially when data of interest hinge on extremely rare events, an estimation of potential risks is highly desirable but a non-trivial task lacking easily applicable methods. In this paper we describe how a quantitative statement for a risk estimation involving extremely rare events can be obtained by guiding simulation based on reinforcement learning. The method draws on variance reduction and importance sampling, yet applies different optimization principles than related methods, like the cross-entropy methods against which we compare. Our rationale for optimizing differently is that in quantitative system verification, a sharper upper bound of the confidence interval is of higher relevance than the total width of the confidence interval.

Our application context is deduced from advanced driver assistance system (ADAS) development. In that context virtual driver simulations are performed with the objective to generate quantitative figures for the safety impact in pre-crash situations. In order to clarify the difference of our technique to variance reduction techniques, a comparative evaluation on a simple probabilistic benchmark system is also presented.

1 Introduction

The global volume of road traffic is growing faster than ever. This contrasts with the ongoing effort to reduce the number of deadly injured people in road traffic. The EU commission announced the ambitious target of halving the overall number of road deaths in the EU by 2020 starting from 2010 at a number of 27.000 [4]. But Eurostat, the statistical office of the EU, states at a total number of 26.100 people who died in road accidents in 2016, which indicate that it is still a long

This research was supported by the Ministry of Science and Culture of Lower Saxony within the research center Critical Systems Engineering for Sociotechnical Systems.

© Springer Nature Switzerland AG 2018
T. Margaria and B. Steffen (Eds.): ISoLA 2018, LNCS 11245, pp. 305–321, 2018.
https://doi.org/10.1007/978-3-030-03421-4_20

way to their target [5]. Many research institutes and the automotive industry are working hard on new Advanced Driver Assistance Systems (ADAS) in particular for the pre-crash phase to reduce the number of traffic victims. While some emergency braking systems from different car manufacturers are already available on the market, harmonized development methods for design, evaluation and assessment of pre-crash systems, which should speed up the development process, are still nascent [11]. Harmonized methods within a model-based design approach shall support the ADAS developer and ensure that the final implementation meets its safety target, thus leading to shorter time-to-market. While exhaustive formal verification of ADAS and their interaction with a human driver is far out of scope due to their complex model structures, which overburden current formal verification frameworks both with respect to the expressiveness of the modeling languages supported and to scalability, a simulation-based approach can in principle be used to validate an assistance system and provide a quantitative estimation of potential risks[1]. The extreme scarceness of actually hazardous situations in human-operated road traffic (e.g., more than 1.64×10^6 km between accidents involving human injuries according to [16]), however, requires adequate identification and statistical treatment of extremely rare situations, which can be achieved by criticality-driven guided simulation [13]. Within this paper, we add quantitative error margins to the quantitative figure provided by such guided simulation. We furthermore demonstrate the superiority compared to naive sampling, especially concerning tightness of the upper bounds of the confidence intervals as relevant to statistical model checking. Additionally we compare different guiding strategies within a rare event simulation by benchmarking them against each other on a simple hybrid-state probabilistic process. The aim is to characterize the performance of different guiding algorithms, providing a rationale for selecting the most appropriate algorithm.

2   Background and Related Work

Estimating rare event frequencies in complex domains is a frequent problem in empirical evaluations. Established approaches employ variance reduction techniques [10] avoiding intractable scaling with respect to the number of samples necessary to characterize rare events. In simulation-based studies, methods like importance sampling, importance splitting, etc., render rare events more likely than in direct Monte Carlo (MC) simulation, because the sample size, i.e., the number of simulations grows too large when the event probability tends to zero. The individual research contributions, however, differ in their application contexts and the transferability to other domains.

In this paper we focus on approaches based on importance sampling (IS). The basic idea of importance sampling is to draw the samples according to a proposal distribution rather than their native distribution and re-normalize the statistics obtained afterwards using importance weights. The expectation $E[g]$

---

[1] Like in formal verification we have to assume the model used for simulation is correct.

of a random variable g estimated by N samples using importance sampling is

$$\hat{E}[g] = \frac{1}{N} \sum_{i=1}^{N} g(X_i) \, w(X_i),$$

where $w(x) = p(x)/q(x)$ is the likelihood ratio with $p(x)$ being the original probability of the sample x and $q(x)$ the probability assigned to the sample when it is generated according to the proposal instead.

The most challenging problem of IS is to find a proposal q such that the variance of the IS estimator is significantly smaller than the variance from pure MC estimation. In [7,8] the authors present different variants of adaptive importance sampling (AIS) for the validation of ADAS illustrated on a simple adaptive cruise control problem. All variants have in common that they draw an initial number of N samples (a batch) before they derive an adapted proposal distribution based on a kernel density estimator. A problem of the approach is that he indicator function used to determine whether a critical event has occurred is only interpreted in a binary way (true or false). Consequently, potential information about the closeness to the rare event cannot be used and adaptation stays uninformed till the first random hits of the rare event. Despite this weakness of the approach, the authors demonstrate that AIS can increase simulation efficiency roughly a tenfold in their problem context.

The work of Zuliani et al. in [20] presents an approach exploiting the cross-entropy (CE) method [14] for generating approximately optimal biasing densities for statistical model checking of hybrid systems. Their approach comprises two steps: First they use the CE to determine a proposal density function which empirically minimizes the Kullback-Leibler divergence to the optimal proposal density. Then importance sampling with that proposal is performed to estimate the expectation $E[g]$ of a random variable g. In order to demonstrate that the proposed method is applicable to stochastic hybrid systems, the authors applied the cross-entropy method to a Simulink-Stateflow example of a fault-tolerant avionics system. It is shown that by increasing the sample size, the relative error (RE) decreases and that with a feasible sample size of 10^4 it is possible to estimate probabilities in the order of 10^{-14} with reasonable accuracy (RE = 0.24). Although CE provides a theoretical basis for selecting proposal distributions adaptively, the effectiveness of such an approach depends heavily on well chosen parameterization of the proposal distributions and additional algorithmic parameters such as batch-size and an appropriately guessed "tilting parameter" providing an initial proposal yielding informative rare-event rates in step 1.

Both the aforementioned approaches do draw on empirical estimates of the variance or cross-entropy obtained from a binary evaluation (satisfaction or violation of a requirement by a sampled trace) of an initial batch of samples, which likely remains uninformative in the case of extremely rare events, which have to be found first before that statistics becomes informative. The focus of our work reported here in contrast is on means helping to find such rare events even in an initial batch. To this end, we employ a continuous approximation of the binary trace evaluation that statistical model checking targets and exploit this approximation in guiding the simulation. Such continuous approximations can either be derived from continuous interpretations of temporal logic [2,6] or from risk functions known from traffic psychology [15].

Jegourel et al. in [9] present an importance-sampling framework combining symbolic analysis with simulation to estimate expected costs in stochastic priced timed automata (SPTA). The framework is integrated into UPPAL SMC. Its first step is a symbolic reachability analysis in order to identify states never leading to trace completions satisfying the desired property. This is feasible as SPTA, in contrast to stochastic hybrid automata, have a decidable qualitative reachability problem which can be represented as a zone-based graph permitting identification of such "dead end" states. In a second step, that knowledge is exploited for pruning expansion of such states in the simulations underlying statistical model checking (SMC). This reduces variance compared to crude Monte-Carlo (MC) simulation as all simulations only expand potentially satisfying states. To estimate effectiveness of the approach the authors compare the empirical variance with that of direct MC simulation. While the empirical variance typically is reduced, the method induces considerable overhead for set-up, state-exploratory analysis of models, and additional storage and simulation costs.

The method does unfortunately not transfer to our problem domain as it, first, would require a full white-box model of the ADAS and environment not normally available when OEMs or tier-1 suppliers cooperate with subordinate suppliers in automotive and, second, as SPTA are not expressive enough to model the full-fledged feedback dynamics involving non-linear system dynamics, non-linear control, and human cognition. The UPPAAL benchmarks provided do also feature a very limited number of discrete locations (some tens of locations) which is considerably below the enormous size of the discrete state-space spanned by cognitive architectures [18] as used in our setting.

3   Application Context

As a specific application context we are interested in estimating the probability of causing a critical situation as a result of the cognitive load induced by cooperation with an advanced driver assistance system (ADAS) in automobiles. This is a crucial question in ADAS design, as the expected positive safety impact of such a system may easily become negated by additional cognitive load induced by the ADAS. Such cognitive load stems from effects like disturbance and distraction, effort for interpretation of system reactions and interventions, effort for mode tracking, or even mode confusion, all of which are standard side effects of assistance and automation. Hazardous effects induced by such systems are, however, a small additive risk and thus at least as rare as fatal hazards in normal driving. Without appropriate importance sampling, model-based simulation studies, as in Monte Carlo statistical model checking, are consequently bound to fail due to the excessive number of simulation traces necessary for a reasonable statistics. The problem with applying importance sampling is that it is in general unclear how to modify proposal probabilities in order to enhance the rare-event statistics in these settings: disturbances by the ADAS, e.g., will only impact safety if occurring at very specific moments, as the human driver (or its substitution by a validated cognitive model) generally is very effective in canceling out temporary deviations from an optimal track. The problem thus is to find and then emphasize in probability those few situations where overall risk is sensitive to interaction with the ADAS.

If we succeed in finding such a proposal distribution, then importance sampling improves our statistics by investigating more samples in "interesting" regions of the sample space. If the goal is enhanced accuracy of the estimated expectation of a random variable, where enhanced accuracy is interpreted as a narrow confidence interval, then the way to go with the proposal distribution is variance reduction. Techniques like adaptive importance sampling under the cross-entropy method or importance splitting address this issue with different algorithmic means.

It should be noted that improving accuracy of an expectation estimate is correlated with, yet not identical to improving the reliability of the related SMC-based quantitative safety verdict: in statistical model checking, we exploit a confidence interval $E \in [a, b]$ with confidence c, where E is the expectation/probability of an outcome violating the requirement specification, to decide with confidence c whether $E \leq \theta$ for a safety target θ. For answering this question, only the upper bound b of the confidence interval is of importance; a confidence interval $E \in [a', b']$ with $b' < b$ would thus convey more information even it were wider than $[a, b]$. We conclude that variance reduction is not necessarily the most effective mode of designing a proposal distribution in importance sampling and design two experiments for benchmarking a reinforcement learning approach more greedily searching for samples violating the safety specification. The benchmarks are as follows:

Cognitive Driver Model in the Loop: In this example, we set up a heterogeneous co-simulation comprising a cognitive architecture instantiated to simulate a human car driver, an off-the-shelf interactive driving simulator providing real-time simulation and rendering of driving dynamics and environment, and a side task representative of ADAS distraction (see [13] for details). The cognitive driver model contains a variety of sub-components ranging from models of perception and motoric action, short-term memory for perceived items, long-term memory for procedural knowledge, driving skills at the control-theoretic layer modeled by differential or difference equations, to rule-based behavior recursively decomposing complex tasks into conditional sub-tasks and finally skills. It has been validated against extensive sets of observed behavior from 17 human drivers [18,19]. In our simulation scenario, it is driving along 1,1 km of a winding road with curve radii between 375 m and 750 m and has the obligation to keep track and a target speed close to the speed limit. The environment for this driving scenario was modeled in the interactive driving simulator SILAB [17] which provides real-time visualization of the environment, visualization of the road, environmental traffic (not used in this experiment), and an interactive car model incorporating a realistic car kinematics which the virtual driver model then steers. During simulation the attention of the driver (model) has

to alternate between three competing goals: (1) Keep the car in the middle of
the lane. (2) Keep a constant speed of 100 km/h as closely as possible. (3) As
soon as possible solve some side tasks displayed in varying time intervals on an
in-vehicle display at the center console. The third goal is a typical proxy used
by cognitive psychologists as a representative for interactions of the driver with
an ADAS installed in the center console of the car.

To meet the requirements of all goals, the visual and cognitive attention has
to alternate between these three tasks and their respective areas of interest (road
through windscreen and mirrors, speedometer, in-vehicle display). If insufficient
attention is paid to keeping the car within the lane, the driver might cross
the lane border which might lead to critical situations. A highly critical point
within the scenario was added by placing a bridge over the road (see Fig. 1). The
pillar of the bridge is placed 2.5 m away from the center of the right lane, which
therefore corresponds to the expected distance between car and pillar when the
car is passing the bridge during normal drive. We learned from naïve sampling
using a pure MC strategy that the distance between the car and the bridge
pillar was above 2.4 m in 7,272 out of 10,000 runs and furthermore that nearly
all (namely 9994 of 10,000) deviations from the middle of the lane stayed well
within the lane boundaries, irrespective of the driver model being distracted by
performing the secondary task. The closest distance to the bridge pillar which
could be observed during the whole simulation batch of 10,000 simulation runs
was about 0.7 m, which is still far from a hit of the pillar and occurred only two
times in 10,000 runs. The likelihood that corrective actions by the driver saves
the situation after a distraction thus is overwhelmingly high; so high indeed that
a simulation time of 1 week, which the 10,000 runs amounts to, cannot reveal a
single accident (not even a near-accident) caused by the side task representing
ADAS interaction. Pure MC simulation consequently is inapt of quantifying the
safety impact of ADAS interaction in this rather typical traffic scenario. Taking
as a verification goal the Signal-Temporal-Logic-like [2] formula

$$\Box(\|(x,y) - (p_x, p_y)\| > 0.5\,\text{m}),\tag{1}$$

where x and y represent the current longitudinal and lateral position of the car
and p_x and p_y the corresponding positions of the bridge pillar, naïve statistical
model checking would after a week simulation time estimate the likelihood of
violation as zero. Unfortunately, this does also mean that such a simulation batch
would remain completely uninformative for adaptive importance-sampling.

In our setting, we instead added a simulation guide into the simulation framework that employs a by-now standard continuous interpretation [2,6] of formula
(1), namely the minimum over time (due to the $\Box$ operator) of the distance
to the bridge pillar (due to term $\|(x,y) - (p_x, p_y)\|$) minus the —in the con-
text of minimization irrelevant— offset 0.5 m, as a continuous objective function
to be minimized. Such minimization then is achieved by modifying the probabilities associated to the various probabilistic elements of the cognitive driver
model, which are introduced to reflect human behavior in a psychologically plausible way. These probabilistic elements serve to emulate the variations in human

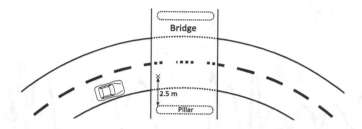

Fig. 1. Distance of bridge pillar to the center of the lane in the driving scenario

behavior which were observed when performing simulator studies with human drivers. They go down to the level of deciding at a rate of 20 Hz between options for gaze attention. Such decision are taken in a goal-directed manner, yet are far from deterministic. They exhibit stochasticity, with the mutual probabilities of the options being assigned situationally based on cognitive priorities between competing processes. The number of probabilistic decisions taken during a car ride of 1,1 km thus is enormous, and it is a search for the needle in the haystack to identify those which actually impact safety. For a deeper look into the underlying concepts and the architecture of the cognitive driver model itself, the reader is referred to [12].

The strategy of the simulation guide is to increase the probability of situations which lead to small distances between the car and the bridge pillar by applying reinforcement learning by the TUTS algorithm [13] explained in Sect. 4. An evaluation of another 10,000 runs using TUTS in the scenario demonstrated that nearly 10% of the simulation runs had a distance smaller than 0.5 m to the bridge pillar, thus being highly critical and violating formula (1). After thus improving the rate of critical situations revealed, we are able to derive a reasonable statistics and thus a quantitative risk statement in a subsequent step, see Sect. 4.

Randomly Bouncing Ball: Since the above simulation setup is rather complex and since it seems useful to compare the approach to other guiding strategies as well as to pure Monte Carlo sampling, we compared different approaches on a much simpler benchmark where we can compute the ground truth and its variance along the stochastic elements. Therefore we took a simple stochastic bouncing ball which starts from an initial height falling down towards a reflective surface. When hitting the floor, the rebound of the ball is scattered due to a rebound angle varying stochastically within a fixed range. Thus the ball can bounce along an axis in a fixed direction but with different heights and horizontal speeds in between resulting from the varying modes of deflection (see Fig. 2).

The ballistic curve of the ball is defined by following the equation:

$$x(t) = x(0) + vt\cos(\theta) \quad y(t) = y(0) + vt\sin(\theta) - \frac{1}{2}gt^2, \tag{2}$$

where θ and v are given by the initial velocity vector $\boldsymbol{v_0}$ as follows:

$$\theta = \arctan(\boldsymbol{v_0}) \qquad v = ||\boldsymbol{v_0}||_2 \tag{3}$$

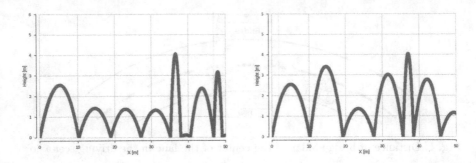

Fig. 2. Two random trajectories of the bouncing ball

Given the initial velocity vector and position, we can therefore calculate when the ball hits the ground $(y(t) = 0)$ the next time. When this happens, we reverse sign of the velocity vector's y-coordinate, damp the speed with a factor ρ and add a random perturbation to the resulting angle to model an irregular surface. More precisely, the velocity vector at any point in time is given by

$$\boldsymbol{v}(t) = \frac{\partial (x(t), y(t))}{\partial t} = (v\cos(\theta), v\sin(\theta) - gt). \tag{4}$$

In particular, we are interested in the next time t_{n+1} of hitting the surface. This time is given by setting the y-coordinate to zero:

$$t_{n+1} = \sqrt{\left(\frac{\sin(\theta)v}{g}\right)^2 + \frac{2y(t_n)}{g}} + \frac{v\sin\theta}{g} \tag{5}$$

To bounce, dampen, and perturb the angle, we simply set the speed and angle at the next time t_{n+1} as follows:

$$||v(t_{n+1})||_2 = ||\boldsymbol{v}(t_n)||_2\rho \qquad \theta(t_{n+1}) = \eta \tag{6}$$

Here, η is a random perturbance. For simplicity, we choose a random (uniform) perturbation from a pre-specified list: $\eta \sim \mathcal{U}\{\eta_1, \ldots, \eta_m\}$.

Next we define the rare event : we are interested in the probability that the ball will hit a small range on the surface (e.g. a hole), described by height 0 and a small interval for the x-coordinate. When the interval is sufficiently small, the probability of reaching this target is equal to the probability of drawing an exactly defined sequence of angles for each bounce on the surface.

4   Simulation Guiding

As mentioned in the previous section, our guiding method explained subsequently differs from variance reduction techniques in that it tries to guide towards rare events even if such have not yet been encountered, while the latter adapt once a non-zero initial statistics has been obtained. In order to explain the difference, we expose the underlying algorithms in the following.

The TUTS Algorithm: In order to obtain a quantitative estimate of the probability that a severe event happens in the driving example, we employed the TUTS algorithm from [13]. TUTS requires a continuous function indicative of (in the sense of roughly correlated to) the criticality $\tilde{c}$ of a simulation run. Such functions can either be designed by the user, or sensible criticality functions from traffic psychology [15] may be used, or quantitative interpretations of temporal logic specifications [2,6] can be employed.

A user-defined criticality threshold τ defines the separation between acceptable and unacceptable situations. The TUTS algorithm attempts to guide the simulation into a region close to the threshold τ, where the variance of satisfaction of the binary verification goal is high if the threshold τ used coincides with the borderline between satisfaction and violation. It therefore employs a tree representing all simulation runs observed so far, and it tries to assign adequately modified probabilities to the decisions in that tree. Note that the use of such a tree allows to assign different probabilities to the same decision at different time instants: a move from state v_1 to state v_2 may happen multiple times along a run, yet may be assigned different probabilities by the guiding algorithm at different times. This property is extremely relevant for the setting of cognitive architectures as, to take our example, the decision whether to address the side task is drawn some thousand times within a single test drive, yet only a handful of those decision points has measurable influence on the risk — some raising risk (distractions in the unknown critical distance before the bridge), others lowering risk (slightly earlier distractions, which reduce the probability of again engaging into the side task during the critical moments).

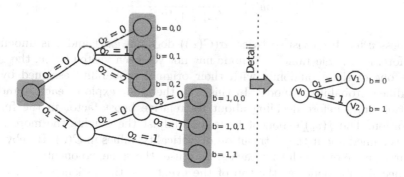

Fig. 3. Event tree spanned by the options o_*. b records the history of the probabilistic choices o_* along the path.

In the course of the simulation, let $C(v)$ be the set of criticality values that have been observed in all simulation runs that passed the node v of the above tree. As an example consider the event tree on the right side of Fig. 3. Being in node v_0, the simulation guide's aim is to give preference, in the sense of boosting its likelihood, to an action (in the example $o_1 = 0$ or $o_1 = 1$ are the possible actions) that more likely results in a criticality close to τ. We measure the closeness to τ using a studentization of the observed deviations according to the distribution of the observations $C(v)$, i.e., calculate the z-score of the distance to τ as follows:

$$z(v) = \frac{\tau - \mu(C(v))}{\sigma(C(v))}$$

To increase the likelihood of observing a criticality of τ when passing v, the guide should prefer options which lead to small absolute z-scores. This is done in a probabilistic way by appropriately putting weight on all options that the guide can select. A weight $w(v)$ is defined for each node v already existing in the tree.[2] The function $t : V \times O \longrightarrow V$ defines the parent-child relationship in the tree: $t(v, o)$ gives the node that is reached when action o is selected while in node v.

The guiding algorithms uses the weights of the nodes to modify the probabilistic selection of actions from the current set of actions $\tilde{O}$. In detail, the probability of selecting action $o \in \tilde{O}$ if the current node is v is defined as:

$$\mathrm{P}_v(o) = \frac{w(t(v, o))}{\sum\limits_{p \in \tilde{O}} w(t(v, p))}. \tag{7}$$

This means that options that lead to highly weighted child nodes are selected with higher probability. Therefore the nodes with low z-values should have high weights. The weights are defined by:

$$w(v) = \frac{1}{(|z| + 1)^{f(v_p)}} \tag{8}$$

Unless v has been visited twice, $\sigma(C(v))$ does not exist and z is undefined. Therefore, if any selectable child node has not yet been visited twice, the guide selects one of these randomly with their original probability assigned by the unmodified probabilistic model. In this way the guide explores each branch at least two times before deciding about its relative boost factor in the further exploration. The $f(v_p)$ exponent is used to adjust the weights the more confidence is gained about the distribution of criticality values in $C(v)$. Hereby v_p is the parent node of v such that each sibling uses the same exponent.

Especially for nodes at the top of the event tree the variance of criticality values $\sigma(C(v))$ is high and sibling nodes often have similar mean values $\mu(C(v))$. These nodes are at the beginning of the simulations. Many subsequent decisions influence the criticality of a simulation. This results in high variances wide confidence intervals for early nodes. In order to take the confidence about the z-values into account the function f is used. This function should rise with the empirical precision of the z-values and lead to a spreading of weights, the more confident

---

[2] Note that hitherto unseen paths in the tree can arise during simulation due to the probabilistic nature of the model being simulated. Therefore, the set of nodes in the tree grows incrementally.

we are in the z-values. For our use case scenario we used a simple definition with free parameters a and b used to adjust the search speed:

$$f(v_p) = a + b \cdot n_{min}, \quad (a, b = 0.5) \tag{9}$$

where n_{min} represents the minimal number of visits of any $v | v_p$ is parent.

Cross-Entropy Method: Cross-entropy [14] is a method which uses adaptive importance sampling (AIS) to adjust the current proposal distribution (denoted by its density, or probability mass function q) such that it converges to the optimal proposal distribution. Here, optimal means that a single sample is sufficient to estimate the expectation of interest exactly. The resulting estimator therefore has zero variance. As this optimal proposal, however, is not available, the cross-entropy method estimates this optimal proposal based on the samples already drawn. To evaluate the proximity of the current proposal to this estimation, the Kullback-Leibler divergence is used. As the Kullback-Leibler divergence is also called cross-entropy, the method is called AIS using cross-entropy.

Instead of reviewing the cross-entropy method in general, we illustrate its application to the bouncing ball. Let p_i denote the probability under the bouncing ball model to draw the i-th possible angle η_i. Under the stochastic bouncing ball model, angles are independent across time-points. Hence the probability of a trace of multiple angles $x_t, t = 1 \ldots, T$ is simply given by the product over $\prod_t p_i \delta(x_t, \eta_i)$. Here δ denotes the Kronecker-delta, which evaluates to 1 if $x_t = \eta_i$ and 0 else. Similarly, we chose q to represent the probability of drawing different angles. As the occurrence of the rare event effectively couples the random events across time, it might be beneficial to allow for inter-time-dependency within the proposal distribution. However, as this increases the number of parameters exponentially, we use the same independence assumption also for the proposal distribution. Specifically, in order to analytically compute the cross-entropy update, we use the following parameterization of q:

$$q(x) = \frac{\exp(\gamma_i \delta(x, \eta_i))}{\sum_k \exp(\gamma_k)} \tag{10}$$

The probability of generating a particular angle $x \in \{\eta_1, \ldots \eta_m\}$ can thus be adjusted by choosing different values of γ. γ can be interpreted as the natural parameter of the exponential family with $\delta(x, \eta_i)$ as the sufficient statistics, which enables us to easily compute updates of the parameters γ, see below.

In the first step, N_0 simulation runs are drawn using the current proposal q^n. Here N_0 is a free parameter of the algorithm, to which we refer to as the batch-size. Each of these simulation runs have an associated criticality value c_i. For the bouncing ball example, we used the Euclidean distance between the vector of sampled angles to the (known) vector of angles that would lead to the bouncing ball hitting the small area associated with the rare event. Using this criticality, the cross-entropy method now selects the α-most critical simulation runs, i.e., the index set

$$I_\alpha := \{i : |\{j : c_j < c_i\}| \leq \alpha N_0\} \tag{11}$$

This index set in turn is used to estimate the optimal proposal distribution q^*, i.e., the proposal that would lead to a zero-variance estimator[3]. Due to the exponential family form of our representation, we only need to compute the empirical means of the sufficient statistics to compute new parameters γ to obtain an updated proposal. This in turn is due to the fact that moment matching is equivalent to minimizing the Kullback-Leibler divergence between the empirical zero-variance distribution and the proposal across different parameter settings of the proposal, see [14].

Hence, the new parameters γ^{n+1} of the proposal distribution can be set by calculating the empirical averages of the sufficient statistics, where we have to account for the re-weighting according to the current proposal distribution q^n.

$$\gamma_i^{n+1} = \frac{1}{|I_\alpha|} \sum_{k \in I_\alpha} \frac{1}{T_k} \sum_t^{T_k} \frac{p(x_t^k)}{q^n(x_t^k)} \delta(x_t^k, \eta_i) \tag{12}$$

Here, x_t^k denote the (random) choices at time k within the k-th trace of the generated batch. Note that we can use the inner sum $\sum_t$ as we assume independence and therefore treat each draw along the k-th trace equally. Having new parameters and thus a new proposal distribution q^{n+1}, we can use this new distributions to generate a new batch of samples of size N_0.

Using this update, the parameters capture the frequencies with which different choices η occurred within the α most critical traces of the generated batch. This information in turn is used to generate those choices more frequently within the next batch. However, even if the certain frequencies have not been observed, due to the exponential structure, the corresponding probability would never be set to zero. Therefore, using this parametrization, we cannot converge to an optimal distribution completely ignoring certain choices unless we use arbitrary large batch-sizes.

5   Confidence Intervals

In order to compare results of different simulation guiding techniques, we need to be able to calculate their confidence intervals (CI), as explained in this section.

Binomial Confidence Interval. For computing the confidence interval of the naïve estimator, we employ the simple binomial CI, also known as the Clopper-Pearson confidence interval, or exact confidence interval [1].

Bootstrap Confidence Intervals. When applying importance sampling, the originally binomial distribution is modified to a multinomial one, as samples are no longer evaluated with just 0 (safe run) or 1 (safe or bad run), but with a plethora of different importance weights. In order to calculate an approximation of the corresponding CI, we compute bootstrap confidence intervals [3]. In order to compute bootstrap confidence intervals for an estimator on samples

---

[3] Note that, due to the finite amount of samples used, this is only an approximation.

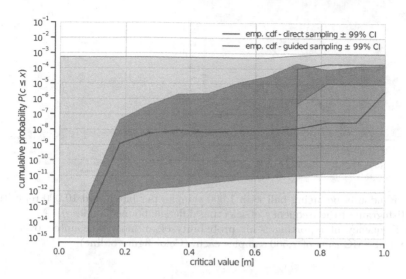

Fig. 4. Estimated probabilities and 99% confidence intervals for approaching the bridge pillar closer than a specified critical distance. Blue: naïve SMC, green: TUTS guiding. (Color figure online)

$S_0 = (x_1, \ldots, x_n)$, one creates multiple samples of the same size by drawing from $\{x_1, \ldots, x_n\}$ with replacement. On these re-sampled samples one then computes the variability of the estimator evaluated on each of the re-samples. Specifically, let $S_1, \ldots S_m$ new samples be obtained via re-sampling and let f be the estimator which takes as argument a sample and provides the estimate as an output. To obtain a $1 - \alpha$ confidence interval, one then orders the estimator outputs $f(S_1), \ldots, f(S_m)$ from lowest to highest. The confidence interval in turn is then given by $[f(S_l), f(S_u)]$, where l and u are the indices corresponding to the $(\alpha/2)m$ and $(1 - \alpha/2)m$ entries in the ordered list respectively.

6   Results

In the driving example, a critical event X_i occurs whenever the distance between car and bridge pillar falls below a specified distance. The likelihood $\hat{p}$ can be computed using the unbiased importance sampling estimator

$$\hat{p} \approx \frac{1}{N} \sum_{i=1}^{N} \left(\begin{cases} 1, \text{ if } x_i \text{ is critical} \\ 0, \text{ else} \end{cases} \right) \frac{p(x_i)}{q(x_i)}, \quad x_i \sim q_i$$

N represents the number of simulation runs, $p(x_i)$ the original probability and $q(x_i)$ the weighted probability of x_i when simulated under measure q.

To show the likelihood of different criticalities, we plot in Fig. 4 the estimated probabilities and 99% confidence intervals for approaching the bridge pillar closer than a specified critical distance. The results have been computed independently

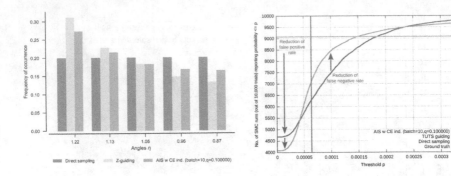

Fig. 5. Randomly bouncing ball with 1,000 samples per batch and 10,000 repetitions.
Left: Histogram of the frequency of selecting different bounce angles η.
Right: Frequency of reporting a hit probability of at most p, counted over 10,000 independent SMC runs of 1,500 samples each. (Color figure online)

using naïve Monte Carlo SMC (blue graph) and TUTS guiding (green graph). The latter obviously presents two significant enhancements:

1. Significantly better assessment of critical distances below 0.7 m, which represent the rare events in the scenario. The smallest distance was recorded at approx. 0.1 m with an estimated probability of 5×10^{-13} and the corresponding 99% bootstrap confidence interval spanning $[10^{-15}, 10^{-11}]$. In the same regime, naïve sampling can only provide 99% confidence that the probability is below 7×10^{-4}.
2. Tighter upper bounds on the likelihood of reaching critical distances above 0.7 m. A quantitative safety specification like "the likelihood of getting closer than 1 m to the bridge pillar should be less than 10^{-4}" can thus be verified with 99% confidence by TUTS, while naïve sampling remains inconclusive. Naïve sampling well reports tighter lower bounds than TUTS, but these are of no use in quantitative verification: both acceptance and refutation of quantitative safety targets depend on whether the threshold is exceeded by the upper bound of the confidence interval.

This comparison demonstrates that deliberately asymmetric CIs can be beneficial within statistical verification: preferring sharp upper bounds of CIs over narrowing the CIs would be a sensible optimization goal for sampling strategies in statistical model-checking.

We can demonstrate this effect also by a threefold comparison on the bouncing ball example, where we compare naïve sampling, adaptive importance sampling driven by cross-entropy, and TUTS guiding. The left part of Fig. 5 demonstrates that TUTS actually employs a significantly different importance sampling strategy than the cross-entropy method. This strategy leads to higher hit rates, as witnessed by Table 1. This higher hit rate, at correspondingly lower importance weight assigned to each hit, generates a steeper increase of the distribution of test outcomes around the true probability, as depicted in the right part of

Table 1. Hits to target achieved over 10,000 batch runs of 1,000 samples each.

Algorithm	Batches featuring ≥ 1 hit	Total number of hits
Naïve Monte Carlo sampling	648	671
AIS driven by cross-entropy	3909	5452
TUTS guiding	4840	25867

Fig. 5. This graph shows for each algorithm the frequency (counted over 10,000 independent runs of 1,500 samples each) of reporting a hit probability below the threshold given on the horizontal axis. Due to quantization, naïve sampling is inapt of computing any positive probability less than $\frac{1}{1500}$. As the actual hit probability is considerably smaller than $\frac{1}{1500}$ at 0.000064 (marked by the red perpendicular line), naïve sampling is likely to report a massive underestimate of 0; this happens on approx. 91.2% of the runs. Being based on importance sampling, both TUTS and AIS can yield probability estimates close to the actual probability and are thus more informative. For the small sample size underlying the graph ($\leq 2,000$ per batch) TUTS is significantly less likely to generate considerable underapproximations below 0.000042, thus reducing the false-positive rate when employing acceptance thresholds in that range. TUTS also has by a fair margin the highest probability of generating relatively exact approximations: Some 3,340 estimates provided by TUTS fall into the range of $\pm 25\%$ around the true probability, while AIS features only 2,065 within that range (and naïve sampling none). As might be expected, the likelihood of massive underestimation by AIS decreases when AIS is given significantly more time for adaptation by increasing batch sizes. For the bouncing ball example we found this to happen when batch sizes considerably exceed 2,000. In that regime, AIS starts to outperform TUTS concerning the number of massive underestimates generated, though TUTS continues to yield the steepest curve around the true probability. Given that the rare events in our actual application domain of ADAS are multiple orders of magnitude more rare than for the bouncing ball, it is, however, unclear whether the corresponding batch sizes guaranteeing convergence of AIS would be a practical option. The faster initial convergence of TUTS seems an interesting property to explore.

7   Conclusion

Within this article, we have extended the TUTS guiding algorithm for identifying extremely rare events in statistical model checking [13] by rigorous confidence bounds. We argue that within quantitative verification contexts, not the actual width of the confidence bounds is relevant, but tightening the single bound relevant to the verification problem. In verification contexts this is the upper bound on violating the requirement or, equivalently, the lower bound on satisfaction. This implies that classical means of variance reduction in importance sampling frameworks tend to aim at the wrong goal, namely achieving a precise probability estimate by reduction of the width of the confidence interval, which is correlated with, yet not identical to the goal of tightening the single bound of the confidence interval that is of relevance to verification. A complex traffic benchmark from the development of advanced driver assistance systems provides witness of this effect: here TUTS guiding provides much sharper upper bounds on accident probabilities throughout the whole regime even though providing relatively wider confidence intervals than naïve sampling in parts of the regime (cf. Fig. 4). As simulation guiding by the optimal adaptive importance sampling method, namely the cross-entropy approach, could not be realized on this complex example, we addressed a second, artificial example of a bouncing ball, where we compared naïve sampling, adaptive importance sampling guided by the cross-entropy method, and TUTS guiding. The results confirm that the TUTS algorithm provides a sampling scheme that converges rapidly even for batch sizes that are small relative to the actual probability. For such small batches, it outperforms both naïve sampling and the cross-entropy method. Beneficial combinations with the latter, where TUTS would foster fast early convergence and the cross-entropy method could then take over, remain an issue of further research.

References

1. Clopper, C.J., Pearson, E.S.: The use of confidence or fiducial limits illustrated in the case of the binomial. Biometrika **26**(4), 404–413 (1934)
2. Donzé, A., Maler, O.: Robust satisfaction of temporal logic over real-valued signals. In: Chatterjee, K., Henzinger, T.A. (eds.) FORMATS 2010. LNCS, vol. 6246, pp. 92–106. Springer, Heidelberg (2010). https://doi.org/10.1007/978-3-642-15297-9_9
3. Efron, B., Tibshirani, R.J.: An Introduction to the Bootstrap. Monographs on Statistics and Applied Probability, no. 57. Chapman & Hall/CRC, London (1993)
4. European Commission: Towards a European road safety area: policy orientations on road safety 2011–2020 (2010). http://eur-lex.europa.eu/legal-content/EN/TXT/PDF/?uri=CELEX:52010DC0389
5. Eurostat: Slightly over 26 000 victims of road accidents in the EU in 2015. Eurostat Press Office Vincent (2016). http://ec.europa.eu/eurostat/documents/2995521/7734698/7-18112016-BP-EN.pdf
6. Fränzle, M., Hansen, M.R.: A robust interpretation of duration calculus. In: Van Hung, D., Wirsing, M. (eds.) ICTAC 2005. LNCS, vol. 3722, pp. 257–271. Springer, Heidelberg (2005). https://doi.org/10.1007/11560647_17
7. Gietelink, O., De Schutter, B., Verhaegen, M.: Adaptive importance sampling for probabilistic validation of advanced driver assistance systems. In: 2006 American Control Conference, vol. 19, 6 pp. (2006)
8. Gietelink, O., De Schutter, B., Verhaegen, M.: Probabilistic validation of advanced driver assistance systems. In: Proceedings of the 16th IFAC World Congress, vol. 19 (2005)
9. Jegourel, C., Larsen, K.G., Legay, A., Mikučionis, M., Poulsen, D.B., Sedwards, S.: Importance sampling for stochastic timed automata. In: Fränzle, M., Kapur, D., Zhan, N. (eds.) SETTA 2016. LNCS, vol. 9984, pp. 163–178. Springer, Cham (2016). https://doi.org/10.1007/978-3-319-47677-3_11

10. Kahn, H.: Use of different Monte Carlo sampling techniques, p. 766 (1955)
11. Page, Y., et al.: A comprehensive and harmonized method for assessing the effectiveness of advanced driver assistance systems by virtual simulation: the P.E.A.R.S. initiative. In: The 24th International Technical Conference on the Enhanced Safety of Vehicles (ESV). NHTSA, Gothenburg (2015)
12. Puch, S., Wortelen, B., Fränzle, M., Peikenkamp, T.: Using guided simulation to improve a model-based design process of complex human machine systems. In: Modelling and Simulation, ESM 2012, pp. 159–164. EUROSIS-ETI, Essen (2012)
13. Puch, S., Wortelen, B., Fränzle, M., Peikenkamp, T.: Evaluation of drivers interaction with assistant systems using criticality driven guided simulation. In: Duffy, V.G. (ed.) DHM 2013. LNCS, vol. 8025, pp. 108–117. Springer, Heidelberg (2013). https://doi.org/10.1007/978-3-642-39173-6_13
14. Rubinstein, R.: The cross-entropy method for combinatorial and continuous optimization. Methodol. Comput. Appl. Probab. 1, 127–190 (1999)
15. Vogel, K.: A comparison of headway and time to collision as safety indicators. Accid. Anal. Prev. 35(3), 427–433 (2003)
16. Vorndran, I.: Unfallstatistik - Verkehrsmittel im Risikovergleich. DESTATIS (2010). https://www.destatis.de/DE/Publikationen/WirtschaftStatistik/Monatsausgaben/WistaDezember10.pdf?__blob=publicationFile
17. WIVW GmbH: Fahrsimulationssoftware SILAB. https://wivw.de/de/silab
18. Wortelen, B., Baumann, M., Lüdtke, A.: Dynamic simulation and prediction of drivers' attention distribution. Transp. Res. Part F Traffic Psychol. Behav. 21, 278–294 (2013)
19. Wortelen, B., Lüdtke, A., Baumann, M.: Integrated simulation of attention distribution and driving behavior. In: Proceedings of the 22nd Annual Conference on Behavior Representation in Modeling & Simulation, pp. 69–76. BRIMS Society, Ottawa (2013)
20. Zuliani, P., Baier, C., Clarke, E.M.: Rare-event verification for stochastic hybrid systems. In: Proceedings of the 15th ACM International Conference on Hybrid Systems: Computation and Control, pp. 217–226. ACM, New York (2012)

Monte Carlo Tree Search for Verifying Reachability in Markov Decision Processes

Pranav Ashok[1], Tomáš Brázdil[2], Jan Křetínský[1(✉)], and Ondřej Slámečka[2]

[1] Technical University of Munich, Munich, Germany
jan.kretinsky@tum.de
[2] Masaryk University, Brno, Czech Republic

Abstract. The maximum reachability probabilities in a Markov decision process can be computed using value iteration (VI). Recently, simulation-based heuristic extensions of VI have been introduced, such as bounded real-time dynamic programming (BRTDP), which often manage to avoid explicit analysis of the whole state space while preserving guarantees on the computed result. In this paper, we introduce a new class of such heuristics, based on Monte Carlo tree search (MCTS), a technique celebrated in various machine-learning settings. We provide a spectrum of algorithms ranging from MCTS to BRTDP. We evaluate these techniques and show that for larger examples, where VI is no more applicable, our techniques are more broadly applicable than BRTDP with only a minor additional overhead.

1 Introduction

Markov decision processes (MDP) [Put14] are a classical formalism for modelling systems with both non-deterministic and probabilistic behaviour. Although there are various analysis techniques for MDP that run in polynomial time and return precise results, such as those based on linear programming, they are rarely used. Indeed, dynamic programming techniques, such as value iteration (VI) or policy iteration, are usually preferred despite their exponential complexity. The reason is that for systems of sizes appearing in practice not even polynomial algorithms are useful and heuristics utilizing the structure of the human-designed systems become a necessity. Consequently, probabilistic model checking has adopted [BCC+14, ACD+17, KM17, KKKW18, DJKV17] techniques, which generally come with weaker guarantees on correctness and running time, but in practice perform better. These techniques originate from reinforcement learning, such as delayed Q-learning [SLW+06], or probabilistic planning, such as bounded real-time dynamic programming (BRTDP) [MLG05].

This research was supported in part by Deutsche Forschungsgemeinschaft (DFG) through the TUM International Graduate School of Science and Engineering (IGSSE) project 10.06 *PARSEC*, the Czech Science Foundation grant No. 18-11193S, and the DFG project 383882557 *Statistical Unbounded Verification*.

T. Margaria and B. Steffen (Eds.): ISoLA 2018, LNCS 11245, pp. 322–335, 2018.
https://doi.org/10.1007/978-3-030-03421-4_21

Since verification techniques are applied in safety-critical settings, the results produced by the techniques are required to be correct and optimal, or at least ε-optimal for a given precision ε. To this end, we follow the general scheme of [BCC+14] and combine the non-guaranteed heuristics with the traditional guaranteed techniques such as VI. However, while pure VI analyses the whole state space, the heuristics often allow us to focus only on a small part of it and still give precise estimates of the induced error. This approach was applied in [BCC+14], yielding a variant of BRTDP for MDP with reachability. Although BRTDP has already been shown to be quite good at avoiding unimportant parts of the state space in many cases, it struggles in many other settings, for instance where the paths to the goal are less probable or when the degree of non-determinism is high.

In this paper, we go one step further and bring a yet less guaranteed, but yet more celebrated technique of *Monte Carlo tree search* (MCTS) [AK87, KS06, Cou07, BPW+12] into verification. MCTS is a heuristic search algorithm which combines exact computation using search trees with sampling methods. To find the best actions to perform, MCTS constructs a search tree by successively unfolding the state-space of the MDP. The value of each newly added state is evaluated using simulations (also called roll-outs) and its value is backpropagated through the already existing search tree.

We show that the exact construction of the search tree in MCTS mitigates some of the pitfalls of BRTDP which relies completely on simulation. Namely, the search tree typically reaches less probable paths much sooner than a BRTDP simulation, e.g., in the example depicted in Fig. 1. We combine MCTS with BRTDP in various ways, obtaining thus a spectrum of algorithms ranging from pure BRTDP to pure MCTS along with a few hybrids in between. The aim is to overcome the weaknesses of BRTDP, while at the same time allowing to tackle large state spaces, which VI is unable to handle, with guaranteed (ε)-optimality of the solution.

While usually performing comparable to BRTDP, we are able to provide reasonable examples which can be tackled using neither BRTDP nor VI, but with our MCTS-BRTDP hybrid algorithms. Consequently, we obtain a technique applicable to larger systems, unlike VI, which is more broadly applicable than BRTDP with not much additional overhead.

Our contribution can be summarized as follows:

- We provide several ways of integrating MCTS into verification approaches so that the resulting technique is an anytime algorithm, returning the maximum reachability probability in MDP together with the respective error bound.
- We evaluate the new techniques and compare them to the state-of-the-art implementations based on VI and BRTDP. We conclude that for larger systems, where VI is not applicable, MCTS-based techniques are more robust than BRTDP.

1.1 Related Work

The correctness of the error bounds in our approach is guaranteed through the computation of the lower and upper bounds on the actual value. Such a computation has been established for MDP in [BCC+14, HM17] and the technique is based on the classical notion of the MEC quotient [dA97].

Statistical Model Checking (SMC). [YS02] is a collection of simulation-based techniques for verification where confidence intervals and probably approximately correct results (PAC) are sufficient. While on Markov chain it is essentially the Monte Carlo technique, on MDP it is more complex and its use is limited [Kre16], resulting in either slow [BCC+14] or non-guaranteed [HMZ+12, DLST15] methods. In contrast, MCTS combines Monte Carlo evaluation with explicit analysis of parts of the state space and thus opens new ways of integrating simulations into MDP verification.

Monte Carlo Tree Search (MCTS). There is a huge amount of literature on various versions of MCTS and applications. See [BPW+12] for an extensive survey. MCTS has been spectacularly successful in several domains, notably in playing classical board games such as Go [SHM+16] and chess [SHS+17].

Many variants of MCTS can be distinguished based on concrete implementations of its four phases: Selection and expansion, where a search tree is extended, roll-out, where simulations are used to evaluate newly added nodes, and back-up, where the result of roll-out is propagated through the search tree. In the selection phase, actions can be chosen based on various heuristics such as the most common UCT [KS06] and its extensions such as FPU and AMAF [GW06]. The evaluation phase has also been approached from many directions. To improve upon purely random simulation, domain specific rules been employed to guide the choice of actions [ST09] and (deep) reinforcement learning (RL) techniques have been used to learn smart simulation strategies [SHM+16]. On the other hand, empirical evidence shows that it is often more beneficial to make simple random roll-outs as opposed to complex simulations strategies [JKR17]. RL has also been integrated with MCTS to generalize UCT by temporal difference (TD) backups [SSM12, VSS17].

2 Preliminaries

2.1 Markov Decision Processes

A *probability distribution* on a finite set X is a mapping $d : X \mapsto [0, 1]$, such that $\sum_{x \in X} d(x) = 1$. We denote by $\mathcal{D}(X)$ the set of all probability distributions on X. Further, the *support* of a probability distribution ρ is denoted by $\mathrm{supp}(d) = \{x \in X \mid d(x) > 0\}$.

Definition 1 (MDP). *A* Markov decision processes (MDP) *is a tuple of the form* $\mathcal{M} = (S, s_{init}, Act, \mathsf{Av}, \Delta, \mathbf{1}, \mathbf{0})$, *where* S *is a finite set of* states, $s_{init}, \mathbf{1}, \mathbf{0} \in S$ *is the* initial *state,* goal *state, and* sink *state, respectively, Act is a finite set of* actions, $\mathsf{Av} : S \rightarrow 2^{Act}$ *assigns to every state a set of* available *actions, and* $\Delta : S \times Act \rightarrow \mathcal{D}(S)$ *is a transition function that given a state s and an action $a \in \mathsf{Av}(s)$ yields a probability distribution over successor states.*

An *infinite path* ρ in an MDP is an infinite word $\rho = s_0 a_0 s_1 a_1 \cdots \in (S \times Act)^\omega$, such that for every $i \in \mathbb{N}$, $a_i \in \mathsf{Av}(s_i)$ and $\Delta(s_i, a_i, s_{i+1}) > 0$. A *finite path* $w = s_0 a_0 s_1 a_1 \ldots s_n \in (S \times Act)^* \times S$ is a finite prefix of an infinite path. A *policy* on an MDP is a function $\pi : (S \times Act)^* \times S \rightarrow \mathcal{D}(Act)$, which given a finite path $w = s_0 a_0 s_1 a_1 \ldots s_n$ yields a probability distribution $\pi(w) \in \mathcal{D}(\mathsf{Av}(s_n))$ on the actions to be taken next. We denote the set of all strategies of an MDP by Π. Fixing a policy π and an initial state s on an MDP $\mathcal{M}$ yields a unique probability measure $\mathbb{P}^\pi_{\mathcal{M},s}$ over infinite paths [Put14, Sect. 2.1.6] and thus the probability $V^\pi(s) := \mathbb{P}^\pi_{\mathcal{M},s}[\{\rho \mid \exists i \in \mathbb{N} : \rho(i) = \mathbb{1}\}]$ to reach the goal state when following π.

Definition 2. *Given a state s, the* maximum reachability probability *is* $V(s) = \sup_{\pi \in \Pi} V^\pi(s)$. *A policy σ is ε-optimal if* $V(s_{init}) - V^\sigma(s_{init}) \leq \varepsilon$.

Note that there always exists a 0-optimal policy of the form $\pi : S \rightarrow Act$ [Put14].

A pair (T, A), where $\emptyset \neq T \subseteq S$ and $\emptyset \neq A \subseteq \bigcup_{s \in T} \mathsf{Av}(s)$, is an *end component* of an MDP $\mathcal{M}$ if

- for all $s \in T, a \in A \cap \mathsf{Av}(s)$ we have $\mathrm{supp}(\Delta(s, a)) \subseteq T$, and
- for all $s, s' \in T$ there is a finite path $w = s a_0 \ldots a_n s' \in (T \times A)^* \times T$, i.e. w starts in s, ends in s', stays inside T and only uses actions in A.

An end component (T, A) is a *maximal end component (MEC)* if there is no other end component (T', A') such that $T \subseteq T'$ and $A \subseteq A'$. The set of MECs of an MDP $\mathcal{M}$ is denoted by $\mathrm{MEC}(\mathcal{M})$. An MDP can be turned into its *MEC quotient* [dA97] as follows. Each MEC is merged into a single state, all the outgoing actions are preserved, except for a possible self-loop (when all its successors are in this MEC). Moreover, if there are no available actions left then it is merged with the sink state o. For a formal definition, see [ABKS18, Appendix A]. The techniques we discuss in this paper require the MDP be turned (gradually or at once) into its MEC-quotient in order to converge to V, as described below.

2.2 Value Iteration

Value iteration (VI) is a dynamic programming algorithm first described by Bellman [Bel57]. The maximum reachability probability is characterized as the least fixpoint of the following equation system for $s \in S$:

$$
V(s) = \begin{cases} 1 & \text{if } s = \mathbb{1} \\ 0 & \text{if } s = \mathrm{o} \\ \max_{a \in Av(s)} \sum_{s' \in S} \Delta(s, a)(s') \cdot V(s') & \text{otherwise} \end{cases}
$$

In order to compute the least fixpoint, an iterative method can be used as follows. We initialize $V^0(s) = 0$ for all s except for $V^0(1) = 1$. A successive iteration V^{i+1} is computed by evaluating the right-hand side of the equation system with V^i. The optimal value is achieved in the limit, i.e. $\lim_{n \to \infty} V^n = V$.

In order to obtain bounds on the imprecision of V^n, one can employ a *bounded* variant of VI [MLG05, BCC+14] (also called *interval iteration* [HM17]). Here one computes not only the *lower bounds* on V via the least-fixpoint approximants V^n (onwards denoted by L^n), but also *upper bounds* via the greatest-fixpoint approximants, called U^n. The greatest-fixpoint can be approximated in a dual way, by initializing the values to 1 except for o where it is 0. On MDPs without MECs (except for 1 and o), we have both $\lim_{n \to \infty} L^n = V = \lim_{n \to \infty} U^n$, giving us an anytime algorithm with the guarantee that $V \in [L^n, U^n]$. However, on general MDPs, $\lim_{n \to \infty} U^n$ can be larger than V, often yielding only a trivial bound of 1, see [ABKS18, Appendix B]. The solution suggested in [BCC+14, HM17] is to consider the MEC quotient instead, where the guarantee is recovered. The MEC quotient can be pre-computed [HM17] or computed gradually on-the-fly only for a part of the state space [BCC+14].

2.3   Bounded Real-Time Dynamic Programming (BRTDP)

BRTDP [MLG05] is a heuristic built on top of (bounded) VI, which has been adapted to the reachability objective in [BCC+14]. It belongs to a class of *asynchronous* VI algorithms. In other words, it differs from VI in that in each iteration it does not update the values for all states, but only a few. The states to be updated are chosen as those that appear in a simulation run performed in that iteration. This way we focus on states visited with high probability and thus having higher impact on the value.

BRTDP thus proceeds as follows. It maintains the current lower and upper bounds L and U on the value, like bounded VI. In each iteration, a simulation run is generated by choosing in each state s

- the action maximizing U, i.e. $\arg\max_a \sum_{s' \in S} \Delta(s, a)(s') \cdot U(s')$,
- the successor s' of a randomly with weight $\Delta(s, a)(s')$ or (more efficiently) in the variant of [BCC+14] with weight $\Delta(s, a)(s') \cdot (U(s') - L(s'))$.

Then the value of each state on the simulation run is updated by the equation system for V. This happens preferably in the backward order [BCC+14] from the last state (1 or o) towards s_{init}, thus efficiently propagating the value information. These iterations are performed repeatedly until $U(s_{\text{init}}) - L(s_{\text{init}}) < \varepsilon$ for some predefined precision ε, yielding the interval $[L(s_{\text{init}}), U(s_{\text{init}})]$ containing the value $V(s_{\text{init}})$.

If the only MECs are formed by 1 and o then the algorithm (depicted in [ABKS18, Appendix C, Algorithm 2] terminates almost surely. But if there are other MECs, then this is not necessarily the case. In order to ensure correct termination, [BCC+14] modifies the algorithm in a way, which we adopt also for our algorithms: Periodically, after a certain number of iterations, we compute the

MEC quotient, not necessarily of the whole MDP, but only of the part formed by the states visited so far by the algorithm.

3   Monte-Carlo Tree Search

Motivation. One of the main challenges in the application of BTRDP are the presence of events that happen after a long time (but are not necessarily rare). For example, consider the simple MDP in Fig. 1, modelling a hypothetical communication protocol. Let s_3 be the goal state, representing a failure state. From each of the states s_0, s_1 and s_2, the MDP tries to send a message. If the message sending fails, which happens with a very low probability, the MDP moves to the next state, otherwise returning to the initial state s_0. BRTDP repeatedly samples paths and propagates ("backs-up") the encountered values through the paths. Even though the goal is reached in almost every simulation, it can take very long time to finish each simulation.

The idea of MCTS is to "grow" a tree into the model rooted at the initial state while starting new simulations from the leaves of the tree. In this example, the tree soon expands to s_1 or s_2 and from then on, simulations are started there and thus are more targeted and the back-propagation of the values is faster.

Generic Algorithm. MCTS can be visualized (see Fig. 2) as gradually building up a tree, which describes several steps of unfolding of the system, collecting more

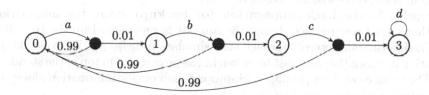

Fig. 1. A difficult case for BRTDP

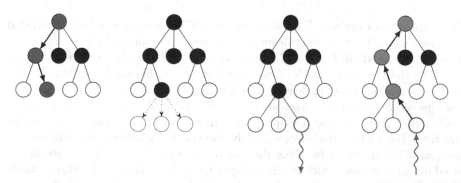

Fig. 2. The four stages of MCTS: *selection, expansion, roll-out* and *back-propagation*

Algorithm 1. The (enriched) MCTS scheme

1: Create a root t_0 of the tree, labelled by s_{init}
2: **while** within computational budget **do**
3:     $t_{parent} \leftarrow$ SELECTNODE(t_0)
4:     $t_{child} \leftarrow$ EXPANDANDPICKROLL-OUTNODE(t_{parent})
5:     $outcome \leftarrow$ ROLL-OUT(t_{child})
6:     BACKUPONROLL-OUT($outcome$)   ▷ Not in the standard MCTS
7:     BACKUPONTREE($t_{child}, outcome$)
8: **return** INDUCEDPOLICY(t_0)   ▷ action with the best estimated value

---

and more information. Note that nodes of the tree correspond to states of the MDP.

The MCTS procedure (see Algorithm 1) proceeds in rounds, each consisting of several stages:

First, in the **selection** stage (line 3), a *tree policy* is followed leading from the root of the tree to the currently most "interesting" leaf.

Second, in the **expansion** stage (line 4), one or more of the successors are added to the tree. In our setting with required guarantees, it turns out sensible to expand all successors, i.e. $\bigcup_{a \in Av(t_{parent})} \mathrm{supp}(\Delta(s_{parent}, a))$. One of the successors is picked, according to the tree policy.

Third, in the **roll-out** stage (line 5) a simulation run is generated, adhering to a *roll-out policy*. In the classical setting, the simulation run receives a certain reward. In our setting, the simulation run receives a reward of 1 if it encounters the goal state, otherwise it receives 0.

Finally, in the **back-propagation** (or **backup**) stage, the information whether a goal was reached during the roll-out is propagated up the tree (line 7). The information received through such simulations helps MCTS to decide the direction in which the tree must be grown in the next step. On top of the standard MCTS, we also consider possible back-propagation of this information along the generated simulations run (line 6).

Next, we discuss a particularly popular way to implement the MCTS scheme.

UCT Implementation. Each stage of the MCTS scheme can be instantiated in various ways. We now describe one of the most common and successful implementations, called UCT [KS06] (abbreviation of "UCB applied to Trees"). Each node t in the tree keeps track of two numbers: n_t is the number of times t has been visited when selecting leaves; v_t is the number of times it has been visited *and* the roll-out from the descendant leaf hit the goal. These numbers can be easily updated during the back-propagation: we simply increase all n's on the way from the leaf to the root, similarly for the v's whenever the roll-out hit the goal. This allows us to define the last missing piece, namely the tree policy based on these values, which is called *Upper Confidence Bound* (UCB1 or simply UCB). The UCB1 value of a node t in the MCTS tree is defined as follows:

$$UCB1(t) = \frac{v_t}{n_t} + C\sqrt{\frac{\ln n_{\text{parent}(t)}}{n_t}}$$

where parent(t) is the parent of t in the tree and C is a fixed *exploitation-exploitation constant*. The tree policy choosing nodes with maximum UCB1 bound is called the *UCB1 policy*.

Intuitively, the first term of the expression describes the ratio of "successful" roll-outs (i.e., hitting the goal) started from a descendant of t. In other words, this *exploitation* term tries to approximate the probability to reach the goal from t. The higher the value, the higher the chances that the tree policy would pick t. In contrast, the second term decreases when the node t is chosen too often. This compensates for the first term, thereby allowing for the siblings of t to be explored. This is the *exploration* term and the effect of the two terms is balanced by the constant C. The appropriate values of C vary among domains and, in practice, are determined experimentally.

It has been proved in [KS06] that for finite-horizon MDP (or MDP with discounted rewards), the UCT with an appropriately selected C converges in the following sense: After n iterations of the MCTS algorithm, the difference between the expectation of the value estimate and the true value of a given state is bounded by $\mathcal{O}(\log(n)/n)$. Moreover, the probability that an action with the best upper confidence bound in the root is not optimal converges to zero at a polynomial rate with $n \to \infty$.

4 Augmenting MCTS with Guarantees

In this section, we present several algorithms based on MCTS. Note that the typical uses of MCTS in practice only require the algorithm to guess a good but not necessarily the optimal action for the current state. When adapting learning algorithms to the verification setting, an important requirement is an ability to give precise guarantees on the sought value or to produce an ε-optimal scheduler. Consequently, in order to obtain the guarantees, our algorithms combine MCTS with BRTDP, which comes with guarantees, to various degrees. The spectrum is depicted in Table 1 and described in more detail below.

Table 1. Spectrum of algorithms ranging from pure MCTS to pure BRTDP

Algorithm	MCTS	BMCTS	MCTS-BRTDP	BRTDP-UCB	BRTDP
SELECTNODE (Tree Policy)	UCB1	UCB1	UCB1	UCB1	BRTDP
ROLL-OUT	Uniform	Uniform	BRTDP		
BACKPUPONROLL-OUT	—	L, U	L, U	v, n, L, U	L, U
BACKUPONTREE	v, n	v, n, L, U	v, n, L, U		

1. Pure MCTS (the UCT variant): The tree is constructed using the UCB1 policy while roll-outs are performed using a uniform random policy, i.e. actions are chosen uniformly, successors according to their transition probabilities. The roll-outs are either successful or not, and this information is back-propagated up the tree, i.e. the v- and n-values of the nodes in the tree are updated.

2. Bounded MCTS (BMCTS): In addition to all the steps of pure MCTS, here we also update the L- and U-values, using the transition probabilities and the old L- and U-values. This update takes place both on all states in the tree on the path from the root to the current leaf as well as all states of visited during the roll-out. The updates happen backwards, starting from the last state of the simulation run, towards the leaf and then towards the root.

3. MCTS-BRTDP: This algorithm is essentially BMCTS with the only difference that the roll-out is performed using the BRTDP policy, i.e. action is chosen as $\arg\max_{a \in \mathsf{Av}(s)} \sum_{s'} \Delta(s,a)(s') \cdot U(s')$, and the successor of a randomly with the weight $\Delta(s,a)(s') \cdot (U(s') - L(s'))$.

4. BRTDP-UCB: As we move towards the BRTDP side of the spectrum, there is no difference between whether a state is captured in the tree or not: back-propagation works the same and the policy to select the node is the same as for the roll-out. In this method, we use the UCB1 policy to choose actions on the whole path from the initial state all the way to the goal or the sink, and back-propagate all information. Note that as opposed to BRTDP, the exploitation is interleaved with some additional exploration, due to UCB1.

5. Pure BRTDP: Finally, we also consider the pure BRTDP algorithm as presented earlier in the paper. This works the same as BRTDP-UCB, but the (selection and roll-out) policy is that of BRTDP.

While MCTS does not provide exact guarantees on the current error, all the other methods keep track of the lower and the upper bound, yielding the respective guarantee on the value. Note that MCTS-BRTDP is a variant of MCTS, where BRTDP is used not only to provide these bounds, but also to provide a more informed roll-out. Such a policy is expected to be more efficient compared to just using a uniform policy or UCB. Since some studies [JKR17] have counter-intuitively shown that more informed roll-outs do not necessarily improve the runtime, we also include BMCTS and BRTDP-UCB, where the path generation is derived from the traditional MCTS approach; the former applies it in the MCTS setting, the latter in the BRTDP setting.

MDPs with MECs. In MDPs where the only MECs are formed by 1 and 0, the roll-outs almost surely reach one of the two states and then stop. Since in MDPs with MECs this is not necessarily the case, we have to collapse the MECs, like discussed in Sect. 2.3. Therefore, a roll-out $w = s_0 s_1 s_2 \dots s_n$ is stopped if $s_n \in \{1, 0\}$ or $s_n = s_k$, for some $0 \leq k < n$. In the latter case, there is a chance that an end component has been discovered. Hence we compute the MEC quotient and only then continue the process. When MECs are collapsed this way, both the lower and the upper bound converge to the value and the resulting methods terminate in finite time almost surely, due to reasoning of [BCC+14] and the exploration term being positive.

Example 1. We revisit the example of Fig. 1 to see how the MCTS-based algorithms presented above tend to work. We focus on MCTS-BRTDP. Once the algorithm starts it is easy to see that in 3 iterations of MCTS-BRTDP, the target state s_3 will belong to the MCTS tree. From the next iteration onwards, the selection step will always choose s_3 to start the roll-out from. But since s_3 is already a target, the algorithm just proceeds to update the information up the tree to the root state. Hence, with just 3 iterations more than what value iteration would need, the algorithm converges to the same result.

While this example is quite trivial, we show experimentally in the next section that the MCTS-based algorithms not only run roughly as fast as BRTDP, but in certain large models that exhibit behaviour similar to the example of Fig. 1, it is clearly the better option.

5   Experimental Evaluation

We implemented all the algorithms outlined in Table 1 in PRISM Model Checker [KNP11]. Table 2 presents the run-times obtained on twelve different models. Six of the models used (coin, leader, mer, firewire, zeroconf and wlan) were chosen from the PRISM Benchmark Suite [KNP12] and the remaining six were constructed by modifying firewire, zeroconf and wlan in order to demonstrate the strengths and weaknesses of VI, BRTDP, and our algorithms. Recall the motivational example of Fig. 1 in Sect. 3, which is hard for BRTDP, yet easy for VI. We refer to this MDP as brtdp-adversary. This hard case is combined with one of benchmarks, firewire, zeroconf and wlan, in two ways as follows.

Branch Models. In the first construction, we allow a branching decision at the initial state. The resulting model is shown in Fig. 3. If action a is chosen, then we enter the brtdp-adversary branch. If action b is chosen, then we enter the standard zeroconf model. Using this schema, we create three models: branch-zeroconf, branch-firewire and branch-wlan.

Composition Models. In the second construction, the models are constructed by the parallel (asynchronous) composition of the brtdp-adversary and one of firewire, zeroconf and wlan. The resulting models are named comp-firewire, comp-zeroconf and comp-wlan.

We run the experiments on an Intel Xeon server with sufficient memory (default PRISM settings). The implementation is single threaded and each experiment is run 15 times to alleviate the effect of the probabilistic nature of the algorithms. The median run-time for each model configuration is reported in Table 2. Note that the measured time is the wall-clock time needed to perform the model checking. We do not include the time needed to start PRISM and to read and parse the input file. An execution finishes successfully once the value of

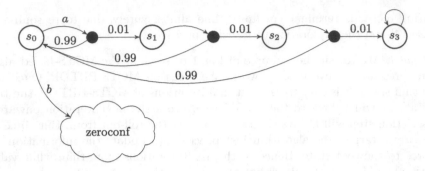

Fig. 3. Combining zeroconf model with the BRTDP adversary in a branching manner.

Table 2. Comparison of the various algorithms. All run-times are in seconds. Cells with '−' denote either running out of memory (in the case of VI) or running out of time.

Benchmark	BMCTS	MCTS-BRTDP	BRTDP-UCB	BRTDP	VI
consensus	5.55	6.48	7.47	6.15	1.13
leader	18.67	15.79	16.33	15.06	8.94
mer	−	4.79	−	3.63	−
firewire	0.07	0.08	0.09	0.09	6.99
wlan	0.09	0.07	0.08	0.08	−
zeroconf	0.93	0.20	0.59	0.20	−
comp-firewire	9.36	9.55	−	−	20.77
comp-wlan	2.51	2.25	−	−	−
comp-zeroconf	−	29.55	−	−	−
branch-firewire	0.09	0.09	0.02	0.09	9.33
branch-wlan	0.10	0.08	0.09	0.07	−
branch-zeroconf	25.90	30.78	35.67	38.14	−

the queried maximal reachability property is known with a guaranteed absolute precision of 10^{-6}, except for `comp-zeroconf` and `branch-zeroconf` where it stops once the value is known with a precision of 10^{-2}. Timeout is set to 10 min.

Table 2 shows that in the cases where BRTDP performs well, our algorithms perform very similarly, irrespective of the performance of VI. However, when BRTDP struggles due to the hard case, our MCTS-based algorithms still perform well, even in cases where VI also times out. In particular, MCTS-BRTDP shows a consistently good performance. The less informed variants BMCTS and BRTDP-UCB of MCTS-BRTDP and BRTDP, respectively, perform consistently at most as well their respective more informed variants. This only confirms the intuitive expectation which, however, has been shown invalid in other settings.

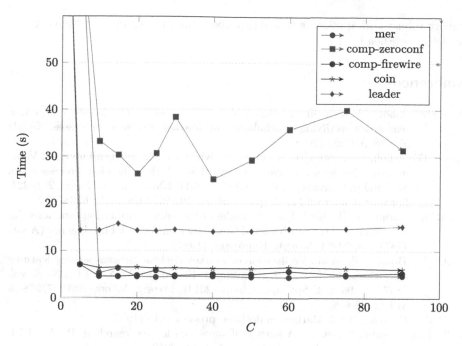

Fig. 4. Dependence of the run-time of MCTS-BRTDP on the exploration-exploitation constant, C

In the experiments, we have used the exploration-exploitation constant $C = 25$, which is rather large compared to the typical usage in literature [KSW06, BPW+12]. This significantly supports exploration. The effect of the constant is illustrated in Fig. 4. We can see that for lower values of C, the algorithms perform worse, due to insufficient incentive to explore.

In conclusion, we see that exploration, which is present in MCTS but not explicitly in BRTDP, leads to a small overhead which, however, pays off dramatically in more complex cases. For the total number of states explored by VI, BRTDP, and our MCTS-based algorithms, we refer the reader to [ABKS18, Appendix D, Table 3].

6   Conclusion

We have introduced Monte Carlo tree search into verification of Markov decision processes, ensuring hard guarantees of the resulting methods. We presented several algorithms, covering the spectrum between MCTS and (in this context more traditional) MDP-planning heuristic BRTDP. Our experiments suggest that the overhead caused by additional exploration is outweighed by the ability of the technique to handle the cases, which are more complicated for BRTDP. Further, similarly to BRTDP, the techniques can handle larger state spaces, where the traditional value iteration fails to deliver any result. Consequently, the method is more robust and applicable to a larger spectrum of examples, at the cost of a negligible overhead.

References

[ABKS18] Ashok, P., Brázdil, T., Křetínský, J., Slámečka, O.: Monte Carlo tree search for verifying reachability in Markov decision processes. CoRR abs/1809.03299 (2018)

[ACD+17] Ashok, P., Chatterjee, K., Daca, P., Křetínský, J., Meggendorfer, T.: Value iteration for long-run average reward in Markov decision processes. In: Majumdar, R., Kunčak, V. (eds.) CAV 2017. LNCS, vol. 10426, pp. 201–221. Springer, Cham (2017). https://doi.org/10.1007/978-3-319-63387-9_10

[AK87] Abramson, B., Korf, R.E.: A model of two-player evaluation functions. In: Proceedings of the 6th National Conference on Artificial Intelligence (AAAI 1987), pp. 90–94. Morgan Kaufmann (1987)

[BCC+14] Brázdil, T., et al.: Verification of Markov decision processes using learning algorithms. In: Cassez, F., Raskin, J.-F. (eds.) ATVA 2014. LNCS, vol. 8837, pp. 98–114. Springer, Cham (2014). https://doi.org/10.1007/978-3-319-11936-6_8

[Bel57] Bellman, R.: A Markovian decision process. 6:15 (1957)

[BPW+12] Browne, C., et al.: A survey of monte carlo tree search methods. IEEE Trans. Comput. Intell. AI Games 4, 1–43 (2012)

[Cou07] Coulom, R.: Efficient selectivity and backup operators in Monte-Carlo tree search. In: van den Herik, H.J., Ciancarini, P., Donkers, H.H.L.M.J. (eds.) CG 2006. LNCS, vol. 4630, pp. 72–83. Springer, Heidelberg (2007). https://doi.org/10.1007/978-3-540-75538-8_7

[dA97] de Alfaro, L.: Formal verification of probabilistic systems. Ph.D. thesis, Stanford University (1997)

[DJKV17] Dehnert, C., Junges, S., Katoen, J.P., Volk, M.: A storm is coming: a modern probabilistic model checker. In: Majumdar, R., Kunčak, V. (eds.) Computer Aided Verification. CAV 2017. Lecture Notes in Computer Science, vol. 10427, pp. 592–600. Springer, Cham (2017). https://doi.org/10.1007/978-3-319-63390-9_31

[DLST15] D'Argenio, P., Legay, A., Sedwards, S., Traonouez, L.-M.: Smart sampling for lightweight verification of Markov decision processes. Int. J. Softw. Tools Technol. Transf. 17(4), 469–484 (2015)

[GW06] Gelly, S., Wang, Y.: Exploration exploitation in Go: UCT for Monte-Carlo Go. In: NIPS: Neural Information Processing Systems Conference On-line Trading of Exploration and Exploitation Workshop, Canada, December 2006

[HM17] Haddad, S., Monmege, B.: Interval iteration algorithm for MDPs and IMDPs. Theor. Comput. Sci. 735, 111–131 (2018)

[HMZ+12] Henriques, D., Martins, J., Zuliani, P., Platzer, A., Clarke, E.M.: Statistical model checking for Markov decision processes. In: QEST, pp. 84–93 (2012)

[JKR17] James, S., Konidaris, G., Rosman, B.: An analysis of Monte Carlo tree search. In: Proceedings of the Thirty-First AAAI Conference on Artificial Intelligence, 4–9 February 2017, San Francisco, California, USA, pp. 3576–3582 (2017)

[KKKW18] Kelmedi, E., Krämer, J., Kretínský, J., Weininger, M.: Value iteration for simple stochastic games: stopping criterion and learning algorithm. In: CAV (1), pp. 623–642. Springer (2018)

[KM17] Křetínský, J., Meggendorfer, T.: Efficient strategy iteration for mean payoff in Markov decision processes. In: ATVA, pp. 380–399 (2017)

[KNP11] Kwiatkowska, M., Norman, G., Parker, D.: PRISM 4.0: verification of probabilistic real-time systems. In: Gopalakrishnan, G., Qadeer, S. (eds.) CAV 2011. LNCS, vol. 6806, pp. 585–591. Springer, Heidelberg (2011). https://doi.org/10.1007/978-3-642-22110-1_47

[KNP12] Kwiatkowska, M., Norman, G., Parker, D.: The PRISM benchmark suite. In: Proceedings of 9th International Conference on Quantitative Evaluation of SysTems (QEST 2012), pp. 203–204. IEEE CS Press (2012)

[Kre16] Křetínský, J.: Survey of statistical verification of linear unbounded properties: model checking and distances. In: Margaria, T., Steffen, B. (eds.) ISoLA 2016. LNCS, vol. 9952, pp. 27–45. Springer, Cham (2016). https://doi.org/10.1007/978-3-319-47166-2_3

[KS06] Kocsis, L., Szepesvári, C.: Bandit based Monte-Carlo planning. In: Fürnkranz, J., Scheffer, T., Spiliopoulou, M. (eds.) ECML 2006. LNCS (LNAI), vol. 4212, pp. 282–293. Springer, Heidelberg (2006). https://doi.org/10.1007/11871842_29

[KSW06] Kocsis, L., Szepesvári, C., Willemson, J.: Improved Monte-Carlo search (2006)

[MLG05] Brendan McMahan, H., Likhachev, M., Gordon, G.J.: Bounded real-time dynamic programming: RTDP with monotone upper bounds and performance guarantees. In: ICML 2005 (2005)

[Put14] Puterman, M.L.: Markov Decision Processes: Discrete Stochastic Dynamic Programming. Wiley, New York (2014)

[SHM+16] Silver, D., et al.: Mastering the game of go with deep neural networks and tree search. Nature 529(7587), 484–489 (2016)

[SHS+17] Silver, D., et al.: Mastering chess and Shogi by self-play with a general reinforcement learning algorithm. CoRR, abs/1712.01815 (2017)

[SLW+06] Strehl, A.L., Li, L., Wiewiora, E., Langford, J., Littman, M.L.: PAC model-free reinforcement learning. In: ICML, pp. 881–888 (2006)

[SSM12] Silver, D., Sutton, R.S., Mueller, M.: Temporal-difference search in computer Go. Mach. Learn. 87, 183–219 (2012)

[ST09] Silver, D., Tesauro, G.: Monte-Carlo simulation balancing. In: Proceedings of the 26th Annual International Conference on Machine Learning (ICML 2009), pp. 945–952. ACM (2009)

[VSS17] Vodopivec, T., Samothrakis, S., Ster, B.: On Monte Carlo tree search and reinforcement learning. J. Artif. Intell. Res. 60, 881–936 (2017)

[YS02] Younes, H.L.S., Simmons, R.G.: Probabilistic verification of discrete event systems using acceptance sampling. In: Brinksma, E., Larsen, K.G. (eds.) CAV 2002. LNCS, vol. 2404, pp. 223–235. Springer, Heidelberg (2002). https://doi.org/10.1007/3-540-45657-0_17

Lightweight Statistical Model Checking in Nondeterministic Continuous Time

Pedro R. D'Argenio[1,2,3], Arnd Hartmanns[4(✉)], and Sean Sedwards[5]

[1] Universidad Nacional de Córdoba, Córdoba, Argentina
dargenio@famaf.unc.edu.ar
[2] CONICET, Córdoba, Argentina
[3] Saarland University, Saarbrücken, Germany
[4] University of Twente, Enschede, The Netherlands
a.hartmanns@utwente.nl
[5] University of Waterloo, Waterloo, Canada
sean.sedwards@uwaterloo.ca

Abstract. Lightweight scheduler sampling brings statistical model checking to nondeterministic formalisms with undiscounted properties, in constant memory. Its direct application to continuous-time models is rendered ineffective by their dense concrete state spaces and the need to consider continuous input for optimal decisions. In this paper we describe the challenges and state of the art in applying lightweight scheduler sampling to three continuous-time formalisms: After a review of recent work on exploiting discrete abstractions for probabilistic timed automata, we discuss scheduler sampling for Markov automata and apply it on two case studies. We provide further insights into the tradeoffs between scheduler classes for stochastic automata. Throughout, we present extended experiments and new visualisations of the distribution of schedulers.

1   Introduction

Statistical model checking (SMC [24,33]) is a formal verification technique for stochastic systems based on Monte Carlo simulation. It naturally works with non-Markovian behaviour and complex continuous dynamics that make the exact model checking problem intractable. As a simulation-based approach, however, SMC is incompatible with nondeterminism. Yet (continuous and discrete) nondeterministic choices are desirable in formal modelling, for abstraction and to represent concurrency as well as the absence of knowledge. Nondeterminism occurs in many popular formalisms, notably in Markov decision processes (MDP). In the presence of nondeterminism, quantities of interest are defined w.r.t. optimal *schedulers* (also called policies, adversaries or strategies) resolving all nondeterministic choices: the verification result is the *maximum* or *minimum* probability

This work is supported by the 3TU project "Big Software on the Run", by ERC grant 695614 (POWVER), by the JST ERATO HASUO Metamathematics for Systems Design project (JPMJER1603), and by SeCyT-UNC projects 05/BP12, 05/B497.

T. Margaria and B. Steffen (Eds.): ISoLA 2018, LNCS 11245, pp. 336–353, 2018.
https://doi.org/10.1007/978-3-030-03421-4_22

or expected value ranging over *all* schedulers. Many SMC tools appear to support nondeterministic models, e.g. PRISM [28] and UPPAAL SMC [13], but use a single implicit probabilistic scheduler that makes all choices randomly. Their results thus lie *somewhere* between the minimum and maximum. Such implicit resolutions are known to affect the trustworthiness of simulation studies [3,27].

Sound SMC in the presence of nondeterminism is a hard problem. For MDP, Brázdil et al. [4] proposed a sound machine learning technique, while UPPAAL STRATEGO [12] explicitly synthesises a "good" scheduler before using it for a standard SMC analysis. Both approaches suffer from worst-case memory usage linear in the number of states. Classic memory-efficient sampling approaches (e.g. [25]) address discounted models only. In contrast, the modes tool [6], part of the MODEST TOOLSET [20], extends the lightweight scheduler sampling (LSS) approach for MDP first implemented in PLASMA [30]. LSS is the only technique that applies to undiscounted properties, as typically considered in formal verification, that also keeps memory usage effectively constant in the number of states.

The effectiveness of LSS depends on the probability of sampling near-optimal schedulers. It works well for discrete-time discrete-state models like MDP, where memoryless schedulers achieve optimal probabilities on a discrete state space. Yet the concrete state spaces of continuous-time models may be uncountably infinite, and optimal schedulers may need real-valued input based on model time. This renders naive applications of scheduler sampling ineffective. However, the use of suitable discrete abstractions makes the approach both feasible and useful for some continuous-time formalisms.

This paper summarises, connects and extends previous work on LSS for continuous-time models. After an introduction to the concept of LSS on MDP in Sect. 2, we summarise recent extensions to probabilistic timed automata (PTA [29]) using regions [22] and zones [9] in Sect. 3. We report extended experimental results, sampling more schedulers and reducing the statistical error compared to our previous work. In Sect. 4 we investigate the challenges in extending LSS to Markov automata (MA [14]), a compositional nondeterministic extension of continuous-time Markov chains. We introduce two new case studies to experiment with modes' support for LSS on MA. In Sect. 5 we turn to stochastic automata (SA [10]), which include general continuous probability distributions. We have recently shown that no simple class of schedulers achieves optimal probabilities on SA [8]. We summarise these results and their effect on LSS, and provide more detailed experimental results to investigate the tradeoffs between restricted classes and discrete abstractions of the state space.

All methods described in this paper are implemented in the modes statistical model checker [6], which was used to perform all the experiments. To investigate the distribution of schedulers, we extended modes to create histograms that visualise the distribution of schedulers w.r.t. the probabilities they induce. We present histograms for all our experiments, providing deeper insights into the character of the nondeterminism in the models and the behaviour of LSS.

2   Lightweight Statistical Model Checking

We summarise the lightweight scheduler sampling approach for Markov decision processes [30], which is the foundation of our techniques for timed systems.

Definition 1. *A (discrete) probability distribution over a set Ω is a function $\mu \in \Omega \to [0,1]$ such that* $\text{support}(\mu) \stackrel{\text{def}}{=} \{ \omega \in \Omega \mid \mu(\omega) > 0 \}$ *is countable and* $\sum_{\omega \in \text{support}(\mu)} \mu(\omega) = 1$. $\text{Dist}(\Omega)$ *is the set of all probability distributions over Ω.*

Definition 2. *A pseudo-random number generator (PRNG) $\mathcal{U}$ can be initialised with a seed $i \in \mathbb{N}$ ($\mathcal{U} := \text{PRNG}(i)$) and then iterated ($\mathcal{U}()$) to produce a new value pseudo-uniformly distributed in $[0,1)$ and pseudo-statistically independent of previous iterates. For a given i, the sequence of iterates is always the same. We denote by $\mathcal{U}(\mu)$ the pseudo-random selection of a value from $\text{support}(\mu)$ according to a value sampled from $\mathcal{U}$ and the probabilities in $\mu \in \text{Dist}(\Omega)$.*

Markov decision processes combine nondeterminism and probabilistic choices. To move from one state to another, first a transition is chosen nondeterministically. Every transition leads into a probability distribution over successor states.

Definition 3. *A Markov decision process (MDP) is a triple $M = \langle S, T, s_{init} \rangle$ where S is a countable set of states, $T \in S \to 2^{\text{Dist}(S)}$ is the transition function with $T(s)$ countable for all $s \in S$, and $s_{init} \in S$ is the initial state. If $|T(s)| \leq 1$ for all $s \in S$, then M is a discrete-time Markov chain (DTMC).*

A *transition* is a pair $\langle s, \mu \rangle$ s.t. $\mu \in T(s)$. A *path* in an MDP is an infinite sequence $\langle s_0, \mu_0 \rangle \langle s_1, \mu_1 \rangle \ldots$ of transitions with $s_0 = s_{init}$. When the current state is s_i, the nondeterministic choice of the next transition is made by a scheduler:

Definition 4. *A (memoryless deterministic) scheduler for an MDP is a function $\mathfrak{s} \in S \to \text{Dist}(S)$ s.t. $\mathfrak{s}(s) \in T(s)$ for all $s \in S$. $\mathfrak{S}$ is the set of all schedulers.*

Once a transition $\langle s_i, \mu_i \rangle$ is chosen, the next state s_{i+1} is selected randomly according to μ_i. Restricting to the choices made by $\mathfrak{s}$ induces a DTMC, and $\mathfrak{s}$ defines the probability measure $\mathbb{P}_{\mathfrak{s}}$ over paths [16]. *Transient properties ϕ are queries for the optimal probabilities* $\text{opt}_{\mathfrak{s} \in \mathfrak{S}} \mathbb{P}_{\mathfrak{s}}(\neg avoid \cup target)$ where $\text{opt} \in \{ \sup, \inf \}$ (for *maximum* and *minimum* probabilities, denoted $p_{\max}$ and $p_{\min}$), *avoid*, *target* $\subseteq S$, and $\neg avoid \cup target$ is the set of paths with at least one state in *target* such that no state in *avoid* has been visited earlier. For these properties, the restriction to memoryless deterministic schedulers preserves optimal probabilities. For a finite *trace* ω, i.e. a path prefix projected to its states, let $\phi(\omega)$ be *undecided* if ω does not contain a state in $\neg avoid \cup target$, *true* if ϕ is satisfied on all paths that have a prefix projecting to ω, and *false* otherwise.

Using MDP to directly model complex systems is cumbersome. Instead, higher-level formalisms like MODEST [18] are used. They provide parallel composition and finite-domain variables. This allows to compactly describe very large MDP. MODEST in fact supports all of the formalisms introduced in this paper.

Input: MDP $M = \langle S, T, s_{init} \rangle$, transient property ϕ, scheduler identifier $\sigma \in \mathbb{Z}_{32}$
Output: Sampled trace ω

```
1  s := s_init, ω := s_init
2  while φ(ω) = undecided ∧ T(s) ≠ ∅ do        // run until φ decided or deadlock
3  │   U_nd := PRNG(H(σ.s))                     // seed U_nd with hash of σ and s
4  │   μ := ⌈U_nd() · |T(s)|⌉-th element of T(s)  // use U_nd to select a transition
5  └   s := U_pr(μ), ω := ω.s                    // use U_pr to select next state, append to ω
6  return ω
```

Algorithm 1. Lightweight simulation for an MDP and a scheduler identifier

Statistical model checking (SMC) [24,33] is, in essence, Monte Carlo integration of formal models. It generates a large number n of simulation *runs* according to the probability distributions in the model and uses them to statistically estimate the probability for a given property. For transient property ϕ on a DTMC, the runs are traces $\omega_1, \ldots, \omega_n$ such that $\phi(\omega_i) \neq undecided$, and the estimate is $\hat{p}_n = \frac{1}{n} \sum_{i=0}^{n} \phi(\omega_i)$ when identifying *true* with 1 and *false* with 0. $\hat{p}_n$ is an unbiased estimator of the actual probability p. The choice of n depends on the desired statistical properties of $\hat{p}$, e.g. that a confidence interval around $\hat{p}$ with confidence δ has half-width w. For a detailed description of statistical methods and especially hypothesis tests for SMC, we refer the reader to [32].

Lightweight scheduler sampling (LSS) extends SMC to the nondeterministic model of MDP by approximating optimal schedulers, i.e. those that realise p_{min} or p_{max}, in constant memory relative to the size of the state space [30]. A scheduler is identified by a single (32-bit) integer. LSS randomly selects m schedulers (i.e. integers), performs standard SMC on the DTMC induced by each, and reports the maximum and minimum estimates over all sampled schedulers as approximations of the actual respective probabilities. We show the core of LSS—performing a simulation run for a given scheduler identifier σ—as Algorithm 1. It uses two PRNGs: $\mathcal{U}_{pr}$ is initialised globally once and used to simulate the probabilistic choices of the MDP in line 5, while $\mathcal{U}_{nd}$ resolves the nondeterministic choices in line 4. We want σ to represent a deterministic memoryless scheduler. Therefore, within one simulation run as well as in different runs for the same value of σ, $\mathcal{U}_{nd}$ must always make the same choice for the same state s. To achieve this, $\mathcal{U}_{nd}$ is re-initialised with a seed based on σ and s in every step (line 3).

The effectiveness of LSS depends on the probability of sampling a near-optimal scheduler. Since we do not know a priori what makes a scheduler optimal, we want to sample "uniformly" from the space of all schedulers. This at least avoids actively biasing against "good" schedulers. More precisely, a uniformly random choice of σ will result in a uniformly chosen (but fixed) resolution of all nondeterministic choices. Algorithm 1 achieves this naturally for MDP.

Bounds and Error Accumulation. The results of LSS are lower bounds for maximum and upper bounds for minimum probabilities up to the specified statistical error. They can thus be used to e.g. *disprove* safety or *prove* schedulability,

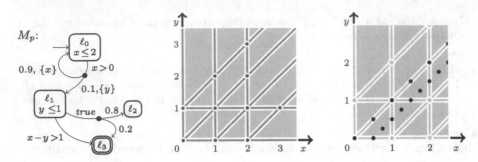

Fig. 1. Example PTA M_p **Fig. 2.** Regions of M_p **Fig. 3.** Representatives

but not the opposite. The accumulation of statistical error introduced by the repeated simulation experiments over m schedulers must also be accounted for, using e.g. Šidák correction or the modified tests described in [11].

Two-phase and Smart Sampling. If, for fixed statistical parameters, SMC needs n runs on a DTMC, LSS needs significantly more than $m \cdot n$ runs on an MDP to avoid error accumulation. The *two-phase* and *smart* sampling approaches can reduce this overhead. The former's first phase consists of performing n simulation runs for each of the m schedulers. The scheduler that resulted in the maximum (or minimum) value is selected, and independently evaluated once more with n runs to produce the final estimate. The first phase is a heuristic to find a near-optimal scheduler before the second phase estimates the value under this scheduler according to the required statistical parameters. Smart sampling [11] generalises this principle to multiple phases, dropping the "worst" half of the schedulers in every round. It tends to find better schedulers faster, while the two-phase approach has predictable performance: it always needs $(m + 1) \cdot n$ runs. We use the two-phase approach for all experiments reported in this paper.

3   Probabilistic Timed Automata

Probabilistic timed automata (PTA [29]) combine MDP and timed automata [1]. We show an example PTA M_p in Fig. 1. It has two *clocks* x and y: variables over $[0, \infty)$ that advance synchronously with rate 1 as time passes. As PTA are a symbolic model, we speak of *locations* (in *Loc*) and *edges* instead of states and transitions. M_p has locations ℓ_0 through ℓ_3. Every location is associated with a *time progress condition*: $x \leq 2$ in ℓ_0, $y \leq 1$ in ℓ_1, and *true* elsewhere. These are *clock constraints*: expressions of the form $\mathcal{C}:: = true \mid false \mid \mathcal{C} \wedge \mathcal{C} \mid c \sim n \mid c_1 - c_2 \sim n$ where $\sim \in \{>, \geq, <, \leq\}$, c, c_1, c_2 are clocks, and $n \in \mathbb{N}$. Every edge is annotated with a *guard* clock constraint and sets of clocks to *reset* to zero. M_p has one edge out of ℓ_0 with guard $x > 0$ that goes back to ℓ_0 with probability 0.9, resetting x, and otherwise to ℓ_1, resetting y. There are two edges out of ℓ_1. The one with guard $x - y > 1$ goes to ℓ_3 with probability 1 and no resets.

Intuitively, the semantics of a PTA is an uncountably infinite MDP: Its states are pairs $\langle \ell, v \rangle$ of the current location ℓ and valuation v for all clocks. In ℓ, time can pass (i.e. the values in v increase) as long as the time progress condition remains satisfied. An edge can be taken if its guard evaluates to *true* at the current point in time. Then a target is chosen randomly, the specified clocks are reset to zero, and we move to the target location. Writing valuations as tuples $\langle v(x), v(y) \rangle$, one concrete trace in the semantics of M_p is $\langle \ell_0, \langle 0, 0 \rangle \rangle \, \langle \ell_0, \langle 0.8, 0.8 \rangle \rangle \, \langle \ell_0, \langle 0, 0.8 \rangle \rangle \, \langle \ell_0, \langle 1.1, 1.9 \rangle \rangle \, \langle \ell_1, \langle 1.1, 0 \rangle \rangle \, \langle \ell_3, \langle 1.1, 0 \rangle \rangle$.

The time spent in ℓ_0 and ℓ_1 is nondeterministic, as is the choice of edge in ℓ_1.

The transient properties defined for MDP in Sect. 2 apply analogously to PTA. In addition, time-bounded properties—where *target* must be reached in $\leq d \in \mathbb{N}$ time units—can be encoded as unbounded ones by adding a new clock c_d that is never reset and replacing *target* by $\{ \langle \ell, v \rangle \mid \ell \in Loc \wedge v(c_d) \leq d \} \cap target$. In M_p, the minimum probability to reach l_3 is 0.2. The maximum is 1; it is only achieved by always waiting in l_0 until $x > 1$ before taking the edge.

A naive extension of lightweight SMC to PTA is to use Algorithm 1 to generate concrete traces like the one given for M_p above. The input to $\mathcal{U}_{nd}$ is then a hash of σ and the current state $\langle \ell, v \rangle$. $\mathcal{U}_{nd}$ selects a delay in $[0, \infty)$ permitted by the time progress condition, followed by an enabled edge, if available. However, this can make (near-)optimal schedulers infeasibly rare. Consider M_p and the maximum probability to reach ℓ_3. An optimal scheduler must *always* select a delay >1 in ℓ_0. Yet, for a fixed σ, we get to make a *new* decision every time we come back to ℓ_0 because $v(y)$ most likely is a different real number in $[0, 2]$ every time. The probability of choosing a σ that *always* makes the *same* decision is zero, and even near-optimal schedulers are rare. The problem is that the number of critical decisions is infinite, such that optimal schedulers have measure zero. To be effective, LSS needs the number of critical decisions to be finite.

3.1 Lightweight SMC with Discrete Abstractions

To model-check transient properties, it suffices to consider the finite *region* graph of a PTA [29], a concept first introduced for timed automata [1]. Since it is too large to be useful in practice, timed automata verification tools instead use *zones*.

Definition 5. *Let $k_c \in \mathbb{N}$ be the maximum constant appearing in comparisons with clock c. A* zone *is a non-empty set of valuations that can be described by a clock constraint in which all comparisons have the form $c_1 - c_2 \sim n_{c_1 c_2}$ for $n_{c_1 c_2} \in \{ 0, \dots, \max\{ k_{c_1}, k_{c_2} \} \}$ or $c \sim n_c$ for $n_c \in \{ 0, \dots, k_c \}$. A* region r *is a minimal zone; its* successor *is the unique first other region encountered when delaying from any valuation in r.*

In M_p we have $k_x = 2$ and $k_y = 1$. The regions of M_p are visualised in Fig. 2: Every gray point, line segment and area is a region. To find a region's successor, follow a 45-degree line from any point within the region up to the next region.

We could use Algorithm 1 on the region graph. However, if the only available operations on regions are to (1) reset a clock and (2) obtain the successor, then performing a long delay needs many simulation steps to sequentially move through several successors. This causes significant performance problems and prevents uniform scheduler sampling: As long as the time progress condition is satisfied, the only reasonable way to implement the scheduler is to let $\mathcal{U}_{nd}$ choose uniformly between delaying to the successor or taking an edge. The total delay thus follows a geometric distribution, biasing towards taking edges early.

A zone-based approach [9] using the standard difference-bound matrix (DBM) data structure solves these two problems. We can easily obtain and represent an entire sequence of regions as a single zone, determine the edges enabled throughout that zone, and use $\mathcal{U}_{nd}$ to uniformly (but deterministically for fixed σ) select one. The resulting algorithm (shown as Algorithm 2 in [9]) is not a simple extension of Algorithm 1 for several reasons that we explore in that paper. In particular, when taking an edge, it needs to select a single region from within the target zone. This is to avoid over-/underapproximating probabilities, since it performs a forwards exploration [29]. The drawback of zone-based LSS is performance: The runtime of most DBM operations, such as intersecting two zones or resetting clocks, is cubic in the number of clocks [2], and selecting a region uniformly at random is exponential [9]. We use a faster quasi-uniform algorithm in our experiments.

Efficient simulation with regions became possible with our new efficient data structure for regions that supports long delays without enumerating successor regions [22]. It implements all operations with worst-case runtime linear in the number of clocks. The problem of efficient data structures for regions had received scant attention as the region graph is too large for exact model checking.

A straightforward symbolic representation of regions consists of a mapping from each clock to the integer part of its value, plus a total order of the fractional parts. Our data structure additionally provides a concrete *representative* value in $\mathbb{Q}$ for every clock, and a function that, given a delay based on a representative valuation, performs that entire delay in one go. The concrete choice of representatives is the main insight. For every clock, the representative value is a multiple of $1/(2 \cdot n_d)$, where n_d is the number of different fractional values among all clocks. We show the representatives of regions of M_p as black dots in Fig. 3: the one of region $x = y = 0$ (which has $n_d = 1$), the one of $0 < x < y \wedge y = 0$ (with $n_d = 2$), their successors, and so on. This choice of representatives is the only one where representatives are equally spaced, allowing an efficient implementation of the delay function. The resulting LSS core is shown as Algorithm 3 in [22].

3.2 Experiments

In [22] we compared the zone- and region-based approaches on PTA models of communication protocols from the literature. We estimated the probabilities of

Table 1. Performance and results for PTA

Model	Clocks	Model checking		Ad-hoc schedulers			LSS with regions			LSS with zones		
		p_{min}	p_{max}	ALAP	Uniform	ASAP	Time	$\hat{p}_{min}$	$\hat{p}_{max}$	Time	$\hat{p}_{min}$	$\hat{p}_{max}$
firewire	1+1	0.781	1.000	0.95	0.98	1.00	20 s	0.79	1.00	27 s	0.79	1.00
wlan	2		0.063	0.05	0.05	0.05	2 744 s	0.04	0.06	3 903 s	0.04	0.06
csmacd₂	4+1	0.729	0.872	0.73	0.75	0.87	108 s	0.73	0.85	398 s	0.73	0.87
csmacd₃	5+1	0.663	0.892	0.71	0.81	0.89	312 s	0.78	0.85	1 185 s	0.77	0.87
csmacd₄	6+1			0.68	0.83	0.90	656 s	0.80	0.85	2 555 s	0.80	0.86

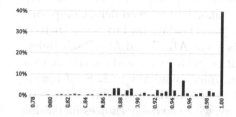

Fig. 4. Histogram for *firewire* (regions)

Fig. 5. Histogram for *wlan* (regions)

- termination in 4000 ns in IEEE 1394 FireWire root contention (*firewire*),
- either of two stations' backoff counters reaching value 2 within one transmission in IEEE 802.11 wireless LAN (*wlan*) using the original timing parameters from the standard (e.g. a maximum transmission time of 15717 μs), and
- all stations correctly delivering their packets within D_n μs on a shared medium via the exponential backoff procedure in IEEE 802.3 CSMA/CD with $n \in \{2,3,4\}$ stations (*csmacd$_n$*), using $D_2 = 1800$, $D_3 = 2700$ and $D_4 = 3600$.

In Table 1 we report the results of a new set of experiments on these models and properties. We have modified the zone-based approach to greedily try to enter/avoid the *target* and *avoid* sets for maximum probabilities (and vice-versa for minimum probabilities) after identifying the set of delays allowed by the time progress condition but before selecting an edge. We also improved the fast quasi-uniform region selection algorithm. Furthermore, we sample more schedulers ($m = 1000$) and have reduced the statistical error: We use $n = 372221$ runs per scheduler for *wlan* and 14889 for the other models. Via the Okamoto bound [31] (as used in the "APMC method" [24]), which relates n to values ϵ and δ s.t. $\mathbb{P}(|\hat{p} - p| > \epsilon) < \delta$ for estimate $\hat{p}$ and actual probability p, this guarantees $\epsilon = 0.001$ for *wlan* and $\epsilon = 0.005$ for the other models with confidence $\delta = 0.95$. We also compare with the probabilities induced by three ad-hoc schedulers:

- **Uniform** selects uniformly at random among the time points where ≥ 1 edge is enabled before uniformly selecting one edge enabled after that chosen delay;
- **ASAP** instead selects the first time point where any edge is enabled; and
- **ALAP** always picks the last time point where at least one edge is enabled.

These are *randomised* schedulers: they may make a different choice every time the same state is visited. They also require the intersections of guards and time progress conditions to be bounded, which is the case for all three models. The Uniform scheduler is similar to the implicit one of UPPAAL SMC [13]. All experiments were performed on a cluster of 10 Intel Xeon E5520 nodes (2.26–2.53 GHz) with 64-bit Ubuntu Linux, providing 40 simulation threads in total (4 per node). Every experiment was performed three times and we report the averages.

Discussion. As expected and previously shown in [22], the region-based approach significantly outperforms the zone-based one as the number of clocks grows. On the larger *csmacd* models, however, the latter finds better schedulers. Comparing with the ad-hoc schedulers reveals that long (short) delays lead to worse (better) performance of the protocol, with the results of the ALAP and ASAP schedulers being closer to the actual optimal probabilities (which we could exactly model-check for the smaller models) than any scheduler found via LSS. So if always scheduling fast or slow indeed is optimal, then near-optimal schedulers are rare: they must *always* pick the min. or max. delay, with the delay choices increasing as the number of stations grows. On *firewire*, ad-hoc schedulers only lead to probabilities near the maximum, while LSS also finds near-minimal schedulers.

Scheduler Histograms. We extended modes to also return the probabilities estimated for *all m* sampled schedulers. This allows us to create histograms that visualise the distribution of schedulers w.r.t. the probabilities they induce. The histograms for *firewire* and *wlan* using regions are shown in Figs. 4 and 5, respectively, with the ones for zones being nearly identical. We see the reasons for the success of LSS as well as the failure of the ad-hoc schedulers reflected in these histograms: For *firewire*, maximal schedulers are very likely while minimal ones are rarer, but still show decent probabilities. For *wlan*, every *deterministic* scheduler sampled by LSS is either near-minimal or near-maximal; the *randomised* ad-hoc schedulers however only realise an average of these two behavioural modes.

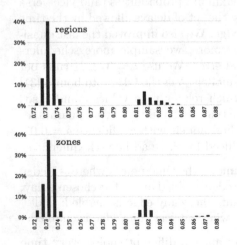

Fig. 6. Histograms for *csmacd*$_2$

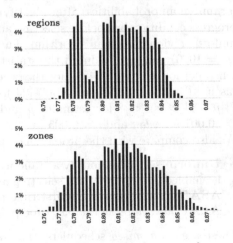

Fig. 7. Histograms for *csmacd*$_3$

For *csmacd*, the distributions of schedulers found with regions and zones are clearly different. With two stations (Fig. 6), there are distinct clusters of similar schedulers, however the region-based approach does not find good ones in the near-maximal cluster. As the number of stations and thus of nondeterministic decisions increases, the average sampled scheduler leads to more average behaviour (Fig. 7), yet the variance among zone-based schedulers is still wider.

4 Markov Automata

Markov automata (MA, [14]) are a compositional model that combines the discrete probabilistic branching of MDP with the exponentially distributed delays of continuous-time Markov chains (CTMC). We show an example MA with states s_0 through s_3 in Fig. 8. It has two types of transitions: *Markovian* ones (as in CTMC) labelled with a rate in $(0, \infty)$ connect s_0 to s_1 and s_2, while *probabilistic transitions* (as in MDP) connect s_1 to s_3 and back to s_0. The *exit rate* of s_0 is $1 + 3 = 4$. Probabilistic transitions are taken immediately when available, with the choice between multiple transitions (like a and b in s_1) being nondeterministic. Markovian transitions become enabled after an amount of time has passed that is exponentially distributed according to the rate of the transition. The choice between multiple of them is resolved by a race between the distributions.

In terms of properties, we are interested in unbounded and time-bounded transient properties, as for PTA. However, due to the absence of clocks, time-bounded properties cannot be encoded as unbounded ones. They instead need to be supported by dedicated analysis methods. We also use expected-time properties to calculate the minimum and maximum expected times $t_{\min}$ and $t_{\max}$ until a set of *target* states is reached for the first time. We require probability 1 for *true* U *target*. For transient property *true* U $\{ s_3 \}$ in M_m, we have $p_{\min} = 0.6$ (always schedule a) and $p_{\max} = 0.75$ (always schedule b). For the expected time to reach $\{ s_2, s_3 \}$, we have $t_{\max} = 0.4$ and $t_{\min} = 0.25$ with the same schedulers.

4.1 Lightweight SMC Possibilities and Challenges

The application of LSS to MA with unbounded transient and expected-time properties is a straightforward adaption to MA of Algorithm 1, since memoryless deterministic schedulers are sufficient to obtain optimal results [17, 23].

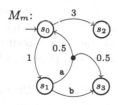

Fig. 8. Example MA M_m

Table 2. Performance and results for MA

Model		m	n	$|\omega|$	Time	$\hat{v}_{\min}$	$\hat{v}_{\max}$
queues	Unif.	1	372 k	25	1 s		0.096
	LSS	100	372 k	25	91 s	0.043	0.144
		1 000	372 k	25	872 s	0.031	0.170
bitcoin	Unif.	1	433	8 k	2 s		26 701
	LSS	1 000	456	14 k	332 s	6 926	249 323
		10 000	433	13 k	2 900 s	6 561	233 745

For time-bounded properties, optimal schedulers need to take into account the amount of time remaining until the time bound is reached. A naive extension of LSS would thus face the same issues as with PTA. The current approaches to perform exact model checking of a time-bounded property with bound d are to use either *digitisation* [23] or *uniformisation* [7]. The former discretises the MA by assuming that ≤ 1 Markovian transitions will fire within any small time interval $(0, \delta]$, where $\delta > 0$ is the digitisation constant such that $\exists k_b \in \mathbb{N}: d = k_b \cdot \delta$. Every state of the digitised model is a pair of the original state in the MA and the amount of time—a multiple of δ—remaining until d. That is, the model is unfolded over the time bound. If the maximum exit rate λ in the MA is known, then we also know that the max. probability computed on the digitised model is at most $k_b \cdot \frac{(\lambda \delta)^2}{2}$ below the actual one. As the digitised model is discrete, a variant of Algorithm 1 could be applied to it directly. However, for the error to be small, a fine digitisation is needed. For example, to achieve error ≤ 0.01 for $d = 0.5$ on M_m requires $\delta = 0.0025$ and $k_b = 200$. That is, the model is unfolded 200 times, so schedulers face the nondeterministic choice between a and b up to 200 times. The probability of sampling an optimal scheduler (i.e. one that always makes the optimal choice) is then 0.5^{200}. Uniformisation, on the other hand, requires global information—the maximum exit rate λ, or an overapproximation thereof—to be applicable in the first place. Furthermore, it does not provide an a priori error bound. When used for model checking, the error is bounded by simultaneously computing an over- and underapproximation of the (max.) probability. However, LSS intrinsically underapproximates and introduces a statistical error. Finally, it is currently not clear how to efficiently apply the method of [7] in an on-the-fly manner as required for simulation. Further research into methods for effective LSS with time-bounded properties on MA is thus needed.

4.2 Experiments

We have implemented LSS for unbounded properties on MA in modes [6]. We evaluate the implementation on two new case studies with properties based on non-rare events (rather than the rare-event *database* model of [6]). We consider

- the queueing system with breakdowns (*queues*) of [26] where ten sources of two types produce packets and fail at different rates. A single server processes the packets and may also fail. We studied a deterministic version of this model in [5]. To experiment with LSS, we now model a single repairman that repairs one broken component at a time instead. If multiple components are broken, the next one to repair is selected nondeterministically. We estimate the probability for $\neg$ *reset* U *buf* $= 8$: starting from a single broken source, what is the probability for server queue overflow before all components are repaired?
- a MODEST MA variant of the model of the *Andresen attack on Bitcoin* presented in [15] where a malicious pool of miners attempts to fork the blockchain to allow e.g. double spending. The malicious pool's strategy is

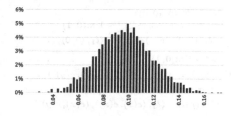

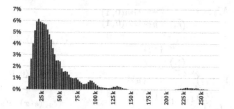

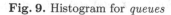

Fig. 9. Histogram for *queues*   **Fig. 10.** Histogram for *bitcoin*

kept open as nondeterministic choices in our model (*bitcoin*), and we estimate the expected time in minutes until the malicious pool succeeds at 20 %
hash rate.

The experimental setup is as described in Sect. 3.2. All results are shown in
Table 2, again including the Uniform ad-hoc scheduler for comparison. v stands
for probabilities p for *queues* and for expected times t for *bitcoin*.

Discussion. To judge the rarity of near-optimal schedulers, we perform two
LSS runs where the second samples 10 times as many schedulers (column m).
For *queues*, sampling more schedulers improves the estimates: extremal schedulers are neither frequent nor excessively rare. This is confirmed by the histogram shown in Fig. 9. The Uniform scheduler again only obtains some average
behaviour. When it comes to the *bitcoin* model, the histogram in Fig. 10 shows
that the most frequently sampled schedulers achieve low expected times, i.e. they
correspond to good strategies for the malicious pool. However, for the "default"
and "optimised" strategies of [15], the expected times are 5403 and 3582 min.
It is clear from the results in Table 2 that the sampled schedulers only come
somewhat close to the default strategy in *absolute* terms. *Relative* to the worst
schedulers found, however, they are still close to both good strategies. Once
more, the Uniform scheduler is mostly useless here. In terms of performance,
simulations for *bitcoin* take relatively long, which is due to the many simulation
steps per run (column $|\omega|$) until the malicious pool wins with a bad strategy.

5   Stochastic Automata

Stochastic automata (SA, [10]) go beyond MA by (1) allowing delays to follow
arbitrary probability distributions and (2) lifting the MA restriction of nondeterminism to (immediate) probabilistic edges. We show an example SA M_1 with six
locations in Fig. 11. It has *stochastic clocks* x and y. The *expiration times* $e(x)$
and $e(y)$ follow the continuous uniform distribution over the interval $[0, 1]$. An
edge in an SA is guarded by a set of clocks: the edge becomes enabled and time
cannot pass further as soon as all clocks in the *guard set* are expired. Thus no
time can pass in ℓ_0 and ℓ_1. When taking an edge, clocks can be *restarted*: their
values are reset to zero and their expiration times are resampled. On entering

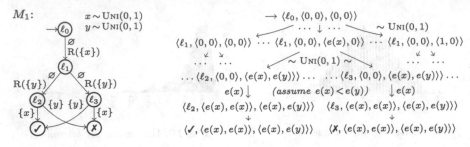

Fig. 11. SA M_1 **Fig. 12.** Excerpt of the semantics of M_1

ℓ_1, x is restarted: its value $v(x)$ becomes zero and $e(x)$ is set to a random value selected from $\mathrm{UNI}(0, 1)$. The choice of going to either ℓ_2 or ℓ_3 from ℓ_1 is nondeterministic, since both outgoing edges become enabled simultaneously. Then y is restarted. In ℓ_2, we have to wait until the first of the two clocks expires. If that is x, we have to move to location ✓; if it is y, we have to move to ✗. The semantics of an SA is an uncountably infinite MDP similar to the semantics of a PTA, but additionally with continuous distributions. The states in the semantics of M_1 are tuples of the form $\langle \ell, \langle v(x), v(y) \rangle, \langle e(x), e(y) \rangle \rangle$: they comprise the current location, the values of the clocks, and their expiration times. Nondeterministic choices are finite since they are between edges only. We illustrate a part of the semantics of M_1 as intuitively explained above in Fig. 12.

5.1   The Power of Schedulers for SA

We consider unbounded transient properties only. On M_1, the maximum probability for $true$ U $\{$ ✓ $\}$ is 0.75. It is achieved by going from ℓ_1 to ℓ_2 iff $e(x) \leq 0.5$: although the scheduler does not know in ℓ_1 what the expiration time of y is going to be after the restart of y, it is more likely to be higher than the (known) expiration time of x if that is low. This example shows that, in order to schedule optimally on SA, schedulers need to know the expiration times. We investigated the power of various restricted classes of schedulers for SA [8] and found that, aside from the history of previously visited states and delays, *all* components of the states are relevant for optimal scheduling. Let us write $\mathfrak{S}^a_{\ell,b,c}$ with $a \in \{\, hist, ml \,\}$, $b \in \{\, v, t, \text{-} \,\}$ and $c \in \{\, e, o, \text{-} \,\}$ to refer to a class of schedulers. Class $\mathfrak{S}^{hist}_{\ell,v,e}$ is the most general one: it sees the entire history (*hist*), clock values (v), and expiration times (e). We considered the following restrictions:

- memoryless schedulers that only see the current state (*ml* instead of *hist*),
- global-time schedulers that only see the total time elapsed since the initial state instead of the values of all individual clocks (t instead of v),
- schedulers that see the relative expiration order, i.e. the order of $e(z) - v(z)$ over all clocks z, in place of the expiration times (o instead of e), and
- schedulers that do not see some of the information at all (indicated by -).

Our findings include that all history-dependent schedulers seeing e coincide with class $\mathfrak{S}_{\ell,v,e}^{ml}$, and that for memoryless schedulers, knowing the expiration order o is incomparable to knowing e but not all of v. Where scheduler classes are not equivalent, we provided small distinguishing SA similar to M_1, which itself distinguishes all pairs of classes that only differ in seeing either e or o. We refer the interested reader to [8] (open-access) for a complete list of these six SA.

5.2   Lightweight SMC Possibilities and Challenges

Clearly, the naive extension of Algorithm 1 to SA fails for the same reasons as for PTA. However, as we explained above and in contrast to MA, not even unbounded properties can be analysed via LSS by relying on a discrete class of schedulers. At the same time, many of the considered classes of schedulers are unrealistically powerful to consider as adversaries in a safety model checking scenario, and need too much information to be useful for implementation as strategies in a planning setup. For example, in many models the expiration times represent information about future events, thus using e or o leads to *prophetic* schedulers [21]. LSS based on some of the restricted classes of schedulers will thus arguably be (more) useful. However, as long as continuous information is involved (such as the values v), some form of discretisation of the state space is needed. As we show below, there is ample room for the development of good discretisations and exploitation of the tradeoffs between classes in LSS for SA.

5.3   Experiments

We have implemented a prototype of LSS for SA in modes. It performs simulation on the exact concrete state space, but provides to schedulers a discretised view: for each real-valued quantity, we identify all values in the same interval $[\frac{i}{q}, \frac{i+1}{q})$, for integers i, q. We report experimental results on M_1 (Fig. 11) and M_2 through M_6 (see [8]) using LSS with $m = 10000$ and $n = 14889$ (so that $\epsilon = 0.005$, cf. Sect. 3.2) for each set of scheduler classes distinguished by the respective SA and discretisation factors $q \in \{1, 2, 4\}$. All models have a structure similar to M_1, and in Table 3 we show the estimated lower bounds on the max. probabilities $\hat{p}_{\max}$ of reaching ✓. We highlight the best result among the discretisation factors.

Discussion. Increasing the discretisation factor or increasing the scheduler power generally also increases the number of decisions the schedulers *can* make. This may also increase the number of *critical* decisions a scheduler *must* make to achieve the max. probability. We clearly see this in the results. Some schedulers achieve the best probability only with the finest discretisation, indicating cases where fine discretisation is important for optimality and optimal schedulers inside the class are not rare. We show the histograms for M_3, $\mathfrak{S}_{\ell,v,-}^{ml}$, and $q \in \{2, 4\}$ in Fig. 13. Indeed many extremal schedulers are found, and the variance appears to depend only on the discretisation. On the other hand, some classes perform worse on some models as the discretisation gets finer, usually

Table 3. Results ($\hat{p}_{max}$) for SA

class	q	M_1	M_2	M_3	M_4	M_5	M_6
$\mathfrak{S}_{\ell,v,e}^{hist}$	1	0.50					
	2	**0.75**					
	4	**0.75**					
$\mathfrak{S}_{\ell,v,o}^{hist}$	1	0.50					
	2	0.50					
	4	0.50					
$\mathfrak{S}_{\ell,t,e}^{hist}$	1			1.00			
	2			0.86			
	4			0.62			
$\mathfrak{S}_{\ell,-,o}^{hist}$	1		**0.90**				
	2		0.83				
	4		0.75				
$\mathfrak{S}_{\ell,v,-}^{hist}$	1						1.00
	2						1.00
	4						1.00
$\mathfrak{S}_{\ell,t,-}^{hist}$	1			1.00			
	2			0.87			
	4			0.78			
$\mathfrak{S}_{\ell,v,e}^{ml}$	1	0.50		0.50			
	2	**0.75**		0.81			
	4	**0.75**		0.81			
$\mathfrak{S}_{\ell,v,o}^{ml}$	1	0.50	**0.82**				
	2	0.50	0.79				
	4	0.50	0.71				
$\mathfrak{S}_{\ell,t,e}^{ml}$	1	0.50		0.50	**0.87**		
	2	**0.75**		**0.64**	0.64		
	4	**0.75**		0.60	0.54		
$\mathfrak{S}_{\ell,t,o}^{ml}$	1	0.50		**1.00**	0.83		
	2	0.50		**1.00**	0.84		
	4	0.50		0.97	**0.85**		
$\mathfrak{S}_{\ell,-,e}^{ml}$	1	0.50		0.50	**0.71**		
	2	**0.75**		0.62	0.66		
	4	**0.75**		**0.66**	0.56		
$\mathfrak{S}_{\ell,-,o}^{ml}$	1	0.50		1.00	0.83		
	2	0.50		1.00	0.83		
	4	0.51		1.00	0.83		
$\mathfrak{S}_{\ell,v,-}^{ml}$	1			0.51		0.50	
	2			0.63		0.50	
	4			**0.78**		0.50	
$\mathfrak{S}_{\ell,t,-}^{ml}$	1			0.50	0.71		
	2			0.50	**0.77**		
	4			0.50	**0.77**		
$\mathfrak{S}_{\ell,-,-}^{ml}$	1				0.71		
	2				0.71		
	4				0.71		

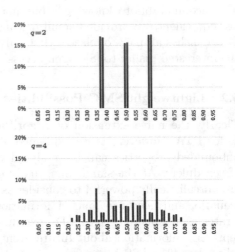

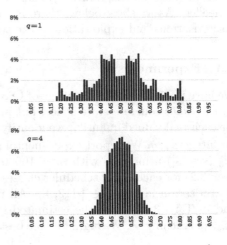

Fig. 13. Histograms for M_3 and $\mathfrak{S}_{\ell,v,-}^{ml}$

Fig. 14. Histograms for M_2 and $\mathfrak{S}_{\ell,v,o}^{ml}$

indicating that optimal schedulers are rare. Several other patterns exist, including a case where $q = 2$ yields the best results, clearly exhibiting the tradeoff between fine discretisation (i.e. a good scheduler is in the class) and rarity of near-optimal schedulers (i.e. the good schedulers will very rarely be sampled).

However, these intuitions do not always match; one interesting case is $\mathfrak{S}^{ml}_{\ell,v,\text{-}}$ for M_2. Its expiration times are drawn from a wide range, up to $\text{UNI}(0,8)$, compared to the other SA that use at most $\text{UNI}(0,2)$. Thus $q = 1$ is already a relatively finer discretisation. Looking at the histograms in Fig. 14, we see that the spread of schedulers is good for $q = 1$, with schedulers on both ends of the spectrum being rather likely, and results being near the actual maximum probability of approx. 0.82. However, as the discretisation gets finer, the increase in the number of decisions dominates the potential to make better decisions, resulting in schedulers almost normally distributed around the "random guess" behaviour that leads to probability 0.5.

The experiments demonstrate that LSS can produce useful and informative results with SA, but that there is a lot of potential for better discretisations.

6 Conclusion

We have taken a tour through the opportunities and challenges in LSS on three continuous-time models. Thanks to discrete abstractions that fully preserve optimal probabilities developed for exact model checking, efficient techniques for PTA now exist. However, tackling time-bounded properties for MA, and any kind of efficient LSS at all for SA, remain open challenges. Our preliminary results for these two continuous-time and continuously stochastic models indicate that LSS shows potential for MA (as evidenced by our case studies), and offers a versatile tool to experiment with different restricted classes of schedulers on SA. We plan to develop better discretisations for SA, and apply LSS on larger case studies for both MA and SA. The ability to visualise the distribution of schedulers provides valuable insights into the character of a model's nondeterminism.

Experiment Replication. We provide an artifact package [19] for independent replication of our experiments. It contains modes, all model files, the raw results, tabular views of those results (from which we derived Tables 1, 2 and 3 and the histograms), and the Linux shell scripts that we used to perform the experiments.

Acknowledgments. The authors thank Yuliya Butkova (Saarland University) for clarifying discussions on uniformisation and the time-bounded analysis of MA.

References

1. Alur, R., Dill, D.L.: A theory of timed automata. Theor. Comput. Sci. **126**(2), 183–235 (1994). https://doi.org/10.1016/0304-3975(94)90010-8
2. Bengtsson, J., Yi, W.: Timed automata: semantics, algorithms and tools. In: Desel, J., Reisig, W., Rozenberg, G. (eds.) ACPN 2003. LNCS, vol. 3098, pp. 87–124. Springer, Heidelberg (2004). https://doi.org/10.1007/978-3-540-27755-2_3
3. Bohlender, D., Bruintjes, H., Junges, S., Katelaan, J., Nguyen, V.Y., Noll, T.: A review of statistical model checking pitfalls on real-time stochastic models. In: Margaria, T., Steffen, B. (eds.) ISoLA 2014. LNCS, vol. 8803, pp. 177–192. Springer, Heidelberg (2014). https://doi.org/10.1007/978-3-662-45231-8_13

4. Brázdil, T.: Verification of Markov decision processes using learning algorithms. In: Cassez, F., Raskin, J.-F. (eds.) ATVA 2014. LNCS, vol. 8837, pp. 98–114. Springer, Cham (2014). https://doi.org/10.1007/978-3-319-11936-6_8

5. Budde, C.E., D'Argenio, P.R., Hartmanns, A.: Better automated importance splitting for transient rare events. In: Larsen, K.G., Sokolsky, O., Wang, J. (eds.) SETTA 2017. LNCS, vol. 10606, pp. 42–58. Springer, Cham (2017). https://doi.org/10.1007/978-3-319-69483-2_3

6. Budde, C.E., DArgenio, P.R., Hartmanns, A., Sedwards, S.: A statistical model checker for nondeterminism and rare events. In: Beyer, D., Huisman, M. (eds.) TACAS 2018. LNCS, vol. 10806, pp. 340–358. Springer, Cham (2018). https://doi.org/10.1007/978-3-319-89963-3_20

7. Butkova, Y., Hatefi, H., Hermanns, H., Krčál, J.: Optimal continuous time Markov decisions. In: Finkbeiner, B., Pu, G., Zhang, L. (eds.) ATVA 2015. LNCS, vol. 9364, pp. 166–182. Springer, Cham (2015). https://doi.org/10.1007/978-3-319-24953-7_12

8. D'Argenio, P.R., Gerhold, M., Hartmanns, A., Sedwards, S.: A hierarchy of scheduler classes for stochastic automata. In: Baier, C., Dal Lago, U. (eds.) FoSSaCS 2018. LNCS, vol. 10803, pp. 384–402. Springer, Cham (2018). https://doi.org/10.1007/978-3-319-89366-2_21

9. D'Argenio, P.R., Hartmanns, A., Legay, A., Sedwards, S.: Statistical approximation of optimal schedulers for probabilistic timed automata. In: Ábrahám, E., Huisman, M. (eds.) IFM 2016. LNCS, vol. 9681, pp. 99–114. Springer, Cham (2016). https://doi.org/10.1007/978-3-319-33693-0_7

10. D'Argenio, P.R., Katoen, J.P.: A theory of stochastic systems part I: stochastic automata. Inf. Comput. **203**(1), 1–38 (2005). https://doi.org/10.1016/j.ic.2005.07.001

11. D'Argenio, P.R., Legay, A., Sedwards, S., Traonouez, L.M.: Smart sampling for lightweight verification of Markov decision processes. Softw. Tools Technol. Transf. **17**(4), 469–484 (2015). https://doi.org/10.1007/s10009-015-0383-0

12. David, A., Jensen, P.G., Larsen, K.G., Mikučionis, M., Taankvist, J.H.: Uppaal Stratego. In: Baier, C., Tinelli, C. (eds.) TACAS 2015. LNCS, vol. 9035, pp. 206–211. Springer, Heidelberg (2015). https://doi.org/10.1007/978-3-662-46681-0_16

13. David, A., Larsen, K.G., Legay, A., Mikučionis, M., Wang, Z.: Time for statistical model checking of real-time systems. In: Gopalakrishnan, G., Qadeer, S. (eds.) CAV 2011. LNCS, vol. 6806, pp. 349–355. Springer, Heidelberg (2011). https://doi.org/10.1007/978-3-642-22110-1_27

14. Eisentraut, C., Hermanns, H., Zhang, L.: On probabilistic automata in continuous time. In: LICS, pp. 342–351. IEEE Computer Society (2010). https://doi.org/10.1109/LICS.2010.41

15. Fehnker, A., Chaudhary, K.: Twenty percent and a few days – optimising a Bitcoin majority attack. In: Dutle, A., Muñoz, C., Narkawicz, A. (eds.) NFM 2018. LNCS, vol. 10811, pp. 157–163. Springer, Cham (2018). https://doi.org/10.1007/978-3-319-77935-5_11

16. Forejt, V., Kwiatkowska, M., Norman, G., Parker, D.: Automated verification techniques for probabilistic systems. In: Bernardo, M., Issarny, V. (eds.) SFM 2011. LNCS, vol. 6659, pp. 53–113. Springer, Heidelberg (2011). https://doi.org/10.1007/978-3-642-21455-4_3

17. Guck, D., Hatefi, H., Hermanns, H., Katoen, J.-P., Timmer, M.: Modelling, reduction and analysis of Markov automata. In: Joshi, K., Siegle, M., Stoelinga, M., D'Argenio, P.R. (eds.) QEST 2013. LNCS, vol. 8054, pp. 55–71. Springer, Heidelberg (2013). https://doi.org/10.1007/978-3-642-40196-1_5

18. Hahn, E.M., Hartmanns, A., Hermanns, H., Katoen, J.P.: A compositional modelling and analysis framework for stochastic hybrid systems. Form. Methods Syst. Des. **43**(2), 191–232 (2013). https://doi.org/10.1007/s10703-012-0167-z
19. Hartmanns, A.: Lightweight statistical model checking in nondeterministic continuous time (artifact). 4TU.Centre for Research Data (2018). https://doi.org/10.4121/uuid:1453a13b-10ae-418f-a1ae-4acf96028118
20. Hartmanns, A., Hermanns, H.: The Modest Toolset: an integrated environment for quantitative modelling and verification. In: Ábrahám, E., Havelund, K. (eds.) TACAS 2014. LNCS, vol. 8413, pp. 593–598. Springer, Heidelberg (2014). https://doi.org/10.1007/978-3-642-54862-8_51
21. Hartmanns, A., Hermanns, H., Krčál, J.: Schedulers are no Prophets. In: Probst, C.W., Hankin, C., Hansen, R.R. (eds.) Semantics, Logics, and Calculi. LNCS, vol. 9560, pp. 214–235. Springer, Cham (2016). https://doi.org/10.1007/978-3-319-27810-0_11
22. Hartmanns, A., Sedwards, S., D'Argenio, P.R.: Efficient simulation-based verification of probabilistic timed automata. In: Winter Simulation Conference, pp. 1419–1430. IEEE (2017). https://doi.org/10.1109/WSC.2017.8247885
23. Hatefi, H., Hermanns, H.: Model checking algorithms for Markov automata. Electron. Commun. EASST **53** (2012) . https://doi.org/10.14279/tuj.eceasst.53.783
24. Hérault, T., Lassaigne, R., Magniette, F., Peyronnet, S.: Approximate probabilistic model checking. In: Steffen, B., Levi, G. (eds.) VMCAI 2004. LNCS, vol. 2937, pp. 73–84. Springer, Heidelberg (2004). https://doi.org/10.1007/978-3-540-24622-0_8
25. Kearns, M.J., Mansour, Y., Ng, A.Y.: A sparse sampling algorithm for near-optimal planning in large Markov decision processes. Mach. Learn. **49**(2–3), 193–208 (2002). https://doi.org/10.1023/A:1017932429737
26. Kroese, D.P., Nicola, V.F.: Efficient estimation of overflow probabilities in queues with breakdowns. Perform. Eval. **36**, 471–484 (1999)
27. Kurkowski, S., Camp, T., Colagrosso, M.: MANET simulation studies: the incredibles. Mob. Comput. Commun. Rev. **9**(4), 50–61 (2005). https://doi.org/10.1145/1096166.1096174
28. Kwiatkowska, M., Norman, G., Parker, D.: PRISM 4.0: verification of probabilistic real-time systems. In: Gopalakrishnan, G., Qadeer, S. (eds.) CAV 2011. LNCS, vol. 6806, pp. 585–591. Springer, Heidelberg (2011). https://doi.org/10.1007/978-3-642-22110-1_47
29. Kwiatkowska, M.Z., Norman, G., Segala, R., Sproston, J.: Automatic verification of real-time systems with discrete probability distributions. Theor. Comput. Sci. **282**(1), 101–150 (2002). https://doi.org/10.1016/S0304-3975(01)00046-9
30. Legay, A., Sedwards, S., Traonouez, L.-M.: Scalable verification of Markov decision processes. In: Canal, C., Idani, A. (eds.) SEFM 2014. LNCS, vol. 8938, pp. 350–362. Springer, Cham (2015). https://doi.org/10.1007/978-3-319-15201-1_23
31. Okamoto, M.: Some inequalities relating to the partial sum of binomial probabilities. Ann. Inst. Stat. Math. **10**(1), 29–35 (1959)
32. Reijsbergen, D., de Boer, P., Scheinhardt, W.R.W., Haverkort, B.R.: On hypothesis testing for statistical model checking. Softw. Tools Technol. Transf. **17**(4), 377–395 (2015). https://doi.org/10.1007/s10009-014-0350-1
33. Younes, H.L.S., Simmons, R.G.: Probabilistic verification of discrete event systems using acceptance sampling. In: Brinksma, E., Larsen, K.G. (eds.) CAV 2002. LNCS, vol. 2404, pp. 223–235. Springer, Heidelberg (2002). https://doi.org/10.1007/3-540-45657-0_17

Statistical Model Checking of Incomplete Stochastic Systems

Shiraj Arora[1](✉), Axel Legay[2], Tania Richmond[2], and Louis-Marie Traonouez[2]

[1] Indian Institute of Technology Hyderabad, Hyderabad, India
cs14resch11010@iith.ac.in
[2] Inria, Rennes, France

Abstract. We study incomplete stochastic systems that are missing some parts of their design, or are lacking information about some components. It is interesting to get early analysis results of the requirements of these systems, in order to adequately refine their design. In previous works, models for incomplete systems are analysed using model checking techniques for three-valued temporal logics. In this paper, we propose statistical model checking algorithms for these logics. We illustrate our approach on a case-study of a network system that is refined after the analysis of early designs.

1 Introduction

Stochastic systems comprise a wide range of applications that use probability distributions to describe the behaviour of a system. For instance, probabilities naturally arise during the execution of many cyber-physical systems to account for the variability of the physical processes connected to computer systems. They are also useful to model uncertainty in communication systems or protocols. The classical formalisms for modelling stochastic systems are Discrete and Continuous Time Markov Chains (DTMC and CTMC).

Formal specification requirements on stochastic systems can be formulated in temporal logics like the Linear Temporal Logic (LTL), the Computational Tree Logic (CTL) or a quantitative extension like the Probabilistic Computation Tree Logic (PCTL) [13]. Many works have studied the probabilistic model checking problem to formally verify these systems [9,13,23]. These works combine classical model checking algorithms with a numerical analysis to compute exact probabilities. These algorithms are however very expensive and often cannot scale to real-life problems.

To circumvent these limitations, one can resort to approximated techniques like Statistical Model Checking (SMC) [11,14,18,25]. These techniques rely on simulations and statistical analysis to evaluate the satisfaction of formal requirements. Requirements are usually expressed in the Bounded Linear Temporal Logic (BLTL). Statistical model checking can solve either quantitative estimation problems that evaluate probabilities, or qualitative analysis problems that perform hypothesis testing. It provides a trade-off between speed and accuracy

T. Margaria and B. Steffen (Eds.): ISoLA 2018, LNCS 11245, pp. 354–371, 2018.
https://doi.org/10.1007/978-3-030-03421-4_23

that can be controlled by the number of simulations. These simulations can be easily distributed on computing grids to increase the speed and accuracy of the analysis.

While probability distributions account for the variability and uncertainty in the system, like the variability of measurements, a precise specification of these distributions is required to analyse a system. This requirement is often hard to meet, especially in the early stages of the design of the system or in highly dynamic systems. Unknown specifications may also arise from the simulation process of the system as some components may be difficult to simulate. It is however of deep interest to have some early evaluation of the requirements of the system, even if it is not completely defined. In particular, a designer would want to know which of the following hypothesis holds: 1. the requirement is satisfied in the current design and in any of the subsequent designs that can be obtained by replacing unknown specifications, 2. the requirement may be satisfied in at least one subsequent design, and 3. the requirement will not be satisfied in any subsequent designs.

Related Works. Solutions for handling unknown specifications in stochastic systems usually imply switching from Boolean logics to three-valued or multi-valued logics. There is a rich theory on multi-valued logics and applications in multiple domains.

Our work is based on the works of Arora et al. [1,2] that introduces a three-valued PCTL logic. In this qPCTL logic *unknown* values are added to the atomic propositions of a DTMC and a qPCTL model checking algorithm is proposed.

Multi-valued extensions of temporal logics have also been proposed by Chechik et al. [5,6]. They introduce three-valued logics for atomic propositions and transitions and they perform model checking of multi-valued CTL.

In probabilistic model checking, multi-valued logics have been used for abstraction of Markov chains models to reduce the complexity of analysis [12,15,16]. Multiple states are combined in order to yield a reduced model. This process may lead to a loss of information that is represented with an *unknown* value. Abstracted models are then often analysed with probabilistic model checker for Markov Decision Processes (MDP).

Finally, Bauer et al. [3] introduced a four-valued semantics for LTL over finite traces. It is used in runtime verification to determine if a property is already satisfied, or if it may be satisfied in the future.

Our Contribution. We extend the works in [1,2] to propose statistical model checking analysis of discrete time Markov chains with unknown values (qDTMC). We address both the quantitative estimation problem and the qualitative analysis problem. For the qualitative analysis problem, we adapt the model checking algorithm of [2] to perform a three hypotheses test and provide bounds on the probability of errors of this test. We finally propose an experiment in which we show how qDTMC and SMC can be used in a refinement process.

Organisation of the Paper. Section 2 gives the basic definitions concerning DTMC and formal logics. Section 3 introduces unknown values in DTMC and extends the semantics of BLTL to a three-valued logic. Section 4 proposes an estimation algorithm for BLTL with unknown values, while Sect. 5 studies the qualitative analysis problem and proposes a three hypotheses testing algorithm. Section 6 presents the implementation of these algorithms in the tool Plasma Lab, and Sect. 7 applies it to a network case-study. Finally, Sect. 8 concludes the paper.

2   Preliminaries

2.1   Discrete Time Markov Chains

Discrete Time Markov Chains (DTMC) are finite automata with a transition probability matrix.

Definition 1 (DTMC). *A DTMC is a tuple $M = (S, \mathbb{P}, s_{init}, AP, L)$ where:*

- *S is a set of states,*
- *$\mathbb{P} : S \times S \to [0,1]$ is a transition probability matrix, such that $\forall s \in S :$ $\sum_{s' \in S} \mathbb{P}(s, s') = 1$,*
- *$s_{init} \in S$ is the initial state,*
- *AP is a set of atomic proposition,*
- *$L : S \to AP$ is a labelling function.*

Definition 2. *A **path** π in a DTMC M is a sequence of states $s_0, s_1, s_2 \ldots$ such that $\forall i \in \{0, 1, 2, \ldots\}$, $\mathbb{P}(s_i, s_{i+1}) > 0$. Let π^i denotes the suffix of π starting at state s_i, that is to say the path $s_i, s_{i+1}, s_{i+2} \ldots.$*

2.2   Bounded Linear Temporal Logic

The Linear Temporal Logic (LTL) allows expressing properties over the paths of a finite state system, such as a DTMC. It extends classical Boolean logic with *temporal operators* that allow reasoning on the temporal dimension of an execution path. These temporal operators express properties over the future of a path, with an unbounded number of states.

The Bounded Linear Temporal Logic (BLTL) is a restriction of LTL that specifies bounds on the temporal operators such that the properties can always be decided on finite executions. This characteristic allows verifying these properties using only simulation based approaches, such as statistical model checking.

Definition 3 (BLTL). *Bounded Linear Temporal Logic (BLTL) is used to express linear-time properties of the system. The syntax for BLTL is as follows:*

$$\Phi ::= T \mid a \mid \neg\Phi \mid \Phi_1 \wedge \Phi_2 \mid \Phi_1 \to \Phi_2 \mid X\Phi \mid F^{\leq k}\Phi \mid G^{\leq k}\Phi \mid \Phi_1 U^{\leq k} \Phi_2 \mid \Phi_1 W^{\leq k} \Phi_2$$

where Φ, Φ_1, and Φ_2 are BLTL formulae, a is an atomic proposition, and $k \in \mathbb{N}$ is the time bound.

Definition 4 (Semantics of BLTL). *Let* $\mathcal{M} : (S, \mathbb{P}, s_{init}, AP, L)$ *be a DTMC. Let* $\pi = s_0 \, s_1 \, s_2 ...$ *be a path in* $\mathcal{M}$ *and* Φ, Φ_1, Φ_2 *be BLTL formulae. Then,* Φ *is said to be satisfied in path* π*, i.e.* $(\pi, \Phi) = \mathsf{T}$*, if one of the following conditions is satisfied. Otherwise, the property is said to be not satisfied and denoted as* $(\pi, \Phi) = \mathsf{F}$.

1. $(\pi, \mathsf{T}) = \mathsf{T}$,
2. $(\pi, a) = \mathsf{T}$ *iff* $a \in L(s_0)$,
3. $(\pi, \neg\Phi) = \mathsf{T}$ *iff* $(\pi, \Phi) = \mathsf{F}$,
4. $(\pi, \Phi_1 \wedge \Phi_2) = \mathsf{T}$ *iff* $(\pi, \Phi_1) = \mathsf{T} \wedge (\pi, \Phi_2) = \mathsf{T}$,
5. $(\pi, \Phi_1 \rightarrow \Phi_2) = \mathsf{T}$ *iff* $(\pi, \Phi_2) = \mathsf{T}$ *whenever* $(\pi, \Phi_1) = \mathsf{T}$,
6. $(\pi, X\Phi) = \mathsf{T}$ *iff* $(\pi^1, \Phi) = \mathsf{T}$,
7. $(\pi, F^{\leq k}\Phi) = \mathsf{T}$ *iff* $\exists i \leq k, (\pi^i, \Phi) = \mathsf{T}$,
8. $(\pi, G^{\leq k}\Phi) = \mathsf{T}$ *iff* $\forall i \leq k, (\pi^i, \Phi) = \mathsf{T}$,
9. $(\pi, (\Phi_1 \, U^{\leq k} \, \Phi_2)) = \mathsf{T}$ *iff* $\exists i \leq k, (\pi^i, \Phi_2) = \mathsf{T} \wedge \forall j < i, (\pi^j, \Phi_1) = \mathsf{T}$,
10. $(\pi, (\Phi_1 \, W^{\leq k} \, \Phi_2)) = \mathsf{T}$ *iff* $[\exists i < k, (\pi^i, \Phi_2) = \mathsf{T} \wedge \forall j < i, (\pi^j, \Phi_1) = \mathsf{T}] \vee [\forall j \leq k, (\pi^j, \Phi_1) = \mathsf{T}]$.

For a BLTL property Φ and a path π, we will write $\pi \models \Phi$ if $(\pi, \Phi) = \mathsf{T}$ and $\pi \not\models \Phi$ if $(\pi, \Phi) = \mathsf{F}$. However, these notations will not be applicable to the three-valued logic that we will present in the next section.

2.3 Statistical Model Checking

Statistical Model Checking (SMC) is an alternative to probabilistic model checking that evaluates the satisfaction of formal properties on any stochastic systems. It combines the formal analysis of linear temporal properties on finite simulations of the system with statistical methods. Contrary to an exhaustive exploration, statistical model checking does not store the state of the system and therefore can even be applied to infinite state systems. It returns approximated results, either quantitative results with confidence intervals or qualitative results with bounds on the probability of error.

Statistical model checking relies on generating a finite number of independent simulations either from a formal model, like DTMC, or even directly from a system simulator. These simulations are formally analysed using a monitor of a linear temporal property like BLTL. The results obtained for each simulation are combined by a statistical algorithm.

Quantitative Estimation. Considering a random path π from a stochastic system, the satisfaction of a BLTL property Φ defines a random variable with a Bernoulli distribution. The goal of a quantitative analysis is to estimate the parameter of this distribution, that is to say the probability $\gamma = Prob(\Phi \models \pi)$. This estimation can be done using a Monte Carlo approach that consists in generating a set of n executions and computes an estimate of the probability using the following formula:

$$\overline{\gamma} = \frac{1}{n} \sum_{i=1}^{n} \mathbf{1}(\pi_i \models \Phi)$$

where **1** is an indicator function that returns 1 if $\pi_i \models \varphi$ and 0 otherwise.

The number of simulations allows to control the precision of the analysis. For instance the Chernoff bound [8] can be used to relate the number of simulations to the absolute error ϵ and the confidence δ with the following formula:

$$Prob(|\overline{\gamma} - \gamma| \geq \epsilon) \leq \delta \quad \text{if} \quad \delta = 2e^{-2n\epsilon^2}$$

Qualitative Analysis. To test if the probability γ is greater (or lower) than a given bound θ, then the problem can be formulated as a hypothesis test with two hypotheses: $H_0 : \gamma \geq \theta$ against $H_1 : \gamma < \theta$. Statistical techniques can then be used to estimate the true hypothesis from the results of the simulations. These techniques do not guarantee a correct result but usually come with two bounds on the probability of making errors. These two bounds are α and β, such that the probability of accepting H_1 (resp. H_0) when H_0 (resp. H_1) holds, called a Type-I error (resp. a Type-II error) is less or equal to α (resp. β).

Statistical tests cannot guarantee a low probability for both types of error (see [25] for details). A solution is to relax the problem with an indifference region that can be defined with a parameter δ, such that the two hypotheses become $H_0 : \gamma \geq \theta + \delta = p_0$ and $H_1 : \gamma \leq \theta - \delta = p_1$. If the true probability γ is between $[p_1, p_0]$ then we are indifferent to which hypothesis is accepted.

A common test to analyse the qualitative problem is the Sequential Probability Ratio Test (SPRT) [24]. This test is based on a variable number of simulations that allows giving results in an online manner, as soon as enough simulations guarantee a decision. The SPRT test computes a ratio based on the last m simulations generated and decide after each new simulation whether a decision can be made or more simulations are needed. The ratio is given by the following formula:

$$ratio = \prod_{i=1}^{m} \frac{p_1^{\mathbf{1}(\pi_i \models \Phi)}(1 - p_1)^{\mathbf{1}(\pi_i \not\models \Phi)}}{p_0^{\mathbf{1}(\pi_i \models \Phi)}(1 - p_0)^{\mathbf{1}(\pi_i \not\models \Phi)}}$$

After each new simulation is generated, the ratio is updated. H_1 is accepted if $ratio \geq (1 - \beta)/\alpha$ whereas H_0 is accepted if $ratio \geq \beta/(1 - \alpha)$. Otherwise, a new simulation is generated.

3   Adding Uncertainty in DTMC and BLTL

To add uncertainty in DTMC models, authors in [1] modified the labelling function of the DTMC such that it may return three values (true, false or unknown) instead of two. This labelling function is then considered as a parameter of the DTMC.

Definition 5 (qDTMC [1]). *A qDTMC $\mathcal{M}(L)$ is a DTMC $\mathcal{M}$ parametrized with a labelling function L allowing unknown values. $\mathcal{M}(L) = (S, \mathbb{P}, s_{init}, AP, L)$ where:*

  – S is a set of states,

- $\mathbb{P} : S \times S \rightarrow [0,1]$ *is a transition probability matrix, such that* $\forall s \in S :$ $\sum_{s' \in S} \mathbb{P}(s, s') = 1$,
- $s_{init} \in S$ *is the initial state,*
- AP *is a set of atomic propositions,*
- $L : S \times AP \rightarrow \{\mathsf{T}, \mathsf{F}, ?\}$ *is a labelling function.*

We define a refinement relation (partial order) between the labelling functions with unknown values, such that a function L_2 refines L_1 if L_2 only replaces some unknown values from L_1 with T or F (and it does not change the values T and F form L_1). Formally,

Definition 6 (Refinement). *Given two labelling functions* L_1, L_2 *of a qDTMC* $\mathcal{M} = (S, \mathbb{P}, s_{init}, AP)$, *we say that* $L_2 \prec L_1$ *iff* $\forall s \in S, \forall p \in AP, (L_1(s, p) = \mathsf{T}) \Rightarrow (L_2(s, p) = \mathsf{T})$ *and* $(L_1(s, p) = \mathsf{F}) \Rightarrow (L_2(s, p) = \mathsf{F})$.

We now extend the semantics of BLTL properties to take care of the unknown information in the path of the qDTMC. The new logic qBLTL has the same syntax as BLTL. Its semantics however may return three values (T, F or ?) instead of a Boolean value. Also, the semantics for a path π of a qDTMC $\mathcal{M}$ now depend on its labelling function L.

Definition 7 (Semantics of qBLTL [1]). *Let* $\mathcal{M}(\mathcal{L}) : (S, \mathbb{P}, s_{init}, AP, L)$ *be a qDTMC. Let* $\pi = s_0\ s_1\ s_2...$ *be a path in* $\mathcal{M}(\mathcal{L})$ *and* Φ, Φ_1, Φ_2 *be qBLTL formulae. The semantics of qBLTL formulae are as follow:*

1. $(\pi, L, \mathsf{T}) = \mathsf{T}$
2. $(\pi, L, a) = L(s_0, a)$
3. $(\pi, L, \neg\Phi) = \begin{cases} \mathsf{T} & \textit{iff } (\pi, L, \Phi) = \mathsf{F} \\ \mathsf{F} & \textit{iff } (\pi, L, \Phi) = \mathsf{T} \\ ? & \textit{iff } (\pi, L, \Phi) = ? \end{cases}$
4. $(\pi, L, \Phi_1 \wedge \Phi_2) = \begin{cases} \mathsf{T} & \textit{iff } (\pi, L, \Phi_1) = \mathsf{T} \wedge (\pi, L, \Phi_2) = \mathsf{T} \\ \mathsf{F} & \textit{iff } (\pi, L, \Phi_1) = \mathsf{F} \vee (\pi, L, \Phi_2) = \mathsf{F} \\ ? & \textit{otherwise} \end{cases}$
5. $(\pi, L, \Phi_1 \rightarrow \Phi_2) = \begin{cases} \mathsf{T} & \textit{iff } (\pi, L, \Phi_1) = \mathsf{F} \vee (\pi, L, \Phi_2) = \mathsf{T} \\ \mathsf{F} & \textit{iff } (\pi, L, \Phi_1) = \mathsf{T} \wedge (\pi, L, \Phi_2) = \mathsf{F} \\ ? & \textit{otherwise} \end{cases}$
6. $(\pi, L, X\Phi) = (\pi^1, L, \Phi)$
7. $(\pi, L, F^{\leq k}\Phi) = \begin{cases} \mathsf{T} & \textit{iff } \exists i \leq k, (\pi^i, L, \Phi) = \mathsf{T} \\ \mathsf{F} & \textit{iff } \forall i \leq k, (\pi^i, L, \Phi) = \mathsf{F} \\ ? & \textit{otherwise} \end{cases}$
8. $(\pi, L, G^{\leq k}\Phi) = \begin{cases} \mathsf{T} & \textit{iff } \forall i \leq k, (\pi^i, L, \Phi) = \mathsf{T} \\ \mathsf{F} & \textit{iff } \exists i \leq k, (\pi^i, L, \Phi) = \mathsf{F} \\ ? & \textit{otherwise} \end{cases}$
9. $(\pi, L, (\Phi_1\ U^{\leq k}\ \Phi_2)) =$
$\begin{cases} \mathsf{T} & \textit{iff } \exists i \leq k, (\pi^i, L, \Phi_2) = \mathsf{T} \wedge \forall j < i, (\pi^j, L, \Phi_1) = \mathsf{T} \\ \mathsf{F} & \textit{iff } [\forall i \leq k, (\pi^i, L, \Phi_2) = \mathsf{F}] \\ & \quad \vee [\exists i \leq k, (\pi^i, L, \Phi_2) = \mathsf{T} \wedge \exists j < i, (\pi^j, L, \Phi_1) = \mathsf{F}] \\ ? & \textit{otherwise} \end{cases}$

10. $(\pi, L, (\Phi_1 \; W^{\leq k} \; \Phi_2)) =$
$$\begin{cases} \mathsf{T} \text{ iff } [\exists i \leq k, (\pi^i, L, \Phi_2) = \mathsf{T} \; \wedge \; \forall j < i, (\pi^j, L, \Phi_1) = \mathsf{T}] \\ \quad \vee \; [\forall j \leq k, (\pi^j, L, \Phi_1) = \mathsf{T}] \\ \mathsf{F} \text{ iff } \exists i \leq k, (\pi^i, L, \Phi_1) = \mathsf{F} \; \wedge \; \forall j < i, (\pi^j, L, \Phi_2) = \mathsf{F} \\ ? \text{ otherwise} \end{cases}$$

The following proposition shows that every qBLTL formula satisfied (resp. unsatisfied) by a qDTMC with a labelling function L_1 is also satisfied (resp. unsatisfied) with any refinement $L_2 \prec L_1$.

Proposition 1. *Given two labelling functions L_1, L_2 of a qDTMC $\mathcal{M}$ such that $L_2 \prec L_1$, and a qPCTL formula Φ. Let π be a path from $\mathcal{M}$. Then,*

$$(\pi, L_1, \Phi) = \mathsf{T} \Rightarrow (\pi, L_2, \Phi) = \mathsf{T}$$

$$(\pi, L_1, \Phi) = \mathsf{F} \Rightarrow (\pi, L_2, \Phi) = \mathsf{F}$$

Proof. This proposition can be easily proved using an induction on the shape of qBLTL formulae. We assume that the proposition holds for sub-formulae Φ, Φ_1 and Φ_2 and we prove that it also holds for any of the formulae that can be built using Eqs. 1. to 10. in Definition 7. We prove below the two base cases, 1 and 2, and the induction for Eq. 9. Other equations are similar.

1. It trivially holds for basic formula 1.
2. For formula 2, if $(\pi, L_1, a) = L_1(s_0, a) = \mathsf{T}$ then by definition of $\prec$ $(\pi, L_2, a) = L_2(s_0, a) = \mathsf{T}$. Conversely, if $(\pi, L_1, a) = L_1(s_0, a) = \mathsf{F}$ also by definition of $\prec$ $(\pi, L_2, a) = L_2(s_0, a) = \mathsf{F}$.
9. For formula 9, if $(\pi, L_1, (\Phi_1 \; U^{\leq k} \; \Phi_2)) = \mathsf{T}$, then there exists $i < k$ with $(\pi^i, L_1, \Phi_2) = \mathsf{T}$ and for all $j < i$, $(\pi^j, L_1, \Phi_1) = \mathsf{T}$. By induction hypothesis, $(\pi^i, L_2, \Phi_2) = \mathsf{T}$ and $(\pi^j, L_2, \Phi_1) = \mathsf{T}$. This proves that $(\pi, L_2, (\Phi_1 \; U^{\leq k} \; \Phi_2)) = \mathsf{T}$. Conversely, if $(\pi, L_1, (\Phi_1 \; U^{\leq k} \; \Phi_2)) = \mathsf{F}$, then either $\forall i \leq k, (\pi^i, L_1, \Phi_2) = \mathsf{F}$. By induction hypothesis, $(\pi^i, L_2, \Phi_2) = \mathsf{F}$ and thus $(\pi, L_2, (\Phi_1 \; U^{\leq k} \; \Phi_2)) = \mathsf{F}$. Or there exists $i \leq k, (\pi^i, L_1, \Phi_2) = \mathsf{T}$ and $j < i, (\pi^j, L_1, \Phi_1) = \mathsf{F}$. Again, by induction hypothesis, $(\pi^i, L_2, \Phi_2) = \mathsf{T}$ and $(\pi^j, L_2, \Phi_1) = \mathsf{F}$, which proves that $(\pi, L_2, (\Phi_1 \; U^{\leq k} \; \Phi_2)) = \mathsf{F}$. □

4   Quantitative Estimation of BLTL with Unknown

In [14], Hérault et al. provided a quantitative estimation of the probability that a BLTL property is satisfied with high confidence by a stochastic system (c.f. Subsect. 2.3). In this section, we propose an efficient extension to qBLTL.

4.1   Three-Valued Estimation Algorithm

In order to estimate the probability that a qDTMC $\mathcal{M}(L)$ satisfies a property Φ in the qBLTL logic, we generate random paths π in the probabilistic space underlying the qDTMC structure of depth k. Let n be the total number of simulations, t the number of T, f the number of F and u the number of ?. Notice that $n = t + f + u$. Then in order to estimate the probability $\gamma = \text{Prob}((\pi, L, \Phi) = \text{T})$, we test if the property Φ holds on each path π_i (for $i = 1, \ldots, n$), and compute a random value t/n, otherwise from the number of paths that do not hold Φ, we compute a random value f/n. Finally we deduce the probability for unknown values from the others, i.e. $u/n = 1 - (t + f)/n$. This is described in Algorithm 1, called three-valued estimation algorithm for True-False-Unknown.

Algorithm 1. Three-valued estimation algorithm

    Data: $\mathcal{M}(L)$ qDTMC model, Φ the property to verify, n the number of
          simulations
    Result: P_T probability of true values, P_F probability of false values and P_U
          probability of unknown values
    begin
        $nb_T = 0;\ nb_F = 0;$
        for $i = 1$ *to* n *do* **do**
            Generate a random path π of length k from $\mathcal{M}(L)$;
            if Φ *is true on* π **then**
              | $nb_T = nb_T + 1;$
            else if Φ *is false on* π **then**
              | $nb_F = nb_F + 1;$
            end
        end
        $P_T = nb_T/n;\ P_F = nb_F/n;\ P_U = 1 - (P_T + P_F);$
        return P_T, P_F, P_U
    end

Remark 1. Algorithm 1 can also be used to verify qualitative statements of the form $\text{Prob}((\Phi \models \pi) \geqslant \theta$. We test whether $t/n > \theta - \varepsilon$. Our decision is correct with confidence $(1 - \delta)$ after a number of samples polynomial in $1/\varepsilon$ and $\log(1/\delta)$. In Sect. 5 we will also present a sequential algorithm for these qualitative statements.

4.2   Correctness

Proposition 2. *The three-valued estimation algorithm is a randomized approximation for the probability* $\gamma = \text{Prob}((\Phi, L, \pi) = \text{T})$ *for a qBLTL formula* Φ, *with* $\gamma \in [0, 1]$.

Proof. Let $X_1, X_2, \ldots, X_k$ be k independent random variables with a multinomial distribution. So each X_i takes value true (let say 1) with probability p_1, false (let say 0) with probability p_2, unknown (let say -1) with probability p_3 in our case. Let X be the random vector $[X_1, X_2, \ldots, X_k]^T$ and μ its mean. Then $\mu = [\mu_1, \mu_2, \ldots, \mu_k]$, with μ_i the mean of X_i, for $i = 1, \ldots, k$. In our case, $k = 3$. Let z_i, for $i = 1, \ldots, k$ be positive integers such that $\sum_{i=1}^{k} z_i = n$. Let z be the vector $[z_1, z_2, \ldots, z_k]^T$. Then the multinomial generalization of the Chernoff-Hoeffding bound [7] gives:

$$Prob(X \geqslant z) \leqslant \prod_{i=1}^{k} \left(\frac{\mu_i}{z_i} \right)^{z_i} \quad \text{provided that } z \geqslant \mu.$$

In our case, $z_1 = nb_T$, $z_2 = nb_F$ and $z_3 = nb_U$, so $n = nb_T + nb_F + nb_U$. Using Stirling's approximation, we can easily check that the minimum bound for n is $4\log(\frac{2}{\delta})/\varepsilon^2$ to get the estimation:

$$Prob(|X - \gamma| \leqslant \varepsilon) \geqslant 1 - \delta.$$

5 Qualitative Analysis of BLTL with Unknown

5.1 Problem

Let Φ be a qBLTL property and $M(L)$ be a qDTMC with labelling function L. Let π be a random path from M. The qualitative analysis problem consists in determining whether one of the two following hypotheses holds: $H_0 : Prob((\pi, L, \Phi) = \mathsf{T}) \geq \theta$ and $H_1 : Prob((\pi, L, \Phi) = \mathsf{F}) > 1 - \theta$. This problem defines a probabilistic qBLTL property $Prob_{\geq \theta}((\pi, L, \Phi) = \mathsf{T})$. It is a subclass of the qPCTL logic presented in [1].

If H_0 holds then Φ is satisfied with at least probability θ using the labelling function L. Consequently using Proposition 1, Φ is also satisfied with at least probability θ for any refinement of L. Conversely, if H_1 holds, Φ can be disproved with at least probability $1 - \theta$ using the labelling function L or any refinement of L.

Contrary to the two-valued qualitative analysis problem presented in Subsect. 2.3, we cannot use a two-valued statistical test to distinguish these two hypotheses, since our simulations results are three-valued. We will therefore combine two statistical tests to design an hypothesis testing algorithm with three potential outcomes.

Remark 2. We present the case for the probabilistic qBLTL property $Prob_{\geq \theta}(\Phi = \mathsf{T})$. To check properties $Prob_{\leq \theta}(\Phi = \mathsf{T})$ we would consider the reverse problem that is checking $Prob_{\geq 1-\theta}(\neg \Phi = \mathsf{F})$ and then use the same algorithm.

5.2 Hypothesis Testing Algorithm

To solve the qualitative analysis problem of a qBLTL property with SMC we propose an hypothesis testing algorithm that may return three values:

- T if the hypothesis $H_0 : Prob((\pi, L, \Phi) = \mathsf{T}) \geq \theta$ is accepted,
- F if the hypothesis $H_1 : Prob((\pi, L, \Phi) = \mathsf{F}) > 1 - \theta$ is accepted,
- ? otherwise (we call this hypothesis H_2).

Algorithm 2 is an adaptation of the model checking algorithm qMC presented in [1]. It follows the same principles. It involves three subroutines. The two subroutines SetToFalse and SetToTrue consist in modifying the original labelling function of the qDTMC in order to replace all uncertainty by F or T, respectively. The results of these transformations are normal DTMC that can be checked with classical SMC algorithms. That is what the subroutine BSMC performs, that is to say it uses the SMC hypothesis test that determines whether a DTMC satisfies a BLTL formula, using the SPRT algorithm presented in Subsect. 2.3, This subroutine returns either T or F.

Algorithm 2. qSMC

Input:
    $\mathcal{M}(L)$: qDTMC with labelling function L
    φ: probabilistic BLTL formula

$L_F \leftarrow$ SetToFalse(L)
if BSMC($\mathcal{M}(L_F), \varphi) = $ T then
  | return T
else
  | $L_T \leftarrow$ SetToTrue(L)
  | if BSMC($\mathcal{M}(L_T), \varphi) = $ F then
  | | return F
  | else
  | L return ?

5.3 Error Bounds for Three Hypotheses Testing

The qSMC algorithm can be seen as a three hypotheses testing algorithm. Therefore the classical error bounds that are used to evaluate the precision of the results in a two hypotheses case, such as the error bounds for the SPRT algorithm, must be extended.

Instead of two types of errors we define three types of errors, one for each hypothesis being wrongly accepted. We say that the qSMC algorithm returns a wrong value when the result is different from the qMC algorithm. In the following we simply write qSMC $= *$ (resp. qMC $= *$) if the qSMC (resp. qMC) algorithm returns the value $* \in \{$T, F, ?$\}$. The three types of errors are:

1. **Type-I error**: H_1 is wrongly accepted: qSMC $=$ F while qMC $\neq$ F
2. **Type-II error**: H_0 is wrongly accepted: qSMC $=$ T while qMC $\neq$ T
3. **Type-III error**: H_2 is wrongly accepted: qSMC $=$? while qMC $\neq$?

We will bound the probability of these errors using the parameters of the binary SMC tests used in the qSMC algorithm. We will write BSMC_T (resp. BSMC_F) to denote the results of the binary SMC algorithm on the qDTMC

$\mathcal{M}(L_T)$ (resp. $\mathcal{M}(L_F)$), and similarly BMC_T and BMC_F to denote the true results of these tests. The bounds on the probability of errors of these tests are:

$$\mathrm{Prob}(\mathrm{BSMC}_F = \mathsf{F} \mid \mathrm{BMC}_F = \mathsf{T}) \leq \alpha_1 \tag{1}$$

$$\mathrm{Prob}(\mathrm{BSMC}_F = \mathsf{T} \mid \mathrm{BMC}_F = \mathsf{F}) \leq \beta_1 \tag{2}$$

$$\mathrm{Prob}(\mathrm{BSMC}_T = \mathsf{F} \mid \mathrm{BMC}_T = \mathsf{T}) \leq \alpha_2 \tag{3}$$

$$\mathrm{Prob}(\mathrm{BSMC}_T = \mathsf{T} \mid \mathrm{BMC}_T = \mathsf{F}) \leq \beta_2 \tag{4}$$

where α_1 and β_1 are the error bounds for the BSMC_F test and α_2 and β_2 the error bounds for the BSMC_T test.

Proposition 3 (Error bounds). *Given a qDTMC $\mathcal{M}(L)$ and a probabilistic BLTL formula φ, the probabilities that the qSMC algorithm returns a wrong answer compared to the qMC algorithm [2] is bounded:*

1. **Type-I error***:* $\mathrm{Prob}(\mathrm{qSMC} = \mathsf{F} \mid \mathrm{qMC} \neq \mathsf{F}) \leq \max(\alpha_1, \alpha_2)$.
2. **Type-II error***:* $\mathrm{Prob}(\mathrm{qSMC} = \mathsf{T} \mid \mathrm{qMC} \neq \mathsf{T}) \leq \beta_1$.
3. **Type-III error***:* $\mathrm{Prob}(\mathrm{qSMC} = ? \mid \mathrm{qMC} \neq ?) \leq \max(\alpha_1, \beta_2)$.

Proof. To compute bounds on the probability of error, we use the following properties on the probabilities between three events A, B and C:

$$\mathrm{Prob}(A \mid B \vee C) \leq \max(\mathrm{Prob}(A \mid B), \mathrm{Prob}(A \mid C))$$
$$\text{if } B \text{ and } C \text{ are disjoint events.} \tag{5}$$

$$\mathrm{Prob}(A \wedge B) \leq \min(\mathrm{Prob}(A), \mathrm{Prob}(B)). \tag{6}$$

$$\mathrm{Prob}(A \vee B) = \mathrm{Prob}(A) + \mathrm{Prob}(B) - \mathrm{Prob}(A \wedge B)$$
$$\leq \mathrm{Prob}(A) + \mathrm{Prob}(B). \tag{7}$$

Bound on Type-I error

$\mathrm{Prob}(\mathrm{qSMC} = \mathsf{F} \mid \mathrm{qMC} \neq \mathsf{F}) = \mathrm{Prob}(\mathrm{qSMC} = \mathsf{F} \mid \mathrm{qMC} = \mathsf{T} \vee \mathrm{qMC} = ?)$
Then according to Eq. 5:
$\leq \max(\mathrm{Prob}(\mathrm{qSMC} = \mathsf{F} \mid \mathrm{qMC} = \mathsf{T}), \mathrm{Prob}(\mathrm{qSMC} = \mathsf{F} \mid \mathrm{qMC} = ?))$
We bound these two probabilities:

$\mathrm{Prob}(\mathrm{qSMC} = \mathsf{F} \mid \mathrm{qMC} = \mathsf{T}) = \mathrm{Prob}(\mathrm{BSMC}_F = \mathsf{F} \wedge \mathrm{BSMC}_T = \mathsf{F} \mid \mathrm{BMC}_F = \mathsf{T})$
According to Eq. 6:
$\leq \min(\mathrm{Prob}(\mathrm{BSMC}_F = \mathsf{F} \mid \mathrm{BMC}_F = \mathsf{T}) , \mathrm{Prob}(\mathrm{BSMC}_T = \mathsf{F} \mid \mathrm{BMC}_F = \mathsf{T}))$
and according to Eq. 1: $\mathrm{Prob}(\mathrm{qSMC} = \mathsf{F} \mid \mathrm{qMC} = \mathsf{T}) \leq \alpha_1$
$\mathrm{Prob}(\mathrm{qSMC} = \mathsf{F} \mid \mathrm{qMC} = ?)$
$= \mathrm{Prob}(\mathrm{BSMC}_F = \mathsf{F} \wedge \mathrm{BSMC}_T = \mathsf{F} \mid \mathrm{BMC}_F = \mathsf{F} \wedge \mathrm{BMC}_T = \mathsf{T})$
According to Eq. 6:
$\leq \min(\mathrm{Prob}(\mathrm{BSMC}_F = \mathsf{F} \mid \mathrm{BMC}_F = \mathsf{F} \wedge \mathrm{BMC}_T = \mathsf{T}),$
$\qquad \mathrm{Prob}(\mathrm{BSMC}_T = \mathsf{F} \mid \mathrm{BMC}_F = \mathsf{F} \wedge \mathrm{BMC}_T = \mathsf{T}))$
and according to Eq. 3: $\mathrm{Prob}(\mathrm{qSMC} = \mathsf{F} \mid \mathrm{qMC} = ?) \leq \alpha_2$

Thus we get $\boxed{\mathrm{Prob}(\mathrm{qSMC} = \mathsf{F} \mid \mathrm{qMC} \neq \mathsf{F}) \leq \max(\alpha_1, \alpha_2)}$.

Bound on Type-II error

$\text{Prob}(\text{qSMC} = \text{T} \mid \text{qMC} \neq \text{T}) = \text{Prob}(\text{qSMC} = \text{T} \mid \text{qMC} = \text{F} \vee \text{qMC} =?)$

$= \text{Prob}(\text{BSMC}_F = \text{T} \mid \text{BMC}_F = \text{F} \wedge (\text{BMC}_T = \text{F} \vee \text{BMC}_T = \text{T}))$

$= \text{Prob}(\text{BSMC}_F = \text{T} \mid \text{BMC}_F = \text{F})$ since $\text{BMC}_T = \text{F}$ and $\text{BMC}_T = \text{T}$ form a total partition of the probability space.

Finally according to Eq. 2 we get $\boxed{\text{Prob}(\text{qSMC} = \text{T} \mid \text{qMC} \neq \text{T}) \leq \beta_1}$.

Bound on Type-III error

$\text{Prob}(\text{qSMC} =? \mid \text{qMC} \neq?) = \text{Prob}(\text{qSMC} =? \mid \text{qMC} = \text{T} \vee \text{qMC} = \text{F})$

$= \text{Prob}(\text{qSMC} =? \mid \text{BMC}_F = \text{T} \vee (\text{BMC}_F = \text{F} \wedge \text{BMC}_T = \text{F}))$

$= \text{Prob}(\text{qSMC} =? \mid \text{BMC}_F = \text{T} \vee \text{BMC}_T = \text{F})$ since $\text{BMC}_F = \text{T}$ and $\text{BMC}_F = \text{F}$ form a total partition of the probability space. Then according to Eq. 5:

$\leq \max(\text{Prob}(\text{qSMC} =? \mid \text{BMC}_F = \text{T}), \text{Prob}(\text{qSMC} =? \mid \text{BMC}_T = \text{F}))$

We bound these two probabilities:

$\text{Prob}(\text{qSMC} =? \mid \text{BMC}_F = \text{T}) = \text{Prob}(\text{BSMC}_F = \text{F} \wedge \text{BSMC}_T = \text{T} \mid \text{BMC}_F = \text{T})$

according to Eqs. 6 and 1:

$\text{Prob}(\text{qSMC} =? \mid \text{BMC}_F = \text{T}) \leq \text{Prob}(\text{BSMC}_F = \text{F} \mid \text{BMC}_F = \text{T}) \leq \alpha_1$

$\text{Prob}(\text{qSMC} =? \mid \text{BMC}_T = \text{F}) = \text{Prob}(\text{BSMC}_F = \text{F} \wedge \text{BSMC}_T = \text{T} \mid \text{BMC}_T = \text{F})$

according to Eqs. 6 and 4:

$\text{Prob}(\text{qSMC} =? \mid \text{BMC}_T = \text{F}) \leq \text{Prob}(\text{BSMC}_T = \text{T} \mid \text{BMC}_T = \text{F}) \leq \beta_2$

Thus we get $\boxed{\text{Prob}(\text{qSMC} =? \mid \text{qMC} \neq?) \leq \max(\alpha_1, \beta_2)}$.   □

6   Implementation Using Plasma Lab

We have implemented our three-valued estimation algorithm and the qSMC hypothesis testing algorithm in the tool Plasma Lab [4, 19]. Plasma Lab is a generic platform for performing statistical model checking of stochastic systems. It provides several SMC algorithms that can be applied to different types of systems and properties using a plugin system. Plasma Lab's algorithms include estimation algorithm with Monte Carlo method, hypothesis testing with SPRT, estimation of rare events with importance splitting and importance sampling [20], and algorithms for Markov decision processes [10]. Plasma Lab includes a simulator for the Reactive Module Language (RML) of the probabilistic model-checker Prism [17] that allows to specify discrete and continuous time Markov chains, as well as Markov decision processes. It also includes interfaces to external simulators such as SystemC [22], LLVM bytecode, or MATLAB/Simulink models [21].

To specify qDTMC in Plasma Lab, we use RML and the simulator plugin implemented in Plasma Lab. RML allows to write DTMC in a compact textual format by writing a set of concurrent modules, each having a set of local variables. These local variables define both the state of the system and its atomic propositions. The system switches from one state to another according to guarded transitions, either involving a single module or a synchronization between several modules. To write qDTMC in RML we add variables that will only be used as atomic propositions. Their values can be 1, for true, 0, for false, or −1, for unknown. With this representation, we do not need to implement a new language and a new simulator.

Plasma Lab also provides several formal logics for analysing paths of stochastic systems. To implement the qBLTL logic we have adapted the BLTL checker of Plasma Lab. The new plugin uses the same parser. It assumes that formulae only use three-valued atomic propositions defined in qDTMC. It implements a new semantics with the rules presented in Definition 7. The analysis of a path by this checker returns a value in $\{-1, 0, 1\}$.

We have implemented the three-valued estimation algorithm and the qSMC algorithm in two new algorithm plugins. The qSMC algorithm implements the subroutines SetToFalse and SetToTrue as syntactic transformations to remove unknowns from the model. It uses the SPRT algorithm and the BLTL checker of Plasma Lab to analyse the RML model after transformation. We summarize the components used in this implementation in Fig. 1.

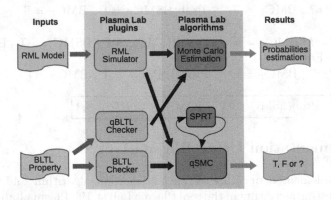

Fig. 1. Plasma Lab implementation of SMC algorithms for qDTMC

7   Experiments

In this section, we illustrate an example scenario wherein a set of nodes are connected to each other in a fixed network topology. A node, called source, wants to deliver a message to another node, called destination, via its neighbouring nodes. The message transfer occurs at discrete time steps. Each node forwards the message to one of its neighbouring nodes with some probability. However, it is possible that the message gets changed or corrupted at one or more intermediary nodes. The information about the nodes that can corrupt the message is incomplete. Thus, the aim is to analyze the probability of delivering an uncorrupted message from the source to the destination.

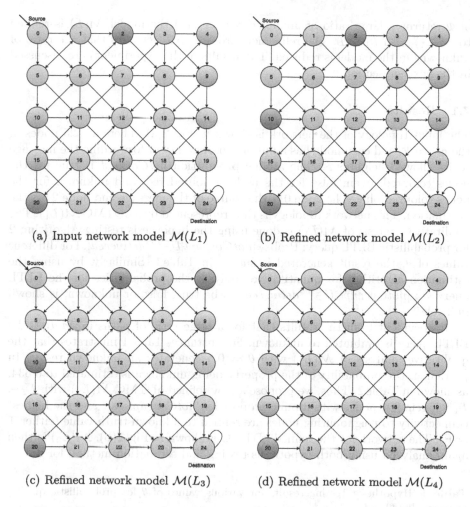

(a) Input network model $\mathcal{M}(L_1)$

(b) Refined network model $\mathcal{M}(L_2)$

(c) Refined network model $\mathcal{M}(L_3)$

(d) Refined network model $\mathcal{M}(L_4)$

Fig. 2. Example network models containing different number of unknowns

We model this network using a qDTMC $\mathcal{M}(L) = (S, \mathbb{P}, s_{init}, AP, L)$. The set of nodes in the network are represented as states in $\mathcal{M}(L)$ and the probability of sending messages between two nodes is governed by the transition probability matrix $\mathbb{P}$. We use an atomic proposition $notCorrupt$ for each state $s \in S$. If the node corresponding to state s does not change the message, the labelling function L assigns true (T) to $notCorrupt$ at s. Similarly, if the node changes the message, then $notCorrupt$ is labelled as false (F) in s. However, if the behaviour of the node is not known, then the atomic proposition $notCorrupt$ is labelled as unknown (?) in the state s. The qDTMC $\mathcal{M}(L)$ can be analyzed to estimate the probability that the message is delivered to the destination within 100 time units and it remains uncorrupted until it is delivered. We formally express this using qBLTL property Φ : $notCorrupt\ U^{\leq 100} delivered$. The qBLTL property Φ is analyzed using both qualitative and quantitative methods. If the analysis of Φ returns a large ratio of unknown results then the model $\mathcal{M}(L)$ is refined to $\mathcal{M}(L_1)$ with $L_1 \prec L$. The refinement from L to L_1 ensures that the ratio of unknowns in the model is reduced. The results of the experiments are discussed in the next subsection.

7.1   Results

The input topology of the network is shown in Fig. 2(a). There are 25 nodes in the network, and each node has a uniform probability of forwarding the message to its allowed neighbours. The atomic proposition *notCorrupt* is true for the nodes coloured green, false for the nodes coloured red, and unknown for the nodes coloured blue. The node 0 is the source of the message and node 24 is the destination. This network topology is thus represented by a qDTMC $\mathcal{M}(L_1)$. The qualitative analysis of $\mathcal{M}(L_1)$ is done using the hypothesis testing Algorithm 2 for probabilistic BLTL query: $\text{Prob}_{\geq \theta}[notCorrupt\ U^{\leq 100} delivered]$. For different values of θ, the result generated is shown in Table 1. Similarly, by using the estimation algorithm for quantitative analysis, the probabilities for the BLTL query $\Phi : [notCorrupt\ U^{\leq 100} delivered]$ to be true, false or unknown, is shown in Table 2.

It is evident from the results that for a large ratio of paths in $\mathcal{M}(L_1)$, the BLTL query is evaluated to unknown. For instance, Table 1 illustrates that the qualitative analysis of $\mathcal{M}(L_1)$ with $\theta = 0.5$ generates an unknown result. In particular, the probability of the property being unknown is estimated to 0.634, as shown in Table 2. Thus, we propose a new refined qDTMC $\mathcal{M}(L_2)$ with $L_2 \prec L_1$ wherein few nodes with atomic proposition *notCorrupt* as ? and the highest connectivity to neighbouring nodes are refined to a known truth value (either T or F). The network for the refined qDTMC is shown in Fig. 2(b). $\mathcal{M}(L_2)$ is then again analyzed using both hypothesis testing and estimation method for Φ.

Table 1. Hypothesis Testing results for various values of θ for probabilistic qBLTL property $Pr(\Phi) \geq \theta$

θ	0.1	0.2	0.3	0.4	0.5	0.6	0.7	0.8	0.9
$\mathcal{M}(L_1)$	T	?	?	?	?	?	F	F	F
$\mathcal{M}(L_2)$	T	T	?	?	?	F	F	F	F
$\mathcal{M}(L_3)$	T	T	T	?	F	F	F	F	F
$\mathcal{M}(L_4)$	T	T	T	T	T	?	F	F	F

Indeed by refining $\mathcal{M}(L_1)$ to $\mathcal{M}(L_2)$, we can see in Table 2 that the probability of unknown result is reduced to 0.273. The qualitative analysis also results in a known result (T or F) for a number of different θ values. To further reduce the uncertainty in the model, we can again refine $\mathcal{M}(L_2)$ to $\mathcal{M}(L_3)$ such that $L_3 \prec L_2$. The network for the refined qDTMC $\mathcal{M}(L_3)$ is shown in Fig. 2(c). The analysis results for $\mathcal{M}(L_3)$ for Φ are also shown in the same tables.

Table 2. Estimated probabilities of qBLTL property Φ being T, F or ?

$\mathcal{M}(L_i)$	$Pr((\mathcal{M}(L_i), \Phi) = T)$	$Pr((\mathcal{M}(L_i), \Phi) = F)$	$Pr((\mathcal{M}(L_i), \Phi) =?)$
$\mathcal{M}(L_1)$	0.122	0.244	0.634
$\mathcal{M}(L_2)$	0.260	0.467	0.273
$\mathcal{M}(L_3)$	0.361	0.507	0.132
$\mathcal{M}(L_4)$	0.597	0.273	0.130

It is evident from the results of analysis of $\mathcal{M}(L_3)$ that the probability of the property being unknown has reduced significantly, thus allowing to make conclusive comments about the behaviour of the network. However, with these refinements $L_3 \prec L_2 \prec L_1$, the probability of Φ being false has also increased to 0.507. Thus, $\mathcal{M}(L_1)$ can alternately be refined to $\mathcal{M}(L_4)$, with $L_4 \prec L_1$, such that we ensure that the nodes with unknown get refined to true only. The network for the qDTMC $\mathcal{M}(L_4)$ is shown in Fig. 2(d). Thus, it can be easily concluded from these results that while properties with low required probabilities can still be verified in incomplete models, the models may need refinements to satisfy properties demanding a higher success rate.

8 Conclusion

In this paper, we proposed a statistical analysis of stochastic systems with incomplete information. These incomplete systems are modelled using discrete time Markov chains with unknowns (qDTMC), and the required behaviour was formalized using qBLTL logic. By doing both quantitative and qualitative analysis of such systems using statistical model checking, we also proposed refinement on the qDTMCs. These refined qDTMCs depict a decrease in the probability of unknown behaviour in the system. The algorithms for both qualitative and quantitative analysis of qDTMC were implemented in the tool Plasma Lab. We demonstrated the working of these algorithms on a case study of a network with unknown information. We plan to extend this work to analyse the behaviour of other stochastic models like Markov decision processes and abstract Markov chains, with incomplete information.

References

1. Arora, S., Rao, M.V.P.: Probabilistic model checking of incomplete models. In: Margaria, T., Steffen, B. (eds.) ISoLA 2016. LNCS, vol. 9952, pp. 62–76. Springer, Cham (2016). https://doi.org/10.1007/978-3-319-47166-2_5
2. Arora, S., Rao, M.V.P.: Probabilistic model checking of incomplete models. CoRR abs/1706.05082 (2017)
3. Bauer, A., Leucker, M., Schallhart, C.: The good, the bad, and the ugly, but how ugly is ugly? In: Sokolsky, O., Taşıran, S. (eds.) RV 2007. LNCS, vol. 4839, pp. 126–138. Springer, Heidelberg (2007). https://doi.org/10.1007/978-3-540-77395-5_11

4. Boyer, B., Corre, K., Legay, A., Sedwards, S.: PLASMA-lab: a flexible, distributable statistical model checking library. In: Joshi, K., Siegle, M., Stoelinga, M., D'Argenio, P.R. (eds.) QEST 2013. LNCS, vol. 8054, pp. 160–164. Springer, Heidelberg (2013). https://doi.org/10.1007/978-3-642-40196-1_12

5. Chechik, M., Easterbrook, S., Devereux, B.: Model checking with multi-valued temporal logics. In: Proceedings of the 31st IEEE International Symposium on Multiple-Valued Logic, pp. 187–192 (2001)

6. Chechik, M., Easterbrook, S., Petrovykh, V.: Model-checking over multi-valued logics. In: Oliveira, J.N., Zave, P. (eds.) FME 2001. LNCS, vol. 2021, pp. 72–98. Springer, Heidelberg (2001). https://doi.org/10.1007/3-540-45251-6_5

7. Chen, X.: Concentration inequalities for bounded random vectors. arXiv preprint: arXiv:1309.0003 (2013)

8. Chernoff, H.: A measure of asymptotic efficiency for tests of a hypothesis based on the sum of observations. Ann. Math. Stat. **23**(4), 493–507 (1952)

9. Courcoubetis, C., Yannakakis, M.: The complexity of probabilistic verification. J. ACM **42**(4), 857–907 (1995)

10. D'Argenio, P., Legay, A., Sedwards, S., Traonouez, L.: Smart sampling for lightweight verification of markov decision processes. STTT **17**(4), 469–484 (2015)

11. David, A., et al.: Statistical model checking for networks of priced timed automata. In: Fahrenberg, U., Tripakis, S. (eds.) FORMATS 2011. LNCS, vol. 6919, pp. 80–96. Springer, Heidelberg (2011). https://doi.org/10.1007/978-3-642-24310-3_7

12. Fecher, H., Leucker, M., Wolf, V.: *Don't Know* in probabilistic systems. In: Valmari, A. (ed.) SPIN 2006. LNCS, vol. 3925, pp. 71–88. Springer, Heidelberg (2006). https://doi.org/10.1007/11691617_5

13. Hansson, H., Jonsson, B.: A logic for reasoning about time and reliability. Form. Asp. Comput. **6**(5), 512–535 (1994)

14. Hérault, T., Lassaigne, R., Magniette, F., Peyronnet, S.: Approximate probabilistic model checking. In: Steffen, B., Levi, G. (eds.) VMCAI 2004. LNCS, vol. 2937, pp. 73–84. Springer, Heidelberg (2004). https://doi.org/10.1007/978-3-540-24622-0_8

15. Huth, M., Piterman, N., Wagner, D.: Three-valued abstractions of Markov chains: completeness for a sizeable fragment of PCTL. In: Kutyłowski, M., Charatonik, W., Gębala, M. (eds.) FCT 2009. LNCS, vol. 5699, pp. 205–216. Springer, Heidelberg (2009). https://doi.org/10.1007/978-3-642-03409-1_19

16. Katoen, J.P., Klink, D., Leucker, M., Wolf, V.: Three-valued abstraction for probabilistic systems. J. Log. Algebr. Program. **81**(4), 356–389 (2012). special Issue: NWPT 2009

17. Kwiatkowska, M., Norman, G., Parker, D.: PRISM 4.0: verification of probabilistic real-time systems. In: Gopalakrishnan, G., Qadeer, S. (eds.) CAV 2011. LNCS, vol. 6806, pp. 585–591. Springer, Heidelberg (2011). https://doi.org/10.1007/978-3-642-22110-1_47

18. Legay, A., Delahaye, B., Bensalem, S.: Statistical model checking: an overview. In: Barringer, H., et al. (eds.) RV 2010. LNCS, vol. 6418, pp. 122–135. Springer, Heidelberg (2010). https://doi.org/10.1007/978-3-642-16612-9_11

19. Legay, A., Sedwards, S., Traonouez, L.-M.: Plasma lab: a modular statistical model checking platform. In: Margaria, T., Steffen, B. (eds.) ISoLA 2016. LNCS, vol. 9952, pp. 77–93. Springer, Cham (2016). https://doi.org/10.1007/978-3-319-47166-2_6

20. Legay, A., Sedwards, S., Traonouez, L.-M.: Rare events for statistical model checking an overview. In: Larsen, K.G., Potapov, I., Srba, J. (eds.) RP 2016. LNCS, vol. 9899, pp. 23–35. Springer, Cham (2016). https://doi.org/10.1007/978-3-319-45994-3_2

21. Legay, A., Traonouez, L.-M.: Statistical model checking of simulink models with plasma lab. In: Artho, C., Ölveczky, P.C. (eds.) FTSCS 2015. CCIS, vol. 596, pp. 259–264. Springer, Cham (2016). https://doi.org/10.1007/978-3-319-29510-7_15
22. Ngo, V.C., Legay, A., Quilbeuf, J.: Statistical model checking for systemc models. In: Proceedings of HASE, pp. 197–204. IEEE Computer Society (2016)
23. Vardi, M.Y.: Automatic verification of probabilistic concurrent finite state programs. In: Proceedings of SFCS, pp. 327–338. IEEE Computer Society (1985)
24. Wald, A.: Sequential tests of statistical hypotheses. Ann. Math. Stat. **16**(2), 117–186 (1945)
25. Younes, H.L.S.: Verification and Planning for Stochastic Processes with Asynchronous Events. Ph.D. thesis, Carnegie Mellon (2005)

Statistical Model Checking of a Moving Block Railway Signalling Scenario with UPPAAL SMC
Experience and Outlook

Davide Basile[1,2], Maurice H. ter Beek[1(✉)], and Vincenzo Ciancia[1]

[1] ISTI–CNR, Pisa, Italy
{basile,terbeek,ciancia}@isti.cnr.it
[2] Department of Statistics, Computer Science and Applications (DISIA),
University of Florence, Florence, Italy

Abstract. We present an experience in modelling and statistical model checking a satellite-based moving block signalling scenario from the railway industry with UPPAAL SMC. This demonstrates the usability and applicability of UPPAAL SMC in the railway domain. We also propose a promising direction for future work, in which we envision spatio-temporal analysis with UPPAAL SMC.

1 Introduction

The railway sector is well known for its robust safety requirements. In fact, the CENELEC EN 50128 standard [31] for the development of software for railway control and protection systems specifically mentions formal methods as highly recommended practices for software systems to be certified at Safety Integrity Levels (SIL) 3 and 4. Indeed, formal methods and tools are widely applied to railway systems [6,12,17,18,34–37,48].

Also the Shift2Rail Joint Undertaking [53] (http://shift2rail.org), the first European rail initiative for focussed research and innovation under Horizon 2020 to increase competitiveness of the European rail industry through the development of safe and reliable technological advances to complete the single European railway area, considers formal methods to be fundamental for its ambitious aim: "double the capacity of the European rail system and increase its reliability and service quality by 50%, all while halving life-cycle costs."

In particular, specific calls were issued concerning the application of formal methods in supporting the transition to the next generation of ERTMS/ETCS signalling systems, which will include satellite-based train positioning, moving block distancing and automatic driving. The European Railway Traffic Management System (ERTMS) is a set of international standards for the interoperability, performance, reliability, and safety of modern European rail transport [30]. It relies on the European Train Control System (ETCS), an automatic train protection system that continuously supervises the train, ensuring to not exceed the

T. Margaria and B. Steffen (Eds.): ISoLA 2018, LNCS 11245, pp. 372–391, 2018.
https://doi.org/10.1007/978-3-030-03421-4_24

safety speed and distance. The current standards distinguish four levels (0–3) of operation of ETCS signalling systems, depending largely on the role of trackside equipment and on the way information is transmitted to and from trains. Full-fledged Level 3 systems are under development, but have not yet been deployed.

In this paper, we report our trial experience in modelling and statistical model checking a Level 3 moving block signalling scenario with UPPAAL SMC. This task was performed in the context of two projects with ample participation from the railway industry, one of which funded under the above mentioned H2020 Shift2Rail initiative. Our experience shows that UPPAAL SMC facilitates an easy transformation of semi-formal UML models into formal models (viz. stochastic timed automata). Furthermore, subsequent analyses with UPPAAL SMC turned out to be very useful in discussions with our industrial partners, demonstrating the usability and applicability of UPPAAL SMC in the railway industry. As an outlook for the future, we envision spatio-temporal analysis based on UPPAAL SMC by exploiting its powerful continuous time analysis capabilities, especially its ODE modelling tools, and its statistical model-checking algorithms in combination with the typically discrete models produced by spatial analysis.

The remainder of the paper is organised as follows. Section 2 introduces the industrial context: next generation ERTMS/ETCS satellite-based moving block railway signalling systems. Section 3 first describes the specific case study, a railway signalling scenario with satellite-based positioning and moving block distancing, after which it presents UPPAAL models of the case study and some preliminary results of applying the statistical model checking features of UPPAAL SMC to the case study. Section 4 discusses a promising direction for future work, spatio-temporal analysis with UPPAAL SMC, after which the contribution of this paper is briefly discussed in Sect. 5.

2   Industrial Context: Railway Signalling Systems

The ERTMS/ETCS signalling systems currently deployed on railways throughout Europe concern at most Level 2. These are characterised by the need for trackside equipment (such as track circuits or axle counters) only for exact train position detection and train integrity supervision, whereas communication of the movement authority (MA), speed information and route data to/from the train is achieved by continuous data transmission via GSM-R or GPRS with a Radio Block Centre (RBC). Moreover, an onboard unit (OBU) continuously monitors the transferred data and the train's maximum permissible speed by determining its position in between the Eurobalises (transponders on the rails of a railway) used as reference points via sensors (axle transducers, accelerometer and radar).

However, the current Level 2 signalling systems are still based on fixed blocks (sections of the railway track between fixed points), which start and end at signals, with their lengths designed to allow trains to operate as frequently as necessary (i.e., ranging from many kilometres for secondary tracks to a few hundred metres for busy commuter lines). The block sizes are determined based on parameters like the line's speed limit, the train's speed, the train's braking characteristics, drivers' sighting and reaction times, etc. But the faster trains are allowed to run, the longer the braking distance and the longer the blocks need to be, thus decreasing the line's capacity. This is because the railway sector's stringent safety requirements impose the length of fixed blocks to be based on the worst-case braking distance, regardless of the actual speed of the train.

The next generation Level 3 signalling systems no longer rely on trackside equipment for train position detection and train integrity supervision, but an onboard odometry system is responsible for monitoring the train's position and autonomously computing its current speed. The OBU frequently sends the train's position to a RBC which, in turn, sends each train a MA, computed by exploiting its knowledge of the position of the rear end of the train ahead. For this to work, the precise absolute location, speed and direction of each train needs to be known. These can be determined by a combination of sensors: active and passive markers along the track, as well as trainborne speedometers.

The resulting moving block signalling systems allow trains in succession to close up, since a safe zone around the moving trains can be computed, thus considerably reducing headways between trains, in principle to the braking distance (cf. Fig. 1). This allows for more trains to run on existing railway tracks, in response to the ever-increasing need to boost the volume of passenger and freight rail transport and the cost and impracticability of constructing new tracks.

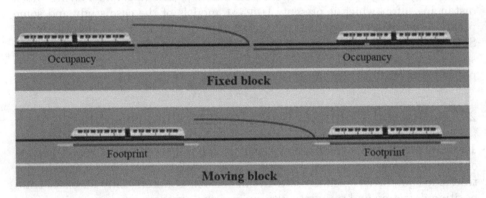

Fig. 1. Safe braking distance between trains for fixed block and moving block signalling (Image courtesy of Israel.abad/Wikimedia Commons distributed under the CC BY-SA 3.0 license)

The envisioned future switch from Level 2 to Level 3 signalling systems would not only optimise the exploitation of railway lines due to the adoption of moving block signalling, but the removal of trackside equipment would result in lower capital and maintenance costs. However, compared with other transport sectors, the railway sector is notoriously cautious about the adoption of technological innovations. This is typically attributed to its well-known robust safety requirements. Therefore, one of the current challenges in the railway sector is to make moving block signalling systems as effective and precise as possible, including

GNSS-based satellite positioning and leveraging on an integrated solution for signal outages (think, e.g., of tunnels) and the problem of multipaths [51].

Requirements analysis followed by safety, hazard and performance analyses of moving block signalling scenarios by means of formal methods and tools are a few of the topics addressed in the EU's H2020 Shift2Rail project ASTRail (SAtellite-based Signalling and Automation SysTems on Railways along with Formal Method and Moving Block Validation) (http://www.astrail.eu) [11]. Moreover, one of the aims of the Tuscany region's project SISTER (SIgnaling & Sensing TEchnologies in Railway applications) (http://stlab.dinfo.unifi.it/sister-project) is to apply innovative signalling solutions in the context of Light Rail Transit infrastructures. In the next section, we describe a concrete case study that has been considered in these projects for a trial application of formal modelling and analysis in order to assess the usability and applicability of formal methods and tools in the railway domain. This assessment is one of the goals of the ASTRail project and currently considered to be an important issue for the successful uptake of formal methods and tools in the railway industry (cf., e.g., [6,11,47,48]).

3   Case Study: Moving Block Signalling Scenario

An important task of a work package of the ASTRail project is devoted to formal verification of a moving block signalling system, based on a model in Real-Time UML (RT UML) [29,52] provided by the project's industrial partners. This model takes as parameters the probability of failures of the different devices involved in the system (e.g. GNSS receivers), to be instantiated with data provided by the vendors of such devices. Hence, our task mainly consisted of translating the semi-formal UML model to a formal one, amenable to formal verification. We chose to use UPPAAL SMC for this task, since it allows for both real-time and probabilistic aspects, which both occur in RT UML models. Moreover, the formalism is similar to UML state machine diagrams, which eased understanding by our partners. The visualisation of message sequence charts helped in this aspect. We now outline the moving block signalling scenario, after which we present the Uppaal models, and some hints on how we obtained them from the RT UML models, in Sect. 3.1 and the results of statistical model checking in Sect. 3.2.

The main components of the Level 3 moving block signalling system that we consider are a trackside RBC and a train's OBU and localisation unit (LU). The OBU measures the train's current speed and verifies the train's integrity, while the LU uses a GNSS-based positioning system to determine the train's location. The RBC is continuously in communication with the train's onboard units to receive data regarding the train's position and its integrity from the train, and to send speed restrictions, route configurations and MAs to the train. The RBC computes the latter by communicating with neighbouring RBCs and by exploiting its knowledge of the positions of switches and other trains (head and tail position) by communicating with a Route Management System (RMS). The model abstracts from the RMS and from the communication between neighbouring RBCs. Instead, it considers the train to communicate with one RBC, based on a seamless handover when the train moves from one RBC supervision area to the adjacent as regulated according to its Functional Interface Specification [54].

A (preliminary) hazard analysis was performed by our industrial partners in order to evaluate the safety level of a moving block signalling system. To this aim, hazards derived from the moving block signalling system in operation, such as GNSS-related errors, communication failures and faulty states, were identified and analysed, after which their risk level was assessed. This safety assessment concerned establishing the probability of the occurrence of a hazard and the severity of its consequences as well as risk qualifying according to the appropriate CENELEC EN 50126 standards concerning Reliability, Availability, Maintainability and Safety (RAMS) [32,33]. This results in a hazard log. We derived a number of safety properties from this hazard log, to be verified on the formal model. One of these will be analysed in Sect. 3.2, where we will provide some details from the log. The full hazard log is omitted for reasons of space.

3.1   Modelling

UPPAAL SMC [28] is a variant of UPPAAL [14], a well-known toolbox for the verification of real-time systems modelled by (extended) timed automata, which was introduced specifically for modelling and analysing cyber-physical systems. UPPAAL SMC models are stochastic timed automata, in which non-determinism is replaced with probabilistic choices and time delays with probability distributions (uniform for bounded time and exponential for unbounded time). As usual, these automata may communicate via broadcast channels and shared variables.

We transformed the RT UML state machine diagrams as provided by our industrial partners into stochastic timed automata. This model transformation was rather straightforward, except for a few issues that mostly concerned the precise meaning of (time-related) modelling choices and which had to be cleared during meetings with our partners. Before presenting our formal UPPAAL models, we list the modelling choices and assumptions that we have made for the specific RT UML model at hand. The model itself is omitted for reasons of confidentiality.

Each parallel region of the RT UML model is translated into a separate automaton. (Pseudo) states and (probabilistic) transitions are in a one-to-one correspondence, except for the addition of urgent states[1] that are used to split communication actions from probabilistic choices. The failure probabilities are currently set to a placeholder value of 10^{-5}, but we recall that these are to be refined based on input from our project partners. Guards and triggers are modelled as input and output broadcast channels, respectively, which implies that we assume the different system components (i.e. the OBU, LU and RBC) to communicate in a synchronous manner. This means that a message is discarded

---

[1] In timed automata, an urgent state (indicated with a '∪' inside the state) is a state with no delay, which allows to reduce the number of clocks in a model, and thus the analysis' complexity.

in case the receiver is not ready (i.e. in the right state) to receive it. The main intuition behind this choice is based on the fact that in this way, a fresh MA sent by the RBC to the OBU will supersede any older MA in case the latter was not yet received.

Time-related aspects are rendered as follows. Timed events `RTat` of stereotype `<<RTevent>>`, typically used to trigger transitions based on the event's timing information, are modelled as invariant conditions and clock guards, which force transitions to be executed when the precise moment in time has been reached. Probabilistic delayed events `RTduration` of stereotype `<<RTdelay>>`, typically used to add durations to actions/transitions, are modelled as probabilistic delays: when an action/transition is enabled, the time at which it is fired is probabilistically distributed. As for failure probabilities and rates of probabilistic distributions, also these will be further refined based on input from our project partners.

We now briefly describe the eight stochastic automata, depicted in Fig. 2, that together make up our UPPAAL model of the moving block scenario.

The automata are screenshots of the automata designed with UPPAAL SMC. In the figures, initial states are indicated by a double circle (e.g. `Idle` in Fig. 2h) and (non-urgent) states have a name (e.g. `Stop`) in purple and an invariant (possibly with clock rates) in pink (e.g. `counter'==1.0 && counter<=timeout`); transitions have guards in green (e.g. `counter>=timeout`), synchronisation actions in cyan (e.g. `ReceiveMA?`, while τ actions are omitted) and updates in blue (e.g. `counter=0`). Exponential distributions rates for states with unbounded delay are depicted in red (e.g. 2 in Fig. 2f), while the values of discrete probabilistic choices (whose transitions are displayed with dashed lines) are depicted in bone (e.g. 99999, i.e. probability $\frac{99999}{1+99999}$). The probabilities are input parameters (originating from the industrial partners), whose values are the result of preliminary evaluations. More fine-tuning of these parameters is awaiting further input from our industrial project partners.

In brief, the automata operate as follows. At fixed intervals of time, given by the parameter `freq_req`, the train's OBU generates a location request (Fig. 2a), which is sent to the train's LU (Fig. 2b). Upon receiving this location request, the LU calculates the train's location (Fig. 2c) and responds to the OBU (Fig. 2d). Upon receiving the train's location, the OBU sends it—together with a requests for a MA—to the RBC (Fig. 2e). Once the RBC has received the location of the train and the request for a MA, it calculates the MA (Fig. 2f) and responds (by sending the MA) to the train's OBU (Fig. 2g). When the OBU has received a MA, it activates a timer to control the freshness of the MA and it activates the emergency stop whenever the current MA has become outdated, recorded by a parameter `timeout` (Fig. 2h). Our industrial partners set `freq_req = 5 s` and `timeout = 3*freq_req = 15 s`. Moreover, we set the initial value of the clock named c1 to `freq_req` and the one named `counter` to 5, i.e. the transition of the automaton depicted in Fig. 2a is enabled initially.

The current model is rather simple, but we anticipate further complexity once we consider more than one train and more than one RBC.

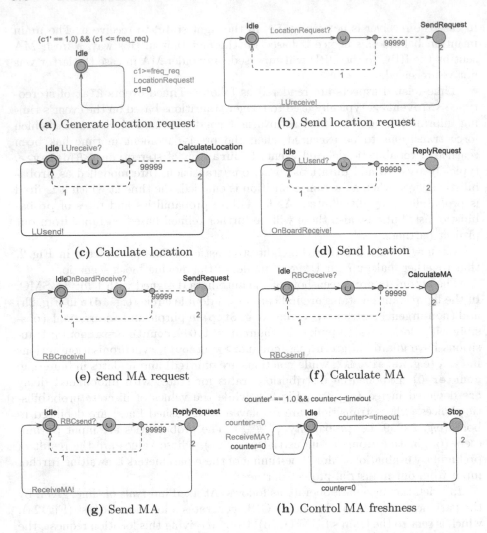

Fig. 2. Complete UPPAAL model of moving block signalling scenario (Color figure online)

3.2 Analyses

Statistical Model Checking (SMC) [1,44,45] is concerned with running a sufficient number of (probabilistic) simulations of a system model to obtain statistical evidence (with a predefined level of statistical confidence) of the quantitative properties to be checked. SMC offers advantages over exhaustive (probabilistic) model checking. Most importantly: SMC scales better, since there is no need to generate and possibly explore the full state space of the model under scrutiny, thus avoiding the combinatorial state-space explosion problem typical of model checking, and the required simulations can trivially be distributed and run in parallel. This comes at a price: contrary to (probabilistic) model checking, exact results (with 100% confidence) are out of the question. Another advantage is its uptake in industry: compared to model checking, SMC is very simple to implement, understand and use, and it requires no specific modelling effort other than an operational system model that can be simulated and checked against (state-based) quantitative properties.

In addition to standard model-checking queries concerned with reachability and deadlock-freeness, UPPAAL SMC allows to check (quantitative) properties over simulation runs of an UPPAAL SMC model (i.e. a network of stochastic timed automata). These properties must be expressed in the Weighted Metric Temporal Logic (WMTL) [19] defined by the grammar

$$\phi ::= p \mid \neg\phi \mid \phi_1 \wedge \phi_2 \mid X\phi \mid \phi_1 U_{x \leq t} \phi_2$$

where p is a state predicate, x is a clock and $t \in \mathbb{N}$. Negation and conjunction are the classical logic operators that yield the full propositional logic. X is the usual neXt operator from temporal logic: $X\phi$ states that in the *next* state of a simulation run, the formula ϕ is satisfied. U is a time-bounded Until operator: $\phi_1 U_{x \leq t} \phi_2$ is satisfied if the formula ϕ_1 holds on a simulation run *until* the formula ϕ_2 is satisfied, and this must happen before the clock x exceeds time t. As usual, it is possible to derive (time-bounded) *eventually* and *always* operators. Let *true* denote $\phi \vee \neg\phi$. Then $\Diamond_{x \leq t} \phi = true\, U_{x \leq t} \phi$ and $\Box_{x \leq t} \phi = \neg\Diamond_{x \leq t} \neg\phi$.

Let $\mathbb{P}_M(\Diamond_{x \leq t} \phi)$ denote the probability that a random simulation run of a model M satisfies ϕ. UPPAAL SMC supports the evaluation of the following three types of queries over a model M:

Probability estimation $\mathbb{P}_M(\Diamond_{x \leq t} p)$?
Hypothesis testing $\mathbb{P}_M(\Diamond_{x \leq t} p) \geq P$? ($P \in [0, 1]$)
Probability comparison $\mathbb{P}_M(\Diamond_{x_1 \leq t_1} p_1) \geq \mathbb{P}_M(\Diamond_{x_2 < t_2} p_2)$?

Additionally, UPPAAL SMC supports the evaluation of expected values of min or max of an expression that evaluates to a clock or an integer value:

Average min $E[bound; N](min : expr)$
Average max $E[bound; N](max : expr)$

where *bound*, for $n \in \mathbb{N}^+$, is either (1) an implicit time bound specified by $\leq n$, (2) an explicit bound by cost specified by $x \leq n$, where x is a specific clock, or (3) a bound on the number of discrete steps specified by $\# \leq n$. Furthermore, N is the number of runs, and *expr* is the expression to evaluate.

Evaluating Safety. Several of the hazards reported in the hazard log provided by our industrial partners report as causes communication failures. Exemplary requirements of such hazards read "Communications between RBC and OBU must be safe and continuously supervised, if the connection is lost an alarm must be triggered" and "OBU device must be SIL 4 device. Once OBU receives the alarm [...] it must immediately send an alarm to RBC", to be mitigated by

"In case of communication loss enter in safe state mode". Each hazard also has an associated so-called Safety Related Application Condition, such as "If train position cannot be received within the maximum time limit, the OBU shall generate an alarm and must transit to degraded mode" and "If Train Integrity cannot be confirmed within the maximum time limit, the train shall be stopped". The recurring aspects in these hazards (viz. communications and safe state) have been modelled, so we can formalise such requirements.

To acquire familiarity with our UPPAAL model, we first checked the property:

$$A\Diamond(\texttt{ReplyMA.ReplyRequest} \parallel \texttt{Controlling.Stop})$$

This CTL formula states that it must always (A) be the case that eventually ($\Diamond$) either (choice operator $\parallel$) a MA is received, i.e. state `ReplyRequest` is reached (cf. Fig. 2g), or the train enters a safe state (i.e. state `Stop` in Fig. 2h). We verified this formula on our model with UPPAAL SMC, which reported its satisfaction. Hence, we know that one of the two aforementioned events happens at some point of any simulation run. However, the formula does not express whether this happens infinitely often. Indeed, compared to full CTL, UPPAAL does not allow nesting of path formulae. Nevertheless, given that our model is cyclic (i.e. it eventually returns to the initial state), in this particular case if the property holds then it will indeed hold infinitely often. We remark that the only reason why a MA may not be received is due to repeated communication failures.

In the remainder of this section, the probability of reaching a safe state and the freshness of a MA are measured using SMC. In particular, we used the academic version 4.1.19 (rev. 5649) of UPPAAL SMC with the following set-up for the statistical parameters (for all evaluated properties): lower and upper probabilistic deviation $(-\delta, +\delta)$: 0.001; probability of false negative and false positive (α, β): 0.005; probability uncertainty (ϵ): 5.0^{-5}.

Evaluating the Probability of Reaching a Safe State. The above property in CTL does not express the time by which the MA must be received, nor the probability of entering a safe state. These aspects are taken into account by the next formula:

$$\mathbb{P}_M(\Diamond_{\leq(\texttt{timeout}-1)} \texttt{Controlling.Stop})$$

where M is the composition of the automata in Fig. 2.

UPPAAL SMC estimates the probability that the train will be in the safe state `Stop` before a `timeout` actually occurs to be in the interval $[0, 9.99994e{-}005]$, with confidence 0.995 and obtained from 59912 runs. This low probability is clearly a result that confirmed our expectations and thus pleased our industrial partners. Note that it is not possible to reach the fail-safe state `Controlling.Stop` before clock `counter` has exceeded `timeout`; hence, the more accurate the statistical parameters the closer to zero this probability will be.

Consequently, we decided to evaluate the following, slightly different, formula:

$$\mathbb{P}_M(\Diamond_{\leq(\texttt{timeout})} \texttt{Controlling.Stop})$$

In this case, the clock does actually reach the `timeout` value and the automaton Controlling in Fig. 2h thus switches to the safe state `Stop`. However, UPPAAL SMC estimates also this probability to be in the interval $[0, 9.99994e{-}005]$, with confidence 0.995 and obtained from 59912 runs. Hence, the probability for this to happen is invariantly low, which again pleased our industrial partners. Both these evaluations took around 5 min.

Evaluating the Freshness of the MA. It is also important to check the 'freshness' of the MA messages. Basically, the older this message is, the less reliable it is considered to be. According to the case study's requirements, the OBU attempts for three times to compute the train's location and receive the MA. In our model, the first attempt takes place at time 0, after which it tries again each 5 s until a timeout occurs at time 15. It is thus of interest to check which of the three attempts has a higher probability of success. In UPPAAL SMC, this can be verified by means of the following formula:

$$E[\leq \text{timeout}; 10000](max : \text{Controlling.counter})$$

which computes, in the interval of time of `timeout` (i.e. 15 s), the average of the maximum value of the clock named `counter`, using 10,000 runs. UPPAAL SMC estimates this average to be in the confidence interval 5.73866 ± 0.0327581, in just over 3 h. As can be concluded from Fig. 2, the clock `counter` is reset each time a new MA is received. Hence, its average value is the average time in which a new MA is received. The cumulative density distribution plot in Fig. 3 provides evidence that the MA messages have a higher probability of being received between the first and the second attempt.

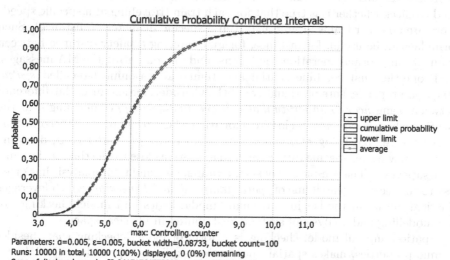

Fig. 3. Analysis of the freshness of the MA

Finally, we observe a trade-off between (1) the freshness of the MA and (2) the probability of reaching a fail-safe state. Indeed, by augmenting timeout an improvement in (2) and a deterioration of (1) is obtained (thus potentially leading to safety issues). Recall that the actual value instantiation for the waiting time (i.e. freq_req = 5 s) and the timeout (i.e. timeout = 3*freq_req = 15 s) were provided by our industrial partners.

The analyses described in this section turned out to be very useful in discussions with our industrial partners concerning the usability and applicability of UPPAAL SMC in the railway domain, as well as to fine-tune the practitioners' semi-formal RT UML model.

4   Future Work: Adding a Spatial Dimension?

An important aspect—currently abstracted away from—in the UPPAAL model of the moving block scenario, presented in Sect. 3.1, concerns using *spatial information* in the case study. An example of such information is the location of trains (their coordinates in a map), calculated by the localisation unit, and used by the RBC to compute the MA messages.

By making the spatial locations of trains explicit, it becomes possible to check whether or not the system satisfies properties of interest of the form "*where* does property ϕ hold?", where property ϕ could be, e.g., "the train is allowed in the current location". Moreover, spatial relationships between different properties could then be checked: "does ϕ hold *near to* where ψ holds?" or "are the locations where ϕ holds *surrounded by* locations where ψ holds?". If, for instance, property ϕ expresses the presence of a single train in a specific area and ψ expresses the absence of trains in a specific area, then such formulae could be used to check whether it is true that for each train (travelling at a specific speed) there are no other trains around it (given a specific diameter of distance). Such formulae can be useful, for instance, for guaranteeing a safety distance between trains during normal operation conditions, and for computing the MA messages.

Properties that combine spatial and temporal reasoning (so-called *spatio-temporal* properties) are particularly subtle. Consider, for instance, the difference between being *near to an entity that will eventually satisfy* ϕ, meaning that the location where we are *now* is close to a location where ϕ will possibly become true in the future, and being *eventually near to an entity that satisfies* ϕ, denoting that we may move, at some future time, to a location close to one that at the same time satisfies ϕ. The complexity of such requirements and their analysis has given rise to the recent research line of *spatio-temporal model checking*, which leverages classical formal methods—in particular, modal logics and model checking—to the modelling and analysis of systems distributed in physical space.

Spatio-temporal model checking is a form of model checking that, besides atomic properties, makes spatial information explicit by providing spatial connectives such as **near** ϕ, interpreted on *points*, which is true at all points that have an edge in common[2] with a point satisfying ϕ. More complex operators can be defined by employing notions of reachability, such as the 'surrounded' operator, or by using spatial metrics (e.g. distance or measure) or by referring to regions of spaces, besides points. Most of these developments have their roots in the field of *topological spatial logics* (cf. [2] for a comprehensive reference). We refer the reader to [22], and the citations therein, for further details.

Although one might think that spatial model checking could be reduced to temporal model checking, this is not the case, due to several differences. For instance, in spatial model checking it is natural to also deal with regions, i.e. contiguous sets of points, which are not usually of interest in temporal model checking. Another point is that 'past' and 'future' modalities are equally relevant in spatial model checking, whereas in temporal model checking it is frequent to deal only with 'future' modalities. Also, the so-called state-space explosion problem is not an issue in current applications of *purely spatial* model checking, since models are explicitly specified state-by-state. However, this does not entail that spatial model checking is inherently limited to small models. Spatial models are often constrained by several factors that limit their complexity, e.g. graphs are typically Euclidean or even just regular grids. A particular case is that of multi-dimensional images (e.g. medical images), where implementations of spatial model checking benefit from very important optimisations that allow several millions of spatial points to be analysed in just seconds.

The state-of-the-art in the computational usage of spatial logics comprises applications of *machine learning*, where the logical operators cater for a machine-readable (and machine-learnable) language with a precise spatial interpretation, and model-checking applications, where the logical language is meant to be easily understandable and hand-written by humans, as for temporal model checking. In the machine-learning research line, some authors (cf., e.g., [5,42]) proposed to employ logical formulae that represent spatio-temporal behaviour as the evolution of a quad-tree representation of a partitioned image. Such formulae may accurately represent complex behaviour; however, these are not meant for human-intelligible specification, but rather tailored to machine learning. In contrast, the topological approach to spatio-temporal model checking, to which one of the authors of the present paper has contributed (cf. [21–23]) is devoted to the study of topological operators (like 'near', 'reachable', 'surrounded'), and to the definition of efficient model-checking algorithms, catering for a simple, albeit expressive logical language that may be used to specify and verify requirements of systems whose behaviour depends on the spatial distribution of components.

Technically, in the approach of [21], a spatio-temporal model over a set of atomic propositions P consists of a graph $G = (N, E)$ with nodes N and edges E, a Kripke structure $K = (S, R)$ with states S and accessibility relation R, and a valuation of atomic propositions $v : (N \times S) \to 2^P$. Consequently, the valuation of a formula ϕ assigns a truth value to each pair n, s consisting of a point $n \in N$ and a state $s \in S$, with the intuitive interpretation that ϕ is true at point n

---

[2] We assume that the considered graphs are symmetric, although this is not generally needed in spatial model checking, especially not in the research line of [22].

in state s. Spatial and temporal formulae can be freely nested, and the computational complexity of the model-checking algorithm is linear in the product of the size of the formula, the number of the temporal states, and the number of points.

Recently, the topological approach was applied in the field of signal analysis [50] and in the context of *smart cities* and *smart transport*, in particular to *statistical spatio-temporal model checking* of bike-sharing systems [24] and to the analysis of networks of *smart buses* [20]). Topological languages can express complex properties of space, as witnessed by their application to the identification of regions of interest in medical imaging (in particular, brain tumours) [15,16].

The tool topochecker[3] is an experimental—but rather feature-complete—model checker capable of analysing branching spatio-temporal models using combinations of the classical temporal operators of CTL [26], the spatial operators of the *Spatial Logic of Closure Spaces* SLCS [23], and the region operators of [22].

The most important aspects of the current paper are indeed related to *continuous* time; this permits the modeller to free herself from discretisation of a temporal domain which is continuous by nature. In the near future, we aim at exploring the same kind of approach to specify spatio-temporal requirements of railway signalling systems. The challenge in pursuing this objective is the combination of *discrete* and *continuous* features that arises from the continuous time model we presented, and the typically discrete models produced by spatial analysis. In this domain, space is usually approximated either as a graph or as a *patch model*, which can be defined as a particular kind of graph model where nodes and arcs are arranged according to a regular grid, denoting adjacency of rectangular region ('patches') that represent a discretisation of physical space.

Using the spatio-temporal model checker topochecker and the UPPAAL toolset separately to analyse space and time is not feasible, since in spatio-temporal analysis the spatial and temporal aspects are intertwined. Our current investigation is therefore focussed on integration of the discrete and continuous world in UPPAAL, in order to exploit its powerful continuous time analysis capabilities, especially its ODE modelling tools, and its statistical model-checking algorithms. Our basic idea is to define and implement a fully automated program, meant to receive as inputs a statistical spatio-temporal logic formula ϕ and an UPPAAL temporal model exhibiting spatial behaviour (e.g. the model we present in this paper, enriched with information about the position and speed of a train at each state, on a railroad map). The program is intended to produce as output a new model, enriched with UPPAAL functions, a set of *observers*—namely, additional parallel processes that do not affect the functionality of the existing ones—and an UPPAAL formula ϕ' predicating on the observers. Statistical model checking of ϕ' is intended to yield the requested result, namely the probability or truth value of ϕ (cf. Fig. 4).

Although we are mostly reporting on work in progress, we can already comment on two possible strategies to address the above challenge. In one approach, the primitives of a spatial-logical language can be encoded as UPPAAL functions

---

[3] cf. https://github.com/vincenzoml/topochecker and http://topochecker.isti.cnr.it.

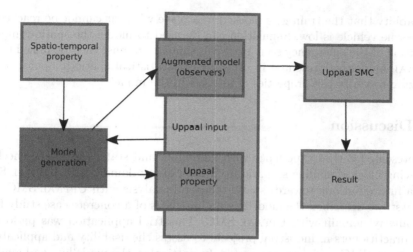

Fig. 4. Envisaged system architecture for spatio-temporal analysis with UPPAAL

and the spatial structure can be represented as a graph directly, using variables of the model checker and a function to identify the neighbourhood relation between points. In this way, spatial properties are used in UPPAAL formulae directly, as if they were atomic properties of temporal states. Such an approach has the advantage of simplicity. However, it requires the reimplementation of a spatial model-checking algorithm (akin to the one used in `topochecker`) in UPPAAL. Moreover, efficiency of such a procedure, and the computational feasibility of this approach with large spatial structures, remains to be demonstrated. Furthermore, this approach is intrinsically limited, as it would be impossible to nest temporal formulae inside spatial connectives.

For the above reasons, an apparently more interesting possibility is to encode space as an UPPAAL process, acting as a primary observer, so that spatial properties (e.g. reachability in space) can be checked by the algorithms of UPPAAL. Continuous clock variables can be used to represent movement in space, with each clock corresponding to a spatial dimension, and ODEs can be tied to spatio-temporal features of UPPAAL processes (position, speed, acceleration) in order to realise complex spatio-temporal analyses. However, this approach requires more work on the side of designing a suitable spatial language, and on defining appropriate observers that permit to represent nested spatio-temporal formulae that need to be encoded in the logical language used by UPPAAL.

We intend to test both approaches in the near future. Possible application scenarios are, e.g., those of *emergency egress* for train control systems. Consider, e.g., the situation in which, by some exceptional event, a train needs to be blocked and passengers ought to be rescued by a wheeled vehicle. This may, or may not, be possible, due to the situation of roads in the emergency situation, and centralised control is expected to instruct the train to stop in an appropriate place. A spatio-temporal property of interest is therefore to check whether the probability that the train gets blocked in a place where it cannot be reached by the rescue vehicle is low. Simulation can be used to model the spatio-temporal evolution of the emergency scenario. Such simulation must then be linked to the UPPAAL model we presented in order to use statistical spatio-temporal model checking to verify the properties of interest in the model.

5 Discussion

We presented a trial experience with modelling and statistical model checking a moving block signalling scenario from the railway domain with UPPAAL SMC and a future outlook towards spatio-temporal analysis with UPPAAL SMC.

First, we described the modelling and analysis of a concrete case study from the railway domain with UPPAAL SMC. This trial application was performed with practitioners in industrial projects to assess the usability and applicability of UPPAAL SMC in the railway sector. In particular, the modelling and analysis experience served to fine-tune their semi-formal model. This has set the stage for a more detailed model, with failure rates and probabilistic delays obtained from other project partners, which is still to be further formalised and analysed.

According to UPPAAL SMC's case study page[4], most of the work on applying UPPAAL SMC concerns the modelling and analysis of communication protocols and scheduling problems. There is another simplistic case study from the railway domain, but—rather than a next generation signalling system based on satellite-based positioning and moving block distancing—it considers a more classical railway control problem: "n trains wanting to cross a single track bridge which may be accessed by just one train at a time". Basically, the so-called *train gate case study* extends the original UPPAAL model of [14] with arrival rates. Plain UPPAAL was used in [41] to model and analyse the MA messages issued by the RBC in an ERTMS/ETCS Level 2 scenario of two trains. In the formal methods community at large, we witness a growing number of attempts at modelling stochastic or hybrid models of advanced ERTMS/ETCS Level 3 scenarios, generally applying 'real', i.e. not statistical, model checking [3,4,27,38–40,46,49].

We used our previous experiences with applying statistical model checking, and UPPAAL SMC in particular, to case studies belonging to the transport domain [10,13,24]. Notably, in [10] we studied the reliability of systems of rail road switch heaters and their energy consumption, with the aim of comparing and tuning different policies of energy consumption [8]. This case study featured continuous physical aspects (heating equations modelled as an ODE) as well as discrete aspects (a communication protocol between the central control unit and the heating devices) and stochastic aspects (failure of a component and weather profiles). Stochastic hybrid automata and UPPAAL SMC proved suitable to model and analyse this particular case study. Previously, in [7], we modelled the system through Stochastic Activity Networks and analysed it with the Möbius tool [25]. Starting from these two different formalisations, we then

---

[4] http://people.cs.aau.dk/~adavid/smc/cases.html.

presented a technique to refine an automata-based discrete representation into a stochastic Petri net model to preserve safety through refinement in [9].

Finally, in this paper we also reported on a preliminary investigation of what we consider to be a promising new direction for the application of formal methods and analysis in the railway domain, and in the transport sector in general. Namely, we envision spatio-temporal analysis with UPPAAL SMC by exploiting its powerful continuous time analysis capabilities, especially its ODE modelling tools, and its statistical model-checking algorithms in combination with the, typically discrete, models produced by spatial analysis, and the related *spatio-temporal model checking* algorithms. To this aim, we may take inspiration from [43], which proposes a methodology to discover potential safety hazards of transport systems already in the design phase, by verifying that the control software prevents collisions and fulfills certain spatio-temporal properties.

Acknowledgements. This work was partially funded by the Tuscany Region project SISTER and by the ASTRail project, which received funding from the Shift2Rail Joint Undertaking under the European Union's Horizon 2020 research and innovation programme under Grant Agreement No. 777561. The content of this paper reflects only the authors' view, and the Shift2Rail Joint Undertaking is not responsible for any use that may be made of the included information.

We thank our colleagues in the Formal Methods and Tools research group at ISTI-CNR, and the partners in these projects, for discussions on the models analysed in this paper.

References

1. Agha, G., Palmskog, K.: A survey of statistical model checking. ACM Trans. Model. Comput. Simul. **28**(1), 6:1–6:39 (2018). https://doi.org/10.1145/3158668
2. Aiello, M., Pratt-Hartmann, I.E., van Benthem, J.F.A.K.: Handbook of Spatial Logics. Springer, Dordrecht (2007). https://doi.org/10.1007/978-1-4020-5587-4
3. Arcaini, P., Jezek, P., Kofron, J.: Modelling the hybrid ERTMS/ETCS Level 3 case study in Spin. In: Butler, M., Raschke, A., Hoang, T.S., Reichl, K. (eds.) ABZ 2018. LNCS, vol. 10817, pp. 277–291. Springer, Cham (2018). https://doi.org/10.1007/978-3-319-91271-4_19
4. Bartholomeus, M., Luttik, B., Willemse, T.: Modelling and analysing ERTMS hybrid Level 3 with the mCRL2 toolset. In: Howar, F., Barnat, J. (eds.) FMICS 2018. LNCS, vol. 11119, pp. 98–114. Springer, Cham (2018). https://doi.org/10.1007/978-3-030-00244-2_7
5. Bartocci, E., Gol, E.A., Haghighi, I., Belta, C.: A formal methods approach to pattern recognition and synthesis in reaction diffusion networks. IEEE Trans. Control. Netw. Syst. **5**(1), 308–320 (2018). https://doi.org/10.1109/tcns.2016.2609138
6. Basile, D., et al.: On the industrial uptake of formal methods in the railway domain. In: Furia, C.A., Winter, K. (eds.) IFM 2018. LNCS, vol. 11023, pp. 20–29. Springer, Cham (2018). https://doi.org/10.1007/978-3-319-98938-9_2
7. Basile, D., Chiaradonna, S., Di Giandomenico, F., Gnesi, S.: A stochastic model-based approach to analyse reliable energy-saving rail road switch heating systems. J. Rail Transp. Plan. Manag. **6**(2), 163–181 (2016). https://doi.org/10.1016/j.jrtpm.2016.03.003

8. Basile, D., Di Giandomenico, F., Gnesi, S.: Tuning energy consumption strategies in the railway domain: a model-based approach. In: Margaria, T., Steffen, B. (eds.) ISoLA 2016. LNCS, vol. 9953, pp. 315–330. Springer, Cham (2016). https://doi.org/10.1007/978-3-319-47169-3_23

9. Basile, D., Di Giandomenico, F., Gnesi, S.: A refinement approach to analyse critical cyber-physical systems. In: Cerone, A., Roveri, M. (eds.) SEFM 2017. LNCS, vol. 10729, pp. 267–283. Springer, Cham (2018). https://doi.org/10.1007/978-3-319-74781-1_19

10. Basile, D., Di Giandomenico, F., Gnesi, S.: Statistical model checking of an energy-saving cyber-physical system in the railway domain. In: Proceedings of the 32nd Symposium on Applied Computing (SAC 2017), pp. 1356–1363. ACM (2017). https://doi.org/10.1145/3019612.3019824

11. ter Beek, M.H., Fantechi, A., Ferrari, A., Gnesi, S., Scopigno, R.: Formal methods for the railway sector. ERCIM News 112, 44–45 (2018). https://ercim-news.ercim.eu/en112/r-i/formal-methods-for-the-railway-sector

12. ter Beek, M.H., Gnesi, S., Knapp, A.: Formal methods for transport systems. Int. J. Softw. Tools Technol. Transf. 20(3) (2018). https://doi.org/10.1007/s10009-018-0487-4

13. ter Beek, M.H., Legay, A., Lluch Lafuente, A., Vandin, A.: A framework for quantitative modeling and analysis of highly (re)configurable systems. IEEE Trans. Softw. Eng. (2018). https://doi.org/10.1109/TSE.2018.2853726

14. Behrmann, G., et al.: UPPAAL 4.0. In: Proceedings of the 3rd International Conference on the Quantitative Evaluation of SysTems (QEST 2006), pp. 125–126. IEEE (2006). https://doi.org/10.1109/QEST.2006.59

15. Belmonte, G., Ciancia, V., Latella, D., Massink, M.: From collective adaptive systems to human centric computation and back: spatial model checking for medical imaging. In: ter Beek, M.H., Loreti, M. (eds.) Proceedings of the Workshop on FORmal Methods for the Quantitative Evaluation of Collective Adaptive SysTems (FORECAST 2016). Electronic Proceedings in Theoretical Computer Science, vol. 217, pp. 81–92 (2016). https://doi.org/10.4204/EPTCS.217.10

16. Belmonte, G., et al.: A topological method for automatic segmentation of glioblastoma in MR FLAIR for radiotherapy. Magn. Reson. Mater. Phys. Biol. Med. 30(Suppl. 1), 437 (2017). https://doi.org/10.1007/s10334-017-0634-z

17. Bjørner, D.: New results and trends in formal techniques and tools for the development of software for transportation systems – a review. In: Tarnai, G., Schnieder, E. (eds.) Proceedings of the 4th Symposium on Formal Methods for Railway Operation and Control Systems (FORMS 2003). L'Harmattan (2003)

18. Boulanger, J.L. (ed.): Formal Methods Applied to Industrial Complex Systems - Implementation of the B Method. Wiley, Hoboken (2014). https://doi.org/10.1002/9781119002727

19. Bulychev, P., David, A., Larsen, K.G., Legay, A., Li, G., Poulsen, D.B.: Rewrite-based statistical model checking of WMTL. In: Qadeer, S., Tasiran, S. (eds.) RV 2012. LNCS, vol. 7687, pp. 260–275. Springer, Heidelberg (2013). https://doi.org/10.1007/978-3-642-35632-2_25

20. Ciancia, V., Gilmore, S., Grilletti, G., Latella, D., Loreti, M., Massink, M.: Spatio-temporal model checking of vehicular movement in public transport systems. Int. J. Softw. Tools Technol. Transf. 20(3) (2018). https://doi.org/10.1007/s10009-018-0483-8

21. Ciancia, V., Grilletti, G., Latella, D., Loreti, M., Massink, M.: An experimental spatio-temporal model checker. In: Bianculli, D., Calinescu, R., Rumpe, B. (eds.) SEFM 2015. LNCS, vol. 9509, pp. 297–311. Springer, Heidelberg (2015). https://doi.org/10.1007/978-3-662-49224-6_24

22. Ciancia, V., Latella, D., Loreti, M., Massink, M.: Model checking spatial logics for closure spaces. Log. Methods Comput. Sci. **12**(4), 1–51 (2016). https://doi.org/10.2168/LMCS-12(4:2)2016

23. Ciancia, V., Latella, D., Loreti, M., Massink, M.: Spatial logic and spatial model checking for closure spaces. In: Bernardo, M., De Nicola, R., Hillston, J. (eds.) SFM 2016. LNCS, vol. 9700, pp. 156–201. Springer, Cham (2016). https://doi.org/10.1007/978-3-319-34096-8_6

24. Ciancia, V., Latella, D., Massink, M., Paškauskas, R., Vandin, A.: A tool-chain for statistical spatio-temporal model checking of bike sharing systems. In: Margaria, T., Steffen, B. (eds.) ISoLA 2016. LNCS, vol. 9952, pp. 657–673. Springer, Cham (2016). https://doi.org/10.1007/978-3-319-47166-2_46

25. Clark, G., et al.: The Möbius modeling tool. In: Proceedings of the 9th International Workshop on Petri Nets and Performance Models (PNPM 2001), pp. 241–250. IEEE (2001). https://doi.org/10.1109/PNPM.2001.953373

26. Clarke, E.M., Henzinger, T.A., Veith, H., Bloem, R. (eds.): Handbook of Model Checking. Springer, Cham (2018). https://doi.org/10.1007/978-3-319-10575-8

27. Cunha, A., Macedo, N.: Validating the hybrid ERTMS/ETCS Level 3 concept with Electrum. In: Butler, M., Raschke, A., Hoang, T.S., Reichl, K. (eds.) ABZ 2018. LNCS, vol. 10817, pp. 307–321. Springer, Cham (2018). https://doi.org/10.1007/978-3-319-91271-4_21

28. David, A., Larsen, K.G., Legay, A., Mikučionis, M., Poulsen, D.B.: UPPAAL SMC tutorial. Int. J. Softw. Tools Technol. Transf. **17**(4), 397–415 (2015). https://doi.org/10.1007/s10009-014-0361-y

29. Douglass, B.P.: Real-time UML. In: Damm, W., Olderog, E.-R. (eds.) FTRTFT 2002. LNCS, vol. 2469, pp. 53–70. Springer, Heidelberg (2002). https://doi.org/10.1007/3-540-45739-9_4

30. EEIG ERTMS Users Group: ERTMS/ETCS RAMS Requirements Specification – Chapter 2 - RAM, 30 September 1998. http://www.era.europa.eu/Document-Register/Documents/B1-02s1266-.pdf

31. European Committee for Electrotechnical Standardization: CENELEC EN 50128 – Railway applications - Communication, signalling and processing systems - Software for railway control and protection systems, 1 June 2011. https://standards.globalspec.com/std/1678027/cenelec-en-50128

32. European Committee for Electrotechnical Standardization: CENELEC EN 50126–1 – Railway applications - The specification and demonstration of Reliability, Availability, Maintainability and Safety (RAMS) - Part 1: Generic RAMS process, 1 October 2017. https://standards.globalspec.com/std/10262901/cenelec-en-50126-1

33. European Committee for Electrotechnical Standardization: CENELEC EN 50126–2 – Railway applications - The specification and demonstration of Reliability, Availability, Maintainability and Safety (RAMS) - Part 2: Systems approach to safety, 1 October 2017. https://standards.globalspec.com/std/10262978/cenelec-en-50126-2

34. Fantechi, A.: Twenty-five years of formal methods and railways: what next? In: Counsell, S., Núñez, M. (eds.) SEFM 2013. LNCS, vol. 8368, pp. 167–183. Springer, Cham (2014). https://doi.org/10.1007/978-3-319-05032-4_13

35. Fantechi, A., Ferrari, A., Gnesi, S.: Formal methods and safety certification: challenges in the railways domain. In: Margaria, T., Steffen, B. (eds.) ISoLA 2016.

LNCS, vol. 9953, pp. 261–265. Springer, Cham (2016). https://doi.org/10.1007/978-3-319-47169-3_18

36. Fantechi, A., Fokkink, W., Morzenti, A.: Some trends in formal methods applications to railway signaling. In: Gnesi, S., Margaria, T. (eds.) Formal Methods for Industrial Critical Systems: A Survey of Applications, Chap. 4, pp. 61–84. Wiley, Hoboken (2013). https://doi.org/10.1002/9781118459898.ch4

37. Flammini, F. (ed.): Railway Safety, Reliability, and Security: Technologies and Systems Engineering. IGI Global, Hershey (2012). https://doi.org/10.4018/978-1-4666-1643-1

38. Fränzle, M., Hahn, E.M., Hermanns, H., Wolovick, N., Zhang, L.: Measurability and safety verification for stochastic hybrid systems. In: Proceedings of the 14th International Conference on Hybrid Systems: Computation and Control (HSCC 2011), pp. 43–52. ACM (2011). https://doi.org/10.1145/1967701.1967710

39. Ghazel, M.: Formalizing a subset of ERTMS/ETCS specifications for verification purposes. Transp. Res. Part C Emerg. Technol. **42**, 60–75 (2014). https://doi.org/10.1016/j.trc.2014.02.002

40. Ghazel, M.: A control scheme for automatic level crossings under the ERTMS/ETCS Level 2/3 operation. IEEE Trans. Intell. Transp. Syst. **18**(10), 2667–2680 (2017). https://doi.org/10.1109/TITS.2017.2657695

41. Ghosh, S., Dasgupta, P., Mandal, C., Katiyar, A.: Formal verification of movement authorities in automatic train control systems. In: Proceedings of the 5th International Conference on Railway Engineering (ICRE 2016), pp. 1–8. IET (2016). https://doi.org/10.1049/cp.2016.0511

42. Grosu, R., Smolka, S.A., Corradini, F., Wasilewska, A., Entcheva, E., Bartocci, E.: Learning and detecting emergent behavior in networks of cardiac myocytes. Commun. ACM **52**(3), 97–105 (2009). https://doi.org/10.1145/1467247.1467271

43. Hordvik, S., Øseth, K., Svendsen, H.H., Blech, J.O., Herrmann, P.: Model-based engineering and spatiotemporal analysis of transport systems. In: Maciaszek, L.A., Filipe, J. (eds.) ENASE 2016. CCIS, vol. 703, pp. 44–65. Springer, Cham (2016). https://doi.org/10.1007/978-3-319-56390-9_3

44. Larsen, K.G., Legay, A.: Statistical model checking past, present, and future. In: Margaria, T., Steffen, B. (eds.) ISoLA 2014. LNCS, vol. 8803, pp. 135–142. Springer, Heidelberg (2014). https://doi.org/10.1007/978-3-662-45231-8_10

45. Legay, A., Delahaye, B., Bensalem, S.: Statistical model checking: an overview. In: Barringer, H., et al. (eds.) RV 2010. LNCS, vol. 6418, pp. 122–135. Springer, Heidelberg (2010). https://doi.org/10.1007/978-3-642-16612-9_11

46. Mammar, A., Frappier, M., Tueno Fotso, S.J., Laleau, R.: An EVENT-B model of the hybrid ERTMS/ETCS Level 3 standard. In: Butler, M., Raschke, A., Hoang, T.S., Reichl, K. (eds.) ABZ 2018. LNCS, vol. 10817, pp. 353–366. Springer, Cham (2018). https://doi.org/10.1007/978-3-319-91271-4_24

47. Mazzanti, F., Ferrari, A.: Ten diverse formal models for a CBTC automatic train supervision system. In: Gallagher, J.P., van Glabbeek, R., Serwe, W. (eds.) Proceedings of the 3rd Workshop on Models for Formal Analysis of Real Systems and the 6th International Workshop on Verification and Program Transformation (MARS/VPT 2018). Electronic Proceedings in Theoretical Computer Science, vol. 268, pp. 104–149 (2018). https://doi.org/10.4204/EPTCS.268.4

48. Mazzanti, F., Ferrari, A., Spagnolo, G.O.: Towards formal methods diversity in railways: an experience report with seven frameworks. Int. J. Softw. Tools Technol. Transf. **20**(3) (2018). https://doi.org/10.1007/s10009-018-0488-3

49. Nardone, R., et al.: Modeling railway control systems in Promela. In: Artho, C., Ölveczky, P.C. (eds.) FTSCS 2015. CCIS, vol. 596, pp. 121–136. Springer, Cham (2016). https://doi.org/10.1007/978-3-319-29510-7_7
50. Nenzi, L., Bortolussi, L., Ciancia, V., Loreti, M., Massink, M.: Qualitative and quantitative monitoring of spatio-temporal properties. In: Bartocci, E., Majumdar, R. (eds.) RV 2015. LNCS, vol. 9333, pp. 21–37. Springer, Cham (2015). https://doi.org/10.1007/978-3-319-23820-3_2
51. Rispoli, F., Castorina, M., Neri, A., Filip, A., Di Mambro, G., Senesi, F.: Recent progress in application of GNSS and advanced communications for railway signaling. In: Proceedings of the 23rd International Conference Radioelektronika (RADIOELEKTRONIKA 2013), pp. 13–22. IEEE (2013). https://doi.org/10.1109/RadioElek.2013.6530882
52. Selic, B.: The real-time UML standard: definition and application. In: Proceedings of the Design, Automation and Test in Europe Conference and Exhibition (DATE 2002), pp. 770–772 (2002). https://doi.org/10.1109/DATE.2002.998385
53. Shift2Rail Joint Undertaking: Multi-Annual Action Plan, 26 November 2015. http://ec.europa.eu/research/participants/data/ref/h2020/other/wp/jtis/h2020-maap-shift2rail_en.pdf
54. UNISIG: FIS for the RBC/RBC handover, version 3.1.0, 15 June 2016. http://www.era.europa.eu/Document-Register/Pages/set-2-FIS-for-the-RBC-RBC-handover.aspx

Mitigating Security Risks Through Attack Strategies Exploration

Braham Lotfi Mediouni[1]([✉]), Ayoub Nouri[1], Marius Bozga[1], Axel Legay[2],
and Saddek Bensalem[1]

[1] University Grenoble Alpes, CNRS, Grenoble INP (Institute of Engineering
University Grenoble Alpes), VERIMAG, 38000 Grenoble, France
braham-lotfi.mediouni@univ-grenoble-alpes.fr
[2] Inria, Rennes, France

Abstract. Security assessment of organization's information systems is
becoming increasingly complex due to their growing sizes and underlying
architectures, e.g., cloud. Analyzing potential attacks is a pragmatic approach that provides insightful information to achieve this purpose. In this
work, we propose to synthesize defense configurations to counter sophisticated attack strategies minimizing resource usage while ensuring a high
probability of success. For this, we combine Statistical Model Checking
techniques with Genetic Algorithms. Experiments performed on real-
life case studies show substantial improvements compared to existing
techniques.

1 Introduction

Modern organizations strongly rely on information and communication technologies in their daily activities. This reliance raises serious questions about the
security threats that may be occasioned because of their inherent vulnerabilities and the way to mitigate the risks accompanying them. The damages that
a cyberattack exploiting such vulnerabilities might cause, e.g. [7], highlight the
urgent need for organizations to integrate risk assessment activities as part of
their main processes. Risk assessment consists of analyzing and evaluating systems vulnerabilities in order to design reliable security policies.

Cyberattacks usually combine various techniques that exploit different vulnerabilities to circumvent deployed defense configurations. Such combinations
are generally referred to as *Attack Strategies*. Reasoning at this level turns out
to be more suitable than trying to fix individual vulnerabilities, especially since
these are difficult to detect. *Offensive security* aims at identifying reliable defense
configurations for a system by exploring attacks exploiting its vulnerabilities.

All is about resources. Both attack and defense actions require resources in order
to be achieved. For instance attack actions require equipment and take time to
be set up. Accordingly, they have some probability of success, i.e. actions that
require a limited amount of resources generally have lower probability of success

T. Margaria and B. Steffen (Eds.): ISoLA 2018, LNCS 11245, pp. 392–413, 2018.
https://doi.org/10.1007/978-3-030-03421-4_25

and conversely. Similarly, defense actions are subject to budgetary considerations (equipment, tools, training, etc.) and do generally provide overlapping protection mechanisms, hence they are not required to be deployed simultaneously. Therefore, it is primordial for organizations to be able to quantitatively analyze and evaluate potential defense actions in order to design configurations that prevent cyberattacks while involving a sufficient set of defense mechanisms.

Diverse attacker profiles can be observed in practice with regard to resources utilization. Some would settle for attack actions requiring limited resources, accepting a low probability of success, while others would privilege actions with high probability of success and allocate resources for that. These profiles are generally the product of various human factors such as experience, budget and motivations. A sophisticated attack strategy would try to optimize these criteria, namely, to find trade-offs requiring an affordable (within a given budget) amount of resources with an acceptable probability of success.

In this work, we propose a risk assessment approach that allows to synthesize defense configurations making sophisticated attacks harder to achieve. Concretely, we consider resources (e.g., the cost) required by an attack to be the hardness criterion. The rational is that since a sophisticated attack tries to optimize the cost with respect to the probability of success, defense actions that increase this cost are expected to prevent those attack strategies from being achieved with high probability. Relevant defense configurations are hence those involving a sufficient set of defenses with the highest impact on the attack cost.

As opposed to [5] that relies on reinforcement learning, our approach combines Statistical Model Checking (SMC) [6,13] with Genetic Algorithms (GA) [10] to synthesize sophisticated attack strategies, which serve as a basis for exploring relevant defense configurations. The proposed approach considers Attack-Defense Tree [8] as a representation of the organization's security breaches, the potential attacks that could exploit them and the deployed defense configuration. Furthermore, the approach takes into account an attacker model that simulates arbitrary attack actions targetting the systems.

The remainder of the paper is organized as follows. We first discuss related work in Sect. 2. In Sect. 3, we formally introduce the considered models for risk assessment. The proposed techniques for attack strategies exploration and for the synthesis of an impactful defense configuration are respectively presented in Sects. 4 and 5. In Sect. 6, we evaluate the proposed methods on four case studies. Finally, Sect. 7 concludes the paper and discusses future directions.

2   Related Work

Attack Trees (AT) [9] are widely used in security to model system vulnerabilities and the different combinations of threats to address a malicious goal. Attack-Defense Trees (ADT) [8] extend ATs with defense measures, also known as countermeasures, to include the organizations defenses and bring into consideration the impact of attacks on these organizations. These defense actions try to prevent an attacker from reaching its final goal. More recently, Attack-Countermeasure Trees (ACT) [11] were introduced to model defense mechanisms that are dynamically triggered upon attack detection.

Different types of analysis are proposed on these variants of trees. In [4] authors focus on the probabilistic analysis of ATs, through the computation of the probability, cost, risk and impact of an attack. A similar analysis is performed on ADTs in [12], called Threat Risk Analysis (TRA), and applied to the security assessment of cloud systems. In addition to the aforementioned probabilistic analysis, Roy et al. [11] make use of the structural and Birnbaum importance measure to prioritize attack events and countermeasures in ACTs.

Authors of [5] propose a reinforcement learning method on ADTs to find a near-optimal attack strategy. In this work, an attacker with a complex probabilistic and timed behavior is considered which makes it more difficult to perform a static analysis. The authors propose to address the security analysis problem from the attacker's viewpoint by synthesizing the stochastic and timed strategy that minimizes the attack cost using UPPAAL STRATEGO tool. The strategy indicates the attack action to perform in each state in order to realize a successful attack with a minimal cost.

In the previous approach, attack actions are also characterized by time duration as intervals. It identifies the sequence of attack actions and associated duration towards satisfying a specified time budget. However, it is not always the case that an attacker can control the duration of an attack action, eg. the time necessary for a brute-force attack. Instead, we consider time as a characteristic of an attack action, i.e., not controlled as it depends on the system, environment, etc. We consider the maximum time bound as a global success condition of an attack, and we propose IEGA, a hybrid Genetic Algorithm to find the stochastic strategy minimizing the attack cost while maximizing the probability of success. This strategy schedules attack actions and tells the attacker which action to perform when a choice is required.

3   Background

In this section, we formally introduce definitions and notations used in the remainder of the paper. We first introduce the models for an attacker and a defender. Then, we recall the definition of an attack-defense tree, and finally, we describe the model used for risk assessment.

For the following definitions, we consider Σ_A to be a set of attack actions, Σ_D is a set of defense actions, and $\Sigma = \Sigma_A \cup \Sigma_D$ the set of all actions. Furthermore, we consider that each attack action $a \in \Sigma_A$ is associated with (1) a time interval $[l_a, u_a]$ that represents lower and upper time bounds allowed to perform a, (2) a cost $c_a \in \mathbb{R}$ which models needed resources to perform a and (3) a probability of success p_a that represents the likelihood for a to succeed when performed. We call environment, denoted env, the success probabilities of attack actions in Σ_A.

3.1   Attacker, Defender and Attack-Defense Tree

Attacker. The attacker model represents all possible attack combinations, given the alphabet of attack actions Σ_A. It is syntactically defined as follows:

Definition 1 (Attacker). *An attacker $\mathcal{A}$ is a tuple $\langle L, l_0, T \rangle$ where:*

- $L = \{l_0, \ldots\}$ *is a set of locations, where l_0 is the initial location,*
- $T \subseteq L \times \Sigma_a \times L$ *is a set of labeled transitions of the form (l_i, a, l_j).*

Intuitively, an attacker $\mathcal{A}$ performs a sequence of attack actions by choosing each time among the enabled ones. At a given state, an attack action a may succeed, leading to a new state where a is no more enabled[1] and where all other actions remain unchanged. In case a fails, the state of the attacker does not change. The success or failure of a selected attack action is not controlled by the attacker, but is determined by the environment *env*. We formally define the behavior of an attacker as follows.

Definition 2 (Attacker semantics). *The semantics of an attacker $\mathcal{A} = \langle L, l_0, T \rangle$ is the labeled transition system $\langle S, s_0, R \rangle$, where:*

- $S = L \times V_{\Sigma_A}$, *where $v \in V_{\Sigma_A}$ is a state vector that contains the status of all the attack actions in Σ_A (succeeded or not), i.e., $V_{\Sigma_A} = \{v : \Sigma_A \longrightarrow \{0,1\}\}$,*
- $s_0 = (l_0, v_0)$ *is the initial state, where $v_0 = [0, \ldots, 0]$ is the initial status of all the attack actions in Σ_A,*
- $R \subseteq S \times \Sigma_A \times S$ *is a set of transitions of the form (s_i, a, s'_i) respecting the following rules:*

  1. *Success:* $\dfrac{(l_i, a, l'_i) \in T, \ v_i(a) = 0, \ v'_i(a) = 1, \ \forall a' \neq a \ v'_i(a') = v_i(a')}{((l_i, v_i), \ a, \ (l'_i, v'_i))}$

  2. *Failure:* $\dfrac{(l_i, a, l'_i) \in T, \ v_i(a) = 0}{((l_i, v_i), \ a, \ (l_i, v_i))}$

We use the notation $status(a, s)$ to denote the status of the attack action a at state $s = (l, v)$, i.e., $status(a, s) = status(a, (l, v)) = v(a)$.

Note that the attacker semantics above is non-deterministic, that is, the choice of an attack action at each state is performed non-deterministically. An attack strategy $\mathcal{S} : \Sigma_A \longrightarrow [0, 1]$ is a mass probability function that associates each attack action with a probability of being selected by the attacker[2]. We denote by $\mathcal{A}|_{\mathcal{S}}$ the attacker $\mathcal{A}$ that applies the strategy $\mathcal{S}$. Thus, the probability $P : S \times \Sigma_A \longrightarrow [0, 1]$ to select an attack action a at any state s_i is defined as

$$P(s_i, a) = \begin{cases} 0 & \text{if } status(a, s_i) = 1 \\ \dfrac{S(a)}{\sum\limits_{a' \in \Sigma_A} S(a') \times (1 - status(a', s_i))} & \text{otherwise} \end{cases}$$

---

[1] This reflects a realistic behavior expressing the monotony of an attack.
[2] In this work, we restrict to static strategies, i.e., the same in any state. Considering dynamic strategies is a future work.

Defender. A defender models the deployed set of defense actions. In this work, it represents a static defense configuration, where a defense action $d \in \Sigma_D$ is either enabled or not in all the states of the system. It is defined as follows:

Definition 3 (Defender). *A defender $\mathcal{D} \subseteq \Sigma_D$ is the subset of enabled defense actions in Σ_D.*

We define a predicate *enabled* $: \Sigma_D \rightarrow \{0, 1\}$ that tells if a defense action is currently enabled. Formally, $enabled(d) = 1$ when $d \in \mathcal{D}$, and 0 otherwise.

Attack-Defense Tree. It represents some knowledge about the system under analysis. For instance, it includes the attack combinations (with respect to the analyzed system vulnerabilities) that may lead to the success of an attack, along defense mechanisms available in the system. In this work, we define it as a Boolean combination of attack and defense actions as follows:

Definition 4 (Attack-Defense Tree). *An attack-defense tree $\mathcal{T}$ is defined by the following inductive grammar:*

$$\phi, \phi_1, \phi_2 :: = true \mid ap \mid \phi_1 \wedge \phi_2 \mid \phi_1 \vee \phi_2 \mid \neg\phi \mid (\phi), \ where \ ap \in \Sigma$$

The evaluation of the attack-defense tree considers the attacker and the defender models. This evaluation is performed as part of the risk analysis procedure based on a Risk Assessment Model introduced below.

3.2   Risk Assessment Model

We now explain how the previous models, namely Attacker, Defender and Attack-Defense Tree are used together to build a complete view for analysis, called *Risk Assessment Model*.

Definition 5 (Risk Assessment Model). *A risk assessment model $\mathcal{M}$ is a composition of:*

- *$\mathcal{A}|_{\mathcal{S}}$ is an attacker following a strategy $\mathcal{S}$,*
- *$env : \Sigma_A \longrightarrow [0, 1]$ is the environment,*
- *$\mathcal{D}$ is a defender,*
- *$\mathcal{T}$ is an attack-defense tree,*
- *$c_{max}, t_{max} \in \mathbb{R}$ are the maximal attacker cost and time resources.*

It allows to simulate attacks represented by an attacker $\mathcal{A}|_{\mathcal{S}}$ – under the constraints c_{max} and t_{max} – on the system (abstracted by the environment *env*) against a fixed defense configuration (modeled by $\mathcal{D}$). The status of an attack is given by the current status of the Attack-Defense Tree $\mathcal{T}$. The evaluation of the status of an attack using the attack-defense tree $\mathcal{T}$ is twofold:

1. the defense configuration $\mathcal{D}$ is used to evaluate the defense part of the tree, (i.e., ap of $\mathcal{T}$ such that $ap \in \Sigma_D$). This phase is done statically since the defense is fixed in our case. For each $ap \in \mathcal{T}$, where ap is a defense action, ap is evaluated to $true$ (respectively $false$) whenever $enabled(ap) = 1$ (respectively $enabled(ap) = 0$).

2. second, the attacker $\mathcal{A}|_S$ is used dynamically to sequentially generate attack actions a_i that may succeed or fail according to the environment vector env. Whenever an attack a_i succeeds, the corresponding atomic proposition in $\mathcal{T}$ is evaluated to $true$. Attack actions in $\mathcal{T}$ are either evaluated to $true$ or not yet.

An execution trace ω of the risk assessment model $\mathcal{M}$ (denoted *attack trace*) is a sequence of timed attack actions (a_i, τ_i), where $\tau_i \in [l_{a_i}, u_{a_i}]$ is the duration of action a_i. We call $\Omega_{\mathcal{M}}$ the set of all attack traces generated by $\mathcal{M}$. Remark that the attacker model is constrained by c_{max} and t_{max} which define a budget of available resources and time to perform a sequence of attack actions. Hence, an attack trace is finite and ends in one of the following scenarios. Let us first introduce the *attack cost* and the *attack duration* as follows. Given a trace $\omega \in \Omega_{\mathcal{M}}$ of length n, the attack cost is $cost(\omega) = \Sigma_{i=1}^{n} c_{a_i}$, where c_{a_i} is the cost associated with action a_i. Similarly, the attack duration is $duration(\omega) = \Sigma_{i=1}^{n} \tau_i$. Thus, an attack trace ends when:

- the attack-defense tree $\mathcal{T}$ is evaluated to $true$ or $false$,
- the attacker has exhausted his resources or time budget, i.e., when $cost(\omega) > c_{max}$ or $duration(\omega) > t_{max}$,
- the attacker cannot select more attack actions based on the strategy $\mathcal{S}$.

It is worth mentioning that the attack-defense tree $\mathcal{T}$ is evaluated to $false$ only when the defense configuration $\mathcal{D}$ prevents all the tree branches from simplifying to $true$. In contrast, the tree evaluates to $true$ when the attacker's goal is fulfilled. The third situation happens when the attacker cannot choose an action according to the strategy $\mathcal{S}$ that could have simplified the attack-defense tree.

Given a trace ω, we interpret it as a successful attack whenever the attack-defense tree is simplified to $true$ in addition to having $cost(\omega)$ and $duration(\omega)$ below the c_{max} and t_{max} respectively, and as a failed attack otherwise.

4   Synthesizing Cost-Effective Attack Strategies

In this section, we present our approach to explore attack strategies. As explained earlier, our goal is to identify the most cost-effective strategy under which an attack is most likely to succeed. Our proposal is based on a hybrid variant of GA and Local Search (LS), called Intensified Elitist Genetic Algorithm (IEGA) that allows to identify a near-optimal attack strategy.

A Genetic Algorithm (GA) is an evolutionary algorithm inspired from natural selection and genetics. It provides an efficient way to explore large solution spaces to select high-quality solutions for optimization and search problems.

An important requirement to achieve an exploration is to be able to quantify solutions in order to establish an order over them. In this work, we rely on SMC to fulfill this goal as explained hereafter.

4.1 Overview

We consider as input a risk assessment model $\mathcal{M}$ composed of an attacker model $\mathcal{A}$, an environment env, a defender model $\mathcal{D}$, an attack-defense tree $\mathcal{T}$ and the constraints t_{max} and c_{max}.

In our approach (IEGA), an individual denoted $\mathcal{I} = \langle \mathcal{S}, cost, p \rangle$ is an attack strategy $\mathcal{S}$ annotated with an expected $cost$ and a probability p of success of an attack when applying it. The $cost$ and the probability p of success for an individual are computed using SMC. More precisely, the probability estimation algorithm (PESTIM) [6] is used to check the risk assessment model against the property $\phi = \lozenge_{t<t_{max}}^{c<c_{max}} \mathcal{T}$. Recall that the precision of PESTIM and its confidence are respectively controlled by the parameters δ and α.

It is worth mentioning that SMC is not only used in a passive way. In some cases, it can lead to update the strategy $\mathcal{S}$ when one or more primordial attack actions were assigned a zero-probability of selection, resulting in a zero-probability of success $(P(\phi) = 0)$. In this case, $\mathcal{S}$ is updated by assigning residual probabilities to actions with a null probability to occur.

$IEGA$ starts by randomly generating N initial strategies (individuals) to constitute the initial population P_0, evolving over M generations, as depicted in Fig. 1. For each generation, $N/2$ new children strategies are generated as follows:

1. **Selection for breeding:** we randomly choose two parent individuals in the current population as candidates for the cross-over operation,
2. **Cross-over operation:** a child individual is built by performing a single-point cross-over,
3. **Intensification with LS:** the resulting individual is intensified using LS, i.e., a heuristic aiming at improving it by exploring its neighbor solutions,
4. **Mutation:** an individual has a p_m probability to be mutated, i.e., altering the selection probability of a randomly chosen attack action.

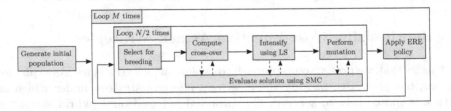

Fig. 1. Workflow of IEGA with a population of N individuals over M generations

The last phase of the outer loop (ERE) in Fig. 1 identifies among parent individuals in population P_i and their $N/2$ children, the ones to keep in the next generation $i + 1$. We use Extreme Ranking Elitism (ERE) [10] as a replacement policy, which aims at selecting the best individuals while keeping some diversity in the population. Concretely, in addition to the best solutions, bad ones are kept to prevent early convergence.

In the next section, we further detail the cross-over, LS and ERE operations. Selection for breeding and mutation are both performed by random sampling in this work, and will therefore not be further detailed.

4.2   IEGA Operations Description

Cross-Over Operation. It consists of building a child $\mathcal{I} = \langle \mathcal{S}, cost, p \rangle$ by combining two randomly selected parents $\mathcal{I}_1 = \langle \mathcal{S}_1, cost_1, p_1 \rangle$ and $\mathcal{I}_2 = \langle \mathcal{S}_2, cost_2, p_2 \rangle$. $\mathcal{I}$ is obtained by performing a single-point cross-over, i.e., inherits the first half of its genes from $\mathcal{I}_1$ and the second half from $\mathcal{I}_2$ as follows:

$$\mathcal{S}[i] = \begin{cases} \mathcal{S}_1[i], & i \leq |\Sigma_A|/2 \\ \mathcal{S}_2[i], & \text{otherwise} \end{cases}$$

Cross-over is followed by a normalization operation to ensure that the obtained strategy $\mathcal{S}$ is a valid mass function, i.e., $\Sigma_i(\mathcal{S}[i]) = 1$.

Intensification with LS. The individuals resulting from the cross-over are intensified, i.e. improved, using a local search (LS) over a set of neighbor solutions.

Individuals are said to be neighbors when their respective strategies are slightly different. More formally, given an individual $\mathcal{I} = \langle \mathcal{S}, cost, p \rangle$, the set of neighbor solutions $V(\mathcal{I}) = \{\mathcal{I}_i = \langle \mathcal{S}_i, cost_i, p_i \rangle\}$ to individual $\mathcal{I}$ is identified by disabling a single attack action a_i, as follows:

- if $\mathcal{S}[i] = 1$ or $\mathcal{S}[i] = 0$ then the ith neighbor individual $\mathcal{I}_i$ does not exist. In the first case, it is because a_i is the only enabled action and disabling it makes $\mathcal{S}$ an invalid mass function. In the second case, a_i is already disabled.
- otherwise, individual $\mathcal{I}_i$ is identified by a strategy $\mathcal{S}_i$ such that:

$$\mathcal{S}_i[j] = \begin{cases} 0, & j = i \\ \frac{\mathcal{S}[j]}{\Sigma_k(\mathcal{S}[k]) - \mathcal{S}[i]}, & \text{otherwise} \end{cases} \tag{1}$$

The normalization in the second case is again to ensure well-formedness of the synthesized strategy (probability mass function). It is worth mentioning that an individual has at most $|\Sigma_A|$ neighbors. Figure 2 illustrates the computation of the neighbors of an individual with a scheduler $\mathcal{S} = [0.3, 0.5, 0.2]$, over 3 attack actions. For example, the first neighbor is obtained by disabling the first attack action in $\mathcal{S}_1$ and then normalizing it.

LS improves the current solution by repeatedly moving to better solutions residing in its neighborhood, until no improvement is possible. A neighbor solution I_i is said to improve the current one I if it has a better fitness value.

The latter is computed using the fitness function $Score$ which is a weighted sum of the $cost$ and the probability of success p. Formally, the fitness function is defined as $Score(cost, p) = a \times p - (1 - a) \times cost$, where $a \in [0, 1]$ represents a linearization factor, used for weighting and scaling the two parameters.

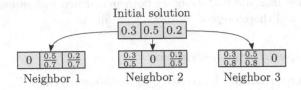

Fig. 2. Illustration of a neighborhood construction

ERE Replacement Policy. A genetic algorithm maintains a population of size N over M generations. The replacement operation rules the survival of individuals through generations. Extreme Ranking Elitist replacement is a balanced solution to provide elitism while avoiding early convergence.

Given a population P_i of N parents and their $N/2$ children, an Extreme Ranking Elitist replacement policy identifies the N candidate individuals for the next generation's population P_{i+1}. This policy is parametrized by p_{ere}, that represents the proportion of the population to be selected by elitism. More precisely, the replacement is performed as follows:

1. We consider an intermediate population P'_i of size $\frac{3N}{2}$ composed of the N parents and their $N/2$ children. Individuals in this population are ranked based on the Pareto dominance principle, and sorted in an ascending order. In the Pareto dominance principle, a solution I_j is known as dominated by another solution I_k if the latter is better for every criterion, in our case, $cost_j \geq cost_k \wedge p_j \leq p_k$ excluding the case where they are all equal. Considering this definition, the ranking consists of assigning rank 1 to non-dominated solutions of the population. Iteratively, we temporarily remove the non-dominated ones and identify the new non-dominated solutions that we assign the next rank, until all the solutions are ranked.

2. To select the N individuals to be part of generation $(i + 1)$, we compute the number of best (elite) individuals $N_b = N \times p_{ere}$, and the number of worst individuals $N_w = N \times (1 - p_{ere})$ kept for diversification. Population P_{i+1} is computed as:

$$P_{i+1} = \bigcup_{j=1}^{N_b} \{P'_i(j)\} \cup \bigcup_{k=\frac{3N}{2}-N_w+1}^{\frac{3N}{2}} \{P'_i(k)\}$$

where $P'_i(j)$ is the jth individual in population P'_i. Therefore, we select the N_b first (best) individuals and the N_w last (worst) solutions in P'_i.

5 Identifying Impactful Defenses

In this section, we explore defense configurations that make the system harder to attack, in the sense that the best attacker – obtained with IEGA – needs more resources to achieve his attack. More precisely, we aim at identifying the defense actions that have the largest impact on the attack cost.

We propose a heuristic, denoted Impact-Optimal Defense (IO-Def), that evaluates the impact of the defenses on the attack cost. A naive approach to security would be to enable all available defense actions. However, some of them may not significantly increase the attack cost. A more pragmatic approach is to look for a good balance between defenses and their impact on the attack cost. This is particularly important if the organization's defense budget is limited.

The heuristic implicitly builds an exploration tree where the root is the defense configuration with all the actions enabled, i.e., $D_1^1 = \Sigma_D$. The defense D_j^i at the ith level of the tree is obtained by disabling the defense action j that was enabled in its parent node. For example, the third child of D_1^1 is $D_3^2 = D_1^1 \setminus \{d_3\}$. Each defense configuration D_j^i is characterized by the cost C_j^i and the success probability P_j^i of the attack strategy obtained with IEGA. The tree is explored in a breadth-first order. For each level $i > 1$, we identify the defense configuration with the minimal impact on the attack cost, and select it for further exploration in the case its impact is lower than a given threshold ϵ.

The impact g_j^i is a measure that scores a defense D_j^i by computing the relative decrease in the attack cost due to the deactivation of the jth defense. It is defined as $(C_*^{i-1} - C_j^i)\,/\,C_*^{i-1}$, where C_*^{i-1} is the attack cost of the selected parent node. The exploration ends whenever all the impacts of level $i+1$

Data: a set of defense actions Σ_D, a threshold ϵ

Result: the optimal subset $\mathcal{D}$ of enabled defenses

$\mathcal{D} = \Sigma_D$;
Boolean *improved* = true;
Integer i = 1;
while *improved* **do**
  i++;
  improved = false;
  Compute the minimal attack cost C_*^{i-1} againt $\mathcal{D}$ using *IEGA*;
  foreach $d_j \in \mathcal{D}$ **do**
    Compute the minimal attack cost C_j^i against $\mathcal{D} \setminus \{d_j\}$ using *IEGA*;
    Compute the impact $g_j^i = \frac{C_*^{i-1} - C_j^i}{C_*^{i-1}}$;
  end
  Find the defense $d_{min} \in \mathcal{D}$ having the lowest impact g_{min}^i;
  if $g_{min}^i < \epsilon$ **then**
    $\mathcal{D} = \mathcal{D} \setminus \{d_{min}\}$;
    improved = true;
  else
    return $\mathcal{D}$;
  end
end

Algorithm 1. Impact-Optimal Defense heuristic for defense exploration

are greater than or equal ϵ, or no more defenses are available, i.e., $D_1^{i+1} = \emptyset$. Finally, the most impactful defense configuration $\mathcal{D}$ is the one in which no defense can be disabled. Algorithm 1 presents the IO-Def heuristic, that identifies the subset $\mathcal{D}$ of defense actions Σ_D such that the individual impact of each enabled defense is above ϵ.

Figure 3 illustrates the exploration of the best defense configuration given three defense actions $\Sigma_D = \{a, b, c\}$, using IO-Def. In this example, the three defense actions are initially enabled, represented in the root node ($i = 1$). Then we disable one defense action at a time, resulting in three new defense configurations $\{a, b\}$, $\{a, c\}$ and $\{b, c\}$, that constitute level $i = 2$. Their impacts are then computed and compared to identify the smallest value, in this case g_2^2. Since $g_2^2 < \epsilon$, $\{a, c\}$ is selected as the new best defense and the exploration is resumed from it. Again, we disable defenses one by one to generate defense configurations of level $i = 3$, and g_1^3 is identified as the smallest impact value. However, in this case, $g_1^3 \geq \epsilon$, which leads to the end of the exploration. Therefore, $\mathcal{D} = \{a, c\}$ is considered to be the most impactful defense configuration.

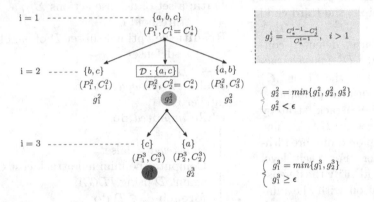

Fig. 3. Illustration of the IO-Def heuristic

In the worst case, Algorithm 1 executes the while loop $n + 1$ times where $n = |\Sigma_D|$. Each iteration computes $m + 1$ attack strategies using IEGA, where $m = |\mathcal{D}|$ (initially $m = n$), and evaluates the impact of defenses. Remark that each iteration decreases m by one (the deactivated defense action). Hence, IEGA is executed, at worst, $\frac{(n+1)(n+2)}{2}$ times. This happens when all the available defenses fail to prevent the identified strategy. Therefore, they are all disabled.

6   Experiments

In this section, we present the experiments performed using IEGA and IO-Def heuristics. We considered case studies addressing security issues at the level of organizations (ORGA, MI), gateway protocols (BGP), and sensor network infrastructures (SCADA). Comparison with the state-of-the-art technique STRATEGO [5] shows that our approach performs better in most of the cases.

6.1   Overview and Experimental Setting

In our experiments, we considered four case studies briefly discussed below[3]:

1. ORGA. In this study, eight cyber and social attack actions can be combined to infiltrate an organization. To prevent such actions, the organization considers different defense actions, namely, train employees for thwart ($t1$) and for tricks ($t2$), threaten to fire them (tf) and authenticate tags (at).
2. Resetting a BGP session. In this case study, an attacker can execute six attack actions to reset a BGP session. The system is protected by three defense actions, i.e. check TCP sequence number by MD5 authentication (au), check trace-route by using randomized sequence numbers (rn), and secure routers with firewall alert (sr).
3. Supervisory Control And Data Acquisition system (SCADA). On these systems, the attacker tries to access some of the thirteen system components and provoke hardware failures in order to disturb the system. The system considers four defense mechanisms: switch the Human-Machine Interface (sw) or restart one of the three system agents ($rst1, rst2, rst3$).
4. A Malicious Insider attack (MI). In this case study, an insider tries to attack an organization system from inside by exploiting seventeen identified vulnerabilities. The system sets up protections by deploying an anti-virus (dva) and a mechanism to track the number of tries on passwords (tpt).

Experimental Approach. For each of the case studies, we performed two kind of experiments. In the first, we manually tried all the possible combinations of available defense actions, synthesized sophisticated attack strategies for them and evaluated their induced costs and probabilities of success. We proceeded as follows: each time, we fixed a defense configuration and applied IEGA in order to synthesize a near-optimal attack strategy. Since IEGA relies on SMC, which is an estimation technique, to synthesize strategies, we performed 25 runs of IEGA each time and measured the expected values and standard deviations of the cost and the probability of success (reported in Table 1). Furthermore, for this first experiment, we compared the results obtained by IEGA with the ones of STRATEGO on the ORGA case study. As stated earlier, our technique synthesizes better attack strategies in terms of cost as reported in Table 2.

The second kind of experiments aims at identifying the most impactful defense configurations against a near-optimal attack strategy obtained in the first experiments. To do so, we rely on the IO-Def heuristic that automatically explores the defense configurations as explained in Sect. 5. The results of this set of experiments are reported in Fig. 5.

For all the experiments, we considered the same budgetary constraints $c_{max} = 50000$ and $t_{max} = 300$ and we set the threshold $\epsilon = 0.05$ for the experiments with IO-Def. We also investigated the performance (exploration time) of the proposed heuristics (IEGA and IO-Def). We observed that IEGA shows a linear growth with respect to the size of Σ_A while IO-Def grows polynomially in the size of Σ_D.

---

[3] Further details are provided in Appendix A.

6.2   Results and Discussion

Manual Exploration of Defenses. We first report in Table 1 the results of IEGA on the BGP, SCADA and MI case studies. In this table, the first column corresponds to the deployed defense configuration, the second and third columns report respectively the average cost $\bar{x}_{cost}$ over 25 runs of IEGA and standard deviation σ_{cost}, the last column shows the average execution time of IEGA. We omit reporting the average probability of success (resp. standard deviation) as it is always 1 (resp. 0)[4]. Note that for each study, we also investigated the setting where no defense action is deployed which allows to see the impact of different defense actions on the attack cost when enabled.

For BGP, we observed that the first three defense configurations lead inevitably to exceed the maximum allowed cost c_{max}. That is, no attack strategy can be synthesized within this budget, whereas in the case of the remaining defense configurations, strategies requiring lower cost can be synthesized.

Moreover, one can see that the cost growth is minor when using *rn* or *au* compared to the case when no defense is used. For SCADA, we notice that the computation of the near-optimal strategy results almost in the same cost for all defense configuration. This can be explained by the existence of a low cost strategy that can always be applied, regardless of the implemented defenses. Furthermore, we observed that the cost induced by using any combination of defense actions does not significantly improve compared to the defenseless case. For MI, we obtained different costs depending on the defenses used. We noticed that defense action *dva* insignificantly increases the attack cost as opposed to *tpt*. The results for the

Table 1. IEGA results with various defense configurations on BGP, SCADA and MI.

Defense	$\bar{x}_{cost}$	σ_{cost}	Runtime (s)
BGP			
au rn sr	50000	0.00	2.65
au sr	50000	0.00	2.54
rn sr	50000	0.00	2.71
au rn	284.31	2.83	3.95
au	285.00	2.38	4.02
sr	428.95	3.60	4.99
rn	284.45	1.97	3.93
None	283.96	1.94	4.09
SCADA			
sw rst1 rst2 rst3	327.71	3.85	40.74
sw rst1 rst2	328.68	3.61	39.49
sw rst1 rst3	328.69	3.00	41.63
sw rst2 rst3	329.20	3.20	42.63
rst1 rst2 rst3	328.57	2.87	42.67
sw rst1	328.09	3.63	39.46
sw rst2	328.48	3.07	38.32
sw rst3	328.29	3.29	39.90
rst1 rst2	327.87	2.91	41.68
rst1 rst3	328.52	4.47	39.43
rst2 rst3	327.78	3.68	39.20
sw	329.03	4.16	38.64
rst1	327.96	3.43	39.29
rst2	326.60	4.38	40.26
rst3	326.95	3.32	42.30
None	330.21	3.11	41.35
MI			
dva tpt	328.83	3.53	49.62
dva	163.04	3.66	48.60
tpt	331.08	3.42	47.84
None	159.85	2.69	49.26

ORGA case study are reported in Table 2 for the sake of comparison with STRATEGO. Except the last two columns, the table presents the same information as

---

[4] Except for the first three cases in BGP where the probability of success is 0.

Table 1. For this study, we observed that varying the enabled defenses significantly affects the minimal attack cost and that the defense action at does not have a great impact on the cost. We actually observed that the attack strategies blocked by this defense action can be also blocked by $t2$.

Detailed results regarding the runtime performance of IEGA are reported in the Table 1 and summarized in Fig. 4. The latter shows a linear evolution of the runtime when increasing the size of Σ_A, i.e., the number of available attack actions. The measures in Fig. 4 correspond respectively to the average runtime on BGP (6 actions, 3.6 s), ORGA (8 actions, 9.9 s), SCADA (13 actions, 40.8 s) and MI (17 actions, 48.8 s). We also observed that IEGA shows a certain stability of the synthesized attack strategy over different runs as testified by the small standard deviation observed in the different experiments.

Finally, we compared the results obtained by IEGA with STRATEGO [5] on the ORGA case study. Comparison results are shown in the last two columns of Table 2 which respectively present the average cost obtained using STRATEGO and the percentage of improvement provided by our approach. This improvement is measured as $\frac{\bar{x}'_{cost} - \bar{x}_{cost}}{\bar{x}'_{cost}}$ where $\bar{x}'_{cost}$ (respectively $\bar{x}_{cost}$) is the minimal cost returned by STRATEGO (respectively IEGA). The obtained results show that our method is able to find attack strategies with lower attack costs than

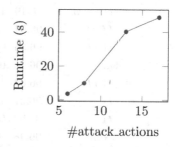

Fig. 4. IEGA runtime variation

STRATEGO within the specified cost budget. In this case study, the improvement induced by our approach –in term of cost reduction– compared to STRATEGO ranged from 3% to 42% depending on the deployed defense configuration.

Automatic Exploration of Defenses. We report in Fig. 5 exploration results using IO-Def for the different case studies. For each of them, we present the identified most impactful defense configuration $\mathcal{D}$ in a separate table showing respectively, the defense actions, their status (on/off), their impact on the attack cost (in percentage) in the context of $\mathcal{D}$ and the IO-Def exploration time.

We recall that identifying a defense action to be impactful or not, is done by comparing its impact to the threshold $\epsilon = 0.05$. We observed that the best defense configuration for ORGA (Fig. 5a) is $\mathcal{D} = \{t1, t2, tf\}$. In this setting, the role played by at was found to be negligible, while the highest impact (+90%) is brought by $t2$. The exploration results for BGP (Fig. 5b) show that the deployment of both rn and sr defenses is mandatory. Both of them have an impact of +99%, i.e., disabling any of them leads to a heavy decrease of the attack cost. In contrast, in the case of SCADA (Fig. 5c), none of the defenses has a significant impact on the attack cost. Basically, this means that the available defenses are

Table 2. IEGA results with various defense configurations on ORGA benchmark.

		IEGA			STRATEGO	Improvement (%)
		$\bar{x}_{cost}$	σ_{cost}	Runtime (s)	$\bar{x}'_{cost}$	
Defenses	t1 t2 tf at	968.08	5.30	9.6	1038.33	7
	t2 tf at	237.97	1.39	10.2	410.52	42
	t1 t2 at	238.37	1.55	10.6	309.35	23
	at t2	237.92	1.27	10.1	359.48	34
	t1 tf t2	967.05	7.90	9.8	1000.90	3
	tf t2	238.18	1.58	10.2	288.53	17
	t1 t2	238.20	1.29	10.2	295.70	19
	t2	238.21	1.59	10.6	298.67	20
	t1 tf at	96.19	1.14	9.4	112.17	14
	tf at	96.04	1.08	9.7	103.37	7
	t1 at	96.35	0.98	9.5	133.60	28
	at	96.15	0.98	9.4	110.00	13
	t1 tf	96.08	1.29	9.8	121.07	21
	tf	96.27	1.14	9.8	105.97	9
	t1	95.99	0.67	9.4	109.33	12
	None	96.48	0.91	10.2	110.57	13

Defense Actions	t1	t2	tf	at
Status	On	On	On	Off
Impact on cost	+75%	+90%	+75%	-
Exploration time	1min 25s			

(a) Results on ORGA

Defense Actions	au	rn	sr
Status	Off	On	On
Impact on cost	-	+99%	+99%
Exploration time	23s		

(b) Results on BGP

Defense Actions	sw	rst1	rst2	rst3
Status	Off	Off	Off	Off
Impact on cost	-	-	-	-
Exploration time	9min 11s			

(c) Results on SCADA

Defense Actions	dva	tpt
Status	Off	On
Impact on cost	-	+50%
Exploration time	4min 7s	

(d) Results on MI

Fig. 5. Results obtained with IO-Def on different case studies

useless against the synthesized cost-effective attack strategy. Figure 5d shows the best defense obtained in the MI case study. In this defense configuration, only *tpt* plays a significant role in increasing the attack cost, with a +50% impact.

Regarding the exploration time of IO-Def, the main observation is that it does not only depend on the size of Σ_D but also on the nature of the system to explore and the IEGA runtime (i.e., the size of Σ_A). In spite of the fact that ORGA and SCADA have the same number of defense actions, they are explored in significantly different amounts of time (respectively 1 min 25 s and 9 min 11 s). This is due to the inefficient available defense actions in the case of SCADA, leading to the worst case exploration time of IO-Def where all the defenses have to be disabled. Moreover, even though MI has the smallest number of defense actions to explore, it is not the fastest. This is explained by the time required for a single run of the IEGA algorithm (48.8s in average) in comparison to the cases of ORGA and BGP (respectively 3.6s and 9.9s in average).

7 Conclusion

In this paper we presented a method for identifying impactful defense actions with respect to sophisticated attack strategies. Our proposal relies on two new heuristics. The first is a bi-objective method to synthesize a cost-effective attacker strategy given a risk assessment model. The second heuristic allows to find the defense configuration with the biggest impact on the attack cost.

It is worth mentioning that the IO-Def heuristic can be adapted for risk assessment from the defense perspective. This can be easily done by extending it to consider a maximal defense budget, which allows to make a more realistic analysis. Other criteria, such as the return on investment (ROI) [11], can be also used to evaluate defense actions. Another investigation would be to synthesize attack strategies for more detailed models, where vulnerabilities and nominal behavior are explicitly described.

A   Case Studies Description

In the following case study descriptions, attack actions are characterized by their lower (LB) and upper (UB) time bounds, the required resources (Cost) and their probability to succeed (Env). In the ADTs, attack actions are represented by ellipses and defense actions by rectangles.

A.1   An Organization System Attack (ORGA) [5]

See (Fig. 6).

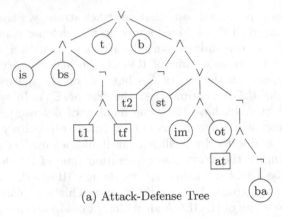

(a) Attack-Defense Tree

Action	LB	UB	Cost	Env
Identify Subject (is)	0	20	80	0.8
Bribe Subject (bs)	0	20	100	0.7
Threaten (t)	0	20	700	0.7
Blackmail (b)	0	20	700	0.7
Send false Tag (st)	0	20	50	0.5
Break Authentication (ba)	0	20	85	0.6
Infiltrate Management (im)	0	20	70	0.5
Order Tag replacement (ot)	0	20	0	0.6

(b) Attack actions characteristics

Defense action	Label
t1	Training for thwart
tf	Threaten to Fire employees
t2	Training for trick
at	Authenticate Tag

(c) Defense actions labels

Fig. 6. ORGA case study description

A.2   Resetting a BGP Session (BGP) [3]

We constructed this case study based on [11], in which detection and mitigation events are attached with success probabilities (resp. P_D and P_M). We transpose these probabilities to the attack actions in a straightforward manner: the probability of an attack action to succeed is computed as the probability that all the implemented countermeasures set to block it, fail. For example, the attack action sa can be blocked by both defense actions au and rn. So, the probability

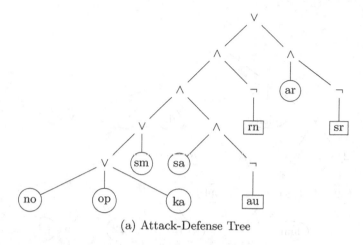

(a) Attack-Defense Tree

Action	LB	UB	Cost	Env
Send RST message to TCP stack (sm)	0	20	50	0.7
Send BGP message: notify (no)	0	20	60	0.7
Send BGP message: open (op)	0	20	70	0.7
Send BGP message: keep alive (ka)	0	20	100	0.7
TCP sequence number attack (sa)	0	20	150	0.42
Alter config. via router (ar)	0	20	190	0.65

(b) Attack actions characteristics

Defense action	Label
au	Check TCP sequence number by MD5 authentication
rn	Check Trace-route by using randomized sequence numbers
sr	Secure routers with firewall alert

(c) Defense actions labels

Fig. 7. Resetting a BGP session description

of sa to succeed equals $Env(sa) = (1 - P_{D1} \times P_{M1}) \times (1 - P_{D2} \times P_{M2})$, where P_{D1}, P_{D2}, P_{M1} and P_{M2} are given in [11]. Note that, in our case, a pair of detection-mitigation events is combined is a single defense action. For example, P_{D1} and P_{M1} are merged into a defense au, and, P_{D2} and P_{M2} into the defense action rn. Also, the defense mechanisms are fixed before starting an analysis and have a probability 1 (Fig. 7).

A.3 Supervisory Control and Data Acquisition System (SCADA) [1]

Similarly to BGP, SCADA is inspired from [11]. This case study represents an example of how attack trees are used to answer the failure assessment problem where attack actions represent the possible hardware/software failures. Since

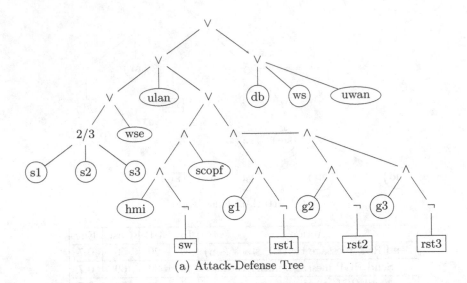

(a) Attack-Defense Tree

Action	LB	UB	Cost	Env
Sensor one (s1)	0	20	100	0.1
Sensor two (s2)	0	20	110	0.1
Sensor three (s3)	0	20	90	0.1
Wrong estimation (wse)	0	20	250	0.25
Unavailable network LAN (ulan)	0	20	275	0.3
Control server one (hmi)	0	20	100	0.15
Control server two (scopf)	0	20	120	0.15
Controlling agent one (g1)	0	20	100	0.09
Controlling agent two (g2)	0	20	30	0.15
Controlling agent three (g3)	0	20	40	0.08
Database (db)	0	20	170	0.5
Unavailable network (uwan)	0	20	160	0.35
Workstation (ws)	0	20	150	0.4

(b) Attack actions characteristics

Defense action	Label
sw	Switch
rst1	Restart agent one if an attack is detected on it
rst2	Restart agent two if an attack is detected on it
rst3	Restart agent three if an attack is detected on it

(c) Defense actions labels

Fig. 8. SCADA system description

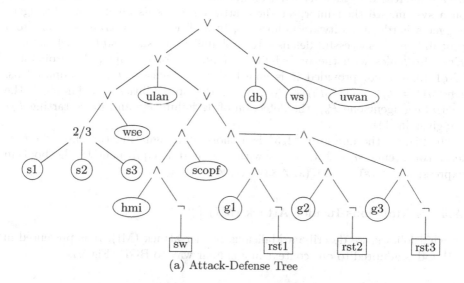

(a) Attack-Defense Tree

Action	LB	UB	Cost	Env
Sensor one (s1)	0	20	100	0.1
Sensor two (s2)	0	20	110	0.1
Sensor three (s3)	0	20	90	0.1
Wrong estimation (wse)	0	20	250	0.25
Unavailable network LAN (ulan)	0	20	275	0.3
Control server one (hmi)	0	20	100	0.15
Control server two (scopf)	0	20	120	0.15
Controlling agent one (g1)	0	20	100	0.09
Controlling agent two (g2)	0	20	30	0.15
Controlling agent three (g3)	0	20	40	0.08
Database (db)	0	20	170	0.5
Unavailable network (uwan)	0	20	160	0.35
Workstation (ws)	0	20	150	0.4

(b) Attack actions characteristics

Defense action	Label
sw	Switch
rst1	Restart agent one if an attack is detected on it
rst2	Restart agent two if an attack is detected on it
rst3	Restart agent three if an attack is detected on it

(c) Defense actions labels

Fig. 9. A Malicious Insider attack (MI) description

we are interested to identify what an attacker can do to reach a malicious goal on a system, we then interpret these attack actions as an attacker trying to trigger a hardware/software failure. So, in addition to the transposition from probabilities of successful defenses to probabilities of successful attack actions, Env also scales with the probability of failures. For example, the probability of $g1$ to succeed, provided it is guarded by a defense $rst1$, is computed as: $Env(g1) = P_{g1} \times (1 - P_D \times P_M)$, where the probabilities of a failure of the controlling agent one P_{g1}, the detection of its failure P_D and its restarting P_M are given in [11].

In Fig. 8a, the operator "2/3" is a shortcut designating the case where at least two events s_i and s_j occur, with $i \neq j$. It is equivalent to the boolean expression $\phi = (s1 \wedge s2) \vee (s1 \wedge s3) \vee (s2 \wedge s3)$.

A.4   A Malicious Insider Attack (MI) [2]

In what follows, we describe a Malicious Insider attack (MI). It is presented in [11] and is adapted to our context in a similar way to BGP (Fig. 9).

References

1. Baker, G.H., Berg, A.: Supervisory control and data acquisition (SCADA) systems. Crit. Infrastruct. Prot. Rep. **1**(6), 5–6 (2002)
2. Butts, J.W., Mills, R.F., Baldwin, R.O.: Developing an insider threat model using functional decomposition. In: Gorodetsky, V., Kotenko, I., Skormin, V. (eds.) MMM-ACNS 2005. LNCS, vol. 3685, pp. 412–417. Springer, Heidelberg (2005). https://doi.org/10.1007/11560326_32
3. Convery, S., Cook, D., Franz, M.: An Attack Tree for the Border Gateway Protocol. Cisco Internet Draft (2002)
4. Edge, K.S., Dalton, G.C., Raines, R.A., Mills, R.F.: Using attack and protection trees to analyze threats and defenses to homeland security. In: Military Communications Conference, MILCOM 2006, pp. 1–7. IEEE (2006)
5. Gadyatskaya, O., Hansen, R.R., Larsen, K.G., Legay, A., Olesen, M.C., Poulsen, D.B.: Modelling attack-defense trees using timed automata. In: Fränzle, M., Markey, N. (eds.) FORMATS 2016. LNCS, vol. 9884, pp. 35–50. Springer, Cham (2016). https://doi.org/10.1007/978-3-319-44878-7_3
6. Hérault, T., Lassaigne, R., Magniette, F., Peyronnet, S.: Approximate probabilistic model checking. In: Steffen, B., Levi, G. (eds.) VMCAI 2004. LNCS, vol. 2937, pp. 73–84. Springer, Heidelberg (2004). https://doi.org/10.1007/978-3-540-24622-0_8
7. Sans ICS: Analysis of the cyber attack on the Ukrainian power grid (2016). Accessed 25 Apr 2018
8. Kordy, B., Mauw, S., Radomirović, S., Schweitzer, P.: Foundations of attack–defense trees. In: Degano, P., Etalle, S., Guttman, J. (eds.) FAST 2010. LNCS, vol. 6561, pp. 80–95. Springer, Heidelberg (2011). https://doi.org/10.1007/978-3-642-19751-2_6
9. Mauw, S., Oostdijk, M.: Foundations of attack trees. In: Won, D.H., Kim, S. (eds.) ICISC 2005. LNCS, vol. 3935, pp. 186–198. Springer, Heidelberg (2005). https://doi.org/10.1007/11734727_17

10. Mediouni, B.L., Niar, S., Benmansour, R., Benatchba, K., Koudil, M.: A bi-objective heuristic for heterogeneous MPSoC design space exploration. In: 2015 10th International Design & Test Symposium (IDT), pp. 90–95. IEEE (2015)
11. Roy, A., Kim, D.S., Trivedi, K.S.: Attack countermeasure trees (ACT): towards unifying the constructs of attack and defense trees. Secur. Commun. Netw. **5**(8), 929–943 (2012)
12. Wang, P., Lin, W.-H., Kuo, P.-T., Lin, H.-T., Wang, T.C.: Threat risk analysis for cloud security based on attack-defense trees. In: ICCM, pp. 106–111 (2012)
13. Younes, H.L.S.: Verification and planning for stochastic processes with asynchronous events. Ph.D. thesis, Carnegie Mellon (2005)

Statistical Model Checking of Processor Systems in Various Interrupt Scenarios

Josef Strnadel[(✉)] [iD]

Faculty of Information Technology, Centre of Excellence IT4Innovations,
Brno University of Technology, Bozetechova 2, 612 66 Brno, Czech Republic
strnadel@fit.vutbr.cz
http://www.fit.vutbr.cz/~strnadel

Abstract. Many practical, especially real-time, systems are expected to be predictable under various sources of unpredictability. To cope with the expectation, a system must be modeled and analyzed precisely for various operating conditions. This represents a problem that grows with the dynamics of the system and that must be, typically, solved before the system starts to operate. Due to the general complexity of the problem, this paper focuses just to processor based systems with interruptible executions. Their predictability analysis becomes more difficult especially when interrupts may occur at arbitrary times, suffer from arrival and servicing jitters, are subject to priorities, or may be nested and un/-masked at run-time. Such a behavior of interrupts and executions has stochastic aspects and leads to the explosion of the number of situations to be considered. To cope with such a behavior, we propose a simulation model that relies on a network of stochastic timed automata and involves the above-mentioned behavioral aspects related to interrupts and executions. For a system, modeled by means of the automata, we show that the problem of analyzing its predictability may be efficiently solved by means of the statistical model checking.

Keywords: Cpu · System · Interrupt · Arrival · Servicing
Execution · Priority · Jitter · Nesting · Masking · Late arrival
Tail chaining · Modeling · Stochastic timed automaton · Predictability
Analysis · Statistical model checking

1 Introduction

Predictability plays an important role in terms of applicability of many systems in practice. Especially, this holds for real-time (RT) systems [1]. They must operate both in a functionally correct way and on time, mostly because of their,

This work was supported by The Ministry of Education, Youth and Sports of the Czech Republic from the National Programme of Sustainability (NPU II); project IT4Innovations excellence in science – LQ1602. Next, it was supported by the project Advanced parallel and embedded computer systems – FIT-S-17-3994.

typically, cyber-physical nature. The problem with analyzing predictability lies in the following facts. Firstly, predictability of a system must be analyzed for various operating conditions. Typically, such an analysis is expected to be performed at the very beginning of the system's development cycle. Practically, it must be done "much earlier" before the system starts to operate or even before its prototype exists (e.g., for specified conditions, it must be analyzed well in advance if some property may never be violated or, if some property always holds). Secondly, a designer of a predictable system must face many sources of unpredictability such as environmental changes, disturbances and anomalies, effects of aging and degradation, defects and damages, operator errors, lack of energy, aperiodicity of events, digitization effects, or drift of a digital clock.

Scope of This Paper. As the problem is too complex to be fully resolved (let alone in this article), we have decided to limit the scope of this paper just to digital, processor (CPU) based systems detecting events through interrupts. The main advantage of such a detection is that no CPU time is consumed regarding an event until the corresponding interrupt is triggered. At a glance, interrupts may look like random variables, adverse effects of which can be neither simply analyzed nor mitigated. However, more careful investigation of interrupt-related aspects reveals new solutions to both the analysis and mitigation. In particular, the predictability analysis of RT systems typically builds on the values of parameters such as the best-case execution time (BCET), worst-case execution time (WCET) or worst-case response time (WCRT). Their values are utilized later, e.g., to facilitate the process of analyzing schedulability of a set of RT tasks constrained, by their deadlines etc., in the time domain [2].

Basically, two approaches to analyzing the parameters, such as WCET, of a system exist [3]: the static timing analysis (e.g., analysis of source codes of the system's software) and dynamic timing analysis (being typically performed using a real platform, its credible simulator or emulator [4]). Some papers, such as [5,6] present a credible simulation model of a CPU system (including architectural elements such as pipelines or caches) to analyze WCET competitively to a real platform or its emulator.

In this paper, we have decided to use the latter approach, but to abstract from architectural details and substitute them by a stochastic model. To meet our expectation, the model must be expressive enough to allow a credible predictability analysis of CPU based systems for various sources of unpredictability. At the input of our approach, we suppose that both the computational platform and the software it executes are known and analyzed precisely, along with parameters such as BCET and WCET. This allows us to focus on further sources of unpredictability (particularly, on those related to interrupts) and on quantification of further important parameters (especially, from the schedulability analysis viewpoint), such as CPU load, WCRT, stack utilization, interrupt service and latency times or throughput of produced/serviced interrupt requests.

Structure of This Paper. The rest of this paper is organized as follows. Section 2 introduces phenomena being modeled and analyzed in this paper.

Section 3 presents our model, basic interrupt scenarios, queries for checking predictability parameters and, finally, representative results. Section 4 concludes the paper.

2 Preliminary

In this section, we present principles playing an important role in understanding the problem solved in this paper. First of all (Sect. 2.1), we remind concepts behind managing the control flow of a program and the CPU context. Secondly (Sect. 2.2), we summarize basic mechanisms and overheads associated with detecting events through interrupts in CPU systems. Finally (Sect. 2.3), we discuss effects of processing interrupt requests (IRQs) to the execution of a program.

2.1 CPU Context and Control Flow of a Program

At this point, we assume that a reader is familiar with technical aspects behind CPUs and their programming, memory and exception/interrupt models, mechanisms they use to execute a program etc. Such an assumption allows us to skip the phase of repeating well-known facts and emphasize further aspects, important from the viewpoint of this paper. For the sake of simplicity, the following emphasizing text focuses just to single-CPU systems, processing instructions in a single operating mode, often denoted as the "run" mode. Aspects of multi-CPU systems and of executing a program in further modes such as test, debug/tracing, wait or (deep) sleep are not discussed – we leave it for further work.

First of all, we would like to emphasize that a CPU is a highly sequential circuit, the inner state of which, denoted as the "context" as well, is a function of many events (a change of the value of an external signal, the start of an instruction etc.) and partial/sub states, e.g., contents of a program/data memory, pipeline and CPU registers such as the stack pointer (SP), program counter (PC) or condition code register (CCR). Both the events in a CPU and its inner state have a significant impact to the control flow of a program executed by the CPU. Events may be either synchronous (e.g., a function call) or asynchronous (e.g., an exception) to the control flow.

To guarantee the correctness of the control flow at run-time (i.e., its consistency with a programmer's intention), a program must be written so that events, temporarily allowed to change the intended control flow, are managed in a way allowing to return the control flow back. Practically, such a management is typically divided into two phases. The goal of the first phase is to store the CPU context (at least, the content of PC) before the control flow changes due to an event (such as a function call). The purpose of the second phase is to restore the CPU context back, i.e., to resume the control flow changed by the event (e.g., by placing the return address of the called function into PC). Let it be noted there that the CPU context may differ for various events; for example, if an exception occurs, further registers, such as CCR, must be stored with PC.

The CPU context is typically stored onto the stack; some CPUs, however, store their context (fully or partially) into special registers as well. Independently on a particular technical solution and if needed, we often denote such a storing as "stacking" and restoring as "unstacking" in this paper.

2.2 IRQ Processing Aspects

Now, let us focus on the execution viewpoint. Ideally, a CPU is continuously busy by processing instructions of a program it executes (we denote the program as "main()" or "main", too). Asynchronously to the program control flow, an interrupt request (IRQ) may occur; for an illustration, see Fig. 1a. At the time of its occurrence, however, the IRQ can be masked (if it is maskable), an instruction may subject to processing etc. Until such a situation is over, servicing of the IRQ cannot start, which delays a reaction to the IRQ. After such an obstacle disappears, stacking of the CPU context starts. Typically, it ends by disabling all (maskable) interrupts followed by the arbitration of IRQs that are pending at that moment. The arbitration fetches the vector of the highest-priority pending IRQ and loads it into the CPU's program counter (PC). By the loading, the associated interrupt service routine (ISR), denoted as "(IRQ) handler" too, starts. Typically, an ISR consists of an application specific prologue, the service itself and an application specific epilogue. An ISR completes by unstacking the CPU context, etc.

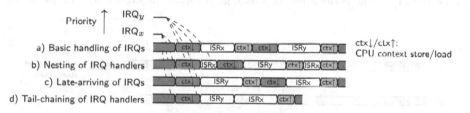

Fig. 1. An illustration to an exception entry, handling and return for ARM® Cortex® and four different interleaving patterns (a, b, c, d) when two IRQs (IRQx, IRQy) are raised consecutively in the order IRQx, IRQy.

If IRQs are unmasked in IRQ handlers, the handlers may nest (embed) in an recurrent way (Fig. 1b). This happens if an IRQ (y), of a sufficiently high priority, pends while an IRQ (x), of lower priority, is being serviced. Then, a handler (ISRx) of the lower-priority IRQ is preempted by a handler (ISRy) of the higher-priority IRQ, where "preempted" means that the execution of the ISRx stops, its CPU context is stacked and then, the execution of the ISRy starts. After the ISRy completes, the CPU context switches back to resume the ISRx, etc. If a higher-priority IRQ (y) occurs after a lower-priority IRQ (x), but during the stacking initiated by the IRQx, the ISRy may start prior to ISRx (Fig. 1c). Such a behavior is possible if the so-called "late-arriving" mechanism is enabled to minimize interrupt response times of higher-priority IRQs.

Further mechanism, denoted as "tail-chaining", may be enabled to minimize the un/stacking overhead regarding IRQ handlers. The mechanism is applicable if a lower-priority IRQ (x) is pending just after a handler of a higher-priority IRQ (y) completes. If it is so, the unstacking after finishing the ISRy and (consequent) stacking before starting the ISRx are not performed. Practically, this mechanism saves the CPU time and minimizes both the interrupt response time and interrupt recovery time of IRQs (Fig. 1d).

2.3   Effects of IRQ Processing to Program Execution

Below, we discuss effects of processing an IRQ to the execution of a program ("main"). For simplicity, we suppose just two unmasked IRQs, the first arriving at t_{IRQ_i} and the second arriving at $t_{IRQ_{i+1}}$, handled by ISR_i and ISR_{i+1}, resp. (see Fig. 2). Because the un/stacking and handling times are typically fixed for an IRQ_i and the given platform (in total, the overhead is $t_{IRQ_i over}$), the CPU spends at most $t_{main_i} = \Delta t_{IRQ_i} - t_{IRQ_i over}$ units of time by executing the program within Δt_{IRQ_i}. In other words, t_{main_i} is proportional to IRQ inter-arrival times (Δt_{IRQ_i}). Ideally, from the program execution viewpoint, it holds $\Delta t_{IRQ_i} \gg t_{IRQ_i over}$ (Fig. 2a). With decreasing Δt_{IRQ_i}, t_{main_i} decreases as well (see Fig. 2b, c), but is nonzero if $\Delta t_{IRQ_i} > t_{IRQ_i over}$. In the worst-case ($\Delta t_{IRQ_i} \leq t_{IRQ_i over}$), no CPU time remains to execute the program, i.e., $t_{main_i} \leq 0$. A system may stop working correctly or collapse suddenly if t_{main_i} drops below an application-specific level. This is typically denoted as the interrupt overload (IOV) effect [7], the seriousness of which grows with the criticality of a program.

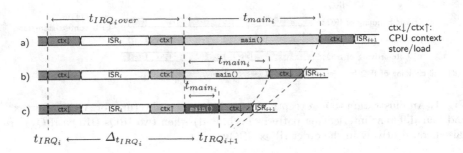

Fig. 2. An illustration to the effect of processing an IRQ to the execution of a program.

2.4   Mitigating Adverse Effects of IRQ-Based Event Detection

Adverse effects, such as IOV, of detecting events through interrupts cannot be always avoided. But, they can be, often efficiently, mitigated to maximize the predictability of a system. Such a mitigation can be done at various levels, depending on the nature of an effect. For example, so-called timing disturbance effects can be efficiently solved in a hardware (e.g., by reconfigurability of IRQ priorities) [7,8] or in a software (e.g., using the common (joint) ISR/task priority space

[9,10] or, resource access protocols [2,12] able to avoid effects such as priority inversion and deadlock). Further effects, implying from the inability of a system to predict IRQ arrival times, can be efficiently mitigated by the so-called event limiters (for an illustration, see Fig. 3). An event limiter [7] is a mechanism constructed to bound the number of event services, i.e. to limit the CPU time consumed for that purpose, within a predefined interval (t_{limit}). Basically, this can be done in four ways (Fig. 3a–d), each characterized by a different approach to detecting an event and to the limiting.

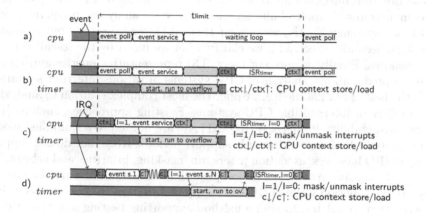

Fig. 3. An illustration to polling based event limiters that measure time by an active, software waiting loop (a) or an on-chip timer (b), resp., and interrupt based event limiters – strict (c), bursty (d); the green slots allow the CPU to execute a useful code. (Color figure online)

The first approach (Fig. 3a) represents a purely software implementation of an event limiter. At the beginning, the limiter detects an event by checking the event flag in a polling loop. If the flag is set, the event service starts. Then, an (well-tuned) active waiting loop starts to disallow checking an event flag before t_{limit} expires. In the second approach (Fig. 3b), the process of measuring time in a loop that wastes the CPU time is replaced by using a timer for that purpose. The timer measures time independently of the CPU and is able to signalize the end of the measurement by issuing an IRQ. This allows the CPU to execute a useful code of a program while the measurement is in a progress. However, using a timer leads to further overheads such as time needed to configure, start or stop the timer, to un/stack the CPU context and to execute the IRQ handler. The approaches from Fig. 3a, b are often denoted as the polling based event limiters. Alternatively, one may use so-called interrupt based limiters (Fig. 3c, d). Such limiters expect that an event is detected by an IRQ. If the IRQ is unmasked etc. (see Sect. 2.2), its handler starts (Fig. 3c, strict limiter). In the handler, further IRQs (except of timer's) are masked, the event is serviced and a timer is configured to generate an IRQ after a predetermined time. In the timer's IRQ handler, IRQs are unmasked again to resume the IRQ based event detection not before t_{limit} expires. The approach from Fig. 3d (bursty limiter, the recent industrial practice [13]) differs in a way it masks IRQs. Rather that (strictly) mask IRQs in each event handler, it masks IRQs in the last from a burst of (N) IRQ handlers. For N = 1, the bursty limiter reduces to the strict one.

3   Our Approach

This section introduces our approach, based on the means of UPPAAL SMC [21], and demonstrates its applicability for the purposes of analyzing predictability of CPU based systems. Firstly, we present (Sect. 3.1) key aspects of our approach (Sect. 3.2). Secondly (Sect. 3.2), we clarify what we mean by the so-called interrupt scenarios. Finally, we present (Sect. 3.3) representative queries and results regarding predictability analysis of CPU systems in various interrupt scenarios.

To the best of our knowledge, we offer the most complex solution to analyzing predictability of interruptible CPU systems. Existing approaches, such as [15], analyze predictability for masked IRQs, [11,16] are limited to a simplified model and an analytical solution – they only support periodic IRQs, but do not support nesting of IRQ handlers, execution jitters, un/masking, priorities and arbitration of IRQs at runtime. Authors of [17] expect that an IRQ occurs not before the so-called hyper-period while in [18], it is supposed that an IRQ occurs each time an instruction completes. In [19], a method supporting nesting and priorities of IRQs is proposed, however, disregarding, unpredictability of IRQ arrival times, un/masking of IRQs at runtime and variability in executing IRQ handlers.

3.1   Proposed Model

Hardware and main(). Our model of hardware consists of three key parts: (Fig. 4a–c): the model of a system (a), of a CPU within the system (b) and of an IRQ controller within the CPU (c) whereas parts b, c have been introduced in [14][1]. In this paper, they are extended (see Fig. 4) by further aspects, such as late arriving, tail chaining, synchronization and measurements by means of stop-watches. To avoid re-publishment of the same ideas, the following text only summarizes main extensions we have made to [14]. For more details about the original models, please consult [14] and the footnote at the bottom of this page.

Simply said, the model of a system (Fig. 4a) generates the reset signal for all CPUs in the system and performs the system-level initialization. Next, the model of a CPU (Fig. 4b) waits until it receives the reset signal. Before it happens all CPU-level stopwatches are forced not to progress (ttotal measures the total time consumed by the corresponding CPU (cpu), tmain measures the time cpu spends by executing main(), tover measures the time cpu spends by managing interrupt limiters and t_e measures the time to dispatch events in a system). Then, it either fetches and processes an instruction of main() or, if an IRQ

---

[1] models are available at http://www.fit.vutbr.cz/~strnadel/publ/2018/dandt/.

pends at the moment, it skips that and moves to `irqPend`. Here it stays while a pending IRQ exists. The control flow of `main()` is given by the `fetch()` function that may reflect a stochastic behavior of `main()` and/or particular aspects of pipelines, caches etc. As a presentation of the aspects is beyond the scope of this paper, please find concepts of their modeling, e.g., in [5]. Consequently, we limit this paper just to the former way of controlling the flow of `main()` in our model. Simply said, we understand instructions of `main()` just as a factor affecting the interrupt latency. Last, the model of an IRQ controller (Fig. 4c) waits until the corresponding CPU is ready to process an IRQ. Then, it either moves to `isrFetch` (to perform the tail-chaining of IRQ handlers, when enabled) or, it captures IRQ flags by calling `captif()` and moves to `exeStop` (to interrupt either `main()` or an IRQ handler, whichever is being executed at the moment). After stacking the CPU context, the model checks (when enabled) if a late arriving IRQ is pending at the moment, masks IRQs for the given CPU and arbitrates pending IRQs. Finally, it fetches the vector of an IRQ handler that has won the arbitration and then, it starts the handler.

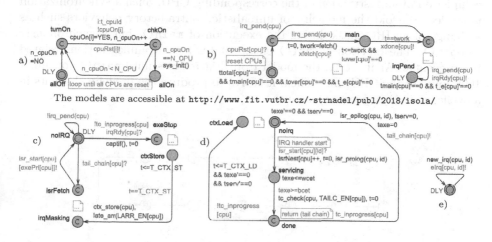

The models are accessible at `http://www.fit.vutbr.cz/~strnadel/publ/2018/isola/`

Fig. 4. Skeletons of revised models: (a) system (the model `Sys`), (b) CPU (`Cpu`), (c) IRQ controller (`irqCtrl`), (d) IRQ handler (`isrSWI`) and (e) IRQ source (`irqRst`).

IRQ Handler and Sources. The basic model of an IRQ handler has been introduced in [14] as well. In this paper, it is extended to cover the tail chaining functionality (see Fig. 4d). Alike in the case of Fig. 4b–c, the following text just summarizes main extensions we have made to [14]. For more details about the original model, please consult [14]. After the servicing completes in the extended model, the function `tc_check()` tests the preconditions for tail-chaining and the model moves to `done`. If the tail-chaining has been activated, the CPU context remains stacked and the corresponding IRQ controller is signaled to start a new (tail-chained) IRQ handler without prior stacking of the CPU context etc. If the tail-chaining has not been activated, the handler completes by unstacking the CPU context and resuming the unstacked execution.

Figure 4e illustrates a simplified skeleton used to model an IRQ source. Basically, the main role of an IRQ source lies in setting the corresponding IRQ flag. In our model, this is done by calling new_irq(). Dynamics of such a setting may be expressed in many ways depending on the nature (one-shot, periodic, aperiodic, sporadic [14] etc.) of a particular source. In our illustration, an IRQ source sets its IRQ flag in random moments, given by the exponential distribution of probability (with its parameter set to DLY).

Events. To facilitate the modeling and analysis of "non-IRQ" events (e.g., of un/masking of IRQs) being produced synchronously to instructions of main(), we have decided to create a separate automaton per a system/CPU (for a simple example, see Fig. 5). Let us note here that each CPU uses a separate clock (t_e[cpu]) to manage the occurrence times of events. For such a clock, it holds that it progresses during the execution of main(). If needed, it may be reset to express relativity (of the occurrence times) with respect to the time being spent in main(). Moreover, an event is synchronized, by xdone[cpu]?, with the completion of an instruction of the corresponding CPU. Such a synchronization is needed to avoid the modeling of unrealistic/contradictory behaviors such as a change of an IRQ mask during the execution of main(), but asynchronously to main(). The function event(e) encapsulates more complex actions related to an event e. At its start, the model from Fig. 5 waits until main() consumes 1000 units of the CPU time. Then, it starts to produce the predefined events in a cyclic, main() dependent, manner.

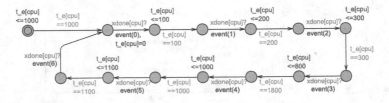

Fig. 5. Illustration to modelling of events in a system/CPU.

Event Limiters. In Fig. 3, we have presented concepts of the so-called event limiters. Below, we present an approach we have utilized to model the limiters. First, let us focus to modeling of a polling based event limiter designed to measure *tlimit* by an active waiting loop (Fig. 6a). It is supposed that the limiter starts at the beginning of main(), so it first waits for entering main(). Then, it stays in sync until an instruction completes. This model expects that the event flag is cyclically checked (in poll) by the first instruction of main(). If the flag is unset, the model moves (via done) to initiate further checking. Otherwise, the model clears both the IRQ request (given by id) and the clock tlim to measure *tlimit*, then moves to service. Here, it loops until the servicing takes BCET to WCET units of the CPU time. Then, the model moves to wait_entry, where it loops actively until *tlimit* is over. Finally, it moves toward starting a new polling instance. Let us note that serv0 and wait0 represent a potential preemption of the servicing/waiting process by an IRQ handler. During such a preemption, neither of the associated clocks progresses because the CPU time is not consumed by the limiter. However, some of the clocks progress in serv1, wait1 to measure the consumption of the CPU time by the limiter.

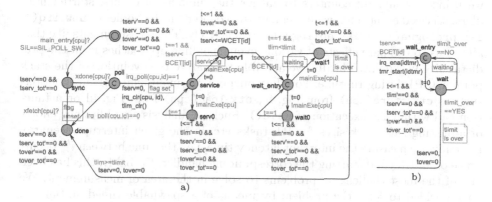

Fig. 6. Models of polling based event limiters that measure *tlimit* time using (a) an active waiting loop (full model), (b) a timer (model cutout).

Figure 6b illustrates a cutout of the model of a polling based event limiter designed to measure *tlimit* by a timer. As this limiter differs from the previous one just in the right part of the figure, nothing but details to that part are presented. Before entering wait_entry, IRQs for the timer are enabled and then, the timer stars to expire after (*tlimit*-tlim) units of time, if greater than zero. Comparing wait1 in Fig. 6a, the CPU time is never consumed while staying in wait in Fig. 6b. The models of the strict and bursty limiters from Fig. 3b, c are absent in Fig. 6 simply because their modeling is trivial. Particularly, it is just necessary to modify the body of isr_prologue(cpu, id) of an IRQ handler to be limited. For the strict limiter, we must modify the body to mask all IRQs (except of timer's) and then, start a timer to unmask the IRQs after it overflows (the unmasking is done in the timer's IRQ handler). For the bursty limiter, we must add further modification, i.e., to increment a counter of events that started within the *tlimit* window and to check if the counter value has reached the burst size (N). If so, we initiate the strict functionality.

Further Aspects. To quantify parameters of predictability, such as WCRT, our models have utilized various instruments that have not been explained yet. The most important ones are discussed in the following text. Firstly, the CPU utilization factor of a *cpu* (U_{cpu}) is quantified as the ratio of tmain[cpu] to ttotal[cpu] (see Fig. 4b). An accurate estimation of that parameter is needed, e.g., to predict the schedulability of (a set of) RT tasks using a schedulability analysis based on the CPU utilization. Secondly, we have utilized the clock `tserv` to measure the CPU time needed to service an event, either in an IRQ (Fig. 4d) or by an event limiter (Fig. 6). Regarding an event limiter, we are interested in further times as well – particularly, in `tserv_tot` (total time needed to service all events detected by the limiter), `tover` (overhead of the limiter per an event) and `tover_tot` (total overhead of the limiter across all detected events). Moreover, we utilize a couple of counters to gather the numbers of events, started handlers, serviced events etc.; we increment the counters in the bodies of `new_irq()`, `isr_prologue()` and `isr_epilogue()`, respectively. The measurements like that allows us to compare effects of various event handling approaches from the predictability viewpoint. Thirdly, we are able to analyze the evolution of the stack pointer (SP) during runtime. For that purpose, we manipulate SP in functions such as `ctx_store(cpu)` from Fig. 4c, `ctx_load(cpu)` from Fig. 4d or a function call within the execution of `main()`. Such an analysis simplifies our efforts of adjusting safe stack sizes for RT tasks etc. in the given interrupt scenario. Fourthly, we measure the interrupt latency time, i.e., the time between i^{th} occurrence of an IRQ and starting the corresponding handler. Probably, this has been one of the most challenging problems to solve in the area of measurement. We have decided to solve the problem by means of a spawnable timed automaton (see Fig. 7). Such an automaton is created dynamically, after an IRQ occurs (the occurrence is detected via the channel `eIrq[cpu][id]`, see Fig. 4d). Then, the automaton measures time (`tilat`) until the corresponding IRQ handler starts (it is signalized via the channel `isr_start[cpu][id]`).

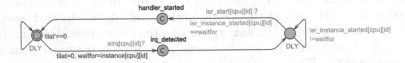

Fig. 7. An illustration to the spawnable automata for measuring the interrupt latency.

3.2 Interrupt Scenarios

We have decided to test and demonstrate applicability of our model from Sect. 3.1 in various interrupt scenarios, details to which follow. The identifier of a scenario is prefixed by "SC". To refer unambiguously to a particular scenario, we have encoded its characteristics into a binary string being situated in the right subscript of "SC". For parts of the string (i.e., base and suffix), see Fig. 8.

The value of a bit within the base part of the string (Fig. 8a) represents a boolean flag that indicates presence (1) or absence (0) of the corresponding feature such as nesting of IRQs or enabling a particular IRQ source. If an event limiter is utilized, then the string is completed with a 2-bit suffix "xy" (Fig. 8b, where xy = 00 for the polling limiter w. an active waiting loop, xy = 01 for the polling limiter w. timer, xy = 10 for the strict limiter and finally, xy = 11 for

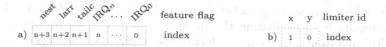

Fig. 8. An illustration to encoding an interrupt scenario: (a) base, (b) suffix.

the bursty limiter. The suffix is separated from the base by a dash ("—"); if needed, the feature flags indexed by n, n+1 may be separated by a dot ("."). If it is necessary to observe impacts of modifying an attribute of a scenario to a system, we prepare a set of modifications for that purpose and identify each of them by Roman numerals in the right superscript of "SC". For an illustration, let us present some representatives of encoding a scenario (for $n=2$): SC_{00001}, $SC_{000.10}$, $SC_{11101-10}$, $SC_{110.11-11}$, $SC_{110.11-11}^{I}$, $SC_{000.10}^{V}$.

During the testing/demonstration, we have utilized four IRQ sources (i.e., $n=3$ in Fig. 8a), referred to as IRQ_0 (non-maskable, highest priority IRQ with arrivals given by the normal distribution of probability), IRQ_1 (maskable, higher-middle priority IRQ with periodical arrivals), IRQ_2 (maskable, lower-middle priority IRQ with periodical arrivals) and IRQ_3 (maskable, lowest priority IRQ with arrivals given by the uniform distribution of probability). For their characteristics, see Fig. 9 please.

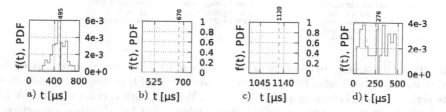

Fig. 9. Characteristics (i.e., probability distribution functions, PDFs) of IRQ sources: (a) IRQ_0, (b) IRQ_1, (c) IRQ_2, (d) IRQ_3. Vertical, dashed red lines do mark mean values. (Color figure online)

3.3 Queries and Results

Due to the limited space, we have restricted this section to just selected representatives of queries and results. For the same reason, we skip herein an introduction to the query language and refer to [20, 21] instead.

Our representative results are summarized in Figs. 10, 11 and 12. They were produced by the toolset UPPAAL SMC [21] based on queries, details to which follow. Figure 10 shows the results of a query in the form `simulate 1 [<= 2500] {exePri, isrNest, ..., cpu(0).main}` being applied to four distinct interrupt scenarios.

Figure 11 presents results of four queries. Firstly, Fig. 11a shows an impact of the IRQ arrival rate to the CPU utilization for various event limiters. The sub-figures (a)–(c) result from a query in the form `E[<= 25000] (max : ...)`. Secondly,

Fig. 11b relies on measuring `tilat` (see Fig. 7) for IRQ_0 and IRQ_3. Thirdly, Fig. 11c results from estimating the maximum of `texe` (see Fig. 4d). Finally, Fig. 11d results from a query in the form $Pr[<= 2500]\{<> \text{isrNest} >= 3\}$. It shows the probability distribution function (PDF) and the mean of time instants when the ISR nesting level exceeds 2.

The last figure (Fig. 12) shows how our approach scales with the number of IRQ sources. We can conclude that it scales about linearly in the time domain and sub-linearly in the space (memory) domain.

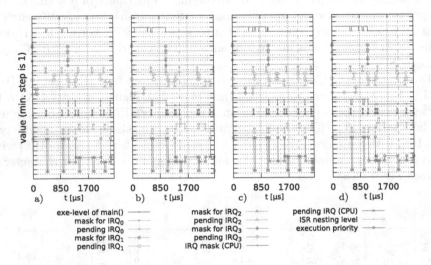

Fig. 10. An illustration to effects of (a) no nesting of IRQ handlers, no late arriving, no tail chaining, (b) nesting of IRQ handlers (c) late arriving (d) nesting of IRQ handlers, late arriving and tail chaining under $SC_{xxx.1111}$. Vertical, dashed violet lines in (b)–(d) do mark the start times of the nesting, late arriving and tail chaining, respectively. (Color figure online)

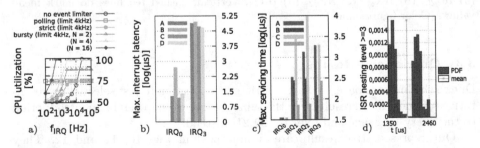

Fig. 11. Representative results of our SMC based predictability analysis. A, B, C and D represent scenarios $SC_{100.1111}$, $SC_{000.1111}$, $SC^{I}_{100.1111}$ and $SC^{II}_{100.1111}$, respectively. The modification I decreases both the mean and deviation of IRQ_0 ten times. Alike, II decreases BCET and WCET of IRQ_1, IRQ_2 ten times. All results, except (d), hold for the 25 ms window.

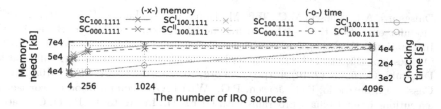

Fig. 12. The scalability of the SMC process as a function of the number of IRQ sources. The modification I decreases both the mean and deviation of IRQ_0 ten times. Alike, II decreases BCET and WCET of IRQ_1, IRQ_2 ten times.

4   Conclusion

This paper presents a simulation model of a processor based system with interruptible executions. To analyze the predictability of such a system, our model copes with adverse phenomena such as processing instructions of a program, arbitrary occurrence times of interrupts, jitters of interrupt occurrence/servicing times, priorities, or nesting and un/masking of interrupts at run-time. Such phenomena have stochastic aspects and lead to the explosion of the number of situations to be considered. In the paper, we show that such an explosion is effectively solvable by means of the statistical model checking. We show that such a checking is able to facilitate the analysis of parameters such as interrupt latency, interrupt servicing time, CPU utilization and to minimize the over/underestimation of their values. In the near future, we plan to move from the single-CPU environment to multi/many-CPU environment and to extend our model to involve the operating system, application and power consumption levels as well.

References

1. Kopetz, H.: Real-Time Systems - Design Principles for Distributed Embedded Applications. Real-Time Systems Series, 376 p. Springer, New York (2011). https://doi.org/10.1007/978-1-4419-8237-7. ISBN 978-1-4419-8236-0
2. Buttazzo, G.: Hard Real-Time Computing Systems: Predictable Scheduling Algorithms and Applications, 376 p. Springer, New York (2011). https://doi.org/10.1007/978-1-4614-0676-1. ISBN 978-1-4614-0675-4
3. Wilhelm, R., et al.: The worst-case execution-time problem - overview of methods and survey of tools. ACM Trans. Embed. Comput. Syst. **7**(3), 36:1–36:53 (2008). https://doi.org/10.1145/1347375.1347389
4. Strnadel, J., Rajnoha, P.: Reflecting RTOS model during WCET timing analysis: MSP430/FreeRTOS case study. Acta Electrotechnica et Informatica **12**(4), 17–29 (2012). https://doi.org/10.2478/v10198-012-0041-3

5. Dalsgaard, A.E., Olesen, M.C., Toft, M., Hansen, R.R., Larsen, K.G.: METAMOC: modular execution time analysis using model checking. In: Lisper, B. (ed.) 10th International Workshop on Worst-Case Execution Time Analysis (WCET 2010). OASIcs, vol. 15, pp. 113–123. Schloss Dagstuhl-Leibniz-Zentrum fuer Informatik, Dagstuhl, Germany (2010). https://doi.org/10.4230/OASIcs.WCET.2010.113

6. Cassez, F., de Aledo, P.G., Jensen, P.G.: WUPPAAL: computation of worst-case execution-time for binary programs with UPPAAL. In: Aceto, L., Bacci, G., Bacci, G., Ingólfsdóttir, A., Legay, A., Mardare, R. (eds.) Models, Algorithms, Logics and Tools. LNCS, vol. 10460, pp. 560–577. Springer, Cham (2017). https://doi.org/10.1007/978-3-319-63121-9_28

7. Regehr, J., Duongsaa, U.: Preventing interrupt overload. In: Proceedings of the ACM SIGPLAN/SIGBED Conference on Languages, Compilers, and Tools For Embedded Systems, New York, United States, pp. 50–58. ACM (2005). https://doi.org/10.1145/1070891.1065918

8. Pellizzoni, R.: Predictable and monitored execution for cots-based real-time embedded systems, Ph.D. thesis, Bonn, Germany. University of Illinois at Urbana-Champaign (2010)

9. Amiri, J.E., Kargahi, M.: A predictable interrupt management policy for real-time operating systems. In: Proceedings of CSI Symposium on Real-Time and Embedded Systems and Technologies (RTEST), pp. 1–8. IEEE (2015). https://doi.org/10.1109/RTEST.2015.7369843

10. Lynx. Lynx Software Technologies Patented Technology Speeds Handling of Hardware Events (2018). http://www.lynx.com/whitepaper/lynx-software-technologies-patented-technology-speeds-handling-of-hardware-events/

11. Leyva-del Foyo, L.E., Mejia-Alvarez, P., de Niz, D.: Integrated task and interrupt management for real-time systems. ACM Trans. Embed. Comput. Syst. **11**(2), 32:1–32:31 (2012). https://doi.org/10.1145/2220336.2220344

12. Cottet, F., Delacroix, J., Kaiser, C., Mammeri, Z.: Scheduling in Real-Time Systems. Wiley, New York (2001). ISBN 978-0-470-84766-4

13. Automotive Open System Architecture GbR (AUTOSAR). Specification of Operating System. Technical report (2018). http://www.autosar.org

14. Strnadel, J.: Predictability analysis of interruptible systems by statistical model checking. IEEE Des. Test **35**(2), 57–63 (2018). https://doi.org/10.1109/MDAT.2017.2766568

15. Chattopadhyay, S., Tresina, M., Narayan, S.: Worst case execution time analysis of automotive software. Procedia Eng. **30**, 983–988 (2012). https://doi.org/10.1016/j.proeng.2012.01.954

16. Kotker, J., Sadigh, D., Seshia, S.A.: Timing analysis of interrupt-driven programs under context bounds. In: Proceedings of Formal Methods in Computer-Aided Design (FMCAD), pp. 81–90 (2012)

17. Kidd, N., Jagannathan, S., Vitek, J.: One stack to run them all. In: van de Pol, J., Weber, M. (eds.) SPIN 2010. LNCS, vol. 6349, pp. 245–261. Springer, Heidelberg (2010). https://doi.org/10.1007/978-3-642-16164-3_18

18. Wu, X., Wen, Y., Chen, L., Dong, W., Wang, J.: Data race detection for interrupt-driven programs via bounded model checking. In: Proceedings of the 2013 IEEE Seventh International Conference on Software Security and Reliability Companion, SERE-C 2013, Washington, DC, USA pp. 204–210. IEEE CS (2013). https://doi.org/10.1109/SERE-C.2013.33

19. Kroening, D., Liang, L., Melham, T., Schrammel, P., Tautschnig, M.: Effective verification of low-level software with nested interrupts. In: Proceedings of the 2015 Design, Automation & Test in Europe Conference & Exhibition, ser. DATE 2015, Jose, CA, USA, pp. 229–234. EDA Consortium (2015). http://dl.acm.org/citation.cfm?id=2755753.2755803
20. Baier, C., Katoen, J.-P.: Principles of Model Checking, ser. Representation and Mind. MIT Press, London (2008). https://mitpress.mit.edu/books/principles-model-checking
21. David, A., Larsen, K.G., Legay, A., Mikucionis, M., Poulsen, D.: UPPAAL SMC tutorial. Int. J. Softw. Tools Technol. Transf. **17**(4), 397–415 (2015). https://doi.org/10.1007/s10009-014-0361-y

RERS 2018

RERS 2018: CTL, LTL, and Reachability

Marc Jasper[✉], Malte Mues, Maximilian Schlüter, Bernhard Steffen,
and Falk Howar

TU Dortmund University, Dortmund, Germany
{marc.jasper,malte.mues,maximilian.schlueter,steffen,
howar}@cs.tu-dortmund.de

Abstract. This paper is dedicated to the Rigorous Examination of Reactive Systems (RERS) Challenge 2018. We focus on changes and improvements compared to previous years. RERS again provided a large variety of verification benchmarks that foster the comparison of validation tools while featuring both sequential and parallel programs. In addition to reachability questions, the RERS Challenge is known for its linear temporal logic (LTL) properties, and RERS'18 extends the portfolio of verification tasks to computational tree logic (CTL). Modifications compared to the previous iteration include an enhanced generation of sequential benchmarks, an improved automation of the construction of parallel benchmarks, a redesigned penalty for wrong answers, and the addition of CTL properties. We illustrate our newly applied generation of parallel benchmarks in detail.

Keywords: Benchmark generation · Program verification
Temporal logics · LTL · CTL · Property-preservation
Modal transition systems · Modal contracts

1 Introduction

The RERS Challenge[1] is an annual international event concerned with the evaluation of program verification and testing tools. In 2018, the 8th installment of RERS once again provided participants with challenging verification tasks that range from reachability queries over linear temporal logic (LTL) [19] model checking tasks to the new addition of computational tree logic (CTL) [4] properties that could be analyzed. As in the two previous iterations, RERS 2018 featured three main tracks: Sequential Reachability, Sequential LTL, and Parallel LTL. This time, a fourth track called Parallel CTL was added as a prototype in order to collect feedback from participants. This new track was therefore not yet part of the regular ranking and achievement structure of RERS.

RERS benchmarks model (reactive) transition systems that strongly resemble PLC controllers, a type of program that is common in industry [5]. Within the Sequential Reachability and Sequential LTL tracks of RERS, benchmark

---

[1] http://www.rers-challenge.org/.

© Springer Nature Switzerland AG 2018
T. Margaria and B. Steffen (Eds.): ISoLA 2018, LNCS 11245, pp. 433–447, 2018.
https://doi.org/10.1007/978-3-030-03421-4_27

programs that need to be analyzed are available as Java and C99 code. Reachability properties are embedded within the source code, whereas LTL properties are specified in an additional text file. For the Parallel LTL and Parallel CTL tracks, the systems that participants need to inspect are provided in three formats: As a Petri net [18], as Promela code [8], and as a parallel composition of labeled transition systems [12,20]. For the Promela version, LTL properties are integrated in the file that describes the model and represented in the corresponding SPIN-syntax. This way, existing tools such as SPIN [8] can be used to analyze these benchmarks without additional transformations. This lowers the entry hurdle for new participants.

A trifold reward structure is used for the RERS Challenge. First of all, each track features one or more achievement categories: Bronze, silver, and gold medals can be earned. A specific medal value is awarded if the corresponding threshold of correctly solved verification tasks is reached, however only if no wrong answers were submitted in that category. Second, RERS features a ranking similar to other competitions. Within this ranking, a participant gets one point for each correct answer, however negative points for wrong answers. Separate rankings exist for each of the three main tracks of RERS'18. Third, RERS features evaluation-based awards for which participants can submit a description of their approach. A jury then reviews these descriptions and rewards outstanding contributions. For more details on the rules and rewards of the RERS Challenge, see [6,9,12].

The main goals of RERS[2] are to:

1. encourage the combination of methods from different (and usually disconnected) research fields for better software verification results,
2. provide a framework for an automated comparison based on differently tailored benchmarks that reveal the strengths and weaknesses of specific approaches, and
3. initiate a discussion about better benchmark generation, reaching out across the usual community barriers to provide benchmarks useful for testing and comparing a wide variety of tools.

Apart from RERS, there exist several other competitions and benchmark suites that evaluate verification or testing approaches [1,2,10,14,16]. The Software Verification Competition (SV-COMP) [2] focuses on programs written in C and the majority of its verification tasks consist of reachability questions. Its benchmarks are hand-selected by a committee and most of them are used again for subsequent challenge iterations. This reuse requires an automatic evaluation and monitoring of participants' tools. SV-COMP therefore features a centralized evaluation approach along with resource constraints where participants submit their tools instead of just their answers to the verification tasks. During the evaluation phase, counterexample traces are also evaluated automatically [3].

Other similar competitions include the Model Checking Contest (MCC) [14] that is concerned with the analysis of Petri nets. Like in SV-COMP, a committee

---

[2] As stated online at http://www.rers-challenge.org/2018/.

selects verification tasks, and the correct solution to provided tasks is not always known to the competition organizers. In such a case, an evaluation is based on a majority voting given the submissions by participants.

In contrast to these competitions, RERS features auto-generated benchmarks that are newly constructed for each iteration of the challenge [23]. This construction is based on formal methods and consists of property-preserving transformations such that the correct solution to verification tasks is known to the challenge organizers, however unknown to participants. The underlying infrastructure to automatically generate benchmarks concerned with program verification is a key feature of RERS that sets it apart from similar events. Moreover, in line with the above-listed goals, RERS is a free-style challenge where participants only need to submit a vector of true/false answers instead of their tools. This type of unmonitored evaluation is only made possible by the fact that the benchmarks of RERS are new each year.

The generator infrastructure of RERS is being improved and extended each year. In 2016, benchmarks that contain parallel programs were newly added to RERS [6]. Within recent years, a new formal framework based on modal contracts was established that allows to generate hard benchmark scenarios which consist of many small parallel components [21,24]. During RERS 2017, this new framework was applied for the first time in order to generate hard benchmarks based on a repeated pattern of modal contracts [12]. The Parallel LTL and Parallel CTL tracks of RERS 2018 build on this concept: Their benchmarks were generated based on randomly selected modal contracts, allowing for a diverse range of communication patterns. This next step in the evolution of our benchmark generation is based on a fully-automatic implementation of the corresponding property-preserving parallel decomposition [24].

Section 2 summarizes the changes and improvements of RERS 2018 compared to its previous iterations. In Sect. 3, the generation of benchmarks for the Parallel LTL and Parallel CTL tracks is explained. Thereafter, Sect. 4 presents a conclusion and an outlook to future developments of the RERS Challenge.

2 Improvements Compared to RERS 2017

As a new addition to the challenge, we introduced an experimental track called Parallel CTL as part of RERS 2018. The goal of this new track was to collect feedback and evaluate if there is demand for benchmarks concerned with CTL model checking. The models were the same as in the Parallel LTL track, and 3 properties (instead of 20 in the Parallel LTL track) could be analyzed by participants per problem. Based on this experimental status, a ranking or achievements were not available in the Parallel CTL track. Section 3 illustrates the generation of the parallel systems that had to be analyzed during RERS 2018. This generation is largely based on the refinement of modal transition systems [15] and therefore preserves considered LTL and CTL properties.

Compared to the previous challenge iteration, the penalty for wrong answers within the ranking evaluation (see Sect. 1) was reduced for RERS 2018. When

RERS started several years ago, this penalty was linear in the number of mistakes. Many participants found such a comparably low penalty to encourage guessing and therefore not ideal for a verification competition. As a result, the penalty for wrong answers was increased to be exponential in the number of mistakes in 2016: If a participant made n mistakes within a certain track, then his or her score was lowered by 2^n. As this severe penalty can lead to very large negative numbers, the penalty was adjusted again for RERS 2018. Given n mistakes in a certain track, the penalty is now n^2.

Since RERS 2017, the generator that is used for our sequential benchmarks has been refactored and hardened. Our long-term goal is a full disclosure of the sequential benchmark generator as an open-source project. Without its input parameters, the benchmark construction process itself must not provide information for solving the generated problems. An open-source generator also opens possibilities for tool developers as they could test their own tools on custom scenarios. Further, we intend to reuse transformation steps used to generate benchmarks from the sequential tracks for the parallel benchmarks. Therefore, we improved the modularity within our generator pipeline.

Some of this refactoring is visible in the generated benchmarks: Variables in the C and Java code for example have new random identifiers. In the past, the chosen names encoded some kind of spatial information unintentionally as names have been picked randomly from a sliding window. They therefore partially exposed the underlying conversion order.

The team from the University of Twente detected a mismatch between the generated reachability solution and the generated sequential system in RERS 2017. For obfuscation reasons, various random choices are required during the conversion described in the past [23]. Due to an incomplete seeding of random values, it was not possible to trace down the problem to a single bug in the generator. The hardening phase of the generator focused on bug fixing in the conversion algorithm and enriching the conversion output with meta data documenting intermediate results. Using seeds for the conversion module allows full reproducibility of a generation run since the refactoring. These countermeasures allow an enhanced debugging experience in the future if this situation should occur ever again.

Another improvement compared to the previous challenge iteration can be found in the generation of parallel benchmarks for RERS 2018. The property-preserving parallel decomposition introduced in [24] has since been implemented as a fully-automatic transformation: Given a so called modal contract which extends a modal transition system [15] with green (always feasible) and red (infeasible) transitions, two modal transition systems are generated that in parallel refine the initial one. For examples, see Sect. 3 and [12,21]. This implementation is planned to be added to the AutomataLib[3], a Java library popular for its use in the LearnLib [11]. Using this new implementation, a well-known input system was expanded fully automatically and in a property-preserving manner, as presented in the following section.

---

[3] https://github.com/LearnLib/automatalib/.

3   Generation of Parallel Benchmarks

This section covers the generation of parallel benchmarks for RERS 2018. Each of these benchmarks contains a parallel composition[4] of labeled transition systems (LTSs) as a model. Each such model is furthermore available as a Petri net and as Promela code. Within the Parallel LTL track of RERS'18, there exist three benchmarks in total: problems 101, 102, and 103. Each of these problems features 20 LTL formulas that participants have to analyze on the given model, more specifically on its expanded parallel composition that considers all parallel interleavings. The number of LTSs as well as their individual size differs among the three benchmarks 101, 102 and 103. For the new experimental Parallel CTL track, three CTL properties could be analyzed for each of the models found in the Parallel LTL track.

All three benchmarks were generated based on the same technique. The generation of each problem starts with an *initial system*: A small parallel composition of LTSs that can be model checked efficiently. Starting with such an initial system, the main generation iteratively applies a sequence of three transformation steps:

1. Randomly define a modal contract I based on some parallel component M.
2. Replace M with two new parallel components that adhere to I.
3. Extend the alphabet of one component.

The generation of each benchmark problem executes these three steps repeatedly while a higher iteration count is used for the harder problems. The parallel component in step 1 is chosen randomly from a pool. This pool is initially filled with the parallel components of the initial system. The modal contract I serves as a tool to decompose the component M into two new ones while preserving all considered temporal properties (step 2). After each iteration, the chosen system is removed from the pool and the two newly generated components are inserted (after step 3).

The alphabet extension of step 3 inserts transitions with new artificial labels in between existing ones and thereby expands the reachable state space of the given parallel system. This alphabet extension can affect the satisfiability of LTL or CTL formulas, for example when the next-time operator is used. We therefore restrict ourselves to a still very expressive subset of temporal properties which are guaranteed to be preserved even under alphabet extensions.

After the desired number of iterations of the above steps is reached, a post-processing takes place until the final benchmark is generated. On the one hand, transitions are randomly yet consistently relabeled in order to obfuscate their meaning. On the other hand, some smaller components are merged by replacing them with their parallel composition. Components that are combined this way are usually chosen from the decompositions of different initial components— intuitively speaking, this step "shuffles" parts of the initial components' behavior

---

[4] Our parallel composition operator will be specified in Definition 1 (Sect. 3.1).

together. This obfuscates the system syntactically and reduces the similarity to the initial system. Semantically, this transformation has no effect.

In the following, Sect. 3.1 explains the initial systems chosen for RERS 2018. Afterwards, Sect. 3.2 presents an example of the modal-contract-based decomposition of steps 1 and 2. Section 3.3 illustrates our alphabet extension before Sect. 3.4 showcases the overall generation of problem 101.

3.1   Initial System

The first step in our generation process is to choose an initial parallel composition of LTSs, the so called *initial system*. Components of this initial composition are then iteratively "split" as mentioned earlier and detailed in Sect. 3.2. For RERS 2018, we chose the well known *dining philosophers problem* as our initial system: Problem 101 is based on three dining philosophers, problem 102 on five, and problem 103 on seven.

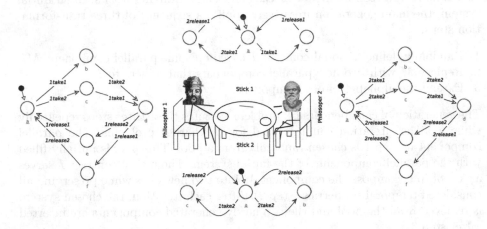

Fig. 1. Two dining philosophers modeled as a parallel composition of LTSs [22].

Figure 1 illustrates how we model the dining philosophers problem as a parallel composition of LTSs. It depicts the LTSs involved in the scenario of two dining philosophers. To give a brief introduction to the dinning philosophers problem: A fixed number of philosophers sit at a table such that everybody has exactly two neighbors. Between two neighbors, exactly one stick can be found on the table. Each philosopher alternates between phases of eating and thinking. A philosopher can only take the sticks located directly next to him or her and needs two of them in order to start eating. Only when finished eating, a philosopher tries to clean and return the two just-used sticks to their original locations. Without additional constraints, the dining philosophers problem contains both deadlocks (every philosopher holds one stick) and resource starvation. To model this scenario, we enumerated both the philosophers and the sticks and then created one parallel component for each of them.

Definition 1 specifies our parallel composition operator based on LTSs. This operator is associative and commutative, implying that the order of parallel LTS components is irrelevant. It is furthermore idempotent, meaning that the duplication of an LTS in the composition has no effect. The reason for this idempotence is that each LTS which features a certain label σ in its alphabet has to synchronize with all others that do so too when triggering transitions labeled with σ.

Definition 1 (Parallel Composition). *Let* $L_1 = (S_1, s_0^1, \Sigma_1, \rightarrow_1)$, $L_2 = (S_2, s_0^2, \Sigma_2, \rightarrow_2)$ *be two labeled transition systems. The **parallel composition***

$$(L_1 \parallel L_2) =_{def} (S_1 \times S_2, (s_0^1, s_0^2), \Sigma_1 \cup \Sigma_2, \rightarrow)$$

is then defined as a commutative and associative operation satisfying the following operational rules with $p, p' \in S_1$ *and* $q, q' \in S_2$:

$$\frac{p \xrightarrow{\sigma}_1 p' \quad q \xrightarrow{\sigma}_2 q'}{(p, q) \xrightarrow{\sigma} (p', q')} \qquad \frac{p \xrightarrow{\sigma}_1 p' \quad \sigma \notin \Sigma_q}{(p, q) \xrightarrow{\sigma} (p', q)}$$

As mentioned earlier, LTL and CTL properties that participants have to analyze on a given benchmark problem need to be analyzed on their expanded parallel composition. We now give some examples of how these properties look like. The following LTL formulas are taken from actual problems of RERS 2018:

$\phi_1 := \mathbf{G}(\text{1release1} \implies \mathbf{X}(\neg\text{1release1} \; \mathbf{W} \; \text{1take1}))$
$\phi_2 := \mathbf{G}(\text{4take5} \implies (\neg\text{5take5} \; \mathbf{W} \; \text{4release5}))$

A philosopher cannot release more sticks than he or she has acquired. An instance of this statement is formalized in property ϕ_1. One can read the formula as follows: It is generally the case that if philosopher 1 releases stick 1, then beginning with the next transition (time step) he will not release the stick again before he took it first or he will never release the stick at all. The second formula ϕ_2 states that if philosopher 4 takes the fifth stick, then philosopher 5 is unable to take this stick until philosopher 4 releases it first. It is also possible that philosopher 5 never takes the fifth stick.

In addition to LTL properties, RERS 2018 featured CTL properties for the first time in the history of the challenge. Regarding property preservation, there is no difference between LTL and CTL in our generation approach as it is based on modal transition systems [15] and the corresponding refinement relation. The following two properties illustrate some CTL formulas of RERS 2018:

$\phi_3 := \mathbf{AG}([\text{1take1}] \; ([\text{2take2}] \; ([\text{3take3}] \; ([\;] \; \text{false}))))$
$\phi_4 := \mathbf{AG}([\text{3take1}] \; (\mathbf{AF}(<\text{3release1}> \; \text{true})))$

Property ϕ_3 states that in every state of the parallel composition, the following holds: If philosopher 1 takes the first stick, then philosopher 2 the second stick, and directly afterwards philosopher 3 the third stick, then a deadlock occurs. A transition label within square brackets means that the remaining sub-formula has to hold in each successor state that is reachable by a transition with that label. No label within those brackets means that all outgoing transitions are constrained. Formula ϕ_3 holds on problem 101 of RERS 2018 as it is based on three dining philosophers. The formula would however be violated by the model of four or more dining philosophers.

Property ϕ_4 requires that whenever the most recent action (state transition) was philosopher 3 taking the first stick, then every possible future eventually ends in or traverses a state from which philosopher 3 can release the first stick. This property does not hold because the system might deadlock in between.

3.2   Contract-Based Decomposition

In order to generate the final benchmarks used for RERS 2018, we expand the initial parallel system of Sect. 3.1. Throughout the generation process, we extend each LTS with modalities and then work on modal transition systems (MTSs) [15]. Intuitively speaking, an MTS extends an LTS with may-only transitions that may or may not be feasible. It therefore allows to express an incomplete component specification. MTSs feature a corresponding refinement relation that preserves temporal properties such as those expressible in LTL or CTL. Our parallel composition operator (Definition 1) can be generalized to MTSs straightforwardly. For more details, see [24].

Each decomposition step is based on a so called *modal contract* [24]. It is the major underlying principle for the modifications of our initial system. Intuitively speaking, a modal contract extends an MTS with green and red transitions: Green transitions express behavior that should always be feasible, whereas red transitions indicate infeasible behavior. A modal contract specifies an automatic parallel decomposition of the MTS that it extends. This decomposition results in two MTSs called context component and system component, respectively. Composed in parallel, context and system refine the MTS that the contract was based on. This guarantees property preservation. For a formal definition and further examples, see [21,24].

Figure 2 shows one modal contract used to generated problem 101 of RERS'18. It extends a component that models one of the sticks. The newly inserted red transition labeled "1take1" extends the system in a way that it might no longer satisfy/violate some LTL properties from problem 101 that it satisfied/violated before. Therefore it should never be triggered, which is expressed by the color red. The infeasibility of this transition also makes sense with the original model in mind: Philosopher 1 cannot take the same stick over and over again without releasing it first.

With the help of this modal contract, two new systems are generated, namely the corresponding context and system components (Fig. 3). Composed in parallel, they behave in the intended way of the contract, meaning red transitions are infeasible while green transitions are feasible. The must transitions of the system component (Fig. 3a) are identical to those of the modal contract (Fig. 2).

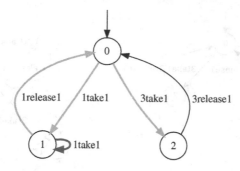

Fig. 2. A modal contract based on the stick between philosophers 1 and 3. Originally existing transitions with labels from {1take1, 1release1, 3take1} are colored green: They must be feasible in order to preserve the semantics of the stick component. The red transition (1 $\xrightarrow{\text{1take1}}$ 1) should never be feasible. (Color figure online)

The dashed transitions come from the red transition labeled "1take1". Overall, the system component barely extends the original model of the stick.

The context component (Fig. 3b) actually implements the guarantees specified by the colors. One can see that all green transitions are represented with must transitions. The infeasibility of the red transition is not as obvious. As seen in Fig. 3c however, the parallel composition of context and system components behaves in this case identically to the original LTS which models one of the sticks.

3.3   Alphabet Extension

After decomposing a component into two parallel ones (Sect. 3.2), namely system and context, we now expand the state space of the corresponding parallel composition. To achieve this, we add new states and new symbols to the context component. This process is therefore called *alphabet extension* (see [24] for a formal introduction).

First, a new component also called alphabet extension is created. For this challenge, such a component consists of just a few states. Figure 4a illustrates an example: Its alphabet is a superset of that of the context component from Fig. 3b. The new alphabet symbol "x9" is choses such that no other component that exists in the parallel composition thus far uses it. Therefore, the transition labeled with "x9" does not require a communication partner to be triggered, which means that it cannot introduce additional deadlocks if composed in parallel with existing components.

When viewing transition labels that occur in the initial system as a visible alphabet, the alphabet extension illustrated in Fig. 4a is furthermore guaranteed to be convergent: It cannot cycle forever following newly added transition labels without giving other components a change to trigger a transition. This is guaranteed by the fact that each loop within Fig. 4a traverses a transition labeled

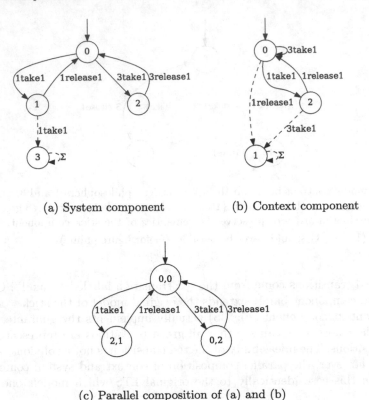

(a) System component   (b) Context component

(c) Parallel composition of (a) and (b)

Fig. 3. The generated system and context components of the modal contract from Fig. 2 and their parallel composition. Solid arrows represent must transitions whereas dashed ones represent may-only transitions. Σ represents the entire alphabet of transition labels that occur within the specific component.

with a symbol from the context component (Fig. 3b). We complete the alphabet extension process by replacing the context (Fig. 3b) by its parallel composition with this extension (Fig. 4b). Semantically, this causes finite sequences of new symbols to occur in traces of our benchmark system, along with new possible interleavings.

3.4   Final Benchmark

We now show how our iterative decomposition that includes alphabet extensions (see earlier parts of Sect. 3) was used to generate problem 101 of RERS 2018. Figure 5 illustrates the involved steps on an abstract level: As opposed to the circles in previous figures which represented nodes in an individual MTS, each square within Fig. 5 stands for one such MTS. Problem 101 is based on three dining philosophers, which is why the generation process starts with six initial

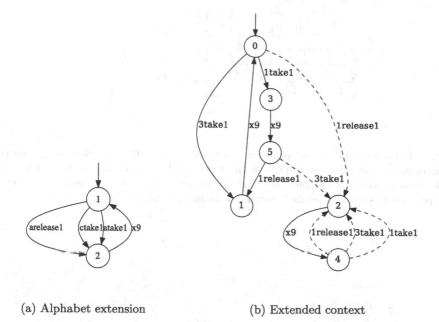

(a) Alphabet extension   (b) Extended context

Fig. 4. Alphabet extension of the component in Fig. 3b and corresponding extended context. The alphabet extension alternates a new symbol "x9" with symbols from the alphabet of the context component in Fig. 3b. The extended context is the parallel composition of context and alphabet extension.

components (similar to the four components in Fig. 1). They are represented by squares in the rectangular box (top row of Fig. 5).

Given these initial components, an iterated parallel decomposition takes place: Each time, a component is split into a system (blue arrow) and context (orange arrow) as presented in Sect. 3.2. The alphabet of the context component is immediately extended as shown in Sect. 3.3. The resulting parallel components of this iterated decomposition are colored gray—they represent the final pool of components after all decompositions have been executed. These gray MTS components were randomly refined to LTSs by discarding may-only transitions or implementing them as must transitions. Afterwards, the resulting LTSs were used to generate the Petri net version of problem 101 (see [12,21] for details on this conversion).

For the final parallel LTSs version of problem 101, some of the gray components were merged: By partially evaluating the parallel composition of gray components in Fig. 5, the original system can be further obfuscated syntactically without altering the semantics of the parallel composition. The final components are represented by squares with an inner octagon. After randomly refining each component to an LTS, the benchmark generation has been completed (except for a random yet consistent transition relabeling). The final parallel LTSs version of problem 101 with original transition labels is illustrated in Fig. 6.

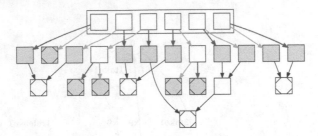

Fig. 5. Generation history of problem 101 from RERS 2018 (see Sect. 3.4). The six squares in the box (top row) represent three philosophers and three sticks (see Fig. 1). Individual parallel components are first decomposed and later merged until a final composition has been generated (squares with inner octagons).

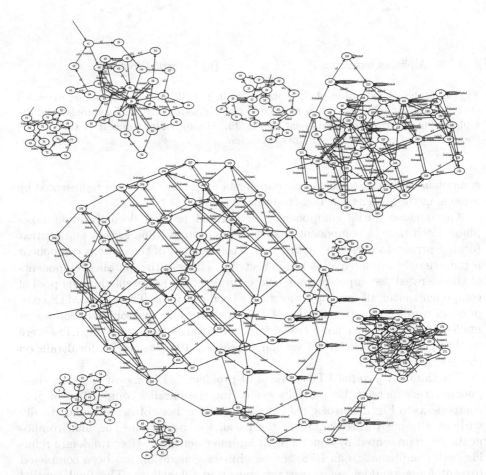

Fig. 6. Problem 101 from RERS 2018 without random relabeling. Except for finite interruptions by symbols x1..x12, the parallel composition of these LTSs is semantically equivalent to that of three dining philosophers (see also Fig. 1).

This version was also translated to Promela code. The initial system of three dining philosophers is no longer apparent, even though regarding the semantics of the corresponding parallel composition, the only difference is that traces are now sometimes finitely interrupted by new artificial transition labels.

4   Conclusion and Outlook

In 2018, the RERS Challenge was once again successful in providing demanding verification benchmarks. As during previous years, an automatic benchmark generation based on formal methods allowed a free-style challenge were participants only need to provide their proposed solution to the given verification tasks. The evolution of RERS has been progressing further: With the addition of an experimental track on CTL properties, RERS explored new areas of automatic benchmark design. The underlying generator infrastructure has been refactored and improved. Furthermore, an efficient implementation of recently conceived formal methods [24] allowed to generate benchmarks with parallel programs of varying communication structure.

For future challenges, we plan to expand our generator infrastructure in order to further automatize the generation of hard parallel benchmarks. A new approach based on multiple LTL synthesis steps has recently been designed that will help to achieve this goal [13]. This new technique furthermore allows to generate benchmarks with hard-to-detect counterexamples for LTL properties. We plan to apply this approach during upcoming iterations of RERS.

Similar to the new Parallel CTL track of RERS'18, we intend to expand RERS with new tracks and target languages for our benchmark generation. One track that is planned has participants check if two parallel programs are bisimulation [17] equivalent. Regarding additional target languages, we intend to investigate a support of C++ with the Message Passing Interface (MPI) [7] for parallel programs. Our long-term goal is to combine existing generator technology for benchmarks with sequential and parallel programs and to provide an open-source tool for benchmark generation. The next iteration of RERS will be part of the TOOLympics[5] at TACAS'19, an event that combines many competitions.

References

1. Bartocci, E., et al.: First international competition on runtime verification: rules, benchmarks, tools, and final results of CRV 2014. STTT, 1–40 (2017). https://doi.org/10.1007/s10009-017-0454-5
2. Beyer, D.: Competition on software verification. In: Flanagan, C., König, B. (eds.) TACAS 2012. LNCS, vol. 7214, pp. 504–524. Springer, Heidelberg (2012). https://doi.org/10.1007/978-3-642-28756-5_38

---

[5] https://tacas.info/toolympics.php.

3. Beyer, D.: Software verification and verifiable witnesses. In: Baier, C., Tinelli, C. (eds.) TACAS 2015. LNCS, vol. 9035, pp. 401–416. Springer, Heidelberg (2015). https://doi.org/10.1007/978-3-662-46681-0_31
4. Clarke, E.M., Emerson, E.A.: Design and synthesis of synchronization skeletons using branching time temporal logic. In: Kozen, D. (ed.) Logic of Programs 1981. LNCS, vol. 131, pp. 52–71. Springer, Heidelberg (1982). https://doi.org/10.1007/BFb0025774
5. Erickson, K.T.: Programmable logic controllers. IEEE Potentials 15(1), 14–17 (1996)
6. Geske, M., Jasper, M., Steffen, B., Howar, F., Schordan, M., van de Pol, J.: RERS 2016: parallel and sequential benchmarks with focus on LTL verification. In: Margaria, T., Steffen, B. (eds.) ISoLA 2016. LNCS, vol. 9953, pp. 787–803. Springer, Cham (2016). https://doi.org/10.1007/978-3-319-47169-3_59
7. Gropp, W.D., Gropp, W., Lusk, E., Skjellum, A.: Using MPI: Portable Parallel Programming with the Message-Passing Interface, vol. 1. MIT Press, Cambridge (1999)
8. Holzmann, G.: The SPIN Model Checker: Primer and Reference Manual, 1st edn. Addison-Wesley Professional, Boston (2011)
9. Howar, F., Isberner, M., Merten, M., Steffen, B., Beyer, D., Păsăreanu, C.: Rigorous examination of reactive systems. The RERS challenges 2012 and 2013. STTT 16(5), 457–464 (2014)
10. Huisman, M., Klebanov, V., Monahan, R.: VerifyThis 2012. STTT 17(6), 647–657 (2015)
11. Isberner, M., Howar, F., Steffen, B.: The open-source LearnLib. In: Kroening, D., Păsăreanu, C.S. (eds.) CAV 2015. LNCS, vol. 9206, pp. 487–495. Springer, Cham (2015). https://doi.org/10.1007/978-3-319-21690-4_32
12. Jasper, M., et al.: The RERS 2017 challenge and workshop (invited paper). In: Proceedings of the 24th ACM SIGSOFT International SPIN Symposium on Model Checking of Software, SPIN 2017, pp. 11–20. ACM (2017)
13. Jasper, M., Steffen, B.: Synthesizing subtle bugs with known witnesses. In: Margaria, T., Steffen, B. (eds.) ISoLA 2018. LNCS, vol. 11245, pp. 235–257. Springer, Cham (2018)
14. Kordon, F.: Report on the model checking contest at Petri nets 2011. In: Jensen, K., van der Aalst, W.M., Ajmone Marsan, M., Franceschinis, G., Kleijn, J., Kristensen, L.M. (eds.) Transactions on Petri Nets and Other Models of Concurrency VI. LNCS, vol. 7400, pp. 169–196. Springer, Heidelberg (2012). https://doi.org/10.1007/978-3-642-35179-2_8
15. Larsen, K.G.: Modal specifications. In: Sifakis, J. (ed.) CAV 1989. LNCS, vol. 407, pp. 232–246. Springer, Heidelberg (1990). https://doi.org/10.1007/3-540-52148-8_19
16. Liao, C., Lin, P.H., Asplund, J., Schordan, M., Karlin, I.: DataRaceBench: a benchmark suite for systematic evaluation of data race detection tools. In: Proceedings of the International Conference for High Performance Computing, Networking, Storage and Analysis, SC 2017, pp. 11:1–11:14. ACM (2017)
17. Park, D.: Concurrency and automata on infinite sequences. In: Deussen, P. (ed.) GI-TCS 1981. LNCS, vol. 104, pp. 167–183. Springer, Heidelberg (1981). https://doi.org/10.1007/BFb0017309
18. Peterson, J.L.: Petri Net Theory and the Modeling of Systems. Prentice Hall PTR, Upper Saddle River (1981)
19. Pnueli, A.: The temporal logic of programs. In: 18th Annual Symposium on Foundations of Computer Science (SFCS 1977), pp. 46–57, October 1977

20. Pnueli, A., Rosner, R.: On the synthesis of a reactive module. In: Proceedings of the 16th ACM SIGPLAN-SIGACT Symposium on Principles of Programming Languages, POPL 1989, pp. 179–190. ACM, New York (1989)
21. Steffen, B., Jasper, M., Meijer, J., van de Pol, J.: Property-preserving generation of tailored benchmark Petri nets. In: 17th International Conference on Application of Concurrency to System Design (ACSD), pp. 1–8, June 2017
22. Steffen, B., Howar, F., Isberner, M., Naujokat, S., Margaria, T.: Tailored generation of concurrent benchmarks. STTT **16**(5), 543–558 (2014)
23. Steffen, B., Isberner, M., Naujokat, S., Margaria, T., Geske, M.: Property-driven benchmark generation: synthesizing programs of realistic structure. STTT **16**(5), 465–479 (2014)
24. Steffen, B., Jasper, M.: Property-preserving parallel decomposition. In: Aceto, L., Bacci, G., Bacci, G., Ingólfsdóttir, A., Legay, A., Mardare, R. (eds.) Models, Algorithms, Logics and Tools. LNCS, vol. 10460, pp. 125–145. Springer, Cham (2017). https://doi.org/10.1007/978-3-319-63121-9_7

Doctoral Symposium

Track Introduction – Doctoral Symposium 2018

Anna-Lena Lamprecht[(✉)]

Department of Information and Computing Sciences, Utrecht University, Utrecht,
The Netherlands
allamprecht@uu.nl

Since 2014 ISoLA has been hosting a Doctoral Symposium as a scientific and networking event specifically targeted at young academics, complementing the different thematically focused research tracks of the main symposium. Master and PhD students are invited to participate and present their research ideas and projects, discuss them with the scientific community, and establish collaborations in their field of research. The Doctoral Symposium is held as combination of poster sessions and short presentations. Posters are on display all along the ISoLA symposium, and the coffee breaks offer plenty of time for elaborate discussion of the posters. Additionally there are Doctoral Symposium sessions in the conference program, where all participants get the opportunity to give a brief presentation and get feedback about their work.

To participate in the Doctoral Symposium, candidates can choose between submitting a full paper or an abstract of up to four pages. Accepted full papers are included in the ISoLA proceedings, while authors of accepted abstracts are invited to submit full-length papers to a post-conference volume. The 2014 post-proceedings were included in a volume in Springer's CCIS series [1], and those for 2016 have been published as independent volume in the open access online journal "Electronic Communications of the European Association of Software Science and Technology" (ECEASST) [2]. At the time of production of the ISoLA 2018 proceedings (this volume), 12 participants have been accepted to the Doctoral Symposium, two of which contribute a full paper to the proceedings:

1. Barbara Steffen (Rotterdam School of Management, Netherlands) will talk about *Industry 4.0 - A Threat or Opportunity?* Industry 4.0 will inevitably lead to technology-push driven business models and solutions in the manufacturing industry as it enables many new opportunities customers would have never dreamt of. Customers and SMEs caught in the traditional system are still thinking "about means of faster horses instead of cars" explaining why this visionary statement is perceived as a threat. A threat to be addressed in the next marketing strategy to stay relevant. However, today SMEs must start to "invasively" integrate the enabling information technology into their operations and offers to stay competitive. It is important to understand that it is the lever to success in the long-term.

T. Margaria and B. Steffen (Eds.): ISoLA 2018, LNCS 11245, pp. 451–456, 2018.
https://doi.org/10.1007/978-3-030-03421-4_28

2. Tim Tegeler (TU Dortmund, Germany) will present his work on *Continuous Practices in the Context of Model-Driven System Development*. He aims to combine the advantages of Domain-specific Modeling (DSM) [3] and Continuous Software Engineering (CSE) [4,5], that is, the domain specific approach of comprehensive code generation with DSM on the one hand, and the continuous build, test and deploy strategies of CSE on the other hand. The goal is an automated pipeline which starts with models and finishes with the deployment of the final program, running through different stages like model validation, code generation, testing and compiling on the way.

3. Julieth Patricia Castellanos Ardila (Mälardalen University, Sweden) will talk about *Enabling Automated Compliance Checking of Processes against Safety Standards*. The development processes of safety-critical systems have to comply to domain-specific safety standards. Checking that the processes fulfill all requirements is tedious and error-prone due to the amount and complexity of the relevant regulations. Ardila's work aims at automating the compliance checking of such processes to reduce the effort that manufacturers have to put into this task. First results include a framework for combined process modelling and compliance checking [6–8], and in this context the formalization of the ISO 26262 standard for functional safety of road vehicles [9].

4. Ashalatha Kunnappilly, Raluca Marinescu and Cristina Seceleanu (Mälardalen University, Sweden) contribute a full paper and talk on *Assuring Intelligent Ambient Assisted Living Solutions by Statistical Model Checking* [10].

5. Georgios Pitsiladis and Petros Stefaneas (National and Kapodistrian University of Athens and National Technical University of Athens, Greece) contribute a full paper and presentation on the *Implementation of Privacy Calculus and its Type Checking in Maude* [11].

6. Alnis Murtovi (TU Dortmund, Germany) will talk about *Model Checking of Procedural Systems*. Procedural model checking allows one to analyse context-free process structures in a compositional fashion. The tool M3C (Modal Meta Model Checker) is designed to not only verify individual context-free systems but entire classes thereof: the model checking results of a modal transition system are valid for each refinement! An interesting application is the validation of properties guaranteed by the structure of domain-specific languages (DSL) alone. In this case, the underlying Context-Free Modal Transition Systems can be regarded as loose syntax specifications for DSLs, and modal refinement as a way to increase the specificity of allowed DSLs by constraining their structure. M3C allows one to verify properties specified in a branching-time logic for all DSLs of a given level of specificity in one go, which is illustrated by looking at variations of an elementary programming language. Technically, M3C is based on second-order model checking which determines how "procedure calls" affect the validity of the properties of interest. The inherent compositionality of the second-order approach leads to a runtime complexity linear in the size of the procedural system representation (whose corresponding transition systems typically have infinitely many states), but exponential in the size of the considered property (a problem that can be dealt with using ADDs in practice).

7. Malte Mues (TU Dortmund, Germany) will present his ideas on *Architectures for Constraint Management*. SMT solvers are powerful tools for constraint solving in program analysis. However, the many heterogeneous languages used by the solvers make it unnecessarily diffult for developers of program analysis tools to exploit their full power. Existing constraint management approaches provide support for managing libraries of constraints, but are mostly limited to a specific technique or language. This work aims to homogenize the current landscape of constraint management approaches across languages in order to eventually open the full power of SMT solvers to program analysis and related applications. It will also involve an evaluation of performance improvements that could be gained by systematic constraint simplification and optimization.

8. Vedran Kasalica (Utrecht University, Netherlands) will present his recent work on *Implementing Efficient Workflow Synthesis Algorithms Using SAT Solving Techniques*. Program synthesis algorithms have been shown to be applicable for the automated composition of workflows according to high-level specifications. The idea enjoys great popularity especially in the eScience community, which cares about scientists without programming training who still have to implement the computational processes to analyze their data. State explosion is a problem inherent so synthesis, however, and uptake in practice is hampered by currently impracticable execution times of the composition algorithms. A new implementation of a workflow synthesis algorithms based on state-of-the art SAT solvers, and applying different bounding techniques and heuristics, has yielded first promising results for a workflow scenario from the geospatial application domain [12].

9. Steven Smyth, Alexander Schulz-Rosengarten and Reinhard von Hanxleden (Kiel University, Germany) contribute a presentation about *Annotated Models in Model-based Compilations*. KiCo (KIELER Compiler) is a model-based compiler as part of the Kiel Integrated Environment for Layout Eclipse Rich Client (KIELER) modeling tools [13]. The core of a model-based compiler is its model-to-model transformations. Models generated by these transformations can be saved and inspected. Since modeling issues, especially causality problems present in synchronous languages, are sometimes hard to spot, Smyth et al. explored methods and appropriate representations/views of the available data. They argue that modern development tools, such as model-based compilers, besides producing the correct result, can and should also guide the modeler to potential issues and provide means to understand what is happening during its transformations. The KIELER framework is going to be adapted according to the findings of their recent studies.

10. Michael Lybecait (TU Dortmund, Germany) will present his work on *Model-Based Code Generators for Domain Specific Tools*. Nowadays domain specific languages (DSL) are more common than years before. With the introduction of language workbenches and meta-tooling suites it has become quite easy to design a DSL for single use. But with the rise of DSL usage the need for adaptable code generators has also experienced an upswing. To reduce the time to market code generators have either to be easy to design for

new DSLs but also need to be easily adapted when the DSL specification is extended. Furthermore the challenges of DSL specialization have also be taken into account. DSLs while usually already focused on a specific problem domain may be specialized even further to address only a part of the original domain thus reducing expressiveness of the new DSL. The presentation will sketch the challenges of code generator design for DSLs and propose a possible solution for overcoming these challenges by introducing a model-based code generator framework that makes the building and adaptation of code generators simple and straightforward.

11. Philip Zweihoff (TU Dortmund, Germany) will talk about *Holistic DSL Web Modeling* and present Pyro, a fully-featured, web based, integrated modeling environment for the rigorous development of user defined graphical domain specific languages (DSLs) [14] that has been built with the CINCO SCCE Meta Tooling suite [15]. It utilizes the DyWA (Dynamic Web Application) framework [16] for data modeling, empowering prototype-driven application development and follows the OTA (One Thing Approach) [17] and XMDD (Extreme Model-Driven Design) paradigm [18] to provide a DSL developer with an automated distribution of their language in the web, accessible by everyone with a browser. As such, it is designed to accelerate a large-area distribution and simultaneously synchronized editing, combined with all features of a local desktop IDE.

12. Alexander Bainczyk (TU Dortmund, Germany) will present his ideas about *Learning-Based Testing in Practice*. Active automata learning [19,20] can be used to infer behavioral models of a system that are suitable for testing. The aim of this work is to integrate learning-based testing methods into DevOps toolchains for automated software construction. Therefore, the web-based ALEX tool [21], which makes learning-based testing technologies available to non-expert users and already comprises traditional test automation capabilities, is going to be extended further. It is planned to use ALEX as part of a continuous integration pipeline in GitLab, and to explore ways that allow developers and testers to use continuous learning techniques easily.

We look forward to meeting all participants of the ISoLA Doctoral Symposium 2018 in November, to another series of interesting posters and presentations, and to lively discussions about the various research topics!

References

1. Lamprecht, A.-L. (ed.): Leveraging Applications of Formal Methods, Verification, and Validation. CCIS, vol. 683. Springer, Cham (2016). https://doi.org/10.1007/978-3-319-51641-7
2. Lamprecht, A.L. (ed.): 7th International Symposium on Leveraging Applications of Formal Methods, Verification and Validation - Doctoral Symposium, 2016 (ISoLA DS 2016), vol. 74. ECEASST (2017)
3. Kelly, S., Tolvanen, J.P.: Domain-Specific Modeling: Enabling Full Code Generation. Wiley, New York (2008)

4. Fitzgerald, B., Stol, K.J.: Continuous software engineering: a roadmap and agenda. J. Syst. Softw. **123**, 176–189 (2017)
5. Bosch, J.: Continuous Software Engineering. Springer, Cham (2014). https://doi.org/10.1007/978-3-319-11283-1
6. Ardila, J.P.C., Gallina, B.: Towards efficiently checking compliance against automotive security and safety standards. In: IEEE International Symposium on Software Reliability Engineering Workshops, ISSRE Workshops, Toulouse, France, 23–26 October 2017, pp. 317–324. IEEE Computer Society (2017)
7. Ardila, J.P.C., Gallina, B., Muram, F.U.: Enabling compliance checking against safety standards from SPEM 2.0 process models. In: The Euromicro Conference on Software Engineering and Advanced Applications, August 2018
8. Ardila, J.C.P., Gallina, B., Muram, F.U.: Transforming SPEM 2.0-compatible process models into models checkable for compliance. In: Stamelos, I., O'Connor, R., Rout, T., Dorling, A. (eds.) SPICE 2018, vol. 918, pp. 233–247. Springer, Cham (2018). https://doi.org/10.1007/978-3-030-00623-5_16
9. Ardila, J.P.C., Gallina, B.: Formal contract logic based patterns for facilitating compliance checking against ISO 26262. In: Rodríguez-Doncel, V., Casanovas, P., González-Conejero, J. (eds.) Proceedings of the 1st Workshop on Technologies for Regulatory Compliance Co-located with the 30th International Conference on Legal Knowledge and Information Systems (JURIX 2017), Luxembourg, 13 December 2017. CEUR Workshop Proceedings, vol. 2049, pp. 65–72. CEUR-WS.org (2017)
10. Kunnappilly, A., Marinescu, R., Seceleanu, C.: Assuring intelligent ambient assisted living solutions by statistical model checking. In: Margaria, T., Steffen, B. (eds.) ISoLA 2018. LNCS, vol. 11245, pp. 457–476. Springer, Cham (2018)
11. Pitsiladis, G., Stefaneas, P.: Implementation of privacy calculus and its type checking in Maude. In: Margaria, T., Steffen, B. (eds.) ISoLA 2018. LNCS, vol. 11245, pp. 477–493. Springer, Cham (2018)
12. Kasalica, V., Lamprecht, A.L.: Automated composition of scientific workflows: a case study on geographic data manipulation (Poster). In: IEEE eScience (2018, to appear)
13. Spönemann, M., Schulze, C.D., Motika, C., Schneider, C., von Hanxleden, R.: KIELER: building on automatic layout for pragmatics-aware modeling. In: 2013 IEEE Symposium on Visual Languages and Human Centric Computing, pp. 195–196, September 2013
14. Zweihoff, P.: Cinco products for the web. Master's thesis, TU Dortmund (2015)
15. Naujokat, S., Lybecait, M., Kopetzki, D., Steffen, B.: CINCO: a simplicity-driven approach to full generation of domain-specific graphical modeling tools. Int. J. Softw. Tools Technol. Transf. **20**(3), 327–354 (2018)
16. Neubauer, J., Frohme, M., Steffen, B., Margaria, T.: Prototype-driven development of web applications with DyWA. In: Margaria, T., Steffen, B. (eds.) ISoLA 2014. LNCS, vol. 8802, pp. 56–72. Springer, Heidelberg (2014). https://doi.org/10.1007/978-3-662-45234-9_5
17. Margaria, T., Steffen, B.: Business process modelling in the jABC: the one-thing-approach. In: Cardoso, J., van der Aalst, W. (eds.) Handbook of Research on Business Process Modeling. IGI Global (2009)
18. Kubczak, C., Jörges, S., Margaria, T., Steffen, B.: eXtreme Model-Driven Design with jABC. In: CTIT Proceedings of the Tools and Consultancy Track of the Fifth European Conference on Model-Driven Architecture Foundations and Applications (ECMDA-FA), vol. WP09-12, pp. 78–99 (2009)

19. Raffelt, H., Merten, M., Steffen, B., Margaria, T.: Dynamic testing via automata learning. Int. J. Softw. Tools Technol. Transf. 11(4), 307 (2009)
20. Steffen, B., Howar, F., Merten, M.: Introduction to active automata learning from a practical perspective. In: Bernardo, M., Issarny, V. (eds.) SFM 2011. LNCS, vol. 6659, pp. 256–296. Springer, Heidelberg (2011). https://doi.org/10.1007/978-3-642-21455-4_8
21. Bainczyk, A., Schieweck, A., Isberner, M., Margaria, T., Neubauer, J., Steffen, B.: ALEX: mixed-mode learning of web applications at ease. In: Margaria, T., Steffen, B. (eds.) ISoLA 2016. LNCS, vol. 9953, pp. 655–671. Springer, Cham (2016). https://doi.org/10.1007/978-3-319-47169-3_51

Assuring Intelligent Ambient Assisted Living Solutions by Statistical Model Checking

Ashalatha Kunnappilly$^{(\boxtimes)}$, Raluca Marinescu, and Cristina Seceleanu

Mälardalen University, Västerås, Sweden
{ashalatha.kunnappilly,raluca.marinescu,cristina.seceleanu}@mdh.se

Abstract. A modern way of enhancing elderly people's quality of life is by employing various Ambient Assisted Living solutions that facilitate an independent and safe living for their users. This is achieved by integrating computerized functions such as health and home monitoring, fall detection, reminders, etc. Such systems are safety critical, therefore ensuring at design time that they operate correctly, but also in a timely and robust manner is important. Most of the solutions are not analyzed formally at design time, especially if such Ambient Assisted Living functions are integrated within the same design. To address this concern, we propose a framework that relies on an abstract component-based description of the system's architecture in the Architecture Analysis and Design Language. To ensure scalability of analysis, we transform the AADL models into a network of stochastic timed automata amenable to statistical analysis of various quality-of-service attributes. The architecture that we analyze is developed as part of the project CAMI, co-financed by the European Commission, and consists of a variety of health and home sensors, a data collector, local and cloud processing, as well as an artificial-intelligence-based decision support system. Our contribution paves the way towards achieving design-time assured integrated Ambient Assisted Living solutions, which in turn could reduce verification effort at later stages.

1 Introduction

The elderly segment of the population often face cognitive decline, chronic age-related diseases, limitations in mobility, vision, and hearing. In this context, Ambient Assisted Living (AAL) solutions can enhance the elderly's quality of life by providing integrated computerized functions aimed to help the users in their independent and safe daily living.

Modern AAL systems are equipped with a wide variety of integrated features, like health monitoring, home monitoring, fall detection, robotic platform support, and support for communication with caregivers [20]. AAL systems are

---

The original version of this chapter was revised: An incorrect version of Fig. 3 was included. This has now been corrected. The correction to this chapter is available at https://doi.org/10.1007/978-3-030-03421-4_31

T. Margaria and B. Steffen (Eds.): ISoLA 2018, LNCS 11245, pp. 457–476, 2018.
https://doi.org/10.1007/978-3-030-03421-4_29

complex safety-critical systems, operating in a dynamic and unpredictable environment (e.g. due to involvement of humans in the loop, like elderly users, caregivers), hence it is desirable that these systems are analyzed to ensure that they meet their functional and extra-functional requirements.

As for any other computerized system, formal techniques such as model checking can also be applied to AAL; however, the task is not trivial due to the complexity of models that include artificial intelligence (AI) techniques, redundant components for fault tolerance, etc.

In this paper, we address this challenge by formally analyzing architectural specifications of integrated AAL solutions. Although here we focus on a particular system, the method is general and can be applied to similar AAL solutions [16]. The AAL system that we model and analyze is developed as part of the project CAMI[1], co-financed by the European Commission under the Ambient Assisted Living Joint Program of H2020. The system consists of various sensors, actuators, user interfaces, cloud services used to store and process data, and also an intelligent decision support system (DSS) that we design and analyze in this work. Our DSS uses a combination of AI reasoning techniques, such as fuzzy logic, rule-based reasoning (RBR), and case-based reasoning (CBR) for efficient decision making.

Our contribution starts with specifying the AAL system architecture in the Architecture Analysis and Design Language (AADL) [11] (see Sect. 3.1). AADL is chosen due to the rich set of modeling constructs and its suitability in specifying real-time systems. In this work, we assume fault-tolerant AAL systems, which we model as a set of interacting *abstract* components in AADL. To specify each component's functional behavior and error behavior, we use the standardized annex sets of AADL, Behavior Annex (BA), and Error Annex (EA), respectively.

Although existing AADL IDE tools like OSATE [1] support initial architecture analysis with respect to latency (timing properties), schedulability, etc., the worst-case timing assumptions are often adopted without considering the component behaviors, which often leads to pessimistic estimations [4]. Thus, there is a need to adopt formal analysis methods like model checking to analyze the functional correctness of an architecture, or the system's timeliness or reliability, within the architectural framework itself. To carry out such analysis and to tackle the latter's scalability, we resort to statistical analysis rather than exhaustive model checking to ensure the system's correctness. Hence, we give semantics to the AADL components in terms of stochastic timed automata (STA) that can be statistically model checked with UPPAAL SMC [8] (See Sect. 3.2). Since our AADL model considers probabilities of failure and recovery of various components, a straightforward encoding would be within a probabilistic framework such as that of PRISM [14], for exhaustive verification. However, the latter does not scale to the size of our model so we resort to an SMC encoding, based on UPPAAL SMC [8]. Although the analysis results are not exact, simulation-based methods are sometimes the only choice for reasoning of complex Cyber Physical Systems [4,19].

In brief, the contributions of this work are as follows: (i) an abstract component-based AADL architectural model of the integrated AAL system

---

[1] http://www.aal-europe.eu/projects/cami/.

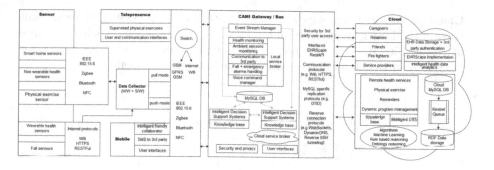

Fig. 1. The CAMI AAL system architecture [18]

CAMI (Sect. 4), (ii) an AI-based DSS and its abstract component-based specification (Sect. 2), (iii) a formal definition of the proposed AADL components in terms of STA (Sect. 5), and (iv) the formal analysis of the STA model against various functional requirements and quality-of-service (QoS) properties with UPPAAL SMC (Sect. 6). We compare to related work in Sect. 7, and conclude the paper in Sect. 8.

2 Use Case: CAMI AAL Architecture

In this section, we describe our use case, the CAMI AAL system architecture [18]. The system architecture is shown in Fig. 1, and follows the structure of many commercial AAL systems with various sensors, data collector, DSS, security and privacy, database systems, user interfaces (UI), local and cloud computing support. The major components of CAMI are briefly described below:

- Sensor unit: Comprises various sensors ranging from health monitoring to home monitoring, physical exercise monitoring, and fall detection.
- Data Collector Unit: Collects data from the sensors and assigns labels and criticality-based priorities for handling events.
- Local processor (CAMI Gateway): Processes the data from the Data Collector Unit. It has two major sub-components:
  - Message Queue (MQ): Queues up the data output from the Data Collector and sorts it according to its priority such that the head of the queue is the sensor data/event with the highest priority. In Fig. 1, the MQ is the Event Stream Manager.
  - Decision Support System (DSS): The brain of the architecture where the data from the MQ gets processed. To handle the complexity associated with the integration of multiple functionalities and to process the interdependencies among simultaneously-occurring events in the AAL environment, we design a novel **intelligent context-aware DSS** system for CAMI that utilizes various AI reasoning schemes to decide on further actions to be taken (e.g., raise an alarm and inform the caregiver, issue a reminder etc.). The DSS architecture is detailed in Sect. 2.1.

– Cloud processor: Is employed for data storage and processing. A redundant copy of the DSS is maintained in the cloud to avoid the single point of failure of the architecture. In this paper, we have considered only one redundant DSS copy in the cloud due to cost and maintenance efficiency.

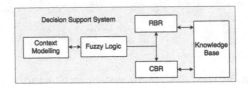

Fig. 2. The DSS architecture

2.1   CAMI's Decision Support System

The DSS architecture that we propose is shown in Fig. 2. Our architecture is inspired by the work of Zhou et al. [27], where the authors have proposed a context-aware, CBR-based ambient intelligence system for AAL applications. In comparison, our DSS combines multiple AI reasoning techniques in an effective way. We employ context modeling (CM) with fuzzy reasoning, RBR in addition to CBR, which help to deal efficiently with multiple AAL scenarios. Context modeling is performed by identifying the context space based on: (i) the personal profile of the user, (ii) the activity of daily living (DA) performed by the user, (iii) spatio-temporal properties, (iv) environment and (v) health parameters. The parameters of context space are either profiled, sensed, or predicted. Fuzzy reasoning is used for detecting DA [23], and also for determining sensor-data deviations. To take decisions in various situations, we employ RBR first, next CBR, that is, upon a context-change, RBR triggers first and checks if there exists a rule to handle that particular context, if not, it allows the CBR system to tackle the context based on its learning from previous scenarios. Developing an efficient case base, case matching and formulating the adaptation rules are the most complex aspects of a CBR system. In our system, each time an RBR outputs a rule, we save it as a *case* in the CBR system with the *case-id* represented by the DA of the user, the *context space* represented by the case features, and the triggered *rule* represented by the solution of the particular case. The Knowledge Base (KB) stores the context, rules, and cases. For detailed description of the internal structure of DSS, the reader can refer to the technical report [16].

2.2   Use Case Scenarios and System Requirements

The CAMI system assists the elderly user in a variety of health, home-related, and social inclusion functionalities. In this paper, we focus on one of the critical scenarios where CAMI comes into assistance of an elderly user, Jim, who falls frequently and suffers from chronic cardiac disease and slight memory loss.

Scenario 1: Jim has sudden pulse variations, detected by the pulse monitoring sensor of CAMI, which are critical for cardiac patients. If the pulse is low, CAMI alerts the caregiver of a low pulse. If the pulse is high, CAMI checks whether the user is currently exercising (if this is the case, a high pulse is considered as normal) and if not, it sends an alert to the caregiver.

Scenario 2: Jim is cooking his breakfast. He suddenly feels dizzy and falls. The gas-based cooker is still on, and eventually starts a fire in Jim's house. In this case, the CAMI system detects the simultaneously-occurring events, and alerts the firefighter and caregiver of both events [17]. Further, if there are any health parameter variations detected for Jim along with the fall (for instance, a low pulse), the fall event can be associated with the low pulse, and the caregiver notified accordingly, which can help a further diagnosis.

This scenario is safety critical and has to be processed in real time.

We present the functional requirement that is derived from the above scenarios and also the QoS requirements that CAMI should satisfy:

R1: If there is a pulse data deviation indicating high pulse, the DA is "not exercising", and the user has a cardiac disease history, then the DSS sends a notification to the caregiver, within 20 s. This relates to Scenario 1.

R2: If fire and fall are detected simultaneously, then the DSS should detect the presence of the simultaneous events and send notifications to both firefighters and caregiver, within 20 s. This relates to Scenario 2.

R3: The decisions taken by the local DSS are updated in the cloud DSS such that they are eventually synchronized. This requirement relates to the data-consistency requirement of CAMI.

R4: If the local DSS fails, then the cloud DSS eventually becomes active. It corresponds to the fault-tolerance aspect of the CAMI system.

The overall goal is to analyze that the CAMI architecture meets the above requirements. We achieve this by first specifying a simplified version of CAMI in AADL, and then by semantically encoding the specification into a network of STA (NSTA) that we statistically model check with UPPAAL SMC.

3 Preliminaries

In this section, we briefly overview AADL, STA and UPPAAL SMC.

3.1 Architecture Analysis and Design Language

AADL [11] is a textual and graphical language in which one can model and analyze a real-time system's hardware and software architecture as hierarchies of components at various levels of abstraction.

AADL component categories like *Application Software*, *Execution Platform* and *System* are used to represent the run-time architecture of the system, however a more generalized representation is possible by specifying it as *abstract*.

A component in AADL can be defined by its *type* and *implementation*: the first defines the interface of the component and its externally observable attributes, whereas the second defines its internal structure. AADL allows possible component interactions via *ports/features*, *shared data*, *subprograms*, and *parameter connections*. In AADL, the input/output ports can be defined as: *event ports*, *data ports*, and *event-data ports*. Based on the component interactions, explicit *data flows* can be defined across the interfaces of AADL components by specifying the components as *flow source*, *flow path* or *flow sink*. The components can also be associated with various *properties*, like the *period* and *execution time* and the *dispatch protocol*. The *dispatch protocol* specifies if the component trigger is *periodic* or *aperiodic*. We also employ various user-defined properties for representing the probabilistic distribution of an aperiodic event and the rate at which a component recovers from the failure.

The AADL core language can be extended via annex sublanguages and user-defined properties. In this work, we employ the standardized annexes of AADL for describing the functional and error behavior of a component, namely the Behavior Annex (BA) [12] and the Error Annex (EA) [9] respectively, which model behaviors as transition systems. Given finite sets of states and state variables, the behavior of a component is defined by a set of state transitions of the form

$$s \xrightarrow{guard, \ actions} s',$$

where s, s' are *states*, *guard* is a boolean condition on the values of state variables or presence of events/data in the component's input ports, and *actions* are performed over the transition and may update state variables, or generate new outputs. Similarly, the EA models the error behavior of a component as transitions between states triggered by error events. It is also possible to represent the different types of errors, recovery paradigms, as well as the probability distributions associated with the error states and events.

In this paper, we focus on abstract components that allow us to defer from the run-time architecture of the system. These generic component categories can be parametrized, and can be refined later in the design process through the "extends" capability of AADL. AADL allows us to archive these components and reuse them. For this, we partition them into two public packages in AADL, namely *component library* and *reference architecture* [10]. A *component library* creates a repository of component types and implementations with simple hierarchy. It can be established via two packages: (i) *Interfaces Library* comprising generic components like sensors, actuators and user-interfaces (UI), and (ii) *Controller Library* that includes the control logic. The *Reference architecture* creates a repository of components of complex hierarchy, e.g. the top-level system architecture.

3.2   Stochastic Timed Automata and UPPAAL SMC

A timed automaton as used in the model checker UPPAAL is a formal notation used in describing real-time systems [2], and is defined by the following tuple:

$$TA = \langle L, l_0, A, V, C, E, I \rangle \tag{1}$$

where: L is a finite set of *locations*, $l_0 \in L$ is the *initial location*, $A = \Sigma \cup \tau$ is a set of *actions*, where Σ is a finite set of *synchronizing actions* ($c!$ denotes the send action, and $c?$ the receiving action) partitioned into inputs and outputs, $\Sigma = \Sigma_i \cup \Sigma_o$, and $\tau \notin \Sigma$ denotes internal or empty actions without synchronization, V is a set of *data variables*, C is a set of *clocks*, $E \subseteq L \times B(C, V) \times A \times 2^C \times L$ is the set of *edges*, where $B(C, V)$ is the set of *guards* over C and V, that is, conjunctive formulas of clock constraints $(B(C))$, of the form $x \bowtie n$ or $x - y \bowtie n$, where $x, y \in C$, $n \in \mathbb{N}$, $\bowtie \in \{<, \leq, =, \geq, >\}$, and non-clock constraints over V $(B(V))$, and $I : L \longrightarrow B_{dc}(C)$ is a function that assigns *invariants* to locations, where $B_{dc}(C) \subseteq B(C)$ is the set of downward-closed clock constraints with $\bowtie \in \{<, \leq, =\}$. The invariants bound the time that can be spent in locations, hence ensuring progress of TA's execution. An edge from location l to location l' is denoted by $l \xrightarrow{g,a,r} l$, where g is the guard of the edge, $c?$ (or $c!$) is a synchronization action a is an update action, and r is the clock reset set, that is, the clocks that are set to 0 by the edge. A location can be marked as *urgent* (marked with a U) or *committed* (marked with a C) indicating that time cannot progress in such locations. The latter is more restrictive, indicating that the next edge to be traversed needs to start from a *committed* location.

The semantics of TA is a *labeled transition system*. The states of the labeled transition system are pairs (l, u), where $l \in L$ is the current location, and $u \in R^C_{\geq 0}$ is the clock valuation in location l. The initial state is denoted by (l_0, u_0), where $\forall x \in C$, $u_0(x) = 0$. Let $u \models g$ denote the clock value u that satisfies guard g. We use $u + d$ to denote the time elapse where all the clock values have increased by d, for $d \in \mathbb{R}_{\geq 0}$. There are two kinds of transitions:

(i) *Delay transitions:* $< l, u > \xrightarrow{d} < l, u + d >$ if $u \models I(l)$ and $(u + d') \models I(l)$, for $0 \leq d' \leq d$, and

(ii) *Action transitions:* $< l, u > \xrightarrow{a} < l', u' >$ if $l \xrightarrow{g,a,r} l', a \in \Sigma, u \models g$, clock valuation u' in the target state (l', u') is derived from u by resetting all clocks in the reset set r of the edge, such that $u' \models I(l')$.

UPPAAL SMC [8] provides statistical model checking for stochastic timed automata (STA). The stochastic interpretation refines the TA with: (i) probabilistic choices between multiple enabled transition, where the output *probability* function γ may be defined by the user, and (ii) probability distributions for non-deterministic time delays, where the *delay density function* μ is a uniform distribution for time-bounded delays or an exponential distribution with user-defined rates for cases of unbounded delays. Formally, an STA is defined by the tuple:

$$STA = \langle TA, \mu, \gamma \rangle \tag{2}$$

The delay density function (μ) over delays in $\mathbb{R}_{\geq 0}$ is either a uniform or an exponential distribution depending on the invariant in l. With El we denote the disjunction of guards g such that $l \xrightarrow{g,o,-} -\ \in E$ for some output o. Then $d(l, v)$ denotes the infimum delay before the output is enabled, $d(l, v) = \inf \{d \in \mathbb{R}_{\geq 0} : v + d \vDash E(l)\}$, whereas $D(l, v) = \sup \{d \in \mathbb{R}_{\geq 0} : v + d \vDash I(l)\}$ is the supremum delay. If the supremum delay $D(l, v) < \infty$, then the delay density function μ in a given state s is the same as a uniform distribution over the interval $[d(l, v); D(l, v)]$. Otherwise, when the upper bound on the delays out of s does not exist, μs is set to an exponential distribution with a rate $P(l)$, where $P : L \rightarrow \mathbb{R}_{\geq 0}$ is an additional distribution rate specified for the automaton. The output probability function γs for every state $s = (l, v) \in S$ is the uniform distribution over the set $\{o : (l, g, o, -, -) \in E \wedge v \vDash g\}$.

A model in UPPAAL SMC consists of a network of interacting STA (NSTA) that communicate via broadcast channels and shared variables. In a broadcast synchronization one sender $c!$ can synchronize with an arbitrary number of receivers $c?$. In the network, the automata repeatedly race against each other, that is, they independently and stochastically decide how much to delay before delivering the output, and what output to broadcast at that moment, with the "winner" being the component that chooses the minimum delay. UPPAAL SMC uses an extension of weighted metric temporal logic (WMTL) [7] to evaluate a property $Pr(*_{x \leq C} \phi)$, where $*$ stands for $\Diamond(eventually)$ or $\Box(always)$, which calculates the probability that ϕ is satisfied within cost $x \leq C$, but also hypothesis testing and probability comparison.

4   AADL Model of CAMI

In this section, we present the modeling framework used for representing the CAMI AAL architecture. We use a generic representation of the components by specifying them as *abstract*, which can be easily extended to specific run-time architecture models.

For developing the abstract model, we classify the AADL components as:

- **Atomic Components** (AC): components that do not have hierarchy in terms of sub-components with interfaces, but might contain sub-components without interfaces.
- **Composite Components** (CC): hierarchical components that contain sub-components with or without interfaces.

For instance, "data" is a sub-component in AADL without interface and it can be part of an AC or CC hierarchy.

In the CAMI architecture, the Sensors, UI, and Data Collector are modeled as AC, whereas the Local Controller, and the Cloud Controller are modeled as CC. The DSS is modeled as a CC with sub-components like CM, CBR and RBR. The fuzzy system is modeled as one of the sub-components of CM. Among all the elements involved in CM, activity recognition (detecting the DA of the user) is highly complex and requires analysis of multiple sensor parameters, so in our current model we have abstracted the module by associating a DA with the user profile in the context model. Similarly, we abstract away the algorithms of the CBR reasoning and only show how RBR outputs can successfully build the case base of the CBR module. We also model a redundant copy of the DSS component in the cloud processor.

An example of an AC in the CAMI architecture is the RBR component of the DSS. In this paper, we illustrate the RBR for **R.1** (Scenario 1), described in Sect. 2.1. The RBR component type, implementation, BA, and EA are shown in Fig. 3. The component type definition specifies its name, category (i.e., "abstract") and interfaces. The RBR component type describes that it gets activated aperiodically according to a probabilistic distribution, has an execution time of 1 s, a failure recovery rate defined by the distribution, and illustrates the data flows between the respective input and output ports. The implementation definition of RBR defines the data sub-components like the fuzzy data output, personal information and daily activity of the user, which form the **context-space** of Scenario 1.

RBR (Component Type + Implementation)

abstract RBR
  features
  input: in event data port;
  output: out event data port;
  flows
  F1 : flow path input -> output;
  properties
  Dispatch_Protocol => Aperiodic;
  property_eventgeneration::AperiodicEventGeneration=>1.0;
  property eventgeneration ::Distribution=> Exponential;
  property_failure_recovery::FailureRecoveryRate=>1.0;
  property_failure_recovery::Distribution=> Exponential;
  Compute_Execution_Time =>1s..1s;
  end RBR;

  abstract implementation RBR.impl
  fuzzy_out_pulse:data fuzzified_data_pulse;
  DA: data ADL;
  u_profile: data user;
  end RBR.impl

RBR (BA+EA)

BA
  states
  Waiting: initial complete final state;
  Operational: state;
  transitions
  Waiting -[on dispatch input]->Operational {if (fuzzyo_pulse ="high" and DA != "exercising" and u_prof =" cardiac_patient"){output := "not_caregiver_highpulse"}
  EA
  states
  Waiting: initial state;
  Failed_Transient: state;
  Failed_Permanent:state;
  LReset: state;
  Failed_ep:state;
  events
  Reset: recover event;
  TF: error event;
  PF: error event;
  Transitions
  t1: Waiting –[PF]->Failed_Permanent
  t2: Waiting -[TF]->Failed_Transient;
  t3: Failed_Transient -[Reset]-> {LReset with 0.9, Failed_Permanent with 0.1};
  t4: LReset-[]->{Waiting with 0.8, Failed_Permanent with 0.2}
  properties
  EMV2::DurationDistribution => [Duration => 1s..2s; applies to Reset;
  EMV2::OccurrenceDistribution =>[ProbabilityValue => 0.9; Distribution => Fixed;]
  applies to Reset;

Fig. 3. An excerpt of the RBR component model

The BA has two states, *Waiting* and *Operational*. *Waiting* represents the initial state where the component waits for an input from the pulse sensor, and *Operational* is the state to which a component switches upon receiving the input (if it has not failed). In the *Operational* state, the system monitors the **fuzzy logic** output to identify any pulse variations. The fuzzy reasoning is not shown in Fig. 4 due to space constraints, however we present the underlying reasoning in a nutshell. First of all, fuzzy data memberships are assigned to the range of pulse data values: Low [40 70], Normal [55 135], and High [110 300], where the numbers represent heart beats per minute. The pulse data read from the sensor are classified as Low, Normal or High.

If a high pulse is detected by the RBR, then the **user context** is tracked by checking the elderly person's activity of daily living and disease history. If the activity is "not exercising" and the user has a cardiac disease history, a notification alert is raised and sent to the caregiver. The information is encoded as a rule in the BA depicted in Fig. 3. Upon triggering a particular rule, the RBR output is stored in the DB as a case input for CBR, where the case-id is represented by DA, case features are the context space and the case solution is the RBR output. The RBR output is also synchronized with Cloud DSS such that data consistency is maintained.

Fig. 4. An excerpt of the DSS component model

The EA uses four states to represent failure: *Failed Transient*, *LReset*, *Failed Permanent*, and *Failed ep*. The state *Failed Transient* models transient failures, from which a recovery is possible via a reset event. Since reset is modeled as an internal event that occurs with respect to a probabilistic distribution, we model an additional location *LReset* to encode a component's reset action upon the successful generation of the reset event. *Failed Permanent* models a permanent failure of the RBR, from which the component cannot recover. *Failed ep* models a failure due to error propagation from its predecessor components. In the EA of Fig. 3, we show two of the states - *Waiting* and *Failed Transient*, plus their transitions based on a *TF* event (event that causes transient failures) and *reset* event. If a *TF* event occurs when the component starts, the latter moves to the *Failed Transient* state. From *Failed Transient*, the system can generate a reset event with occurrence probability of 0.9 and moves to *LReset*. If the recovery is successful with the reset event, the system moves to *Waiting* state with probability 0.8, else it moves to *Failed Permanent* with probability 0.2. In this work, we have considered the *Waiting* state in the EA and BA to be similar. In

Fig. 4, we present an excerpt of the DSS component, as an example of CC. The component type definition is similar to that of an AC, except that we do not define explicitly properties like execution time of a CC (it is considered based on the execution time of each component, respectively). However, component implementation shows the prototypes used to define sub-components and connections between them. The EA shows the composite error behavior of DSS and shows that the DSS moves to *Failed Transient* or *Failed Permanent*, if all of its sub-components move to these states, respectively. No BA is created for the DSS since the behavior is defined by the BA of the sub-components.

The assumptions of CAMI's AADL model are: (i) all the system components have a reliability of 99.98%, (ii) each sensor has a periodic activation, (iii) all the system components interact via ports without any delay of communication, and (iv) the output is produced in the *Operational* state, without any loss of information during transmission.

In the following, we define the syntax of AAL-relevant AADL components as tuples, and their semantics in terms of stochastic timed automata.

5   Semantics of AAL-Relevant AADL Components

In this section, we introduce the tuple definition of an AADL component, for which we provide formal semantics as a network of STA.

An AADL component that we employ in this paper is defined by the following tuple:

$$AADLComp = \langle Comptype, Compimp, EA, BA \rangle, \qquad (3)$$

where *Comptype* represents the component type, *Compimp* represents the component implementation, *BA* the behavioral annex specification, and *EA* the error annex.

The RBR component of DSS is an AC defined by its type, implementation, BA and EA (Fig. 4), as follows:

$$RBRAADL = \langle ComptypeRBR, CompimpRBR, EARBR, BARBR \rangle \qquad (4)$$

As a whole, the DSS in our CAMI architecture is a CC, and hence it is defined by its type, implementation and EA (no BA) as shown in Fig. 5. Formally, it can be represented as follows:

$$DSSAADL = \langle ComptypeDSS, CompimpDSS, EADSS \rangle \qquad (5)$$

In the following we present the semantic encoding of RBR abd DSS, respectively, in terms of STA.

Definition 1. (Formal Encoding of RBR). *Let us assume an RBR component defined by Eq. 4. We define the formal encoding of RBR as the following network of synchronized STA: $RBRNSTA = RBRiSTA\|RBRaSTA$, where RBRiSTA is the "interface" STA of the RBR component and RBRaSTA is the "annex" STA that encodes both the behavior and the error annex information.*

- **RBRiSTA** is defined as an [16] STA of the form: $\langle L, l_0, A, V, C, E, I, \mu, \gamma \rangle$, where:
  - $L = \{Idle, Start, Op, Fail\}$, $l0 = Idle$;
  - $A = \{start\_RBRi?, start\_RBR!, stop\_RBR!, stop\_RBRi!\} \cup \{x = 0\}$, where A comprises the set of synchronization channels associated with its input-output ports (start_RBR!, stop_RBR!), plus the synchronization channels to concord with DSS (start_RBRi?, stop_RBRi!) and the reset actions on clock x;
  - $V = out\_port \cup in\_port \cup \{PF\_RBR, TF\_RBR\}$, where out_port and in_port represent the set of output and input ports, respectively, and the boolean variables, PF_RBR, TF_RBR, represent the error events;
  - $C = \{x\}$ is the clock that models the execution-time of RBR (Te = 1);
  - $E = \Big\{ Idle \xrightarrow{start\_RBRi?} start, start \xrightarrow{start\_RBR!, x=0} Op,$
    $Op \xrightarrow{TF\_RBR==1 \vee PF\_RBR==1 \wedge x==1} Fail, Op \xrightarrow{x==1, stop\_RBR!} stop,$
    $stop \xrightarrow{stop\_RBRi!} Idle, Fail \xrightarrow{TF\_RBR==0 \wedge PF\_RBR==0} Idle,$
    $Fail \xrightarrow{TF\_RBR==1 \wedge PF\_RBR==1} Fail \Big\}$;
  - $I(Op) = x \leq 1$;
  - $P(Idle) = 1$, $P(Fail) = 1$, given by γ, where $P(Idle) = 1$ represents the occurrence distribution of aperiodic events and $P(Fail) = 1$ represents the probability of leaving location Fail;

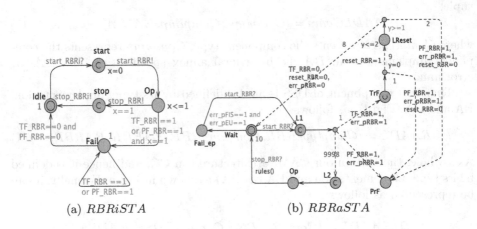

(a) RBRiSTA   (b) RBRaSTA

Fig. 5. The NSTA for the RBR

- The **RBRaSTA** is created in a similar way with:
  - $L = \{Wait, Op, TrF, PrF, Fail\_ep, LReset, L1, L2\}$, $l0 = Wait$, where L comprises the set of states in the EA and BA, respectively, plus additional committed locations (L1, L2) that ensure that receiving is deterministic in UPPAAL SMC;

- $A = \{start\_RBR?, stop\_RBR?\} \cup \{rules(), TF\_RBR = 0, TF\_RBR = 1, PF\_RBR = 1, reset\_RBR = 0, reset\_RBR = 1, err\_pRBR = 0, err\_pRBR = 1, err\_p = 1, y = 0\}$, where A is composed of the actions defined in the BA and EA, plus the synchronizations channels to concord with RBRiSTA (start_RBR?, stop_RBR?), and the reset of clock y;
- $V = \{PF\_RBR, TF\_RBR, reset\_RBR, err\_pRBR, err_p\}$, where V consists of the set of error events defined in the EA;
- $C = \{y\}$ models the duration of the "component reset";
- $E = \Big\{ Wait \xrightarrow{start\_RBR?} L1, L1 \xrightarrow{TF\_RBR=1, err\_pRBR=1} TrF, L1$

  $\xrightarrow{PF\_RBR=1, err\_pRBR=1} PrF, L1 \rightarrow L2, L2 \rightarrow Op, Op \xrightarrow{stop\_RBR?, rules()}$

  $Wait, TrF \xrightarrow{reset\_RBR=1, y=0} LReset,$

  $TrF \xrightarrow{PF\_RBR=1, err\_pRBR=1, reset\_RBR=0} PrF,$

  $LReset \xrightarrow{TF\_RBR=0, err\_pRBR=0, reset\_RBR=0} Wait,$

  $LReset \xrightarrow{PF\_RBR=1, err\_pRBR=1, reset\_RDR=0} PrF,$

  $Wait \xrightarrow{err\_p==1} Fail\_ep\}$, where E consists of the transitions in EA, BA and those between L1 and L2;
- $I(LReset) = y \leq 2$;
- $P(Wait) = 10$, given by γ, that is the occurrence-distribution of Wait;
- $L1 \xrightarrow{0.9998} L2, L1 \xrightarrow{0.001} TrF, L1 \xrightarrow{0.001} PrF$, assigned by μ, where μ is the occurrence-distribution of error events.   □

Figure 5 depicts the NSTA for the RBR, as described by Definition 1.

Definition 2 (Formal Encoding of DSS).   The formal encoding of the DSS defined by the tuple in Eq. 5 is also a network of two synchronized STA, $DSSNSTA = DSSiSTA \| DSSaSTA$, where $DSSiSTA$ is the "interface" STA of the DSS component, and $DSSaSTA$ is the "annex" STA that encodes the information from the error annex in AADL.

– **DSSiSTA** is defined as follows:
  - $L = \{Wait, CM, RBR, CBR, Fail, L1Sync, L2Sync, L3Sync, L4Sync\}$, $l0 = Wait$, where L comprises the the sub-components of the DSS (CM, RBR, CBR), plus additional locations to ensure synchronization (L1Sync, L2Sync, L3Sync, L4Sync), and location Fail to model the component failure.
  - $A = \{start\_DSSLC?, start\_CMi!, stop\_CMi?, start\_RBRi!, stop\_RBRi?, start\_CBRi!, stop\_CBRi?, stop\_DSSLC!, start\_DSSCC!\} \cup \{iCM\_in = iDSSLC\_in, iRBR\_in = iCM\_out, iCBR\_in = iRBR\_out, iDSSLC\_out = iCBR\_out, iDSSCC\_in = iDSSLC\_out\}$, where A consists of the synchronizations actions with DSS sub-components, and the assignments associated with the corresponding connections and flows;
  - $V = \{iDSSLC\_in, iCM\_in, iRBR\_in, iCBR\_in, iDSSCC\_in, iDSSLC\_out, iCM\_out, iRBR\_out, iCBR\_out, iDSSLC\_out, PF\_DSS, TF\_DSS\}$, where V is defined in the similar way as that of RBRiSTA;

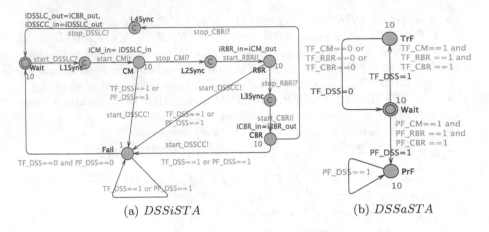

(a) *DSSiSTA*   (b) *DSSaSTA*

Fig. 6. The NSTA for the DSS

- $E = \{Wait \xrightarrow{start\_DSSLC?} L1Sync, L1Sync \xrightarrow{start\_CMi!, iCM\_in=iDSSLC\_in}$
  $CM, CM \xrightarrow{stop\_CMi?} L2Sync, L2Sync \xrightarrow{start\_RBRi!, iRBR\_in=iCM\_out} RBR,$
  $RBR \xrightarrow{stop\_RBRi?} L3Sync, L3Sync \xrightarrow{start\_CBRi!, iCBR\_in=iRBR\_out} CBR,$
  $CBR \xrightarrow{stop\_CBRi?} L4Sync, L4Sync$
  $\xrightarrow{stop\_DSSLC!, iDSSLC\_out=iCBR\_out, iDSSCC\_in=iDSSLC\_out} Wait,$
  $CM \xrightarrow{(TF\_DSS=1 \vee PF\_DSS=1), start\_DSSCC!} Fail, RBR$
  $\xrightarrow{(TF\_DSS=1 \vee PF\_DSS=1), start\_DSSCC!} Fail, CBR$
  $\xrightarrow{(TF\_DSS=1 \vee PF\_DSS=1), start\_DSSCC!} Fail, Fail$
  $\xrightarrow{(TF\_DSS==1 \vee PF\_DSS==1)} Fail, Fail \xrightarrow{(TF\_DSS==0 \wedge PF\_DSS==0)} Wait\},$
  where E is defined with respect to the connections between the respective
  sub-components and their synchronizations;
- $P(Wait)=10$, $P(CM)=10$, $P(RBR)=10$, $P(CBR)=10$, $P(Fail)=1$,
  defined by γ.
- The **DSSaSTA** is defined in a similar way as RBRaSTA, except that the
  encoding is done with the elements of the EA. (Note: There is no BA defined
  for CC)
  - $L = \{Wait, TrF, PrF\}$, $l0 = Wait;$
  - $A = \{TF\_DSS = 0, TF\_DSS = 1, PF\_DSS = 1\};$
  - $V = \{TF\_DSS, TF\_CM, TF\_RBR, TF\_CBR, PF\_CM, PF\_RBR,$
    $PF\_CBR, PF\_DSS\};$
  - $E = \{Wait \xrightarrow{TF\_CM==1 \wedge TF\_RBR==1 \wedge TF\_CBR==1, TF\_DSS=1} TrF,$
    $Wait \xrightarrow{PF\_CM==1 \wedge PF\_RBR==1 \wedge PF\_CBR==1, PF\_DSS=1} PrF, PrF$
    $\xrightarrow{PF\_DSS==1} PrF, TrF \xrightarrow{TF\_CM==0 \vee TF\_RBR==0 \vee TF\_CBR==0, TF\_DSS=0}$
    $Wait\};$
  - $P(Wait) = 10, P(TrF) = 10, P(PrF) = 10$, defined by γ.   □

Figure 6 depicts the NSTA for the DSS, as described by the Definition 2.

6   Statistical Analysis of CAMI with UPPAAL SMC

In this section, we check if the STA encoding of CAMI satisfies the requirements introduced in Sect. 2.2.

Table 1. Verification results

Req.	Query	Result	Runs
R1	$Pr[<= 1000]([]((M\_pulse.pulse\_not == 3)$ $imply(110 <= sd\_w.data\_val <= 300$ and $M\_pulse.FIS\_out == 3$ and $DA == 1$ and $upro.disease\_history == 3$ and $M\_pulse.s1 <= 20))$	Pr [0.99975,1] with confidence 0.998	3868
	$Pr[<= 1000](<> (M\_pulse.pulse\_not == 3))$	Pr [0.99975,1] with confidence 0.998	4901
R2	$Pr[<= 1000]([](M\_firefall.fire\_not == 2$ and $M\_firefall.fall\_not == 2$ imply $((se\_w.fall == 1$ or $sd\_nw.data\_val == 1)$ and $se\_nw.fire == 1$ and $M\_firefall.s1 <= 20))$	Pr [0.99975,1] with confidence 0.998	3868
	$Pr[<= 1000](<> (Pr[<- 100](<> (M\_firefall.$ $fall\_not == 2$ and $M\_firefall.fire\_not == 2))$	Pr [0.99975,1] with confidence 0.998	7905
R3	$Pr[<= 1000]([](M\_consistency.stop$ imply $(RBR\_om == iCBRCC_m)))$	Pr [0.99975,1] with confidence 0.998	3868
	$Pr[<= 1000](<> (M\_consistency.stop))$	Pr [0.99975,1] with confidence 0.998	5777
R4	$Pr[<= 1000]([](INT\_CC.DSSCC$ imply $PF\_DSS == 1))$	Pr [0.99975,1] with confidence 0.998	3868
	$Pr[<= 1000](<> (INT\_CC.DSSCC))$	Pr [0.01,0.04] with confidence 0.998	2885

We verify the system requirements using UPPAAL SMC [8]. To check that our CAMI DSS meets its requirements, we employ a monitor STA that monitors the sensor values, the respective DSS output, and the corresponding clock. The verification results are tabulated in Table 1. The system satisfies all the functional requirements corresponding to Scenarios 1 and 2 (R1 and R2) with high probabilities (close to 1) and with high confidence. Requirements R3 and R4 are related the QoS attributes of the CAMI architecture. R3 checks the data consistency of Local DSS and Cloud DSS and requires that the RBR outputs of the local DSS get stored in the case-base of the cloud DSS. This requirement is satisfied with a high probability of [0.99975, 1] and high confidence of 0.998. Query R4 is related the fault-tolerance of CAMI. We see from Table 1 that the probability of cloud DSS to become activated (R4) is [0.01, 0.04]; this is because it gets activated only when the local DSS has failed and the failure probability of local DSS is between [0.01, 0.04] for a simulation over 1000 time units. However, if the local DSS has failed, we see that the probability of cloud DSS getting activated is very high [0.99975, 1] with a confidence of 0.998, which satisfies our requirement. Most of the requirements are verified with queries that contain terms of the form *A imply B*, therefore a pre-check of each corresponding "A", being reachable is first carried out.

7   Related Work

In recent years, there has been a lot of work in the area of AAL due to the need of supporting an increased elderly population [20].

Moreover, many functionalities that need to be tackled by AAL solutions are of a safety-critical nature, e.g., health emergencies like cardiac arrest, fall of the elderly, and home emergencies like fire at home, etc. [25], therefore work on their modeling and analysis is fully justified.

The formal assurance of AAL systems has been the focus of some related research in the recent years. Parente et al. provide a list of various formal methods that can be used for AAL systems [24]. In another interesting work, Rodrigues et al. [26] perform a dependability analysis of AAL architectures using UML and PRISM. Other interesting research work uses temporal reasoning [3,22] and Markov Decision Processes to formally verify the reliability of AAL systems [21]. Although these approaches target the formal analysis of AAL systems, most of the above work addresses only simple scenarios and are not used to analyze complex behaviors resulting from integrating critical AAL functions (e.g. fire and fall), as well as their decision making. In addition, these approaches do not aim to develop an overall framework for the verification of AAL systems, starting from an integrated architectural design, their design specifications, followed by a verification strategy, as proposed in this paper.

The use of Architecture Description Languages (ADL) to specify AAL designs has not been exercised previously, yet this is common when designing automotive or automation systems. There have also been approaches to formally verify AADL designs in other domains. The transformation approach from AADL to TA or variants has been already addressed by related work [5,13,15]. Although these approaches are automated verification techniques, there is a lack of focus on abstract components/patterns with stochastic properties. In addition, these approaches also suffer from state-space explosion, therefore they might not scale well to complex AAL designs.

Nevertheless, there is interesting research that deals with stochastic properties and statistical model checking for the analysis of extended AADL models. One such example is in the work of Bruintjes et al. [6], where the authors have used SMC approach for timed reachability analysis of extended AADL designs. Although our approach also focuses on linear systems, it is different from the mentioned work in the fact that we focus on abstract components, and also introduce BA modeling for capturing the functional behavior of our modules, specifically for modeling the behavior of intelligent DSS. In their work, Bruintjes et al. use the SLIM Language, which is strongly based on AADL and is specific to avionics and automotive industry, including the error behavior and modes. However, we use the AADL core language with its standardized annex sets (EA and BA) for the architecture specification, thereby enabling us to represent the functional and error behaviour with the architecture model. The abstract component based modeling also brings extensibility and reusability to our approach. Moreover, the authors only consider the event occurrences or delay variations using uniform or exponential distributions, whereas by employing our user-defined properties, we can also specify other distributions. Furthermore, the approach of Bruintjes et al. only deals with evaluation of time-bounded queries, however we also evaluate properties like reliability, data consistency, etc., along with timeliness. Another interesting work [4], possibly carried out in parallel with our work, employs statistical model checking using UPPAAL SMC to evaluate the performance of nonlinear hybrid models with uncertainty modeled in extended AADL. Although the approach is not specific to the AAL domain, it is promising to specify complex CPS systems considering uncertainties from physical environment. Unlike our model, the authors use Priced Timed Automata (PTA) models.

In comparison, our approach considers only linear models that evolve continuously (yet the analysis is carried out in discrete time due to sampling of continuous data). In brief, the two approaches resemble, yet our approach is all contained in the core language of AADL (as different from the mentioned work where the authors resort to other annexes integrated in OSATE), is tailored to systems that contain AI components, and assumes the random failure of various components, which is not considered in the related work.

8   Conclusions and Future Work

In this paper, we have presented a framework for the formal modeling and analysis of integrated AAL systems, instantiated on CAMI that includes a variety of sensors, data collector unit, intelligent decision support system, user interfaces, and local and cloud processing schemes.

As a first step, CAMI is represented as interacting abstract components in AADL, using a commercially available tool, OSATE [1]. To provide scalable formal analysis of the AAL system, we have semantically encoded the AADL CAMI model into a network of stochastic timed automata. The resulting formal model has been analyzed with UPPAAL SMC to ensure that the required functional behavior with timeliness, reliability and fault-tolerance is enforced with high probability and accuracy. The framework is intended to augment existing AAL solutions with formal analysis support and provide analysis prior to implementation. Such an analysis is beneficial for AAL systems, which are real-time, safety-critical systems, and require high levels of dependability.

Due to the heterogeneity of components available in the AAL domain, the component failure probabilities, periods and execution times are not chosen with respect to any specific category of components, nevertheless the results presented in the paper are promising as the components that have been proposed can be refined further. The verification results are specific to our CAMI architecture, however one can use the approach to verify any set of requirements for various architecture types defined by the generic architectural model documented in the extended technical report of this work [16]. It is worth mentioning that the results are derived assuming high reliability of individual architecture components and considering specific values for the periods and execution times. However, taking into account the wide variety of available sensors and other components, we can easily adapt the values to account for requirements of any specific architecture.

In the future, we plan to enhance our DSS model with more rules for RBR and full functionality support of CBR and activity recognition, thereby providing an extensive analysis of AAL systems behaviors in possible critical scenarios. Another interesting direction to proceed with is providing automated tool support for the semantic encoding.

Acknowledgement. This work has been supported by the joint EU/Vinnova project grant CAMI, AAL-2014-1-087, which is gratefully acknowledged.

References

1. OSATE-Open Source AADL Test Environment. http://osate.github.io/. Accessed 15 May 2018
2. Alur, R., Courcoubetis, C., Dill, D.: Model-checking in dense real-time. Inf. Comput. **104**(1), 2–34 (1993)
3. Augusto, J.C., Nugent, C.D.: The use of temporal reasoning and management of complex events in smart homes. In: Proceedings of the 16th European Conference on Artificial Intelligence, pp. 778–782. IOS Press (2004)
4. Bao, Y., Chen, M., Zhu, Q., Wei, T., Mallet, F., Zhou, T.: Quantitative performance evaluation of uncertainty-aware hybrid AADL designs using statistical model checking. IEEE Trans. Comput. Aided Des. Integr. Circuits Syst. **36**(12), 1989–2002 (2017)
5. Besnard, L., et al.: Formal semantics of behavior specifications in the architecture analysis and design language standard. In: Nakajima, S., Talpin, J.-P., Toyoshima, M., Yu, H. (eds.) Cyber-Physical System Design from an Architecture Analysis Viewpoint, pp. 53–79. Springer, Singapore (2017). https://doi.org/10.1007/978-981-10-4436-6_3
6. Bruintjes, H., Katoen, J.P., Lesens, D.: A statistical approach for timed reachability in AADL models. In: 45th Annual IEEE/IFIP International Conference on Dependable Systems and Networks (DSN), pp. 81–88. IEEE (2015)
7. Bulychev, P., David, A., Larsen, K.G., Legay, A., Li, G., Poulsen, D.B.: Rewrite-based statistical model checking of WMTL. In: Qadeer, S., Tasiran, S. (eds.) RV 2012. LNCS, vol. 7687, pp. 260–275. Springer, Heidelberg (2013). https://doi.org/10.1007/978-3-642-35632-2_25
8. David, A., Larsen, K.G., Legay, A., Mikučionis, M., Poulsen, D.B.: Uppaal SMC tutorial. Int. J. Softw. Tools Technol. Transf. **17**(4), 397–415 (2015)
9. Delange, J., Feiler, P.: Architecture fault modeling with the AADL error-model annex. In: 2014 40th EUROMICRO Conference on Software Engineering and Advanced Applications (SEAA), pp. 361–368. IEEE (2014)
10. Feiler, P.H., Gluch, D.P.: Model-Based Engineering with AADL: An Introduction to the SAE Architecture Analysis & Design Language. Addison-Wesley, Boston (2012)

11. Feiler, P.H., Lewis, B., Vestal, S., Colbert, E.: An overview of the SAE architecture analysis & design language (AADL) standard: a basis for model-based architecture-driven embedded systems engineering. In: Dissaux, P., Filali-Amine, M., Michel, P., Vernadat, F. (eds.) IFIP WCC TC2 2004. IFIP The International Federation for Information Processing, vol. 176. Springer, Boston (2005). https://doi.org/10.1007/0-387-24590-1_1

12. Frana, R., Bodeveix, J.P., Filali, M., Rolland, J.F.: The AADL behaviour annex-experiments and roadmap. In: 2007 12th IEEE International Conference on Engineering Complex Computer Systems, pp. 377–382. IEEE (2007)

13. Hamdane, M.F., Chaoui, A., Strecker, M.: From AADL to timed automaton-a verification approach. Int. J. Softw. Eng. Appl. **7**(4), 115–126 (2013)

14. Hinton, A., Kwiatkowska, M., Norman, G., Parker, D.: PRISM: a tool for automatic verification of probabilistic systems. In: Hermanns, H., Palsberg, J. (eds.) TACAS 2006. LNCS, vol. 3920, pp. 441–444. Springer, Heidelberg (2006). https://doi.org/10.1007/11691372_29

15. Johnsen, A., Lundqvist, K., Pettersson, P., Jaradat, O.: Automated verification of AADL-specifications using UPPAAL. In: 2012 IEEE 14th International Symposium on High-Assurance Systems Engineering (HASE), pp. 130–138. IEEE (2012)

16. Kunnappilly, A., Marinescu, R., Seceleanu, C.: A Statistical Analysis Framework for Ambient Assisted Living Solutions. Technical report. http://www.es.mdh.se/publications/5125-17

17. Kunnappilly, A., Seceleanu, C., Lindén, M.: Do we need an integrated framework for ambient assisted living? In: García, C.R., Caballero-Gil, P., Burmester, M., Quesada-Arencibia, A. (eds.) UCAmI/IWAAL/AmIHEALTH -2016, Part II. LNCS, vol. 10070, pp. 52–63. Springer, Cham (2016). https://doi.org/10.1007/978-3-319-48799-1_7

18. Kunnappilly, A., Sorici, A., Awada, I.A., Mocanu, I., Seceleanu, C., Florea, A.M.: A novel integrated architecture for ambient assisted living systems. In: 2017 IEEE 41st Annual Computer Software and Applications Conference (COMPSAC), vol. 1, pp. 465–472. IEEE (2017)

19. Legay, A., Delahaye, B., Bensalem, S.: Statistical model checking: an overview. In: Barringer, H., et al. (eds.) RV 2010. LNCS, vol. 6418, pp. 122–135. Springer, Heidelberg (2010). https://doi.org/10.1007/978-3-642-16612-9_11

20. Li, R., Lu, B., McDonald-Maier, K.D.: Cognitive assisted living ambient system: a survey. Digit. Commun. Netw. **1**(4), 229–252 (2015)

21. Liu, Y., Gui, L., Liu, Y.: MDP-based reliability analysis of an ambient assisted living system. In: Jones, C., Pihlajasaari, P., Sun, J. (eds.) FM 2014. LNCS, vol. 8442, pp. 688–702. Springer, Cham (2014). https://doi.org/10.1007/978-3-319-06410-9_46

22. Magherini, T., Fantechi, A., Nugent, C.D., Vicario, E.: Using temporal logic and model checking in automated recognition of human activities for ambient-assisted living. IEEE Trans. Hum. Mach. Syst. **43**(6), 509–521 (2013)

23. Medjahed, H., Istrate, D., Boudy, J., Dorizzi, B.: Human activities of daily living recognition using fuzzy logic for elderly home monitoring. In: 2009 IEEE International Conference on Fuzzy Systems, FUZZ-IEEE 2009, pp. 2001–2006. IEEE (2009)

24. Parente, G., Nugent, C.D., Hong, X., Donnelly, M.P., Chen, L., Vicario, E.: Formal modeling techniques for ambient assisted living. Ageing Int. **36**(2), 192–216 (2011)

25. Rashidi, P., Mihailidis, A.: A survey on ambient-assisted living tools for older adults. IEEE J. Biomed. Health Inform. **17**(3), 579–590 (2013)

26. Rodrigues, G.N., Alves, V., Silveira, R., Laranjeira, L.A.: Dependability analysis in the ambient assisted living domain: an exploratory case study. J. Syst. Softw. 85(1), 112–131 (2012)
27. Zhou, F., Jiao, J.R., Chen, S., Zhang, D.: A case-driven ambient intelligence system for elderly in-home assistance applications. IEEE Trans. Syst. Man Cybern. Part C (Appl. Rev.) 41(2), 179–189 (2011)

Implementation of Privacy Calculus and Its Type Checking in Maude

Georgios V. Pitsiladis[1,2]([⊠]) and Petros Stefaneas[2]

[1] National and Kapodistrian University of Athens,
Panepistimiopolis, 15784 Ilissia, Greece
`gpitsiladis@mail.ntua.gr`
[2] National Technical University of Athens,
Heroon Polytechniou 9, 15780 Zografou, Greece
`petros@math.ntua.gr`

Abstract. Philippou and Kouzapas have proposed a privacy-related framework, consisting of (i) a variant of the π-calculus, called Privacy Calculus, that describes the interactions of processes, (ii) a privacy policy language, (iii) a type system that serves to check whether Privacy Calculus processes respect privacy policies. We present an executable implementation of (a version of) it in the programming/specification language Maude: we give an overview of the framework, outline the key aspects of its implementation, and offer a simple example of how the implementation can be used.

Keywords: Maude · Privacy · Privacy policies · π-calculus
Type systems

1 Introduction

1.1 Related Work

In recent years, the advancement of technology has posed a great threat to privacy. As a result, privacy enforcement needs relevant tools that protect user privacy and detect potential or actual breaches. A long-term goal that follows from these concerns and has attracted some interest recently is to have sound and efficient formal systems that can be used in practice to reason about privacy-related properties of information systems and enforce privacy requirements.

[6] defines a framework which uses type checking and a custom variant of the π-calculus, in order to reason about data on the Web, particularly the data expressed with standards such as RDF. [13] defines a rather expressive formal system based on epistemic logic, tailored to reasoning about the privacy policies of social networks. Another formal framework for privacy, which is the basis of the present paper, is described in [8] and its extensions [7,9,15]; it consists of privacy policies and processes/systems of a variant of π-calculus, bridged with a type checker. Moreover, since privacy policies share some common properties with access control policies, there have been attempts to extend access control

© Springer Nature Switzerland AG 2018
T. Margaria and B. Steffen (Eds.): ISoLA 2018, LNCS 11245, pp. 477–493, 2018.
https://doi.org/10.1007/978-3-030-03421-4_30

policies, in order to be usefully applicable for privacy purposes; such an extension, which has influenced our work, is P-RBAC [1, 11, 12].

Maude is a powerful tool with many uses. We opted for it due to its firm mathematical foundations (equational and rewriting logic), its executable semantics, and its reflective character, which simplifies proving properties of specifications in the same framework they are defined; it is also claimed to be rather efficient [10]. We believe that having executable implementations of the frameworks defined can aid in applying them at greater scale and, thus, in spotting difficulties in their widespread use. In addition, one could use automatic theorem proving on such implementations to mechanically prove useful properties of their specifications.

1.2   Overview

The work we present here has mostly been carried out as part of a diploma thesis [16] in the School of Applied Mathematical and Physical Science of the National Technical University of Athens, supervised by Prof. Petros Stefaneas. The main contributions of the thesis were (i) the extension of the framework of [7] (privacy policy language, processes/systems of π-calculus, type checker), mostly by the incorporation of the concept of conditions and (ii) the implementation of the (extended) framework in Core Maude. The first part has been presented in [15], but the essential parts of it will be summed up here (in some cases, there have been improvements; we indicate them and compare them with [15]).

The code of the specification is not included in this paper (for lack of space), but can be found in http://users.ntua.gr/gpitsiladis/isola2018/privacy.maude. It is split into several modules in order to facilitate its reading and its future examination with Maude tools, such as the Church-Rosser Checker and the Sufficient Completeness Checker [4, Sect. 1.3]. The code of the running Example (Examples 1, 2, and 3 below) is in http://users.ntua.gr/gpitsiladis/isola2018/example-sales.maude.

As depicted in Fig. 1, the framework (and, hence, the tool) is split into three parts: Privacy Calculus, privacy policy language, and type system. The Privacy Calculus, using the construct of Systems, models the code of the application whose privacy properties are under scrutiny. The privacy policy language models rules and policies regarding privacy as Privacy Policies. The type system, using the construct of Γ-Environments to model information about the environment the code is running in, checks (using the function $\vdash$) syntactic well-formedness of Systems and, more importantly, with the help of the internal construct of Θ-Interfaces (which are the types of Systems), checks (using the relation $\models$) compliance of Systems (hence application code) to Privacy Policies.

The structure of the paper closely follows the structure of the framework: Sect. 2 describes the privacy policy language, Sect. 3 describes the Privacy Calculus, and Sect. 4 describes the type checker that can be used to test systems of the Privacy Calculus for policy compliance; each of these sections is split into a subsection describing the mathematical specification of the respective part of the framework and a subsection describing its implementation in Maude (design choices, sort and operator declarations, and example of usage). Finally, Sect. 5 contains concluding remarks and possible directions for future work.

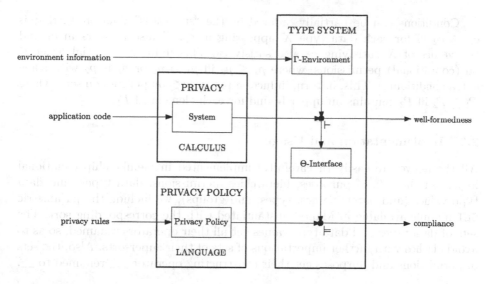

Fig. 1. The structure of the framework. It is comprised of three parts: the Privacy Calculus, a privacy policy language, and a type system. Each contains a construct to model application code, privacy policies, and execution environment respectively. The framework can check for the syntactic well-formedness of code and for its compliance to a privacy policy.

2 The Privacy Policy Language

The privacy policy language of our tool is a slightly more mature version of the one in [15, Sect. 2], which itself extends the language of [7, Sect. 3] with conditions and splits the notion of groups into users and roles, in the spirit of [11].

2.1 Mathematical Specification

Policies are specified on top of some basic notions: (i) *groups* (split in *users* and *roles*), (ii) *purposes*, and (iii) *data types* (or *basic types*). Groups are characterisations of entities that can act upon private data. The concept of purposes is vital when dealing with privacy issues [2, Sect. 1]. Data types are types (such as Age, Time) of private or not private data. Each data type X can be granted with a finite *data value set* D_X that serves for the formation of conditions; a condition is either a statement that a data type has (or has not) a specific value or a conjunction of such statements; for example, $\texttt{AgeRange} \neq \texttt{under18} \wedge \texttt{Consent} = \texttt{Yes}$.

A policy maps each of the (private) basic types in its domain to a hierarchy of purpose-endowed groups and a permission function, which grants permissions to group-purpose pairs; the available permissions in our tool (which can easily be adapted to the needs of different applications) are read, write, access, disc G where G can be any group. All (unconditional) permissions can become conditional, by appending to them the keyword if and a condition.

Conditions can be partially ordered by the "strictness" relation $\leq$, that is $c_1 \leq c_2$ iff for each data type X appearing in c_2, X also appears in c_1 and the values of X satisfying c_1 also satisfy c_2. This induces a partial order $\leq$ on (conditional) permissions, where $p_1 \leq p_2$ iff $p_1 = p_2$ or p_1 is p_2 with some extra condition(s). This, in turn, induces a preorder $\lesssim$ on permission sets, where $P_1 \lesssim P_2$ iff P_2 contains an upper bound for each element of P_1.

2.2   Implementation and Usage

All the above are easily (if carefully) implemented in membership equational logic. For the sets of purposes, hierarchies, permissions, data types, and data type values (and, later, names, types, and groups), we include the parametric SET module available in Maude, instantiated with the corresponding sort. The sets of data types and data type values get all their operators renamed, so as to avoid clashes with further importations of sets of their supersorts. Also, the sets of permissions and purposes get their constructing operator _,_ renamed to __.

Example 1. Suppose we are modelling a company whose privacy policy with regard to marketing contains the clause "Personal information of customers may be disclosed to third parties if the customer gives their consent. Personal information of customers under thirteen years old will never be disclosed to third parties." and we consider the private data of a single user named Alice. The entities that interest us in this case are of course Alice and the marketing department, but also the server and database of the company. Alice and the server act for the purpose of purchasing a product, the database acts for the purpose of storage, and the marketing department acts for the purpose of marketing.

First, we have to start a new module (or several modules) that includes those components of the tool that we wish to use. The main modules of interest are:

- PRIVACY-TYPE-CHECKER, a functional module that provides everything needed for type checking Privacy Calculus systems against policies,
- UNIVERSE, a functional module that defines the sorts containing application-specific information (Group, DataType, Purpose, etc.), so we have to extend it when using the tool.

Inside our module, we have to define the groups, purposes, and data types we are going to use. In our example, the groups are: a user Alice, the roles of the company (Company, Server, DB, MarketingDpt), and the roles Clients, ThirdParty; since hierarchies need to have a single root, we employ the role Comp&Clients. So, we declare

```
ops Company Comp&Clients DB MarketingDpt ThirdParty Server
     Clients : -> Role [ctor] .
op Alice : -> User [ctor] .
```

The declaration of purposes is simple:

```
ops purchase storage marketing : -> Purpose [ctor] .
```

As for data types, we have Alice's private data: Age and Consent, with specific value sets, and OrderData, with no specific value set. OrderData is declared as op OrderData : −>PrivateDataType [ctor], Age is declared as

> op Age : −> PrivateDataType [ctor] .
> sort AgeValues .
> subsort AgeValues < PrivateDataValue .
> ops under13 over13 : −> AgeValues [ctor] .
> eq domain(Age) = under13 over13 .
> eq var(under13) = Age .
> eq var(over13) = Age .

and Consent (with values yes and no) is similar. If we had a non-private data type (such as Time), we would follow the same procedure, using DataType instead of PrivateDataType and DataValue instead of PrivateDataValue.

We can now model the policy at hand. For ease of presentation, we will use the same hierarchy for all private data types. Hierarchies are built with the operator _:_‘[_‘] : Group Set{Purpose} NeSet{Hierarchy} ~> Hierarchy, but shorthands are provided for cases where there is no purpose or no subhierarchy. Thus, the hierarchy of our example can be defined as follows:

> op H : −> Hierarchy . eq H =
>   Comp&Clients[
>   Clients : purchase [Alice []],
>   Company [
>   DB : storage,
>   Server : purchase,
>   MarketingDpt : marketing
>   ],
>   ThirdParty [MarketingDpt : marketing]
>   ].

Note that hierarchies can have cycles, but a group is not permitted to appear in its subhierarchy. The privacy policy of the company can be defined as follows:

> op sales-policy : −> Policy . eq sales-policy =
>   OrderData >> H,
>   p(marketing, MarketingDpt) = access
>   disc ThirdParty if Age =/= under13 /\ OwnerConsent ==
>   yes,
>   p(purchase, Server) = read access write disc Company,
>   p(purchase, Alice) = read write access disc Comp&Clients
>   ; Age >> H,
>   p(marketing, MarketingDpt) = access read,
>   p(storage, DB) = access write disc Company,
>   p(purchase, Alice) = read write access disc Comp&Clients
>   ; OwnerConsent >> H,
>   p(marketing, MarketingDpt) = access read,

p(storage, DB) = access write disc Company,

p(purchase, Alice) = read write access disc Comp&Clients .

Note that conditions bind to the nearest permission; for example, sales-policy states that the marketing department can access order data (for marketing purposes) unconditionally, but can only disclose it to third parties (for the same purpose) if two conditions hold. Note also that any permission not given explicitly is not allowed by the policy.

3   The Privacy Calculus

Privacy Calculus is a version of (typed) π-calculus with the group construct of [3]. In our tool, we use it as presented in [15, Sect. 3], with the addition of CINNI [18] and some alterations in its semantics described below.

3.1   Mathematical Specification and Implementation in Maude

Syntax. For *names* of channels, hereafter ranged over by x, y, z, in order to tackle the usual issues with name binding, we employ CINNI: consider an (infinitely countable) set of *name IDs* (ranged over by a, b); each name ID can be turned into an (indexed) name by subscripting it with a non negative integer, referring to the bindings for the same ID we have to skip. In the Maude implementation, we use Qid as the source of name IDs (by specifying **subsort** Qid < NameId) and add an operator _'{_'} : NameId Nat −>IndexedName [ctor] to signify subscripting. We also include all data values as names in our calculus, thinking of them as constants: **subsort** DataValue < Name.

One of the principal goals of CINNI is to define name substitution (declared as **op** '[_:=_'] : NameId Name −>Subst [ctor] and **op** __ : Subst Name −>Name) elegantly; it also defines the **shiftup**, **shiftdown** and **lift** operators, behaving is as described in Table 1, all of which are constructors of the sort Subst.

Table 1. Behaviour of the operators shiftup, shiftdown and lift. a and b are different name labels. subst is some term of sort Subst. It is defined in [18, p. 6] and also described in [19, Table 1].

[shiftup a]	[shiftdown a]	[lift a subst]
a{n} ↦ a{n+1}	a{n} ↦ a{max(n-1, 0)}	a{n+1} ↦ [shiftup a] (subst a{n})
b{m} ↦ b{m}	b{m} ↦ b{m}	a{0} ↦ a{0}
		b{m} ↦ [shiftup a] (subst b{m})

Types, hereafter denoted by T, are defined recursively: data types are types and for each group G and type T, $G[T]$ is a type; intuitively, $G[T]$ means a channel belonging to group G carries data of type T. For example, the term Company[Comp&Clients[Age]] is a channel (to be used by members of group Company) that carries names of channels (to be used by members of group Comp &Clients) carrying data of type Age.

Programmes of privacy calculus are defined in two levels: *processes* (denoted by P) and *systems* (denoted by S):

1. The processes $\mathbf{0}, P_1|P_2, !P, (\nu a : T)P, x(a : T).P, \overline{x}\langle y\rangle.P$ and $[x = y](P_1 ; P_2)$ are standard constructs of π-calculus: the empty process (does nothing), the parallel composition of two processes, the (unbounded) replication of a process, the binding of a name (thought of as creation of a channel), the input process (a is a placeholder for a name to be received by P through x), the output process (output y through x and then continue as P), and the conditional (if the names x and y are equal, then proceed as P_1, else proceed as P_2).

2. The system $G : u [P]$ declares that a process P is running on behalf of group G for the purpose u (the group G is bound). The system $R [S]$ declares that the system S is running on behalf of role R (the group R is bound). Finally, the systems $\mathbf{0}, (\nu a : T)S, S_1 \parallel S_2$ act like the respective processes (we use $\parallel$ instead of $|$ for the parallel composition of systems).

The declaration of the above definitions in Maude is mostly straightforward. As explained in [4, Sect. 14.2.6], $\mathbf{0}$ being the identity element of parallel composition could (and would) lead to non termination, so we use sorts NeProcess and NeSystem of non empty processes/systems to avoid this issue. We then have to declare how operators behave with respect to these subsorts; for example:

```
op ('(v_:_')_) : NameId Type Process -> Process [frozen(3)] .
op ('(v_:_')_) : NameId Type NeProcess -> NeProcess [ctor ditto] .
```

Notice the usage of **frozen** in all the declarations of operators that form processes and systems. As seen later, in the operational semantics of π-calculus, the next step of a process/system happens at the root of its syntactic tree (of course, it may then propagate to subterms). Without the **frozen** attribute, rewriting (that is, operational steps) could be triggered in subterms of a process/system.

In the declaration of parallel composition, we also use the equational attributes **assoc comm id**, which specify properties that normally are part of the structural congruence of π-calculus. These attributes allow Maude to identify processes/systems with the same behaviour; since they are built-in, using them is more computationally efficient than specifying explicitly the corresponding rules of structural congruence.

For ease of usage, when defining processes/systems, we sometime want to write a instead of a_0; since NameId is not a subsort of Name and we do not wish to introduce an extra operator, we add special cases of constructor operators; for example:

```
op ('[_==_']'(_;_')) : NameId Name Process Process -> NeProcess
    [frozen(3 4)] .
eq [A == X](P1 ; P2) = [A{0} == X](P1 ; P2) .
```

For ease of reading, some operators are written differently in Maude: $\mathbf{0}$ become OP and OS, $x(a : T).P$ becomes in x(a : T). P, and $\overline{x}\langle y\rangle.P$ becomes out x(y). P. For the conditional, we declare shorthands for cases where one of the branches is the empty process. Finally, we define a normal form for condition checking: if a name is compared to a constant, the constant is written after the name.

As usual, we define the operator fn that collects the names free in a process/system. Its declaration is simple, except for name binders, where we have to use shifting; for example:

eq fn((v A : T) P) = [shiftdown A] delete(A{0}, fn(P)) .

Moreover, we define the operators fg and bg for free and bound groups.

For name substitution and other CINNI operations, we have an operator __ : Subst Process −>Process (similarly for systems) that carries CINNI operations to free names. As specified by CINNI, name binders need lifting; for example: eq SUBST (in X(A : T). P) =in (SUBST X)(A : T). [liftup A SUBST] P.

Semantics. As is usual, our discussion of π-calculus semantics commences with structural congruence, i.e. a relation that identifies syntactically different processes/systems with identical intended behaviour. The structural congruence of our calculus is simple: it states that (i) α-equivalent constructs are congruent, (ii) parallel composition is associative commutative, with the empty process/system as identity element, (iii) binding a name or group in the empty process/system leaves us with the empty process/system, and (iv) replicating the empty process leaves us with the empty process. As explained above, we included part (ii) in the declaration of some operators; since CINNI takes care of name bindings, α-equivalence can be silently ignored with no problems; the rest can be dealt with by adding some equalities, such as **eq** ! 0P =0P and **eq** (v A : T) 0S =0S.

Note that the structural congruence of [3] includes rules regarding group binding; as explained in [8, pp. 3–4], since we give extra privacy-related meaning to the binding of a group, we have to omit the one stating that the binding of a group in a (non-empty) system can be omitted when the group is not used in the system. Due to this peculiarity of our structural congruence, the operational semantics of privacy calculus is better defined as a labelled transition semantics.

In all its other versions, privacy calculus is presented with early semantics, but its implementation would either lead to a state explosion (since the possible messages that can be received by a process are infinite) or require some workaround, as in [19, pp. 7–8]. As a consequence, we employ late semantics, which avoids this issue; incidentally, [14, p. 35] states "experimental evidence indicates that proof systems and decision procedures using the late semantics are slightly more efficient".

Labels for labelled transition semantics are built as follows: τ is the silent/internal action, $x(a)$ is input, $\overline{x}\langle y \rangle$ is output and $(\nu y : T)\overline{x}\langle y \rangle$ is bound output; all names are free, except for y in $(\nu y : T)\overline{x}\langle y \rangle$. The rules of our semantics are presented in Fig. 2.

The primary aim of our tool is to statically check whether a system adheres to a policy; as a consequence, we need not have implemented the semantics of Privacy Calculus in Maude. However, we did implement it, aiming for a more complete tool and for the ability to study the behaviour of a Privacy Calculus

$$x(a : T).P \xrightarrow{x(a)} P \qquad \text{(In)} \qquad \frac{P \xrightarrow{l} P'}{!P \xrightarrow{l} P' \, \| !P} \qquad \text{(Repl)}$$

$$\bar{x}\langle y \rangle.P \xrightarrow{\bar{x}\langle y \rangle} P \qquad \text{(Out)}$$

$$\frac{P \xrightarrow{l} P'}{[x = x] (P \, ; Q) \xrightarrow{l} P'} \quad \text{(CondT)} \qquad \frac{Q \xrightarrow{l} Q' \qquad x \neq y}{[x = y] (P \, ; Q) \xrightarrow{l} Q'} \quad \text{(CondF)}$$

$$\frac{F \xrightarrow{\bar{x}\langle a_0 \rangle} F'}{(\nu a : T)F \xrightarrow{(\nu a_0 : T)\bar{x}\langle a_0 \rangle} F'} \quad \text{(Open)} \qquad \frac{F_1 \equiv F_2 \qquad F_2 \xrightarrow{l} F}{F_1 \xrightarrow{l} F} \quad \text{(Congr)}$$

$$\frac{F_1 \xrightarrow{x(a)} F_1' \qquad F_2 \xrightarrow{\bar{x}\langle z \rangle} F_2'}{F_1 \mid F_2 \xrightarrow{\tau} ([a := z] \, F_1') \mid F_2'} \quad \text{(Comm)} \qquad \frac{F_1 \xrightarrow{l} F_1' \qquad bn(l) \cap fn(F_2) = \emptyset}{F_1 \mid F_2 \xrightarrow{l} F_1' \mid F_2} \quad \text{(Par)}$$

$$\frac{F_1 \xrightarrow{x(a)} F_1' \qquad F_2 \xrightarrow{(\nu b_n : T)\bar{x}\langle b_n \rangle} F_2'}{F_1 \mid F_2 \xrightarrow{\tau} (\nu b : T)(([a := b_n] \, F_1') \mid F_2')} \quad \text{(Close)} \qquad \frac{S \xrightarrow{l} S'}{R \, [S] \xrightarrow{l} R \, [S']} \quad \text{(ResGS)}$$

$$\frac{F \xrightarrow{l} F' \qquad a_0 \notin fn(l)}{(\nu a : T)F \xrightarrow{[\text{shiftdown } a \, l]} (\nu a : T)F'} \quad \text{(ResN)} \qquad \frac{P \xrightarrow{l} P'}{G : u \, [P] \xrightarrow{l} G : u \, [P']} \quad \text{(ResGP)}$$

Fig. 2. The rules of labelled transition semantics.

system using Maude's **search** command [4, Sect. 5.4.3], something that might turn out to be useful in applications. The semantics can be found in a rewrite module called PRIVACY-CALCULUS-SEMANTICS. For its implementation, we use some ideas from [19, Sect. 3–4]:

1. A one-step transition $F \xrightarrow{l} F'$ is encoded as a rewrite F =>{1} F'; in order for this kind of expressions to be well-defined, we have to define a sort ActProcess, as follows (and similarly for systems):

   sort ActProcess . subsort Process < ActProcess .
   op '{_'}_ : Label ActProcess -> ActProcess [frozen(2)] .

   The interesting cases of (Congr) are taken care of by CINNI (which reduces α-equivalence to bound name selection) and Maude (via the equations and equational attributes defining structural congruence). The other rules of Fig. 2 are just transcribed in the chosen form; for example:

   crl [CondF] : [X == Y] (P1 ; P2) => {1} P2'
       if X =/= Y /\ P2 => {1} P2' .

2. The operator that builds objects of ActProcess is declared using the **frozen** attribute, so as to control rewrites (as described above on page 7). Consequently, a mechanism must be provided explicitly for multi-step transitions; for processes, it suffices to provide the following code, with AP a variable of ActProcess (transitions of systems are similar):

```
sort TraceProcess .
subsort TraceProcess < ActProcess .
op '[_'] : Process -> TraceProcess [frozen] .
crl [reflP] : [ P ] => {1}P' if P => {1}P' .
crl [transP] : [ P ] => {1}AP
      if P => {1}P' /\ [ P' ] => AP /\ AP =/= [ P' ].
```

Objects of sort TraceProcess trigger rules transP and reflP. Operator [_] prevents infinite regressions where rules are used as conditions to themselves, a situation that would result if we just defined Process to be a subsort of TraceProcess.

3.2   Usage

In applications, Privacy Calculus will most probably be used as an intermediate language between the code in need of privacy analysis and the modules that will check adherence to policies. However, at this stage, one has to model the situation directly in π-calculus and provide the resulting system to the framework. This is achieved by defining (as in Example 1) the groups, purposes, data types, and data values in use and then synthesising the system that describes the behaviour to be analysed.

As discussed above, one can use Maude's **search** (or **rewrite**) command to find possible transitions of a system, although searching can take a lot of time for large system. Of course, this requires that the module specifying the system includes the rewrite module PRIVACY-CALCULUS-SEMANTICS.

Example 2. In the context of Example 1, the system S below contains (among other subsystems that have been replaced with ellipses for ease or presentation) a subsystem for the marketing department that reads the consumer's age and consent, checks their values, and (if the conditions hold) gets the order data and forwards it through an unknown channel.

```
op S : -> System . eq S =
Comp&Clients[(v 'order : Comp&Clients[Comp&Clients[OrderData]])(
    Company[
        (v 'userage : Company[Company[Age]])
        (v 'usercons : Company[Company[OwnerConsent]])
        (v 'orderdata : Company[Company[OrderData]])(
            ... || ThirdParty[MarketingDpt : marketing [
                in 'userage('age : Company[Age]). in 'age('x : Age).
                in 'usercons('cons : Company[OwnerConsent]).
                in 'cons('y : OwnerConsent).
                ['x =/= under13]['y == yes]
                    in 'orderdata('d : Company[OrderData]).
                    out 'linktotp('d). 0P
            ]] || ... )]
    || Clients[Alice : purchase[...]]
)] .
```

The **search** command may be used as follows (after loading the tool and the module(s) defining S):

> search S =>! S':ActSystem .

gives all the possible single-step transitions of S, while

> search [10,1] [S] =>+ {silent}S':ActSystem .

gives 10 possible multi-step transitions of S with a silent transition as their last step. Due to the rule of transitivity in our specification of multi-step transitions, the second numerical argument to **search** is irrelevant, since the search tree always has depth 1; for the same reason, using =>! may lead to non-terminating computation (since there are non-terminating systems), so one has to use =>+ for searching multi-step transitions.

4   The Type Checker

The type checker enforces the well-formedness of processes/systems and statically extracts their types, which describe the permissions needed in a structured form that also logs the relevant groups and purposes. The extracted information can then be compared to a privacy policy to check the adherence of a system to it. In [7], it is proved that the type checker is safe, in the sense that it does not flag non-adherent systems as adherent; as argued in [15], this property is not violated by the addition of conditions in the manner presented here.

4.1   Mathematical Specification

Type checking is based on Γ-Environments, Δ-Environments, and Θ-Interfaces.

Γ-*Environments* map (free) channel names to types and store the groups and conditions in scope; they serve to check the syntactic well-formedness of processes/systems and extract their type. Γ-Environments can be appended (if they contain different names and groups) with the operator $\cdot$.

Δ-*Environments* are the types of processes; they map private data types to permission sets. Δ-Environments can be appended (if the types in their domain are different) with $\cdot$ and combined with $\uplus$. A condition can be added to a Δ-Environment with $\oplus$. Functions Δ_r and Δ_w create default Δ-Environments, according to the type T given as argument; these should probably be tailored for specific applications, depending mainly on the basic permissions included; in our tool, where the basic permissions are **read**, **access**, **write**, and **disc** , we have opted for the following definitions, where t signifies some private data type:

$$\Delta_r(T) = \begin{cases} t : \texttt{read} & \text{if } T = t \\ t : \texttt{access} & \text{if } T = G[t] \\ \emptyset & \text{otherwise} \end{cases}, \quad \Delta_w(T) = \begin{cases} t : \texttt{write} & \text{if } T = G[t] \\ t : \texttt{disc } G & \text{if } T = G[G'[t]] \\ \emptyset & \text{otherwise} \end{cases}$$

Θ-*Interfaces* are the types of systems; they map private data types to pairs of a linear single-purpose group hierarchy and a permission set. They can be appended with ;. We can add a group to their hierarchies with $\odot$. Given a group G, a purpose u, and a Δ-Environment Δ, we can form the Θ-Interface $G\,[u]\oplus\Delta$.

The rules of the type system, presented in Fig. 3, are mostly as in [15, Fig. 3]. Rules (Out), (ParP), (ParS), (Nil), (Rep), (ResGP), and (ResGS) remain as before. CINNI affects (In), (ResNP), and (ResNS). Rules (CondC) and (GCond) have replaced the equivalent (CondA), (CondB). Comparison of two arbitrary names (note that this does not provide any information about the condition holding) is handled by (CondV). Finally, (Name) is split to (VName), (CName), since types of constants are known a priori.

$$\frac{x\in \mathrm{D}_X}{\Gamma \vdash x \triangleright X}\ \text{(CName)} \qquad \frac{[\textsf{shiftup}\,a\,\Gamma]\cdot a_0 : T \vdash P \triangleright \Delta \qquad \Gamma \vdash x \triangleright G[T]}{\Gamma \vdash x(a:T).P \triangleright \Delta \uplus \Delta_{\mathrm{r}}(T)}\ \text{(In)}$$

$$\frac{\mathrm{fg}(T)\subseteq \mathrm{dom}(\Gamma) \qquad x\notin \bigcup_X \mathrm{D}_X}{\Gamma \cdot x : T \vdash x \triangleright T}\ \text{(VName)} \qquad \frac{[\textsf{shiftup}\,a\,\Gamma]\cdot a_0 : T \vdash P \triangleright \Delta}{\Gamma \vdash (\nu\,a : T)P \triangleright \Delta}\ \text{(ResNP)}$$

$$\frac{\Gamma \vdash P \triangleright \Delta \qquad \mathrm{op}\in\{=,\neq\}}{\Gamma \cdot (x\,\mathrm{op}\,y)\vdash P \triangleright (x\,\mathrm{op}\,y)\oplus\Delta}\ \text{(GCond)} \qquad \frac{[\textsf{shiftup}\,a\,\Gamma]\cdot a_0 : T \vdash S \triangleright \Theta}{\Gamma \vdash (\nu\,a : T)S \triangleright \Theta}\ \text{(ResNS)}$$

$$\frac{\Gamma \cdot (X=y)\vdash P_1 \triangleright \Delta_1 \qquad \Gamma \cdot (X\neq y)\vdash P_2 \triangleright \Delta_2 \qquad \Gamma \vdash x \triangleright X \qquad y\in \mathrm{D}_X}{\Gamma \vdash [x=y]\,(P_1\,;\,P_2)\triangleright \Delta_1\uplus\Delta_2}\ \text{(CondC)}$$

$$\frac{\Gamma \vdash P_1 \triangleright \Delta_1 \qquad \Gamma \vdash P_2 \triangleright \Delta_2 \qquad \Gamma \vdash x \triangleright T \qquad \Gamma \vdash y \triangleright T \qquad x,y\notin \bigcup_X \mathrm{D}_X}{\Gamma \vdash [x=y]\,(P_1\,;\,P_2)\triangleright \Delta_1\uplus\Delta_2}\ \text{(CondV)}$$

$$\Gamma \vdash \mathbf{0}\triangleright\emptyset\ \text{(Nil)} \qquad \frac{\Gamma \vdash P \triangleright \Delta}{\Gamma \vdash !P \triangleright \Delta}\ \text{(Rep)} \qquad \frac{\Gamma \vdash P \triangleright \Delta \qquad \Gamma \vdash x \triangleright G[T] \qquad \Gamma \vdash y \triangleright T}{\Gamma \vdash \bar{x}\,\langle y\rangle\,.P \triangleright \Delta \uplus \Delta_{\mathrm{w}}\,G[T]}\ \text{(Out)}$$

$$\frac{\Gamma \vdash P_1 \triangleright \Delta_1 \qquad \Gamma \vdash P_2 \triangleright \Delta_2}{\Gamma \vdash P_1\mid P_2 \triangleright \Delta_1\uplus\Delta_2}\ \text{(ParP)} \qquad \frac{\Gamma \vdash S_1 \triangleright \Theta_1 \qquad \Gamma \vdash S_2 \triangleright \Theta_2}{\Gamma \vdash S_1\mid S_2 \triangleright \Theta_1;\Theta_2}\ \text{(ParS)}$$

$$\frac{\Gamma \cdot G\vdash P \triangleright \Delta}{\Gamma \vdash G[P]\,\langle u\rangle \triangleright G[u]\odot\Delta}\ \text{(ResGP)} \qquad \frac{\Gamma \cdot R\vdash S \triangleright \Theta}{\Gamma \vdash R[S]\triangleright R\odot\Theta}\ \text{(ResGS)}$$

Fig. 3. The rules of the type system.

Once extracted, a Θ-Interface can be tested for conformance to a policy with the operator $\models$ of [15, Sect. 4]. In effect, given a policy $\mathcal{P}$ and a Θ-Interface Θ, $\mathcal{P}\models\Theta$ iff for each private data type in Θ used by a set of groups for a purpose, the set of permissions exercised is bounded above (according to $\lesssim$) by the permissions granted by the policy to the game groups for the same purpose and data type.

As proved in [15, Sect. 5], the operators $\models$ and $\vdash$ can be jointly used to test a process for errors, in a suitable sense of the terms "error" and "test". In particular, define a system S to be an error with respect to policy $\mathcal{P}$ and Γ-Environment Γ (notation error$_{\mathcal{P},\Gamma}(S)$) iff it does not type-check or it is going to violate the policy in its next operation (this can be decided statically, by inspecting the outermost input/output subterms of S; see [15, Definition. 4] for a formal definition). Then, by the definitions of error, $\models$, and $\vdash$, it follows that

$\models$ and $\vdash$ offer a semi-decision procedure that ensures error-free behaviour (with respect to Γ and $\mathcal{P}$).

Theorem 1. *Let S be a system and $\mathcal{P}$ a policy. If there is a Γ-Environment Γ such that $\Gamma \vdash S \triangleright \Theta$ and $\mathcal{P} \models \Theta$, then $\neg\text{error}_{\mathcal{P},\Gamma}(S)$.*

Moreover, the above property survives transitions, as demonstrated by the following theorem.

Theorem 2. *Let S be a system and $\mathcal{P}$ a policy. Suppose that, after an arbitrary number of transitions, S becomes S'. If there is some Γ-Environment Γ such that $\Gamma \vdash S \triangleright \Theta$ and $\mathcal{P} \models \Theta$, then there is an extension Γ' of Γ such that $\neg\text{error}_{\mathcal{P},\Gamma'}(S')$.*

Proof sketch. The ordering $\leq$ of permission sets induces an ordering $\lesssim$ of Δ-Environments and Θ-Interfaces, with the property that if a Θ-Interface respects a policy, then all "smaller" Θ-Interfaces respect the same policy. Moreover, if $\Gamma \vdash S \triangleright \Theta$ and $S \xrightarrow{l} S'$, then there exists some extension Γ' of Γ such that $\Gamma' \vdash S' \triangleright \Theta'$ and $\Theta' \lesssim \Theta$.

4.2 Implementation and Usage

For the implementation of the above, one mostly has to translate the specification to Maude. For the operators $\uplus$, $\oplus$, and $\odot$ we use the plain symbol $+$. The empty Γ-Environment, Δ-Environment, and Θ-Interface are identity elements of their respective appending –and, moreover, the empty Δ-Environment is also the identity element of $\uplus-$, so we use sorts of non empty environments, for the reasons explained in [4, Sect. 14.2.6]. Type checking is implemented as a partial function that given a Γ-Environment and a name (resp. process; system) returns its resulting type (resp. Δ-Environment; Θ-Interface); for example, (ParP) becomes:

```
eq GAMMA |- NEP1 | NEP2 =
        (GAMMA |- NEP1) + (GAMMA |- NEP2) [label ParP] .
```

and (CondC), stating that the type of a condition check is the combination of the types that result from its branches if we add to the Γ-Environment the (positive or negative, according to the branch) condition holding, but only in case y is a data value and the type of x is the data type of y, becomes:

```
ceq GAMMA |- [X == Y] (P ; P') =
        (GAMMA . cond:((GAMMA |- Y) == Y) |- P )
    + (GAMMA . cond:((GAMMA |- Y) =/= Y) |- P')
        if Y :: DataValue /\ GAMMA |- Y = GAMMA |- X [label CondC] .
```

We can then specify an operator `compatible : Policy GEnvironment System` $->$`Bool` that tries to extract the type of the given system and, if successful, checks its satisfaction against the given policy using the operator $\models$.

Example 3. Suppose we want to know whether the system of Example 2 abides to the privacy policy of Example 1.

First, we have to specify a proper Γ-Environment, giving a type to all names free in the system and containing all groups and conditions within the scope of which we are implicitly working; in our case, we use `Gamma` $=$'`linktotp{0}` `: ThirdParty[Company[OrderData]]`, since '`linktotp{0}` is free in S. We then load the tool and our module(s) and write

> `red compatible(sales-policy, Gamma, S) .`

to the Maude prompt, which in our case returns

`rewrites: 10962 in 4ms cpu (3ms real) (2740500 rewrites/second)`
`result Bool: true`

and, thus, we are confident that our system respects the policy. If we remove the condition checks of S above (making it violate the policy), we observe that `compatible` returns `false`.

Several factors can cause the outcome of `compatible` to be `false`:

- The policy, the Γ-Environment, or the system may be syntactically invalid; in this case, either (probably) our module will not be accepted by Maude or the problematic term will have a kind but not a sort.
- The policy may be ill-formed (i.e. containing multiple subpolicies for the same data type or a subpolicy for a non-private data type or an ill-formed hierarchy); in this case, it will have a kind but not a sort.
- The system may be ill-formed; in this case, the outcome of `Gamma |- S`, where `Gamma` is our Γ-Environment will have a kind but not a sort; in particular, it will be a `fail` term pointing to the problematic subterm of S.
- The system may not respect the policy.
- The system may respect the policy (semantically), but its syntax may falsely indicate otherwise (for example, it may contain a branch that violates the policy but will never be reached).

5   Conclusion

5.1   Successes and Limitations

As (hopefully) is demonstrated by the running example, the framework we present can be used to check conformance of privacy-related applications with a wide range of (conditional) policies. The type checker can assure the user that a system is safe to use (in the context given, modelled by a Γ-Environment), a property that has been proved as a (meta)theorem of our type system. The specification in Maude is fully executable and closely follows the mathematical one, making it easier to reason about.

However, the privacy policy language is still less expressive and realistic than might be needed in practice. The language we described is not well-suited for multi-user environments, although this can probably be alleviated by introducing variables in policies and hierarchical data. [9] has already extended the framework to better accommodate anonymised data, identification, and storage of private data in databases.

Powerful as they may be, verification techniques, such as type checking, require non-trivial effort from the user, who has to model the real-world scenario in a way that fits the language of the formal framework in use. This severely restricts their application outside critical systems and calls for solutions bridging theory with practice.

Admittedly, the Privacy Calculus is too abstract for use in actual applications. In order for our framework to be useful, one must find some solution to bridge actual code-writing with this level of abstraction. One possibility would be to provide a compiler that transforms programmes in widely used languages, such as Java, to Privacy Calculus. In environments where it can be enforced that all private data will be handled by a specific (software) entity, it might be possible to include Privacy Calculus in the design of the libraries that manage private data handling. Certainly, some aspects, such as the particular groups, purposes, and data types, but also the specific permissions that can be reasoned about, will always have to be adapted to each case (or kind of cases) separately.

Of course, static verification has limits. An issue that has been mentioned in [8, p. 15] is that, in principle, group membership may change over time in ways that can interfere with static analysis. In addition, complex cases may render type checking impractical. Also, it is possible that a system may be safe for reasons having to do with its semantics, but static analysis alone may flag it unsafe. For such reasons, static and runtime approaches to verification should be combined.

5.2   Future Work

The work we presented here can be extended in many directions.

Maude is a very powerful tool, whose capabilities are far wider that what we have used so far. Its reflective character (that is, the fact that specifications can themselves be handled as data in other Maude modules) has been used to create a number of useful tools for the examination of the properties of modules [5, Sect. 21.1]. We could use these tools to mechanically prove that our specification has some desirable properties (for example, termination of type checking, validity of equational properties corresponding to soundness of type checking), even while it gets extended with more features.

Besides the features added in [9] we mentioned above, the framework can be extended in many ways. For example, Universal P-RBAC [12] uses the construct of obligation (that is, an action that must precede or follow the usage of private data) and gives hierarchical structure to purposes and data; both ideas are certainly useful in real-world situations regarding privacy. [17] provides a taxonomy of kinds of privacy violations; it can be (and has been) used as a source of inspiration for the creation of policies.

Eventually, that is when the framework and the tool have reached a certain maturity, it will be valuable to empirically evaluate their expressibility and their efficiency in a real-world scenario.

References

1. Byun, J.W., Bertino, E., Li, N.: Purpose based access control of complex data for privacy protection. In: Proceedings of the Tenth ACM Symposium on Access Control Models and Technologies, SACMAT 2005, pp. 102–110. ACM, New York (2005). https://doi.org/10.1145/1063979.1063998
2. Byun, J.W., Li, N.: Purpose based access control for privacy protection in relational database systems. VLDB J. **17**(4), 603–619 (2008). https://doi.org/10.1007/s00778-006-0023-0
3. Cardelli, L., Ghelli, G., Gordon, A.D.: Secrecy and group creation. Inf. Comput. **196**(2), 127–155 (2005). https://doi.org/10.1016/j.ic.2004.08.003
4. Clavel, M., et al.: Maude Manual (Version 2.7). Technical report, SRI International Computer Science Laboratory (2015). http://maude.cs.uiuc.edu/maude2-manual
5. Clavel, M., et al.: All About Maude - A High-Performance Logical Framework: How to Specify, Program, and Verify Systems in Rewriting Logic. Programming and Software Engineering. Springer, Heidelberg (2007). https://www.springer.com/la/book/9783540719403
6. Jakšić, S., Pantović, J., Ghilezan, S.: Linked data privacy. Math. Struct. Comput. Sci. **27**(1), 33–53 (2017). https://doi.org/10.1017/S096012951500002X
7. Kokkinofta, E., Philippou, A.: Type checking purpose-based privacy policies in the π-Calculus. In: Hildebrandt, T., Ravara, A., van der Werf, J.M., Weidlich, M. (eds.) WS-FM 2014-2015. LNCS, vol. 9421, pp. 122–142. Springer, Cham (2016). https://doi.org/10.1007/978-3-319-33612-1_8
8. Kouzapas, D., Philippou, A.: Type checking privacy policies in the π-calculus. In: Graf, S., Viswanathan, M. (eds.) FORTE 2015. LNCS, vol. 9039, pp. 181–195. Springer, Cham (2015). https://doi.org/10.1007/978-3-319-19195-9_12
9. Kouzapas, D., Philippou, A.: Privacy by typing in the π-calculus. Logical Methods Comput. Sci. **13**(4) (2017). https://doi.org/10.23638/LMCS-13(4:27)2017
10. Meseguer, J.: Twenty years of rewriting logic. J. Log. Algebr. Program. **81**(7), 721–781 (2012). https://doi.org/10.1016/j.jlap.2012.06.003
11. Ni, Q., et al.: Privacy-aware Role-based access control. ACM Trans. Inf. Syst. Secur. **13**(3), 24:1–24:31 (2010). https://doi.org/10.1145/1805974.1805980
12. Ni, Q., Lin, D., Bertino, E., Lobo, J.: Conditional privacy-aware role based access control. In: Biskup, J., López, J. (eds.) ESORICS 2007. LNCS, vol. 4734, pp. 72–89. Springer, Heidelberg (2007). https://doi.org/10.1007/978-3-540-74835-9_6
13. Pardo, R., Schneider, G.: A formal privacy policy framework for social networks. In: Giannakopoulou, D., Salaün, G. (eds.) SEFM 2014. LNCS, vol. 8702, pp. 378–392. Springer, Cham (2014). https://doi.org/10.1007/978-3-319-10431-7_30
14. Parrow, J.: An introduction to the π-calculus. In: Bergstra, J.A., Ponse, A., Smolka, S.A. (eds.) Handbook of Process Algebra, pp. 479–543. Elsevier Science, Amsterdam (2001). https://doi.org/10.1016/B978-044482830-9/50026-6
15. Pitsiladis, G.V.: Type checking conditional purpose-based privacy policies in the π-calculus. Limassol, Cyprus (2016). http://users.ntua.gr/gpitsiladis/files/documents/2016-11-fmpriv-conditions.pdf

16. Pitsiladis, G.V.: Type Checking Privacy Policies in the π-calculus and its Executable Implementation in Maude (in Greek). Diploma thesis, National Technical University of Athens, Greece (2016). http://dspace.lib.ntua.gr/handle/123456789/44439

17. Solove, D.J.: A Taxonomy of Privacy. SSRN Scholarly Paper ID 667622, Social Science Research Network, Rochester, NY, February 2005. https://papers.ssrn.com/abstract=667622

18. Stehr, M.O.: CINNI - A generic calculus of explicit substitutions and its application to λ- ς- and π-calculi. Electron. Notes Theor. Comput. Sci. **36**, 70–92 (2000). https://doi.org/10.1016/S1571-0661(05)80125-2

19. Thati, P., Sen, K., Martí-Oliet, N.: An executable specification of asynchronous π-calculus semantics and may testing in Maude 2.0. Electron. Notes Theor. Comput. Sci. **71**, 261–281 (2004). https://doi.org/10.1016/S1571-0661(05)82539-3

Correction to: Assuring Intelligent Ambient Assisted Living Solutions by Statistical Model Checking

Ashalatha Kunnappilly, Raluca Marinescu, and Cristina Seceleanu

Correction to:
Chapter "Assuring Intelligent Ambient Assisted Living
Solutions by Statistical Model Checking" in:
T. Margaria and B. Steffen (Eds.): *Leveraging Applications*
of Formal Methods, Verification and Validation, **LNCS 11245,**
https://doi.org/10.1007/978-3-030-03421-4_29

In the original version of this chapter, Fig. 3 was incorrect. This has now been corrected.

The updated version of this chapter can be found at
https://doi.org/10.1007/978-3-030-03421-4_29

© Springer Nature Switzerland AG 2019
T. Margaria and B. Steffen (Eds.): ISoLA 2018, LNCS 11245, p. C1, 2018.
https://doi.org/10.1007/978-3-030-03421-4_31

Author Index

Printed in the United States
By Bookmasters